MIDDLE EAST PATTERNS : PLACES,
DS44.95 .H45 1994

~~AC 08 97~~		
~~MR 12 98~~		
~~'02~~		
~~MY 2 7 07~~		

MIDDLE EAST
PATTERNS

SECOND EDITION

MIDDLE EAST PATTERNS

Places, Peoples, and Politics

Colbert C. Held
Baylor University

With the assistance of
Mildred McDonald Held

Cartography by John V. Cotter

WESTVIEW PRESS

Boulder • San Francisco • Oxford

The calligraphy on pp. ii, 1, and 201 (which means "Over every learned one is the One more learned") is taken from Mohamed U. Zakariya, *The Calligraphy of Islam: Reflections on the State of the Art* (Washington, D.C.: Center for Contemporary Arab Studies, Georgetown University, 1979) and is used by permission of the Center.

All photos are by the author unless otherwise attributed. FRONT COVER PHOTOS: *Center:* Gallery at University of Petroleum and Minerals, Dhahran, Saudi Arabia; *Clockwise from top right:* Village in Turkey's Pontic Mountains; Palmyra, Syria; shoppers at *suq* in Nazwa, Inner Oman; Housing Bank Center, Amman, Jordan; ancient citadel of Aleppo (Syria) in background, modern Aleppo in foreground; Asir house, Saudi Arabia; Bedouins in Saudi Arabia; modern apartment buildings, Jidda, Saudi Arabia; wind-rippled dunes in Saudi Arabia's Rub al-Khali. BACK COVER PHOTO: Mosaic of space images of Middle East (courtesy USGS/NMD Eros Data Center).

Published in 1994 in the United States of America by Westview Press, 5500 Central Avenue, Boulder, Colorado 80301-2877, and in the United Kingdom by Westview Press, 36 Lonsdale Road, Summertown, Oxford OX2 7EW

Library of Congress Cataloging-in-Publication Data
Held, Colbert C.
Middle East patterns : places, peoples, and politics / Colbert C.
  Held, with the assistance of Mildred McDonald Held ; cartography by
John V. Cotter. — 2nd ed.
    p.   cm.
  Includes bibliographical references and index.
  ISBN 0-8133-8220-3. — ISBN 0-8133-8221-1 (pbk.)
    1. Middle East—Geography.   I. Held, Mildred M.   II. Title.
DS44.95.H45   1994
915.6—dc20
                                                                                        93-4447
                                                                                            CIP

Printed and bound in the United States of America

   ∞   The paper used in this publication meets the requirements of the American National Standard for Permanence of Paper
       for Printed Library Materials Z39.48-1984.

10   9   8   7   6   5   4   3   2   1

Contents

PART ONE: PHYSICAL AND CULTURAL GEOGRAPHY

PART TWO: REGIONAL GEOGRAPHY

Tables

Tables

Country Facts

Illustrations

Maps

Figures (Photographs)

Graphs

Preface and Acknowledgments
to the Second Edition

Developments in the Middle East since the publication of the first edition of *Middle East Patterns* have once more underscored the volatility, internal disparity, and significance of the region. After the failure of a dozen tentative efforts between various pairs of states to achieve unity during the 45 years following World War II, the Yemen Arab Republic and the People's Democratic Republic of Yemen successfully merged in 1990. President Saddam Husayn of Iraq once again misjudged a situation and precipitated the Gulf war of 1990–1991 and later military echoes in early 1993. A significant minority of Muslims especially, but also Jews and Christians, pushed ever deeper into radicalism and employed religion as an excuse for internal and external belligerence and terrorism. Nearly everywhere, economic development continued apace. The ongoing Middle East peace talks launched in Madrid in October 1991 appeared to achieve few tangible results after ten rounds by mid-1993. However, they showed that bitter enemies could negotiate, and both positively and negatively they set the stage for the secret negotiation of the momentous Israeli-Palestinian accord of September 1993.

These and other aspects of the Middle East required a complete revision of the first edition of this book, and all are treated in this second edition. This revision includes 39 new, updated, or otherwise revised maps and 55 new photographs, most taken during my field trip to the Middle East in 1990. (Photographs not otherwise attributed are printed from some of the 20,000 Kodachrome slides I shot in the Middle East between 1957 and 1990.) The bibliography and the notes have been expanded to provide more detailed source information and background comments.

Middle East Patterns is still the only geography of the Middle East by an American geographer since 1960. A geography in the broad sense of the word, the revision is also designed for reference and general reading as well as college course use.

As with the first edition, my greatest appreciation for assistance in the preparation of this revision is due and is warmly extended to my wife, Milly. No words can express my affectionate gratitude for her faithful, unstinting, and unselfish support and full participation over the years involved in the research, writing, and editing that produced the final result.

I am also grateful to the numerous U.S. and local government officials, oil company representatives, and academicians who contributed so vitally to the success of my several months of fieldwork in fifteen countries of the Middle East in 1990. Many former Foreign Service colleagues and new Foreign Service friends were of inestimable assistance in arranging interviews with various officials, facilitating field trips, and aiding in the acquisition of statistics and other information. I offer warm thanks especially to Ambassador April Glaspie, Baghdad; Economic Counselor Clay Nettles, Ankara; and Consul General and Mrs. Philip Griffin, Jiddah. I am also grateful to Ambassadors Charles Dunbar, Sana, and his deputy Georgia DeBell Craig; Edward Walker, Abu Dhabi; Richard Boehm, Muscat, and his political-economic counselor Anthony Benesch and economic-commercial officer Henry Enscher; Mark Hambley, Doha, and his vice-consul Michelle Bernier-Toth and political-economic officer Donald Roberts; Charles Hostler, Manama, and his vice-consul Stephanie Kronenburg; Charles Freeman, Riyadh, and his administrative assistant Alice Boynton; Nathaniel Howell and his wife, Marjorie; and Roscoe Sudarth, Amman, and his deputy Patrick Theros and assistant Charles Heffernan. Dr. and Mrs. John Cummings of the U.S.-Saudi Joint Economic Commission in Riyadh, my son-in-law and daughter, were again very helpful, as was my daughter Melinda Brunger.

Political officer David Litt, Embassy Damascus, and his colleagues gave insightful briefings and helped rescue lost rolls of film. Consul General Thomas Carolan, Istanbul, was helpful in absentia even though he was on home leave. David Winn, deputy principal officer in Jerusalem, generously shared his time and experience. Among several embassy employees, Nadia Riszk in the Embassy Library, Cairo, has been helpful on many occasions. Douglas Silliman and James Eighmie in NEA, Department of State, Washington, D.C., coordinated many essential aspects of the 1990 trip.

Local government officials were impressively helpful in virtually every country in the region, particularly in Qatar, Kuwait, Jordan, and Turkey. Turkish State Hydraulic Works deputy regional director Raif Özenci gave me a lengthy and detailed briefing on the Atatürk Dam and the Southeast Anatolia Project.

Oil companies in several countries extended courtesies that permitted unusual observations in remote areas: They include Yemen Hunt Oil Company (especially General Manager Richard Davis), Crescent Oil Company in Sharjah (especially President Hamid Jafar and his administrative assistant, Maggie Magdesian), Petroleum Development Oman, Qatar Petroleum Company, Bahrain National Oil Company, and Saudi Aramco. As in the past, Aramco was especially helpful in the persons of Robert Norberg, Shafiq Kombargi, Ismail Nawwab, James Mandaville, and Jim Ragland.

I should like to express my very warm appreciation to geographers too numerous to name, in universities in thirteen of the fifteen countries visited, who were unfailingly cordial and helpful. Many of the departments have an admirable vitality and play important roles in their respective schools. Two geographers to whom I am especially grateful are Dr. Mansoor al-Ohaly of the University of Riyadh and Dr. Amal al-Sabbagh, dean of Faculty of Arts of the University of Kuwait.

Baylor University has been as strongly supportive of this second edition as it was of the first. Documents Librarian John Wilson and his staff as well as others at Moody Library deserve specific thanks, as do consultants in the Center for Computing. Westview Press staff members, especially Barbara Ellington and the magic-weaving production editor Libby Barstow, continue to be a pleasure to work with. Copy editor Cheryl Carnahan's sharp eyes, sharp grammarian's mind, and sharp pencil wrought wonders in a very complicated manuscript. I also continue to be grateful to the individuals and institutions that contributed so much to the success of the first edition and that, by extension, have contributed to this revision. As before, I accept full responsibility for any errors in the book.

Colbert C. Held
Waco, Texas
September 1993

Preface and Acknowledgments
to the First Edition

This book is one outgrowth of my sixteen years of residence, travel, and fieldwork in the Middle East for the U.S. Department of State. I went to my first assignment, in Beirut, from the University of Nebraska as an academic geographer and returned with both a practical bent and an urge to share my observations with other people interested in the Middle East. Hence this survey of the region and its states, a survey that I contemplated for nearly 30 years and have been writing for six. Along with description and analysis, I have tried to infuse some of the sheer fascination I have always found in the various cultural and physical patterns of the area.

Middle East Patterns is aimed at both midlevel college students and general readers who seek information on and insights into the spatial dynamics of the Middle East. I have tried to reduce technical terminology to a minimum, without sacrifice of scholarship, so as to aid understanding by readers with little or no background in academic geography. Although the focus of the survey is mainly on spatial patterns, I interweave historical, economic, political, and ethnographic elements because they are inherent in the geographical mosaic.

The two parts of the book reflect the two basic approaches to geographical analysis: The first eleven chapters are a topical (systematic) examination of the Middle East—historical, biophysical, ethnographic, economic, and geopolitical. The other eleven chapters are a country-by-country study of the region. Both parts are classic approaches, and both are consistent with the renewed academic emphasis on regional studies. The physical environment receives appropriate attention, but emphasis in both the topical and the country chapters is on human and cultural aspects of the area.

This is the first geography of the Middle East by a U.S. geographer since 1960. This lapse of nearly 30 years between such studies is astonishing in view of the vital role of the Middle East in U.S. affairs and the equally vital role of the geographical perspective. In the book, I have incorporated field research and observations from repeated assignments to every country in the Middle East, except South Yemen, and I have also drawn on studies by colleagues and other scholars, some of whom I mention below and some in the notes.

The contribution to this work by my wife, Milly, is so great that the least I can do is acknowledge it on the title page. Our older daughter, Melinda Brunger, gave invaluable, massive editorial assistance on most chapters, and our geographer younger daughter, Joanne Cummings, and her economist husband, Dr. John T. Cummings, critiqued several chapters. The Arabian American Oil Company (Aramco) gave corporate logistical support on several trips in Saudi Arabia, but equally important was the generous and indispensable help by former and present members of the company as individuals: Peter C. Speers, retired from many years in Saudi Arabia, evaluated most chapters and checked place-name transliterations with a meticulous scholarship matched only by his patience and humor. James Mandaville, Jr., company geographer-planner, checked several topic chapters and the Saudi chapter line by line with his own geographer's carefulness and scholarship, and Dale E. Garrison gave helpful suggestions on several chapters. Geologists Syd Bowers and Ellen Herron critiqued the geomorphology discussions, and Dr. Glenn Brown and Roy O. Jackson, longtime Middle East geologists with the U.S. Geological Survey, also gave patient assistance in this area. The late Arthur B. Allen, a Foreign Service colleague, commented on the first few chapters, as did my lawyer nephew, John Charles Held.

U.S. government specialists too numerous to single out were generous with advice, data, and documents, especially members of the Departments of State, Agriculture, Defense, and Commerce along with the Geological Survey, Library of Congress (including the Map Division), National Aeronautics and Space Administration (NASA), Central Intelligence Agency (CIA), and Bureau of Mines. A score of oil companies in the Middle East gave vital assistance in supplying information and logistical support, particularly Aramco, Crescent Petroleum Company (Sharjah), Bahrain Petroleum Company (Bapco), Continental Oil Company, Dubai Petroleum Company, Petroleum Development (Oman) Ltd., and Yemen Hunt Oil Company. Virtually every government information office in the Middle East responded to my requests for official data, as did many substantive ministries and agencies. Baylor University assisted in several ways, especially the staff of the Moody Memorial Library; Professors Bruce C. Cresson, James Breckenridge, O. T. Hayward, and Donald M. Green, who critiqued chapters; photographer Chris Hansen, who made most of the photographs that appear in the book from my color slides; and departmental secretary Mrs. Pat Bibb. Several graduate assistants helped in searching out data, and more than a score of class students gave invaluable suggestions about various chapters.

Among many Foreign Service colleagues, I am especially beholden to Ambassadors James E. Akins, Andrew J. Killgore, George M. Lane, David G. Newton, and Marshall W. Wiley as well as the late Consul General Robert B. Houghton and the late Harry N. Howard, and their respective wives, for generous hospitality and invaluable insights. Richard W. Buro and Hartwell Robinson helped guide me through the pitfalls of word processing. Westview Press staff members have been a pleasure to work with for six years, and I am indebted to a series of editors that included Lynne Rienner, Holly Arrow, and last, but especially, Jennifer Knerr. The contributions by copy editor Megan Schoeck and production editor Libby Barstow are marvels I especially appreciate. All have been patient and encouraging. I am grateful to Encyclopaedia Britannica, Inc., for permission to use statistics from the recent (since 1985) *Britannica World Data,* published each year in the *Britannica Book of the Year.* My thanks also to the Wissenschaftliche Verlagsgesellschaft mbH, Stuttgart, for climate data and to the Survey of Israel and Syracuse University Press.

All the brainpower in aid of this work notwithstanding, I assume responsibility for any errors in the book, realizing that there would have been many more without the critiques of family, friends, colleagues, editors, and students. I am grateful to these critics and invite others to join them.

C.C.H.

A Note on Transliteration

For transliteration of place-names from Arabic, Hebrew, and Greek, I have generally followed the recommendations of the U.S. Board on Geographic Names (BGN), except that I elected to omit diacritical marks on transliterations from those three languages. (I retained diacritics in Turkish words, since Turkish uses a basically Roman alphabet in which diacritics are an integral part of the written language.) Indicating the *ain* and the *hamza* in Arabic words merely confuses the general reader who knows no Arabic and adds little of essence for readers who do. I have deliberately accepted inconsistency in using conventional forms and spellings for certain names—Cairo (rather than al-Qahirah), Damascus (al-Dimashq), Yemen (al-Yaman), Bab el-Mandeb (Bab al-Mandab), Dubai (Dubayyah), Medina (al-Madinah), Doha (al-Dawhah), Bekaa (Biqa), and others. I have also dropped the definite article (*al*) in many names: Aqabah, Riyadh, Qatif; and where I have retained it I have used it only in the basic form, not in the form modified by "sun letters" (Sharm al-Shaykh, not Sharm ash-Shaykh; Jabal al-Ruwaq, not Jabal ar-Ruwaq). I have also retained certain spellings that have become ingrained through use by oil companies.

Some names create certain problems. For example, the Gulf is called the Persian Gulf by Iran and many other countries and the Arabian Gulf by Arab states and some other countries. Many names in former Palestine—and the use of the name *Palestine* itself—imply particular biases: West Bank versus Samaria and Judea, Gulf of Aqabah versus Gulf of Elat, al-Quds or Jerusalem versus Yerushalayyem, and others. Jordan's disengagement from the West Bank in July-August 1988 has rendered even the applicability of the term *West Bank* a question mark. Revolutionary Iran has changed dozens of place-names because they connoted the Pahlavi royal family: for example, Bandar-e Pahlavi is now Bandar-e Anzali, Rezaiyeh is Urumiyeh (conventional: Urmia), and Bandar-e Shahpur is Bandar-e Khomeyni. I have used the new names that have been publicly announced.

C.C.H.

MIDDLE EAST
PATTERNS

PART 1

Physical and Cultural Geography

1

Tricontinental Junction: An Introduction

Middle East Preview

Located at the tricontinental hub of Europe, Asia, and Africa, the Middle East possesses unique geopolitical significance. It is the cradle of civilization, birthplace of the three great monotheistic religions, crossroads of movement and trade, base of extensive empires, resource area for 67 percent of the world's petroleum, home to 241.5 million people in sixteen countries, fountain of political and ideological ferment, and locus of some of the most persistently explosive conflicts since World War II. No country on earth can be unconcerned with the course of major developments in the region.

The Middle East has been in the news, often treated at length, almost daily since 1947. It was the center of attention of the world media not only during the wars of 1956, 1967, 1973, 1980–1988, 1982, and especially 1990–1991 but also during peace negotiations in 1991–1993. Yet the vast amount of routine reporting has rarely included in-depth objective background information about the area's complex patterns of regions, peoples, and problems—until the 1990–1991 Gulf war. Even then, the almost continuous detailed coverage naturally focused on news—the hour-by-hour events in the Gulf and, often, in Israel. Background information was often more pejorative than objective, not only concerning Iraq, the aggressor, but also regarding many members of the coalition. Fortunately, the media responsibly displayed maps of relevant areas, so that the world—especially the U.S. public—was generally better informed about the Middle East after the Gulf war than ever before. Nevertheless, much of the public perception of the fundamental nature of the Middle East continued to be sketchy at best and continued to include stereotypes and prejudices that have roots as far back as the Crusades.

More balanced and analytical media focus was devoted to the dramatic accord between Israel and the Palestine Liberation Organization (PLO) signed in Washington on September 13, 1993. Many long-neglected aspects of the region and its profound problems received unusually intensive attention from many quarters for the several weeks before and after the climax of the negotiations. The historic signing ceremony on the White House lawn permitted presentation of full and uncensored statements and ceremonial actions by both Palestinians and Israelis. Even so, comments by many persons on television and in the print media during the unfolding of the drama often revealed prejudice or limited understanding regarding the basic problems.

Rational decisions and actions on the part of governments, as well as intelligent participation by citizens in those decisions and actions, require objective knowledge and understanding of the interactions among the basic enduring patterns in this vital region of the world. Decision makers and citizens must depend on sources other than the three-minute sound bites of the daily news for the background information necessary to comprehend an area with the complexity and significance of the Middle East.

The fate of much of the world, including that of the industrialized countries, is inextricably bound up with developments in the Middle East. It is important, therefore, to recognize that the region's peoples and states have their own

3

histories, aspirations, value systems, problems of development and change, regional and global relationships, and agendas. With the transformation of the former Soviet realm in the early 1990s and the shuffling of transnational relationships in Eurasia, the Middle East assumes a changed but still vitally significant role. It is the aim of this book to examine the natural and cultural patterns of the Middle East and their influence on political and economic developments, to analyze and interpret the more significant regional and global relations, and thus to afford a greater knowledge of and insights into this crucial region.

Political and religious confrontations, military conflicts, and economic influence have given the Middle East an increasingly central role in world affairs. Because of its tricontinental location (Map 1-1) and its central position in the World-Island (see Chap. 11), the region has historically been a world crossroads, and the late Professor George B. Cressey titled his 1960 study of Middle East geography *Crossroads* to emphasize that important function.

However, the region is often perceived in particularistic terms—of petroleum or the Islamic Revolution or Israel or Arab nationalism or other single issues—which clouds the greater significance of this exceedingly complex area. Short-term and simplistic perceptions are also misleading—for example, that the Middle East has only recently become important or that it is typified by the Iranian revolution of the late 1970s, by the Iraqi aggression of 1990, or by rich oil *shaykhs* (sheikhs) in desert kingdoms. In fact, the Middle East blends diverse geographical elements, rich historical traditions, and complex cultural and national groupings to produce kaleidoscopic patterns that continue to evolve and change. Inevitably, the impact of rapid change and of the continued search for legitimacy and identity induces stress and resultant antagonisms. The maps and photographs in this book depict some of these complexities and contrasts (see, for example, Figs. 1-1 and 1-2).

The significance of the location of the Middle East derives partly from its irregular shape. Seas penetrate deeply into the land and alternate with peninsulas and land bridges around the Syrian-Mesopotamian core. These seas, including the

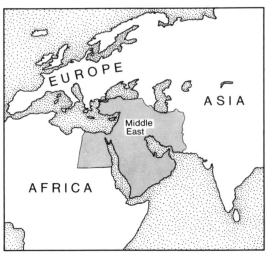

Map 1-1. *The Middle East as tricontinental hub, the heart of the World-Island.*

Red, Mediterranean, Black, and Caspian (actually an inland lake), and the Persian/Arabian Gulf have made maritime movements of the peoples of the area relatively easy for more than 5,000 years, provide access to the region, and conversely, serve as natural insulation between regional cultural groups.

The Middle East is commonly known as the "cradle of civilization." Evidence of the earliest known humans has been found in East Africa, and very old human skeletons and tools have been found in other areas; but the Middle East had human inhabitants very early and seems to have produced the earliest integrated civilizations, agricultural villages and developed towns, and religious-political systems. These civilizations evolved in the Fertile Crescent, an arc of fertile land that extends from the Mediterranean around the Syrian Desert to the Gulf, and particularly the Mesopotamian Basin, the depression occupied by the Tigris and Euphrates rivers. From this geographical core, the ideas, techniques, and implements of the Fertile Crescent diffused to other similar environments—westward to the Nile Valley in Egypt, eastward to the Indus Valley in present-day Pakistan, and beyond—and mixed with impressive civilizations in those areas.

More than 5,000 years ago, this seminal culture hearth of Mesopotamia produced the earliest known writing and high levels of science and

Figure 1-1. *Barren, wind-rippled dunes in Saudi Arabia's Rub al-Khali (Empty Quarter).*

mathematics. The Middle East thus became a matrix for later Western and Oriental civilizations. The cultural complex that spread outward from the Mesopotamian core also gave rise to successive confrontations among expanding ancient empires. The high level of civilization achieved by successive empires suggests a resilience and capacity for adaptation that is still evident in the region. Several power foci, which will be discussed later in this book, emerged through the centuries and have persisted for more than 4,500 years to the present.

In addition to the clashes between successive empires, there also evolved in the Middle East the three major monotheistic religions—Judaism, Christianity, and Islam. Each is rooted in earlier religions, yet each is distinctive. Their respective origins within the region provide one measure of the cultural richness and unique significance of the Middle East.

Just as Christianity gave rise through the centuries to a general civilization referred to as Christendom, so Islam engendered the Islamic

civilization. The cradle of both the religion of Islam and the culture of Islam, the Middle East remains the heartland of the Islamic culture realm, the original core area of which—Mecca and Medina in western Saudi Arabia—is the goal of the annual Muslim hajj, or pilgrimage, and is a religious focus for most Muslims.

The Islamic civilization is the single most pervasive unifying factor in the Middle East, and the correlation between religion and culture on the one hand and geographical area and environment on the other is a major element in any study of the region. Two important functions of the Middle East region during medieval times relate to the bond between the area and Islam. During the centuries of the so-called Dark Ages in Europe, and while the Byzantine Empire was absorbed in political and theological disputes, the Islamic Middle East was translating and interpreting classical writings—literary, philosophical, and scientific—thus preserving the classical heritage, much of which might otherwise have been lost. Also, contemporaneously,

Figure 1-2. *Village surrounded by green fields of corn (maize) and well-forested slopes in Turkey's Pontic Mountains, an area of moderately heavy precipitation just south of the Black Sea.*

the Middle East was a remarkable commercial crossroads, maintaining contacts with potent East Asian civilizations, partly through Muslim missionaries, and later linking those civilizations with a revived Mediterranean area and Renaissance Europe.

Significant as the foregoing traditional aspects of the Middle East are, four contemporary aspects dominate the world's perception of the area: enormous petroleum resources, the political tensions arising from the Arab-Israeli confrontation, the bewildering rivalries among leaders and states, and the extremism among zealous Muslims, Jews, and Christians. Most of the petroleum—two-thirds of the world's known reserves—lies along a broad depression extending southeastward from near Elazığ, Turkey, along the axis of the Gulf, to the Arabian Sea coast of Oman. Of the roughly 60 million barrels of petroleum produced daily in the world in 1991, approximately 17 million barrels, or more than 28 percent, originated in the countries on the Gulf.

In 1979, at the height of Middle East production, the region's percentage of the world's total was more than half. In addition to selling oil to the West, the Middle East oil-producing countries depend heavily upon imports of goods and technical/managerial expertise from the industrialized countries. The resultant interdependence between industrialized countries and oil-producing countries has increased as the former grow more concerned with stable energy supplies and as the latter continue to require Western technology for development.

The Arab-Israeli wars in 1948–1949, 1956, 1967, 1973, and 1982 resulted in thousands of casualties and the diversion to armaments of billions of dollars needed for development. The oil boycott in 1973, periodic outbreaks of fighting in the Levant, and regional and international obsession with the Arab-Israeli problem all attest to the destabilizing effects of the Arab-Israeli conflict. Although less protracted, the internecine Gulf wars of 1980–1988 and 1990–1991 resulted in many more casualties than the earlier battles in the Levant and were immeasurably more devastating.

The Middle East: Definition

That the Fertile Crescent is the core of the Middle East is universally accepted, and that the region comprises the general area from northeast Africa to south Asia is also widely approved. There is, moreover, a broad consensus that the Middle East extends from the western border of Egypt to the eastern border of Iran and from the Black Sea to the Arabian Sea. However, the precise limits of the region are still variously conceived by scholars and media. All the attention devoted to the region has not ended the uncertainty about what the Middle East includes, and only recently has the area's name been generally accepted. What is the proper designation of the Middle East? What is its actual extent? And what criteria best determine the region's name and limits?

Nomenclature

Changes in terminology in recent decades reflect underlying changes in Western perceptions of the region. Earlier toponyms implied a Eurocentric viewpoint: the East, Orient (Latin for "east"), Levant (also "east"), Near East, or Nearer East. Thus, the East was obviously named by the West, specifically Western Europe. During the thirteenth century, the Italians, at the beginning of the Renaissance the most active European traders with the Mediterranean lands, referred to the eastern Mediterranean as the Levant—the "rising" (of the sun), signifying the East. Levant was taken into other European languages and has long been used to designate the lands near the coasts of the eastern Mediterranean and is used in that sense in this book.

Increasing contacts between Western Europe and the Ottoman Empire during the sixteenth and seventeenth centuries—as a consequence of voyages of discovery, increased commercial ties, and later, European imperialism—produced a new name for the eastern Mediterranean region. "East" applied to lands of the Ottoman Empire, from the Balkan Peninsula eastward and southeastward, whereas "Far East" designated the newly opening lands of China, Japan, and Indo-China. Later in the nineteenth century, with increasing involvement in Persia and India by Britain and France, "Near East" became the designation for Ottoman territories, including those in the Balkans, and "East" applied to India and adjacent areas. The breakup of the Ottoman Empire after World War I disrupted the political unity of the Near East, as it had come to be defined by Europeans, and thus the term lost its geographical exactness.

In 1902, the advocate of expanded U.S. sea power, Captain Alfred T. Mahan, employed the name "Middle East" for an indefinite area around the Gulf. Potential applicability of the designation was reinforced in the late 1930s when the British government applied "Middle East Command" to military forces in the area that extended from the central Mediterranean into the Indian subcontinent. Gradually, especially after the Middle East Command Headquarters was moved to Cairo, the designation for the military command came to be applied to the area itself. Books, journals, and organizations showed a growing preference for Middle East, as did the Washington-based Middle East Institute and its *Middle East Journal,* founded in 1946.

The National Geographic Society entitled its map of the area in the early 1960s "Lands of the Eastern Mediterranean (Called the Near East or the Middle East)." By the mid-1970s, however, the society's maps of the region carried unqualified "Middle East" titles. The official designation of the U.S. Department of State geographic bureau responsible for the area is Bureau of Near Eastern Affairs (NEA), but informal usage favors Middle East. The U.S. military services followed the British precedent and used Middle East after World War II, and the Central Intelligence Agency has long used that designation in its public reports. Current British usage is predominantly Middle East, and the United Nations generally uses that designation, although some UN statistical series use Near East.

In an effort to avoid the implication of a Eurocentric perspective, some specialists have sought more objective terminology, favoring the designation "Southwest Asia." Taking this effort one step further, Cressey urged use of the portmanteau word "Swasia," as short for Southwest

Map 1-2. *Map delineating the Middle East as defined for this book. Only international boundaries, country names, capital cities, and seas are shown. Radius of the circle is 1,250 miles/2,012 km.*

Asia.[1] Southwest Asia is used to some extent, but Swasia is rarely employed. The toponym "Middle East" is used in this book, both because it is well accepted in international usage and also because "middle" connotes the region's central location, its function as a tricontinental hub, and its role as a strategic bridge. Moreover, Egypt, an essential part of the region, lies in northeast Africa.

Delimitation

The geographical limits of the region are more debatable than is its toponym, and areas ac-

cepted as integral elements of the Middle East vary somewhat from study to study. The problem is periodically explored if not settled.[2]

Following the reasoning of the Department of State geographer in the 1950s, this book defines the Middle East as shown in Map 1-2, which includes sixteen countries. However, Cressey added Afghanistan, to the east of Iran; Fisher also included part of Libya, to the west of Egypt;[3] and Beaumont, Blake, and Wagstaff included all of Libya.[4] The sixteen countries that are the focus of this book are considered as the Middle East on the latest maps published by the National Geographic Society, Department of State, Central Intelligence Agency, John Bartholomew (leading British map agency), and other international agencies.

Current histories of the Middle East vary still more in coverage. A few include not only Libya but also the Sudan, and like some geographers and anthropologists, some historians include all of North Africa.

There is appreciable validity in including the countries of North Africa, as since the early years of Islam, that region has been linked in many ways with the Near East. This link has meant inter alia that North Africa is also Arab and Muslim. Arabs often refer to the area of northwestern Africa as the Maghrib (Maghreb, west) and to the Arab lands east of Libya as the Mashriq (east). Even Turkey has past links with the Maghrib because of onetime Ottoman holdings in North Africa, and Iranian lands were a core area of the Abbasid Empire when it controlled the Maghrib. If land links between the Maghrib and the Mashriq faltered, maritime links along the Mediterranean could sustain the commercial and cultural ties.

Nevertheless, despite the religious and historical links, certain differences have existed between northwestern Africa and the Middle East proper. The Mashriq has had more intimate relations with Turks and Persians, given that Byzantine and then Ottoman political control was both stronger and lasted longer in the Mashriq than in the Maghrib. Christian influence has persistently been appreciable in the Fertile Crescent, much less so in the Maghrib. Lands west of the Nile have had their own regional influences and, unlike the Mashriq realm, were subject to direct European colonization in the nineteenth century. Especially since World War II, the Arab states of the Mashriq have been increasingly interactive with one another, despite periodic divisive influences; and although each is locked in hostility rather than cooperation with its Arab neighbors, Israel on the west and Iran on the east are increasingly involved in the region. Turkey is similarly becoming interlinked with its pre-1918 imperial provinces.

Although the Middle East is the core of the Islamic culture realm, the "Muslim world" must be clearly differentiated from the Middle East and from the Middle East–North Africa area. Lands in which the Islamic religion and civilization are dominant extend well into West Africa on the west and far into central and southern Asia and Australasia on the east. Central Asia, with its famous Islamic urban centers of Samarkand, Tashkent, Merv (Mary), Bukhara, and Balkh, was more closely linked with Middle East core areas from the seventh to the eighteenth centuries than was the Maghrib. However, conquest of central Asia by Russia during the late nineteenth century broke virtually all of the links, and the five new (since 1991) independent states of Kazakhstan, Kyrghyzstan, Tajikistan, Turkmenistan, and Uzbekistan—even though Muslim—cannot categorically be included in the current Middle East region. It is, nevertheless, noteworthy that Iran especially, but also Turkey and Saudi Arabia, is vigorously seeking to interconnect with the new Muslim states that were formerly Soviet constituent republics, including Azerbaijan in the Caucasus.

Regional Unity of Empires

Interwoven historical-political-geographical developments have, over many centuries, exercised integrating influences on the region. For 4,000 years, up to the end of World War I, the Middle East experienced varying degrees of control by a series of great empires centered in several power cores or foci in the region. The empires echo many familiar names: Babylonian, Hittite, Egyptian, Assyrian, Chaldean, Persian, Seleucid, Ptolemaic, Roman, Byzantine, Parthian, Sassanian, Umayyad, Abbasid, and Ottoman. A score of other smaller empires are less familiar: Aramaean, Phoenician, Sabaean, Nabataean, and others.

Except for the Roman Empire, which was governed from outside the Middle East, the major empires centered successively in four focal points of power: Mesopotamia, Asia Minor, Nile Valley, and Iranian Plateau, with the Syrian realm a possible fifth. Each of the power foci has functioned two or three times as an imperial power center over the millennia, and at one time or another, each major part of the Middle East has controlled most or much of the rest of the region;

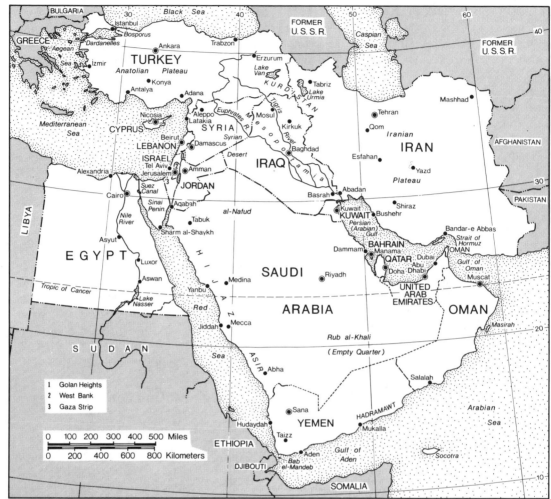

Map 1-3. *Reference map showing most of the names frequently used in this book. Note latitudes and interpenetration of land and water.*

conversely, almost every part of the Middle East has been controlled by each of the other major parts. During periods of close political unity, an interchange of ideas, mores, goods, and people among areas added to a unifying cultural identity. The roles of these power foci and of additional minor cores are a major theme of this book and will be analyzed in both their historical and geopolitical contexts (see Chaps. 2 and 11).

Aims and Concepts: A Glance

In recognition of the reciprocal relationships between geography and history, this book integrates historical highlights with a geographical analysis of patterns, particularly cultural patterns. These cultural patterns, very much emphasized in this study, are especially influenced by time, so that process becomes an essential element in the analysis. Biophysical patterns generally change less slowly but likewise yield to noteworthy processes. We shall, therefore, examine the interaction of people and biophysical phenomena not only in the context of their spatial relations but also in the context of their historical processes.

Further, geography emphasizes the complementary character of the patterns of human activity and natural elements, revealing its dual character—cultural and physical. Human or cultural elements include both people (their number, distribution, ethnic types, and other group characteristics, including their sense of identity) and their great variety of works (settlements, agriculture and related facilities, transportation routes and facilities, industries, and other cultural features). Major biophysical or natural elements include landforms, water resources, climate, soils, vegetation, animal life, and mineral resources.

After a discussion of the historical foundations (Chap. 2), the patterns of the foregoing elements are examined from both a systematic and a regional perspective. Chapters 3 through 11 examine the area from a broad systematic or topical perspective, examining a succession of element patterns, both natural and cultural. Chapters 12 through 22 then shift perspective and examine the regions of the Middle East. In this regional approach, the overall Middle East region is subdivided into meaningful segments (subregions or minor regions) that are interpreted both as individual units and as interrelated parts of the whole. For the purposes of this book, the main regional unit of analysis is the sovereign nation or state (Map 1-3). Thus, we shall study the Middle East not only as a whole, in terms of the elements or topics, but also as sixteen state/regions. Within each state (or country), the component "landscapes" or third-order regions (that is, sub-subregions) receive attention and are clearly numbered on the respective country maps.

Perceptions of environment vary from one cultural group to another and change over time. For example, to the Bedouins of eastern Saudi Arabia during the early twentieth century, their habitat was a typical desert area in which they, as nomadic pastoralists, could wander with their flocks in search of pasturage. By contrast, the petroleum geologists and engineers at midcentury, concentrating on subsurface features, perceived that same desert as an area of potential petroleum resources. This book also gives consideration to such varying environmental perceptions.

In summary, this geographical study of the Middle East focuses on spatial relations among peoples, human activities, and biophysical elements—their overall configuration and also microlevel interactions. In the process, the analysis reveals both variations and similarities within the region, its unity and diversity, with a focus on those factors that are most influential in giving the contemporary Middle East its remarkable mosaic of interacting patterns.

2

Patterns of Time: Historical-Geographical Foundations

Persistence of Patterns

A Succession of Landscapes

Having evolved over thousands of years and a wide range of environments, the Middle East's cultural mosaic and political patterns are exceedingly complex. Chronologically successive cultures and empires have partially erased and yet partially preserved preceding patterns, creating by this long development a geographical palimpsest. This sequential development and its traces in the modern Middle East are the themes of this chapter, which deals with the historical political geography of the region.

Evidence of sequent occupance,[1] or the settlement and exploitation of the same region by successive cultures, dates from prehistoric times and characterizes many Middle Eastern landscapes. In the narrow coastal plain of southern Lebanon, for example, a modern oil pipeline extends along or over Ottoman Turkish buildings, medieval Muslim mosques, a Crusader castle, Byzantine mosaics, Roman tombs, ruins of the Phoenician port of Sidon, Bronze Age pottery shards, and Neolithic flints. The wrinkled hand of the past has fashioned much of the landscape of the Middle East.

Even if ruins and artifacts from the distant past are not visible on the surface, they are often stratified in successively older layers beneath the surface. In the more favorable environments of the Middle East, few excavations fail to yield some kind of evidence of ancient human occupa-

tion or use of the land. The past is nearly always present.

Heritage of Patterns

Prior to surveying the evolution of the regional palimpsest, we can gain appreciation of the significance of the region's long heritage by glancing at six selected topics as examples of that heritage. These examples underscore the relevance of even the distant past to present-day patterns and problems.

1. Religion. Certain sites and towns settled in ancient times had religious motivations or gained religious importance for later groups. Many of the centers have retained their significance or have achieved even greater emotional impact, so that they attract hundreds of thousands of pilgrims and secular tourists annually, thereby maintaining major economic importance. For example, before the development of Saudi Arabia's oil fields, pilgrims to Mecca and Medina provided the major basis for the kingdom's economy. Similarly, control over Jerusalem generated foreign exchange for the Ottoman Empire, later for Jordan, and after 1967 for Israel. Religious sites often hold significance for multiple religious groups, leading to disputes over which historical "layer" is to be recognized or preserved or excavated. Such controversies center on several sites in and around Jerusalem.

2. Infrastructure. Infrastructural features—basic facilities that support other development, including irrigation systems, caravan routes, and hillside terracing to facilitate farming—have evolved over many centuries. Numerous ancient infrastructures still survive and continue to enhance the value of particular areas and to influence relative levels of prosperity in the region. The middle and lower Tigris-Euphrates Valley, the Nile Valley and Delta, and the Jordan Valley, for example, have been developed over thousands of years into productive irrigated farming areas. Such development required enormous efforts by earlier peoples to achieve the clearing of dense vegetation, drainage, leveling, cultivation, irrigation by means of an elaborately engineered system of canals, and restoration after periodic flooding. Thus, modern economies rely on ancient infrastructures and on the cultural heritage of ancient technologies.

3. *Natural Resources.* Settlements and human activities have long correlated with patterns of natural resources in the Middle East, notably those of water, fertile soils, and more recently, oil. Natural resource sites often show signs of a remarkable sequent occupance, exhibiting infrastructural elements from Roman aqueducts to modern pipelines. In addition, however, certain ecological problems persist. Increasingly serious difficulties are associated with salt-impregnated soils resulting from faulty irrigation of poorly drained areas or from soil erosion caused by cultivating steep slopes or by overgrazing. Stone implements found along former lakeshores in deserts of the Arabian Peninsula signal later environmental deterioration. Meanwhile, new areas have become habitable, with oil providing an economic base and with new technologies such as pumping and desalination providing the necessary water. The long history of civilization in the Middle East yields practical information about the area's patterns of natural resources and their evolution over time.

4. *Strategic Features.* The strategic significance of Middle East seas, straits, coastal plains, mountain passes, river valleys, and major trade and invasion routes was displayed in ancient times and persists in the late twentieth century despite modern technology. For example, the Strait of Hormuz and the Gulf are both still important despite sophisticated military aircraft and missiles.

5. *Culture and Art.* Virtually every contemporary city in the Middle East has developed on the site of an ancient town. Excavations for foundations of modern buildings commonly uncover statues, monuments, or ruins of earlier occupation. Logically enough, certain locational factors exercise a persistent attraction for human occupation and certain cross-country routes. Ruins of monuments and other structures, found by the thousands throughout the settled Middle East, have become major sources of tourist revenues for many countries in the region, and transportable artifacts, inscriptions on stone and clay, documents on papyrus and vellum, and other antiquities are preserved in museums both within and outside the Middle East. Such items are valuable for research, their economic benefits, and understanding of the historical evolution of the area.

6. *Conflict.* Sequent occupance over the millennia has resulted in competing claims to the same lands and pressure on inhabited areas to accommodate high population growth, refugees, and new immigrants. The founding of the modern state of Israel, in which a Jewish population has largely displaced a Palestinian—primarily Muslim—one, exemplifies this type of conflict. The war between Iran and Iraq in the 1980s echoed numerous territorial and religious conflicts of earlier periods. Thus, any analysis of modern conflicts in the region must take cognizance of the roots of those conflicts in the area's historical political geography.

Early Patterns

Primitive People and Pristine Environments

The more favorable Middle East environments attracted human habitation as early as the Paleolithic, or Old Stone Age, contemporary with Pleistocene glaciation (about 1.6 million years ago to 12,000 BC). Primitive Paleolithic human (or humanoid) groups were environmentally bound to sites that offered fresh water, easily gathered food, and natural shelters, especially caves. Particularly favorable sites were found in the areas marked by the western and eastern limbs of the Fertile Crescent (Map 2-1). The ear-

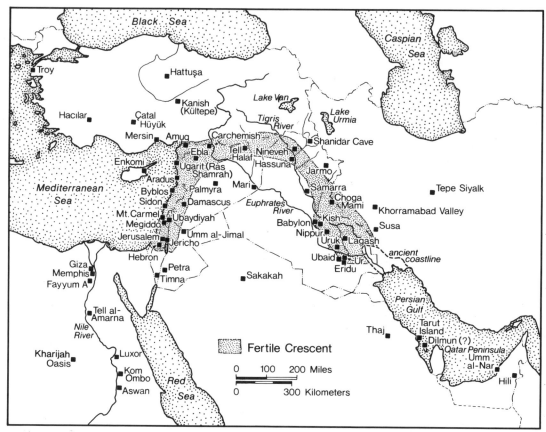

Map 2-1. *Selected major ancient sites. The Fertile Crescent (stippled) is often referred to in the text.*

liest known humanoid occupance site in the region, dating from more than one million years ago, is in northern Saudi Arabia, near the village of Shuwayhitiyah. The study of this site in the mid-1980s introduced an entirely new concept of human migration from the generally accepted area of hominid origin in East Africa into Asia. Stone tools from several of these extremely ancient sites in Arabia have now been found.[2] Until the 1980s, the earliest site studied dated from 600,000 years ago and is at Ubaydiyah, on an ancient lakeshore in the Jordan Valley just south of the Sea of Galilee. Numerous Paleolithic sites more than 100,000 years old are scattered from the Nile Valley to the piedmont arc around Mesopotamia.

Climatic changes that caused the northward retreat of the last ice sheets in Eurasia about 15,000 years ago also modified the regional ecol-

ogy of the Middle East. Open woodlands and grasslands soon characterized the Fertile Crescent, in contrast to the damp forests that invaded Eurasian areas uncovered by the melting and retreating glaciers. As one consequence, the Fertile Crescent population increased and developed, ushering in the Mesolithic period, or Middle Stone Age—sometimes called Epipaleolithic—which began about 12,000 BC.

Neolithic Revolution in a Special Environment

Ameliorating climatic conditions after 9000 BC brought further steady improvements in the Fertile Crescent environment, which encouraged not only an increase in the number of Mesolithic peoples but also the growth and spread of wild plants and animals that constituted the humans' food supply. This favorable environment of grasslands with scattered trees became the native habitat of early forms of wheat and barley, varieties of which still grow along field borders in the northern Fertile Crescent. After wild varieties of the two cereals had been widely harvested for many centuries, they were gradually domesticated and cultivated along with other major food plants, including vegetables and nut trees. At about the same time, animals that still dominate the farm scene were domesticated—sheep, goats, cattle, pigs, and dogs.

Thus, a particular environment, a special plant community, and an adaptive population combined to initiate the Neolithic—the New Stone Age—in the Fertile Crescent about 8000 BC. Heralded especially by the agricultural revolution, the Neolithic period also saw the systematic development of organized settlements. Such settlements were not feasible prior to the planned cultivation of plants and domestication of animals, so that the agricultural and urban revolutions functioned reciprocally. Moreover, these stimulated, or at least were accompanied by, a further complex of cultural processes: political administration, organized religion, trade, and writing in both Mesopotamia and Egypt.

The Archaeological Tell

Giving mute, fascinating, and vital testimony regarding Neolithic and later settlements is the archaeological mound, a common feature of the Middle East landscape. Usually referred to by the Semitic name *tell*,[3] an archaeological mound marks an ancient site on which successive settlements were established on the debris of earlier ones. Typical mounds, or tells, contain layers of cultural remains accumulated over thousands of years, the height of the mound generally indicating the length of time the site was occupied. With characteristically flat tops and sharply sloping sides, tells are prime targets for archaeological excavations. Correlation of finds among tells reveals patterns of cultures and settlement, including economic and political relations, that existed more than 5,000 years ago.

Of the thousands of tells scattered over the Middle East, several score are world renowned and attract hundreds of scholars and tourists annually. Familiar examples include: Troy, in northwestern Asia Minor; Babylon, in central Mesopotamia; and Jericho, in the Jordan Valley (all shown on Map 2-1).

Agriculture, Cities, and Civilization

The human advance from food gathering to food producing about 7000 BC[4] and the consequent expansion of the food supply accompanied a great increase in population in more favorable areas. As well as providing a more balanced diet, agriculture also permitted production of a food surplus for nonproductive seasons and famines. In addition, farming permitted and encouraged experimentation, cooperative planning, and a concentration of people into villages, which resulted in a widening of social exchange, organization, and trade within and among settlements. Food-storage facilities, key evidence of early agriculture, and food-preservation techniques required group planning.

About 5500 BC, Fertile Crescent farmers took another giant step forward and minimized their dependence on local rainfall: They extended, then gradually shifted, farming from the Zagros piedmonts above the Tigris-Euphrates Basin down to the Mesopotamian plain along the riverbanks. The new agriculture was irrigated cultivation, utilizing a system of canals to feed river water to the cultivated fields.

Along with the earlier rainfed farming advances, irrigation farming accompanied or had a "feedback" effect on key social developments in Mesopotamia: cooperative planning; organized engineering; expanded storage facilities for harvest surpluses; trade relations to exchange excess food for other items; cities to accommodate people, goods, and expanded activities; defenses for the protection of food supplies, irrigation works, settlements, and temples; centralized administration to apportion water and to coordinate activities; and for inventories and trade, a system of writing,[5] the basis for future law, literature, and long-distance communication.

Evidence of origins of agriculture in areas outside Mesopotamia is contradictory. Rather than having been borrowed from the Tigris-Euphrates Basin, systematic agriculture in the Nile Valley may have had independent beginnings. Certainly, farming began very early in Egypt, as it did also in Southeast Asia. However, evidence for Mesopotamia as the source area for the diffusion of settled agriculture remains strong.

Specific innovations developed as Mesopotamian irrigation agriculture evolved. The plow appeared about 3000–4000 BC; the wheel was well known in Mesopotamia by 3500 BC, but apparently not in Egypt until 1700 BC; and stamp and cylinder seals (ancestors of writing) had appeared in some quantity by 3500 BC. Impressive temples had been constructed in Uruk (Erech of the Old Testament, Warka in modern Iraq) by 3200 BC; earliest evidences of writing appeared about 3200 BC, and cuneiform (wedge-shaped) writing on clay was common by 2400 BC; and a dozen major Sumerian cities, and many more villages, existed in Mesopotamia by 2700 BC.

Excavated remains of some of the early Mesopotamian cities reveal cultural achievements that were remarkably advanced for their time (4000–3500 BC). Areal extents and estimated populations of the cities, as well as the architecture and artistic decorations of temples and palaces, have fascinated both specialists and casual observers. The ruins of Uruk, visible under a mantle of sand southeast of present-day Baghdad (Map 2-1), suggest an ancient population of 50,000, and the outline of the walls extends for 5.6 miles/9 km. Terraced tower temples, or ziggurats, dominated several of the cities on the Mesopotamian plain, and the Hanging Gardens of Babylon and the Tower of Babel of the Old Testament were almost certainly ziggurats. The building of terraced or stepped towers in Mesopotamia was generally contemporary with pyramid construction in Egypt, and the stepped design of the oldest known pyramid along the Nile suggests that it was borrowed from the Mesopotamian ziggurat concept (Fig. 2-1).

Thus, evidence from 5,000 years ago clearly shows a remarkable interaction between people and environment in the Tigris-Euphrates Basin. Irrigation farming and urban development were twin manifestations of the evolving and expanding early culture.

One major factor in the human-environmental relationship was the availability of building materials for the growing number of structures erected in Mesopotamia. In the southern part of the basin, only the clays and silts laid down by the Tigris and Euphrates rivers on their lower alluvial plain were directly available for use as building materials. Unshaped river mud (*tawf*) supplied the material for the earlier structures in the area, and it is still a common construction material for houses in villages of southern Iraq. Later structures were of sun-dried mud brick, and still later buildings were faced with fired brick. Southern Mesopotamian ziggurats, temples, and palaces of the third and second millennia are, therefore, less well preserved than are the massive Egyptian temples and pyramids, which were constructed of the limestone that was plentiful along the Nile Valley. Similarly, Assyrian palaces in northern Mesopotamia, built of limestone from nearby quarries, have survived wonderfully well (Fig. 2-2).

Historical-Political Evolution

The rise and expansion of Middle East empires after 4000 BC display pattern dynamics that are still relevant to the modern region. For this reason, the following condensed survey of the evolution of ancient and medieval patterns serves as a prelude to studying the modern region.

Early Mesopotamian States

Middle East recorded history begins in the fourth millennium BC in southern Mesopotamia with the Sumerians, whose origins are unknown and whose written language is unrelated to any other known language. The earliest records show them in control of the irrigation works and related settlements in ancient Sumer, whether or not they built the impressive installations. Functioning as city-states, the major cities of Sumer in the middle of the third millennium BC were Eridu, Uruk, Ur (later Ur of the Chaldees, home of Abraham of both the Old Testament and the Quran [Koran]), and others shown on Map 2-2. The partially excavated ruins of these famous settlements of 4,500–5,000 years ago now lie well away from any river, but the towns were originally established along the banks of the Euphrates, which later changed course. The banks of the slower and more manageable Euphrates offered

Figure 2-1. *The step pyramid of Zoser at Saqqara, a few miles southwest of Cairo, is considered to be the oldest of the large Egyptian pyramids (dating from about 2723 BC), predating the great Giza pyramids by at least a century.*

Figure 2-2. *The ruins of Nineveh, across the Tigris River from Mosul, Iraq, are one of the world's great archaeological sites. Recent digs directed by Dr. David Stronach found new evidence at the southeast gate (Halzi Gate) regarding the fall of the Assyrian capital. Dr. Stronach and the gate are shown here.*

Map 2-2. *Mesopotamia and adjacent lands showing earliest known states as well as earliest known cities—Uruk, Eridu, Ur, Lagash, and others. Dashed line indicates approximate limits of the Old Babylonian Empire.*

greater advantages for the siting of Sumerian cities and fields than did the banks of the more rapidly flowing Tigris, advantages that are still factors in urban locations in the late twentieth century.

North of the Sumerians lived the Akkadians, first of numerous Semitic groups to enter Mesopotamia. They probably originated in the Arabian Peninsula, a source region for successive waves of Semitic peoples into the Fertile Crescent for 3,000 years. The Akkadians overwhelmed the Sumerians about 2335 BC, unified the former city-states, and developed the first known empire. The Akkadian Empire quickly spread into the Zagros Mountains on the east and to the Mediterranean Sea on the west, and the Akkadian language became the lingua franca, or common language, of the civilized Middle East for several centuries. After a short but productive period, the Akkadian heartland was overrun about 2200 BC by the Gutians from the Zagros

Mountains. A precursor of many later invasions of Mesopotamia from the mountains and plateau east of the Tigris—the latest in the 1980s—the Gutian adventure collapsed after less than a century.

Reemerging as a culturally mixed people, the Sumerians established a United Sumer and Akkad with a capital at Ur. This Sumerian Empire reached its peak of brilliance about 2000 BC, developing a thriving trade with the Indus Valley peoples and establishing ports of trade on the sea route to the Indus. Ruins of such ports have been found on islands in the Gulf, especially on Bahrain, where excavations have uncovered well-preserved ruins of what is believed to have been the Dilmun referred to in Sumerian records.[6]

The first Babylonian Empire emerged soon after 2000 BC and absorbed Sumer. It was created by another Semitic group, the Amorites ("westerners"), who immigrated into central Mesopotamia from the Syrian Desert about 2000 BC. Having established a power center in Babylon, they expanded their control over all of Mesopotamia. Between 1792 and 1750 BC, Babylonia was ruled by one of the most famous kings in oriental history, Hammurabi the Great. Hammurabi's famous legal code collected and systematized Sumerian and Akkadian laws from earlier centuries and brought a new sophistication to political administration and control. Babylon and Babylonia played important roles in Mesopotamia for more than 2,000 years.

Other noteworthy power centers evolved and expanded in several parts of the Middle East and adjacent areas after 1700 BC, emphasizing the persistence of the ebb and flow of imperial realms. Mesopotamia lost its isolated self-sufficiency as peoples with new languages and new cultures immigrated into Asia Minor, the Iranian Plateau, the Levant, and the Caucasus. Such groups included the Indo-European Hittites, who controlled Asia Minor for more than 400 years from their stronghold of Hattusa on the Anatolian Plateau. The Hittites destroyed Babylon during an incursion in the sixteenth century BC, after which the Indo-European Kassites emerged from the Zagros Mountains to rule the weakened Babylonian area for more than four centuries. Another group, the Hurrians (biblical Horites), spoke a language that was neither Semitic nor Indo-European and relied on an Indo-European warrior aristocracy and horse-drawn chariots to build the Kingdom of Mitanni about 1500 BC. Hurrian military power pushed the borders of Mitanni control westward to the Mediterranean and eastward to the Zagros.

However, of all the ancient Middle East civilizations and empires outside Mesopotamia, none could match the fabled culture of the Nile, the Pharaonic kingdoms of Upper and Lower Egypt.

Early Egypt

The steadily evolving Mesopotamian culture of the late Neolithic and early Bronze Age extended its influence not only eastward to the Indus Valley and beyond but also westward to the Nile Valley. Ancient cultures to which the Nile was already host adapted Mesopotamian influences and made them distinctly "Egyptian." For example, writing developed in Sumer as a practical method of recording inventories and trade transactions, and the relatively simple technique required quick incisions with a reed stylus on damp clay, both the reed and the clay being widely available. This concept of writing was apparently borrowed by the Egyptians, who used their own familiar materials, a bronze chisel and stone, to carve elaborate hieroglyphics for religious or royal inscriptions. Indeed, "hieroglyphic" means "sacred carving."

Basic environmental differences between Mesopotamia and Egypt influenced other historical and cultural differences. Both rivers of Mesopotamia, Tigris and Euphrates, have irregular flow regimes, flow in shallow beds, flood unpredictably (or did so especially before the hydraulic works of the twentieth century), shift courses, and generally lack dependable rhythm. The Nile, in contrast, has eroded a wall-bounded valley in the rock desert, has a regular floodplain and flood time (late summer), seldom shifts course, and follows a regular rhythm documented over centuries.

Although caution is necessary in seeking links between culture and environment, certain correlations can be drawn for the early Nile civilization. Egyptian cultural stability followed the rhythm of the river and was influenced by the relative isolation enforced by the desert beyond the Nile Valley. The Nile's physical unity facili-

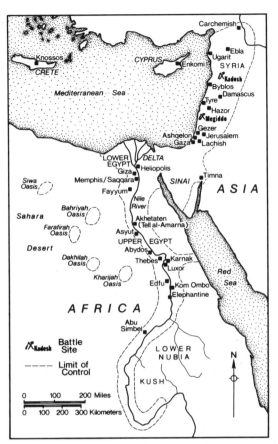

Map 2-3. *Ancient Egypt and the Levant showing major ancient sites. Dashed line shows approximate maximum limit of New Kingdom control.*

tated early political unity after a certain cultural level developed along the river (Map 2-3). Well before 3000 BC sailboats proceeded upstream, blown by the northeast trade winds, and downstream, carried by the river's current. Only limited east-west traffic left the Nile Valley, since regular commercial movement over the deserts flanking the valley was hazardous.

Also, united administration coordinated efforts to construct and maintain major canals, allocate water, protect riparian rights of access to the Nile, resurvey fields after the annual floods that deposited the fertile silt, and maintain a god-king leadership figure. The continuity and stability of the cosmos was a dominant concept among the ancient Egyptians; their perception of life as a benevolent rhythm was influenced by their observing preservation of wood, cloth, and papyrus, even the desiccated remains of people and animals, in their hot, dry climate.

The Egyptians constructed advanced architectural works in the form of tombs and temples. They created sophisticated jewelry, inlaid ornaments, vases, and sculpture. To obtain such materials as gold, ebony, cedar, and turquoise, the Egyptians carried on an active trade, especially in the eastern Mediterranean, northern Red Sea, and upper Nile. Trade relations among Egyptians, Minoans on Crete, Mycenaeans in several locations, Hittites in Asia Minor, Canaanites along the Levant coast, and other peoples in the Sinai and to the south engendered a cross-fertilization of ideas and techniques. Enriched by contacts with Mesopotamia, Anatolia, and Syria-Palestine (modern coastal Syria, Lebanon, and Palestine), Egyptian culture in its turn influenced Greek and Roman development, and thereby Western civilization.

Egyptian power declined after about 1090 BC and surrendered to outside control as Libyans, Ethiopians, and Assyrians imposed their respective dynasties. The Persians then conquered Egypt in 525 BC and held it, with only a brief interruption, for 200 years until it was seized by Alexander the Great in 332 BC. Under Alexander's Hellenistic successors, the Greek-Macedonian Ptolemies, Egypt achieved independence again for 250 years. It experienced a cultural resurgence before passing to Roman control in 30 BC after the suicide of Cleopatra, last of the Ptolemaic line. Egypt was not to be completely independent again under indigenous regimes for almost 2,000 years, until after World War II.

Mesopotamia to the Roman Conquests

Assyrian Empire. Along with Babylonia, Assyria was one of the most persistent of Fertile Crescent imperial states. It emerged in the mid-1350s BC, centered in the upper Tigris Basin, and dominated the Middle East for 300 years after 935 BC as the prototypal oriental monarchy (Map 2-4A). Assyrian cruelty is legend, but the empire also maintained control by means of its organization, efficiency, engineering, commerce, communications, and record keeping. During its eighth-century expansion, Assyria mastered the Syria-Pal-

estine realm, conquered the biblical kingdom of Israel, and in the latter case dispersed the population, a practice the Assyrians often followed with conquered peoples. The Assyrians themselves disappeared from history after being overwhelmed by Babylonians and Medes, who took Nineveh in 612 BC (Fig. 2-2). Modern-day Assyrians have a different religion and are not known to have any connection with the ancient Assyrians.

Discoveries in the ruins of Assyrian capitals and other cities—Assur, Nineveh, and the palace complexes at Khorsabad and Nimrud—in the early nineteenth century launched modern systematic archaeology and stimulated an appreciation of ancient Mesopotamian history as it emerged from the translation of some of the 22,000 clay tablets found in the palace library at Nineveh.

Neo-Babylonian (Chaldean) Empire. With Assyria destroyed, Babylonia once again became the dominant power in Mesopotamia. This Neo-Babylonian Empire was led for almost a century by the Chaldeans, a Semitic people from the Syrian Desert, like the Semitic Amorites of the Old Babylonian Empire 1,400 years earlier. The great imperial capital, Babylon, was revitalized by the Chaldean king Nebuchadrezzar the Great (also known as Nebuchadnezzar), who reigned 604–562 BC. Its Hanging Gardens (a ziggurat with planted terraces) were considered one of the Seven Wonders of the Ancient World, and the Ishtar Gate remains impressive even in ruins. The extensive ruins of Nebuchadrezzar's palace were very impressive but were somewhat depreciated by unduly extensive reconstruction by the Iraqi government during the 1980s. In any case, Babylon's excavated ruins afford significant insight into the life of 2,000 to 4,000 years ago. The biblical account of the destruction of Jerusalem and other Judean cities by Nebuchadrezzar and of the deportation of the Judeans into Babylonian exile in 586 BC provided an enduring record of this monarch and his empire.

Persian (Achaemenid) Empire. After its brilliant Chaldean revival, Babylonia fell to the Persian king Cyrus the Great in 539 BC. The city of Babylon itself, captured without a struggle, survived

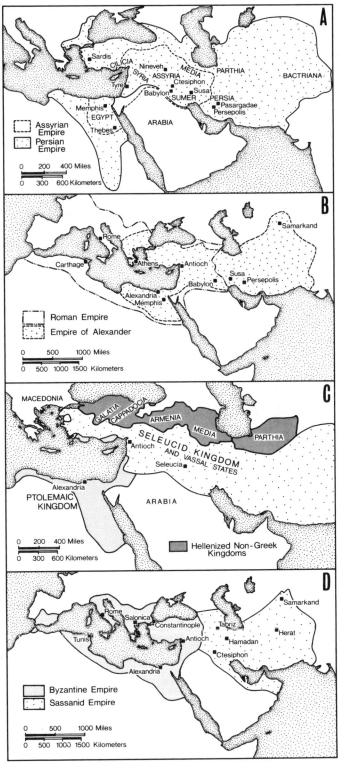

Map 2-4. *Major Middle East–Mediterranean empires from before 1000 BC to the rise of Islam.*

for another six centuries—Alexander the Great died there in 323 BC—but by AD 100 it had been abandoned. The Chaldean Babylonian Empire was the last native Mesopotamian state of antiquity. The Tigris-Euphrates Basin was ruled by outside powers for the next 2,500 years, well into the twentieth century, and the strategic narrow interfluve (area between the rivers) between Babylon on the west and Baghdad on the east served repeatedly as a location for successive imperial capitals.

The Persians were members of an Indo-European tribe who swept down on Babylonia from their stronghold on the Iranian Plateau. The plateau had already disgorged the Gutians and the Indo-European Kassites and Medes, and from it later erupted other conquering Persians and Persian-related groups—Parthians, Sassanians, and Safavids. Thus, the Iranian Plateau has been the source area for Indo-European conquerors and immigrants into the Fertile Crescent as the Arabian Peninsula has been for Semitic invaders.

Having merged with the Medes, the Persians during the Achaemenid dynasty swiftly established an empire that was more extensive than any of its predecessors. Their territories reached from the Balkan Peninsula–Aegean Sea and Nile Valley on the west to the Indus Valley and Turanian Basin on the east (Map 2-4A). Thus, for the first time, one Middle East power center controlled all the other power centers, excepting only the barren and inaccessible Arabian Peninsula.

In addition, Persia profited from, inherited, and improved on Assyrian efficiency and communications. The Persian Royal Road from Susa (in southwestern Iran) to Sardis (in western Asia Minor, see Map 2-4A) permitted the rapid transportation of goods and messages and served as an early Middle Eastern Pony Express. Some already established cities played more powerful roles, especially Susa, Ecbatana (modern Hamadan), and the legendary Persepolis. Modern excavations, reconstructions, and studies of Persepolis are especially revealing (Fig. 2-3). The Persian Empire continued for more than 200 years until it was conquered by Alexander the Great between 334 and 326 BC. Although Persia never regained the territorial dominion of Achaemenid times, Iranian peoples again controlled the plateau within a century after Alexan-

der's death. They have shown themselves for 2,300 years to be a culturally and politically significant power.

Empire of Alexander. Leaving his small Macedonian home base in northern Greece in 334 BC, Alexander the Great had conquered the entire Persian Empire by 326 BC and had established his eastern frontier beyond the Indus (Map 2-4B). Alexander founded cities, brought about cultural interchange, and spread Hellenistic ideas and practices in the process of expanding his own empire beyond the limits of the preceding Persian borders. His death in Babylon at the age of 33 left a power vacuum that disrupted the carefully crafted unity of the Hellenistic Empire, and imperial lands were parceled out among Alexander's top generals. Ultimately, a threefold division emerged that, alongside revived Persian power, survived for 250 years.

Seleucid and Ptolemaic Empires. With slightly shifting boundaries, the two most important Hellenistic states in the Middle East were the Seleucid and the Ptolemaic (Map 2-4C), and ruins and other vestiges of these empires are still evident in scores of sites in Egypt and the Levant. Asia Minor fragmented into a complex mosaic of kingdoms. An Armenian state persisted for centuries and became the base for an Armenian national identity that still endures. The northeastern Iranian Plateau area embraced the Iranian Parthian kingdom, and a Hellenized Greco-Bactrian kingdom dominated lands farther east.

Hellenistic cultural influences continued into the Roman and Byzantine empires in the Middle East, spanning a period of almost 1,000 years. Two Hellenistic cities in the Middle East are noteworthy: Antioch became a prominent city and regional center in the Seleucid realm, and in the Ptolemaic kingdom, Alexandria, founded by Alexander near the mouth of the Nile, became a brilliant center of Hellenism with a large Greek population. Descendants of these Greeks still live in Alexandria, although most of them emigrated during the 1950s. Alexandria's lighthouse (Pharos), built about 300 BC, was one of the Seven Wonders of the Ancient World and aided navigation for 1,600 years. The Ptolemaic Empire ended with Cleopatra's suicide in 30 BC, when Egypt en-

Figure 2-3. *Persepolis in modern Iran. Wonderfully detailed bas-reliefs on staircase and platform of the Apadana (fifth century BC), built by Darius the Great and his son Xerxes, depict representatives of subject peoples and reveal much about the social and political situation of the time.*

tered 673 years of control by the Roman and eastern Roman empires. The Seleucid Empire also collapsed before the advancing Romans, and Syria became a Roman province in 64 BC.

Smaller Semitic Kingdoms. Other noteworthy cultures contemporaneous with the extensive empires just reviewed include those of the Canaanite-Phoenicians, Hebrews, and Aramaeans. The Hebrews, a Semitic tribe, appear to have emerged from the Arabian Desert, as did other Semites mentioned earlier. Legends of their early culture and migrations, typical of many tribal groups of the time, are recorded in the book of Genesis. These accounts include the exodus from Egypt, generally dated in the thirteenth century BC, and the entry into southern Canaan. The accounts yield valuable insights into both the Hebrew culture and also many of the attitudes of the time. In Canaan, the Hebrews not only confronted the native Canaanites in the hill country but also were long kept from the southern coast by other recent arrivals—the Philistines, one of the Sea Peoples. (It was from the Philistines that the later name of the area, Palestine, was derived.)

The biblical record indicates that a unified Israelite kingdom finally emerged (about 1020 BC) and lasted almost a century, dividing in 922 BC after the death of Solomon. The northern kingdom, Israel, lasted less than 200 years and was conquered by Assyrians in 722 BC, its people dispersed as the ten lost tribes. Judah, the southern kingdom, with Jerusalem as its capital, survived Israel by 136 years but fell to Nebuchadrezzar in 586 BC, when thousands of Judeans were deported to Babylon. Many returned to Judea after the 50 years of the Babylonian captivity, but hundreds remained, to form a thriving Jewish colony in Mesopotamia that lasted 2,500 years. For the returnees, Judea became a core of territorial contention among Ptolemaic Egypt, the Seleucids, Rome, and local kingdoms. It is interesting to note that from 922 BC until the present time, the Palestine area was a sovereign state under a native administration in de jure control of a unified territory for only a few decades under the Hasmoneans (Maccabees), a reign that was ended by the Romans in 63 BC. Most of the Jews of Palestine had been dispersed over the Mediterranean Basin and the Middle East by the middle of the second century after Christ.

The "land of Canaan" comprised the general area of the western Syria-Palestine realm. Although the individualistic Canaanite city-states maintained active cultural and economic relations, including language, religion, and trade, they failed to unify politically or militarily. Thus, they were vulnerable to invading Amorites, Israelites, Assyrians, and others, and the Canaanite civilization declined after the thirteenth century BC.

The north Canaanite Phoenicians, however, developed remarkable city-states around ports at Tyre, Sidon, Beirut, Byblos, Tripoli, and Aradus. (It is interesting to note that Tyre, Sidon, Beirut, and Tripoli reverted to some extent to their ancient roles of autonomous city-states during the breakdown of the political-territorial unity of Lebanon in the 1980s.) The Phoenicians developed an aggressive maritime trade, which reached as far as the western Mediterranean, and founded colonies over a wide area. Their most powerful colony, Carthage, challenged Rome itself for supremacy in the three Punic (Phoenician) Wars of the second and third centuries BC. While conducting their wide-ranging trade, the Phoenicians simplified and carried with them the first true alphabet, developed by Semitic peoples in the Levant. This alphabet was subsequently adapted by the Greeks, Etruscans, and Romans.

The Aramaeans were inland traders who diffused their culture along with their Semitic language. The Aramaic tongue spread along land trading routes and became the lingua franca of commerce and diplomacy from Egypt to Mesopotamia. It was still spoken in Syria and Palestine at the time of Christ. Damascus and other Aramaean city-states, biblical Aram, were overcome by the Hebrew King David, but they regained their independence and continued as Aramaean centers until conquered by the Assyrians in 732 BC. The Aramaean culture gradually faded, but dialects of the Aramaic language continued into the twentieth century in several church liturgies.

Roman and Successor Empires

Roman. Although Hellenistic control over much of the Middle East originated from an outside area (Macedonia), Rome was the first power from outside the region to maintain hegemony over large areas of the Middle East for a lengthy period. However, extensive as it was, Roman territorial control in the Middle East never equaled that of the Persian and Hellenistic empires (Map 2-4). Even so, Egypt and Syria-Palestine felt the lingering Roman influence until the seventh century after Christ, and Asia Minor did so for several centuries longer.

Roman legions failed to venture beyond Mesopotamia. They contended with Iranian-based armies along the Euphrates and in Armenia but were never successful in sustained desert operations. To symbolize their military presence, however, the Romans constructed lines of forts and boundary markers to form the Limes Arabicus (Arabian Boundary), similar to the Roman *limes* constructed in central Europe. In northwestern Syria, well-preserved stretches of Roman roads still exist, a part of ancient infrastructure underlying the modern Middle East. Hundreds of vestiges of Roman occupation—roads, theaters, temples, aqueducts, baths—are prominent features in the landscapes of Asia Minor, the Levant, and parts of Egypt, partly because Roman construction in those areas was monumental and well engineered (Fig. 2-4). Some structures combine Hellenistic, Roman, and Byzantine construction from different periods, and these Greco-Roman ruins attract many visitors to areas from Istanbul in the northwest to Dura Europos on the upper Euphrates in the east.

Parthian. Although Alexander destroyed the Persian Empire, the Iranian identity reasserted itself a century later through the Iranian Parthians. Emerging as a native kingdom in 248 BC, the Parthian Kingdom became an empire within 75 years, extending over the Iranian Plateau and Mesopotamia. Observing the historic strategic value of the narrowest width of the middle Tigris-Euphrates interfluve, the Parthians established twin capital cities, Seleucia and Ctesiphon—near the location of modern Baghdad in Iraq.

Sassanian. The Parthian Empire was overthrown and was succeeded in AD 226 by another Iranian empire, the Sassanian. The powerful Sassanians expanded northeastward across the Oxus River (modern Amu Darya, between the new republics

Figure 2-4. *Colonnaded street in the ruins of Jerash, a great Roman provincial city north of Amman. Note the well-paved street, which has a well-engineered storm drain underneath it.*

of Turkmenistan and Uzbekistan) and eastward to the Indus, as well as across the Gulf into the Qatif area of Arabia and into Oman (Map 2-4D). They maintained Ctesiphon as a capital and also inherited Rome as a perennial territorial adversary in Syria-Mesopotamia. The Sassanian Empire collapsed entirely under the assault of invading Arab Muslims in the 630s and 640s.

Byzantine. Although the western Roman Empire and its formerly great capital declined after the fourth century, the eastern empire and its capital thrived. Founded by the first eastern emperor, Constantine, and named after its founder, Constantinople was earlier Byzantium and later Istanbul. Steadily orientalized, the eastern empire became less Latin and more Greek and was finally referred to as the Byzantine Empire. Holding extensive lands for many centuries (Map 2-4D and Fig. 2-5), it gradually contracted until the only remaining territory was Constantinople and its environs, which fell to the Ottomans in the watershed year of 1453. Allowing for its ex-

pansions and contractions, the Byzantine Empire survived for 1,100 years, longer than any other empire in the Middle East.

Having battled the Sassanians to a standstill for control of the Fertile Crescent, the weakened Byzantines lost Egypt and the Levant in the 630s to the same Arab assault that overwhelmed the Sassanians. The Byzantines, however, were able to hold on to their Anatolian stronghold while the Sassanians lost not only Mesopotamia but also their entire Iranian Plateau power base. The Middle East had entered a new era, that of Islam.

Islamic Empires

The Arab eruption into Mesopotamia and Syria-Palestine in AD 633 was another in the series of Semitic waves from interior Arabia extending back over 3,000 years. This particular Arab invasion, however, involved many more people and far more territory than had previous incursions, and it had incalculably greater ramifications. With this invasion, the present cultural patterns of the Middle East began to emerge.

Figure 2-5, *Ruins of the large St. Sergius Basilica in Rasafah, a Byzantine city built on the site of a much older city mentioned in the Old Testament In lower right, the author seeks another angle from which to photograph. (Mildred M. Held photograph)*

The founder of Islam, the Prophet Muhammad, had unified the Arabs of the Hijaz (western Arabia) and then of the Arabian Peninsula. He achieved unification on three levels: a new religion (whose adherents were called Muslims—see Chap. 6), a political organization (virtually a theocracy), and ethnic identity. Precepts for all three are found in the Muslim scriptures, the Quran. After Muhammad's death in 632, dedicated Muslims poured northward to spread the faith and to seize new lands for its flowering. Within a century, Muslim forces appeared before Tours in France, the high point of their westward spread, and other Muslims held central Asia. At its maxi-

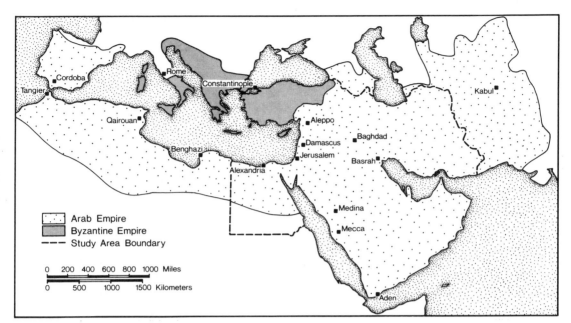

Map 2-5. *Arab Empire at its maximum extent, late eighth century. Arabs never succeeded in conquering Asia Minor.*

mum extent in the eighth century AD, the Arab Empire exceeded in size all previous Middle East empires and compared with the Roman Empire at its maximum (compare Maps 2-4 and 2-5). The Muslim invasion marked the first Semitic conquest of the Iranian Plateau, although the conquerors imposed only the religion of Islam and their alphabet, not their Semitic language or their racial (physical) characteristics.

However, even more than the Roman Empire, the Arab Empire and its successor Muslim empires and kingdoms shifted capitals and cores, broke into parts, recombined in different patterns, and changed composition. But unified or fragmented, the region retained one enduring characteristic—Islam as religion and culture. The development of Islam and the Muslim state were two highly integrated aspects of the same phenomenon.

With the founding of the Umayyad Empire in AD 661, power shifted from the Hijaz to Syria, and the new capital was Damascus. The character of the Muslim state altered accordingly, from a religion-centered theocracy to an empire imitative of Byzantine and Persian courts.

In AD 750, the Abbasid dynasty seized control of the Arab Empire and moved the center from Damascus to Mesopotamia. The Abbasids built their new capital, Baghdad, on the Tigris-Euphrates interfluve, which had been occupied by a succession of imperial capital cities earlier. The next century brought the reign of the Abbasid caliph, Harun al-Rashid, of *Arabian Nights* fame.[7] During the same century, however, evidence of the decline of the Abbasids appeared, as the court weakened and breakaway kingdoms rose, expanded, and were absorbed.

Seljuks, Crusaders, Mongols

Seljuks. Besides the breakaway states, several other kingdoms were established by invaders from outside the Middle East. During the tenth century, Seljuk Turks from central Asia moved onto the Iranian Plateau. The Seljuks entered Baghdad in 1055 but left the Abbasid caliphs as figureheads, from Mesopotamia they forced their way westward and, in the watershed battle of Manzikert north of Lake Van (1071), defeated Byzantine armies and carried Islam into inner Anatolia for the first time. Islam gradually expanded over all of Asia Minor and has remained entrenched there ever since. With the way open into Anatolia, the Seljuks established the Sultanate of Rum and indirectly paved the way for the later expansion of the Turkish Ottoman Empire.

Crusaders. The second group of states established by outside invaders arose primarily because of the Seljuk incursions and their threat to the Byzantines. After their defeat at Manzikert and with Seljuk territorial control continuing to expand, the Byzantines petitioned for help from the Roman Catholic feudal states of western Europe. Successive waves of Christians—French, English, German, Italian, and other Europeans, all labeled "Franks" by the Middle East Muslims—were sent in response to the Byzantine request. The human waves became known as the Crusades, the first beginning in 1096, succeeding ones in 1147, 1189, 1202, 1218, and 1228, and there were others unconnected with the original purpose. The First Crusade established the Crusader kingdoms, which occupied a relatively small area along a coastal strip at the eastern end of the Mediterranean. The last Crusader foothold fell in 1291. Although the Crusades had only a modest impact on the Middle East at the time, the reverse effects were momentous, since they were a major stimulus for the European Renaissance. In the Levant, numerous ruined Crusader castles remain as romantic symbols of early European imperialism in the Middle East. Some castles, like other more ancient Middle East monuments, served military purposes intermittently into the twentieth century because of their massive walls and strategic sites.

Mongols. In the thirteenth century, invading horse-mounted Mongol and Tatar-Mongol archers made far-ranging territorial conquests in the Middle East to add to their vast empires in Asia. Generally short-lived, the conquests nevertheless yielded the Il-Khanid dynasty in Persia (1256–1349) through Genghis Khan's grandson, Hulagu. Genghis Khan, Hulagu (who sacked Baghdad in 1258), and Tamerlane (Timur Leng, who took Baghdad in 1393) all laid waste extensive areas of the Middle East. So devastating was Hulagu's ravaging of Mesopotamia that the centuries-old complex irrigation system and the road system were not restored to their former efficiency until the twentieth century.

Ottoman Empire and Contemporaries

Like the Seljuks, the Ottomans were a Turkish tribe who converted to Islam in central Asia and then migrated onto the plateaus of Iran and Anatolia. Beginning in the early fourteenth century, the Ottomans expanded from a small principality in northwestern Asia Minor until they controlled a vast area from the Danube to Yemen. The Ottoman Middle East holdings remained fairly constant from the early 1600s until World War I—with the notable exception of Egypt, which gradually disengaged itself. Like the Byzantines, whom they displaced, the Ottomans gained and lost territories but were remarkable for their political longevity, as an unbroken dynasty held the sultanate for 600 years.

Reviving Persian political organization once again, a kingdom under the Safavids emerged in the Iranian Plateau in 1500. With changes in dynasty in 1736 (Afshars), 1750 (Zands), 1794 (Qajars), and 1925 (Pahlavis), Persia survived—periodically contending with the Ottomans over Mesopotamia—as a monarchy until early 1979 (its name was changed to Iran in 1935) and still survives as a dynamic Islamic republic.

Thus, from about 1500 until World War I, two major Middle East powers, each based in one of the two strongest power foci, contended with each other, primarily along the line of the Zagros piedmont: the Ottoman Empire, based in Anatolia, and the Persian Empire or Kingdom, based on the Iranian Plateau. Still occupying a third power focus, but with limits on its former greatness, Egypt gradually eased away from Ottoman control during the early nineteenth century and had passed under British protection by World War I. The interior of the Arabian Peninsula escaped Ottoman control and remained tribally fragmented until most of the peninsula was unified as Saudi Arabia in the 1930s.

Some Inferences

The foregoing review of the evolution of political-geographical patterns of the Middle East suggests several general observations. Lessons to be drawn from the review are significant and relevant not only as a basis for the rest of this book but also as guidelines for determining practical foreign policies in the region.

1. Four major power foci and two minor ones have appeared and reappeared in the Middle East throughout history: The Anatolian Plateau (Asia

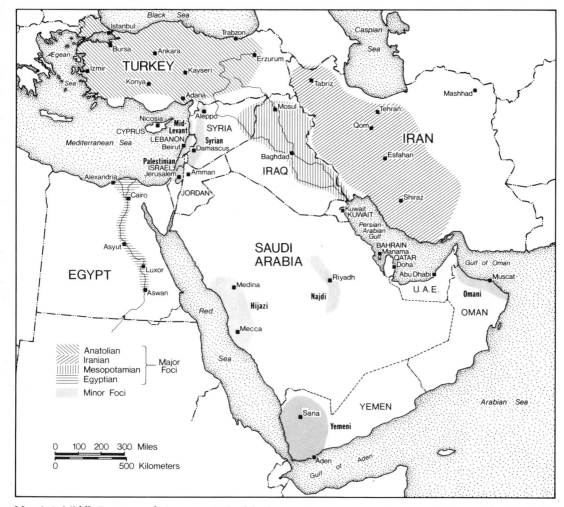

Map 2-6. *Middle East power foci or cores. Each of the four major power centers has controlled most of the Middle East at some time, but none has controlled all other centers simultaneously.*

Minor), Iranian Plateau, Mesopotamia (Tigris-Euphrates Basin), and Nile Valley are the four major foci, and the western Fertile Crescent and central and western Arabian Peninsula are the two minor foci. The Yemen and Oman areas have also served as centers of strength (Map 2-6).

2. The two most persistently powerful foci, and the two from which the greatest geographical areas have usually been controlled, have been the two intermontane plateaus, Anatolia and Iran. These two centers now host two of the three most populous states—which are also among the most powerful states—in the Middle East: Turkey, Iran, and Egypt.

3. No one power has ever succeeded in conquering and occupying the entire Middle East as the region is defined in Chapter 1. Regardless of the existing imperial power at any given point, some other part of the region maintained its independence.

4. The one area that has always been able to maintain its independence, or at least its separateness from outside powers, is the interior of the Arabian Peninsula (Najd). The peninsula was a focus of imperial territorial control during the middle of the seventh century, but otherwise the area has maintained its separateness except as a source of migrants who appeared in Syria and Mesopotamia between 2500 BC and AD 700.

5. Although Mesopotamia was the earliest power focus and remained the one focus for 1,700 years, it gradually weakened as a separate

center and later functioned as a focus of power only when connected to the Iranian Plateau center. Under the sovereignty of Iraq, Mesopotamia demonstrated renewed potency beginning in the 1980s.

6. The political-geographical history of the Middle East has, to a great extent, been centered on the interaction of the powers occupying Asia Minor and the Iranian Plateau. Each power often sought control of Mesopotamia, with Mesopotamia sometimes being used as a springboard against the power on the other side of the basin.

7. Powers centered in the three northern foci have controlled the Nile Valley at various times, but never has the Nile Valley power controlled any one of the three major northern foci. Rather, Egyptian control outside Egypt has been limited to the western limb of the Fertile Crescent (Syria-Palestine realm) plus some brief inroads into southeastern Anatolia by Egyptian forces in the 1830s.

Neither history nor geography can dictate the future. Changing technology, outside influences, or other developments might alter the relative significance of the several power foci in the Middle East. Since the 1950s, the emergence of Israel and the rise of the Middle East's petroleum age have unquestionably reorchestrated political, military, and economic influences. Yet to consider historical and geographical factors in the region's role as mere academic curiosities is to misread vital lessons and to risk repetition of the mistakes of the past. The roles of the centers in the twentieth century are considered in Chapter 11, which examines contemporary Middle East political-geographical development.

3

The Lands and
the Waters

An Overview

A basic tenet of geography is that physical features on the earth's surface and their related bioclimatic elements mutually interact with patterns of population, peoples, and human activities. This chapter and Chapters 4 and 5 focus on the biophysical elements of the Middle East; Chapters 6–11 consider peoples and their activities. Since the related factors of geomorphology (landforms) and climate (see Chap. 4) have the broadest effects on cultural and economic patterns, they are examined first.

Map 3-1 reveals that land and sea areas alternate like broad spokes around the Middle East hub, with four land areas forming great promontories into the seas and, conversely, four seas penetrating into the land. In the northwest, Asia Minor, embracing the Anatolian Plateau, comprises a peninsular bridge to southeastern Europe. Southeastward from eastern Anatolia, the Iranian Plateau extends into Asia proper. Continuing clockwise, there is a massive rectangular Arabian Peninsula, which split from Africa along the axis of the Red Sea. The southwestern quadrant of the Middle East is occupied by Egypt, the square northeastern corner of the continent of Africa. Finally, the regional hub consists of the Fertile Crescent area, which occupies the zone between the northern (Anatolian-Iranian) and southern (Egyptian-Arabian) belts of the region.

Alternately, five bodies of water touch or reach far into the Middle East land area. The deep Mediterranean Sea on the west washes the shores of six of the Middle East states. The Black Sea, to the north of Asia Minor, lies between Turkey and the other five littoral states and overflows to the Mediterranean through the straits of the Bosporus and Dardanelles. The Caspian Sea to the northeast is really an inland lake with no outlet to the sea, and its surface is well below sea level. The Persian/Arabian Gulf—or simply "the Gulf"—occupies the drowned, downbuckled tectonic trough between Arabia and Iran. The Red Sea, with its two extensions to the north and the related Gulf of Aden to the south, floods the great rift that separates the Arabian Peninsula from Africa.

Penetration of seas into the land has several major consequences. Physically, the seas—the Mediterranean especially—intersperse sources of moisture in areas that would be far more desertic without the seas. In addition, penetration of the seas means a great deal more coastline, which increases the number of outlets to and contacts with the outside world. The seaways provide, as they have for millennia, major routes for trade and movement of peoples, and the sailing of tankers up and down the Gulf, even during the 1980s war, exemplifies one utility of Middle East seas.

Major landform provinces and features of the Middle East originated generally because of a shifting of large segments of the earth's outermost shell. These earth crust pieces, or "plates," in the lithosphere[1] jostle one another periodically and in so doing profoundly affect one another's adjacent edges. According to the theory of plate tectonics,[2] at least four and perhaps six or more plates have collided or pulled apart to create the present pattern of the Middle East (Map 3-2). Typically, several plate contact zones are

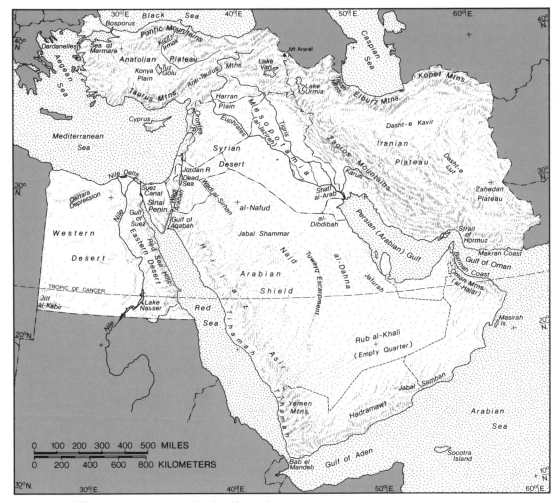

Map 3-1. *Middle East: Major geomorphic (landform) features.*

marked by major faults, some of which are still active and periodically cause destructive earthquakes. Other contact areas have resulted in compression-folded mountain ranges (the Zagros, for example) or downfolded troughs (the Gulf).

Although most of the gross landforms of the Middle East have evolved directly or indirectly from regional plate movements, smaller and more local forms have been shaped by other factors. Local earth movements, erosion by water or wind, and combined wind erosion and deposition are some typical factors. For example, some of the extensive sand deserts of Arabia are reshaped deposits of sand blown in from appreciable distances, sometimes hundreds of miles.

Elsewhere are extensive plains areas of "desert pavement." Here the surface is blanketed with a layer of pebbles that lag behind after finer particles have been blown away by persistent winds. This pavement of pebbles serves as an armor for the underlying sand particles so long as the deceptively delicate ecological balance is undisturbed. Unfortunately, that equilibrium has been completely upset in extensive areas by modern development, with its wheeled vehicles, construction equipment, bulldozers, and—most destructive of all—military tanks and the installation of trenches and bunkers. Wartime operations in Sinai and in northeastern Arabia, Kuwait, and southern Iraq especially destroyed the protective pebble pavement, exposing the under-

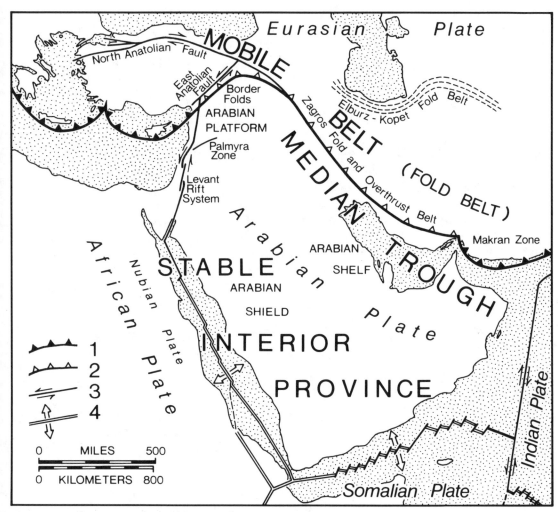

Map 3-2. *Tectonics in the Middle East are very complex, so many features are uncertain, but this map shows the better-defined aspects. Note the concentration of tectonic zones in eastern Turkey. Symbols: 1 = collision zone apparently involving subduction of seafloor along arcuate plate contacts; 2 = collision zone involving continental overthrusting; 3 = horizontal displacement along transform faults (arrows indicate left-lateral or right-lateral); 4 = seafloor spreading, the moving apart of the ocean's crust.*

lying sand to wind erosion and the new evolution of sand dunes.[3]

Running water, even though relatively limited, has profoundly altered some of the desert areas of the Middle East, although many forms shaped by streams were developed in earlier ages when rainfall was higher and streams were larger. Weathering and erosion of rock in arid areas have resulted in a greater angularity and sharpness of outline than are typically found in more humid areas, such as northern Turkey, where the silhouettes are more rounded.

Usually the result of tectonic plate shifts, significant seismic activity and effects of volcanism are widespread in the Middle East. The map of earthquakes (later in this chapter) both indicates zones of actively colliding plates and illustrates the high incidence of seismic events in Anatolia, Iran, and Cyprus. Colliding plates, separating plates, and some shearing plates generate outpourings of lava either explosively from volcanoes or quietly through vents and fissures. Anatolia especially has numerous classic volcanic cones, including Mount Ararat; and extensive areas of southwestern Syria, central Jordan, and especially western Saudi Arabia are buried under extensive lava flows.

Survey of Landforms

On a broad scale, the landform patterns of the Middle East may be grouped into three general structural and macro landform provinces: the Stable Interior Province, the Mobile Belt, and intermediate between the two, the Median Trough (see Map 3-2). This threefold division serves as a basis for a survey of major Middle Eastern landforms that will, in turn, aid in understanding the region's cultural patterns. Map 3-1 shows most of the features mentioned below, but use of a more detailed map is recommended.

Stable Interior Province

The Stable Interior Province lies in the southwest of the Middle East, its core an extensive area of ancient metamorphic basement rock composing the Nubian-Arabian Shield. Planed down during millions of years, the shield is primarily plateau in character but has been uptilted to mountains on either side of the Red Sea rift.

The shield's ancient basement rocks, some more than 1 billion years old but most 890–560 million years old by radiometric dating, have split open along the Red Sea axis and are exposed along both uptilted coasts of this slowly widening rift. The shield was depressed around its flanks except to the southwest, and the flanks were covered by thousands of feet of sedimentary rocks, principally limestones. These sedimentaries now outcrop in and underlie the great arc of territory sweeping from northern Egypt through the Fertile Crescent countries and around the eastern and southeastern flanks of the Arabian Peninsula.

Egyptian Deserts. Between the Red Sea and the Nile Valley, the Eastern Desert of Egypt culminates in the Red Sea Hills, a moderately rugged and barren mountain mass of dominantly basement rocks of the Nubian Shield. West of the Nile, in the Western Desert, the shield is blanketed with relatively thin sedimentary strata to the south and additional, thicker, younger strata to the north. Depressions along the contact between the two different sets of thicknesses of sedimentary cover cradle five oases, and a much deeper depression, the Qattara, south of the Mediterranean coast, reaches 436 ft./133 m below sea level. (The significance of these depressions is examined in Chap. 20.) The Nile River flows along the separation between the two major deserts, and its great delta lies in a former embayment of the Mediterranean coast.

Arabian Peninsula. A narrow coastal plain, Tihamah, extends virtually the full length of the peninsula's Red Sea coast and is backed by a formidable mountain range. This linear barrier, the Hijaz Mountains, averages 7,000 ft./2,135 m and forms the uptilted western edge of the Arabian Shield. Back of the Hijaz, the ancient basement rocks of the shield extend in a semicircle concave westward, to the heart of the Arabian Peninsula. There the Central Arabian Arch bowed up the shield, causing increased erosion to force an eastward retreat of the edge of the older sedimentary cover that formerly blanketed much of western Arabia.

The opening of the Red Sea rift, plus faulting along the edges, induced the extrusion of several extensive flows of basaltic lava—one as large as 7,720 miles^2/20,000 km^2—from both fissures and vents in the shield. Successive older lava series reach thousands of feet in thickness in the peninsula's southwestern corner and constitute the rugged mountains that give the High Yemen its character.

To the north, northeast, and southeast of central Arabia, the basement is depressed and is buried under layers of sedimentary rock, the Arabian Shelf. These sedimentaries have a vital significance in the world economy, since around and under the Gulf they contain the world's greatest known oil resources.

Sand, wind, aridity, and open space have combined to create three large and several small sand deserts in the Arabian Peninsula. In the south center lies the Rub al-Khali (Empty Quarter), the world's largest single sand dune area (see Fig. 1-1). In the north is the Nafud (or the Great Nafud), one-fifth the size of the Rub al-Khali. Extending in a great arc from the Nafud to the Rub al-Khali is a belt of red sand known as the Dahna.

At the southeastern corner of the Arabian Peninsula are the rugged and curious Oman Mountains (or Jabal al-Hajar), with elevations typically around 5,000 ft./1,525 m but peaking at 10,000 ft./3,048 m. Also a product of collision between the Arabian Plate and the Iranian subplate, the range is more related structurally and petrologically to the mountains of southwestern Iran than to neighboring parts of Arabia.

Syrian Desert. The same general sedimentary sequence found in the eastern Arabian Peninsula overlies the basement rocks in the Syrian Desert area in the heart of the Middle East. However, the dip of the strata in the central area is gentler, and large expanses of eastern Jordan, eastern and southern Syria, and western Iraq show level to undulating surfaces of Cretaceous limestones.

Jordan Valley and Related Features. A major geomorphic feature of the western Fertile Crescent is the Levant Rift System, a great trench that extends from the northwestern end of the Red Sea up the Gulf of Aqabah and along the axis of the Wadi al-Arabah, Dead Sea, Jordan Valley, and Bekaa of Lebanon to the Ghab Depression in northwestern Syria (Fig. 3-1). It thus extends through or along parts of Egypt, Saudi Arabia, Israel, Jordan, Lebanon, and Syria. This feature is considered by most specialists to be primarily a transform fault, similar to the San Andreas Fault in California, that resulted chiefly from rotation of the Arabian Plate away from the African Plate during the Miocene epoch, with further rifting during Plio-Pleistocene times.

The system, called by several other names— Dead Sea Fault, Jordan–Dead Sea Rift, West Arabian Fault Zone, and others—is a left-lateral fault (showing a leftward shear when viewed across the fault line) that resulted in a total horizontal displacement of 66.5 miles/107 km during two main stages. Thus, the igneous and metamorphic rocks north of Aqabah were formerly adjacent to the center of the east coast of the Sinai Peninsula. The four deeper basins along the fault—the Gulf of Aqabah, Dead Sea, Sea of Galilee, and Huleh Basin—are "pull-apart zones" in which elongated depressions were formed as lo-

cal grabens. The bottom of the trench is below sea level from north of the Sea of Galilee to well south of the Dead Sea, with the Dead Sea the lowest body of water on the globe (see "Middle East Lakes" section later in this chapter).

The first of the system's three main segments comprises the trench and related features extending from the Gulf of Aqabah north to and including the Huleh Basin. A second segment begins at the southern border of Lebanon, where the Levant Rift bends to the northeast. This segment consists of a less profound trench but still constitutes a prominent linear depression through eastern Lebanon, the Bekaa (Fig. 3-1). This segment of the Levant Rift is the Yammunah Fault, which exhibits a significant vertical displacement along its western side that is still continuing, creating frequent but minor earthquakes. In the third segment, beginning at the northern border of Lebanon, the fault zone turns north again and finally disappears just beyond the Ghab Depression in northwestern Syria, the northernmost feature of the system.

The belt west of the three-segment fault is upwarped along a north-south axis for most of its length and is considered by some geologists to be a sliver subplate related to the African Plate. The highlands formed by the upfolded and faulted structures west of the Levant Rift include, from south to north, the Judean and Samarian hills, the upper Galilee highlands, Mount Lebanon, and the Jabal al-Nusayriyah. East of the Bekaa are the Anti-Lebanon Mountains, beyond which extend the prominent splayed ridges of the Palmyra Folds (clearly visible in Fig. 3-1, top), crumpled up and faulted by rotation of the Arabian Plate.

Mobile Belt

The Mobile Belt (or Fold Belt) is a continuous band of folded and faulted mountains extending from western to eastern Anatolia and then southeastward across Iran and eastward into the Himalayas. This belt, the middle segment of the Alpine-Himalayan mountain system, makes Turkey, northeastern Iraq, and Iran structurally extraordinarily complex.

Asia Minor (Anatolia). South of and generally parallel to the Black Sea coast, the Pontic Moun-

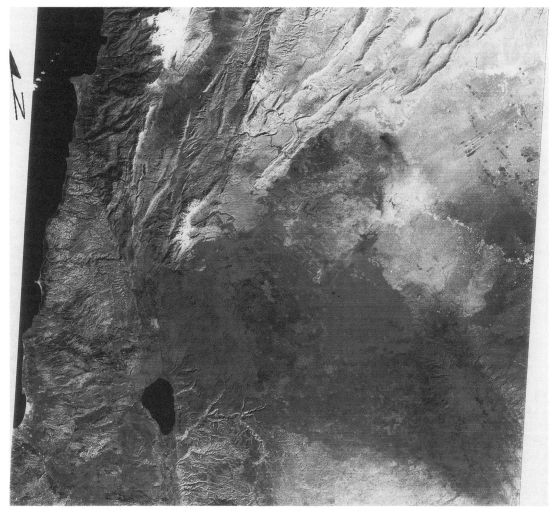

Figure 3-1. *Portion of Levant Rift System showing junction of Lebanon, Syria, Jordan, and Israel, including the Sea of Galilee (black harp-shaped area). (U.S. Geological Survey–NASA image)*

tains (5,000–13,000 ft./1,524–3,962 m) extend virtually the full length of Turkey. For much of their length, they lie north of the great North Anatolian Transform Fault, the eastern end of a 4,000-mile/6,440-km fault that begins at the Mid-Atlantic Rift. Periodic slippage along this right-lateral fault has produced devastating earthquakes.

Rimming the southern side of Asia Minor are the Taurus Mountains (7,000–9,000 ft./2,135–2,745 m), whose complexity reflects the severity of the compression that formed them. The slightly offset Anti-Taurus Mountains extend eastward to merge with folds that in turn bend

southeastward to become the Zagros Mountains. The Anti-Taurus generally parallel the East Anatolian Transform Fault, which in turn partially parallels the Southeast Anatolian Suture Zone between the former northern edge of the Arabian Plate and the southeastern edge of the Anatolian subplate (see Map 3-2).

At its western end, the East Anatolian Transform Fault links with both the northern end of the Levant Rift System and the eastern end of the Cyprus Subduction Zone. At its eastern end, it intersects the North Anatolian Fault. The proximity of these several seismic belts results in frequent and severe earthquakes (Map 3-3), such as

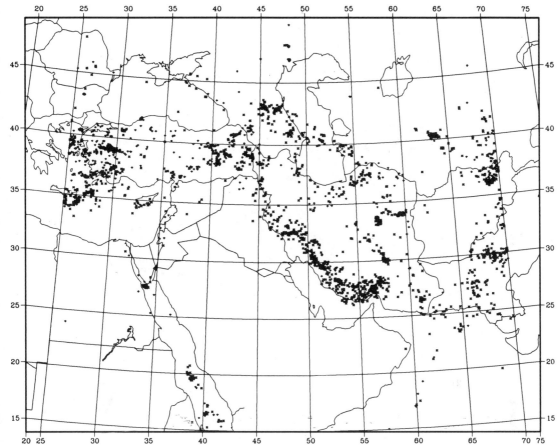

Map 3-3. *Major Middle East earthquakes 1966–1986 (magnitude of more than 4.5 and depth less than 31 miles/50 km). Note the frequency of tremors along Zagros Fold and Overthrust Belt and in western and eastern Turkey (compare with Map 3-2). (Map by special courtesy of National Earthquake Information Center, U.S. Geological Survey)*

the three catastrophic quakes in the Erzincan area in 1938, 1983, and 1992. South of the suture zone is a complex foreland in which moderate Border Folds merge into the Harran Plain along the Turkish-Syrian boundary.

Extreme western Anatolia is an area of block mountains, alternating uplifted and down-dropped masses (horsts and grabens). These structures have produced a series of rugged east-west promontories and deeply indented bays on the Aegean coast, where Ionian Greeks settled in the sixth century BC. In the northwest, a large foundered block flooded to form the Sea of Marmara. More than 600 miles/965 km to the east, the East Anatolian Accretionary Complex is a jumble of mountains and tilted plateaus (Fig. 3-2), the area where the junction of plates and

compression create severe seismic movements. Volcanic vents have also opened and are now marked by massive volcanoes (Mount Ararat near the Turkish-Iranian border reaches 16,948 ft./5,166 m), lava flows, and crater lakes. Mineralization along these various plate contacts gives Turkey more nonfuel mineral wealth than any other country in the Middle East. In between this East Anatolian complex and the western mountains is the exceedingly complex central Anatolian intermontane plateau, with its lowest part an almost flat-floored basin occupied by the shallow Tuz Gölü ("salt lake").

Off the Mediterranean coast of Turkey, the island of Cyprus is believed to have been formed as a result of the same plate collision that produced the Taurus range. An exposed granitic intrusion

Figure 3-2. *Eastern Anatolian mountains—rugged, snow-covered, cloud-shrouded, and complex mountains west of Lake Van. Heavy precipitation makes this a hydrographic center spawning such major rivers as the Tigris and the Euphrates.*

forms the core of the Troodos (6,407 ft./1,953 m), the highly mineralized mountain mass of southern Cyprus, whereas a limestone reef was uplifted to produce the narrow Kyrenia range (3,360 ft./1,025 m), which parallels the northern coast of the island. The depression between the Troodos and Kyrenia highlands is a sediment-filled basin, the Mesaoria, Cyprus's breadbasket.

Iranian Plateau. Folding in the Mobile Belt extends farther eastward and southeastward into the Iranian mountain and intermontane plateau regions. From the junction of Turkey, Iran, and Iraq to the Arabian Sea, compression between the Arabian Plate and the Iranian subplate has crumpled, faulted, and thrust-faulted mostly sedimentary rocks along the longest and most prominent fold belt in the Middle East, the Zagros Mountains (10,000–14,000 ft./3,000–4,300 m). In the southern Zagros, scores of salt plugs have been pushed to or near the surface, creating stratigraphic structures that in many instances have entrapped large quantities of petroleum and natural gas. Farther southeast, the Makran range, which lies behind Iran's coast on the Gulf of Oman, is the result of uplift of oceanic crust

and exhibits forms that are distinctly different from the Zagros geomorphology.

Compressed between the rigid core blocks of Iran and the Russian Platform of the Eurasian Plate, high linear ridges were folded sharply upward across northern Iran. The Elburz Mountains south of the Caspian Sea and the series of ridges in the Kopet Mountains along the Iran-Turkmenistan border reach elevations of 12,000–15,000 ft./3,660–4,575 m in the Elburz and somewhat less in the Kopet. As in eastern Turkey, plate collision in the Elburz belt squeezed lava out of the vent of the Mt. Damavand volcano (18,600 ft./5,669 m, the highest point in the entire Middle East). Along the eastern Iranian border, near Pakistan, scattered volcanoes—including Iran's only recently active vent—and complex fold mountains around the Zahedan Plateau enclose the third side of the triangular Iranian Plateau core. As in central Anatolia, the lowest part of Iran's inner basin contains ephemeral salt lakes (playas), known in Iran as *kavirs*.

Median Trough

The Mesopotamian-Gulf trough, which is technically the northeastern edge of the Stable Interior Province, lies along the median axis between the Arabian Plate and the Iranian subplate and is a major geomorphic feature of the Middle East. It is a zone of downbuckling and subsidence on the flanks of the Arabian Shield. The northwestern half of the trough is above water and is partly a low plateau northwest of Baghdad and an alluvial-deltaic plain from Baghdad to the Gulf. The southeastern half of the structural trough has been invaded by the shallow waters of the Gulf, entering from the Indian Ocean through the Strait of Hormuz. The strait is thus as significant physically as it is economically and strategically.

Middle East Seas

Even after the sea basins of the main water bodies of the Middle East reached their approximate present contours, major modifications occurred in response to slight crustal adjustments and to climatic variations. Especially during the Pleistocene glacial period, sea level fell more than 395 ft./120 m below its current level during periods of ice advance, when millions of cubic meters of ocean water were frozen into the ice sheets. During those same periods of glacial maxima, the Middle East enjoyed pluvial periods, when precipitation increased appreciably. The increased rainfall charged the regional aquifers and induced environmental conditions more favorable for human cultural development during the long Paleolithic period. Eustatic (sea level) changes during glacial retreats, when the melting of the ice sheets freed water that had been previously locked in the glaciers, brought seas 180–195 ft./55–60 m higher than at present, giving a total differential of more than 590 ft./180 m over the 1.3 million years of the glacial Pleistocene.

The great drop in sea level during glacial maxima dried up the Strait of Gibraltar, connecting the Mediterranean and the Atlantic; the Bosporus and Dardanelles, connecting the Mediterranean and the Black Sea; and the Strait of Hormuz, connecting the Gulf and the Indian Ocean. With their main water supplies cut off, the basins of the three inland seas became extensive desert basins, large-scale versions of today's Death Valley in California, and some of the salt deposited during the periods of evaporation still affects the chemical composition of rocks, water, and soil in the region. As the interglacial thaw induced a rise in sea level, the mounting water crested the dried-up straits and roared into the empty basins in thunderous cascades, refilling the huge depressions to their former, and approximately present, configurations.

Red Sea and the Gulf of Aden

The Red Sea occupies an elongated, escarpment-bounded depression 1,220 miles/1,965 km long and 155–280 miles/250–450 km wide. Rifting opened the Red Sea in two phases, one 30 million–15 million years ago and a more recent one beginning 5 million years ago and still continuing along the sea's entire length. South of 21° N Lat, the sea's main trough, 2,000–3,000 ft./600–1,000 m deep, is bisected by a deeper axial trough, which is usually less than 30 miles/50 km wide and about 6,500 ft./2,000 m deep, formed by seafloor spreading during the past 4 million years. By contrast, north of 25° N Lat, the inner axial trough is lacking, and the floor has an irregular, faulted surface. Between the shores and the center axis, continental shelf extends all along both coasts.

Seafloor spreading, especially in a series of eighteen deeps in the transition zone between 24° and 21°, brings molten lava into the bottom of the trench. The lava heats the seawater above it and stimulates the formation of hot brines and the development of a sludge with high concentrations of zinc, copper, silver, gold, and other metals. Facing each other across these deeps, Saudi Arabia and Sudan formed a Red Sea Commission in 1975 to consider exploitation of the metals. The sludge is not a commercially feasible source at present, but it will be a major source for the metals in the future.

Rifting along both branches of the Red Sea at the northern end, along the Gulf of Suez west of the Sinai Peninsula and the Gulf of Aqabah east of the Sinai (Fig. 3-3), is of two different types and ages. With great depths, exceeding 5,900 ft./1,800 m, the Gulf of Aqabah is a pull-apart zone associated with the Levant Rift and is morphogenetically related to the Dead Sea, Sea of Galilee, and Huleh Basin. Much shallower, only about 150 ft./45 m, and a much older structure, the Gulf of Suez split from the Red Sea Hills to the West and subsided over a long period.

Figure 3-3. *Looking northeast across the Sinai Peninsula with Gulf of Suez on the west and the Gulf of Aqabah on the east. Note rugged, dark basement rocks in southern Sinai and along eastern coast of the Gulf of Aqabah. (Photograph courtesy of National Aeronautics and Space Administration)*

Opening by seafloor spreading along a rift at right angles to that widening the southern Red Sea, the Gulf of Aden has proceeded further and can be considered as an example of a young ocean basin. It exhibits well-defined continental margins, small ocean basins, an oceanic crust floor, an active midocean ridge (Sheba Ridge), and a spreading center characterized by a rift valley and transverse fracture zones. This triple junction of the rifts (see Map 3-2) creates a magnificent laboratory for observing the mechanics and processes of seafloor spreading.

Persian/Arabian Gulf

Lying in a tectonic basin of Late Pliocene to Pleistocene age, the shallow Gulf is a marginal sea that exhibits striking contrasts with the Red Sea and the Gulf of Aden. It covers approximately 87,000 miles^2/226,000 km^2 and is about 620 miles/1,000 km long and 125–185 miles/201–300 km wide. Although it reaches depths of more than 330 ft./100 m near the Strait of Hormuz, its average depth is only 115 ft./35 m. Since the floor slope and depth are greater on the Iranian side, the basin has a marked bathymetric asymmetry across its axis, reflecting the downfolding between the Arabian Plate and Iranian subplate. Because the Gulf's elongated axis defines this separation between two different geomorphic provinces, the opposite coasts, Arabia to the west and Iran to the east, reflect the contrasting structures. The low surface of the eastern half of the stable Arabian Shelf is a generally level coastal area that slopes gently under the shallow Gulf waters and is fringed with offshore sand islands and sand spits. One such sand spit is Ras Tanura, location of three of the world's largest oil installations. To the east of the anticlinal Qatar Peninsula is a broad, shallow area 33–66 ft./10–20 m deep studded with numerous shoals and salt-dome islands, around which huge petroleum accumulations are exploited. Formerly the world's greatest natural-pearl fishing area, the Great Pearl Bank Barrier extends eastward across this embayment. The concave southern coast of the Gulf is typified by low, evaporitic, supratidal flats (*sabkhahs*), some of which, along the coast of the United Arab Emirates, are more than 6 miles/10 km wide. On the east, in contrast, the Iranian coast rises steeply and quickly merges with the folded ridges of the Zagros Foreland.

The Gulf shows a wide variation in temperature and salinity because of its shallowness and limited connection with the ocean. In summer, the surface waters are warm, and evaporation is high. Even in winter, water temperature is about 68°F/20°C. Salinity varies from 7 percent (twice that of average seawater) in protected Arabian lagoons to less than 3.7 percent near the Strait of Hormuz. The major freshwater influx into the Gulf is that of the Shatt al-Arab (the combined Tigris and Euphrates rivers), but water also enters from the Karun River in Iran and from short streams descending the western ridges of the Zagros Foreland. Tidal ranges in the western Gulf are moderate, with average maximums of about 8 ft./2.5 m. When the sea level fell during the later Pleistocene glaciation to empty the Gulf, the Tigris-Euphrates river system flowed across the dry basin and emptied into the Arabian Sea through the Strait of Hormuz. Seawater began to pour back into the basin about 18,000 years ago, and the present level was reached about 5,000 years ago.

With more than a score of major oil export terminals in operation in the Gulf virtually around the clock, and with 40 to 50 large tankers sailing up or down the Gulf daily, pollution of the waters and beaches has long been a grave concern around the littoral. Despite government monitoring and caveat, and despite appreciable care taken by oil companies and shippers, as many as a quarter of a million barrels of oil pollute the Gulf annually. The rapidly growing population around the littoral discards many tons of waste into the water daily. However, the greatest blow to the Gulf came in January 1991, when Iraqis occupying Kuwait dumped several million barrels of crude oil (the exact amount is uncertain) into the Gulf off the coast of the amirate. This oil spill, the largest ever in the world, spread to cover more than 600 miles²/1,554 km² of sea surface and to foul 300 miles/483 km of the Gulf's west coast. With the Gulf's counterclock-wise circulation, the slick spread south to the Qatar coast within 60 days, killing countless fish, shrimp, crabs, and birds, as well as fouling sea grass beds and beaches and posing a threat to desalination plant intakes. Although reasonable revival may well take place in less time than the more pessimistic predictions, the Gulf coast of Saudi Arabia, the sea bottom on the west side of the Gulf, and the fish and wildlife of the area will require several years to achieve a moderate recovery.[4]

Caspian Sea

Unlike the other "seas," the Caspian has no outlet, and its surface averages about 92 ft./28 m below sea level. The Caspian bottom has two basins connected by a channel east of the Baku Peninsula. The shallower of the basins is at the northern end and eastern side; the greatest depth is in the southwestern quadrant, 3,363 ft./1,025 m. With most of the fluviatile inflow coming from the Volga at the northern end, the level of the Caspian was slowly dropping until the late 1970s as the Russians increasingly utilized Volga water for irrigation purposes. The trend was reversed in 1977, and during the early 1980s the level rose steadily. A railroad ferry crosses from Baku to Krasnovodsk, and other freight and passenger vessels utilize the sea; however, most boats on the Caspian are fishing vessels, seeking especially the famous Caspian sturgeon, source of the valuable Russian and Iranian caviar.

Black Sea

The deeply foundered subplate of the Black Sea is of major importance to the littoral states that fringe its coasts. Relatively shallow near the Danube Delta in the northwest, the Black Sea depth exceeds 7,000 ft./2,135 m across much of its southern extent. The northern slopes of Turkey's Pontic Mountains plunge steeply into the Black Sea, giving deep water access to Turkey's many northern ports. Receiving a plentiful freshwater inflow from rivers in the north and several smaller rivers in the south, the Black Sea is only moderately salty. Virtually tideless, it overflows freely through the Bosporus into the Sea of Marmara and thence through the Dardanelles into the Aegean. The Black Sea is also known as the Euxine Sea, the ancient Pontus Euxinus.

Mediterranean Sea

Of complex origin, the Mediterranean is partially a western remnant of the pre-Miocene Tethys Sea and partially a collapsed structure along the collision zone between the African and Eurasian plates. Its greatest depth (15,072 ft./4,594 m) is west of Crete, and the basin off the Levant coast is 4,787 ft./1,459 m. Except in the southeast, where Nile sediments extend seaward and have been carried eastward and northeastward by currents, most Mediterranean coasts descend sharply under the Mediterranean waters. Most ports, therefore, generally face few dredging problems, unlike virtually all Gulf ports. The extensive, deep Mediterranean waters exercise profound effects on the climate of much of the Middle East, and the sea has carried ships of many nations for thousands of years.

Middle East Lakes

Few natural freshwater lakes of any considerable size and significance occur in the Middle East outside the Tigris and Euphrates valleys, where the lakes tend to be shallow and are more similar to marshes than to lakes. However, five are noteworthy here, and these and others are discussed in more detail in the relevant country chapters. Although not large, the Sea of Galilee in Israel (also called Lake Tiberias and Lake Kinneret) has both religious-historical significance and crucial contemporary economic and political importance. Covering 64 miles^2/165 km^2, the lake's surface varies between 685 and 710 ft./209 and 214 m below sea level, and its maximum depth is 138 ft./42 m. The lake occupies one of the enlarged basins in the Levant Rift System (see Fig. 3-1) and is now regulated as the control basin for Israel's national water system. Its generally fresh water is locally briny owing to underwater salt springs, especially near Tiberias on its west coast.

Farther south in the Levant Rift lies the Middle East's most famous salt lake, the Dead Sea. Its surface is more than 1,310 ft./400 m below sea level (lowest water body on earth), and its maximum depth is an additional 1,300 ft./396 m lower. Like other inland lakes with no outlet, the Dead Sea has become increasingly saline because of the evaporation from its surface—roughly 96.8 million ft.^{3}/2.74 million m^3 per day—and because of the addition of salt from surrounding springs. Its water shows the highest salinity of all the world's water bodies, 35 percent, ten times that of average seawater. As a result, fish cannot survive in the water (hence the name of the lake), and buoyancy of the water is so great that people cannot sink while swimming in the Dead Sea.

Another result is that dissolved salts are present in such quantities that they are precipitated naturally or can be precipitated in evaporation pans, so that they are "mined" on a large scale in Israel and Jordan. This evaporation and a rapidly diminishing inflow of water from the Jordan River in the north—the lake's main supply of fresh water—owing to an increasing use of the river basin's water for irrigation mean that the lake's surface is steadily dropping. At present the southern basin has shrunk to half its former size and, now separated from the larger and deeper northern basin by the sill extending from the Lisan Peninsula, is only a few feet deep.[5]

Numerous large saltwater lakes occupy closed tectonic basins in northwestern Iran and on the Anatolian Plateau. The two largest are Lake Urmia and Lake Van, the two lying on either side of the Iranian-Turkish boundary. Relatively shallow, not more than 66 ft./20 m deep, the very salty Lake Urmia expands in size by one-third with the spring runoff to cover 2,317 miles^2/6,000 km^2. Nestled in the rugged eastern Anatolian highlands, the much deeper Lake Van, whose water is bitter because of several salts, has a surface elevation of 5,400 ft./1,646 m and covers 1,434 miles^2/3,714 km^2. The structurally and topographically complex southwestern part of Anatolia cradles a dozen salt lakes between Konya on the east and Denizli on the west. In northwestern Anatolia, lakes also occupy inland extensions of grabens east and south of the Sea of Marmara. Tuz Gölü is a shallow evaporation pan in the central Anatolian sump that expands and contracts markedly according to seasonal precipitation.

Major River Systems

Aridity in the southern and eastern sectors of the Middle East precludes any large-scale, local perennial runoff, and the river systems in these regions rise in nearby areas of significant water surplus. Structural conditions in some of the more humid sectors interrupt drainage lines to divert a considerable percentage of the interior runoff into closed basins. Thus, the major river systems in the Middle East are limited both qualitatively and quantitatively. The two largest stream systems are the Nile in the southwest and the Tigris-Euphrates in the center, with all three rivers crossing deserts but originating in highlands with a water surplus. Escalating disputes between the countries controlling the sources of the three streams and the downstream consuming countries are among the potentially serious confrontations faced by the Middle East in the 1990s and the new century (see Chap. 11). Not one perennial stream drains any part of the Arabian Peninsula, which serves as compelling confirmation of the stark aridity of this vast realm.

With the major exception of the Nile, virtually all Middle East rivers have a maximum runoff in late spring and a minimum flow in early fall. Most rivers at flood time are fed by snowmelt, which comes later than the actual precipitation maximum (November through February); and their minimum flow after the hot, dry summer is supplied primarily by springs and other groundwater discharge. The Nile regime is precisely the reverse, as it floods in late summer and early fall after the heavy summer monsoon rains in the river's source highlands and is at its minimum in the spring.

Tigris and Euphrates Rivers

Although the Tigris (Arabic, Dijlah; Turkish, Dicle) and Euphrates (Arabic, al-Furat, Turkish, Fırat) rivers enter the Gulf through a common 100-mile/160-km channel (the Shatt al-Arab), each is otherwise a separate stream. Both rise in the eastern Anatolian highlands hydrographic center of Turkey, their headwaters only a few miles from each other (Map 3-1). In the highlands, additional tributaries augment their flow, but as they course across the flat desert they lose water through evaporation and diversion for irrigation purposes. With diminished flow, they lose carrying capacity, drop some of their loads of silt, and continue to build up a common vast deltaic plain, with each channel also building natural levees.[6]

The longer of the two and the one with the greater drainage basin, the Euphrates proper begins at the confluence of the Kara and Murat rivers near Keban, northeast of Malatya in eastern Turkey, and ends with its junction with the Tigris at Qurnah, at the head of the Shatt al-Arab. This river, 1,700 miles/2,700 km long, drains a basin of 171,430 miles²/444,000 km². About 28 percent of the basin is in Turkey, 17 percent in Syria, 40 percent in Iraq, and 15 percent in Saudi Arabia. However, more than 90 percent of the actual water flow is from runoff in Turkey. The Balikh and Khabur left-bank tributaries, rising in the Anti-Taurus foothills, join the Euphrates as it flows across Syria, and no tributaries enter it in Iraq. Mean annual flow at Hit, in central Iraq, was formerly 31,820 million cubic meters (m³) per year; however, damming of the Euphrates at four places in Turkey and at Tabaqah (renamed al-Thawrah) in Syria has greatly diminished the river's mean flow and will reduce it much more from the mid-1990s onward.

Although shorter than the Euphrates, the Tigris (1,150 miles/1,850 km) formerly carried an average 42,230 million m³ per year, 25 percent more water than did the Euphrates; and since the Turkish and Syrian diversions of the Euphrates, the differential is even greater. To compensate for the dwindling lower Euphrates, water can be diverted by the Samarra barrage from the Tigris to the Euphrates by way of Lake Tharthar, a flood control facility occupying a depression between the two rivers. Other aspects of water management have been enhanced with the completion in late 1992 of Iraq's so-called third river, a 350-mile/563-km canal that extends from Baghdad to Basrah. Draining an area of more than 43,110 miles²/111,655 km² above Samarra, the Tigris, unlike the Euphrates, receives significant contributions from tributaries in Iraq. Bringing snowmelt and rainwater from the high Zagros in northeastern Iraq, all the tributaries enter along the left bank and include, from north to south, Great Zab, Little Zab, Udhaym, and Diyala. The Karkheh joins the Tigris at Amarah, upstream from Qurnah. More than the upper Tigris, the lower Tigris is subject to sudden flooding, especially when the Zab rivers flood simultaneously. However, flood control measures, such as the Tharthar Project, have done much to alleviate the impact of floods. Neither river is satisfactory for regular navigation, although the Tigris carried shallow-draft boats earlier in the century.

The building of the Tigris-Euphrates Delta has long been a subject of debate among geomorphologists. The enormous load of silt carried by the Tigris (about 40 million m^3 annually past Baghdad) and formerly by the Euphrates (whose silt now largely settles in Turkish and Syrian reservoirs and in flood control basins between Ramadi and Karbala in Iraq) has built a huge delta beyond Hit on the Euphrates and beyond Samarra on the Tigris. The rivers could logically be expected to continue rapid construction of a contemporary common delta; however, building from the east, the much more rapidly advancing combined fan and delta of the Karun River has, in effect, dammed the outlet of the Tigris-Euphrates system into the Gulf. The Karun fan-delta barrier causes the Tigris-Euphrates streams to drop their silt load prior to overflowing the barrier, a process that has created a maze of marshes and channels northwest of Basrah. Thus, the shoreline of the head of the Gulf during Sumerian times, for example, is uncertain. Whereas Ur seems to have been a port during its heyday, 3000 BC, it may have been a river port, like modern Basrah. Problems regarding delta building and early coastlines at the head of the Gulf require further investigation.

Nile River

With a length of 4,145 miles/6,669 km, the Nile is the world's longest river. Its drainage basin of 1.15 million miles^2/2.98 million km^2 is almost one-tenth the land area of Africa, although the Amazon, Mississippi, and Congo rivers have still larger watersheds. Seen anywhere along its lower course, the Nile, with an average annual flow at Aswan of 83,570 million m^3 per year, is an amazingly large stream to have traversed the full width of the eastern Sahara, yet 32 other major rivers carry more water than does the Nile during an average year.

The Nile's main tributary, the White Nile, is born in the lake district of East Africa and channels the overflow from Lake Victoria. From this lake, whence the river's alternate name of Victoria Nile, the White Nile descends into the Sudd, the world's largest freshwater swamp, in south-

ern Sudan. After dropping its silt load in and being regulated by the Sudd, the river flows northward and crosses progressively more desertic terrain to join the Blue Nile at Khartoum.

The Blue Nile is fed by heavy summer monsoon rains on the high Ethiopian Plateau and has a slightly different regime from that of the more uniform White Nile. It was primarily the Blue Nile floods that, prior to the two Aswan dams, caused the annual Nile flood in Egypt. From Khartoum, the Nile flows over a series of six cataracts, numbered upstream from the first cataract at Aswan, and 200 miles/322 km below the Khartoum confluence (still in the Sudan), it receives the intermittent Atbara, the river's last tributary. Debouching into the Mediterranean 1,680 miles/2,705 km below the Atbara confluence, the Nile has dropped a great silt load for thousands of years to build up the extensive delta that is an integral part of the country. However, the Aswan High Dam has changed the river regime, and the Nile no longer adds significantly to its delta (Chap. 20).

Fold Belt Rivers

Asia Minor and the western Iranian highlands have many perennial streams, a limited number of which carry sufficient volume to be noteworthy. Clockwise, they include the Büyük Menderes in southwestern Anatolia; Gediz, debouching just north of Izmir; Sakarya, draining the highlands between Ankara and Istanbul and reaching the Black Sea west of Zonguldak; Kızıl, or Kızılırmak (Turkish *ırmak* = "river"), the ancient Halys, with its basin comprising much of north-central Anatolia, making a broad loop before reaching its appreciable delta between Sinop and Samsun; and Yeşil, debouching across its delta east of Samsun. Most of these Anatolian rivers have been dammed for power generation.

Farther east is the Aras, which forms the Turkish-Armenian and Iranian-Azerbaijanian borders and empties into the Caspian Sea over the combined Kura-Aras delta south of Baku. In Iran, the Qezel Owzan–Safid drains a considerable area between Tehran and Tabriz and then cuts through a steep-sided gorge in the western Elburz (where it has been dammed) to empty into the southwestern Caspian over an appreciable delta; the Zayandeh, or Zayandeh Rud (Per-

Figure 3-4. *The Jordan River meandering across its floodplain (al-Zor), flowing sluggishly from upper right to lower left. The higher terrace level is the* Ghor.

sian *rud* = "river"), has an importance beyond its physical volume as it irrigates a considerable area around Esfahan before losing itself in a sump southeast of the city; and the Karun carries the largest volume of all Iranian rivers across a huge delta built jointly with its tributary, the Dez, and the nearby Karkheh. In Turkey, the two parallel Ceyhan and Seyhan rivers drain into the northeastern corner of the Mediterranean across the extensive Çukurova (Turkish *ova* = "plain"), the combined deltaic plain built by the two rivers.

Three Levant Rivers

Three modest rivers in the Levant have economic and political significance far beyond their physical dimensions. The Jordan River (al-Urdunn) has several headwaters draining southeastern Lebanon, southwestern Syria, and northern Israel; and its major tributary, the Yarmuk, enters on the east bank just south of the Sea of Galilee. The Zarqa enters from the plateau south of the Yarmuk. Meandering along the rift valley floor, the Jordan cuts through old lake bed deposits laid down in the late Pleistocene pluvial periods when the ancestral Dead Sea was as much as 655 ft./200 m higher than at present (Fig. 3-4). Increased diversion of the Jordan and its tributary waters for irrigation purposes by Israel and the

Kingdom of Jordan utilizes most of the river's water, except at flood time, before it reaches the Dead Sea. Thus, both the Jordan River and the Dead Sea are shrinking.

The two other Levant rivers of note arise within a few hundred meters of each other in the northern Bekaa of Lebanon, both fed by springs. The Litani flows southward, and below the Qirawn Dam it enters a rapidly deepening gorge before turning westward to the Mediterranean. Israeli water planners have long sought methods by which to divert some of the Litani's water from Lebanon into the upper Jordan basin to increase irrigation supplies for Israel. North of Baalbak, the Orontes River (Arabic, Asi) flows northward along the bend in the Levant Rift and enters the reclaimed Ghab Marshes, a graben at the north end of the rift valley. The lower Orontes flows through Antakya (Antioch) and then debouches into the Mediterranean.

Groundwater

In addition to surface water, underground water is of vital significance in the Middle East and has been for thousands of years. Some groundwater comes to the surface in natural springs—artesian springs (*ayns* in the Arab lands), or contact springs—or by emerging from caverns dissolved in limestone. Other water is tapped by hand-dug wells, many 50–100 ft./15–30 m deep. Wells in desert areas may be only a few feet deep, dug into the sand and gravel of a broad wadi or an alluvial fan. Especially in Iran, but also in other Middle Eastern areas, water in alluvial fans is tapped by a remarkable *qanat* system (also called *foggara, falaj, karez*), underground tunnels with spaced access wells reaching the surface (see Chap. 7). Thus, oases in the desert may be supplied by river water (Nile, Tigris, Euphrates), natural springs (in Egypt's Western Desert and in Saudi Arabia's Hofuf and Qatif oases), or dug wells (many in Iran and Saudi Arabia's Najd).

Greatly increased supplies of capital, rapidly growing populations, and increased exploitation of the environment in the Middle East have focused regional and national attention on water resources in general. Vast areas have no dependable surface runoff, but despite their desert character, modern hydrogeological studies have discovered that they have surprisingly large underground water supplies. Since World War I, and especially since World War II, technology has been applied to the search for and exploitation of underground water, with the result that supplies beyond any earlier expectations have been found and are being pumped by deep wells. It is now known that some of this water, usually in the deeper aquifers, is fossil water that was accumulated thousands of years ago, especially during the pluvial periods of the Pleistocene. Other aquifers are inexplicably recharged in the short term, even in areas that receive only minimum amounts of precipitation. The problem is that modern technology might permit such an overuse of these limited water supplies that critical shortages will develop within two or three decades.

In the central Arabian Peninsula, outcropping sedimentary strata of the Arabian Shelf contain aquifers that are recharged by the low annual rainfall in Najd and that carry the water at increasing depths underground very slowly toward the Gulf coast. Some of this water emerges in artesian springs in Hofuf, Qatif, and Bahrain; some is tapped by wells. Some is pumped in the recharge area itself, and enormous amounts of fossil water in the Cretaceous Wasia and Biyadh aquifers are being heavily exploited in central Saudi Arabia. In the Western Desert of Egypt, the widespread Nubian sandstone, which overlies the Nubian Shield, also contains huge amounts of fossil water that is being considered for possible pumping. Some of this water emerges in the five oases of the area. Groundwater plays a major role in the water supplies of the coastal plain of Israel, Mount Lebanon, western Jordan, and, indeed, every country of the Middle East.

Thus, the significance of the patterns of physical features goes beyond that of the landforms as such. Great concern focuses on the features' influence on and interaction with other patterns, cultural and biophysical. Topography has always influenced and will always influence where people cultivate their fields, build their settlements, align their transportation routes, construct their ports, fight their battles, and conduct their other activities. Similarly, landforms have interacted with climate, soils, and vegetation to create the natural environment. Above all, the utilization of water has been and is the single most critical aspect of the human experience in the Middle East. Economic and political aspects of the water problem are discussed further in Chapter 11.

4

The Skies and
the Winds: Climate

Middle East
Climate Factors

Climate has as much direct and indirect impact on people and their activities as any other geographic factor. It affects the clothes people wear, the design of their houses, the vigor of their outdoor labor, the need for energy to cool or heat their homes, and virtually all of their daily activities. In its interaction with other biophysical elements, the role of climate in a given environment is of great significance. Temperature, precipitation, and winds, for example, influence other natural elements in the landscape—vegetation especially but also soils, landforms, and animal life.

Whereas weather is the sum of day-to-day conditions of the atmosphere, climate is the long-term average of those conditions. Thus, climate may be thought of as "statistical weather." Six basic factors of climate in the Middle East control climates in general, although they have their own regional characteristics and balance. These six factors are latitude, seasonal pressure belts, passing pressure systems, land-water relationships, ocean currents, and landforms.[1] All of these except ocean currents, which are not of major importance in this area, are examined in their Middle East context.

Latitude

The latitudinal location of a place has two critical direct influences that in turn exercise major indirect influences. First, the latitude determines the angle at which the rays of the sun strike the earth and thus basically determines the amount of in-

solation, or solar radiation, a place receives. Second, as the vertical rays of the sun at noon shift latitudinally with the seasons, belts of atmospheric pressure and winds shift accordingly. Located between 13° and 42° N Lat, the Middle East lies in the lower to middle latitudes. For comparison purposes, all of the United States lies north of 25° N Lat.

Seasonal Pressure Belts

Atmospheric pressure, whether in a belt or in a "cell," influences both horizontal airflow (winds) and also whether air in a given belt is descending or rising. Most of the arid southern two-thirds of the Middle East lies much of the year under a subtropical high-pressure belt, a discontinuous east-west zone in which descending dry air heats adiabatically and desiccates by compression. The belt itself is marked by calms; however, once the subsiding air reaches the surface, it pours outward both northward and southward. The airflow toward the equator becomes the northeast trade winds, and the flow toward the pole joins the westerlies. The dry high pressure and the dry trade winds result in desert belts that extend from the Atlantic Ocean eastward across North Africa, such as the great Sahara (Arabic *sahra* = "desert"), then across Arabia and Iran to merge with the interior, midlatitude deserts of central Asia.

The more humid northern third of the Middle East, extending from the Aegean and Mediterranean seas to central Iran, is primarily a zone of transition between pressure belts and generally has a typical Mediterranean climate. In this climate type, conditions alternate between hot, dry summers and cool or cold, relatively moist winters. In summer, this zone lies under dry continental trade winds or descending hot, dry air, a seasonal extension of the full desert conditions farther south. In winter, this same zone lies under a belt of stormy westerlies and passing atmospheric depressions that migrate southward during the low-sun season. An added contrast between winter and summer conditions in the southernmost Middle East results from the seasonal reversal of the great Asian pressure systems. It is this reversal, from prevailing high pressure in winter to low pressure in summer, that produces the conditions known as the monsoons ("seasons," from the Arabic *mawsim*).

When the Asian atmospheric conditions reverse in spring with the northward migration of the vertical rays of the sun, the shift in pressure and winds brings with it an equatorial low-pressure belt, or doldrums, technically the Intertropical Convergence Zone (ITCZ). Extending across the extreme southern Arabian Peninsula, the ITCZ results in late spring and early fall precipitation in Asir and Yemen in the southwestern part of the peninsula and in Dhufar in southern Oman in the southeast.

Passing Pressure Systems

Passing low-pressure systems—depressions or cyclones—are the winter weather makers for the northern and central parts of the Middle East. In autumn, as the vertical rays of the sun at noon shift southward, the belt of the stormy westerlies and the mean position of the polar front also shift southward over the northern half of the region. Within that belt, in response to positioning of the jet stream, cyclonic depressions move periodically from west to east, following several regular tracks through the eastern Mediterranean.

The main paths meet near Cyprus and continue across Lebanon, Syria, and Iraq into Iran, although one track goes north of Asia Minor through the Black Sea. Because of the barrier effect of the north-south mountain ranges in the Levant, plus the frictional effect of the island of Cyprus, the lows tend to pause near that island. This delay gives rise to an average low-pressure center over the eastern Mediterranean during winter months, the Cyprus low, which produces the considerable precipitation in the area. Less

frequently, depressions cross Israel and Jordan and veer southeastward into the Arabian Peninsula. In most of the region, these weather makers bring the winter precipitation, much of it in the form of snow in the highland areas, that is characteristic of the Mediterranean climate.

Land-Water Relationships

Land-water patterns in the Middle East are major influences on climatic conditions in the region. Since the sea is the ultimate source of all moisture, the presence of water bodies, especially on the windward side, increases the potential for precipitation and humidity. Because of the high specific heat of water, large bodies of water also moderate the temperature of the air above them, warming onshore winds in winter and cooling them in summer in a heat exchange. This phenomenon especially affects the more northern areas, along the Black Sea and Caspian coasts, and along the eastern Mediterranean shores.

Landforms

Topography influences every aspect of climate. Highland areas have lower temperatures; mountain barriers intercept winds and wring moisture from them; mountain masses shunt storms to one side or the other; and open plains give full play to prevailing winds. Highland masses such as the Anatolian Plateau divert passing storms to the north or south, influencing the storm tracks and other climatic elements. Since in the normal lapse rate temperature decreases 3.3°F/1.9°C for each 1,000 ft./305 m of elevation, highland areas in the Middle East enjoy temperatures lower than those of adjacent plains. Many favored mountain areas become resort centers during the hot summers.

Highlands may also produce orographic (mountain-induced) precipitation from moisture-laden winds. Mount Lebanon is a classic example: Moist winds from the Mediterranean blow against the western slopes of the mountains behind Tripoli, Beirut, and Sidon. As the winds move upslope they are rapidly cooled adiabatically at 5.5°F/3.1°C for each 1,000 ft./305 m, reach cloud stage and then dew point, and precipitate rain at middle elevations and snow on the upper slopes. Similar orographic influences operate on the slopes north and south of Mount Lebanon, as well as in the Anatolian, Zagros, Elburz, and Yemen mountains.

Elements of Middle East Climate

The climate factors just reviewed combine to produce various climate characteristics: temperature, winds, precipitation, humidity, and evaporation. Each of these elements is examined for the region as a whole, and in the next section, we look at how they combine in specific areas to produce certain climate types: deserts, steppes, and humid temperate climates. Temperature and precipitation patterns are shown in two maps, and data for those same elements at selected stations are given in the table at the end of the chapter. The table also gives elevation, latitude and longitude, and climate type for each of the stations, and the patterns of the climate types are given in a third map.

Temperature

Markedly high temperatures prevail more than half of the year in most of the lowland areas of the Middle East. Although July and August are the hottest months, the period from April through October is warm to hot in most of the region. Afternoon temperatures of 100°F/38°C are registered in the middle Nile Valley and in the interior of Arabia by early March, and such temperatures may continue well into November.

Lowland desert areas that are located in the interior or are subject to airflow from the interior have the highest average summer temperatures (Map 4-1A). Means of more than 90°F/32°C for the hottest months are common for extensive areas in Iraq, Iran, and especially the Arabian Peninsula. The cloudless summer skies, typical of desert and Mediterranean climate conditions, add to elevated daytime temperatures.

At one desert station—Abqaiq, an oil-production center in eastern Saudi Arabia 27 miles/43 km from the Gulf coast—the averages mask the extremes of temperature. The mean daily temperature for July and August at Abqaiq is a broiling 98°F/37°C—compared, for example, with 91°F/33°C for Yuma, Arizona, in July, one of the highest monthly means in the United States.

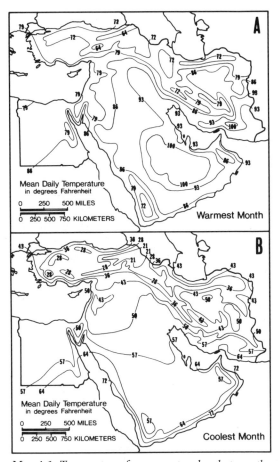

Map 4-1. *Temperatures for warmest and coolest months.*

However, even more revealing is the average of Abqaiq's daily *maximum* temperatures (afternoon highs) for July, August, and October—112°F/44°C, 113°F/45°C, and 114°F/45.5°C, respectively. An absolute maximum of 125°F/52°C has been recorded, in July, at Abqaiq, and in many years, fifteen or twenty consecutive weeks will pass during which afternoon highs are never less than 100°F/38°C.

Before the installation of evaporative coolers and then full air conditioning, many older homes in the Middle East included an underground room (known as a *sirdab* in Iraq) in which the family sought relief from the summer heat. In the hotter areas, especially along the humid coasts, summer nights bring little respite from the heat of day, either because of a small diurnal range of temperature (difference between day and night) or because of high humidity, or both. In low-income neighborhoods of crowded cities such as Cairo, Baghdad, Abadan, and Aden and in many villages, families often sleep on the flat roof of the home. By contrast, in open deserts or at considerable elevations, summer nights can be cool or even chilly.

Despite the prevalence of high summer temperatures in the Middle East, the temperature of some interior locations is moderated by elevation. Midsummer afternoon readings exceed 100°F/38°C in Damascus, Tehran, and Amman; but the mean of the warmest month, which includes the lowest daily temperature, is moderate. At these interior locations and elevations, the heat accumulated during the day radiates back into the cloudless sky and dry air, dropping the predawn minimum temperatures to levels 35–40°F/20–22°C below the afternoon maxima. This appreciable diurnal range provides a respite from the enervating, dehydrating heat of the day. Coastal localities generally experience smaller diurnal and seasonal ranges.

Several mountain areas have become prosperous summer resorts not only for local lowlanders but also for visitors from the Gulf states, Saudi Arabia, and elsewhere. Resorts in the mountains behind Beirut were crowded with summer residents prior to the outbreak of internal warfare of the mid-1970s, and similar climate areas in the mountains of Syria, Turkey, and Iran offer temperature relief, especially in the evenings. Hamadan, at 5,822 ft./1,775 m in western Iran, served as a summer capital for early Persian kings; and Taif, at about the same elevation in the Hijaz, serves as a Saudi summer capital and resort area.

Cities on the Anatolian and Iranian plateaus combine characteristics of dry highland summers, and thus clear nights, with the effects of lying at a more northerly latitude. For example, the highest mean at Ankara is 25°F/14°C cooler than that at Dhahran near sea level in Saudi Arabia. At Mashhad, in northeastern Iran (3,232 ft./985 m and 36° N Lat), the July mean is 79°F/26°C.

The degree of contrast between summer and winter temperatures depends primarily on latitude, interior location, and elevation. Samsun, on Turkey's northern coast, and Ankara, 115 miles/185 km inland, have the same August mean temperature; but Samsun's January mean is 12°F/7°C higher than Ankara's because of the warming effect of the Black Sea. The uplands of Anatolia and Iran, with higher elevations and more northerly and continental influences, register the coldest winters of the Middle East. These cold conditions are reflected in the data for Erzurum in eastern Anatolia and for Tabriz in northwestern Iran (see Table 4-1).

Winds

Wind is both a factor and an element in climate. As it transfers large amounts of air from one place to another, wind influences temperature, humidity and precipitation, evaporation, and bodily responses in both people and animals. Higher-velocity winds create or reduce sand dunes by shifting large amounts of sand, and, using sand and other rock particles as tools, they are major agents in desert erosion. On Middle Eastern waterways, mariners have depended upon the steady winds for centuries. The influence of wind on precipitation is of particular significance. Therefore, it is necessary to examine several aspects of winds in the Middle East, especially their role in influencing precipitation, and to discuss the more significant specific winds.

The ITCZ equatorial low-pressure belt, displaced and intensified in its May–August persistence over the Indian subcontinent, controls winds over the entire Middle East for more than four months during the summer monsoon. Whereas wind direction in the Arabian Sea area is prevailingly northeasterly in winter (the northeast monsoon), the summer flow of air is the opposite and is referred to as the southwest monsoon. When the Indus Valley low is deepest in July, the monsoon winds reach gale force over the sea. These winds are so strong that they pull the surface waters away from the south shore of the Arabian Peninsula, causing an upwelling of cool water from the deeps next to the coast and enhancing fishing conditions. Sailors have traditionally followed the summer winds eastward to the Indian subcontinent.

North of the low-pressure belt, air circulation pulls in the northeast trade winds toward the ITCZ. Blowing on clear, cloudless summer days, these strong northerly winds in the Aegean and the Mediterranean are called *etesian* ("annual") winds by the Greeks and *meltimi* by the Turks.

Useful to sailors when moderate, the *meltimi* become hazardous when their velocity is higher.

These prevailing winds continue over the low relief of Egypt as normal northeast trade winds, and they blow steadily through the Nile Valley for most of the year. They are of considerable economic value to Egypt, since they fill the sails of hundreds of Nile River boats, *faluqas* (feluccas), as they sail upstream against the Nile current. The *faluqas* then furl their sails for the return trip and drift downstream. On the other side of the Arabian Peninsula, blowing down the Mesopotamian trough and the Gulf basin, is the early summer *shamal* (Arabic for "north"). This dry wind blows at 25–30 mph/40–50 kph in June and early July, bringing frequent dust storms from Mesopotamia before moderating to 15–20 mph/25–32 kph in late summer. At its higher velocities, the *shamal* poses hazards to small sailing dhows and even to terminal loading operations of the huge oil tankers in the Gulf. One of the factors that prompted coalition commanders to decide on the starting date of Desert Storm operations in January 1991 was the intention to expel Iraqi forces from Kuwait before the onset of *shamal*-season sandstorms. If goals were achieved rapidly, such a starting date would also allow completion of the campaign before the winter rains and the ensuing spring and summer heat. Wind-borne dust is common in all seasons, primarily in the most barren desert areas, which have a minimal vegetative cover to hold the loose soil.

In various other parts of the Middle East where the strong flow of air during the summer monsoon is especially constant, the wind has many local names. For example, in the eastern Iranian province of Sistan, just west of the low-pressure center, it is called *bad-e sad-o-bist* ("the wind of 120 days"). The prevailing winds are often put to practical use by people. In southern Iran and along the Gulf coasts a traditional and practical architectural feature of many homes is the *badgir*, the so-called Persian wind tower, which uses vertical ducts on a square tower to direct the air downward into rooms below. These wind towers are disappearing, however, as older homes are razed for newer structures and as artificial air-conditioning becomes commonplace (Fig. 4-1).

Cool-season conditions originate in a standard set of meteorological occurrences. As a depression, with its counterclockwise circulation, approaches the eastern Mediterranean from the west, winds are southerly or southeasterly on the front of the low and will pull warm or even hot air out of the Sahara into the Mediterranean coastal areas. The southerly winds in the southeastern quadrant of the low are often dry and dusty as well as warm. Such conditions are especially likely in spring and autumn.

Through much of the Mediterranean Basin, the hot, dry wind on the front of a passing low is called a *sirocco,* originally an Italian word derived from the Arabic *sharq* ("east"). Sirocco-type winds, similar to the Santa Anas in California, desiccate the landscape, wither leaves and fruit on trees, render the brush vegetation susceptible to fires, and cause respiratory difficulties for people. As the depression tracks eastward, the winds have local names in the areas through which the system moves: *Jibli* ("south" or "southeast") in Libya, *khamsin* (Arabic for "fifty," probably suggesting the average number of days it might blow) in Egypt, *shlur shluq* in Lebanon and Syria, *sharqi* in Iraq, *kaws* ("the archer") in the Gulf, and *simoon* (Arabic for "poison") in parts of the Gulf area are examples. In the Gulf, strong southwestern winds known locally as *swahili* ("coastal") replace the *kaws*.

Some winds can start out quite cold in winter when the air is pulled out of the elevated northern plateaus, but they warm by compression in descending from the plateaus and can raise temperatures rapidly at the foot of the slope. Such winds are known as foehn winds in the Alps and as chinook winds on the eastern slopes of the Rocky Mountains in North America. Strong foehn-like winds known as *raghiehs* blow along the coasts of Turkey and Syria in the northeastern Mediterranean, originating from the plateau north of the Taurus Mountains. *Nashi*, northeasterly winds along the southern coast of Iran, likewise come from a plateau behind the coast and have a foehn effect.

Precipitation

Climate is the single most influential factor among Middle East biophysical patterns, and of the various climatic elements, the significance of

Figure 4-1. *Persian wind towers (badgirs) on picturesque old buildings erected in the early core of Dubai City before the oil boom (also note dhows in foreground).*

precipitation must be emphasized. One clear indication of its significance is the immediately apparent evidence of the correlation between the areas of heavier precipitation (or runoff from heavy precipitation) and the areas of concentrations of population in the Middle East. Water plays a vital role even in those regions of the world in which it is plentiful, but its role in the Middle East, where water supplies are marginal in so much of the region, is critical. Water is life.

High seasonal temperatures in much of the Middle East typically accompany low seasonal precipitation. Thus, dryness is the key word for the climate in most of this region. At the extreme, the interior of the southern half of the Arabian Peninsula, the Rub al-Khali, is probably as dry as any area of comparable size on earth.

In the remaining interior of the peninsula, called Arabia Deserta (although the Roman term actually was applied to far northern Arabia), as well as in northern Egypt and in the Syrian Desert, vast areas have only 1–5 in./25–125 mm of precipitation annually (Map 4-2). This zone of aridity is too far south to benefit from the invasion of the westerlies in winter and too far north to receive rain from the ITCZ in summer. Map 4-2 also shows, however, that much of the north-

ern quarter of the Middle East receives 15–40 in./380–1,015 mm of precipitation. Obviously, a rather sharp contrast exists in rainfall amounts, and thus in vegetation and agriculture, between the northern one-fourth and the southern three-fourths of the region. Except in the southern Arabian Peninsula and in limited areas in the north, by far the most of the Middle East's precipitation falls during the months October–April, which is typical of the Mediterranean climate (cf. Beirut, Jerusalem, and Mosul in Table 4-1).

Precipitation at desert stations varies greatly from year to year, so that the percentage variation can be high because of the limited amounts involved. By its very nature, desert rainfall tends to be sporadic, often coming in sudden, brief downpours that are sharply restricted in area; however, broad frontal rains do occur and are also important. The sudden rains penetrate quickly into the porous ground in a sand desert area to produce a prompt growth of grass and flowers, which soon attract Bedouin herdsmen with their camels, sheep, or goats. In a rocky area with only a limited sand sponge and with no vegetation to absorb the rain, the runoff quickly concentrates into the local wadis—dry drainage

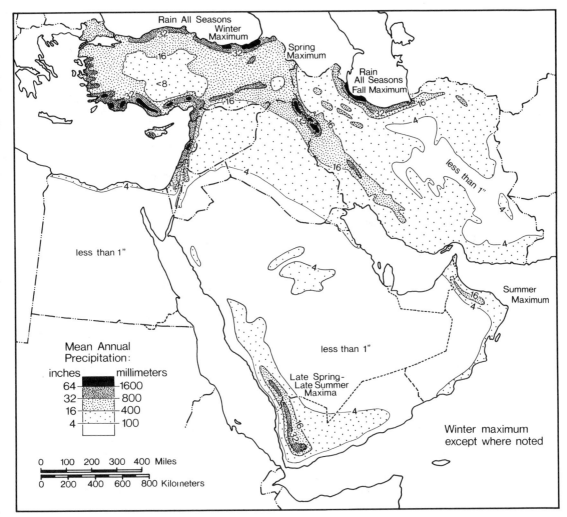

Map 4-2. *Middle East precipitation. Note heavy orographic precipitation on mountains rimming Asia Minor and on other mountain ranges.*

channels, sometimes so broad and flat that they are hardly perceptible as drainage lines—and causes flash floods.

Typical desert precipitation conditions exist at Dhahran, the oil center in eastern Saudi Arabia and a station with good climate records. With an average annual rainfall of 3.4 in./86 mm (slightly less than that of Yuma, Arizona), the station had a 93 percent negative departure from "normal" in 1970 when only 0.24 in./6 mm of rain fell during the entire year. Similarly, it had a 322 percent positive variation in 1976 when 10.9 in./277 mm fell. In 1974 nearly 5 in./118 mm fell at Dhahran in the month of December.

North of the zone of maximum aridity in the Egyptian and Arabian deserts, precipitation nearly everywhere is concentrated in the winter season, and annual totals generally increase with increasing latitude, elevation, and western exposure. The effect of latitude is exemplified by the south-to-north increase in rainfall shown by the data for Luxor, Cairo, Alexandria, Gaza, Tel Aviv, Haifa, and Beirut.

Rarely is there measurable rainfall in the central third of the Middle East between May and September. In Dhahran, no rain has been recorded between late May and early November since the station opened in the late 1930s—

although there was one freak heavy summer rain in Abqaiq. Thus, the hottest time of the year is rainless, with all that implies for people and vegetation, including crops.

The mountains in the southwestern corner of Turkey are an example of the orographic influence of west-facing slopes as they receive more than 60 in./1,525 mm of precipitation during the winter. The mountains of northern Lebanon also receive about the same amount, much of it as heavy snows, the basis for several ski resorts such as the Cedars. Depressions reaching the southeastern corner of the Black Sea rise up mountain slopes and yield more than 90 in./2,285 mm at Rize, probably the highest total precipitation in the Middle East. Inland, 25–40 in./635–1,015 mm of precipitation, much of it as snow, falls on the upper ridges of the Zagros Mountains and the higher slopes of the eastern Anatolian mountains. The slow melting of the deep snows in the eastern Anatolian hydrographic center during the spring and early summer supplies the runoff for the Tigris and Euphrates rivers and other streams that have their headwaters in these highlands.

Snow falls every winter in the uplands of the Middle East north of about 33° N Lat. Once or twice in most winters it also falls as far south as the Jerusalem hill country (which received 3 ft./0.9 m of snow in 1920) and the southern highlands of Jordan. In early 1992, heavy snow—from 12 to 20 in./350 to 508 mm—fell in Damascus, Jerusalem, and Amman in January and again in February. The Syrian and Mesopotamian deserts receive occasional snowfalls, and it has snowed in Riyadh and even—in 1987, for the first time in memory or records—in the Buraymi Oasis on the United Arab Emirates–Oman border.

In the southwestern corner of the Arabian Peninsula, the Yemen Mountains and their extension northward into the Asir of Saudi Arabia intercept moisture-laden southwest monsoon winds between April and September, producing 20–40 in./500–1,000 mm of orographic rain on the west-facing slopes. Because of this relatively abundant rainfall, the area earned the ancient designation Arabia Felix (Fortunate Arabia). Lying between 13° and 17° N Lat, the Yemen Mountains receive monsoon rains in two periods during the shifting of the vertical rays of the sun, northward in late April–early May, southward in

August. Thus, the area has a double-maximum precipitation regime, with rain in spring and again, more plentifully, in late summer with a dry early summer in between. Such a regime reveals the role of the migrating equatorial low pressure zone, the ITCZ (see Sana, Table 4-1).

Humidity

Three generalizations can be made about humidity in the Middle East. First, generally low humidity characterizes deserts and higher elevations—the year-round low humidity in Egypt has preserved human and animal mummies and delicate inlaid wood for more than 5,000 years. At stations in the interior deserts, the average relative humidity for the three summer months varies between 12 and 18 percent, with minima falling to 5 percent and occasionally even to an extreme 3 percent. With temperatures of 100°–120°F/38°–50°C and winds of 10–20 mph/16–32 kph, such low humidity parches the skin, causes nosebleeds, and scorches vegetation.

Second, the humidity along the coasts, even in arid areas, tends to be quite high, causing an uncomfortable combination of heat and humidity in summer. Such coastal cities as Beirut, Tel Aviv, and Alexandria on the Mediterranean; Ramsar on the southwestern Caspian coast; Jiddah on the Red Sea; and Kuwait, Manama, Dammam, and Abu Dhabi on the Gulf are very humid (70–75 percent average relative humidity) during August and early September. In comparison, Riyadh, in the interior of Saudi Arabia, has humidities of 49 percent in January and 15 percent in August. As one consequence of the high coastal humidity, heavy dew accompanies the predawn drop in temperature resulting from nighttime heat radiation into the clear air. Along the Mediterranean coast near Tel Aviv, dew falls an average of 200 nights each year, reaching a cumulative total equal to 1.2 in /30 mm of rain.

The third generalization is that humidity is moderate and exercises no remarkable effects in much of Asia Minor. Ankara, Sivas, and Erzurum all have percentages within a moderate range.

Evaporation

Evaporation plays a key role in determining aridity, but unlike temperature and precipitation, it is difficult to measure precisely, and no universally practiced system has been adopted to record it. If the mean water loss exceeds the mean precipitation annually, conditions tend toward aridity. Measurements of evaporation in central Saudi Arabia show rates ranging from 35 to 100 times the local mean annual rainfall. Actual evaporation in al-Sulayyil, in the southern Najd, for example, averages 207 in./5,250 mm annually,[2] more than 100 times the mean annual rainfall. Similar conditions exist in southern Egypt—where evaporation from Lake Nasser is a major problem—and southern Iran. However, other influences—season of precipitation, temperature, soil conditions—can be of major importance and can affect the ecology. Other factors being equal, natural vegetation is indicative of aridity and indirectly of evaporation.

Climate Regions

The preceding analysis of factors and elements in the climate of the Middle East and description of sample areas permit a synthesis of the elements into specific regional climate types. Such a synthesis requires both a system to determine the climate types and also the drawing of approximate boundaries between the regional types. The widely used classification developed by W. Koeppen and R. Geiger can be meaningfully applied to the Middle East (Map 4-3).[3] Each of the stations listed in Table 4-1 is assigned its Koeppen climate classification, and it is instructive to see how individual stations (shown on Map 4-3 by initials) fit into the patterns of climate types.

More than 85 percent of the Middle East is dominated by dry or summer-dry climates. In Koeppen's year-round dry (B) climates, evaporation exceeds precipitation; but degrees of dryness separate B climates into arid (BW) and semiarid or steppe (BS), which is characteristic of a short grassland vegetation area. Nearly half the Middle East is actual desert, BW; another 18–20 percent is steppe, BS. The division is economically important, since nomadic herding predominates on the dry side of the steppe whereas barley and even wheat can be grown in most years on the moist side of the steppe. Most of the BW/BS climates are hot in summer and either warm or mild in winter, thus falling into the Koeppen cat-

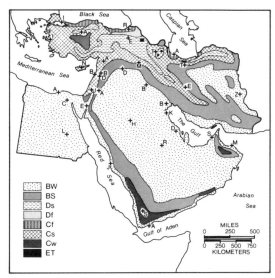

Map 4-3. *Climate types according to modified Koeppen system. BW = desert, BS = steppe. Initials indicate climate stations listed in Table 4-1. See text for explanation of other symbols.*

egory of BWh or BSh ("h" signifies hot or warm). The dry climates in areas of high elevation fall below the boundary between hot and cold and are therefore BWk or BSk.

Still another third of the region receives sufficient precipitation to balance or outweigh evaporation, although nearly all of it falls during the cool months, November–April. This cool-season precipitation evaporates less than summer moisture and is therefore more effective. These areas of Mediterranean-type climate are designated Cs by Koeppen ("C" indicates a mesothermal, temperate climate; "s" indicates summer dry). The warmer areas of Cs climate are classed as Csa, the cooler areas Csb. The Csa climate is the typical Mediterranean climate, continuous along the shores of the Levant and western and southern Asia Minor. An upland Cs extends along the highland Fertile Crescent, along the Zagros, and into northeastern Iran.

The climate of a small area in Yemen is similar to the Csa except that its rain comes mostly in summer, during the summer monsoon, a condition identified by Koeppen as Cwa ("w" indicates winter dry), a cooler version of the savanna climate. If sufficient data were available, a small area of Cwa might also be identified in southern

Oman. Tundra climate occurs on a few high mountaintops in eastern Anatolia and northern Iran (ET on Map 4-3).

Adding to the complexity of the climates of the Anatolian and Iranian plateaus are four limited areas with conditions unusual for the Middle East. Two areas along the southern coast of the Black Sea and two along the southern coast of the Caspian receive sufficient precipitation in sum-mer as well as in winter to be recognized as year-round moist climate areas, Cfa ("f" indicates moist all year). Also unusual for the Middle East are several interior mountain areas in Turkey and Iran with sufficiently cold winters to place them in the Koeppen D category (microthermal, continental climates). Whereas these types of cli-mate cover two-thirds of North America, they are relatively limited in the Middle East.

TABLE 4-1: SELECTED MIDDLE EAST TEMPERATURES AND PRECIPITATION (°C and mm)

CLIMATE STATION		JAN	FEB	MAR	APR	MAY	JNE	JLY	AUG	SPT	OCT	NOV	DEC	ANNUAL
Istanbul, Turkey	40 m	5	4	5	10	15	20	22	22	18	14	10	7	13°C
40°58'N/29°05'E	Csa	88	80	61	37	32	28	27	22	49	62	87	96	669 mm
Izmir, Turkey	25 m	9	9	11	15	20	25	28	27	23	18	14	10	17°C
38°26'N/27°10'E	Csa	141	100	72	43	39	8	3	3	11	41	93	141	695 mm
Ankara, Turkey	894 m	0	1	5	11	16	20	23	23	18	13	7	2	12°C
30°57'N/32°53'E	Csa	37	36	36	37	49	30	14	9	17	24	30	43	362 mm
Rize, Turkey	4 m	7	7	8	11	16	20	22	23	20	16	12	9	14°C
41°02'N/40°30'E	Cfa	259	215	187	97	97	131	150	211	270	299	278	246	2440 mm
Erzurum, Turkey	1863 m	-9	-7	-3	5	11	15	19	20	15	9	2	-6	6°C
39°55'N/41°16'E	Dfb	29	32	41	53	78	55	31	19	27	49	38	25	476 mm
Anzali, Iran	-15 m	8	8	9	13	19	22	26	25	23	18	14	10	16°C
37°28'N/49°28'E	Cfa	133	125	111	75	56	57	45	131	298	326	227	173	1757 mm
Tabriz, Iran	1362 m	1	1	5	11	16	21	24	25	21	14	6	0	12°C
38°08'N/46°15'E	BSh	15	32	45	47	43	23	11	1	9	14	29	16	285 mm
Esfahan, Iran	1598 m	4	6	10	16	20	25	28	26	23	16	9	4	16°C
32°37'N/51°40'E	BWh	19	16	18	16	8	1	5	1	0	3	19	20	126 mm
Tehran, Iran	1519 m	4	5	10	15	21	26	30	28	25	18	11	5	16°C
35°37'N/51°40'E	BSh	37	23	36	31	14	2	1	1	1	5	29	27	207 mm
Zahedan, Iran	1370 m	6	12	15	19	23	27	28	26	22	18	12	7	18°C
29°28'N/60°53'E	BWh	30	24	14	16	7	0	0	0	0	0	13	9	113 mm
Nicosia, Cyprus	217 m	11	11	12	17	21	26	28	28	25	21	16	12	19°C
35°09'N/33°17'E	Csa	74	43	37	17	21	9	1	2	7	21	32	75	339 mm
Aleppo, Syria	392 m	6	7	10	16	21	25	28	29	24	19	12	8	17°C
36°11'N/37°13'E	Csa	63	46	36	35	14	4	0	2	0	18	27	74	319 mm
Damascus, Syria	729 m	8	9	12	17	21	25	27	28	24	21	14	9	18°C
33°29'N/36°14'E	Csa	54	39	29	15	6	0	0	0	0	5	26	60	234 mm
Dayr al-Zawr, Sy	203 m	8	10	13	19	24	30	32	32	28	21	14	8	20°C
35°20'N/40°09'E	BSh	35	33	32	20	7	2	0	0	0	3	12	33	177 mm
Beirut, Lebanon	16 m	14	14	15	18	21	24	26	27	26	23	19	16	20°C
33°47'N/35°29'E	Csa	113	80	77	26	10	1	0	0	7	20	78	105	517 mm
Bhamdun, Leb	1130 m	7	7	9	13	17	20	22	22	19	17	13	9	15°C
33°46'N/35°39'E	Csa	302	262	194	95	40	1	1	1	3	54	132	239	1324 mm
Jerusalem, Israel	810 m	9	10	12	16	20	22	23	24	22	20	15	11	17°C
31°47'N/35°13'E	Csa	128	106	85	17	4	0	0	0	1	8	61	76	486 mm

CLIMATE STATION		JAN	FEB	MAR	APR	MAY	JNE	JLY	AUG	SPT	OCT	NOV	DEC	ANNUAL
Elat, Israel	11 m	16	18	20	24	29	32	34	34	31	27	22	17	25°C
29°33′N/34°57′E	BWh	2	5	5	3	0	0	0	0	0	0	2	9	26 mm
Amman, Jordan	771 m	8	9	12	16	21	24	25	26	23	21	15	10	18°C
31°57′N/35°57′E	Csa	68	59	44	13	5	0	0	0	1	4	31	48	273 mm
Mosul, Iraq	222 m	6	9	12	17	24	30	34	33	30	20	13	8	20°C
36°19′N/43°09′E	Csa	70	67	65	55	20	1	0	0	0	7	43	62	390 mm
Baghdad, Iraq	34 m	10	12	16	22	28	33	35	34	31	25	17	11	23°C
33°20′N/44°24′E	BWh	25	25	29	16	7	0	0	0	0	3	22	26	153 mm
Basrah, Iraq	2 m	12	14	18	24	29	32	34	33	31	26	19	14	24°C
30°34′N/47°47′E	BWh	26	17	25	22	7	0	0	0	0	1	28	38	164 mm
Kuwait, Kuwait	11 m	14	16	20	26	31	35	37	37	33	27	21	15	26°C
29°20′N/47°57′E	BWh	15	7	8	11	3	0	0	0	0	0	25	41	110 mm
Hayil, Saudi Arabia	914 m	12	13	17	20	25	29	30	31	28	23	19	12	22°C
27°31′N/41°44′E	BWh	9	8	6	11	7	0	0	0	0	11	22	3	77 mm
Dhahran, Saudi Ar	25 m	17	17	22	27	32	35	36	37	34	29	24	18	27°C
26°16′N/50°10′E	BWh	26	15	12	2	3	0	0	0	0	0	4	24	86 mm
Riyadh, Saudi Arab	609 m	16	16	21	26	30	34	40	36	32	25	20	16	26°C
24°42′N/46°43′E	BWh	24	6	6	11	15	0	0	2	0	0	11	7	82 mm
Jiddah, Saudi Arab	12 m	23	23	24	27	30	31	32	31	30	29	27	26	28°C
21°30′N/39°12′E	BWh	17	2	13	11	13	1	0	2	0	0	6	12	77 mm
Sharjah, UAE	2 m	18	18	22	25	28	30	33	34	31	28	24	20	26°C
25°21′N/55°23′E	BWh	34	13	9	18	1	0	2	0	0	0	18	21	116 mm
Muscat, Oman	5 m	22	22	25	29	33	34	33	31	31	30	26	23	28°C
22°37′N/58°35′E	BWh	28	13	10	10	1	3	1	1	1	3	10	18	99 mm
Aden, Yemen	3 m	26	26	27	29	31	33	32	32	32	29	27	26	29°C
12°50′N/45°02′E	BWh	7	3	6	0	1	0	3	2	7	1	3	6	39 mm
Sana, Yemen	2350 m	12	15	16	18	19	20	20	20	18	14	12	11	16°C
15°23′N/44°11′E	BWh	0	4	21	46	46	0	20	102	3	9	0	0	251 mm
Alexandria, Egypt	7 m	15	15	17	19	20	24	26	27	26	24	21	17	21°C
31°12′N/29°57′E	BSh	44	25	11	3	2	0	0	1	1	7	30	48	172 mm
Cairo, Egypt	74 m	14	15	18	21	25	28	29	29	26	24	20	16	22°C
30°08′N/31°34′E	BWh	4	4	3	1	1	0	0	0	0	1	1	7	22 mm
Luxor, Egypt	89 m	14	16	20	25	30	32	32	32	30	27	21	16	25°C
25°40′N/32°42′E	BWh	0	0	0	0	0	0	0	0	0	0	0	0	0 mm

Table includes station latitude and longitude, elevation in meters, and Koeppen classification. See text for explanation of Koeppen symbols. Source: Willy Rudloff. *World Climates.* Stuttgart: Wissenschaftliche Verlagsgesellschaft mbH, 1981 (except Bhambdun and Hayil). (With permission)

5

Soils, Vegetation, and Animal Life

Ecological Relationships and Soils

Elements of the environment exert complex reciprocal effects—between topography and climate, between climate and vegetation, between vegetation and soils, between climate and soils—and the human element adds still other types and degrees of reciprocal influences. These ecological interactions constitute a fundamental dynamic in the geographic system, and it follows that a change in any one element in the ecosystem generates a change in the system as a whole.

A soil is the product of several environmental factors: climate, parent material, vegetation, fauna (especially including man), relief, and time. A comparison of Maps 3-1, 4-2, 4-3, and the second map in this chapter suggests a pattern among the factors that influence the general character of soils in the Middle East.

For example, predominant aridity and heat are two of the strongest general influences on the soils of the vast area from western Egypt to eastern Iran, excluding Asia Minor and the Levant. Limited vegetation cover in this same general area, also largely a consequence of aridity, deprives soils of humus. Extensive limestone and sandstone outcroppings, as well as loose sand, also profoundly affect soil characteristics. Mountain soils are especially influenced by relief, specifically the slope on which they develop. Proper management is important for all soils, and one characteristic that is amenable to management is soil salinity, a serious problem especially in southern Mesopotamia but also in most desert areas where crops are irrigated on poorly drained land.

Middle East soils are as varied as other aspects of the regional environment. Not only do soils of the Turkish forests differ from those of the Syrian steppes, but the prevailing types of desert soils over extensive desert areas also exhibit subtle but important variations. Moreover, large desert areas are totally lacking in true soils—widespread expanses of sand and virtually bare rock are obvious examples. The surface materials in much of the Middle East have not developed a soil "profile," a cross section that reveals identifying horizons (the vertical sequence of colors and textures that differentiate soils).

Lack of a mature profile results from several ecological conditions, including extreme aridity. In arid areas, there is no soil water to move downward and leach chemicals and other materials into the lower horizons of the soil profile. Also, where a vegetation cover is limited, sudden heavy but infrequent rains and frequent strong winds cause surface materials to erode rapidly, thus preventing profile development.

With little or no organic matter on the surface or in the upper horizon of soils, especially those of desert areas, soils of light color predominate in the region. Light color likewise prevails in soils that have an accumulation of salt near the surface. Around the desert margins, in semiarid and subhumid environments, most of the soils have an elevated calcium content, often from the underlying limestone that is frequently the parent material. However, soil calcium also builds up in moisture-deficient areas because soluble products of weathering accumulate within the upper

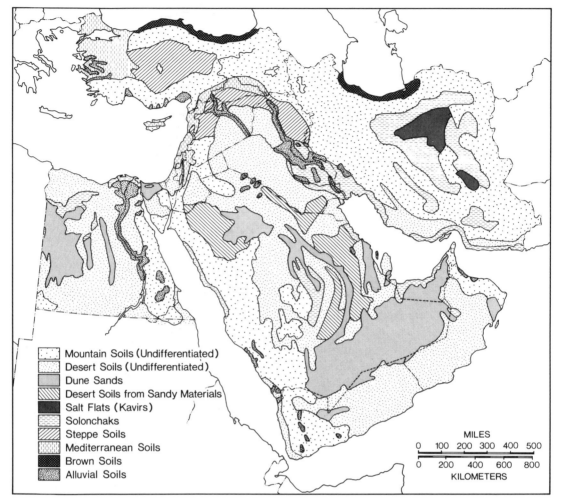

Map 5-1. *Middle East soils. (Adapted from several sources, especially the UNESCO world soils map and Clawson et al. 1971)*

horizons of the soil to form calcium carbonate and soluble salts. In moderate amounts, both salt and gypsum reduce soil productivity, and in large quantities they render soils unfit for cultivation.

Thus, agriculture in desert areas is limited not only directly by aridity but also indirectly by the effects of aridity on soil development. There are, nevertheless, exceptionally productive soils in certain desert areas—in numerous oases, the Nile Valley and Delta, and the floodplains of the Tigris and Euphrates rivers, for example (Map 5-1).

However, it is in the coastal plains, plateaus, and rolling lands of the northern and northwest-

ern areas of the Middle East that soils have reached mature development because of humid, temperate conditions. In Asia Minor, western Iran, and the Fertile Crescent, where annual precipitation exceeds 10 in./255 mm and averages perhaps 25 in./635 mm, there are extensive areas of well-developed and productive soils (Map 5-1). These regions exhibit greater varieties of soil groups as well as greater variations within the groups.

Middle East Soil Patterns

Soil taxonomy—the systematic classification and nomenclature of soils—has been a problem ever

Figure 5-1. *Typical desert soil and vegetation in eastern Saudi Arabia. (The oil rig shown is old-style equipment, now replaced with shorter, collapsible rigs.) (Aramco photograph)*

since the burgeoning of soil science. Unlike flora, fauna, rocks, and similar landscape elements, soils were often classified and named by different soil scientists according to different characteristics and genetic factors. A general ecological-genetic system developed by the Russians was widely used—but also widely debated—for several decades before the 1970s. Of several national systems that have emerged, the U.S. "Seventh Approximation," published by the Department of Agriculture in 1975 in its *Soil Taxonomy,* has been the most influential. Based on inherent soil characteristics, the classification is highly scientific and precise. However, since its precision introduces technical detail that is confusing to the nonspecialist, the following discussion utilizes a simpler taxonomy based on the traditional ecological-genetic concept.

Barren Sands and Rock and Other Non-Soils

Generally speaking, the area of barren land and desert soils in the Middle East extends southward, southeastward, and eastward from the 10-in./250-mm rainfall line (compare Map 4-2). Approximately half of the surface of the roughly 2 million miles²/5.2 million km² extending from western Egypt across the Arabian Peninsula and the Syrian Desert to eastern Iran is so barren that

it lacks either true soil or appreciable vegetation cover. Much of the barren area is gravel and loose sand, including dune sand (see Figs. 1-1 and 5-1); much of the rest is virtually bare rock. Prominent sand areas include western Egypt and, on the Arabian Peninsula, the Great Nafud in the north and the enormous Rub al-Khali in the south, with the arc of Dahna sands connecting the two. Huge gravel plains lacking true soils extend across the north of the Arabian Peninsula and appear in extensive patches in the eastern third of the peninsula.

Large areas of Lithosols (rock soils) extend along the east side of the Levant Rift System–Red Sea rift on the basaltic lava outpourings. A particularly common type of landscape in this area is the *hamadah,* typically an extensive plain with a surface cover of stones and pebbles. Actual soil development is limited, and vegetal cover is generally lacking. Even larger areas of Lithosols extend over the limestones of eastern Syria and Jordan, of Iraq west of the Euphrates, and along the axis of the north-south escarpments in central Arabia. Soils of the Lithosol group are also intermixed with varied Mountain soils in all the mountainous areas of the Middle East, especially those in the southern and southwestern sectors. These soils are grouped with Undifferentiated Mountain soils on Map 5-1.

Figure 5-2. *Sabkhat Matti, a typical* sabkhah *("tidal salt flat") in eastern Arabia. With a white crust of silty salt, such flats are inviting to vehicles and aircraft, but using them can be risky, especially after a rain. The soil on the* sabkhah *is a Solonchak, as the salt crust suggests.*

True Soils of the Desert

The other half of the desert areas referred to above contains true soils, with developed profiles and vegetation cover: Desert soils, Red Desert soils, Sierozem soils, and Solonchak (salty) soils. All except Solonchaks are grouped as Undifferentiated Desert soils on Map 5-1. Some profiles are weakly developed, and some of the vegetation is thin and scattered; but the landscape is less barren than the desert areas of Egypt, the Nafud, and the Rub al-Khali.

Desert soils are light gray or light brownish-gray, are low in organic matter, and closely overlie calcareous (calcium-containing) material, typically limestone. They normally support scattered shrubby desert plants but can be quite productive when irrigated. Much the same may be said of the Red Desert soils, although they are reddish in the upper part of the profile, as the name suggests, and they tend to develop in the hotter parts of the deserts. Sierozems are more widely scattered but are found in two large areas: on the floor of the great central basin of Turkey, around Tuz Gölü, and in much of northern Syria, where they support scattered short grass and brush as well as desert shrubs.

Solonchak soils are especially found in large interior undrained basins and low-lying areas: the Dasht-e Lut and the even saltier Dasht-e Kavir (Salt Desert) on the Iranian Plateau; the Qattara Depression in northwestern Egypt; southern Mesopotamia back from the river floodplains; in the tidal flats (*sabkhahs*) along low coastlines on both sides of the Arabian Peninsula; and over the inland coastal plain of the Gulf (Fig. 5-2 and Map 5-1). Either because of interior drainage or periodic tides, all these areas have high saltwater tables that supply salty water to the surface, evaporation of which forms the typical salt crust of Solonchaks. Most Solonchaks are useless for agriculture, but some can be made reasonably productive by artificially flushing the soil with fresh water and then applying proper fertilization. The area suffering most seriously from salt accumulation in otherwise irrigable and cultivable soils is southern Iraq.

Alluvial Soils

Alluvial soils—or, more properly, soils on alluvium as a parent material—appear in only relatively limited areas in the extensive desert lands of the area. However, these limited alluvial soil

Figure 5-3. *Looking north across the deeply entrenched Wadi Zarqa just south of Jerash. In the center are olive and nut tree groves, and elongated white structures are hothouses for growing early vegetables. Note Mediterranean maquis vegetation.*

areas are among the most intensively cultivated and productive in the world, certainly in the Middle East. They include the rich soils of the Nile Valley and Delta, floodplains of the Tigris and Euphrates rivers, valleys of west-central Iran, and small scattered oases and larger wadi bottoms of the Arabian Peninsula (see Map 5-1). They possess young profiles, are usually of good texture and tillability, and display most of the other characteristics of an ideal agricultural soil. Moreover, water for irrigating the soils is typically nearby.

Soils of the Humid Areas

Except for the irrigated alluvial soils, most of the cultivated and agriculturally productive soils of the Middle East are those of Asia Minor, the Fertile Crescent proper, and western Iran. On the inner, less humid side of the curve of the Fertile Crescent, there is an irregular belt of grassland soils that have developed in a zone receiving 6–10 in./150–250 mm of annual precipitation. They belong, in groups of decreasing aridity, to the traditional Reddish-Brown, Chestnut, and Reddish-Chestnut groups (grouped as steppe soils on Map 5-1). Such soils vary from well-developed and deep to poorly developed and thin on hill-

sides (see Fig. 5-3). Most are calcareous, especially since many overlie the widespread limestones of Jordan, Syria, southeastern Turkey, and Iraq. They receive sufficient precipitation to permit grain farming without irrigation.

In a major portion of the Mediterranean climate areas, a particular group of soils develops because of the regime of cool, wet winters and hot, dry summers. Usually called Mediterranean soils (as on Map 5-1), they are of a reddish-brown color, because of their iron content, and are referred to as *terra rossa* ("red earth"). In recent years, *terra rossa* has received increasing consideration as more of a red clay parent material for the true soil. Especially in early spring, this soil contrasts dramatically with the white limestone hills that surround pockets of the soil in southern Turkey and the Levant. Although this soil has eroded badly on the limestone slopes in many areas, it has been productive for thousands of years throughout the Mediterranean Basin.

Rendzina soil is also derived from limestones, usually the softer types such as marls, and it is often associated with *terra rossa*. Usually gray or black, in contrast to the rust of the *terra rossa*, it is also calcareous, clayey, and productive. It alternates with *terra rossa* in the uplands inland from the Levant coast from northwestern Syria south to Beer Sheva in Israel (its occurrences are too limited to show on Map 5-1).

Most of the remaining soil pattern is a complex one, forming a mosaic of Noncalcic Brown soils, Brown Forest soils, and Lithosols and other Mountain soils of Anatolia, northwestern Iran, and the mountains behind the eastern Mediterranean coast. These soil associations produce a great variety of foods, fodder, and industrial crops, including timber forests and tree crops of nuts or fruits, on moderate slopes in the better climate areas.

Vegetation

As an effective product of interacting influences on landscape, the natural vegetation of an area is often indicative of the general character of the local precipitation, temperature, soil, animal life, pressure of human population, and other aspects. Like the region's topography and soils, Middle East vegetation has also undergone natural changes during recent geological times. Certain plants are survivals from earlier periods; other plants from those periods have completely disappeared, from either natural or human causes, and their former presence is indicated only by seeds, spores, fruits, or leaves in old lake beds or in archaeological mounds.

Human activities, including agricultural exploitation, have decisively altered vegetation, soil, drainage, and other aspects of the environment in the millennia since the first Neolithic settlements, and the human impact on natural vegetation in the Middle East has been one of destruction as well as change. People have cleared forests not only to gain land for agricultural purposes but also to obtain timber and fuel. Cedars of Lebanon and other trees of the Levant supplied timbers for Egyptian and Phoenician ships, as did trees from Anatolia for ships of the Greeks, Romans, Byzantines, and Ottomans. Wood has also been employed in the Middle East for making charcoal, long used in heating and cooking and in lime and pottery kilns. Not only trees but also grasses, shrubs, and other low vegetation have been degraded or destroyed because of hu-

man activity and because of overgrazing by sheep and goats.

Humans have also changed vegetation without destroying it, as, for example, by exploiting a particular tree or plant and/or altering the floristic composition or geographical range of a species. Only in the remotest areas of the Middle East does the original type of vegetation remain; and, except in cultivated areas, the change has primarily been one of vegetal degradation.

Middle East Vegetation Patterns

Varied vegetation types extend from the dense high forests inland from the Black Sea and Caspian coasts to the scattered desert shrub of the Arabian Peninsula and the barren, salty *kavirs* of the interior Iranian Plateau (Map 5-2). Notwithstanding extensive forests in several northern mountain areas, the vegetal formations occupying the greatest expanses of the region are annual grasses and broadleaf annuals and shrubs of the steppes and deserts. Rather specialized scrub forms, known by their French names *maquis* and *garigue,* are typical of the Mediterranean areas with their cool, wet winters and hot, rainless summers.

The phytogeographical (phyto = "plant") patterns examined in this section are the plant associations, inferred from existing vegetation in noncultivated areas, that would exist without human interference.[1]

Desert Shrub

The desert is the product of aridity, and its xerophytic (dry plant) vegetation gives the desert its true expression. The desert environment supplies plants with favorable warmth and light but then imposes unfavorable moisture conditions. Some desert plants tolerate drought, some resist it, and some avoid it. When water occasionally does become available, plants respond immediately and profusely.

Areas that are barren of vegetation are generally coextensive with the areas of barren sands, rock, and salt surfaces on the soil map (Map 5-1), as well as with the areas that receive less than 1

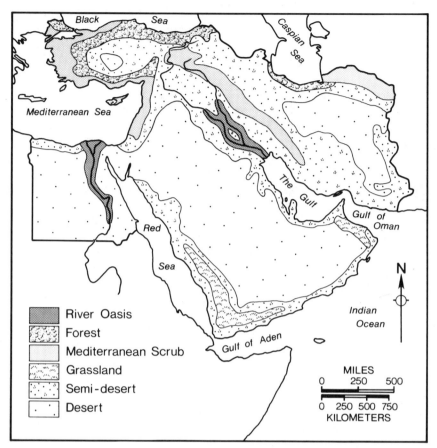

Map 5-2. *Middle East vegetation. Both "Grassland" and "Semi-desert" may be roughly equivalent to steppe.*

in./25 mm of annual rainfall—even so, the Rub al-Khali has areas that have a surprisingly well-developed vegetation. Deserts that are truly barren of vegetation are less common than is often supposed, and the typical desert exhibits at least a scattering of especially equipped dry bush or shrub (see Fig. 5-1).

Beginning with its small size—3–5 ft./1–1.5 m—and the wide spacing among individual plants to accommodate the limited supply of moisture, xerophytic vegetation has an impressive array of survival devices. With low shoot-to-root ratios, some shrubs have root systems that extend to depths of 30–50 ft./9–15 m. Their leaves are small, are often coated against excess transpiration (moisture loss), and in some species curl or even drop during unusually dry periods.

Tough stems resist drought, and the shrubs often have thorns for protection against grazing animals. Some of the lower bushes, 6–18 in./15–46 cm high, have woody or wiry stems and tiny leaves but a deep root system. By contrast, other desert plants, such as *Euphorbia,* store water in expandable succulent parts.

Scattered among the perennial and often long-lived shrubby plants are other low vegetal forms (4–12 in./10–30 cm) that sometimes constitute more than two-thirds of the typical desert plant community, including some species of grasses and many herbaceous forms. Some of these small plants are perennial, some are annual, and a few are both, depending upon their ecology. Most of the herbaceous annuals have an ephemeral life cycle of six to ten weeks, after which they lie dormant as seeds that burst into sprouts with the next rain, sometimes several years later. Along with a few of the xeromorphic perennial shrubs, they "avoid" the dry season instead of trying to endure it.

Shrubs in extensive fields of eolian (wind-blown) sand may be passive sand dwellers or sand binders; the latter hold the sand around extensive root systems and thus build prominent phytogenic (plant-created) mounds or hillocks. The resulting landscape, usually called *dikakah* or *marbakh* in Arabia, makes cross-country travel difficult. Some salty soils support halophytic (salt plant) vegetation. Over much of the eastern Arabian Peninsula, a common saltbush, popularly called *rimth*—useful for fodder and dietary salt for camels and other animals—is usually associated with at least slightly salty groundwater in poorly drained areas. However, on the true *sabkhahs* along the eastern Arabian Peninsula coast and on the *kavirs* of interior Iran, with their salt crust and briny subsurface, not even the most salt-tolerant plants can survive (see Fig. 5-2).[2]

The acacia, one of the largest desert shrubs, grades into a modest tree—up to 20 ft.—in moister soils. With its characteristic umbrella crown, it is a prominent and readily identifiable vegetative form in the silts, sands, and gravels in drainage channels or sheets from the central to the southern Arabian Peninsula. Where no other shade is available, it offers shade to animal and man in the broiling sun.

Grasslands (Steppes)

The change from desert to grassland is actually a zone of transition, and the exact boundary between the two is difficult to delineate because many of the desert species carry over into the adjoining grasslands. As moisture increases away from the desert, the more xerophytic species increasingly yield to plants adapted to the greater precipitation and better developed soils. More important, plant population density increases until the grasses form a virtually continuous vegetal cover.

The steppes constitute a discontinuous belt extending from the Sinai Peninsula northward through western Jordan and Syria, across southeastern Turkey and northern Syria, in an arc around northern Iraq, and along the Zagros piedmont. There are also many areas of considerable size in central Anatolia and in scattered locations in west-central Iran. (Steppe and semidesert are much the same in many areas, as is noted in the caption for Map 5-2.) With their short-grass vegetation, the steppelands are thus the core of the Fertile Crescent, with all that fact implies historically and agriculturally.

Mediterranean Zone

Whereas desert and steppe plants are especially equipped to survive a drought that lasts even many years, Mediterranean flora survive the characteristic summer drought of two to six months and then take advantage of the winter rain. Such flora appears as a low evergreen forest with scattered small trees and more closely spaced bushes and scrub. The height of the plants and the density of their growth increase from the dry side (approximately along the 15-in./380-mm isohyet) to the more humid part of the habitat, where the summer drought is also shorter. On the dry side, the Mediterranean vegetation zone is similar to the wooded steppe. On the humid side, the zone grades into the full forest of the highlands across the northern sector of the Middle East.

In between is the typical Mediterranean flora that may be divided into two main groups: garigue, the lower and more degraded of the flora, and maquis, the taller and better developed association. Some plant geographers also distinguish a third category of Mediterranean vegetation, *batha,* a kind of subgarigue. Both maquis and garigue are found in Mediterranean climate areas across southern Europe and elsewhere. In southern California, for example, similar vegetation is called "chaparral."

Garigue includes primarily a sclerophyllous (hard-leafed) scrub about 3 ft./1 m in height and also smaller shrubs, grass, and in spring, many colorful flowers—anemone, ranunculus, crocus, iris, and others. Commonly found on steeper, uncultivated hillsides in the Levant and in western and southern Asia Minor, garigue is a last safeguard against soil erosion. Maquis, which is typical of more favorable habitats than is garigue, forms a woodland dominated by low sclerophyllous evergreen trees and shrubs up to about 12 ft./3.7 m in height. In better stands of maquis, one finds trees—oaks, pistachios, and pines, especially the widespread Aleppo pine. Culinary herbs, such as thyme, marjoram, and laurel, and flowering bushes, such as oleanders, are associated with both garigue and maquis.

Forests

Few areas in the Middle East now have woodlands as well developed as those in Europe and North America, but historical evidence indicates that 2,500–3,000 years ago, forests clothed slopes that are now almost bare or are ragged—forests such as the Cedars of Lebanon or the forests of Asia Minor. Current reforestation and afforestation programs in several Middle East states are demonstrating that many previously treeless habitats can, given proper care, produce impressive forests of selected species.

The region's most extensive high forests extend along the Pontic Mountains from Istanbul eastward to the Iranian border and include impressive stands of beech, mixed with areas of spruce (especially *Picea orientalis*) in the east. On the southern, inner slopes of the Pontic Mountains, and especially in the western highlands, there are extensive areas of oak and pine (*Pinus nigra* and *P. silvestris* in the north and *P. brutia* in the west). *P. nigra* and *P. brutia* dominate the forests of the Taurus Mountains across southern Anatolia, and oaks predominate in the southeastern mountains west and south of Lake Van.

The great Euxinian Forest of northern Anatolia extends, with some discontinuity, into northern Iran to link up with the Hyrcanian or Caspian Forest in the Elburz Mountains. This humid forest facing the Caspian Sea is almost tropical in its luxuriance, with a rich variety of undergrowth as well as tall trees: linden, ash, oak, beech, elm, hornbeam, walnut, maple, and evergreens. Beech, dominant on the lower open slopes, is gradually replaced higher up, so that at 6,000–8,000 ft./1,830–2,440 m one finds the most magnificent trees in the Middle East—primarily oaks (*Quercus macranthera* and others) but also elm, ash, hornbeam, and maple.

In the higher elevations of the Zagros chains there is a somewhat dry, deciduous forest in which oaks dominate. With smaller and more widely spaced trees, and with a limited number of species, this Zagrosian Forest differs appreciably from the humid Euxinian and Hyrcanian forests.

In the west, scattered woodlands survive in areas of former extensive forests in the Levant highlands—in Israel, Jordan, Lebanon, Syria—and on the island of Cyprus. Most of these forests are either small remnants of great expanses of trees in the past, the Cedars of Lebanon, for example, or are woodlands planted in recent decades through government programs of reforestation or afforestation.

The endemic Aleppo pine, *Pinus halepensis,* is the tree most frequently planted in these programs. Sometimes called the "umbrella pine," it has come to be identified with the Levant highlands. Efforts to regenerate forests of Cedars of Lebanon (*Cedrus libani*) have encountered many problems, especially slow growth. The broadleaved tree most often used in plantation programs is a rapidly growing oak, *Quercus ithaburensis*. In drier areas, the pistachio serves well in planted woodlands; in still more arid areas, the tamarisk is utilized. *Tamarix aphylla* is used in group plantings and *T. gallica* as windbreaks.

Animal Life

Historical Changes

The variety of Middle East environments supports a rich variety of fauna; Iran alone has approximately the same number of species of mammals as all of Europe west of the pre-1991 Soviet border. Unfortunately, to judge by biblical and other early writings, many larger species have become extinct in the Middle East. Still others have been reduced to a fraction of their former count, are nearing extinction, or now occupy only a remnant of their original range. The residual effects on fauna of the area from the heavy fighting during the two wars between 1980 and 1991 are still not clear. Certainly the decimation of fish and bird life caused by the pollution of the upper Gulf was appalling, but it may not have been as catastrophic as was originally feared.

Appreciably different environmental conditions in the Middle East during the Tertiary period and the Pleistocene epoch supported animal groups unlike those of modern times. For example, although the ancestor of *Bos taurus,* wild and domesticated cattle, came from the Taurus Mountains of southern Anatolia, there is fossil evidence of *Bos* in the Rub al-Khali during pre-Pleistocene times. Some gazelle were numerous in the steppes and more vegetated deserts, and several species of deer grazed the wooded steppe and open forests. Wild sheep and goats kept to the heights. Lions, tigers, leopards, cheetahs, and other felines were formerly common in parts of the Fertile Crescent and Iran, and other carnivores, such as the wolf, fox, jackal, and hyena, roamed much of the same area.

All of these larger mammals have been decimated by nature and people, and the lion and tiger have virtually disappeared from the region. The crocodile disappeared about 1900, the ostrich in the early 1930s. The ruggedness of the north and the aridity of the south have given refuge to individual survivors and to small groups of gazelle, deer, mountain sheep and goats (including ibex), wild boar, and similar mammals, along with an occasional leopard, wolf, jackal, hyena, and fox. A considerable baboon population is found in the woodlands of Asir in southwestern Arabia. Hundreds of hamadryas baboons scurry through the brush among the granite knobs of the national park along the escarpment west of Abha; they are heedless of park visitors but nimbly steal any food left unattended. The gazelle population of the Syrian and Arabian deserts has declined precipitously, primarily as a result of hunting with rifles from cross-country vehicles. As endangered species, gazelle and oryx (a type of antelope) are now protected. In small numbers oryx, who require no water except moisture in leaves they eat or the dew they take in with the leaves in early morning, can survive in the arid Rub al-Khali.

The numerous domesticated animals of the Middle East—sheep, camels, goats, donkeys, cattle—are of great economic significance and are discussed in connection with land use in Chapter 7.

Some Common Types

The smaller mammals are much more numerous than the larger animals in both species and population, including hare, squirrel, hedgehog, honey badger, mongoose, and many species of rodents (jerboa, gerbil, hamster, field mouse,

sand rat). The many species of reptiles include few harmful types, but there are a few vipers, cobras, and adders.

Lizards, represented by dozens of species, are common in all parts of the Middle East. One common lizard of the Arabian Desert is the burrowing *dabb,* or spiney-tailed lizard, a heavy-bodied herbivorous species that grows to 18–20 in./45–50 cm and is eaten by the Bedouins. The longer but slimmer *waral,* or desert monitor, is carnivorous and more aggressive; unlike the *dabb,* it is not considered edible. The small *tuhayhi,* an agamid lizard, seeks protection by vibrating its body and sinking into loose sand. The sand-swimming skink and other lizards also use submergence in sand as a temperature-regulating device, since lizards—and many other animals—must maintain body temperature within a fairly narrow range. Stinging scorpions are especially numerous in the more arid areas. Since they are nocturnal, they can generally be avoided by the exercise of reasonable care.

Birds

The Middle East has traditionally been rich in bird life and is estimated to have at least 500 species. During spring and fall, the great eastern Mediterranean flyway is used by many flocks of migrating birds. The narrowness of the corridor affords an exceptional opportunity for bird observation but also adds to the vulnerability of the migrating birds to hunters. Marshes along the many coasts attract thousands of waterfowl, and many game birds are present, although now in reduced numbers. Among the common birds of prey are the falcons, traditionally used by Bedouins for hunting. The sport of hunting with falcons has increasingly become a popular pastime in the Arabian Peninsula and the drier areas of the Fertile Crescent. Field birds are especially numerous along the Nile Valley, and cotes for pigeons and doves are a common sight around villages. Doves, which are rarely hunted, are seen everywhere outside the cities in Israel. A variety of songbirds frequent the forests of the Pontic Mountains of northern Turkey.

Insects

Some insects in the region are major pests. There were formerly plagues of locusts, sometimes catastrophic ones, but concerted action has reduced the locust danger to a minimum. Malaria-spreading mosquitoes remain a serious problem despite pesticide programs, and flies (Diptera) are a widespread nuisance and also serious threat, since they spread eye diseases as well as gastrointestinal disorders. Incredibly, passengers in a vehicle traveling the open desert far from any settlement who stop for a picnic will almost immediately find themselves besieged by dozens of persistent flies.

6

Patterns of Peoples
and Cultures

The exceedingly complex patterns of distribution of population and peoples in the Middle East are shaped by many interacting biophysical, cultural, and historical influences. As has already been noted, the correlation between the pattern of population concentration and the pattern of precipitation and available water is especially high, and complex ethnic patterns often suggest alternating mountains and valleys that give refuge to or compartmentalize different groups of peoples.

Enumerating populations is difficult in most Middle East countries, and quantifying religions and linguistic groups is even more of a problem because such quantification often confronts very sensitive issues. Governments often attempt to obscure the number—and therefore the influence—of minority ethnic groups, such as Kurds in Turkey (and other countries involved in "Kurdistan") or Druzes in Lebanon. Similarly, official enumerators sometimes manipulate data concerning religious minorities, as has occurred in Egypt regarding the Copts and in Iran regarding Armenians and Zoroastrians. Therefore, figures vary widely, even in the best reports, and the following discussion and related tables represent a careful compromise among several authoritative sources. Data in the text are usually kept consistent with those in the tables and the country summaries, although more recent figures are occasionally introduced.

Census taking in some Middle East countries may face these various problems: Nomads may be difficult to locate; technical difficulties may interfere with accuracy, and the perceived sensitivity of data may cause some results to be sup-

pressed. Lebanon, for example, with its multiplicity of antagonistic religious communities and associated political factions, has avoided a census since the count in 1932 under the French mandate. Saudi Arabia conducted only basic demographic sampling until its 1974 partial census and is reticent about data on the high percentage of foreign resident workers.

Rapid growth in such oil states as Kuwait, the United Arab Emirates, and Saudi Arabia rendered statistics obsolete even before they were published during the 1970s and early 1980s. The physical destruction and human misery inflicted on Kuwait by the Iraqi invasion in August 1990 prompted the exodus of hundreds of thousands of the amirate's inhabitants, and the population will inevitably take several years to stabilize so that reenumeration would be meaningful. Qatar took its first census in 1986, and Oman has never had one. Even the statistics-conscious State of Israel experienced difficulty in maintaining a reliable count of its population during the influx of Jews from the Soviet Union and its successor states beginning in 1989. Also, in encouraging the immigration of Jews to Israel, the government of Israel has suppressed data on emigration from the state. Bahrain, Cyprus, Israel, and Turkey, however, regularly collect and publish generally good country statistics. All Middle East governments have made enormous and admirable improvement since the 1960s and 1970s in gathering statistical data and making at least most of these data available to the public. Devastated Lebanon continues to lag in this regard. In view of the foregoing, it is obvious that extensive quantitative analyses of the region are impossible and

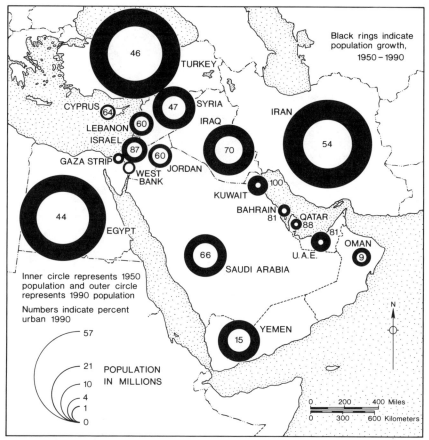

Map 6-1. *Middle East demography. Note dominance of population size in Turkey, Iran, and Egypt, as well as great growth in Kuwait and the UAE.*

that there is appreciable statistical unevenness among the different areas of the Middle East.

The sixteen countries of the Middle East had an estimated 1991 population total of 241.5 million, about 4.5 percent of the estimated world population of 5.3 billion. The 1990 total was more than three times the 1950 total of 79.7 million, prior to explosive population growth accompanying the oil boom. During the 40-year period after 1950, population increased by 15 times in Kuwait and by more than 27 times in the United Arab Emirates, and the population in most of the other states increased three or four times.

Two comparisons regarding Muslim and Arab populations may be noted. First, of approximately 935 million Muslims in the world, about one-fourth are in the Middle East. Second, of the estimated 1990 total population of all 20 Arab League states of 222.5 million, 121.3 million are in

the 12 Middle East member states. For these and other reasons, the Middle East constitutes the center of Islamic and Arab identity.

The following discussion of patterns of Middle Eastern peoples reveals the richness and complexity of the region's cultural patterns and gives some insight into the human dynamics behind major trends and events in the area: the fundamental political patterns, historical and contemporary conflicts, traditional group hostilities, changing cultural patterns, migrations of ethnic and religious groups, and certain irredentist claims.

Patterns: Population

Distribution

The pattern of distribution of population in the Middle East (see Maps 6-1, 6-2, and the second

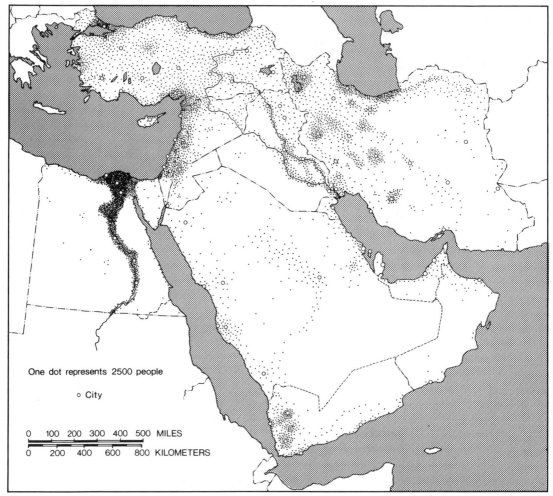

Map 6-2. *Distribution of population. The proverbial concentration of population in the Nile Valley and Delta is clearly shown.*

map in Chap. 10) is not only of great significance in itself; it also indicates the locations of more favorable environments and greater economic opportunities—twin magnets that attract people. The degree of urbanization indicated on Map 6-1 reflects both the historical role of the city in the Middle East and the rapid urbanization after 1950. The Middle East is more urbanized than is often assumed. At least 155 cities in the region have populations that exceed 100,000, and perhaps 15 cities exceed 1 million. Cities with populations between 100,000 and 500,000 have become relatively numerous during the second half of the twentieth century and are found in almost all Middle East countries. Nevertheless, despite

the trend of increasing urbanization, most of the people of the Middle East still live in villages.

Some of the scattered dots on Map 6-2 represent groups of nomadic pastoralists, whose numbers can only be estimated. The high mobility of nomads makes them difficult to count, but the numbers of all types of nonsedentary peoples have been found to be steadily decreasing. Several hundred thousand Bedouins of the Arabian Peninsula deserts are known to have settled between 1960 and 1990, and Bedouins elsewhere are becoming more settled, partly because of government pressures and incentives. Rough estimates of the numbers of nonsedentary peoples in the Middle East are 800,000 Bedouins, 2,000,000

Figure 6-1. *Bedouins in Saudi Arabia, watering their camels at wells in the broad Wadi Sahba, west of Haradh, enjoy a joke.*

other nomads, and 2,750,000 who move their livestock between mountain and lowland pastures with the seasons—transhumance, or vertical nomadism (Fig. 6-1).

Populations of the sixteen Middle East states vary greatly, as Table 6-1 and Graph 6-1 indicate. As is true in any region, population variations among states can be traced to six major factors: quality of the basic geographical environment, range and quality of natural resources, effectiveness of the national economy (and outside aid)—including food supply and health care—social and political pressures for or against population increase, incidental or planned (and even forced) immigration and emigration, and size of the state territory. In Part 2 these factors are explored within each Middle East country, but some quantitative comparisons can be made here.

The three largest populations are close to the 55 million total and have evolved in three of the four largest countries: Turkey, Iran, and Egypt (Graph 6-1), which also occupy three of the four major power foci (Map 2-6). Similarly, the fourth-largest population, that in Iraq, is found in the fourth major power focus. The fifth-largest population, estimates of which are variable, inhabits the largest state in the region—Saudi Arabia. Syria and Yemen have comparable populations of 12–13 million people and exhibit moderately large populations for their partly rugged and partly arid environments. Israel's population growth is highly dependent on periodically explosive immigration and capital transfers. Of the remaining countries, Jordan, Oman, and the UAE have relatively small populations for their size because they include extensive barren areas with minimal numbers of nomadic occupants. Kuwait, Qatar, Cyprus, and Bahrain are smaller states with smaller but prosperous populations.

Density

In addition to the basic patterns of distribution of population, patterns of density of population—the number of persons per unit of area—are also of significance. The density figures for most Middle East countries are not, however, comparable to similar data for countries in Western Europe, where few areas are actually uninhabited. As the dots in Map 6-2 show, population in the Middle East congregates in favorable areas, and there are extensive intervening areas that are uninhabited or dotted by a few nomads or widely

TABLE 6-1: AREA AND DEMOGRAPHY, 1990

COUNTRY	1 AREA IN SQ MI	2 AREA IN SQ KM	3 POP IN 000s	4 DENSITY PER SQ MI	5 DENSITY PER SQ KM	6 % POP URBAN	7 % ANNUAL GROWTH
Bahrain	267	692	503	1,883.9	726.9	80.7	3.4
Cyprus	3,572	9,251	739	206.9	79.9	63.5	1.1
Egypt	385,229	997,739	53,170	138.0	53.3	43.9	2.7
Iran	636,372	1,648,196	56,293	88.5	34.2	54.3	3.7
Iraq	167,975	435,052	17,754	105.7	40.8	70.2	3.1
Israel[a]	7,992	20,700	4,666	583.8	225.4	86.9	1.6
Jordan[b]	34,343	88,946	3,169	92.3	35.6	59.5	3.7
Kuwait[c]	6,880	17,818	2,143	311.5	120.3	100.0	4.6
Lebanon	3,950	10,230	2,965	750.6	289.8	60.1	2.1
Oman	120,000	300,000	1,468	12.2	4.9	8.8	3.4
Qatar	4,412	11,427	444	100.6	38.9	88.0	5.3
Saudi Arabia	865,000	2,240,000	14,131	16.3	6.3	65.9	4.1
Syria	71,498	185,180	12,116	169.5	65.4	47.0	3.4
Turkey	300,948	779,452	56,941	189.2	73.1	45.9	2.5
UAE	30,000	77,700	1,903	63.4	24.5	80.8	4.1
Yemen	205,356	531,869	11,546	56.2	21.7	15.2	2.6
Gaza	140	363	608	4,342.9	1,674.9	---	3.2
West Bank	2,270	5,900	908	400.0	153.9	---	2.5
TOTAL/AVG.	2,846,204	7,360,515	241,467	84.8	32.8	51.3	3.2
United Kingdom	94,251	244,110	57,384	608.8	235.1	89.6	0.3
Spain	194,898	504,783	38,959	199.9	77.2	72.8	0.2

Area includes internal waters. Population data are estimates for mid-1990. Percentage of annual growth rate (Column 7) is average for period 1985-1990. [a]Excludes territories occupied by Israel since 1967 (West Bank, Gaza, Golan). [b]Excludes West Bank, formerly under Jordanian administration. [c]Data for pre-Iraqi occupation period; population is now less than half that in Column 3 (see Chap. 18). Data for U.K. and Spain given for comparison. Source: *Britannica World Data 1991*. (With permission)

scattered villages. Thus, except in relatively favored areas like Asia Minor and the Levant, people concentrate in "islands" of better environments.

Some small oases may be widely scattered, with only a few families occupying each, as in the Jiwa (Liwa) Oases in western Abu Dhabi; by contrast, scores of thousands of people may be crowded into a narrow, intensively cultivated valley, as along the Nile River. In both cases, only a small percentage of the country's total area is actually occupied. In Egypt, for example, 53.2 million people have an overall density of 138 per mile^2/53 per km^2. However, population density based on the area actually inhabited and cultivated, about 3 percent of Egypt's total area, soars to more than 4,600 per mile^2/1,775 per km^2.

Rates of Birth, Death, and Increase

Statistics reveal a sharp decline in crude death rates (deaths per 1,000 population) in the Third World in the twentieth century. Better hygiene, health education, and health care facilities have increased live births, lowered the infant death rate, and lengthened the average human life. An increase in the birthrate (births per 1,000 population), certainly in the live birthrate, has accompanied the decrease in the death rate in many countries. The result has been a marked rise in the net population increase.

As shown in Table 6-1, the growth rates of the sixteen countries in the Middle East follow this trend in population increase, both because of high birthrates and because of high immigration. The birthrates of Syria, Oman, Iran, Iraq,

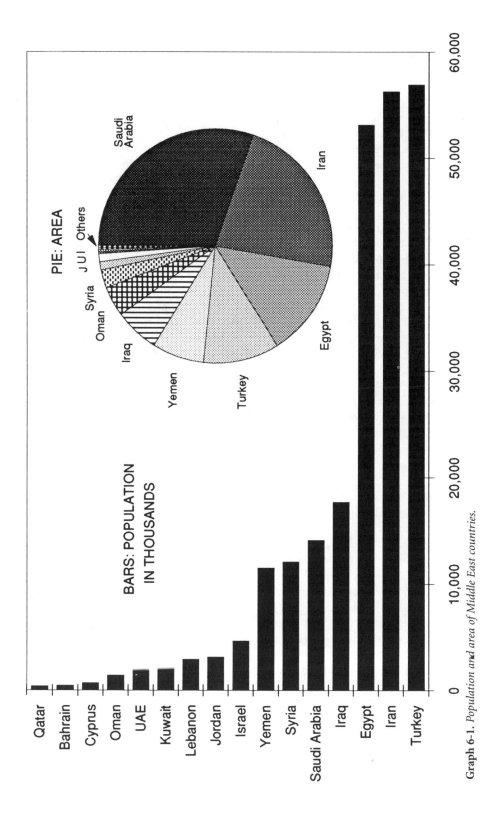

PIE: AREA

BARS: POPULATION
IN THOUSANDS

Graph 6-1. *Population and area of Middle East countries.*

and Yemen all exceed 44 per 1,000 and are among the highest in the world. Some countries, particularly Egypt, Turkey, and prior to 1979, Iran, have adopted systematic programs to inhibit the high rate of population increase by discouraging large families, but some groups resist family planning programs because their traditional customs encourage large families. In Israel, where as a group Jews have one of the lowest birthrates in the Middle East, the government encourages Jewish families to have more children, with the aim of matching the higher Arab birthrate. For the most part, however, family size in the region is tending to decrease.

Birthrates vary both from country to country and from group to group. For example, they differ among religious groups and ethnic groups (sometimes equivalent to economic classes) in all Middle East countries. The birthrate is substantially lower among Coptic Christians than among Muslims in Egypt, lower among Maronites than among Shiis in Lebanon, lower among European Jews than among Oriental Jews in Israel, and lower among Greek Cypriots than among Turkish Cypriots in Cyprus. Birthrate differentials accentuate political antagonisms because they might lead to a change in the balance of power.

Migration

All three basic aspects of migration—immigration, emigration, and internal migration—play a significant role in defining the contemporary pattern of peoples in the Middle East. For example, immigration into the region (by Jews, Indians, and Pakistanis, for example) and migration within the region (by Palestinians, Jordanians, Egyptians, Jews, Lebanese, Kurds, and others) have dramatically increased some populations and profoundly altered the ethnic composition of some states. The extraordinary influx of Jews into Israel between 1945 and 1951 and of Jews from the former Soviet Union after 1989 completely reconstituted the population, character, and political orientation of the Palestine realm.

As a general rule, people have not emigrated from the region in large numbers in modern times. However, since the middle of the twentieth century, tens of thousands of emigrants have fled conflict and limited economic opportunity in the Levant, emigrating to the United States, Canada, Western Europe, and Australia. This emigration has included many Palestinian Arab refugees, Christian Lebanese, some Syrians and Jordanians, and by the late 1970s, many thousands of Israelis.

Patterns of Peoples

It is the cultural differentiation among peoples—variations in language, religion, common memories of a shared historical past, shared customs and dress, consensus of values—that creates separate group identities and nations. Thus, examination of the mosaic of peoples, or ethnic groups, is a major component of this analysis of Middle East patterns. Cultural patterns are, in effect, shuffled three times. The two dominant cultural patterns, language and religion, deserve individual attention, and sections on those patterns are then followed by a survey of ethnic groups. Two salient points to be noted in the following discussion are the fact that half of the population of the region is non-Arab, although twelve of sixteen countries are Arab states, and the fact that within its essential unity, Islam carries ethnic and political imprints and also has a number of sectarian variations. Thus, within its regional unity, the Middle East possesses great cultural diversity.[1]

Patterns: Languages

Language is the principal criterion for defining ethnic groups, particularly if the distinction is an ethnolinguistic one. Thus, Map 6-3 summarizes one of the most revealing patterns in the cultural geography of the Middle East. The depiction of only six main linguistic groupings—Arabic, Turkish, Farsi (Persian), Kurdish, Hebrew, and Greek—should not obscure the presence of approximately 25 other language groups in less accessible basins, valleys, and plateaus. Some of these other languages appear on Map 6-3, but many others are covered in the listing of ethnic groups later in the chapter, and some of them are discussed in this section.

Semitic and Berber

The Semitic language group includes Arabic, the numerically predominant regional language; He-

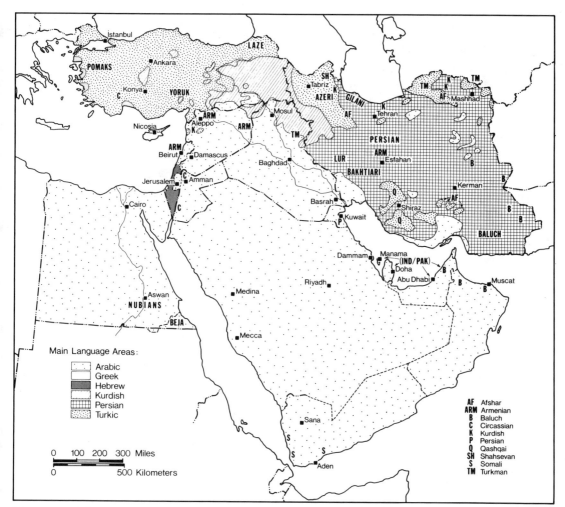

Map 6-3. *Middle East languages, indicating ethnolinguistic groups. This pattern is the basis for political patterns and for numerous regional conflicts. Note that the complexity of the pattern of languages is greatest in mountain areas, especially in Iran.*

brew, spoken in Israel; and vestiges of Aramaic, formerly spoken widely throughout the Middle East for more than 2,000 years. The North African Berber and Coptic languages are grouped here with the Semitic languages, although they belong to different subfamilies.

Arabic. Arabic is the national language of twelve of the sixteen countries of the region and is spoken by approximately 115 million Middle Easterners, nearly half the total population. Three levels of usage have emerged: (1) colloquial, informal spoken Arabic; (2) modern standard Arabic, or "newspaper Arabic," the more formal Arabic used in books and lectures; and (3) classical

Arabic, the formal and highly conventionalized style based on the language of pre-Islamic poetry, the Quran, and the writings of the first few centuries of the Islamic era. Educated Arabs understand all three, but uneducated Arabs have difficulty understanding the two more formal usages. In addition, four major dialects of Middle East Arabic are generally distinguished: those of Egypt, Syria (western Arabic), Iraq (eastern Arabic), and the Arabian Peninsula. Significant differences of vocabulary and pronunciation exist among and even within these four dialects.

Speaking Arabic as a mother tongue is the hallmark of being an Arab. Since it is the language of the Quran, the holy book of the Muslims, Arabic has a mystical quality for many Arabs. It has additional emotional overtones as the language in which speeches and documents on Arab nationalism are prepared. The written language even plays a central role in Middle East art, since it is used in traditional decorative motifs in lieu of the sometimes proscribed human, animal, and vegetal motifs. Calligraphy is one of the highest forms of the fine arts in Islam.

Hebrew. Compared with Arabic, Hebrew is spoken in a relatively limited area by a comparatively small number of people, approximately 3.8 million. It should be noted that not all Jews in the region—not even all Israeli Jews—speak Hebrew. An ancient language, it was a major vernacular for more than 1,000 years in the traditional Old Testament area of Israel. It ceased to be used as a working language centuries ago, but it was studied by biblical scholars and was used in Jewish communities as a ritual language, much as Latin, Greek, and Syriac are used in Christian church liturgies. It is also a scriptural language and has a mystical quality for religious Jews similar to that Arabic has for devout Muslims. Ultrareligious Jews consider Hebrew so sacred that they reserve it for ritual use only and refuse to use it as a vernacular, employing Yiddish or other languages for everyday use.

Hebrew was revived in the late nineteenth century under the stimulus of Jewish nationalism, the Zionist movement, and because of the need for a unifying national language for the new Jewish immigrants to Israel in the twentieth century. Contemporary usage has required adaptation of old terms and the coinage of new scientific terms.

Aramaic. Now primarily of historical interest, Aramaic (not to be confused with Armenian) served for more than 1,500 years as the lingua franca of the Fertile Crescent and was the language of Palestine by the time of Christ. Like Latin to the west, Aramaic was used for translations of the Bible. The Syriac form of Aramaic is used in the scriptures and liturgies of several Oriental Christian churches—Maronite, Nestorian, Chaldean—and by such sects as the Mandaeans and Samaritans. It is also still spoken by a few hundred Christians in three mountain villages northwest of Damascus.

Berber. A subfamily language in the Afro-Asiatic language family, Berber is spoken by many millions of North Africans. It is spoken in the Middle East by only a few thousand Berbers who live in oases in northwestern Egypt.

Coptic. With its name derived from *Qibt*, a corruption of the Greek word *Aigyptos* (Egypt), Coptic was the latest form of the ancient Egyptian language. With the addition of some Greek during the Hellenistic period, Coptic served as a vernacular in Egypt until over the centuries it was gradually supplanted by Arabic after the Muslim conquest. The discovery that many Coptic words were taken directly from the ancient Egyptian aided in the deciphering of Egyptian hieroglyphics. By the sixteenth century, Coptic was used primarily in the liturgy of the Coptic Christian church in Egypt.

Altaic Turkic Languages

The Altaic family includes a large number of languages spoken in the former Soviet Union and in China, as well as Magyar (Hungarian) and Finnish in Europe and more than a score of Turkic languages spoken in central Asia and the Middle East.

Turkish. The best known of the Turkic languages, Turkish is spoken by the largest number of Turkic language speakers. The national language of the Republic of Turkey, it was brought into the Middle East by Turkish tribes migrating from central Asia in the tenth to thirteenth centuries. As Turkish speakers adopted Islam and settled Asia Minor, the language absorbed loanwords from Arabic, the language of the Quran, and also from literary Persian.

Lacking a standard alphabet of its own, for 800–900 years Turkish was written in the Arabic alphabet of the Quran. In 1928, the Latin alphabet, with a number of diacritical marks borrowed from German and French, officially replaced the Arabic alphabet, and the language was "purified" of Arabic and Persian terms. In the Middle East, it is spoken throughout the Republic of Turkey and by the 170,000 Turkish Cypriots in northern

Cyprus; otherwise, it is spoken by only small, scattered family-size groups in the Fertile Crescent area.

Azeri. Azeri (or Azerbaijani) is the second major Turkic language spoken in the Middle East, centered in northwestern Iran and adjacent areas in Iraq and the Republic of Azerbaijan. Regional variations of Azeri appear in the western Elburz and the southern Caspian littoral among the Afshar, Shahsavan (now called Ilsavan), and Qajar ethnic groups. Like Turkish, Azeri was carried by migrating Turkic tribes during the Abbasid Empire.

Other Turkic languages spoken by several hundred thousand people each in Iran and Turkey include Qashqai (spoken by Turkic tribes in the southern Zagros Mountains of Iran) and various Turkmen dialects spoken by scattered peoples in the Anatolian-Iranian mountains and basins and in small areas in northeastern Iraq.

Indo-European Languages

The Indo-European languages of the Middle East include more than a score of Indo-Iranian tongues, the main ones being Farsi (Persian), Kurdish, Baluchi, and Luri with its related dialect of Bakhtiari. Armenian and Greek are other languages in the main Indo-European family that are spoken in the region.

Farsi (Persian). The primary Indo-Iranian language of the Middle East is Farsi, a name taken from the ancient Iranian province of Fars. After Arabic and Turkish, Farsi is spoken by the third-largest language group in the region. The Persian languages were brought to the Iranian Plateau more than 1,500 years before Turkic languages were heard in the area. After the Muslim conquest of Iran in the seventh century, Persian, like Turkish, incorporated hundreds of Arabic loanwords and adopted a slightly modified Arabic script.

Farsi is the primary language of Iran, although more than a third of the Iranians speak a mother tongue other than Persian—Azeri, Kurdish, Gilaki, Luri, Baluchi, Arabic, and others. However, as the official language and the language used by the mass media, government, educational institutions, and most Iranian writers, Farsi is increasingly used as a second language by minority groups. Persian literature has a rich history dating from the Zoroastrian scriptures, the Avesta, written before 500 BC.

Kurdish. The Indo-Iranian language spoken by the second-largest number of people in the Middle East, Kurdish is used across a geographical range from the streets of Beirut eastward through its main concentration in the mountains of Kurdistan and into the remote valleys of Afghanistan. It is grammatically and lexically distinct from Persian. Reflecting the extension of Kurdistan into several hegemonies, Kurdish is written with the Arabic alphabet in Iraq, the adapted Arabic alphabet in Iran, and the Latin alphabet in Turkey.

Other Indo-Iranian Languages. *Baluchi* is spoken by the Baluch of Baluchistan in southeastern and eastern Iran but even more so outside the Middle East proper in Pakistan and Afghanistan. It is also spoken by several thousand Baluch who have migrated across the Gulf to the United Arab Emirates and to Oman. *Luri,* a dialect of Persian, is spoken by nomadic tribes in the central Zagros, both by the Lur themselves and also, as a slightly different dialect, by their Bakhtiari neighbors. Sometimes called "Caspian" languages, a half-dozen Indo-Iranian dialects, mixed with one or two Turkic tongues, are spoken along the southern coast of the Caspian Sea and on the northern slopes of the Elburz Mountains back of the Caspian coast.

Armenian and Greek. Armenian and Greek, two Indo-European languages, were formerly spoken over more extensive areas in the Middle East than they are at present. Armenian was the dominant language for more than 2,000 years in the area still referred to by the regional name Armenia, the highlands at the junction of Turkey, Iran, and the new Republic of Armenia. However, the decimation of Armenian speakers and their migration from Turkey have reduced the area of the language's use to scattered pockets in Anatolia and urban centers such as Beirut, Damascus, Aleppo, Tehran, and Cairo.

Similarly, Greek had been a major language in western Asia Minor 2,000 years before Turks arrived in significant numbers, and early Greeks also settled several Mediterranean islands, including Cyprus. As the urban and intellectual language of the Levant for more than two centuries after Alexander the Great, Greek was used by some of the Christian missionaries and writers of books of the New Testament. By the mid-1920s, however, only a few thousand Greek speakers remained in Asia Minor, primarily in Istanbul and coastal cities of the Mediterranean and Aegean. The main concentration of Greek speakers in the Middle East is now found in southern Cyprus, with small family-size pockets in cities in the Levant.

Patterns: Religions

Complexity of Patterns of Religion

At first glance, the pattern of religions appears simple: Islam embraces all but about 8 percent of the people of the Middle East. This pattern, however, is complicated by basic divisions within Islam between Sunni and Shii Muslims and also by the splintering of Shii sects.

Divisions within the general Christian religion, which developed its early structure in the Middle East, are even more numerous. Differing theological interpretations resulted in schisms, which were later only partly mended by the church in Rome, until more than a dozen sects claimed sole possession of Christian truth.

Several million Jews are now concentrated in Israel, where ethnic and sectarian subdivisions periodically dispute over such issues as conversion and observation of the Sabbath. Ancient or syncretic religions—Zoroastrian, Yazidi, Mandaean, Bahai—constitute small Middle Eastern minorities.

Religious divisions have long played, and at the present time increasingly play, significant cultural-political-geographical roles in the Middle East. In recent decades political instability and social violence have increasingly devolved from intensification of religious and ethnic consciousness. In turn, political polarization resulting from religious fervor has inflamed communal feelings and weakened national bonds. Most significant during the 1970s and 1980s was the increasing politicization of religion, which is explored in Chapter 11.

The pattern of religions has been strongly influenced by two historical factors in modern times. First, at the time of the Muslim conquest of the area from the Nile River to the Iranian Plateau in the seventh century, there were millions of Christians and Zoroastrians, scores of thousands of Jews in both Mesopotamia and Palestine, thousands of Mandaeans, and other smaller groups. In general, the Muslim invaders proselyted these conquered peoples. However, those who practiced Judaism and Christianity were considered *ahl al-kitab* ("people of the book") and were permitted to maintain their own religions and communities under certain conditions. Later, Mandaeans, Zoroastrians, and even Berbers were accepted as people of the book. Therefore, religious groups possessed a strong group identity linked with their courts, areas of residence, occupations, and usually language as well as religion. This early group identity still persists, and it continues to affect regional relationships and the internal politics of Middle East states.

In a second historical development, the Islamic concept of people of the book was codified by the Ottoman Empire into the *millet* system (from *millah*, "religion" or "religious community"), and *millets* further imprinted group consciousness on the non-Muslims of the Middle East. Religious affiliation assumed great cultural-political significance, and identity cards in Lebanon, Israel, and other states still specify the individual's religion.

Three Monotheistic World Religions

A familiar and significant aspect of the Middle East is that it is the birthplace of the world's three major monotheistic religions: Judaism, Christianity, and Islam (Map 6-4; Fig. 6-2). Judaism and Christianity both originated in the hill area between the Mediterranean coastal plain and the Jordan Valley, and Islam originated 700 miles/1,125 km to the southeast in hills that lie inland from the Red Sea coast. As Judaism borrowed from Mesopotamian and Canaanite traditions, so Christianity evolved from Judaic

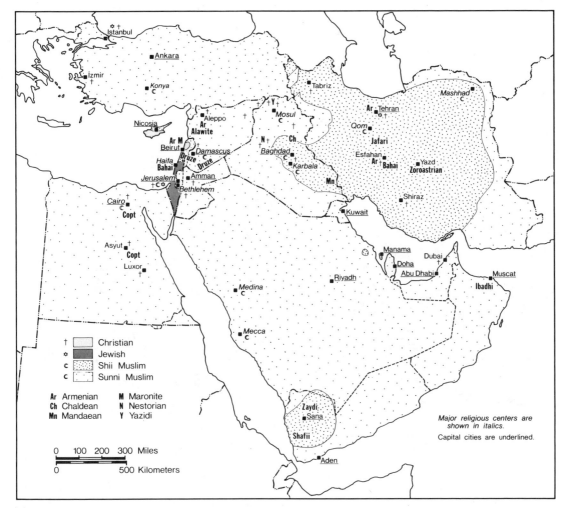

Map 6-4. *Middle East religions. Note the overwhelming dominance of Islam and the extension of Shiism into southern Iraq.*

traditions and others of the region, and Islam borrowed heavily from Judaism, Christianity, and local traditions in the Hijaz. In the Middle East in 1992, Muslims numbered about 223 million, more than 92 percent of the population of the region. Christianity was the second-largest religion, with approximately 12 million adherents, and Judaism third with approximately 4.1 million.

The following discussion focuses on spatial relations rather than historical evolution or theology. Islam is examined in somewhat more detail because of its greater geographical and quantita-

tive importance in the region and because it is less well known or understood outside the Muslim world.

Islam

The name *Islam* is Arabic for "submission," that is, submission to God's will, and a Muslim is "one who submits." The term *Muhammadan* is sometimes used instead of Muslim; however, the usage may be misleading, since it may suggest a parallel with "Christian" in the sense of worship of Christ, whereas Muslims do not worship Muhammad. They do revere his teachings and

Figure 6-2. *Mosque of St. Sophia (Greek, Haghia Sophia; Turkish, Aya Sofya—Divine Wisdom) in Istanbul. Originally a Byzantine church, it was converted into a mosque when Constantinople was captured by the Ottomans in 1453. Deconsecrated in the 1930s, it is now a museum.*

consider him the last and greatest of the prophets, the Seal of the Prophets.

The origins of Islam reflect a regional character. Mecca, the Arabian town in which Islam first evolved, was an important midway caravan post between Yemen and Syria. The importance of Mecca was enhanced by the presence of the Well of Zamzam, since water was scarce along Tihamah, the barren Red Sea coastal plain followed by the caravans. The town was also the site of an ancient shrine, the Kaabah, which contained an array of idols and also housed the Black Stone of Mecca, a meteorite. Mecca's rapid development in the sixth century stimulated intellectual exchange, as townspeople and Bedouins from the Hijaz mingled with the caravan travelers from Syria, Yemen, and other trade areas.

One Mecca merchant who was inspired by the ideas being discussed was Muhammad ibn Abdullah, a member of the Hashim clan of the Quraysh tribe. While meditating in a cave near Mecca, he received what he later explained were dictations from the Angel Gabriel of the Holy Word of the one God. Preaching his revelations, Muhammad denounced the idols in the Kaabah shrine and thereby reduced Mecca's tourist trade. Harassed by Mecca merchants, Muhammad and his followers, the original Muslims, emigrated to Yathrib, 210 miles/340 km north of Mecca. Yathrib later became known as *al Madinat al-Nabi* (the City of the Prophet), or simply *al-Madina* (the City) and is known commonly as Medina. The year AD 622, when the migration to Medina occurred, became the first year of the Islamic calendar. Muslim years, reckoned on the lunar system (which makes them eleven days shorter than Gregorian calendar years), are designated as *anno Hegirae* (AH), year of the Hegira (Arabic, *hijrah,* "flight").

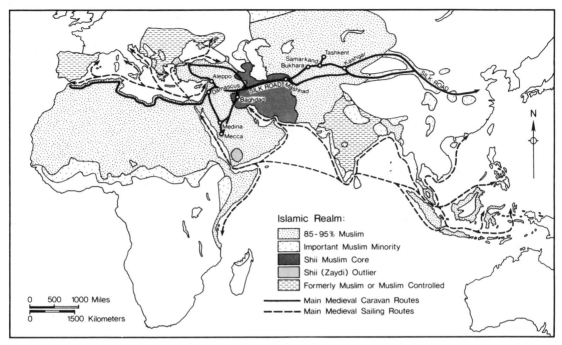

Map 6-5. *Present extent of Islam, with major medieval caravan and sea routes that contributed to the spread and maintenance of Islam.*

In Medina, dictations from the Angel Gabriel were recited by the Prophet to his followers until his death in AD 632. These recitations were assembled in 651 into the Muslim scriptures, the Quran (Koran), meaning "recitation," which plays a central role in Islam. As the precise Word of God, the Quran links God and man, and its poetic language echoes the Hijaz desert area and village and Bedouin traditions, as the Old and New Testaments refer to the desert and nomadic traditions of Sinai and the Syro-Palestinian area.

Translation of the Quran from Arabic was long forbidden, since that would mean altering the direct Word of God, and converts to Islam perforce learned the Arabic language in order to understand the Quran. As Islam spread throughout the Middle East to Spain and into central Asia (Map 6-5), the Arabic language also spread, with crucial historical and political-geographical consequences.

Although, like all religions, Islam has been elaborated into a complex and subtle body of theology, both its essential message and practice are simple and straightforward. Its one basic essential is that a new convert express and believe

the *shahadah,* or profession of faith: "There is no god but God; Muhammad is the messenger of God," a translation of the euphonious Arabic *La ilaha illa Allah; Muhammadun rasulu Allah.* The *shahadah* and four additional primary obligations constitute the five pillars of Islam, which have profoundly affected regional character in the Islamic world: *salah,* devotional worship or prayer five times a day while facing toward the Kaabah, the House of God, in Mecca; *zakah,* religious tax (and *sadaqah,* voluntary almsgiving, as additionally meritorious); *sawm,* fasting during the holy month of Ramadan, ninth month of the Muslim year; and the *hajj,* the pilgrimage to Mecca.

The Quran also underlies the Shariah, the sacred law of Islam, which covers all aspects of the lives of Muslims—not only religious and private but also political and public, social and economic. Shariah still plays an important role in the law of several Middle East countries (Saudi Arabia, Qatar, Iran) and complements the more westernized legal codes of countries such as Egypt, Syria, and Iraq. Resurgent Islamic fundamentalism has brought a renewed interest in

Shariah law, which has at various times been in conflict with modern secular trends in the region.

Islam was for many centuries both religion and government, and when the Shariah was compiled, it combined religious and civil matters. The caliph (Arabic, *khalifah,* "successor") thus led both the community of believers (the *ummah*) and the Islamic state. Subsequent schisms within Islam have placed severe strains on this unity of religion and state.

The most momentous schismatic dispute within Islam occurred with the seventh-century division between Sunni and Shii. This split has precipitated wars, assassinations, civil conflict, and rancor in the Middle East and North Africa for more than 1,300 years and still has grave repercussions in the area today. Part of the bitterness between Iran and Iraq during their 1980s war may be traced to the Sunni-Shii differences. The Sunnis (or Sunnites)—*ahl al-sunnah wa-l-jamaah,* "the people of custom and community"—consider themselves the original, Orthodox Muslims and have always been in the overwhelming majority. They believe that caliphs could be chosen by leaders of the *ummah* and were secular leaders only. The Shiis (or Shiites or Shiah)—*shiat Ali,* "partisans of Ali"—evolved as a separate sect beginning in AD 657 because they believe that only descendants of Muhammad's daughter Fatima and his son-in-law Ali were legitimate successors to Muhammad. To Shiis, these successors are divinely guided, sinless, infallible religious leaders (imams) with authority to interpret the Prophet's spiritual knowledge. This fundamental theological schism has accentuated the political and cultural cleavages that have long divided Arabs and Persians, especially since Safavid shahs adopted dormant Shiism as the imperial religion in the early 1500s.

After the initial split from Sunni Islam, Shiis experienced further divisions over the issue of succession (Table 6-2).

1. The predominant Shii group accepted Ali and eleven of his descendants as the true imams and became known as Twelvers (also Ithna Ashari, Imamis, and Jafaris). They are concentrated in Iran and Iraq, but considerable numbers are found in every Middle East country, including Lebanon.

2. A smaller group preferred a different seventh imam, Ismail, and became known as Seveners (also Ismailis). Greatly reduced in numbers, most are now divided into heretical sects such as the Druze and the Alawi. The Ismailis developed their political power between the tenth and thirteenth centuries. Early Ismaili dynasties ruled in Syria and Bahrain, and the Ismaili Fatimids, named for Muhammad's daughter, achieved an Egyptian renaissance in Cairo during the tenth to twelfth centuries. Ismaili "assassins" engaged in political sabotage and murder, primarily in northern Iran, until they were decimated in the thirteenth century, but contemporary Ismailis are a mild sect found in India, Syria, the Gulf area, and along the coast of eastern Africa.

Two offshoots of the Ismailis mentioned above became newsworthy in the 1970s and 1980s during the Lebanese civil war and Syria's involvement in Lebanon's troubles. The larger sect, the Druze, originated in 1017 in Cairo with followers of the Fatimid caliph al-Hakim. Although they called themselves Muwahhidun (Unitarists), outsiders called them Druzes after the name of an early missionary. The Druzes won especially large numbers of converts among isolated mountain peoples in southern Lebanon and adjacent areas, where the Druzes, an esoteric and nonproselyting sect, are still concentrated.[2]

The second offshoot sect, the Alawis (or Alawites, also known as Nusayris and sometimes Ansariyahs) are concentrated in northwestern Syria. Although the name "Alawi" indicates "followers of Ali," the rituals of their esoteric religion are known to include pre-Christian, Christian, and Sabian elements as well as Shii Islamic practices. Using neither mosques nor churches, Alawis conduct rites around shrines near revered tombs and sacred groves.

3. A third group of Shiis chose a different fifth imam, Zayd, and became known as Fivers (also Zaydis). They are concentrated in Yemen, where a broken line of Zaydi secular imams held power until the overthrow of Imam al-Badr in the mid-1960s. Yemeni links with the Shiis originated in the support given Ali by Yemeni tribesmen who, settling in southern Mesopotamia after the Arab Muslim conquest of the area, allied themselves with the supporters of Ali.

TABLE 6-2: RELIGIONS OF THE MIDDLE EAST

RELIGION, CHURCH, SECT (INCLUDING ALTERNATE NAMES)	MAIN CENTER OR PAT. SEAT	LITURGICAL LANGUAGE	MAIN AREAS IN WHICH FOUND IN MIDEAST
———— ISLAM ————			
Sunni Islam (largest sect by far)	None (Mecca)	>Ar; Turk, Farsi	Most of Mideast
Shii Islam (second-largest sect by far)	None (Mecca, Karbala)	Farsi, Arabic	Iran, Southern Iraq, South Lebanon
Imamis (Jafaris, "Twelvers," Ithna Ashari)	——	Farsi, Arabic	Iran, Iraq
Ismailis ("Seveners")	——	Arabic	Levant
Zaydis ("Fivers")	——	Arabic	Yemen
Alawis (Alawites, Nusayris, Ansaris)	None	Arabic	Western Syria
Druzes (Muwahhidun ["Unitarians"])	None	Arabic	S Syr, C Leb, N Isr
Ibadhis	Nazwa, Oman	Arabic	Inner Oman, <Iran
———— CHRISTIANITY ————			
Churches with no outside affiliation			
Coptic Orthodox Church (C O C, Alexandria)	Cairo	Coptic, Arabic	C and N Egypt
Armenian Orthodox Ch. (Arm. Georgian Church)	Antilyas, Leb	Armenian	C Middle East
Syrian Orth. Ch. (Jacobite Ch., W Syr. Church)	Damascus	Syriac, Arabic	Syria, Iraq
Ethiopian Orthodox Church (Ethiopian Church)	Addis Ababa	Geez	Egypt
Church of the East (Nestorian Church, East Syrian Church, Assyrian Church)	Baghdad (official)	Syriac	Syria, Iraq
Churches affiliated with the Patriarchate of Constantinople			
Orthodox Patriarchate of Constantinople (Greek Orthodox Church of Const., The Great Church)	Istanbul	Greek	Levant
Greek Orth. Church of Antioch (Rum Orth., etc.)	Damascus	Arabic	Levant
Greek Orth. Church of Alexandria (Ch. of Alex.)	Alexandria	Greek, Arabic	Egypt
Greek Orth. Church of Jerusalem (Ch. of Jerus.)	Jerusalem	Arabic, Greek	Levant
Greek Orthodox (several other names)	(Several)	(Several)	Levant
Uniate Churches: Churches united with the Roman Catholic Church			
Coptic Catholic Church (Coptic Cath. Ch. of Alex.)	Cairo	Coptic, Arabic	Egypt
Maronite Church (Maronite Church of Antioch)	Bkirke, Leb	Syriac, Arabic	Central Lebanon
Syrian Catholic Ch. (Patriarchate of Antioch)	Beirut, Leb	Syriac, Arabic	Levant
Armenian Cath. Church (Arm. Cath. Ch. Cilicia)	Bzummar, Leb	Armenian	Levant
Chaldean Catholic Church (Chaldean Church)	Baghdad	Syriac, Arabic	Iraq
Melkite Church (Rum Catholic Church, Greek Catholic Church of Antioch)	Damascus	Arabic	Syria
Western Churches			
Roman Catholic Church	Rome	(Various)	Mideast exc Arabia
Protestant Churches (Presbyterians, Methodists, Baptists, Anglicans, several others)	———	English, others	Mideast exc Arabia
———— JUDAISM ————			
Orthodox Judaism	(Jerusalem)	Hebrew	Israel, <other ME
Hasidic Judaism [ultra-Orthodox Judaism]	(Jerusalem)	Hebrew	Israel
(Samaritanism [offshoot of Judaism])	Nablus (WB)	Aramaic	West Bank, Israel
———— OTHERS ————			
Yazidism (erroneously: "Devil Worship")	None	Kurdish, Ar	NW Iraq, NE Syria
Mandaeism (Sabianism, Mendaism)	None	Aramaic dial.	Baghdad, S Iraq
Bahaism	Haifa	(Several)	Iran, Levant
Zoroastrianism	None	Farsi	Central Iran

"Pat." = Patriarchal. "WB" = West Bank. Some liturgies use local languages (Arabic, Turkish, Farsi [Persian]) in addition to the traditional languages. Syriac is a form of Aramaic. Memberships vary widely, from more than 223 million Muslims to about 528 Samaritans. (From various sources, including Joseph 1983, *Britannica World Data 1991*, and author's field research.)

Figure 6-3. *Young shoppers at an outdoor* suq *in Nazwa, famous ancient town in Inner Oman. Note the handsomely embroidered, typically Omani headwear of the young men.*

An isolated, little-known group of Muslims, the Ibadhis, live in Inner Oman, where they were banished from southern Iraq in the seventh century. They are descendants of the Kharijites ("seceders"), who assassinated Ali and withdrew from the belief systems of both the Sunnis and the other Shiis regarding the right of caliphal succession. The Ibadhis intermittently maintained their own imamate in Inner Oman and periodically fought for control of Muscat and all of Oman into the mid-twentieth century. With Nazwa as their main center, they are now a conservative, dignified group and are joining in the development of modern Oman (see Fig. 6-3).

Christianity

Middle East Christianity embraces more than a dozen sects centered on the spiritual and ethical teachings of Jesus of Nazareth, who is believed to have lived and taught in Palestine 2,000 years ago. In the Occidental world, calendar years are designated, with an inadvertent error of about four years, as *anno Domini* (AD), indicating years that have lapsed since the birth of Jesus.

Although other religions believe in the messianic concept, the Christian religion preaches, as a central belief, that Jesus was the long-awaited Messiah (Greek, *Christos,* "the anointed," anglicized to Christ). The early apostles compiled his teachings in the Gospels ("good tidings") and added their own preachings and letters. Assembled, these writings form the New Testament (New Covenant), the main scriptures of the Christian religion, which is coupled with the Old Testament to constitute the Holy Bible of Christianity. Even in its early years, Christianity incorporated influences from the region's several cultures—Jewish, Greek (Hellenistic), Roman, and Aramaic.

By New Testament accounts, Jesus was acclaimed during his three-year ministry in the area of Judea, Galilee, and neighboring places. However, only a few of his followers, mainly converted Jews, remained faithful after his crucifixion by the Roman authorities (Fig. 6-4). In AD 66, when the Christian Jews of Jerusalem refused to support the Jewish revolt, Jewish leaders rejected the Christians and their concepts.

After this breach between Christians and Jews, the apostle-missionaries decided to preach to the Gentiles (Greeks) in Asia Minor and Syria. Antioch became the first Christian center, soon fol-

Figure 6-4. *View in the Old City of Jerusalem: The Via Dolorosa in the Christian Quarter. To the left is the Ecce Homo Arch. The church is part of the Convent of the Sisters of Zion.*

lowed by Edessa (modern Urfa) farther east. Suppressed for 200 years by Roman authorities as inimical to their own religion and positions, Christianity was officially permitted by the Edict of Milan (313), was accepted by Emperor Constantine after he moved his imperial capital from Rome to Constantinople in 330, and was made the state religion of the Roman Empire in 380. A series of ecumenical councils, convened in or near the eastern imperial capital of Constantinople, debated heresies and sought unity but engendered fragmentation. Christianity was the dominant religion of the Middle East outside Iran and the Arabian Peninsula between the fourth and the sixth centuries, but today it is a minority faith in an overwhelmingly Muslim area.

The approximately 12 million Christians in the Middle East are divided among more than a dozen Orthodox and Catholic sects, with a minority divided among a number of Protestant churches (see Table 6-2). The largest group, the Coptic Christians, live in Egypt. The second-largest group, the Maronites, are concentrated in Lebanon, where a variety of Christian groups constitute about 28–32 percent of the population. The third-largest number are in Syria, where they constitute about 10 percent of the population. The fourth-largest number of Christians are found among a variety of sects in northern and northeastern Iraq, where mountains shelter numerous relict groups—non-Christian as well as Christian. The fifth-largest number of Christians, and the greatest concentration of Greek Orthodox in the region, are in Cyprus, where they constitute about three-fourths of the island's population and nearly 100 percent of the population in south Cyprus. Finally, Turkey, Iran, and Jordan each have Christian minorities that number more than 400,000 in Turkey and Iran and 200,000 in Jordan.

Judaism

Oldest of the three great monotheistic religions, Judaism evolved over a period of more than 1,500 years, a development that is the theme of the Old Testament. It takes its name from Judah, the southern kingdom associated with the northern kingdom of Israel, from which the term *Jew* is also derived. The patriarch Jacob, through his religious name, Israel, became the traditional eponymous ancestor of the Bnai Yisrael, children (literally, Sons) of Israel.

Judaism's roots lie in traditions of a seminomadic Aramaean tribe that is personified in the patriarch Abraham. In the Old Testament account, the original group migrated from southern Mesopotamia, Ur of the Chaldees, up the Euphrates Valley to the Harran and then, probably about 1700 BC, southwestward to the southern hills of Canaan. Out of the tribal growth and development of the Bnai Yisrael evolved the elements of the monotheistic religion that came to

be known as Judaism. It revolved around the one God (Yahweh), the covenant between God and the people of Israel, the comprehensive law, and for many Jews, the land.

Missionary activity among the Hebrews (called Jews after the 50-year Babylonian Exile) following the return of many exiles in 538 BC reflected the belief in Israel's election by God to mediate divine blessings to all nations. By the time of the birth of Jesus, Judaism was winning many converts in the Roman Empire. However, after the Romans destroyed the temple in Jerusalem in AD 70 and dispersed the Jews from Palestine, missionary activity by Jews almost ceased. Particularism and separatism, as opposed to universalism, increasingly characterized Judaism, which became a token religion in its original territory for more than eighteen centuries.

Different interpretations of the Torah (the Law, the first five books of the Old Testament, also called the Pentateuch) and the Talmud (a body of commentary and guidance) have led to various groupings within Judaism. In modern times, Judaism embraces such groups as the ultraorthodox Hasidim ("those who are pious"), the Orthodox, the Conservative, the Reform, and the Reconstructionists. Neither Reform Judaism, which seeks to liberalize orthodoxy and bring Judaism into modern Western life, nor Conservative Judaism, seeking a middle position, achieved recognition in Israel until the 1970s, and attempts continued in the early 1990s to place restrictions on citizenship granted to Jews converted by a nonorthodox rabbi. Nevertheless, Judaism has not experienced the degree of institutionalized sectarian fragmentation suffered by Christianity and Islam. Reimplanted in its native locale in the mid-twentieth century, Judaism has become for many of its adherents a belief system that is quite different from its original theology. Surveys have shown that only a minority of Israeli Jews actually practice Judaism, and distinctions must be drawn among Jews, practitioners of Judaism, Zionists, and Israelis.

Other Religions

The primarily Kurdish *Yazidis* (or Yezidis) call themselves Dawasin and are called Dasnayis by the Syrians. Their highly syncretic religion, which borrowed heavily from Zoroastrianism as well as Christianity and Islam, revolves around a supreme benign deity and a lord of all evil, the Peacock King. The Yazidi practice of "prudent propitiation" of the Peacock King has been mistakenly interpreted as worship of the devil.

Zoroastrianism is named after its traditional founder, Zoroaster (or Zarathustra), who is believed to have lived in the sixth century BC. It was widespread in the Iranian-Mesopotamian realm and was the major religion of the Achaemenid Empire and then the Sassanian Empire. Essentially monotheistic in its early stages, it exercised significant influence on Judaism and on Christianity. Taught by magi (magians) as priests, Zoroastrianism emphasizes the eternal cosmic contest between good and evil, falsehood and truth, darkness and light. Zoroastrian practices include fire worship and exposure of the dead to vultures on "towers of silence" (*dakhmes* or *qala-e khamushan*), many ruins of which remain in central Iran. The Zoroastrian scripture is the Avesta, which has been supplemented by the commentary Zend-Avesta. Disfavored during the seventh-century Muslim invasion, many Zoroastrians converted to Islam. Zoroastrianism is also opposed by the current Islamic fundamentalist government in Iran but does survive primarily in the Yazd and Kerman areas of central Iran as well as among the Parsees in India, especially in Bombay.

A minor religious group concentrated in Iraq is the *Mandaeans* (from Aramaic *manda*, "knowledge"), also called Sabians ("baptizers") and John the Baptist Christians—although they are not Christians. John the Baptist is a central figure in this highly syncretic religion, which includes Jewish, Iranian, Babylonian, Gnostic, and Christian elements. Because Mandaeans stress the importance of immersion and regular ablutions, they live near running water, mostly along the lower Tigris River. Their scriptures and liturgy are in Syriac

A fairly recent, eclectic faith, *Bahaism* evolved in Iran in the 1840s as an offshoot of Shii Islam. Babist mysticism spread rapidly after a Shii religious leader was acclaimed the *bab* ("gate") between the worldly and the spiritual. Advocating a universalistic faith synthesizing Islam, Judaism, and Christianity, Bahaism has spread widely in Europe and North America. The Bahai world center is on Mt. Carmel, in Haifa, Israel (photo in Chap. 15), and its members number tens of thousands in the Middle East, chiefly in central Iran, where they have been persecuted since the revolution of 1978–1979.

Patterns: Ethnic Groups

Aspects of Middle East language and religion patterns may now be merged in a survey of ethnic groups of the region (Table 6-3). This survey of peoples examines six major ethnic aggregates—Arabs, Turks, Persians, Jews, Armenians, and Greeks—and briefly discusses related smaller groups associated with each major group. The relationship between primary group and associated groups may involve language, religion, cultural affinity, or geographical proximity, including shared nationality. For example, the Lur and the Bakhtiari are considered with the Persian group, since all three live in Iran, speak Indo-Iranian languages, and belong to the Shii sect of Islam. Similarly, the Maronites and Druzes are considered with the Arabs, since both groups are associated with Lebanon and speak Arabic, even though the Maronites are Christians and the Druzes are a heretical sect of Shii Islam. Because of cultural and historical complexities, the categories used are not always exclusive.

Arabs and Related Groups

Arabs. Even with the diversity of traits and the distribution over vast distances of this largest Middle East group, the ethnic identity of the Arabs is one of the basic realities of the pattern of peoples in the region. Not only are Arabs the overwhelmingly dominant ethnolinguistic group in twelve of the sixteen countries, they also include several hundred thousand nationals in three more of the countries—Israel and the areas it occupies, Turkey, and Iran—and are numerically negligible only in Cyprus.

All Arabs share two cultural elements, and most share a third. First, the Arabic language provides an element common to all Arabs, despite variations in dialect. As the language of the Quran, it has deep religious and cultural significance for most Arabs. Second, the Islamic cultural heritage embodied in architecture, design, calligraphy, and art provides a common history

TABLE 6-3: ETHNIC GROUPS OF THE MIDDLE EAST (WITH ETHNOLINGUISTIC GROUPING)

ETHNIC GROUP (AND ALT. NAMES)	MAIN LANGUAGE	MAIN RELIGION	NO., 000s	MAIN AREAS/COMMENTS
——— AFRO-ASIATIC: Semitic and Berber ———				
ALAWIS (Alawites, Nusayris)	Arabic	Alawi	1,450	W Syria, N Lebanon
ARABS	Arabic	Islam (>Sunni)	115,000	Mid East, N Africa
ASSYRIANS (Aissores)	Syriac, Arabic	Christian (Nestorian)	? 350	NE Syria, N Iraq
CHALDEANS ("Assyrians")	Arabic, Syriac	Christian (Chaldean)	? 200	N Iraq, B'dad, E Syria
COPTS	Arabic	Christian (Coptic)	4,250	C and N Egypt
DRUZES (Muwahhidun)	Arabic	Druze	900	S Syr, C Leb, N Israel
JEWS (Yahudis)	Hebrew, Ar.	Judaism	3,800	Israel, Iran, Turkey
MANDAEANS (Sabians, Mendai)	Ar., Aramaic	Mandaean	5	Baghdad, S Iraq
MARONITES	Ar., French	Christian (Maronite)	730	NC and C Lebanon
(MUTAWALIS) (Metouali)	(Arabic)	(Shii Islam)	1,000	(C and S Lebanon)
SAMARITANS	Ar., Aram. di.	Samaritan	<1	528 in Nablus & Holon
BERBERS	Berber	Sunni Islam	8	NW Egypt (mils. to W)
——— URAL-ALTAIC: Turkic ———				
AFSHAR (include several groups)	Azeri	Shii Islam	250	NW Iran, SC Iran
AZERIS (Azerbaijanis)	Azeri	Shii Islam	13,000	NW Iran
QAJARS (include several groups)	Azeri	Shii Islam	? 200	SE Caspian Coast
QASHQAI	Qashqai	Shii Islam	845	Iran: C Zagros Mts.
ILSAVAN/SHAHSAVAN (sev.)	Azeri	Shii Islam	410	NW Iran, other Iran
TATARS ("Tartars")	Tatar Turkic	Sunni Islam	? 90	E Turkey, N Iran
TURKS	Turkish	Sunni Islam	47,000	Turkey
TURKMEN (Turcomans)	Turkmen	Sunni Islam	1,900	N Iran, NE Iraq, Trky
YORUK	Turkish	Sunni Islam	390	W and SE Turkey
——— INDO-EUROPEAN: Indo-Iranian, Armenian, and Greek ———				
BAKHTIARI	Luri	Shii Islam	950	Iran: C Zagros Mts.
BALUCH (Baluchis)	Baluchi	Sunni Islam	2,000	SE Iran (& Pak & Afgh)
GILANI (include several groups)	Gilaki	Shii Islam	? 2,300	SW Caspian Coast
HAZARAS (Berberis)	Hazaragi	Shii Islam	250	E Iran; >in Afgh, Pak
KURDS	Kurdish	Sunni Islam	18,100	Iran, Iraq, Syria, Trky
LUR (include several groups)	Luri	Shii Islam	1,125	C Zagros Mts., E Iraq
MAZANDARANI (incl. sev. grps)	Mazandarani	Shii Islam	? 2,200	SW Caspian Coast
PERSIANS	Farsi (Persian)	Shii Islam	28,900	C & N Iran; <Iraq, UAE
PUSHTUN (Pukhtun, Pathans)	Pashto	Sunni Islam	85	E Iran (mils. to E)
YAZIDIS (Dasnayi, Asdais)	Kurdish	Yazidi	? 125	N Iraq, NW Syria
ZOROASTRIANS (Parsis,Gabres, Zardoshti)	Farsi (Persian)	Zoroastrian	110	SC Iran (Yazd), Tehran (also many in India)
ARMENIANS (Hai)	Armenian	Christian (Arm Orth)	1,200	Leb, Syria, Iran, Trky
GREEKS (Elleniki)	Greek	Christian (Orthodox)	780	Cyprus, Istanbul, Egypt
——— CAUCASIC ———				
CIRCASSIANS (Adyghe,Cherkes)	Circassian	>Sunni Islam	300	Trky, Syria, Jrdn, Israel
GEORGIANS	Georgian	>Sunni	? 75	N Turkey, WC Iran
LAZE (Laz, Tchan)	Laz	Sunni Islam	40	SE Black Sea Coast
——— MISCELLANEOUS ———				
BEJA	Beja	Sunni Islam	<20	<SE Egypt (>NE Sudn)
GYPSIES (Romanies, many others)	Romany, etc.	Various	?>1,000	Scattered
NUBIANS	Nubian, Ar.	Sunni Islam	150	<S Eqypt (>N Sudan)

Groups may overlap and are, therefore, not necessarily mutually exclusive (e.g., Druzes and Alawis are Arabs). Mutawali are Lebanese Shii Muslims; the name dates from the nineteenth century. Numbers can be only rough estimates in some cases. See text regarding Armenians, Azeris, and Georgians. (Data from *Britannica World Data 1991; World Factbook 1991*; Weekes 1984; and author's field research.)

for Arabs—Muslim and Christian, orthodox and heretic, Bedouin and city dweller, Syrian and Qatari. The region's Islamic heritage underlies modern Arab political identity, a relevant factor in many modern problems and conflicts (Chap. 11). Third, since more than 92 percent of Middle East Arabs are Muslim, Islam as a religion unites the majority of them.

Copts. Coptic ethnic identity derives primarily from the Coptic religion. Numbering about 10 percent of the population of Egypt, Copts are the largest non-Muslim ethnic group in the Middle East, a remnant of the ancient Hamitic Egyptians who converted to Christianity. Practicing endogamy and segregation from other Egyptians and from invaders, they have preserved their Monophysite Christianity as well as a physical kinship with the early Egyptians. The Coptic language survived as the vernacular until supplanted by Arabic 1,000 years after the Islamic conquest. Outside the urban centers of Cairo and Alexandria, the Copts are concentrated in Upper Egypt, in Asyut and Luxor. Friction with the majority Muslims in Egypt is discussed in Chapter 20.

Maronites. Like the Copts, Maronites are differentiated primarily on the basis of their religion. However, their geographical isolation in the Lebanon Mountains has encouraged independence and endogamy, and has produced a cultural differentiation and substantial political autonomy. Arabic supplanted Syriac during the eighteenth century as a working language, and ties with the French (Franks) during the Crusades and the mandate years (1920–1943) promoted the use of French as a second language. The determined separatism of the Maronites has been a compelling dynamic in Lebanese political-geographical events (see Chap. 13).

Oppressed for their adherence to a Christian heresy, the Maronites left Syria in the tenth century and concentrated in the Lebanon Mountains around Qadisha Gorge. Their cooperation with the Crusader invaders alienated them from the Muslim population, and a small group of Maronites left with the retreating Crusaders to settle in Cyprus, where a small community remains. Thousands of Maronites emigrated from

Mount Lebanon around 1900, and emigration increased after the 1950s because of the civil conflict in Lebanon. An estimated 700,000 Maronites—many claiming Phoenician descent—remain in the Levant, the overwhelming majority of them in Lebanon but a few in Cyprus and in Syria.

Druzes. Druze identity also originated in religion, with cultural and physical differentiations developing over the centuries. Although originating in Egypt, the Druzes won adherents in the Mount Hermon area, where they are still centered. Additional contemporary concentrations are in the Shuf area in central Mount Lebanon and in the Jabal al-Druze of southern Syria.

As heretics, the Druzes were alienated from other Shii Muslims, as well as from their Sunni Muslim neighbors, and clashed with the Maronite Christians as both groups migrated into central Mount Lebanon 1,000 years ago. Rejected by their neighbors, the Druzes separated themselves through endogamy. The Druze sense of independence and separatism contributed to their military orientation, which has been exhibited against the Crusaders, against the Maronites in the 1840s–1850s and 1958, and in the 1975–1991 civil conflict in Lebanon. On the other hand, Druzes in Israel generally accepted the new Jewish government in 1948–1949 and have been the only Arabs permitted to serve in the Israeli army. However, Druze-Israeli relations have deteriorated as a result of Israel's annexation of the Golan Heights in 1981, the Israeli army's occupation of southern Lebanon, and the uprising (*intifadah*) in the occupied territories beginning in 1987.

Alawis. The Alawis are also primarily distinguished by their religion, and they too have developed distinct cultural attributes through segregation and endogamy. They are concentrated in a mountainous refuge area in northwestern Syria, Jabal al-Nusayriyah, and constitute about 12 percent of the population of that country.

The Alawis have preserved no ancient language and use Arabic regularly. Although criticized by other Syrians for their cooperation with French mandate authorities between the two world wars, after World War II the Alawis were trusted in the army and in government because of their minority status. A climax of their group's role came in 1969, when Syrian Air Force General Hafiz al-Asad, an Alawi, seized power in Damascus and retained the presidency into the present time.

Chaldeans. The Chaldeans are differentiated primarily on the basis of religion, forming an Arabic-speaking Christian collectivity within a dominantly Sunni Muslim area of Iraq. Named after (but not descended from) the ancient Chaldeans of southern Iraq, the Chaldeans are the largest Christian group in Iraq and are centered in the northeastern part of the country and in Baghdad. Many emigrated to the United States after World War II.

Assyrians. The Assyrians are not descendants of the ancient imperial Assyrians, as many of them claim. Syriac remained their vernacular until recent times, and older Assyrians retain some fluency in the traditional language, but Arabic is the modern vernacular of the group. Dating only from the dispersion of the Assyrians in 1932, their present pattern of distribution has three concentrations: in approximately a score of villages on the upper Khabur River in northeastern Syria; in Baghdad, Kirkuk, and the hills north of Mosul in Iraq, where they were pushed by Mongols in the Middle Ages; and in extreme northwestern Iran, west of Lake Urmia. By the early 1980s more Assyrians probably lived in North America than in the Middle East.

Circassians. Half a million Circassians migrated into the Middle East from the Caucasus Mountains when czarist Russia took over their homeland after the Congress of Berlin in 1878. The Ottoman sultan permitted them to settle along the axis from Damascus southward to Amman and beyond, as well as in Asia Minor and in the mountains of Kurdistan. They still live in these areas and play modest roles in Syria, Jordan, and northern Israel. Prior to its destruction by the Israelis, Qunaytirah, in the Golan Heights, was a center of Circassian settlement.

Yazidis. The Yazidis have Kurdish ethnic roots. They are settled farmers concentrated in the Jabal Sinjar west of Mosul and in the hills northwest of Aleppo. Yazidis do not interact with neighboring tribes; they practice endogamy and prohibit conversion into the group—membership is only by birth.

Nubians. Nubians lived in the area between Aswan, Egypt, and the Dongola region of Sudan for perhaps 3,000 years before the construction of the Aswan High Dam. More African in appearance than the Egyptians farther down the Nile, the Nubians converted to Christianity in the sixth century AD and resisted Islam until 1366. Nearly all speak the Nubian language, but most of them also speak Arabic. Of the total Nubian population in Egypt and the Sudan, about one-third live in Egypt and are Sunni Muslims.

Others. Smaller ethnic groups interrelate with the dominant Arab group because of geographical proximity. Some are differentiated by language, some by religion, and some by both.

The *Beja* are nomadic pastoralists who migrate seasonally into the southeastern corner of Egypt from northeastern Sudan. The *Berbers* are a major ethnic group in North Africa and in the Arab World, numbering more than 11 million from Egypt westward to the Atlantic. However, only a few thousand live in the Middle East as defined in this study, primarily in the Siwa Oasis of northwestern Egypt. Their name comes from *barbari* ("barbarians"), as they were called by the Romans. The *Mandaeans* are a dwindling relict group in Iraq, and its members live in al-Amarah, Suq al-Shuyukh, and Baghdad. The *Shabak* form another small group in the "ethnic shatter zone" of northern Iraq. Originally Sufi mystics in the fourteenth and fifteenth centuries, they became secretive and heretical, practiced endogamy, and became a closed and isolated community.

The *Sulaba* (or *Sulayb*) are a gypsylike people in the Arabian Peninsula who, in small groups, follow Bedouin tribes in their nomadic migrations and serve as tinkers, musicians, and entertainers for the Bedouins and villagers. They are not considered Arabs, and they are so ostracized that their group origins and traditions are little known. *Gypsies* wander by the thousands in many parts of the Middle East as traditional migrants. Many claim to be Muslims, but others engage in varied religious practices. Like all true gypsies, they originated in northwestern India and speak dialects of Romany, an Indic branch of Indo-Iranian. They often also speak local languages.

Chechens migrated into the Middle East from the northern Caucasus in the mid-nineteenth century. In 1865, 40,000 arrived in Turkey, where most have been assimilated. Later, other small groups of Chechens settled farther south in the Ottoman Empire; and more than 2,000, sometimes called Shishanis, still live in west-central Jordan alongside their fellow Caucasians, the Circassians.

Turks and Related Groups

Turks. The second-largest ethnolinguistic group in the Middle East (after the Arabs), ethnic Turks number about 51 million, somewhat more than one-third of the total number of Turkic-speaking peoples of the world. Generally, Turks speak Turkish as a primary language, are Muslims (90 percent are Sunni), claim a Turkish heritage, and are patriotic about the Republic of Turkey. Culturally, the Turks combined Persian, Arab, Byzantine, and Anatolian cultural elements with their former nomadic central Asian culture. Turks, Tatars, and Turkmen are difficult to differentiate, despite distinctive characteristics, partly because of intermarriage and cultural assimilation.

Four groups of Turks in the Middle East can be identified on the basis of cultural and geographical differentiations. First, the Anatolian Turks in Asia Minor are a thorough biological mixture of earlier Anatolian peoples. Second, the Rumelian Turks (from Rum, meaning Roman or European), are European Turks who remained in Europe after Ottoman days and who later returned to Turkey. More than 400,000 were expelled from Greece in exchange for a similar number of Greeks expelled from Turkey after World War I, and many other scores of thousands later arrived in Turkey from Bulgaria, Romania, and Yugoslavia. Along with ethnic Turks from Bulgaria came about 150,000 Pomaks, most of whom were Bulgars who converted to Islam during Ottoman control of the Balkans. Now highly Turkified, they live in western Anatolia.

The third group is made up of descendants of the Ottoman Turks who stayed in areas of the Middle East when they were detached from the Ottoman Empire after World War I. They live in small groups in Syria, Lebanon, Jordan, and Iraq but are steadily becoming Arabized. Similar to this group is the fourth, the 170,000 Cypriot Turks, who live in the northern third of Cyprus and most of whom are descendants of Ottoman Turks who moved to the island after the Ottoman conquest in the early sixteenth century. Cypriot Turks have been joined by Turks from Turkey since 1974, augmenting their numbers appreciably.

Azeris. The Azeris form the second-largest Turkic group (after the Turks themselves) and the fifth-largest ethnolinguistic group in the Middle East. They live to the north and east of the more numerous Kurds, and some related Turkic groups—including the Ilsavan/Shahsavan, Afshar, and Qajars—live to the east of the main group. Some Azeris also live in Turkey. They are the dominant group in the Azerbaijan region of northwestern Iran, where they live primarily as settled farmers and herders. Another several million live in the Azerbaijan Republic, adjacent to northwestern Iran. Like the Persians, and unlike most Turks, the Azeris are Shii Muslims. Tabriz serves as an Azeri center, although its population is ethnically complex.

Turkmen. Despite a common Turkic language, Turkmen are distinct from true Turks and from Tatars. Most of them remain in Turkistan, primarily in the Republic of Turkmenistan, adjacent to Iran and east of the Caspian. They are highly tribalized, and their tribal names serve as familiar designations for their traditional hand-knotted rugs. Although they are one of the most widely scattered ethnic groups in the region, main concentrations appear in central Anatolia, eastern Anatolia, northeastern Iraq in the foothills near Mosul and Kirkuk, and across northern Iran, particularly in the northeastern mountains of Khorasan. They tend to live in mountainous areas and to preserve their nomadism for both economic and defensive reasons; however, as with most nomadic groups, the Turkmen are becoming settled and are integrating into the sedentary economy and society. They are all Muslims, about two-thirds Sunni and one-third Shii.

Yoruk. The Yoruk are apparently descendants of some of the earliest Turkish tribes to enter Asia Minor. As one evidence, their Turkish language has been less influenced by Arabic and Persian than has the national Turkish language. Nominally Muslim, their Islam is unorthodox, with neither clergy nor mosques. Rug knotting is a traditional skill among the Yoruk.

The changes in Yoruk areas and life-style are indicative of development in the Middle East. Under the Ottomans the Yoruk maintained a nomadic existence in western Anatolia in the uplands between Konya and Bursa. Intensive government projects during the 1920s and 1930s to develop pastures and to improve agricultural practices in western Asia Minor interfered with their seasonal migrations, producing gradual sedentarization. The changing agricultural economy diminished the Yoruk livelihood, and in the mid-twentieth century, several thousand migrated to southeastern Turkey, where they resumed nomadic pastoralism. Many Yoruk now migrate by truck rather than by camel or on foot.

Ilsavan/Shahsavan. The name *Shahsavan* ("shah lovers") was impolitic after the 1979 overthrow of the shah of Iran, and the designation was changed to Ilsavan ("tribe lovers"). The Ilsavan are a large nomadic group who are closely related to the Azeris and Afshars, traditionally sharing territory and nomadic migrations to some extent. Like those groups, the Ilsavan are also Shii Muslim. They were given special tribal status in the seventeenth century because they were loyal to the shah, and they traditionally supported the ruling dynasty; however, they seem to have accepted the revolutionary republican government.

Qashqai. The Qashqai are descendants of Turkic tribes who left central Asia in the eleventh century and moved into the Zagros Mountains in the fifteenth century. Like the great majority of ethnic groups in Iran, the Qashqai are Shii Muslim. The persistence of their nomadism, both horizontal and vertical (transhumance), is legendary. Herding large flocks of sheep, they make an arduous seasonal migration, sometimes over

distances of as much as 350 miles/560 km, between their summer and winter pastures. Herding is supplemented by making knotted rugs, kelims (woven rugs), and bags in traditional Qashqai patterns.

Afshars. The Afshars are another Turkic group who are assumed to have migrated onto the Iranian Plateau from Turkistan during the Middle Ages. Like the Ilsavan (with whom they at times migrate), they are sometimes considered a subdivision of the Azeris: All three groups speak related Turkic dialects, practice Shii Islam, and engage to some extent in nomadism. The Afshars are widely distributed in the northern Zagros Mountains from north of Tabriz to Hamadan, and there are two other concentrations, one in Iran in the mountains south of Kerman and the other in Turkey east of Kayseri.

Qajars. The Turkic-speaking Qajars are one of several interlocked ethnic groups in northwestern Iran and the southern Caspian coast area, with some of the related groups belonging to the Turkic family and others the Iranian language family. The Qajars supplied a dynasty that ruled Persia for 131 years (1794–1925). Mostly settled farmers, with small groups of seasonal nomads, the Qajars form a small enclave among the more numerous Mazandarani along the southeastern Caspian coast.

Tatars. Sometimes incorrectly called "Tartars," the Tatars ("archers") were named after (but not directly descended from) the Ta-Ta Mongols who invaded the Middle East along with other Mongols in the thirteenth century. In succeeding centuries, Turks and Tatars intermarried, creating a widespread Turko-Tatar group. Turks, Turkmen, Tatars, Turko-Tatars, and Mongols are often confused in historical writings. The Tatars north of the Black and Caspian seas are far more numerous than in the Middle East and number in the millions. Although scores of thousands of Tatars emigrated from Russia into Turkey during the nineteenth century, they have since become assimilated. Tatars speak a Turkic Kipchak language rather than a Mongolic tongue, and virtually all are Muslim, most of them Sunni.

Persians and Related Groups

Persians are numerically the third-largest ethno-linguistic group in the Middle East, after the Arabs and Turks. Indo-Iranians immigrated into the mountains and basins south and southwest of the Caspian Sea during the second millennium BC. One branch migrated southeastward into the Indus Valley and evolved into the Hindus, and other groups halted in the rugged folds of the Zagros Mountains and settled in western Iran. Those south of the Caspian evolved as Medes (or Medians), and those in the southern Zagros became Persians. They called themselves Aryans ("nobles") and named their new mountain and basin homeland after themselves—Iran.

Persians. Evolving for a thousand years in the folds of the Zagros, the Persians emerged as a unified sedentary people in the sixth century BC and built an unprecedented empire (see Chap. 2). Although they were later defeated by Alexander the Great and were overwhelmed by Arab Muslims in the seventh century, the Persians repeatedly restored a power base on the intermontane Iranian Plateau. Since World War I, the Persians have become the leading ethnic group in the Iranian nation and fill most government, industrial, professional, and cultural positions. By the 1970s most educated Persians spoke French or English in addition to Farsi, and many have been educated in the United States or France; however, after the Islamic Revolution, the authorities discouraged Westernization and forced a return to Islamic fundamentalism.

More than 95 percent of Persians adhere to the Twelver, or Jafari, sect of Shii Islam, for nationalistic as much as for theological reasons. A small but significant number of Persians are Zoroastrians and Bahais. Although Persians live throughout Iran, by far the majority of the population in the foothills, valleys, basins, and plateaus in the area from Hamadan to Qom to Tehran to Shiraz to Kerman is true Persian, and Persians also predominate in those cities.

In addition to the approximately 28 million Persians in Iran (nearly half the population of the country), another million live on the west side of the Gulf and, as Arabized Persians, in the Qatif and al-Hasa oases in the Eastern Province of Saudi Arabia, as well as around the Shii shrines in Iraq. Pro-Iranian sentiments among some of these Persians outside Iran have been a matter of concern to their host countries since the early 1980s. Wherever they live, but especially in Iran itself, Persians proudly differentiate themselves by their language, Shii religion, history, 2,000 years of literature, and distinctive arts. The cleavage between Persians and Arabs along the Zagros piedmont exhibited its vitality after 1979 when the mutually aggressive Iran and Iraq entered eight years of bitter warfare.

Kurds. The fourth-largest ethnolinguistic group in the Middle East, the Kurds occupy a centuries-old mountain homeland, Kurdistan, which embraces an irregular area at the junction of Turkey, Iraq, and Iran (see Map 6-3). The Kurds not only predominate in Kurdistan but also intermingle with neighboring Azeris and Armenians and with Turks, Turkmen, Arabs, and others. Both the total Kurdish population and its distribution among the three countries that share most of Kurdistan can only be estimated and are debatable. Kurdish leaders claim much higher numbers than are accepted by officials and scholars. Reasonable figures as of late 1992 suggest a total of 17.3 million Kurds in "Kurdistan"—9 million in Turkey, 3.8 million in Iraq, and 4.5 million in Iran. In addition, perhaps another 1 million Kurds live in northern Syria, central Anatolia, Lebanon, the central Zagros Mountains, and the Elburz and Kopet mountains.

Retaining a tribal structure, the Kurds are settled farmers, herdsmen, and townsmen. Formerly nomadic, Kurds are becoming settled and even urbanized. Especially in their core mountain home area, the Kurds resist outside authority. Although Kurdish nationalism evolved with Arab, Turkish, and Persian nationalism in the late nineteenth century, the Kurds have failed to achieve political independence, despite periodic rebellions against the central government in Turkey, Iran, and especially Iraq.[3]

Language and heritage define Kurdishness rather than physical derivation; many consider themselves descendants of the Medes, while others believe they were formerly part of the Lur. Most Kurds are Sunni Muslims, which separates them from the Shii Persians, but some Kurds in

Iran and parts of Iraq have become Shii. Both the historical and contemporary plights of the Kurds became the focus of intensive media coverage after the Gulf war of 1990–1991. Further details on the situation of the Kurds in the respective countries that share Kurdistan are given in the chapters on Iraq, Turkey, and Iran.

Baluch. Like the Kurds, the Baluch are primarily Sunni Muslims, speak an Indo-Iranian language, live in an isolated mountain environment, and have a traditional homeland—Baluchistan—at the junction of three countries—Iran, Pakistan, and Afghanistan. However, Baluchistan is an arid realm, and the Baluch are much more nomadic or seminomadic, with only a few settling in the impoverished villages of the area. Although tribal organization does remain strong among the Baluch, the various tribes are not closely integrated. Isolated in their spare desert and mountain environment, the Baluch are the poorest and most neglected major group in Iran. Probably a mixture of Dravidians of the Indian Peninsula and seventh-century Arab invaders, the Baluch are culturally more closely related to the Pakistanis and the Pushtun of Afghanistan than to the Persians.

Emigrants from Baluchistan have crossed the Gulf of Oman to both Oman and the present United Arab Emirates, where their round tents have provided a contrast to the rectangular Arab tents. The Baluch serve in large numbers in the various military forces of the southeastern Arabian Peninsula.

Lur. Of uncertain origin, the Lur speak a dialect of Persian and are linguistically and culturally related to the Persians and to the nearby Bakhtiari. They occupy Lorestan, a homeland in the central Zagros Mountains between Bakhtaran (Kermanshah) and Shiraz, and are racially mixed.

The basic social organizational unit among the Lur is the tribe (*il*). Some nomadic tribes migrate to the high mountains in the summer, but other Lur tribes have become sedentary or semisedentary, especially in the eastern valleys. The sedentary tribes have adopted Persian (Farsi) as a second language. Tribal structure has gradually become less rigid as the power of the tribal chiefs (khans) has been undermined by the central gov-

ernment. Most Lur are Shii Muslims but hold some beliefs that are inconsistent with Persian and Bakhtiari Shiism. Of the Lur who have spilled over into Iraq, a few roam the Zagros piedmont in the Mandali area east of Baghdad while others work in towns along the Tigris. Estimates of the number of Lur vary greatly.

Bakhtiari. Tribes in the Il-e Bakhtiari confederation relate geographically and culturally not only to the nearby Lur but also to the Turkic Qashqai. Like the Qashqai, the Bakhtiari are tribally organized, disciplined, and still largely nomadic. Traditionally playing a powerful role in Iranian politics, Bakhtiari leaders periodically held high government positions until the 1920s. Bakhtiari tribesmen have served in the Iranian army for centuries, but the political influence of the khans was restricted by the central government after World War I. Like many Iranian tribes, the Bakhtiari produce handmade rugs with distinctive design. Their ethnic costumes evoke statues and bas reliefs of Parthians of 2,000 years ago.

Zoroastrians. Zoroastrians are probably the least physically mixed ethnic Persians in Iran, comparable to the Copts in Egypt, and they are so sharply distinguished by their religion that they constitute an ethnic group as distinct as the Maronites or Druzes in the Levant. By adhering to a definite geographical area, practicing endogamy, and exercising group determination, Zoroastrians have survived and preserved their identity despite persecution. The several thousand who fled to western India during the Arab invasion of the 630s became known as Parsees, who are now concentrated in Bombay and make up some of the major industrialist families of southern Asia.

Others. Another score of ethnic groups related to the Persians are found in pockets on the Iranian Plateau, further illustrating the complexity of the ethnic pattern in the eastern Middle East. Two such groups, neither sharply differentiated from their neighbors, live as farmers and fishermen along the shores of the Caspian Sea—the *Gilani* along the southwestern shore around Rasht and the *Mazandarani* in the coastal lowlands and adjacent mountains southeast of the Caspian. Two other Persian ethnic groups are listed in Table 6-3; the others are too small to be distinguished.

Jews and Samaritans

Jews. After an early history chronicled in the Old Testament, Jews were deported in the first century AD from most of Palestine by the Romans. In this second phase of the Jewish Diaspora (the first was the Babylonian Exile), Jews settled around the shore of the Mediterranean Basin, and sizable communities developed in several major Mediterranean coastal cities, including Alexandria, Egypt, which had a major Jewish community for more than 2,000 years until after World War II. Under the Ottoman Empire, Jews (like Christians) constituted a *millet,* and Jewish minority rights were sufficiently protected so that after 1492, tens of thousands of Sephardic (Spanish) Jews who fled the Spanish Inquisition settled in the Ottoman Empire. They thus became citizens of successor Arab states after 1918 and continued to receive the rights of *ahl al-kitab.*

Ashkenazi (German) Jews from central and eastern Europe have migrated to the Middle East comparatively recently, in the late nineteenth and twentieth centuries, especially in waves of immigration (aliyah) after World War II. After the establishment of Israel in 1948, most of the Jews in Middle East Arab countries emigrated to Israel, and an estimated 300,000 Jews had left Egypt, Lebanon, Syria, Iraq, and Yemen by the early 1990s.

In spite of generally endogamous traditions, Jews arriving in Israel have exhibited physical differences related to their countries of origin in addition to variations in linguistic, political-geographical (or national), and ideological backgrounds. Subethnic divisions have emerged between Ashkenazi Jews and Oriental or Eastern Jews, including Sephardim, with the Sabras, or native-born Israelis, forming another subgroup. The continuing question, Who is a Jew? and the distinctions among observant Jews, nonobservant (or nonpracticing) Jews, halakic Jews (strictly adherent to religious law), assimilated Jews, and even Christian Jews complicate problems of Israeli citizenship, especially in connection with the Israeli Law of Return. Of a world total of 18 million Jews, about 4.4 million lived in Israel, and about 75,000 in the rest of the Middle East, mainly in Iran and Turkey, in 1992.

Samaritans. The Samaritans, mentioned in the New Testament, are a small but particularly interesting group that originated among Israelites who remained in Samaria during the Babylonian Exile and, through intermarriage with other groups, emerged as a new people. They found themselves irreconcilably estranged from the Jews who returned from Babylon, and the two groups remain incompatible even today. Decimated in battles with the Romans and Byzantines, the Samaritans numbered only 528 in early 1987, about half in Nabulus, north of Jerusalem, and the other half in Holon, near Tel Aviv (later official figures are not available). This relict group scarcely reproduces itself but rejects contacts with outsiders.

Armenians, Greeks, and Others

Armenians. The Armenian people date back more than 3,000 years, to about the time the Hittites disappeared from Anatolia. Prior to World War I, they were centered in the Lake Van area and surrounding eastern Anatolian mountains, long referred to as Armenia. The ancient kingdom of Armenia, located in the same area, was the first state to adopt Christianity as its official religion.

Although Armenians constituted an influential *millet* during the Ottoman Empire, relations between Armenians and Turks became hostile after 1878, and there were battles in 1895–1896, 1909, 1915–1917, and 1920–1921. In a confused, complex, and disputed series of circumstances involving local relationships (including Kurdish-Armenian-Turkish-Russian relations), reciprocal attacks, Russian interference, and European entanglements, hundreds of thousands of Armenians in central and eastern Asia Minor were persecuted, massacred, and deported; thousands more fled into adjacent lands for safety. A post–World War I Armenian republic was proposed by the Allies at the Paris Peace Conference, but it never materialized.

Although the Armenians, who call themselves Hai, lost their traditional homeland in the early 1920s, they maintain a strong ethnic identity, language, and religion, partly through a tradition of endogamy. Armenian communities in the Middle East and elsewhere center on the church (usually Armenian Orthodox), school, newspaper, and businesses and have a cultural emphasis on education and achievement. Armenians in the Middle East total about 1.2 million and are generally concentrated in western Turkey (especially in Istanbul), Lebanon, Syria (especially in Aleppo and Damascus), Iraq, Iran, and Egypt. The new Armenian Republic, successor to the former Soviet Armenian SSR, has a population of more than 3 million, and thousands of Middle East Armenians have emigrated there as well as to the West since World War II. Beginning in 1988, in another expression of their strong sense of identity, Armenians took advantage of glasnost and forcibly sought the union of Nagorno-Karabakh, a heavily Armenian-populated area of the Azerbaijan Republic, with the Armenian Republic.

Greeks. Greeks occupied the Aegean Sea fringe of western Asia Minor from 1000 BC until they fled, were expelled, or were exchanged for Turks in Greece in the mid-1920s following the failure of a Greek military expedition against the new Turkish Republic in 1922, which was another in a centuries-long series of hostilities between Greeks and Turks. From about 2 million Greeks in Asia Minor before World War I, only a few score thousand remain in Turkey—mostly in Istanbul. Groups of Greeks remained in Egypt and Syria-Palestine after the time of Greek (Hellenistic) control, although many of Alexandria's thou-

sands of Greeks finally left because of Egyptian nationalist pressure during the 1950s and 1960s. Jerusalem maintains a small Greek colony, considerably Arabized. The largest concentration of Greeks in the Middle East today, about 570,000, lives on the island of Cyprus and constitutes the sole national group in the Republic of Cyprus. Greek Cypriots maintain their strong identity not only through continued use of the Greek language but also through close ties with Greece, with which many Greek Cypriots sought *enosis* ("union") during the civil war of the 1950s.

Georgians. Originally a Christian group in the southern Caucasus Mountains, the Georgians were dispersed over Asia Minor and Iran during the seventeenth century and later, when many of them became Muslims. Like the Armenians and Azeris, the Georgians had their own soviet socialist republic in the former USSR and also converted it into an independent republic in 1991. The small group of Georgians in the Middle East live mostly in Turkey and are being gradually assimilated.

Laze. Many Laze left the southern Caucasus following Russia's seizure of the area after 1878 and settled just across the border in northeastern Turkey. Traditionally seafarers and fishermen living on or near the Black Sea coast, where Rize is a Laze center, the Laze often serve on Black Sea ships or on Turkish naval vessels. They speak their own language, Laz, which is akin to Georgian.

7

The Desert and
the Sown: Land Use

Agricultural conditions, systems, and products differ strikingly from one area of the Middle East to another. Agricultural landscapes vary from the irrigated gardens of the Nile Valley to the Mediterranean croplands and fruit orchards of the Levant and from the extensive wheat fields of interior Anatolia to the desert rangelands of the wandering herdsmen. Valleys and slopes of the mountains of northern Anatolia and Iran are reminiscent of the European Alps. By contrast, vast arid expanses appear to be barren wasteland. Although some desert areas, such as the Rub al-Khali, have little to offer agriculturally, other large desert stretches are effectively utilized by nomadic herders.

Agricultural lands in the Middle East fall into three broad types—not all mutually exclusive—according to the availability of moisture: (1) subhumid and humid areas suitable for rainfed crops, from wheat and barley on the drier margin to maize and tea on the high rainfall margin; (2) irrigated areas located primarily in deserts and semideserts but also increasingly as enclaves in the more humid areas; (3) arid and semiarid lands used by pastoralists for grazing their animals. This chapter surveys these patterns of land use (see Table 7-1), forestry and fishing, and land tenure and reform from a regional perspective.

Agriculture

Before the boom in oil production after the mid-1950s, the Middle East was by every criterion overwhelmingly an agricultural area. Even with only modest agricultural yields, the region was a net exporter of food. By the early 1990s, however, the sixteen Middle East states were importing more than 50 percent of their food requirements; and this percentage will rise as the population maintains its growth curve, acquires greater purchasing power, and shifts increasingly from agricultural employment to more varied economic activity.

The relative decline in agricultural employment has been especially marked in the petroleum-producing areas, most significantly in the areas around the Gulf. Several Gulf coastal city-states with fishing economies prior to World War II still engage in fishing, but the percentage contribution of that activity to the national economy is now negligible, as is the percentage of the work force employed in fishing. (The percentage of workers in the various economic sectors of the sixteen states is shown in a table in Chapter 9, which indicates the relative importance of agriculture statistically in each country.)

Even in those countries in which a high percentage of the economically active population is still engaged in agriculture, such activity may contribute only a small percentage of the gross domestic product (GDP). For example, in Egypt, with 43 percent of the work force engaged in agriculture, only about 21 percent of the GDP comes from this source. In Turkey, where the 45 percent of the work force engaged in agriculture contributes 7 percent of the GDP, the 14 percent engaged in manufacturing and mining contributes 26 percent of the GDP. Moreover, manufacturing now surpasses agriculture as the leading employer in some formerly agricultural countries.

TABLE 7-1: LAND USE, GENERAL

COUNTRY	1 TOTAL AREA UNDER CULTIVATION	2 AREA UNDER IRRIGATION TOTAL	3 % OF CULT. AREA	4 PERCENTAGE OF TOTAL AREA UNDER CULTIVA-TION	5 PERM. PASTURE	6 FOREST, WOODLND	7 WASTE, OTHER
Bahrain	2	1	50	3	6	<1	91
Cyprus	157	33	21	17	<1	13	69
Egypt	2,583	2,580	100	3	---	<1	97
Iran	14,830	5,750	39	9	27	11	52
Iraq	5,450	2,538	47	12	9	4	74
Israel	433	216	50	21	7	5	65
Jordan	374	57	15	4	9	<1	86
Kuwait	4	2	50	<1	8	<1	92
Lebanon	301	86	28	29	1	8	61
Oman	48	41	85	<1	5	<1	95
Qatar	5	4	80	<1	5	<1	95
Saudi Arabia	1,185	430	36	<1	40	<1	59
Syria	5,560	650	12	30	44	3	22
Turkey	27,730	2,200	8	36	11	26	26
UAE	39	5	13	<1	2	<1	97
Yemen	1,479	310	21	3	30	6	61
Gaza	---	---	---	---	---	---	---
West Bank	---	---	---	---	---	---	---
TOTAL/AVG.	60,180	14,903	25	8	23	6	61

Several figures are Food and Agriculture Organization (FAO) estimates. Data in Columns 1 and 2 are in thousands of hectares. Percentages calculated from FAO data. Source: UN FAO *Production Yearbook 1989.*

The relative decrease in the percentage share of agriculture may obscure government efforts to develop a nation's agricultural potential. Agriculture is such a vital element in the national economies that all Middle East states are conducting systematic, wide-ranging agricultural development programs. Oil income will cease in a few decades, but meanwhile it can be invested in agricultural projects that will have a long-range benefit.

Some General Aspects

By its very nature, agriculture is highly interactive with ecological factors and cultural traditions, so it differs from one area to another as well as within an area. For example, mixed farming as practiced in the United States and Western Europe is not well developed in the Middle East; a system in which the farmer grows feed grains and then feeds them to animals is in any case poorly adapted to an environment with more grazing land than grain surpluses. Income from

livestock, including that from milk and egg production as well as that from meat and meat by-products, accounts for less than one-third of the agricultural income in the Middle East. Nevertheless, domestic animals play a significant role in the agricultural cycle, since they provide farm income between harvests. Traditional herding of livestock by nomadic pastoralists, however, is steadily declining not only in the deserts of the oil states but also in the mountains of Iran and Turkey.

Wheat is found throughout the region and leads all crops in terms of area sown. Highly specialized crops are produced in scattered small areas: coffee and the mildly narcotic *qat* in Yemen, frankincense in southern Oman and Yemen, tea in northeastern Turkey and northwestern Iran, dates around the Gulf, licorice in southern Iraq, and pine nuts in Lebanon.

Food crops occupy most of the cultivated area in the Middle East, but industrial crops (cotton, tobacco, sugarcane, sugar beets, linseed, sesame)

TABLE 7-2: LAND USE: MAJOR GROUND CROPS AND NUMBER OF TRACTORS

COUNTRY	1 WHEAT AREA	2 WHEAT PROD.	3 ALL VEGE-TABLES	4 TOBAC-CO	5 COTTON LINT	6 GRAPES	7 TRACTORS
Bahrain	---	---	12	---	---	---	---
Cyprus	5	8	122	---	---	30	13,600
Egypt	630	3,148	10,793	---	346	48	46,000
Iran	6,000	5,800	4,265	18	122	170	113,000
Iraq	500	491	3,117	2	5	57	43,000
Israel	90	201	1,023	1	40	5	24,500
Jordan	117	50	603	4	---	6	5,673
Kuwait	---	---	124	---	---	---	120
Lebanon	10	23	430	3	---	20	3,000
Oman	1	1	237	---	---	---	137
Qatar	---	---	22	---	---	---	90
Saudi Arabia	645	3,100	1,206	---	---	7	1,850
Syria	871	1,020	1,826	15	155	110	54,900
Turkey	9,300	15,729	16,869	290	555	600	654,636
UAE	1	1	174	---	---	---	---
Yemen	86	165	610	4	7	15	5,320
Gaza	1	2	106	---	---	1	272
West Bank	---	---	---	---	---	---	---
TOTAL/AVG.	18,257	29,739	41,539	337	1,230	1,069	966,098

Many of the data are Food and Agriculture Organization (FAO) estimates or are unofficial figures. Wheat area is in 000s of hectares. Crop production is in 000s of metric tons. Tractors are units. Numbers of tractors are from 1988, all other figures are from 1989. Source: UN FAO *Production Yearbook 1989.*

have also been locally important for more than a century. Cotton and flax have been major crops in Egypt since pharaonic times. Where ecological conditions are especially favorable, industrial crops have been promoted by government agencies since the 1950s—for example, sugar beets in Syria and Turkey and cotton in Israel and Turkey.

With the exceptions of the intensively irrigated lands, parts of Israel, and a few other scattered areas, low crop yields still typify regional agriculture, although yields have increased ·notably since the 1950s. Until the 1960s, mechanization was uncommon, but coordinated programs are increasing the number of machines, especially tractors (see Table 7-2, col. 7). Farming in Israel is highly mechanized.

Small farms that are primarily tenant operated characterize the region. Along with efforts to improve yields, farmers and governments have made systematic attempts to improve the quality of crops, the quality of the produce that reaches the consumer, conservation, efficiency, and other

agricultural practices. Such programs produce a region-wide dynamic of change, with uneven but sometimes excellent results.

Physical Factors

1. *Climate.* Moisture supply is the main problem in much of the region, and except in parts of Turkey and in some mountain areas it is inadequate, seasonally concentrated, and unreliable. In areas with a widespread marginal climate, drought years are frequent and severe, and such areas experience wide swings in grain production. For example, in the locally dry year of 1984, Jordan produced only 15,000 mt (metric tons) of wheat; in 1980, which was unusually wet, Jordan's wheat crop was 134,000 mt—893 percent greater.

Only 7 percent of the region can regularly support rainfed (unirrigated) agriculture (note isohyets on Map 4-2 and see Table 4-1). Approximate precipitation parameters for agriculture in the region are the 5-in./125-mm isohyet as the minimum for regular grain production and the

12-in./300-mm isohyet as the lower limit for other crops. Irrigation can extend the cultivated area, but only to a limited extent, and it must be developed at great expense and effort for the most intensive and effective methods of water use. Available water is finite, and irrigable land is limited. Despite the problem of aridity, crops benefit from the long growing season, prevailingly clear skies, and favorable light for plant growth.

2. *Soils.* Because the area with naturally productive soils is limited, higher crop yields require good farm management, including intensive fertilization, good drainage, improved fallowing in lieu of the traditional procedures, and good crop rotation. Salinity buildup is an ever-present problem in drier areas.

3. *Relief.* The wide distribution of mountainous areas and rough terrain reduces the amount of land that is naturally suitable for cultivation. Although valuable for their cooler climate and as major sources of runoff for irrigation water, mountains can be adapted to only limited agricultural production (see Fig. 3-2). However, in places, laborious terracing and other techniques have made a moderate production of specialty crops possible. Nevertheless, population pressure on the land long ago induced cultivators to plow highland slopes, which has resulted in soil erosion and loss of forests. For their part, most of the low-lying plains and plateaus, which do have a relief that is appropriate for cultivation, are the areas of inadequate moisture and less productive soils.

Traditions, Techniques, and Technology

Improvement in agriculture has been hindered by the persistence of traditional practices that are inimical to better farming and marketing. Until recently, the cost of farm inputs (fertilizer, pesticides, machinery) was only 25 percent of the gross value of output, in contrast to 70 percent in the United States. Thus, the value added per agricultural worker has been generally low, and total farm production has also been low as a result, but the situation is improving markedly. The rapidly increasing production of horticultural crops in plastic greenhouses impresses even the casual observer, not only in the Fertile Crescent but also in Egypt, Saudi Arabia, and the Gulf amirates. Although more expensive, greenhouse or hothouse production of tomatoes, beans, peppers, eggplant, strawberries, and similar crops permits earlier marketing, much higher yield, more attractive produce, and higher pricing.

Ironically, the countries that have the wealth to supply the highest capital inputs to agriculture have, with one or two exceptions, the lowest agricultural potential: Oman, Saudi Arabia, and the smaller Gulf states. Iraq and Iran have both oil income and agricultural potential but have spread their income thinly, especially during the wars of the 1980s and 1990–1991. Iraq particularly squandered enormous capital resources on armament production and purchases. However, every Middle Eastern government has an active, if not uniformly effective, national program for upgrading agriculture, and oil-producing Arab states with a limited agricultural potential have given financial assistance to their less wealthy Arab neighbors who have a greater crop potential. Such aid is mutually beneficial, as it produces a multiplier effect, and agricultural progress has been appreciably stimulated.

Mechanization on any perceptible scale has come late and slowly, and because mechanization requires a systems approach that has been neglected, the mere adoption of machines has not achieved an optimum benefit. Even the greatly increased use of the internal combustion engine, which is common even in remote areas for pumping irrigation water, is a mixed blessing because of overpumping. The use of tractors is steadily increasing; their number quadrupled between 1970 and 1984. That increase is mainly attributable to the quintupling of the number of tractors in Turkey, which has two-thirds of the tractors in the Middle East. More sophisticated and expensive machines are still unusual—cotton pickers, corn (maize) pickers, and wheat combines. Milking machines are rare, except in Israel, which uses nearly three times as many as does all the rest of the region combined.

With financial aid from the United States and from international Jewish agencies, Israel devotes even higher capital inputs per unit area to land reclamation and improvement than do the Gulf states. In proportion to its size, Israel has executed the most intensive land improvement programs in the region, and one of its major land reclamation projects, the drainage and cultivation of the Huleh Marshes in extreme northern Israel, was undertaken as early as the 1950s. Whereas "making the desert bloom" has been accomplished only in limited "oasis" areas in the dry Negev of Israel, scores of projects have improved cropland or rangeland, irrigated cultivated areas, drained marshes, and installed systems for drip irrigation.

Some areas, especially in Turkey, give good rainfed yields in an average year; but in most parts of the Middle East, irrigation is either essential, as in Egypt, or highly beneficial, as on the Levant coastal plains. Thus, for most of the region the critical resource is water. Accordingly, states have undertaken engineering projects to harness more of their water resources, to distribute that water to improved cultivable areas, and to utilize more efficient irrigation techniques. Some of the world's major irrigation projects, involving construction of world-class dams, were undertaken in the Middle East during the late 1970s and the 1980s: the Southeast Anatolia Project in Turkey, the Jazirah Project in Syria, and the older Aswan High Dam Project in Egypt. Some political problems ensuing from these projects are examined in Chapter 11.

Landholdings and Land Reform

Land Tenure

Land tenure is an essential socioeconomic aspect of agricultural patterns and is extraordinarily complex in the Middle East. The complexity arises partly from the number of national systems in the region and partly from the varied legal systems introduced into much of the area by earlier regional governments. The prevailing land tenure system developed in an Islamic context after the Muslim conquests of the seventh century and was modified over four centuries under the Ottoman Empire (which excluded

Iran). With many land regulations rooted in Islamic law, some relationships with land are traditionally revered as religious in nature.

Highly simplified, landholdings everywhere, except Cyprus and parts of Israel, fall into three major categories: (1) state-owned land, the most common type, with strong usufruct rights vested in the occupant (*miri* lands, called *khaliseh* in Iran); (2) freehold land or land under private ownership (*mulk*); and (3) land in a religious trust (*waqf*), a unique Islamic form of trusteeship for the endowment of some religious or other social purpose, such as a mosque or school. The amount of *waqf* land is steadily decreasing, with the trusts being discouraged by governments because they are difficult for the state to control or tax. Thus, despite traditional reverence for the institution, *waqf* land has been widely expropriated under recent land reform programs.

Two communal subcategories of land tenure play important roles in Middle East agriculture. The nomadic tribal grazing range (*dirah*) is based on the concept of land as territory rather than land as property. However, a major tribe considers that it has priority rights in its *dirah* as its communal range, along with tribal water sources. Hundreds of thousands of square miles are included in nomadic tribal ranges in the Middle East as a whole. A second subcategory, the communal village—*musha* in the Syria-Palestine realm—permits villagers in marginal environments to shift between sedentarism and nomadism as circumstances dictate.[1]

Some large state landholdings quietly passed into private control during the post–World War I confusion that accompanied the transfer of former Ottoman territories. Under many different designations, some trustees gradually assumed private ownership of tracts of *miri* land, especially tribal leaders who might have been registered as "owners" of extensive communal areas.

Traditional land tenure systems changed sharply in Palestine after World War I as land acquired by the Jewish National Fund (JNF) from Arab owners was occupied by Zionist immigrants. Under a new Jewish system, suggestive of combined aspects of the Islamic *miri* and *waqf* systems, the JNF took over the land "in the name of the Jewish people" and leased it for nominal sums to the colonists. More significantly, during the fighting in 1948 and 1949, Israeli agencies expropriated approximately 1,112,000 acres/450,000 ha of cultivated land from Palestinian Arab owners who became refugees. Such lands were absorbed by the new state or by the quasi-official JNF and similar agencies, then were leased to new Jewish settlers. As the occupying power, the Israeli government has expropriated scores of plots of lands in the West Bank, primarily for installation of Jewish settlements.

Holdings and Reform

The size of landholdings is another significant aspect of land tenure and of agricultural patterns and has also had major impacts on the social and political stability of several countries in the region. Since World War II, reform-minded governments have conducted land reform programs to break up landholdings that were considered to be excessively large and to lessen the influence of powerful landlords.

Even before land reform, small holdings were typical in the Middle East, especially in irrigated areas where land is scarce, highly desirable, and expensive because of its improvements. In Egypt, for example, where all cultivated land must be irrigated, farms of less than 10 acres/4 ha embrace 97 percent of all agricultural land. Such small holdings occupy only 34 percent of the nonirrigated areas in Syria.

Prior to land reform programs that began in the mid-1950s, small numbers of wealthy landlords possessed huge holdings in Egypt, Syria, Iraq, and Iran. In Iraq, for example, a study by the UN's Food and Agriculture Organization (FAO) revealed that 2 percent of the landowners held 66 percent of the land in the mid-1950s; in Iran, large owners and tribal leaders controlled 50 percent of the land. Following the model of revolutionary republican Egypt under Gamal Abd al-Nasser, Syria and Iraq conducted land reform programs during the late 1950s and early 1960s. As one result of these land redistribution programs, the number of great landlords in the Middle East has declined sharply and is still decreasing. The same reforms changed landowning patterns: Individual ownership has replaced many of the tribal rights to planting and pasture, and land consolidation programs have reduced fragmented, scattered holdings.

Rainfed Crop Farming

Extensive Grain Farming

As the mean annual rainfall increases to about 5 in./125 mm along the inner margin of the Fertile Crescent, desert and semiarid grasslands give way to subhumid cropland (Map 7-1). The cereal grains grown in this subhumid belt—wheat, barley, and millet—are in fact highly bred grasses. Here, despite frequent negative deviations from the average annual precipitation, grains grown without irrigation yield moderately good crops in occasional wet years, as in 1991–1992, and at least minimum crops in the frequent drought years. Wheat yields might range between 15 and 2.5 bu. per acre/1,000 and 165 kg per ha, and barley does as well or better. Both the production and yields of wheat are increasing significantly in the Middle East as the new dwarf wheats are planted.

Crop failures in the marginal lands are frequent. The more drought-prone areas could be better utilized for growing high-quality forage grasses in a comprehensive range management program to increase meat production, but changing from grains to grass might be difficult, since some nomadic groups on the margins of grain-farming areas operate as both wandering herdsmen and part-time grain farmers. In a wet cycle, they tend to settle down, only to shift back to nomadic herding in a dry cycle, as in the *musha* village. Yet in each cycle, a few families tend to remain sedentary, so that the nomads gradually suffer a net loss.

Whether on the dry margins or in the more humid areas, all wheat grown in the Middle East is winter wheat, planted in the autumn to take advantage of the cool-season rainfall and harvested in the early days of the warm, dry summer.

Mediterranean Agriculture

Wheat and Other Cereals. In the rainfed agriculture of the more humid Mediterranean climate areas, wheat is still the dominant crop in

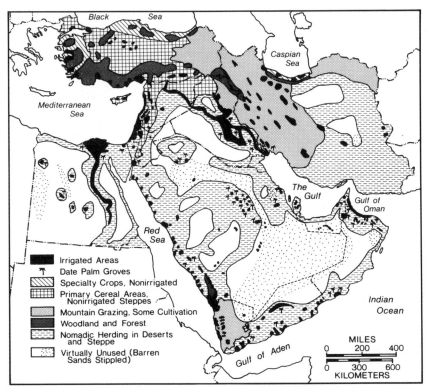

Map 7-1. *Middle East land use.*

area planted, but Mediterranean agriculture is typically varied and includes specialized arboriculture (tree crops), viticulture (grape cultivation), and a great range of irrigated crops. Wheat is more intensively cultivated in this wetter area where yields are higher and more reliable than in the steppes (14–17 bu. per acre/940–1,145 kg per ha as a representative range). Millet and barley are also common in the area.

Vegetables and Fruits. Mediterranean-type agricultural conditions are ecologically suitable, particularly with supplementary irrigation, for a variety of vegetables and fruits, many of which evolved in the area (Table 7-3). Coastal plains fringing the eastern Mediterranean, from western Turkey to southern Israel and around Cyprus, are veritable vegetable gardens and fruit orchards. Irrigation helps support citrus groves, especially oranges, in favorable segments all along this coastal belt, and bananas are grown in southern Turkey, Lebanon, and Israel. Oranges from Lebanon, Israel (the Jaffa orange), and Gaza are prime

products. Many soft fruits—peaches, apricots, plums, pears, and cherries—and vines are grown higher up, at cooler and more humid elevations. Two especially important perennial crops, olives and grapes, occupy 40 percent of the fruit area of the region. Less favorable lower hillsides are clothed with olive groves well into the interior, even east of the Jordan Valley. On dry, stony slopes in much of the eastern Mediterranean, as well as on slopes of the Zagros in Iran, tree nuts such as almonds, walnuts, and pistachios thrive, despite the hot, dry summers. The fig appears frequently where irrigation permits its survival. Smyrna (Izmir) figs, rich and purple and large as lemons, are world renowned.

Fruits, vegetables, and nuts are also specialties of favorable areas well away from the coasts and far into the interior of Anatolia (Fig. 7-1), Syria, and Iran. The Bekaa-Galilee-Jordan trench shelters fruit orchards, including those for bananas in Israel and Jordan. The Damascus oasis, the Ghutah, is a fabled garden, and well-tended orchards flourish in protected basins and valleys in

TABLE 7-3: LAND USE: TREE CROPS, TIMBER (ROUNDWOOD), AND FISH

COUNTRY	1 ALL FRUITS	2 ORANGES	3 TREE NUTS	4 OLIVES	5 DATES	6 TIMBER (m^3)	7 FISH
Bahrain	50	---	---	—	46	---	6.7
Cyprus	411	50	2	9	---	76	2.5
Egypt	3,795	1,370	4	32	560	2,211	250.0
Iran	3,415	150	197	10	440	6,817	156.0
Iraq	1,359	175	5	4	375	149	18.0
Israel	1,508	546	4	27	9	118	28.4
Jordan	162	40	1	30	---	8	0.1
Kuwait	2	---	---	—	1	---	10.8
Lebanon	649	179	7	30	---	488	1.8
Oman	197	---	---	—	121	---	166.1
Qatar	8	---	---	—	5	---	3.1
Saudi Arabia	630	---	---	—	500	6	46.8
Syria	1,149	148	45	132	---	48	5.6
Turkey	8,732	738	767	650	8	16,809	627.9
UAE	108	---	---	—	68	---	86.4
Yemen	331	5	---	—	28	312	73.1
Gaza	134	90	1	2	2	---	0.5
West Bank	---	---	---	—	---	---	---
TOTALS	22,640	3,491	1,033	926	2,163	27,042	1,483.8

Many of the data are Food and Agriculture Organization (FAO) estimates or are unofficial figures. All crops are for 1989, fish for 1988, and both are in metric tons; roundwood is for 1988 and is in cubic meters. Column 1 excludes melons. Sources: Crops from UN FAO *Production Yearbook 1989*. Roundwood timber and fish from *Britannica World Data 1991*. (With permission)

Turkey and Iran, where harvested fruits are spread on rooftops and roadsides to dry under the summer sun. Dried apricots and a variety of pistachios from Iran are widely marketed. Oilseeds, including sunflower, sesame, and safflower, are more commonly grown in large fields in the all-season rain areas of northwestern Turkey.

Industrial Crops. To compensate for the dry conditions in summer, farmers in Mediterranean climate areas of the region use supplementary irrigation to produce substantial quantities of industrial crops—cotton, tobacco, sugar beets, sugarcane (more common in warmer, irrigated Upper Egypt), linseed, and hemp. Egyptian long-staple cotton, an improved variety of a crop cultivated in Egypt for thousands of years, is in wide demand on world markets. Cotton production has also been expanded in Turkey, Syria, and Israel along with sugar beet production in Turkey and Syria.

The Olive: A Special Note. The most widespread tree crop in the Mediterranean climate lands is the olive, the hallmark of true Mediterranean conditions (Fig. 7-2). With a very long taproot, as deep as 30 ft./9 m, and a small, waxy leaf, the olive tree is well adapted to the cool, wet winters and the warm, rainless summers. Likewise adapted to the chemical and physical characteristics of the Mediterranean soils, the olive requires no irrigation and only modest attention to produce plentiful crops for 200–300 years and more. The olive yield varies according to soil moisture, but appreciable amounts of fruit are grown even in dry years. One result is that people of the Mediterranean Basin have depended upon the olive for both food and oil: Olive oil is the basic oil for cooking, soap, even greasing wagon wheels.

Figure 7-1. *Agriculture in Anatolia: Harvesting chickpeas (garbanzos) in the Euphrates basin near the Atatürk Dam. Turkey is a regional leader in the production of many crops and in the variety of crops produced.*

Carob, or "locust trees," grow on dry, uncultivated hillsides. A major crop in southern Cyprus, carob beans are exported for use as cattle feed, varnish base, and a health food substitute for chocolate. Smaller numbers of the trees also grow along the southern coast of Turkey and in the Levant.

Agriculture in Year-Round Rain Areas

Compared with the steppe and Mediterranean areas, a different crop ecology characterizes northern Turkey and northwestern Iran where appreciable amounts of summer rain complement the Mediterranean winter rain. The agricultural landscape exhibits fields of corn (maize) in Turkey (Fig. 1-2), tea plantations in both Turkey (along the southeastern Black Sea coast) and Iran (south of the Caspian Sea), rice (with supplementary irrigation) in those same areas, and the world's greatest hazelnut (filbert) groves on the seaward-facing slopes around Trabzon in Turkey. The famous Turkish tobacco predominates farther west along the Black Sea coast, and still farther west are extensive fields of sunflowers, grown for their oilseeds.

The High Yemen also benefits from summer precipitation as does the Asir to the north. Taking advantage of the monsoonal rains to grow grain sorghum (milo maize), a summer crop, Yemen is the Middle East's leading producer of sorghum. The highlands also produce small amounts of the famous Yemen coffee, which, however, is yielding place to *qat*, another specialty crop of the steep Yemen terraces. Two other specialty crops of the Middle East are narcotic—opium poppies in western Turkey and Iran, grown under government control, and hashish grown illegally in Lebanon and Iran. Opium poppies and hashish were, unhappily, important cash crops for farmers of the Bekaa of eastern Lebanon, especially during the civil warfare of the period 1975–1990.

Water in the Desert: Irrigation

Irrigation plays a vital role in the life of the Middle East, where aridity and semiaridity prevail in more than 80 percent of the land area. Irrigation helps remedy the deficiency, seasonality, and variability of rainfall, so that agriculture can gain

Figure 7-2. *Huge olive groves on Turkey's Aegean coast, one of the world's most ideal olive environments. These groves constitute a valuable* waqf, *religious endowment.*

the greatest advantage from a long, frost-free growing season. Much of the irrigation is supplementary rather than the sole source of water, and rainfed and irrigated cultivation intermingle in many sectors of the region. Where primary irrigation is possible year-round in an area with a long growing season, two and even three crops a year are grown, as in parts of Egypt.

Sources of Water

Life from the Rivers. Most of the water for irrigation in the Middle East comes from rivers (see Chap. 3). The Nile, Tigris, and Euphrates are the three main sources of river irrigation water, but scores of smaller rivers and hundreds of streamlets also supply water for irrigation. Fed by runoff from rains and snows on highlands adjacent to the desert valleys, the flow of these rivers depends on the timing of the rainfall and snowmelt. Some river water is tapped indirectly—from dammed reservoirs, shallow wells in alluvium adjacent to the riverbanks, underground tunnels, or canals carrying diverted water—but the river remains the primary source.

Groundwater. The second most important source of irrigation water in most of the area is groundwater from underground aquifers tapped primarily by wells. Some wells are only a few feet deep, some ancient hand-dug wells reach 300–400 ft./90–120 m, and thousands of modern drilled wells reach 2,000–3,000 ft./610–915 m. In many instances, underground aquifers have been discovered through petroleum exploration, as was the great Wasia aquifer in central Saudi Arabia. Elsewhere, modern hydrogeological technology has found moderately productive aquifers in areas long considered hopelessly waterless—the Western Desert of Egypt, western and eastern Arabia, and Inner Oman.

Springs. Naturally flowing springs are a third source of water for irrigation. Such springs usually occur where the water table intersects the ground surface, often in a series along a stratum outcrop or fault line. Nearly every Middle East state has at least some springs, thousands of which are used to irrigate plots ranging in size from a few square feet to a score or more acres. Some springs issue from horizontal solution channels, as in Mount Lebanon, others from vertical solution shafts in limestone karst regions, as in eastern Arabia. Artesian springs bring groundwater up the solution pits from appreciable depths to support several extensive oases. Saudi Arabia's three largest oases—Hofuf, Qatif, and al-Kharj—are irrigated in this way, as are large oases on Bahrain.

Methods of irrigation depend on the water source as well as on the technology available. Since World War II, huge dams, elevated concrete water chutes, drilled wells, mechanical pumps, and other modern equipment have rapidly been replacing traditional techniques, yet the old methods survive in many areas. Gravity-flow canals, hand-bucket transfer of water, counterpoised buckets (called *shadufs* in Egypt), Archimedes screws, and water wheels (the picturesque *noriahs* of Hamah, Syria, on the Orontes) are all traditional methods.

A more complicated traditional method for transporting irrigation water under certain conditions is the *qanat* system (shown in Fig. 22-3), which taps water at an upslope source and conducts it downslope through an underground tunnel. The ideal environment for a *qanat* is a large alluvial fan, the cone of gravel deposited by a stream emerging from a constricted valley onto a piedmont. Originating in Persia centuries before the Christian era, the *qanat* concept spread eastward to central Asia and westward through Arabia and North Africa to Morocco—and, indeed, eventually was applied by Spanish colonists on a small scale in the Western Hemisphere. It has been given different names in different places—*karez, falaj, foggara.*

Excavation of a *qanat* involves both horizontal and vertical digging: carefully controlled burrowing of a gently sloping tunnel to carry the water and also opening a series of regularly spaced vertical shafts from the surface to the tunnel. The initial shaft, the "mother well," taps the source of the water, usually a stream disappearing into the gravels at the apex of an alluvial fan, and other shafts serve several purposes: as air vents, pits for access and for disposal of excavated material, clean-out shafts, and wells. A *qanat* can thus be identified on the surface by a telltale alignment of holes, each surrounded by a circular spoil ridge. Scores of thousands of *qanats* tunnel through alluvial fans at the foot of mountains in Iran and surrounding countries, especially Oman. Although many still supply water to towns, villages, and fields, increasing numbers are abandoned each year for cheaper and more convenient pipelines.

Modern irrigation technology has introduced more efficient methods of applying water directly to crops, including overhead sprinkler systems and, more recently, drip irrigation. The latter system, also known as trickle irrigation, supplies moisture—sometimes mixed with fertilizer—to each individual plant through appropriately spaced openings. Although expensive initially, this system makes more efficient use of water, fertilizer, and labor, and it is certain to be utilized on an increasing scale. Overhead sprinklers, more efficient than basin and furrow methods, nevertheless waste some water through evaporation both in the air and on the surface. They require appreciable investment, but both movable impulse sprinklers and self-propelled center-pivot circular sprinklers are nevertheless widely used, with the latter utilized on a grand scale in the wheat fields of central Saudi Arabia.

Irrigated Lands

In 1980, irrigated cropland covered 55,360 miles^2/143,380 km^2, which was 1.9 percent of all the land and 20 percent of the agricultural land in the sixteen states of the Middle East. Four years later, irrigated area had *decreased* to 53,734 miles^2/139,170 km^2, despite efforts in all states to increase irrigation. With the opening of extensive new water projects in Iraq, Egypt, Turkey, and Saudi Arabia, by 1988 irrigated area increased to 57,540 miles^2/149,030 km^2. A similar increase is likely by 1993. The value of crops raised by artificial watering constitutes a disproportionate percentage of the value of total crop production, perhaps as much as three-fourths. One explanation is that all cultivated land is irrigated in Egypt, agriculturally the second-most overall productive country in the Middle East (Turkey is first). From a half to a quarter of the cultivated land in most other major agricultural countries in the region is irrigated (see Table 7-1), and even in Turkey, with 8 percent, and Syria, with 12 percent, of the cultivated land under irrigation, irrigated crops amount to more than 26 and 52 percent of production, respectively.

Although expansion of irrigation is an obvious step toward increasing crop production, such expansion encounters four serious obstacles: decreasing availability of water; increasing expense in terms of cost-effectiveness; competition for land availability; and conflicts over riparian rights. Although high expenditures per unit area in Israel, Saudi Arabia, and some of the Gulf states have produced excellent returns, such levels of expenditure are of questionable cost-effectiveness in realistic terms, and they are not practicable in most other parts of the region. In such areas as southern Iraq, expanding irrigation presents its own problems, including salination. Drainage, both surface and underground tile, may offer more benefit than irrigation in some areas.

Role of Animals

Livestock raising, practiced in the Middle East as early as 8000 BC, is common in all three types of land, although it differs from one environmental area to another; and nomadic herding on the desert or in the Zagros Mountains is quite different from raising animals on farms, especially on irrigated farms. Since agricultural statistics for the Middle East do not distinguish between farm animals and those herded by nomads, data in the following discussion pertain to all types of livestock.

Commercial animal raising is at its most intensive in specialized agricultural settlements in Israel. In addition, systematic commercial raising of small animals has made rapid strides in several countries since 1950. Chicken raising, for example, increased sharply during the 1970s—166 percent for the region as a whole, and up to 2,100 percent in the United Arab Emirates (UAE). The number of chickens increased by 82 million—15 percent—between 1986 and 1988 alone. Although no figures are available on the subject, pigeons are raised in large numbers by individuals in towns and villages as well as by farmers in many areas of the Middle East, especially in Egypt (Fig. 7-3). Fish farming is an important aspect of land use in the Huleh Basin of Israel and is beginning on an experimental basis in Saudi Arabia and other Gulf countries.

Meat animals are produced in large numbers (Table 7-4). Chickens, sheep, goats, and cattle (*Bos taurus*) are the most numerous (Fig. 7-4). Hogs are raised in Cyprus, Israel, Egypt, Turkey, and Lebanon, although they cannot be marketed in conservative Muslim or Jewish areas where the

Figure 7-3. *An Egyptian specialty: Dovecotes on a small farm in the Fayyum Depression. Doves and pigeons are raised for their meat, specialty eggs, and manure.*

animal is ritually prohibited. Sheep have been relatively numerous for millennia and are an important source not only of a favorite meat, wool, and skins but also of milk and cheese. Of the total number of sheep, Turkey and Iran together have almost 65 percent.

Goats are 38 percent as numerous as sheep. Despite its reputation for destroying vegetation, the goat, properly managed, is hardly more damaging to forage than the sheep or cow, and it is a uniquely valuable animal for grazing the poorer types of forage. Vegetation can best be protected through progressive exclusion of goats from designated areas, and goat exclusion laws have been very successful in Cyprus, Israel, and Turkey. The Angora goats of Turkey are especially valuable for their unique hair, used in making mohair.

The number of camels was slowly declining, falling from more than 1 million in 1969–1971 to 763,000 in 1985; however, it rose to nearly 1 million during the late 1980s as interest in camels re-

TABLE 7-4: FARM ANIMALS (000s of head)

COUNTRY	1 CAMELS	2 CATTLE	3 SHEEP	4 HOGS	5 CHICKENS	6 GOATS	7 BUFFALOES
Bahrain	1	6	8	---	1,000	16	---
Cyprus	---	46	300	284	3,000	205	---
Egypt	77	1,950	1,320	15	30,000	1,650	2,650
Iran	27	8,000	34,000	---	115,000	13,500	230
Iraq	58	1,650	9,500	---	77,000	1,600	145
Israel	10	357	375	130	23,000	125	---
Jordan	15	29	1,225	---	60,000	500	---
Kuwait	8	29	320	---	30,000	43	---
Lebanon	---	55	145	22	12,000	475	---
Oman	83	136	220	---	2,000	770	---
Qatar	22	8	128	---	1,000	78	---
Saudi Arabia	405	250	7,698	---	70,000	3,700	---
Syria	5	756	13,903	1	13,000	1,053	1
Turkey	3	12,000	34,850	10	59,000	13,100	540
UAE	100	48	250	---	7,000	575	---
Yemen	144	1,179	3,681	---	27,000	3,125	---
Gaza	1	4	10	---	2,000	20	---
West Bank	---	---	---	---	---	---	---
TOTALS	959	26,503	107,933	462	532,000	40,535	3,566

Most of the data are Food and Agriculture Organization estimates; a few are unofficial figures. Source: UN FAO *Production Yearbook 1989.*

Figure 7-4. *Anatolian shepherd with sheep and goats near Boğazkale. Some of the goats are of the famous Angora breed.*

vived—for the sport of camel racing, for example. The traditional significance of the camel, including its use for religious feasts, suggests that it will continue to play an important, if diminished, role well into the twenty-first century.

The number of cattle in the Middle East, along with the population and standard of living, increased steadily from the early 1960s into the mid-1980s. In the late 1980s, however, cattle decreased dramatically in Turkey and sharply in

Egypt as farmers turned more to raising crops and concentrating on smaller animals. The quality of cattle has improved as farmers have turned to better breeds; especially in the case of dairy cattle, better breeds have greatly improved the milk yield. A growing awareness of the nutritional benefits of milk has encouraged dairying in many areas, and Ras al-Khaymah, one of the United Arab Emirates, now produces cow's milk for the UAE urban areas. Israel has imported and bred some of the best dairy cattle in the world, and it leads the Middle East in milk production per animal by a wide margin. Egyptian farms, with plenty of water in which buffalo can submerge themselves, have three-fourths of the region's buffalo (*Babalus babulis,* or water buffalo, quite different from the American bison) and have more buffalo than sheep, cattle, or goats. Water buffalo are also common in the marsh area of southern Iraq.

Horse populations have declined sharply in every Middle East state, with the special exceptions of Saudi Arabia and Qatar, as the work horse is displaced by the tractor and the automobile. Fine Arabian show horses constitute only a small percentage of the regional equine population; after becoming rare in the Middle East in the mid-twentieth century, they are again being bred by a few wealthy Saudis and other Arabs.

Nomadic Pastoralism

Nomadic pastoralism is an essential aspect of the Middle East in the popular perception and also in fact. Animal herding by nomads involves a wide range of periodic horizontal and vertical migrations by tribal groups and their animals in search of grass and water. It is these periodic movements, both across country and vertically to higher or lower elevations, that have led to the interrelated triad of nonsedentary herding—nomadism, pastoralism, and tribalism. Nomadic pastoralism extends over a larger area than any other type of agricultural activity—more, in fact, than all other types combined. It dominates the dry area from the Western Desert of Egypt across the Arabian Peninsula and interior Iran to Baluchistan and also is practiced in extensive mountainous areas in west-central Iran. Major nomadic pastoral groups include the Bedouins of the deserts and steppes except in Iran (see Fig.

6-1), Qashqai and Bakhtiari of the High Zagros, Turkmen of the Kopet ranges, Baluch of southeastern Iran, and other smaller groups. Although the number of people engaged in nomadic herding is steadily decreasing, it remains a significant aspect of tradition, culture, and economic life, especially in the Arabian Peninsula and Syrian Desert.

Using marginal resources and very basic technology, Bedouins are well adjusted to their desert environment, primarily through a symbiotic relationship with their animals. Alone on the open desert in summer, a Bedouin family could survive only a day or two as there would be no water, no food, no shelter. But the family's camels, which feed on salty shrubs, supply milk for consumption as liquid, yogurt, or cheese; supply hair for certain weaving; supply hides and leather; serve as transportation, including transport to a water supply; supply dung for fuel; and in dire emergency, provide meat when slaughtered.

Most contemporary Bedouins also herd sheep and goats for wool, milk, hides, and meat. The essential characteristic of the Bedouins is their geographically cyclic movements to find grass for their herds and flocks. Other nomads follow similar cycles that may vary in frequency of migration, types of animals herded, and other details.

The Remarkable Camel

The domesticated camel appeared about 2000 BC. Although the Bactrian camel (*Camelus bactrianus*), with two humps, is common in parts of Anatolia and in northern and northeastern Iran, the Arabian camel, or dromedary (*C. dromedarius*), with one hump, has long been herded in the Arabian Peninsula, North Africa, and adjacent lands. Nomads in the Syrian Desert, Mesopotamia, Anatolia, and Iran, on the other hand, herd sheep and goats and raise fewer camels—indeed, none at all in mountainous areas.

The camel adapts especially well to life in the desert environment, as it has a remarkable ability to conserve water in hot weather and a low requirement for water in winter (Fig. 7-5). Its long neck allows the camel to graze both surface vegetation and tree leaves. The soft, padded feet of the animal operate like snowshoes and enable it

Figure 7-5. *Camels being watered by Bedouin herdsmen in Saudi Arabia.*

Figure 7-6. *Timber from forests in the Taurus Mountains stacked on the south coast of Turkey near Mersin.*

to walk over drift sand without sinking and over hot surfaces without pain.

Traversing terrain that other beasts cannot, the "ship of the desert" can carry heavier loads through greater heat and aridity for a longer working life than oxen, horses, or donkeys. Using camel caravans, the early Arabs monopolized ancient trade routes and laid the bases for mercantile cities over a wide area. The use of the camel actually delayed the evolution of desert roads, since wagons and carts drawn by oxen or horses were less efficient than camels. However, after the mid-twentieth century, motor vehicles, aircraft, and railroads displaced the camel as transport, certainly for long distances, and some modern Bedouins even transport their camels and other animals by pickup truck.[2]

Forest Products

Forestry plays a minor role in Middle East agriculture, as is suggested by the sparse forest vegetation (see Map 5-2). Only Turkey and Iran have noteworthy forest industries, and extensive, systematic timber exploitation is practiced only in Turkey (Fig. 7-6). Timber production in the high Pontus in the north, the high Taurus in the south, and the highlands between Istanbul and Ankara yields 593.3 million ft.^{3}/16.8 million m^3 of roundwood a year, 62 percent of Middle East production (see Table 7.3). Iran's production is 240 ft.^{3}/6.8 million m^3, and Egypt's 77.7 million ft.^{3}/2.2 million m^3. No other country in the region produces even 0.5 million m^3.

Fishing

Surrounded and deeply penetrated by seas, and with a total length of coastline exceeding 14,585 miles/23,470 km, the Middle East countries have an appreciable potential for a fishing industry. However, other factors inhibit progress toward reaching that potential, including overfishing and pollution.

With its long coastlines on three seas and its vigorous maritime activity, Turkey leads the sixteen Middle East countries in fish landed. Its total of 628,000 mt is more than twice that of its nearest competitor, Egypt, and nearly four times that of the next competitor, Oman (see Table 7-3). Access to rich fisheries associated with the upwelling waters along the southern coast of the Arabian Peninsula provides Oman and neighboring Yemen with their considerable catches. Iran exploits its long coastline on the Gulf, as well as its coastline on the Gulf of Oman and the Caspian Sea, for fishing. From all three it takes more than 156,000 mt, and it reaps a notably valuable harvest of caviar (fish roe) from the Caspian. All the leading fishing states sharply increased their landings during the late 1980s.

8

Riches
Beneath the Earth

Underground Resources

In its enormous wealth in petroleum and natural gas resources, the Middle East is without equal and perforce has a unique role on the world scene. Moreover, the region's percentage of the world's oil reserves, as well as its percentage of the world's production, is certain to increase, since the relatively limited reserves elsewhere are being more rapidly depleted by intensive exploitation. In income benefits, never before in history has a region achieved such explosive large-scale economic development in such a short time as the Gulf oil-producing area of the Middle East did during the four decades following the end of World War II.

The importance of the Middle East's petroleum reserves notwithstanding, it should not obscure other significant aspects of the region. The Middle East also possesses historical, geopolitical, political, human, geographical, and other nonenergy economic significance. The importance of these other aspects is often overlooked or is subordinated to petroleum and more limited regional interests. Although this chapter focuses on oil, one major aim of this book as a whole is to weigh the various phases of the region in order to achieve a more balanced perspective.

Petroleum is the sole item produced and exported on any scale by several Middle East countries. At the average rate of production during the 5 years 1985–1990, Middle East petroleum resources will last for about 120 years if no additional resources are found. Unlikely as the lack of new discoveries may be, the oil-producing countries themselves are alert to the singularity of the basis of their wealth and to its eventual depletion. They are also aware of the external forces that influence the production, transportation, and marketing of their most important exchangeable product. In view of the relatively rapid exhaustibility of this singular resource, and with the lessons of numerous boom-and-bust producing areas to guide them, Middle East oil producers have sought ways to control their own destinies—through the Organization of Petroleum Exporting Countries (OPEC), for example. In an effort to maintain economic viability for a longer period, they are also conducting intensive programs of economic diversification.

With certain exceptions, the overall percentage of the world's supply of underground resources other than petroleum in the Middle East is relatively minor. Nevertheless, the exploitation of nonenergy minerals is a major item in the economies of several countries with limited oil output. Nonoil mineral industries are or have been of noteworthy importance in Turkey, Iran, Jordan, Cyprus, Egypt, Syria, and Israel.

Petroleum: Historical Development

Asphalt, gas, and oil seeps from underground hydrocarbon deposits have been known for millennia at numerous sites in the Middle East—in northern Mesopotamia, near Hit on the Euphrates, in western Iran, under the Dead Sea, at the northern end of the Gulf of Suez, and in a dozen other places in the region.[1] Bitumen (asphalt, pitch, tar) is mentioned several times in the Old

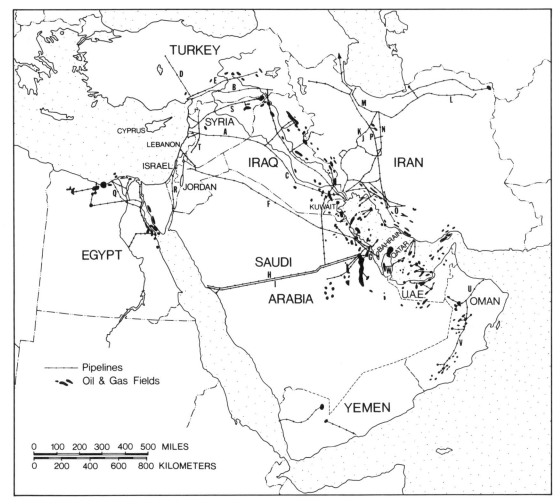

Map 8-1. *Major petroleum and natural gas fields and pipelines, early 1990s. (Adapted from Exxon 1984 and recent volumes of* International Petroleum Encyclopedia*)*

Testament: Noah used pitch in constructing the ark, and Moses' mother used bitumen and pitch to line the basket in which she floated the baby Moses on the Nile. Bitumen was used as mortar in the construction of brick walls, ziggurats, and other buildings in Sumerian and Babylonian times and can still be identified in many ruins in Iraq and western Iran.

The Old Testament "fiery furnace" of Shadrach, Meshach, and Abednego was likely the still-burning gas seepage known as the "eternal fires" near Kirkuk in northern Iraq. Flaming gas seepages were the focal points of fire-worshiping religions of ancient Persia, and fire temples became numerous there. Oil from seeps and oozes was collected for lamps, and it was used in warfare long before the Christian era. Thus, twentieth-century oil explorers had certain indicators for siting their early wildcat wells.

William Knox D'Arcy, a British subject, obtained a concession in 1901 to drill for oil in western Iran. Financed by a British syndicate, his crew made the first major oil strike in the Middle East in 1908. The initial discovery was in the Masjed-e Soleyman field, the first of many fabulous Middle East reservoirs (Map 8-1). The next year the D'Arcy group formed the Anglo-Persian Oil Company (APOC), which later became British Petroleum, and the first shipment of oil from the Middle East was made by APOC in 1912 from

Abadan, on the Shatt al-Arab. Further development was limited until World War I, when events proved the superiority of fuel oil over coal for firing boilers on naval vessels and commercial steamers. The demand for oil spiraled upward and has never ceased.

Other European entrepreneurs sought exploration rights across the border in Mesopotamia as soon as oil was found in Iran. The Turkish Petroleum Company, formed before World War I by British, French, and Dutch interests, found oil in 1927 by drilling only a few hundred meters from the "eternal fires." The discovery near Kirkuk opened one of the major oil fields of the world. In 1928, the United States made its first entry into the Middle East oil race when the Near East Development Corporation (NEDC) obtained an equity interest in Turkish Petroleum, renamed Iraq Petroleum Company in 1929. NEDC originally comprised five companies but later was equally divided between Standard of New Jersey (now Exxon) and Socony Vacuum (now Mobil).

From the early years of oil exploration in the Middle East, agreements among countries and companies divided up areas of operations and marketing. One accord was the Red Line Agreement, reached in 1928, which covered former Ottoman Empire possessions, excluding Kuwait and Egypt. It provided that any oil deals involving areas within the Red Line must be unanimously approved by all companies operating inside that line. Although later rescinded, this agreement regulated patterns of concessions in much of the Middle East for several critical years.

Neither the worldwide depression nor discoveries of other large supplies of oil, as in the East Texas field, slowed intensive exploration in the Middle East during the 1930s. By World War II, exploration had revealed the presence of oil in huge quantities beyond southern Iraq in the Mesopotamian-Gulf trough (Map 8-2).

The modest but important Bahrain field, found in 1932, was the first field discovered in the Gulf area proper, outside Iran and Iraq. Bahrain Island was also the scene of the first all-American oil venture in the Middle East. First a subsidiary of Standard Oil of California (Socal) and later jointly owned by Socal and Texaco, the Bahrain Petroleum Company (Bapco) was, however, chartered in Canada in order to fulfill a requirement that oil concessions in British territories be granted to "British companies." From the hills on the upturned strata of the geologic dome on Bahrain, U.S. geologists using binoculars studied Dammam Dome on the Arabian mainland 20 miles/32 km away and became convinced that a likely oil structure lay under it.

Urged by the geologists on Bahrain, Socal obtained a concession in 1933 for the eastern part of the Kingdom of Saudi Arabia and assigned the concession to California Arabian Standard Oil Company (Casoc). Casoc found oil in 1938 in Dammam Dome, as predicted. The company changed its name in 1944 to the more appropriate Arabian American Oil Company and is now widely known by the acronym Aramco. Even after it became a national oil company and was quietly renamed Saudi Arabian Oil Company, it continued to use the famous short form in the designation "Saudi Aramco," sanctioned in an early 1989 guideline.

During approximately the same 1930s period, the Kuwait Oil Company discovered and developed the rich Burgan reservoir in Kuwait. Both Saudi Arabia and Kuwait were able to produce only minor amounts of oil before the outbreak of World War II required reduction of operations. However, Saudi Arabia did export 12,000–15,000 barrels per day (bpd) to the refinery on Bahrain during the war, and some exploration continued. Wartime requirements permitted construction of a small refinery at Ras Tanura on the Saudi coast, which later expanded to become one of the world's largest refining facilities.

Growing realization of the region's oil potential accelerated exploration in the lower Gulf, and after the war, more than a score of new enterprises received concessions to explore various areas both on land and offshore. Whereas British, Dutch, French, and American "majors" had dominated the Gulf industry for four decades, they were now joined by national and private companies from Italy, Germany, Spain, Japan, Brazil, India, and elsewhere. Still later, producing countries formed their own national companies and gradually took over most or all of the controlling interest in the oil operations in their respective countries.

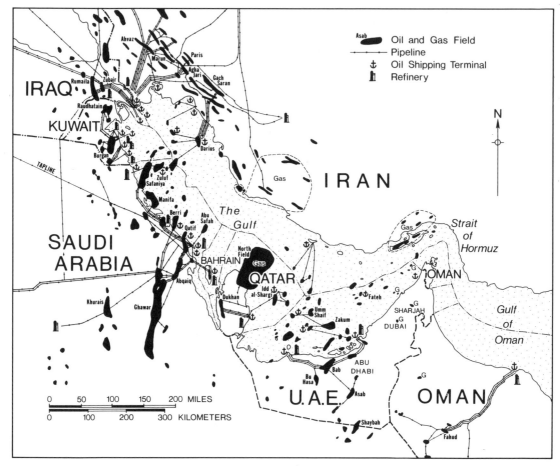

Map 8-2. *Gulf region petroleum and natural gas fields, pipelines, oil export terminals, and refineries. Ghawar in Saudi Arabia is the world's richest known oil field. (Adapted from Exxon 1984 and recent volumes of* International Petroleum Encyclopedia*)*

The Dukhan field in western Qatar was discovered in 1940 by Qatar Petroleum Company, an Iraq Petroleum Company subsidiary, but production was delayed until 1949. The offshore Umm Shaif field, in Abu Dhabi territorial waters, was the first of many major offshore discoveries to complement the onshore fields in the lower Gulf. The Umm Shaif field was found in 1958, but it did not produce until 1962 because of the difficulties of producing, transporting, and storing offshore oil in the area. Abu Dhabi's large onshore Bab field began production in 1963, and other amirates began production several years later, primarily with the help of smaller companies (Fig. 8-1). The first discoveries in Oman came in 1963 and 1964, and production began in 1967.

In the western areas of the Middle East, exploration—which began early in Egypt—indicates that petroleum resources are comparatively modest. Oil seepages near the mouth of the Gulf of Suez, known as early as Roman times, attracted exploration attention soon after the opening of the petroleum age, and indeed, the first well drilled in Egypt (1886) was the earliest in the Middle East. However, commercial production did not begin until 1913, a year after the first oil shipment from Iran, and major output levels were not achieved until the 1960s.

In adjoining Israel, hydrocarbon indications in and around the Dead Sea attracted surveys, but only minor resources have been found. Exploration in Lebanon, including a test well in 1947–1948, showed no likely prospects, and no

Figure 8-1. *Pump station in the Marib Alif oil field at the beginning of the 24–26-in./61–64-cm pipeline over the Yemen highlands to the export terminal at Salif on the coast of the Red Sea.*

development has been undertaken in that country. Syria finally found a small field in 1956 and commercial quantities in 1959, both in the extreme northeast in segments of the fold belt in which the Kirkuk field had been found in Iraq; but production was delayed for several years until pipeline outlets could be laid. After new finds in the mid-1980s, Syria undertook an intensive and successful search for new oil and gas fields, especially in the east around Dayr al-Zawr. To the south, exploratory drilling in Jordan in the mid-1950s found nothing in either the West Bank or the East Bank. Limited finds in the 1980s raised some hopes that had not, however, been realized by late 1992.

The latest discoveries in new areas were made in the Yemens in 1984 and 1985 before their merger in 1990. Earlier tests in the west of the then Yemen Arab Republic (YAR) by U.S. interests had been negative, but another U.S. company (Hunt) made a major oil strike in 1984 in the Marib Basin area. Production and export began in late 1987. The Marib success encouraged the People's Democratic Republic of Yemen (PDRY) to drill an extension of the structure south of the border, and tests found oil in appreciable quantities that by the early 1990s far exceeded the reserves found in the original strikes to the north.

Turkey found oil in 1940, and development there achieved a steady pace in the 1960s and is continuing, but with only limited results, since the extreme folding and faulting typical of this area fragment the reservoirs and cause the individual fields to be small and scattered. Shell and Mobil have each joined efforts with the Turkish national oil company, as have other smaller companies. Finally, exploration on Cyprus during the 1940s and 1950s found no promising structures on the island and indicated that Cyprus, like Lebanon, is unlikely to have oil resources.

Patterns of Reserves

As of 1991, 668 billion barrels of oil—67 percent of the world's proved reserves of petroleum—lay under the Middle East, most of it around and under the Gulf and under the Gulf of Suez in Egypt (Maps 8-1 and 8-3). Despite the fact that exploration in past decades has been reasonably intensive, new discoveries during just the years 1987–1991 augmented the already huge Middle East petroleum reserves by nearly 40 percent. UAE reserves tripled, from 33 billion barrels to

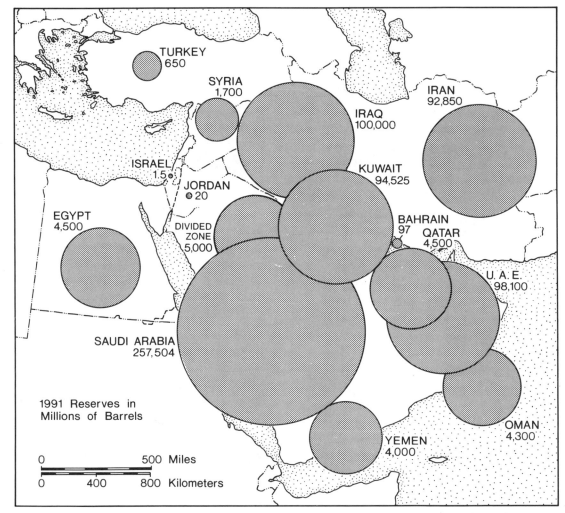

Map 8-3. *Middle East proved petroleum reserves, by country. Proportional circles show amount of proved reserves in millions of barrels.*

98.1 billion; those in Iraq more than doubled, from 47.1 to 100 billion; those in Iran almost doubled, from 48.8 to 92.9; and, on a smaller scale, reserves in the merged Yemen soared from 0.3 to 4 billion barrels, mostly in the former South Yemen. In addition, Saudi Arabia's vast reserves rose 65 percent, from 167 to 258 billion barrels, even after the country had produced 63 billion barrels between 1938 and 1992. By far the largest in both the Middle East and the world, the Saudi reserves equal those of all the rest of the world outside the Middle East, except for the former Soviet Union and Europe, combined. After Saudi Arabia, the second through fifth greatest

known reserves in the Middle East and the world are, in order, considered to be those of Iraq, UAE, Kuwait, and Iran (Table 8-1 and Graph 8-1). In fact, these four producers shift in rank among themselves every year or two. These five countries are followed in rank by four non–Middle East states: Venezuela, 59 billion barrels of proved reserves; successor states of the former Soviet Union, 57 billion; Mexico, 52 billion; and the United States, 26 billion. Probable reserves add billions of additional potential.[2]

Of the region's petroleum, eastern Saudi Arabia contains nearly half, distributed over 50 fields, onshore and offshore, extending from Ku-

TABLE 8-1: PETROLEUM: RESERVES AND RECENT PRODUCTION

COUNTRY	1 OIL RESRVS 1991 000s BBL	2 GAS RESRVS 1991 BILLS FT ^{3}	3 PRODUCTN 1989 000s BPD	4 PRODUCTN 1990 000s BPD	5 PRODUCTN 1991 000s BPD	6 AVERAGE 1986-90 000s BPD
Bahrain	97,460	6,250	42.2	42.0	38.2	43.1
Cyprus	---	---	---	---	---	---
(Divided Zone)[a]	5,000,000	10,000	396.6	315.0	129.7[b]	350.6
Egypt	4,500,000	12,400	854.3	873.0	885.0	850.3
Iran	92,850,000	600,350	2,934.3	3,120.0	3,342.0	2,482.0
Iraq	100,000,000	95,000	2,830.0	2,083.0	280.0[c]	2,295.1
Israel	1,400	10	0.3	0.3	0.2	0.4
Jordan	20,000	400	0.3	0.4	0.3	1.0
Kuwait	94,525,000	48,600	1,542.6	1,080.0	126.3[b]	1,234.9
Lebanon	---	---	---	---	---	---
Oman	4,300,000	7,200	622.7	658.0	705.0	596.6
Qatar	4,500,000	163,200	394.6	387.0	390.0	349.5
Saudi Arabia	257,504,000	180,355	4,935.6	6,215.0	8,157.7	4,926.6
Syria	1,700,000	5,500	300.6	385.0	473.0	275.1
Turkey	650,000	1,150	55.5	70.0	86.7	54.9
UAE	98,100,000	200,400	1,844.6	2,101.0	2,405.3	1,643.1
Yemen	4,000,000	7,000	186.6	179.0	200.8	111.6
TOTAL/AVG.	667,747,860	1,337,815	16,940.8	17,508.7	17,220.2	15,214.8
Abu Dhabi	92,200,000	182,800	1,359.0	1,587.0	1,945.8	1,175.4
Dubai	4,000,000	4,800	410.6	469.0	434.0	393.2
Ras al-Khaymah	400,000	2,000	10.0	10.0	0.8	15.1
Sharjah	1,500,000	10,800	65.0	35.0	24.7	59.4

[a]Divided Zone production is normally divided between Kuwait and Saudi Arabia. [b]Kuwait and Divided Zone production was down sharply because of Iraqi sabotage of their wells. [c]Iraq production was at one-tenth of normal because of UN sanctions against exports from Iraq. Note that petroleum reserves are in thousands of barrels (bbl). Natural gas reserves are in billions of cubic feet. Production figures are in thousands of barrels per day (bpd). The last four rows give data on the four amirates of the UAE that produce petroleum. Source: *International Petroleum Encyclopedia 1992*.

wait south to the Abu Dhabi border (Map 8-2). Prominent is the large, linear Ghawar field, the world's greatest single oil reservoir. The gently folded and domed structures of northeastern Arabia continue northward into Kuwait, with which Saudi Arabia shares the world's greatest offshore field, Safaniya-Khafji.

The Arabian-Kuwait structures extend across the Kuwait-Iraq border and join the northwest-southeast trend of the Zagros fold reservoirs in southern Iraq. One particular field, the Rumaila, straddles the Kuwait-Iraq border and became a matter of conflict in the Iraqi invasion of Kuwait in August 1990 and in discussions of boundary

revisions in 1992. In Iraq, which claims 100 billion barrels of reserves—second-largest in the region—oil reservoirs have been found in subsurface folds from Ain Zalah in the extreme north through the Kirkuk and Baghdad reservoirs to Rumaila and Zubair in the extreme south. The next-largest reserves lie offshore and onshore in the southernmost Gulf area (Fig. 8-2). Most of the major fields lie in Abu Dhabi, largest and westernmost of the seven component shaykh-doms of the United Arab Emirates. By the early 1990s Abu Dhabi alone had three and a half times the oil reserves of the United States. Onshore, Kuwait possesses the fabulous Burgan field, with

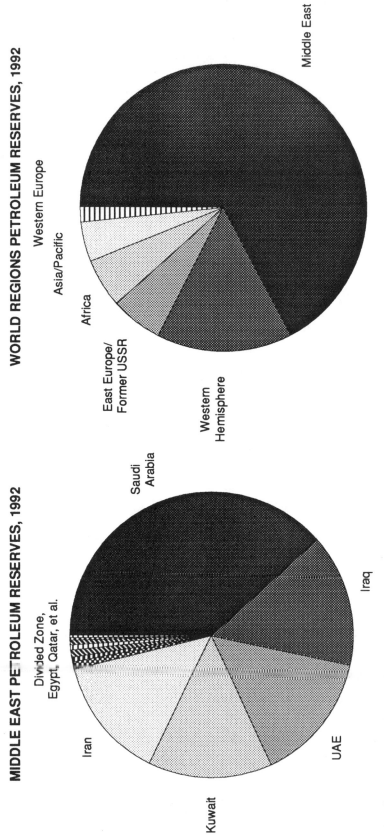

MIDDLE EAST PETROLEUM RESERVES, 1992

Divided Zone,
Egypt, Qatar, et al.

Saudi
Arabia

Iran

Kuwait

UAE

Iraq

WORLD REGIONS PETROLEUM RESERVES, 1992

Western Europe

Asia/Pacific

Africa

East Europe/
Former USSR

Western
Hemisphere

Middle East

Graph 8-1. *1992 petroleum reserves of Middle East countries* (left) *and of world regions* (right).

Figure 8-2. *Helicopter view of Dubai's main oil field, Fateh, located 56 miles/90 km offshore. Smoke plumes are from flares burning nonmarketable natural gas separated from petroleum.*

more oil per unit of surface area than any other field known. With Saudi Arabia and Kuwait holding undivided half shares in the oil of the Divided Zone (the former Neutral Zone), Kuwait's 94 billion barrels of reserves accord it fourth rank in reserves in the Middle East and the world. Iran possesses the fifth-largest reserves in the Middle East and the world, even after having produced 39.2 billion barrels since oil was first discovered in Iran in 1908. Virtually all of Iran's 40 oil fields follow the trend of folds in the Zagros Mountains in western Iran from Kermanshah in the northwest to Bandar-e Abbas in the southeast at the Strait of Hormuz. Lying in the southeastern part of the sedimentary basin, opposite the Qatar Peninsula and east toward the Strait of Hormuz, are more than a dozen rich gas fields. Like Saudi Arabia and Kuwait, Iran also possesses offshore fields with impressive reserves and production.

Qatar's reserves in its onshore Dukhan field and its three offshore fields give it proved petroleum reserves approximately equal to those of Egypt, Yemen, and nearby Oman. However, Qatar's relatively modest oil reserves are richly supplemented by the North gas field, the world's largest, which alone gives Qatar the sixth-great-

est gas reserves in the world after those of the former Soviet lands, Iran, UAE, Saudi Arabia, and the United States (Table 8-1).

The Sultanate of Oman is the latest of the Gulf area states to achieve significant levels of petroleum production. The original discoveries in 1963 and 1964 were followed by more than 50 other scattered, modest field discoveries by 1991. Although none are as rich as the fields in less intensively folded and faulted structures farther northwest up the great Gulf trough, Oman is now estimated to have 4.3 billion barrels of proved reserves.

Bahrain, although the earliest of the actual Gulf producers, has proved to possess the smallest reserves. However, during deep-test drilling for additional oil resources in 1949, the Bahrain Petroleum Company discovered the large gas reservoir in the Khuff formation (Permian age), which has since been found to have enormous reserves in Gulf offshore fields, in several Iranian fields, and in other neighboring fields. Commercial development of Bahrain's Khuff deep gas began in 1969.

Turkey's numerous small fields lie at the upper end of the great series of structures reaching northwestward from Oman up the Gulf trough and through the Mesopotamian depression. In about 60 minor fields that have been discovered on the upper Tigris and, more recently, on the upper Euphrates, total reserves are only 450 million barrels.

Although petroleum reserves on the western side of the region are only a minor segment of the Middle East total, sizable fields have been found and are yielding roughly 1.5 million bpd. Production is primarily from Egypt and Syria, with limited output from Turkey and with increasing output from the recent finds in Yemen. Israel's reserves are almost depleted, and Jordan's known reserves are negligible.

Egypt ranks sixth in reserves, along with Qatar, among the Middle East oil states. Petroleum is found in more than 70 fields in and on both sides of the Gulf of Suez, on the Mediterranean coast west of Alexandria, and in small fields south of the Mediterranean coast in the Western Desert. These Egyptian reservoirs are in completely separate basins from those of the Gulf region.

Syria's older fields lie in the extreme northeastern corner of the country, just west of the Tigris River, and are an integral part of the structures containing the Batman fields of southeastern Turkey and the fields of northern Iraq. A significant discovery in late 1984 near Dayr al-Zawr initiated a modest "oil boom" in eastern Syria that spread to the center of the country and opened a score of small new fields.

Jordan's recently found Hamzah field, near al-Azraq, has shown only limited potential. By contrast, reserves in new fields in the recently formed Republic of Yemen already exceed 4 billion barrels, ranking Yemen with neighboring Oman as well as Egypt and Qatar. This poorest corner of the Middle East desperately needed oil income, and the future of the Yemen oil industry is bright.

Petroleum Production

Some Influences on Production

Whereas reserves reveal the production potential of individual fields and countries, the trend of actual production reflects the combination of a variety of complex factors. Production may trend steadily upward as new reserves are exploited, as in Saudi Arabia for 35 virtually unbroken years after World War II. Conversely, production may drop steadily as reserves are depleted, which happened in Bahrain after 1970. Production may drop in a country because of wartime conditions, as happened in Iran and Iraq in the early 1980s and in Iraq and Kuwait in the early 1990s (see Table 8-1, col. 5). Iraq's output dropped to a fraction of its normal level in 1991–1992 because of UN-imposed sanctions. Daily production may be deliberately reduced by government fiat so as to extend the life of the reserves, as in Kuwait after 1972.

However, along with the status of reserves, market demand is obviously a crucial factor influencing level of production. Middle East production curves became erratic in the early 1970s, after more than 25 years of steadily and even dramatically increasing production during the unparalleled industrial development in much of the world after World War II. Noteworthy influences on the region's production included the impact of the 1973 Arab-Israeli war and the Arab oil boycott; the sharp rise in the price of oil as the OPEC nations increasingly assumed control of the production and marketing of their own resources; the growing realization among industrialized oil-consuming nations that they must both conserve and substitute for petroleum and natural gas; the slightly shifting pattern of producing areas as North Sea production sharply increased and as increasing Soviet production had its effect on world markets; and, partly as a consequence, the decision by OPEC nations to cut production in an effort to sustain the OPEC price. The production cut halved the output of Middle East OPEC members from 21 million bpd in 1979 to 10.7 million bpd in 1986. The marketing strategy failed, and, ignoring their quotas, OPEC members pushed their output to more than 22 million bpd in late 1988; and they continued to escalate production despite falling prices, reaching 24 million bpd in mid-1990 even after prices dropped to less than $15/barrel. The consistent OPEC goal of $21/barrel has been elusive except during the 1990–1991 Gulf war, when the price shot up to $35 and $40/barrel for several weeks in late 1990.

Two forces during the mid-1980s tended to depress Middle East oil production. The war be-

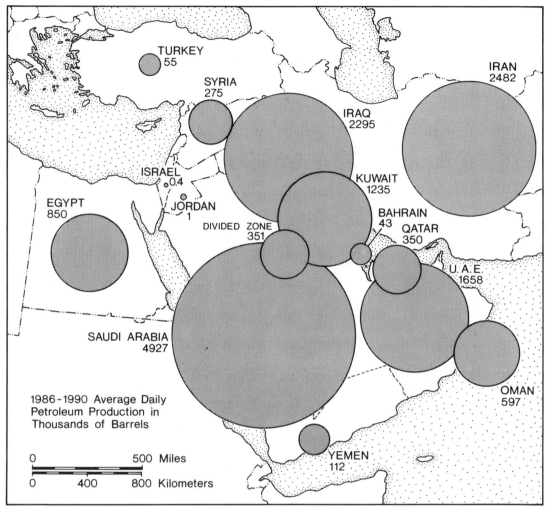

TURKEY
55

SYRIA
275

IRAQ
2295

IRAN
2482

ISRAEL
0.4

KUWAIT
1235

EGYPT
850

JORDAN
1

BAHRAIN
43   QATAR
350

DIVIDED ZONE
351

U.A.E.
1658

SAUDI ARABIA
4927

OMAN
597

1986-1990 Average Daily
Petroleum Production in
Thousands of Barrels

0   500 Miles

0   400   800 Kilometers

YEMEN
112

Map 8-4. *Middle East petroleum production by country, in thousands of barrels per day. To avoid weighting any single year, an average of annual production during the five years 1986–1990 was chosen as the figure to represent in the proportional circles.*

tween Iran and Iraq caused the output by the combatants, both members of OPEC, to be erratic. On the other side, Saudi Arabia played a swing role in the operation of the OPEC quota system for several years and dramatically reduced its output from nearly 10 million bpd in 1980 to about 3.3 million bpd in 1985 as part of the effort by OPEC to decrease the supply of oil that reached the market. It then shifted strategy and substantially increased production to persuade other Gulf producers to adhere more closely to the OPEC quotas. Output in Oman and Egypt continued to climb, but neither country is a

member of OPEC. Map 8-4 shows a meaningful production comparison for Middle East producers—the average output in bpd for the years 1986–1990 (also see Table 8-1).

Also noteworthy is the fact that an oil or gas field has a certain optimum level of production that theoretically permits the maximum production over the maximum number of years. This reservoir optimum can be more readily determined and followed in the Middle East than in the United States. In virtually all Middle East fields, exploration and production are controlled by one operator, whereas U.S. fields are developed by multiple companies that compete for the oil underlying the checkerboard of leases. A statistical comparison shows the significant consequence: Twelve producing countries in the Middle East averaged 17.2 million bpd from 8,905 wells in 1991 for an average of 1,931 bpd per well, while the United States produced 7.37 million bpd from 597,320 wells for an average of 12.3 bpd per well. U.S. production costs are thus appreciably higher, and percentage recovery of oil in the U.S. reservoirs is lower without expensive secondary recovery procedures.

Natural Gas

Natural gas reserves include both "associated" and "nonassociated" gas. The former is found with petroleum and reaches the surface along with the oil in which it is dissolved. Nonassociated gas occurs separately in underground reservoirs and is produced only as gas. The distinction is significant in several ways, including the availability to consumers of one kind of gas or the other.

Associated gas must be separated from crude oil as soon as the mixture reaches the surface. In the early years of Middle East production, the demand was for oil, and since associated gas had no market, it was separated and immediately burned off. Gradually, as increased population and economic development created a major market demand for gas, flaring diminished, and separated gas was piped to nearby consumers. In time, rapidly increasing oil production made available enormous amounts of associated gas after separation from the primary product, oil. These seemingly inexhaustible gas supplies came to be taken for granted by consumers—power companies, fertilizer companies, water desalination plants, aluminum smelters, and residential consumers. Also, the gas was utilized in more sophisticated ways, for example, after being broken down into its major components of methane, ethane, propane, butane, and heavier hydrocarbons.

Therefore, when oil prices and production decreased sharply in the early 1980s, not only did the producing areas suffer from reduced oil-sale income, they also suddenly had insufficient supplies of the natural gas that had become a fringe benefit of the high level of oil production. The main recourse was to increase the search for and production of nonassociated gas, which could be exploited without reference to the demand for oil.

When Bahrain found a large gas reservoir in the deep Khuff formation in 1949, its neighbors also drilled into the Khuff and likewise found enormous nonassociated gas reservoirs. In addition to Qatar's huge North Field reservoir of nonassociated gas in the Khuff zone, all Gulf states are finding large reserves of gas both in the Khuff and in other deep reservoirs. When added to the country's nonassociated gas reserves, the large gas fields found in southwestern Iran in the late 1970s and early 1980s, many of them in the Khuff zone, give Iran 600.4 trillion ft.^{3}, by far the largest gas reserves outside the area of the former Soviet Union. In 1992, total Middle East gas reserves constituted nearly one-third of all known world gas reserves. An ironic twist in the search for nonassociated gas came in the early 1980s when exploration for deep gas in Kuwait coincidentally found additional oil reserves equal to the total known oil reserves of the United States.

Production Comparisons

Saudi Arabia has led Middle East states in petroleum production since it overtook Kuwait in 1966. Indeed, it has ranked second or third in world production since the mid-1970s (the then Soviet Union and the United States were usually first and second), peaking at 9.64 million bpd in 1981, falling to 3.3 million bpd in 1985, then rebounding to 8.1 million bpd in 1991 (Table 8-1). The 1991 figure may be considered abnormally high, since the Saudis produced at a high level to compensate for the loss of Kuwaiti and Iraqi production and to supply the needs of the coalition forces operating out of Saudi territory during the Gulf crisis. However, the kingdom was still producing more than 8 million bpd in early 1993 and was gearing up for an output of more than 10 million bpd. Ranked second in production in the early 1990s, Iran reached peaks of more than 6 million bpd in 1974 and 5.9 million bpd in 1976 before tumbling to 1.37 million bpd in the war year of 1981. Under stable conditions, Iran, which hovered around 3.2 million bpd in the early 1990s, could sustain an average daily production of 5 million barrels for many years.

Iraq ranked fourth in Middle East production until 1975, when it replaced Kuwait in third place; and it exceeded 1 million bpd from 1960 to the early 1980s, with a peak of 3.4 million bpd in 1979. Its production dropped periodically during the early 1970s, when confrontations with Syria interrupted Iraq's oil throughput to terminals on the Mediterranean coast via pipelines crossing Syria. Iraq's production again suffered during the early 1980s, dropping below 1 million bpd in 1981–1983. Output was poised at the 3 million bpd level in mid-1990, when Iraq expressed sharp rancor toward its OPEC comembers about quotas and over-quota production. Placed under UN sanctions after it invaded Kuwait, Iraq suffered heavy damage during coalition bombing and was forced to shut down all exports. It was still producing only for its own needs and for limited supplies to Jordan well into late 1992.

The next-largest producer in the Gulf and in the Middle East is the United Arab Emirates, whose production rose from a negligible amount in 1963 to 2 million bpd in 1977 before joining the regional downward trend. Prior to the independence of the UAE in 1971, oil was produced only in Abu Dhabi, which has continued to be the federation's major producer. Production from Dubai's offshore Fateh field has contributed an increasingly greater share of the UAE total. Regularly accused of exceeding its OPEC quota, the UAE produced between 1.8 and 2.4 million bpd at the beginning of the 1990s. The high 1991 figure may be ascribed to the UAE's joining Saudi Arabia in supplying petroleum to the allied coalition.

Kuwait led in Middle East production from 1954 to 1966; its production peaked in 1972 at 3 million bpd, was intentionally reduced for several years for conservation purposes (dropping Kuwait to fourth or fifth place), fell to 675,000 bpd in 1982 as a result of the oil crisis, and rebounded to well over 1.5 million bpd in 1989. Production, of course, dropped sharply after the Iraqi invasion in August 1990 (see Chap. 18) but recovered to 1.6 million bpd in early 1993 en route to a goal of 2 million bpd by late 1993.

Production in Oman, which is not a member of OPEC, quickly reached stride in the late 1960s and, after faltering briefly, then maintained a steady production of 300,000–400,000 bpd. New discoveries and improved recovery techniques have recently led to a sustained curve of increasing production, from 283,000 bpd in 1980 to 705,000 in 1991.

Egypt, also not constrained by OPEC quotas, has varied between 800,000 and 900,000 bpd most years since 1984. Syria's production of very heavy crude varied from 160,000 to 175,000 bpd in the late 1970s and early 1980s, but the discovery in eastern Syria of a light sweet crude oil in the mid-1980s afforded a basis for nearly tripling output from 161,000 bpd in 1985 to more than 473,000 bpd in 1991. Syria can now export one-third of its production but needs further experience to determine if such output can be maintained. Far to the south, production in Yemen's new fields was approaching 200,000 bpd in early 1992 and will undoubtedly, like Syria, double within a few years. Israel's negligible production is by far the smallest of all Middle East producers.

In an assessment of the long-range significance of Middle East oil, two production ratios are important: the ratio of an area's annual production to its reserves and the ratio of its percentage of world production to its percentage of world reserves. It is noteworthy that Middle East production in 1991, for example, was 0.9 percent of the region's reserves, the corresponding ratio for the United States was 10.2 percent, and that for Mexico was 2 percent. In the same year, Middle East production amounted to 29 percent of the world total, with 67 percent of the world's petroleum reserves at that time; North American production was 14 percent of the world total, with only 3.2 percent of the world's reserves; and corresponding figures for other areas showed the same high ratio of production to reserves. The vital lesson is that intensive exploitation of oil will exhaust reserves more rapidly in areas outside the Middle East. Thus, the world will be even more highly dependent on the Middle East for oil by the end of the century than it is at present.

Major Oil Facilities

Raising petroleum and gas to the wellhead is only the beginning of a complex handling and processing procedure. The crude oil must be gathered from the wells in the field, and associated gas must be separated from the petroleum and either flared in the field or else piped to a consuming or processing facility. The degassed crude oil may then require "sweetening" before it is transported by pipeline to an export terminal or to a nearby refinery. Refining "cracks" the crude into a series of hydrocarbons from the lightest fractions at one end (naphtha and gasoline) through the middle distillates (kerosene and aviation jet fuel) to such heavy fractions as fuel oil and asphalt. Each product requires separate handling and has its own market. Some products may be further processed in petrochemical plants.

In the early years of oil production in the Middle East, most of the degassed crude petroleum was pumped directly to tank farms at export terminals and then pumped onto tanker ships for delivery to overseas consumers, primarily in Western Europe, Japan, and the United States. Most Middle East production is still exported in the same way. However, over the years, increasing amounts of petroleum have been refined in the producing countries and the products either consumed locally by the larger and more affluent populations or else exported in a more valuable refined form. Refineries were built in Iran, Bahrain, and Saudi Arabia soon after production began in each country, and oil refining is now a significant industry in every Middle East state.

A fairly high correlation exists between the pattern of producing fields and the pattern of handling and processing facilities—particularly with regard to pipelines and export terminals, but not necessarily refineries and petrochemical industries. Crude feedstock can be transported hundreds of miles by pipeline to refineries far distant from an oil field; more frequently it is transported by tanker ship to coastal refineries in more heavily populated industrial states. Pipelines, export terminals, and refineries are shown on Maps 8-1 and 8-2.

Pipelines

Pipelines are the arteries of the petroleum industry. Indeed, they are a unique land transportation system for oil and related products from the time the oil approaches the surface of the ground until it arrives at the interconnected refinery or shipping terminal. Since oil is of little value until it is moved from the well to an export or processing facility, pipelines are integral and vital links in the oil industry.

Environmental factors greatly influence the routes and costs of long-distance pipelines in the Middle East: topography, surface rock, density of population, and others. Equally important is security of the pipelines and of the oil passing through them, the attitude of authorities concerned, and the political stability of the areas traversed. International pipelines have been particularly susceptible to shutdowns because of disputes among states along the routes, as well as subject to sabotage by dissident groups.

More than 8,000 miles/12,875 km of large-diameter pipelines transport crude petroleum from major fields in the Middle East to regional shipping terminals and refineries. Three systems merit attention because of the leading roles they play or have played and because they exemplify the problems faced by pipelines as a result of the regional crosscurrents.

The successive pipeline systems used by Iraq to export its oil illustrate the problems of an interior location and the importance of relations with neighboring states. For more than 40 years, Iraq exported its crude production through Iraq Petroleum Company (IPC) lines from Kirkuk across Syria to the Mediterranean coast. The first lines, opened in 1934, ran parallel from Kirkuk to Hadithah on the Euphrates, where they divided. One line terminated at Haifa, in the British mandate of Palestine, and the other at Tripoli, in the French mandate of Lebanon.

After World War II, new Middle East political patterns forced abandonment of the Haifa line, and the IPC built new lines to Baniyas in Syria. A series of disputes between Iraq and Syria forced indefinite closure of the system in April 1982, but not before Iraq had initiated projects to lessen its dependence on the export system through Syria.

In the mid-1970s, Iraq undertook construction of two new pipeline outlets. In 1975, it opened a strategic internal line to its own terminals at the head of the Gulf, where the export facilities were highly concentrated at the narrow outlet of Iraq's corridor to the coast. This arrangement was soon disrupted when the terminals were destroyed in 1980–1981, early in the war with Iran. However,

Iraq had already supplemented its Gulf export capacity with a new pipeline from Kirkuk through Turkey to Yumurtalık on the Mediterranean coast near Iskenderun, which opened in 1977. The capacity of this line was increased in 1984, and a parallel 40-in./102-cm line was opened in 1987, giving the system through Turkey a capacity of 1.5 million bpd.

Still concerned about its total dependence on one neighboring country for the export of its one major product, Iraq discussed with both Jordan and Saudi Arabia the possibility of extending pipelines through their territories to export terminals at Aqabah and Yanbu, respectively. Iraq eventually rejected the proposal for an export line to Aqabah, just across the border from Elat, Israel, since the system would be an easy target for Israeli artillery or air strikes; but by September 1985, contractors had completed construction of a 500,000-bpd 48-in./122-cm pipeline (IPSA-I) across northern Saudi Arabia to connect with Petroline, the huge Saudi crude oil line. Thus, balked at exporting through Syria and through its own terminals at the head of the Gulf, Iraq could export oil through Turkey and Saudi Arabia for the remaining years of its war with Iran. Later, the line from Iraq was continued as a separate 48-in./122-cm line, IPSA-II, parallel to the Saudi lines across the peninsula to a separate Red Sea export terminal, Muajjil, 30 miles/48 km south of Yanbu. The line was officially opened January 9, 1990, with a capacity of 1.65 million bpd.

Thus, Iraq had an export capacity of 3.15 million bpd through Turkey and Saudi Arabia, plus 800,000 bpd through its Gulf terminals when they were in operation, plus another potential 1.25 million bpd across Syria through the old IPC lines. However, Iraq's dependence on the goodwill of its neighbors in order to export its oil became dramatically evident once again in 1990 when Iraq invaded Kuwait. Complying with UN sanctions against Iraq, both Turkey and Saudi Arabia closed the lines crossing their territories and vowed to keep them shut in as long as the UN sanctions were in force. Thus, Iraq had no lines through which to export its production— which is the price of being virtually landlocked and of failing to maintain friendly relations with neighbors on which it is highly dependent.

A second international petroleum pipeline of major significance was the Trans-Arabian Pipe Line (Tapline), which extended 1,068 miles/1,718 km from the east coast of Saudi Arabia to the Mediterranean coast in southern Lebanon. Although throughput to the Mediterranean terminal was shut in by the early 1980s, Tapline had played a noteworthy role in Middle East oil developments for three decades, and it is an excellent case study in geographic petroleum economics.

Plans considered during World War II and completed by 1946 for a Gulf-to-Mediterranean pipeline envisioned a shortcut for oil from eastern Arabia to the eastern Mediterranean to avoid the long, slow voyage around the Arabian Peninsula and through the Suez Canal. Compared with the route of the original IPC lines across the Syrian Desert, the proposed route for Tapline was much longer and its environment much more barren, virtually uninhabited except for small numbers of Bedouins, and almost unknown. Tapline's diameter of 30–31 in./76–79 cm was also much larger than that of any of its predecessors.

When the line was opened in December 1950, it crossed Saudi Arabia, Jordan, Syria, and Lebanon (see Map 8-1). Five main pump stations were needed to move the eventual capacity of 500,000 bpd: Qaysumah, Rafha, Badanah, and Turayf in Saudi Arabia and Qaryatayn in Jordan. A given barrel of oil required eleven days to transit the line from eastern Arabia to the Zahrani loading terminal near Sidon. Although most of the oil was exported, the line also supplied crude feedstock to a refinery in Zarqa, Jordan, and to a smaller refinery at Sidon in Lebanon. The line operated with signal success for many years, but problems mounted during and after the Arab-Israeli war in June 1967, when a segment of the line across the Golan Heights passed to Israeli control. Problems ranged from sabotage to disputes over royalties and were exacerbated after the 1973 Arab-Israeli war.

Another difficulty was that closure of the Suez Canal after the 1967 war stimulated the construction and use of increasingly large oil tankers. Very Large Crude Carriers (VLCCs) could transport crude from the Gulf around southern Africa to Western Europe and North America even more cheaply than could the smaller tankers that

Figure 8-3. *One of the world's largest tank farms, on a sand spit at Saudi Aramco's Ras Tanura export terminal on the Gulf coast. The terminal is likewise one of the world's largest. (Aramco photograph)*

had formerly followed the Red Sea–Suez Canal–Mediterranean route. More important for Tapline, VLCC per-barrel costs were even cheaper than those of the smaller tankers lifting crude from Tapline's Zahrani terminal. With mounting operational problems and expenses, Tapline finally ceased supplying the Zahrani terminal in February 1975, when oil lifted at Ras Tanura (Fig. 8-3) could be landed at English Channel ports by VLCCs more than $2.00 per barrel cheaper than oil lifted from Zahrani. Thus, technology, economics, politics, and geography combined to render Tapline obsolete after 25 years of operation. Tapline did continue for several years to pump less than 100,000 bpd to supply the Jordanian refinery at Zarqa, in accordance with the Saudi government's goodwill efforts to maintain shipments to Jordan into the late 1980s, using only a small fraction of the pipeline's capacity. Saudi goodwill shipments gradually lessened, partly because of nonpayment for the oil, and they stopped entirely in August 1990 when Jordanians expressed opposition to the UN actions against Iraq. After 1990, Tapline was virtually unused.

A third noteworthy line began as an internal facility but gained international connections. In 1981, the Saudis opened the largest-diameter long-distance crude oil line in the Middle East, a 48-in./122-cm line that extends from the oil fields of the Eastern Province to Yanbu on the Red Sea coast, with a new export facility, refinery, and industrial center. The original capacity of 1.85 million bpd was raised to 3.3 million bpd with opening of a 56-in./142-cm parallel interconnected (looped) line in 1987. Originally called Petroline, this East-West crude oil pipeline system was upgraded during the early 1990s to a capacity of 4.8 million bpd, primarily to ensure a protected export outlet during crisis periods in the Gulf. The amount it normally carries is only a fraction of its capacity but is sufficient to feed refineries and petrochemical plants in Yanbu and have small amounts for exports. During crises, the East-West line would deliver nearly 5 million bpd of crude to the Red Sea for export via tanker, northward either through the Suez Canal or to the Gulf of Suez for delivery to the Egyptian "Sumed" lines, or southward through the Bab el-Mandeb.

Other Pipelines, Terminals, and Refineries

In addition to the major long lines just described, several internal pipelines are of major regional importance and have a significant impact on international movements of Middle East petroleum. Both Egypt and Israel have pipelines that permit transportation of oil from the Red Sea to the Mediterranean, and these lines serve

TABLE 8-2: PETROLEUM: REFINERIES AND PRODUCING FIELDS AND WELLS

COUNTRY	1 NO. OF REFIN-ERIES	2 TOTAL REF. CAPACITY (B/D)	3 LARGEST REFINERY IN RESPECTIVE COUNTRY	4 MAIN REF. CAPACITY (B/D)	5 PRO-DUCING FIELDS	6 PRO-DUCING WELLS
	1991	1991	1991	1991	1990	1991
Bahrain	1	243,000	Sitra	243,000	1	317
Cyprus	1	18,600	Larnaca	18,000	---	---
(Divided Zone)	0[a]	---	---	---	5	499
Egypt	8	523,153	Mostorod	156,750	70	907
Iran	5	720,000	Tehran[b]	210,000	37	361
Iraq	8	318,500	Baiji	150,000	20	820
Israel	2	180,000	Haifa	110,000	4	12
Jordan	1	100,000	Zarqa	100,000	1	4
Kuwait	4	819,000	Mina al-Ahmadi	370,000	8	363[c]
Lebanon	2	37,500	Tripoli	20,000	---	---
Oman	1	76,932	Mina al-Fahal	76,932	54	1,237
Qatar	1	62,000	Musayid	62,000	4	238
Saudi Arabia	8	1,862,500	Ras Tanura	530,000	50	1,235
Syria	2	237,394	Banyas	120,000	13	963
Turkey	5	728,644	Izmit	267,325	61	684
UAE	2	192,500	Ruways	120,000	21	1,178
Yemen	2	171,500	Little Aden	161,500	5	87
TOTALS	53	6,291,223	---	2,715,507	354	8,905
Abu Dhabi	2	192,500	Ruways	120,000	13	1,001
Dubai	0	---	---	---	5	150
Ras al-Khaymah	0	---	---	---	1	7
Sharjah	0	---	---	---	2	20

Columns 1-4 show numbers of refineries in Middle East countries, the total average throughput capacity for 1991 in barrels per calendar day for each country, the refinery with the largest capacity in each country, and its capacity. Columns 5 and 6 show numbers of producing fields and wells. The last four rows give data on the four amirates of the UAE that produce petroleum. [a]Divided Zone refinery data divided between Kuwait and Saudi Arabia. [b]Iran's largest refinery prior to its destruction in the early 1980s was in Abadan. [c]More than half of Kuwait's wells had not resumed production after the Iraqi sabotage (see Chap. 18). Source: *International Petroleum Encyclopedia 1991* and *1992*.

tankers that are too large for the Suez Canal or that prefer to avoid the canal. Egypt's Suez-Mediterranean system (Sumed) consists of twin parallel 42-in./107-cm lines that transfer oil from the northern end of the Gulf of Suez to the Mediterranean Sea coast just west of Alexandria. Israel's 42-in./107-cm Trans-Israel Pipeline (Tipline) runs from Elat to a terminal at Ashqelon. Details on the more important oil export terminals and refineries are given in the individual country chapters. However, Table 8-2 gives comparative data on refineries.

Markets and Marketing

Early commercial developers of Middle East petroleum fields envisaged exploiting the resources for export to their respective home countries or for fuel for naval ships. Local consumption was limited. However, as the pace of regional economic development increased, demand for the petroleum products mounted in the Middle East as elsewhere, and governments in successive oil-exporting countries achieved control over the exploitation and marketing of their highly valuable and sometimes sole resource and then contracted for local basic oil-processing facilities.

Marketing of large amounts of petroleum has traditionally been on long-term contracts. Concessionary companies operating in a producing country were often the direct sellers, disposing of their share of the product within a stable if highly complex world marketing system. For several decades, the system was virtually controlled by a small number of major oil companies, primarily the "Seven Sisters": Jersey Standard (Exxon), British Petroleum, Royal Dutch/Shell, Texaco, Standard of California (Chevron), Socony-Vacuum (Mobil), and Gulf (which merged with Chevron in 1984). National oil companies of Italy, Spain, and Brazil, as well as Japanese companies, joined in the programs to explore for, produce, and market Middle East oil. They thereby gained international marketing influence.

Until 1970, the main importers of Middle East crude were industrial countries that required supplies beyond their own production capacity and included those countries that held major concessions in Middle East producing countries. Some of the importers had only limited or even no known petroleum resources of their own. Virtually every major oil exporter in the Middle East during the 1960s and 1970s counted the same half-dozen leading purchasers among its top ten customers: Great Britain, France, West Germany, Japan, the Netherlands, and the United States. Main secondary buyers included Italy, Spain, Canada, and Brazil; and such countries as Australia, India, Sweden, and Switzerland also regularly made noteworthy purchases of Middle East crude.

After 1970, steadily increasing production from developing offshore fields on the continental shelves of Great Britain and other North Sea countries afforded northwestern Europe a large supply of local oil and gas, and the demand for Middle East crude by North Sea countries dropped by more than 3 million bpd as both Great Britain and Norway became net exporters. After the early 1970s, the trend of oil exports from the Middle East from year to year has been markedly more variable than that during the 1950s and 1960s. The import pattern of the United States also changed: In 1977 the United

States imported 46 percent of its oil needs, about 18 percent from the Middle East; in 1983 it imported only 28 percent of its oil requirements, just 4 percent from the Middle East; in 1988 it imported about 41 percent of its oil consumption, about 11 percent from the Middle East; and in 1992 it imported 50 percent of its needs, about 28 percent from the Middle East.

In addition to an increased local use of petroleum, consumption of natural gas in the Middle East has also grown dramatically. Whereas in 1972 more than two-thirds of the gas produced in association with Middle East oil was either flared or reinjected (pumped back into the oil reservoir), by 1982 only half of the gas was being flared, and utilization had increased by 38 percent. Industry forecasts suggest that flaring may drop to as low as 10 percent of gross production in the early 1990s.

OPEC: Pricing and Participation

In the early years, companies operating concessions in the Middle East generally determined production and price levels, taking into account Middle East costs of production and the world demand for petroleum. Posted prices were periodically set and publicly stated by oil companies as the "list" prices at which various grades of crude would be sold at Gulf terminals. Highly complex arrangements, royalties, taxes, deductions, and discounts affected government revenue levels and company profits.

When various factors combined to precipitate a reduction in posted prices in 1960, the governments of major producing countries, in a continuing effort to gain greater control over the pricing system, met in Baghdad in September 1960 and created the Organization of Petroleum Exporting Countries (OPEC). Charter members were Saudi Arabia, Iran, Iraq, Kuwait, and Venezuela; and by 1975, membership had expanded to include Qatar, Indonesia, Libya, Abu Dhabi (later the United Arab Emirates), Algeria, Nigeria, Ecuador (withdrew in 1992), and Gabon. Of the 12 current members, 6 are in the Middle East, and 5 of these are Arab countries (2 additional Arab members are in North Africa). Bahrain,

Oman, Egypt, and Syria are not OPEC members. Eight years after the formation of OPEC, Arab oil exporters, partly as a result of the impact of the 1967 Arab-Israeli war, formed a parallel group, the Organization of Arab Petroleum Exporting Countries (OAPEC), which included all Arab members of OPEC and also Bahrain, Egypt, and Syria. Oman has not joined either organization.

With prices of virtually all other commodities and services having risen steadily since the late 1940s, petroleum was increasingly underpriced into the early 1970s. Not until late in 1973 was the FOB price of the benchmark Arabian Light crude at Ras Tanura to surge decisively above $3.00 per barrel (all prices and sales were, and still are, in U.S. dollars). Indeed, late 1973 was the turning point in company-government relations in the region, as company-set posted prices were abandoned in late 1973 because of the OPEC-announced price levels. At the beginning of 1974, OPEC set a price of $11.65, almost three times what it had been three months earlier, and the price then rose through a series of gradual increases to $13.34 at the beginning of 1979, doubled in one year to $26.00, and peaked at $34.00 a barrel in October 1981. Unified pricing, however, was often disregarded by some OPEC sellers—increasingly so into the middle and late 1980s, until the price fell to about $13.00 a barrel. Mounting determination by OPEC members to strengthen their hold on the pricing and handling of their petroleum was sharpened, especially for members of OAPEC, by the impact of the 1973 Arab-Israeli war, and OAPEC members embargoed oil shipments to the United States and the Netherlands in retaliation for actions or policies considered supportive of Israel in that war.

The 1973–1974 escalation of oil prices (which was proceeding independently of the OAPEC embargo) broke, for virtually the first time, the previously steady and often rapid growth of world petroleum consumption since 1945. Shaken by a tenfold price increase per barrel of petroleum from late 1973 to early 1981, major consuming countries attempted to minimize the shock of the increases not only by conservation and more efficient use of oil but also by utilizing alternate forms of energy. In addition, the price increases stimulated a greater development of oil resources in non-OPEC countries, depressing demand for OPEC oil. The seemingly insatiable demand for oil into the late 1970s, despite escalating prices, created a surplus productive capacity, which, in turn, exerted a downward pressure on market prices and caused financial stress in several OPEC states. By the end of 1981, OPEC's emphasis had shifted from setting oil prices to enforcing decreased production quotas for individual member countries in order to keep prices up. The economic booms in petroleum-producing areas elsewhere also gave way to recessions after the collapse of the OPEC-set prices.

In the early 1990s, OPEC continued to struggle with the delicate problem of the fair apportionment of production quotas among its members and hence with the problem of price maintenance. As in any such arrangement, members sought high prices, but some were unwilling to adhere to the assigned production quota limit— the sine qua non for achieving higher prices. In early 1993, OPEC strove to reduce members' total output from 25 million bpd to 23.6 million bpd and thus, by limiting supply, to lever the market price up from the current $18 to $21 per barrel. Whereas OPEC efforts regularly fell short of its goals, the organization continues to be a major factor in petroleum marketing.

OPEC became not only the bête noir of the late 1970s but also a scapegoat for many of the accumulated ills of the world economy. For decades much of the industrial world had enjoyed rapidly expanding economic growth while relying heavily on a steadily increasing and seemingly inexhaustible supply of incredibly cheap energy from beneath the sands and seas of the Middle East. Continuation of such an incongruous economic arrangement should not have been expected, and OPEC became the channel for an inevitable reversal of the economic trend. Realizing that their petroleum supplies are a nonrenewable resource serving as a crucial energy source worldwide, the Middle East producers naturally insist on receiving a maximum return on their sole export and thereby conserving their supplies.

While Middle East producers pooled their marketing efforts in OPEC, each individual government steadily increased its "participation" in the private companies holding concessions in its

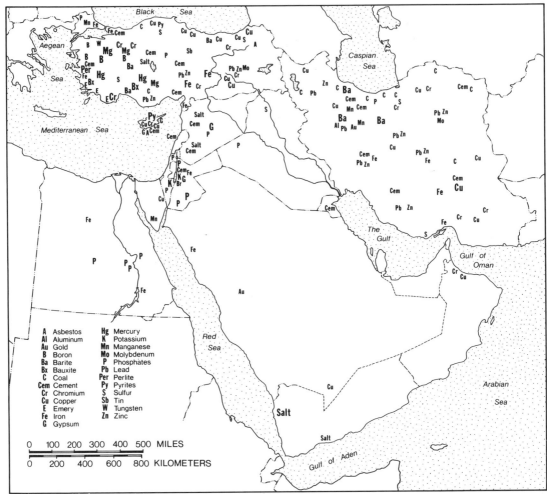

Map 8-5. *Distribution of more important deposits of solid minerals in the Middle East. Note the richness of mineral occurrences in the zones of tectonic plate contacts in Turkey, Iran, and Cyprus. (Adapted from several maps in Bureau of Mines 1984, 1986, and 1989)*

country. By 1980, most OPEC countries had raised their share of ownership of local producing operations to 100 percent and had turned their interests over to national oil companies. By the late 1980s, the national oil companies were increasing their downstream operations (refining, distributing, retailing) both domestically and in customer countries, thus expanding a healthy interdependence.

Other Minerals

The production and utilization of petroleum and natural gas have been the focal point of eco-

nomic mineral activity in the Middle East for several decades. However, several areas are highly mineralized, have produced limited to modest quantities of ores for many centuries, and are now the focus of intensified mineral exploration activities (Map 8-5). The oil-producing countries have joined their neighbors in intensively searching for commercially useful ores and rocks.

Even limited production can bring significant benefit to a local area, especially one lacking petroleum resources; and the processing of ores in areas such as western Iran and northern Oman can be relatively economical because of the availability of large amounts of local natural gas.

Thus, income from mining and quarrying industries is expected to increase significantly by the end of the century.

Turkey and Iran, which occupy extensive segments of the mineralized Fold Belt, have long produced the greatest amounts and variety of solid minerals. Cyprus also is part of the mineralized belt and has been a considerable mineral producer historically, but it faces approaching depletion of its formerly appreciable resources of copper, iron pyrites, and chromite. Jordan, Syria, Israel, Egypt, and Iraq have achieved significant production of phosphate rock, and Israel and Jordan produce noteworthy amounts of potash from the Dead Sea. Both Saudi Arabia and Egypt hope to revive and expand mining in the crystalline shield areas in their respective territories.

Solid Fuels

Although a deficiency in coal resources contributed to the retardation of industrial development in the Middle East during the nineteenth century, the effects of this deficiency have diminished since World War II. Only Turkey, Iran, and—to a minor extent—Egypt have noteworthy coal reserves, and only Turkey's production is significant.

Turkey compensates for its small petroleum output by intensively exploiting its considerable resources of coal (1.4 billion mt) and lignite (8 billion mt). Solid fuels production by the early 1990s exceeded 55 million mt per year. Although Iran possesses modest coal reserves in some of the same structures that contain coalbeds in Turkey, neither the imperial government nor the revolutionary government after 1979 has encouraged coal production in view of Iran's enormous petroleum and gas resources. The Islamic Republic's 1989 coal production was only 1.2 million mt. Egypt's coal production is useful locally but is very modest.

Metals

Most (although not all) metallic ores occur in mineralized igneous and cyrstalline rocks. They cannot, therefore, be normally expected in the extensive sedimentary areas of the Fertile Crescent countries or the Arabian Peninsula. Certain metals may be found in either class of rocks, and, indeed, some limited deposits of iron, lead, and zinc are found in the sedimentary strata just mentioned. Therefore, it is primarily in (1) the complex rocks of the Anatolian and Iranian plateaus, (2) the shield blocks on either side of the Red Sea, and (3) the unusual Oman Mountains that concentrated mineralization has been found and is exploited.

As is the case for solid minerals in general, Turkey possesses by far the greatest variety and greatest quantity of metal ores, and Iran is second. Turkey's production of chromite and ferrochrome has contributed a significant share of the world total for several decades, ranking third in the world. Iran ranks well below Turkey in chrome production but still produces significant amounts. Middle East production of several ferroalloys—tungsten, vanadium, manganese, and antimony—is of minor importance; and for all four, Turkey's small output leads the region.

The Middle East's known iron ore resources are modest and are distributed among Turkey, Egypt, and Iran, the same states that also share leadership in the production of pig iron and steel. Iron was exploited in Anatolia before 1800 BC by the Hittites, who maintained a near-monopoly on ironworking for several centuries. By the 1970s and 1980s, Turkish production of iron ore moved irregularly upward to a 1988 peak of more than 5.5 million mt, much of it from Divriği southeast of Sivas. With reserves equal to those of Turkey, Egypt produces only about half of Turkey's tonnage from deposits near Aswan and southwest of Cairo. Iran's iron reserves are twice those of Turkey and Egypt combined, but production is about equal to that of Egypt, 2.5 million mt in 1989.

Nonferrous metals regularly produced in noteworthy quantities in the region include notably copper but also lead, zinc, mercury, and bauxite (aluminum ore). Although Turkey, Cyprus, and Iran have traditionally been the leading copper producers, Iran became the distinct leader in 1982 after more than a decade of developing its copper resources. Oman appeared as a copper producer for the first time in 1983 and ranks third, after Turkey, in output. Production from Cyprus's ancient mines varies and in some years ceases to be commercially worthwhile.

Iran normally leads in the output of lead and zinc, with Turkey in second place. Turkey is the

Figure 8-4. *Open-pit mining of phosphates and a phosphates processing plant near Palmyra in central Syria.*

region's only producer of bauxite and mercury worth noting, and it has significant reserves of uranium, unexploited at the present time. Israel, however, produces small amounts of uranium from its Negev phosphate deposits for supplementary use in the nearby Dimona reactor. Although gold was apparently available in impressive amounts in ancient Egypt, Persia, Asia Minor, and western Arabia, none of the precious metals are produced in significant amounts in the Middle East today. For several years, Saudi Arabia has conducted an intensive search to identify and map ancient gold-mining sites, both for historical reasons and for possible reexploitation of the deposits.

Nonmetals

Certain types of nonmetallic minerals may be found in several different rock environments, others are found only in sedimentary rocks, and still others occur only in igneous rocks. Thus, the Middle East's nonmetallic ores are more widely distributed over the region than are its metallic resources and may even be processed from sea- or lake water.

The most widely produced solid mineral is salt, produced in virtually every country in the region but in especially large quantities in Turkey, Egypt, and Iran. Lebanon, Yemen, Egypt, and Iraq produce salt by evaporating seawater in small ponds or evaporation pans along the shore. Other producers evaporate surface or underground brines, and Iran and Yemen mine rock salt from underground salt plugs that have pushed their way toward the surface from deep subsurface strata.

The region's production of phosphate rock, valuable for making chemical fertilizers, is of considerable significance on the global scale, as the world demand for phosphate rock has mounted sharply with the growing need for soil fertilizers to increase soil productivity. Middle East resources have, therefore, been more vigorously exploited, with production steadily growing through the late 1970s and 1980s. The region's leading producer is Jordan, which also usually ranks fourth or fifth in the world, with a 1990 output of 6.1 million mt. Four neighboring states are, in 1990 order of production, significant producers from similar rock strata: Israel, Syria (Fig. 8-4), Egypt, and Iraq.

Other nonmetallic minerals of the region may be noted, especially with regard to the unusual aspects of several of them. For example, meerschaum is found in significant commercial quantities only in Turkey. Despite its name ("sea foam" in German), it is a hydrous magnesium silicate—a fine white clayey mineral—used to make special kinds of smoking pipe bowls, many of which are elaborately carved. Turkey's great diversity in minerals also includes production of about 35 percent of the world's boron, and Turkey, Iran, and Egypt mine modest amounts of barite, bentonite, kaolin, feldspar, fluospar, magnesite, and talc. Potash is produced in large amounts from Dead Sea water by both Israel and Jordan, with Israel's output constituting about 4 percent of the world output. Among other minerals Israel produces from the Dead Sea, the bromine output is about one-third of the world total. Asbestos has long been a major product of the metamorphic rocks of Cyprus (Fig. 8-5) and is produced from related structures in Turkey and Egypt. Output has decreased sharply since revelation of asbestos fiber dangers to health.

Gypsum is produced by the thousands of tons in many parts of the region, to be used primarily in the making of cement. The other cement ingredients, lime and clay, are also widespread. Millions of tons of cement were consumed by building construction in the explosively growing towns in much of the Middle East from the mid-1950s to the mid-1980s, with more yet to come.

Figure 8-5. *The large Amiantos asbestos mine in the Troodos Mountains, southwestern Cyprus. Concerns over the environmental risks in using asbestos have reduced world demand for the mineral, and this mine is in jeopardy.*

A significant portion of the world's sulfur production is exported from the Middle East as a by-product of petroleum gas processing. Saudi Arabia alone has a production and export capacity of 1.5 million mt per year, and Iraq has one of the world's largest deposits of native sulfur at Mishraq.

9

Manufacturing and Transportation

Preliminary View

The Stimulus of Oil

The unparalleled petroleum development surveyed in the previous chapter naturally stimulated expansion in other economic sectors. The entire Middle East benefited from the ripple effect on a grand scale, but the expansion was most remarkable in the Gulf states. Rapidly developing Gulf areas soaked up surplus labor from Yemen, Egypt, Lebanon, Jordan, and Syria. At the same time, a reverse flow of cash in grants, loans, and remittances transferred a share of oil profits to nonproducing areas or smaller producers. From Baghdad to Beirut, Kuwait to Cairo, Dubai to Damascus, capital and development fever became the common denominator. Contractors, artisans, and consultants came by the hundreds to take advantage of the boom.

Along Gulf coasts tiny fishing villages became wealthy national capitals with some of the world's largest per capita incomes. Farther inland, splendid paved highways threaded their way across rolling deserts, replacing caravan trails and rutted tracks. By the early 1990s, the Gulf states, including Saudi Arabia, had achieved stunning material progress that was awesome to local inhabitant and outside specialist alike. The splendor and even opulence of public buildings, hotels, airport terminals, shopping centers, and universities were matched by the number and complexity of technologically advanced gas-oil separating facilities, shipping terminals, oil refineries, petrochemical plants, drydocks, aluminum smelters, and similar installations that appear to sprout from deserts and beaches. The insatiable demand for labor in the boom economy guaranteed the indigenous population full employment, favored treatment, many free benefits, and a high standard of living.

Despite the general advancement, the Middle East still has contradictions and inequalities in its standards of living and development patterns. Several states have laid modest-to-appreciable industrial foundations and have developed several diversified producing areas. Even so, none of the Gulf oil producers is a true "industrial" state, in the Western sense, although prerevolutionary Iran sought a high level of industrialization. Development of modern manufacturing started earlier in the eastern Mediterranean, especially in Egypt, where it began in the early 1800s under Muhammad Ali, and in Turkey, where it originated under the nineteenth-century Ottoman new order. Economic evolution during the regional oil boom and the emergence of Israel contributed to the pattern of manufacturing discussed later in this chapter, which reveals the importance of manufacturing in the older areas of Turkey, Iran, and Egypt, as well as the later belts in Syria, Israel, and Iraq. On a smaller scale are Cyprus and, in normal times, Lebanon, which was one of the most intensively developed areas in the Middle East in the early 1970s.

Exact quantification of the industrialization of states in the region is difficult to impossible because of the lack of meaningful and comparable statistics. Determining the values of the usual criteria used to analyze the degree of industrialization—percentage of the gross national product (GNP) derived from manufacturing and other industrial output, percent of the work force

Figure 9-1. *Women and young girls knotting an especially large and fine carpet in an Esfahan workshop. Rug making continues to be a major industry in Iran.*

employed in manufacturing and other industry, and per capita energy consumption, steel output, and other indicators—is thus problematic. Moreover, the Middle East is unique because it has a high output of electrical energy regardless of industrial output. In another connection, much of its industry is capital intensive, highly automated, and labor extensive: A refinery, for example, is a huge facility with high output, but it employs few workers.

Since the overwhelming emphasis is on petroleum exploitation in the Gulf region, that area's recently evolved economic patterns and activities differ from those of neighboring non-oil areas. There are considerable gaps in the gross domestic product (GDP) and in per capita income between the Gulf and the eastern Mediterranean, but the ripple effect of oil income in part of the region has been noteworthy in other parts. Development in Cyprus, Jordan, and—before 1975 Lebanon has been impressive because of the ripple effect. The dramatic development in Israel has been largely independent of the regional oil boom but has been heavily financed by capital transfers of aid, especially from the United States and Germany. Capital availability from oil income has set the pace for all Middle East countries, even though development has been uneven

among the several states and among sectors of the economy. In any given recent year, Saudi Arabia expended $250–275 billion for development in a large area with a relatively small population, whereas Egypt spent one-tenth that amount on a small inhabited area with a population four times that of the Saudi kingdom.

Historical Perspective

During the golden age of Islam, in the ninth and tenth centuries, the Middle East boasted the world's best-developed economy and flourishing trade. High-quality textiles were a specialty—linens from Egypt, damask from Damascus, silks from Kufah, brocades from Shiraz, and muslin from Mosul, as well as carpets from Iran, Bukhara, and other centers (Fig. 9-1). Colored glass from Syria, decorated ceramic tiles from several areas, pottery, porcelain, inlaid and decorated wood, paper, engraved and inlaid brass and copper (damascene), engraved gold and silver jewelry, leather wares, and fine soaps and perfumes were produced in the small workshops of the *suqs* or bazaars. Products moved between Spain on the west and Samarkand on the east as well as into Scandinavia, India, and China.

Some goods moved by sea, and Basrah became a preeminent port of the time. However, much of the traffic was overland, and great dromedary caravans often moved eastward from Baghdad through Hamadan, Rey, and Merv (Mary) to Samarkand, where loads were transferred to the Bactrian camels of the Mongols and Chinese (see Map 6-5). Towns favorably located as trade centers thrived during the period, and some of them have maintained their prosperity into the present.

But with the age of discovery, Western European ships sailed around southern Africa and gained control of the trade routes between their home countries and southern and eastern Asia. Middle East arts and crafts declined, and, their markets lost, continued only at a survival level. By the seventeenth century, the great caravans between the Islamic world and China were only a memory.

Renewed European interest in the Middle East in the nineteenth century revived some aspects of the region's economic activity—carpet making, metalworking, and woodworking. Steamships transported far greater loads than had the earlier small sailing vessels, and European investors built railways from ports into interiors under concessionary terms.

Cooperation and Aid

Arab Coordination

The concept of Arab unity has always had an economic component, but economic coordination has been inhibited by recurrent political conflict. Successive economic agreements and institutions have been arranged, only to become ineffective in reality. Similar friction has precluded regionwide cooperation, and Israel, Iran, and Turkey are generally excluded from Arab groupings.

Two Gulf efforts, on the other hand, have been quite successful: (1) the Gulf Organization for Industrial Consultancy (GOIC), established in Doha in 1976, and more important, (2) the Cooperation Council of the Arab States of the Gulf, better known as the Gulf Cooperation Council (GCC), created in 1981 (see Chap. 11).

Economic Aid

A further influence on Middle East economic patterns is that of direct transfers of capital into

and within the region. Huge amounts of petrodollars flowed to the OPEC states for oil payments after 1972 and were used for development projects in the oil states as well as for aid to non-oil states.

From the 1950s to the present, industrialized states have made large grants and loans to many governments and agencies in the Middle East. The United States has extended the largest amounts, primarily to Israel, Turkey, Egypt, and Jordan, although virtually every country in the region—other than the Gulf amirates—received substantial U.S. aid at some point between 1940 and 1989, including Iran, Iraq, and Saudi Arabia. Israel received by far the largest amounts along with indirect grants and loans of many types. Most Western European countries—especially Great Britain, Germany, and France but also some of the smaller states—have also granted and lent large amounts to Middle East countries. The former Soviet Union gave its client states assistance, primarily military but also economic for dams and related projects in Egypt and Syria. Japan is the leading Asian donor, although the People's Republic of China has built major highways and a textile mill in Yemen.

In addition to these bilateral amounts, technical and development aid has also been given to all non-oil Middle East states through the United Nations, and the United Nations Relief and Works Agency (UNRWA) has funneled large amounts of aid to Palestinian refugees from 1949 to the present. Technical assistance has also been given to the oil states on a reimbursable basis.

Intraregional aid after the 1960s became a wealth-sharing process. In 1961, Kuwait created the Kuwait Fund for Arab Economic Development (KFAED), which has given hundreds of millions of dollars in loans and grants for economic development not only in the Arab world but also in African countries. Similar funds were created later by other oil states—the Abu Dhabi Fund for Arab Economic Development, the Iraqi Fund for External Development, and the Saudi Fund for Development. Large grants are regularly made by oil states to non-oil states outside the channels of the funds, especially on an emergency basis. Financial aid to countries that assist in the military defense of Gulf producers is especially substantial. After the 1973 Arab-Israeli war, for example, Arab oil producers transferred $3 billion to Egypt, $1 billion to Syria, and $125 million to Jordan.

During Iraq's war with Iran in 1980–1988, Kuwait, Saudi Arabia, Qatar, and the UAE contributed more than $55 billion to Iraq's wartime expenses. When Iraq invaded Kuwait in 1990, Kuwait, Saudi Arabia, and the UAE helped defray the costs of the coalition's rollback of the Iraqis with cash reimbursements over several months that totaled $84 billion and with material support worth another $51 billion. They also contributed several billion dollars toward losses and costs incurred by Turkey, Jordan, and Egypt because of the UN sanctions and coalition actions.[1]

Regional Development Problems

Remarkable though it has been, regional development in the Middle East has been hindered by several fundamental problems. The initial shortage of skilled labor required time for the training of indigenous workers and managers to replace expatriate workers. The original dependence of the Gulf oil states on northwestern Europeans and Americans for exploration and development of oil resources has evolved into a mutual relationship involving oil supplies, dollar payments, technological needs, and petrodollar recycling. Nearly everywhere, the shortage of water—and in places, the actual lack of water—has had a serious negative impact on the pattern of economic development.

Therefore, despite its energy resources, the Middle East faces serious problems in trying to bring about comprehensive economic development. Progress in certain sectors has been dramatic, but the achievement of long-term self-sufficiency in a balanced economy will be more difficult.

Labor and Skills

The lack of a sufficient and trained work force was the most serious single deterrent to initial development in most of the Middle East, especially in the Gulf oil states, and the various steps taken to meet the labor demand have had profound spatial implications. During the 35 years before 1992, there was a sharp contrast in the labor available between the northwestern part of the Middle East and the southeastern part. The northwest had a labor surplus and a small supply of technical and managerial people. By contrast, the Gulf area possessed a sparse and primarily pastoral/fishing population, which was inadequate in number and unequipped in skills to meet the labor demands of a booming oil economy.

The demand for labor in the Gulf states was both qualitative and quantitative. The supply of unskilled workers from nearby areas and southern Asia was almost unlimited, but the number of available engineers, technicians, business managers, and similar professionals was small. As the pace of development increased during the 1960s, workers at all levels came from Jordan, Egypt, and Lebanon to Saudi Arabia and the smaller Gulf states. Yemenis filled hundreds of semi-skilled jobs in Saudi Arabia, and Indians, Pakistanis, and Baluch poured into the lower Gulf to work.

Cultural affiliations were important, since Arabic speakers and Muslims tended to adapt most easily in the Gulf. However, Pakistanis and Indian Muslims often adapted more readily than cosmopolitan Lebanese. In addition, managerial positions generally required fluency in English, the lingua franca of the oil industry. As a consequence, the work force was transformed in size and composition throughout the Gulf within a few years (Table 9-1).

The situation of Palestinian workers in the Gulf is a special one. The demand for skilled workers and professionals was rapidly escalating in Kuwait just when the Palestinian Arabs were forced to leave their homeland. Many moved to Kuwait, and by 1986, the number of Palestinian/Jordanians there had climbed to more than 350,000. In Kuwait, as was true to a greater extent in Jordan, the Palestinians helped create the economy that absorbed them. However, Kuwait later became concerned about the growing political power of the Palestinians in that country and discouraged further Palestinian immigration. During the Iraqi occupation of Kuwait from August 1990 to February 1991, many Palestinians, among others, evacuated their homes and went elsewhere for the duration of the conflict. Many of the Palestinians and other expatriate evacuees

TABLE 9-1: ECONOMICALLY ACTIVE POPULATION: TOTAL AND SECTOR DISTRIBUTION

COUNTRY	1 ECON ACTIVE POP TOTAL NO. IN 000s	2 % TOTAL POP	3 AG, FOR, FISHING	4 MFG, MNG, QG	5 CNSTRC-TION	6 TRNSP, COMM	7 TRADE, HTL, RT	8 SERVS, OTHER
			% OF ECON ACTIVE POP IN SELECTED SECTORS					
Bahrain	183	42	2	13.4	21.0	9.4	13.4	36.5
Cyprus (1989)[a]	263	37	13.6	19.0	8.4	5.1	20.5	28.2
Egypt	12,095	15	42.7	16.6	4.7	4.9	8.5	21.6
Iran	12,820	26	24.9	12.3	9.4	4.9	6.8	40.8
Iraq (1987)	3,956	24	12.5	8.8	8.6	5.7	5.4	58.3
Israel (1989)	1,604	36	4.4	21.7	5.2	6.1	14.0	39.1
Jordan	524	20	6.2	7.7	10.7	8.6	10.5	53.1
Kuwait (1988)	699	33	1.3	9.0	15.4	5.3	11.4	54.5
Lebanon	694	23	19.1	18.9	6.2	7.0	16.5	28.8
Oman	468	32	23.3	3.3	27.5	1.4	26.4	16.5
Qatar	201	45	3.1	11.9	20.1	3.7	10.9	48.6
Saudi Arabia	3,032	21	14.3	14.9	18.7	6.9	12.3	29.8
Syria	2,488	21	30.0	14.5	15.5	6.3	10.4	24.4
Turkey (1988)	20,617	36	45.3	13.7	4.9	3.7	10.0	20.3
UAE	891	47	5.0	10.4	24.8	7.4	13.6	35.7
Yemen	2,043	18	56.6	6.9	7.9	5.3	12.2	11.1
Gaza (1987)	102	17	18.0	17.8	23.4	5.4	14.8	8.1
West Bank ('87)	182	20	19.8	16.6	24.4	5.6	13.8	7.7
TOTAL/AVG.	62,862	29	19.0	13.2	14.3	5.7	12.9	30.0
U.K. (1987)	27,896	49	2.1	21.1	5.6	5.4	18.1	29.8
Spain (1989)	14,819	38	12.3	21.4	9.0	5.0	18.5	29.2

Sectors include agriculture, forestry, fishing; manufacturing, mining, quarrying; construction; transportation, communications; trade, hotels, restaurants; and services and other. Data for 1986 unless indicated otherwise. [a]Cyprus data for Republic of Cyprus (Southern Cyprus) only. Corresponding data for United Kingdom and Spain given for comparison. Source: *Britannica World Data 1991*. (With permission)

were neither invited back nor permitted to return, and some of the Palestinians who stayed were accused of collaboration with the enemy. By late 1992, the Palestinian population of Kuwait was, although not accurately known, estimated to be under 20,000, less than 6 percent of the number before August 1990. More Asians are being brought in to replace departed Arabs.

The migration of hundreds of thousands of people to the Gulf area between 1945 and 1985 exerted a profound effect on the work force in both the supplying and the receiving countries. For example, more than 20 percent of the population of then North Yemen was working in Saudi Arabia during the 1970s and early 1980s. However, about 800,000 Yemenis employed in Saudi Arabia were expelled during the Gulf crisis of 1990–

1991, since the Yemen government maintained an anticoalition stance.

Remittances

One measure of the magnitude of the labor migration to the Gulf oil states is the amount of money the migrant workers sent back to their home countries. For example, in 1981, Jordanians working outside their own country sent back more than $1.23 billion, which was equal to 28 percent of the kingdom's GNP, 39 percent of its imports, and 168 percent of its exports. Similarly, in 1982, Egyptians remitted $1.87 billion. Illustrative of the increase in Pakistani workers in the Gulf is the fact that remittances to Pakistan totaled $339 million in 1974–1975 and $2 billion in 1980–1981, a sixfold increase in six years. Remittances to then North Yemen also exceeded $2 billion annually in the early 1980s. With the recession in the oil states after the mid-1980s, many of the expatriates lost their jobs and returned home, and others who remained had lower incomes and sent smaller remittances home. This reduction in income inevitably created economic difficulties for the labor-supplying countries. Even after the partial recovery in the late 1980s, the demand for labor in the Gulf did not return to its earlier levels, since the peak of the construction boom had passed. The service sector imported South and Southeast Asians to staff its large number of hotel and restaurant positions and similar jobs. Even more acute than the 1980s recession were the economic blows that struck many Gulf expatriate workers as direct and indirect results of the Iraqi invasion of Kuwait in 1990. Hundreds of thousands of workers and professionals found themselves without jobs and no longer welcome in their adopted lands, and they were forced to return to depressed economic conditions in their home countries—Jordan, Lebanon, Egypt, and Yemen.

Patterns of Industry

Factors of Industrial Location

Patterns of manufacturing in the Middle East are determined by the classic geographical factors of raw materials, labor supply, transportation, market, and power (energy) along with such intangibles as financial incentives, momentum, tradition, and technology. Concentrations of the greatest number of factors attract the largest ensembles of manufacturing.

Distribution of Centers

Despite the great economic development of the Middle East since 1950, industrial regions tend to be relatively modest on a world scale. Designed in early years to serve domestic requirements, more of the plants now export some of their output. The numerous petrochemical plants are highly export oriented. Many more textile mills (in Turkey, Egypt, and Israel), clothing factories (not only in the Levant but even in the UAE), wineries (in the Levant and Cyprus), and similar operations are catering to the export market. Is-

rael is especially dedicated to export industries, from diamond cutting to armaments. In absolute terms, not considering per capita output, Iran is by far the leading Middle East manufacturing country in total manufacturing value-added ($44.5 billion in 1988), followed by Turkey, Saudi Arabia, Israel, and Egypt. Iraq was formerly sixth but lost many of its producing units in 1991.

Certain types of industries—including such basic production as processed foods and beverages, construction materials, and clothing—are widespread and are found in every country and in many parts of the larger countries. Less widespread but nevertheless found in virtually every country are such manufacturing industries as textiles, leather, wood products, cement, printing, cigarettes, metalworking, ceramics, and jewelry. Less common is the production of glass, plastics, chemicals, tools, small appliances, and irrigation pipe and sprinklers. States with significant oil and gas production have evolved a typical ensemble of industries that use oil and gas as feedstock or as fuel—oil refineries, water distillation plants, electricity generating plants, fertilizer and other petrochemical plants, and in two Gulf states, such energy-dependent facilities as aluminum smelters.

Only in the major producing countries are there industries making or assembling motor vehicles, ships, machine tools, major appliances, electronic items, and armaments. Only in Egypt and Israel is there aircraft production, and only in Israel is there diamond cutting. Few countries engage in basic research and development on any noteworthy scale, and Israel, which ranks on the world scale, is far in the lead. However, Turkey, Egypt, Iran, Saudi Arabia, Iraq, and others are steadily increasing their research efforts.

Seven general economic zones may be geographically differentiated within the area (Map 9-1). They form a rough arc following the trend of the Fertile Crescent but extending beyond and below it, and each area is examined in the various country chapters.

1. Nile Delta. The Egyptian manufacturing sector is one of the two earliest and most diversified centers in the Middle East and comprises the area Alexandria-Cairo-Suez–Port Said–Alexandria. Cairo and Alexandria are the centers of the

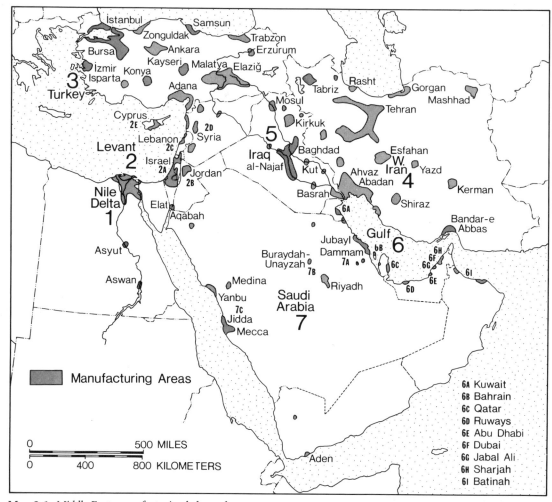

Map 9-1. *Middle East manufacturing belts and centers.*

most important production areas in Egypt, along with the great textile towns in the central Delta. Served by a dense road and railway net and embracing one of the highest densities of population in the world, this sector is based on creative traditions of the ancient, medieval, and modern ages. In addition to prized handcraft items, the products range from processed foods and textiles, through aluminum and iron and steel, to metal products, fertilizers, refined petroleum products, motor vehicles, light armaments, and assembled helicopters.

   2. Levant. Northeast of the first zone is a grouping of five neighboring but unconnected manufacturing concentrations in the four Levant states and on the island of Cyprus.

   2A. Israel. The dense concentration of highly varied plants in Israel constitutes the most nationally balanced and systematized range of manufacturing facilities in the Middle East. One reason for the varied facilities is that the Israeli economy is basically isolated, with few materials moving into or out of the zone on the land side, which requires self-sufficiency. Moreover, Israel must perforce develop industry to provide employment for its influx of technological immigrants and to maintain a basis for a high standard of living. By the mid-1980s, most categories of manufacturing were represented in Israel, from food processing to the fifth- or sixth-largest armaments industry in the world, including a controversial nuclear facility at Dimona. Tel Aviv and Haifa are the main concentrations of industry, but industries have been dispersed for both development and security purposes. Many specialty factories—electronics plant, for example—are being developed in smaller settlements around the country.

2B. Jordan. The industrial area of Jordan has only a modest range of light manufacturing facilities concentrated primarily in the Amman-Zarqa-Irbid triangle in the northwestern part of the country. However, Aqabah, Jordan's only port, is a growing center of production. Percentage growth has been great since 1960, but Jordan started from a very low industrial base.

2C. Lebanon. Traditionally, manufacturing in Lebanon has been primarily consumer oriented, often related to the retail trade. As in Egypt and Syria, handcrafted articles are produced in great variety, from inlaid wood furniture to jewelry. Other manufactured products include textiles, clothing, leather items, paints, chemicals, cement, glasswares (a tradition from Phoenician times), cigarettes (a state monopoly), and raw steel and other metal products. Lebanon's open economy attracted huge amounts of investment capital between 1950 and 1975, but industrial production dropped sharply and at best limped along after the late 1970s. Even after a return to peacetime, which looked reasonably promising in early 1993, Lebanon will lack the capital flow that prompted the industrial development of the period from the early 1950s to the early 1970s.

2D. Syria. Damascus has been famous for more than 1,200 years for its handcrafted metals, inlaid woods, textiles, and glass; and since the 1960s, more modern factory-made goods have been produced: machine-made textiles, clothing, appliances, machinery, cement, chemicals, cigarettes, and similar items. The ancient trade center of Aleppo is likewise a modern production center. Homs and Hamah, on the Damascus-Aleppo axis; the coastal centers of Latakia, Baniyas, and Tartus; and the modest newly developing centers of Raqqah and Dayr al-Zawr in the Euphrates Valley are also worth noting.

2E. Cyprus. The main producing areas on Cyprus are in the Nicosia area and on the south coast. Despite the separation of northern Cyprus after 1974, the vitality of the Republic of Cyprus

has encouraged the emergence or expansion of establishments producing cigarettes, processed foodstuffs, wine, paper products, clothing, shoes, textiles, and cement.

3. Turkey. Endowed with many elements conducive to industrial development equal to that of India or Argentina, Turkey has the largest number of industrial workers, probably the largest number of industrial establishments, and the second-highest total value-added by manufacturing. Food processing is by far the single most important producing activity and is on a much greater scale than that of the other states of the region. Textiles, handmade and machine-made rugs, leather goods, tobacco products, wood and paper products, ceramics, appliances, chemicals, pharmaceuticals, heavy and light machinery, assembled automobiles, railway equipment, and small ships are some of the broad range of Turkish factory products. Manufacturing is widespread, and most of the larger cities have several factories. Major production centers are Istanbul, Izmir, Zonguldak, Ankara, Kırıkkale, Divriği, Mersin, Adana, and Erzurum, plus the other cities shown on Map 9-1.

4. Western Iran. Like Turkey, Iran has a large population, work force, and domestic market and numerous raw materials and other advantages for manufacturing. Unlike Turkey, Iran also has huge oil resources, and it leads the Middle East in value-added by manufacturing. It has a long and distinguished history of manufacturing, traditionally producing rugs, textiles, handcrafted metalwares, jewelry, ceramics (especially tiles), and similar items. Iran's highly diversified modern industrial products—many made in small five- to ten-employee shops—include fabricated metals (utilitarian wrought iron as well as traditional copper and brass), jewelry, plain and art textiles and leather goods, hand-knotted rugs, petroleum products and chemicals, and a wide range of food products. Several major areas are dispersed over western Iran: Tehran, the Ahvaz-Khorramshahr-Abadan-Bandar-e Khomeyni triangle area at the head of the Gulf, Kharg Island, Shiraz, Sar Cheshmeh, Arak, Esfahan, Tabriz, and Gorgan. Iran has clearly demonstrated that it has achieved world rank with the moderately large industrial producers.

5. *Iraq.* The amount and variety of manufacturing in Iraq increased steadily and, during the late 1980s, impressively after Iraq's modest start in the mid-1950s. However, the share of manufacturing in the country's economy was still only 12 percent of the GDP by 1988. In the early 1990s this share was skewed by the highly atypical economic situation in the country, including the shutdown of most of the crude petroleum production. Additionally, much of the country's industrial complex was heavily damaged by coalition bombing in early 1991, appreciably more so than by Iranian bombing and shelling from 1980 to 1988. Still under UN sanctions in early 1993, Iraq faces grave problems in restoring its pre-1990 factory output, much less developing to the level it sought in its economic planning in the 1989–1990 timeframe. Nevertheless, the Iraqis made much more determined and rapid progress toward recovery during 1992 than expected. Traditional handcrafts include silversmithing, copper and brass working, textile weaving, and rug making. Baghdad is the main center of the sprawling modern Mesopotamian industrial zone, which proved to be much more developed and sophisticated than expected when UN inspectors checked it in early 1991 for nuclear, chemical, and biological production. Government planning has spread facilities to Mosul, Irbil, Kirkuk, and the area of Basrah and al-Zubayr. The Basrah and al-Zubayr areas and other southern centers were the most heavily damaged in 1980–1988 and 1991, and reconstruction has proceeded only slowly in the south in comparison with the rebuilding of the capital area. Petrochemicals and other petroleum-related products make up a considerable share of the country's industrial output, but 1980s wartime demands and the Baath party military ambitions also mandated the rapid development of a large and varied armaments industry. The considerable scale of that industry became clear during UN inspections of Iraqi military plants in 1991–1992. Many smaller establishments produce processed foods and beverages, cigarettes, textiles, clothing, shoes, furniture, and metal goods.

6. *Gulf.* The Gulf industrial zone, including Oman—but excluding Saudi Arabia, Iraq, and Iran—might be subdivided into subzones based partly on national boundaries, as was the case with the Levant zone. However, the Gulf facilities have a substantial degree of similarity and have developed almost entirely since the 1960s, after petroleum development stimulated dramatic economic and population growth. The core economic activity in every subcenter of the Gulf zone is petroleum production and processing, and the main satellite facilities produce petroleum-related products—petrochemicals, fertilizers, liquefied natural gas derivatives, secondary sulfur, and a range of refinery products.

However, there is an array of manufacturing in several parts of the area, and further diversification is under way (see Chap. 18). Since construction has been a major aspect of the economy since the mid-1950s, production of construction materials has been, but is decreasingly, a major industry. It includes cement, cement blocks, bricks, steel reinforcing rods, and metal frames for windows and doors. Dhow building is still carried on in traditional centers: Kuwait, Bahrain, Ajman, and Ras al-Khaymah. Most of the larger new industries are capital intensive as well as large energy users.

Major subcenters include (6A) the Kuwait Bay and Gulf coast area; (6B) northeastern Bahrain, which has locational advantages and the earliest industrial development among the smaller Gulf states; (6C) east-central Qatar, primarily around Musayid (Umm Said) and Doha; (6D-6H) the five United Arab Emirates (UAE) main industrial developments of (6D) al-Ruways near the shipping terminal of Jabal Dhanna, (6E) Abu Dhabi Island with its light production, (6F) Dubai City with a wide range of small plants that produce consumer goods, (6G) Jabal Ali as a heavy industrial center south of Dubai, and (6H) Sharjah with modest manufacturing establishments; and finally (6I) the Batinah coast of Oman, which produced only a few handcrafted articles until the mid-1960s but which now has a group of copper-centered plants near Suhar and other plants west of Muscat.

7. *Saudi Triad: al-Hasa, Najd, Hijaz.* From a pre-1935 manufacturing production level below that of any other major country in the Middle East, Saudi Arabia by the early 1990s had developed a vigorous and diversified range of production. Latest available data on value-added by manufacturing show Saudi Arabia ranking third

in the Middle East, after Iran and Turkey. Initially, development focused almost entirely on the oil industry in the Eastern Province, but there are now diversified industries in both mid-Arabia and the west. The latest developments include an industrial city and port on each side of the peninsula—Jubayl on the Gulf coast and Yanbu on the Red Sea coast. Therefore, Saudi Arabia now has three main producing centers: (7A) on the Gulf coast along the Jubayl–Dammam–al-Khobar axis, with outliers in the Hofuf-Abqaiq area; (7B) the two centers of Qasim and Riyadh in Najd; and (7C) the Jiddah-Mecca area in the Hijaz, with an outlier in Yanbu.

Transportation

Roads were of limited significance in the Middle East before World War I because of centuries of preference for cross-country transport via camel caravans. In early road construction in 1859–1863, a French company built a 69-mile/111-km road from Beirut port to Damascus, and an additional 258 miles/415 km of roads had been built in Lebanon by 1900. With the approach of the twentieth century, the French, British, Germans, and—in Iran—Russians were involved in building roads, railroads, and ports in and around the Middle East, mostly under concessionary terms. The Dutch, Portuguese, and British successively controlled the main sea lanes after the sixteenth century, and British steamships played a major role in the Gulf until World War II.

Consequently, the mandates and recently independent states of the Middle East had a basic transportation net by the late 1920s that was appreciably improved by the end of World War II. However, it was the huge petrodollar influx after the early 1960s that permitted transformation of the regional communications network—road net, seaports and airports, pipeline network, and to a lesser extent, rail net.

Two aspects of the pattern of Middle East communications are worth noting. First, the Middle East exhibits a coarse pattern of "islands" or cores of development that are widely separated by uninhabited or sparsely populated deserts, mountain masses, or seas. Before the mid-nineteenth century, these various cores were linked by land caravans and, if coastal, by small sailing ships, with flexible schedules and capacities and minimum costs. Railway and road nets were not required, nor would they have been profitable, since there was little cargo traffic along the routes between the centers. Even today the two main rail nets, in Turkey and Iran, and two secondary nets, in Egypt and Iraq, are primarily internal, with relatively limited international movement of freight or passengers. On the other hand, the three most extensive road nets, in Turkey, Saudi Arabia, and Iran, are increasingly linked with neighboring nets, and both cargo and passengers cross frontiers along roads in steadily growing numbers. In peaceful periods, the main highway border crossings are, especially on weekends and holidays, normally crowded—between Lebanon and Syria, Syria and Jordan, Turkey and Bulgaria, Turkey and Iran, Kuwait and Iraq, and Saudi Arabia and Bahrain.

Second, airways in most of the Middle East developed to a significant level before railroads were built, and airlines serve the region very well. Aircraft can fly over and thereby ignore both the physical-environmental hazards and the political perils—the expanses of desert, sea, and mountains when flying Istanbul-Bahrain, Beirut-Tehran, or Cairo-Muscat, and the political obstacles of an isolated Israel, a warring Lebanon (at least during 1975–1991), or a sanctioned Iraq after August 1990. And where airlines are locally unavailable or inadequate, the highway net serves most purposes. Therefore, at the present time, railways are of less regional importance than are the other available means of transportation (Map 9-2).

Highways

Prior to midcentury, most of the road systems in the Middle East were scattered webs around capitals or other primary cities in the Fertile Crescent countries or in the three large states of Egypt, Turkey, and Iran. Only a few miles of surfaced roads existed anywhere in the Arabian Peninsula. By the early 1990s, the Middle East had 491,893 miles/791,589 km of roads, of which more than one-third were paved highways (Fig. 9-2). Barring unexpected frontier closures, a motorist can now drive on paved roads—mostly first-class highways—from Istanbul over the Bosporus Bridge to the Pakistan border via Erzurum, Tabriz, Tehran, and Yazd; or from Istanbul to Aden

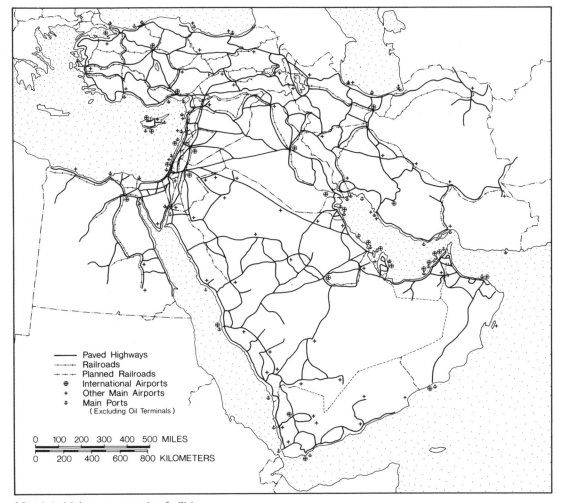

Map 9-2. *Major transportation facilities.*

Figure 9-2. *Highways old and new. When I made a consular visit into remote areas of the Trucial States in the Oman Mountains in 1964, the already rugged track (maximum speed, 10 mph/16 kmph) degenerated into a rocky streambed (maximum speed, about 3 mph/5 kmph), as shown on the left. During a 1979 visit to the same area, I enjoyed one of the many blessings of the oil boom in the UAE: a first-class, well-built highway (right).*

Figure 9-3. *A stretch of the 15.5-mile/25-km causeway linking Saudi Arabia and Bahrain (seen in distance). Completed in 1986 at a cost of more than $1 billion, the causeway is especially heavily traveled on the local weekend (Thursday-Friday).*

via Adana, Damascus, Amman, and Jiddah; or turn east at Jiddah and reach Abu Dhabi and Muscat via Dhahran. Even the Gulf island state of Bahrain can now be reached by highway via a causeway opened in 1986 (Fig. 9-3).

The regional road network is also being linked to the Trans-European Motorway (TEM), especially in Turkey. Now under construction, this special integrated, high-grade motorway will run north and south through eastern Europe, from Gdansk on Poland's Baltic coast to Istanbul, then east to Ankara and the Iranian border, about 6,215 miles/10,000 km. Spur roads in Anatolia will extend the main TEM to the borders of Syria and Iraq. Turkey will thus have 2,235 miles/3,600 km of the motorway, but the project may take the remainder of the century to finance and complete.

Israel's very dense network of roads is isolated. Before 1967, there were no open connections with the country's neighbors, and in 1992, there were only uncertain connections with Egypt. Pedestrians can usually cross the Allenby Bridge over the Jordan River, and Israeli military vehicles cross into southern Lebanon.

Cyprus, where driving on the left side of the road is a British legacy, has a road net and ad-ministration that were divided between north and south in 1974. The island is integrated with the Levant road system by frequent car ferry, and other ferries that connect several eastern Mediterranean ports transport private cars and trucks among Istanbul, Izmir, and Mersin in Turkey; Latakia, Syria; Beirut and Juniyah in Lebanon; and Alexandria, Egypt. A special truck ferry from Volos in Greece to Tartus in Syria enables truckers to avoid the long drive over winding mountain roads in Anatolia.

Predictably, the most densely inhabited areas, if reasonably prosperous, have the densest highway networks, as can be seen in Table 9-2 and Map 9-2. Israel, Cyprus, and Lebanon have the region's densest nets, but these countries are small and have a limited absolute length of roads. Turkey, Iran, and Saudi Arabia, in that order, have the longest total length of roads.

Some segments of the road net in the Middle East are noteworthy both for their engineering and for their scenic impact. The paved 62-mile/100-km highway from Hudaydah, on Yemen's Red Sea coast, up the steep, rugged escarpment to the capital, Sana, affords magnificent vistas as it winds past terraced fields and picturesque villages to reach the plateau, 9,000 ft./2,743

TABLE 9-2: TRANSPORTATION: ROADS, RAILROADS, MERCHANT MARINE

COUNTRY	1 ROADS: LENGTH IN KM	2 % OF ROADS PAVED	3 KM OF ROADS PER KM^2	4 NUMBER OF VEHICLES (ALL TYPES)	5 PERSONS PER VEHICLE	6 RR TRACK IN KM	7 KM OF RR PER KM^2	8 MERCHANT MARINE 000s DWT
Bahrain	243	---	0.35	107,347	4.1	---	---	64.7
Cyprus	9,824	43	1.00	233,930	3.1	---	---	32,698.8
Egypt	45,500^a	68^a	0.05	1,377,564	38.0	5,355	0.005	1,795.7
Iran	139,368	48	0.08	2,681,087^b	17.0^b	4,601^c	0.003	8,685.3
Iraq	45,554	84	0.10	1,040,730	17.0	2,457^c	0.006	1,812.7
Israel	12,823	100	0.62	837,064	5.3	594	0.03	586.0
Jordan	5,625	100	0.06	223,301	13.0	788^c	0.009	47.7
Kuwait	4,273	100	0.24	564,514	3.6	---	---	2,886.6
Lebanon	7,370	85	0.72	522,932^b	5.0^b	222	0.02	593.1
Oman	20,749	20	0.07	226,464	5.9	---	---	13.1
Qatar	1,080	63	0.09	141,724	2.8	---	---	459.1
Saudi Arabia	92,802	36	0.04	4,268,407	2.9	893	0.0004	3,535.4
Syria	30,452	95	0.16	248,309	46.0	2,078	0.01	102.5
Turkey	320,611	14	0.41	2,063,049	26.0	8,430^c	0.01	5,477.1
UAE	4,360^b	61^b	0.06	77,764^b	18.0^b	---	---	1,315.7
Yemen	50,905^b	12^b	0.10	403,495	58.0	---	---	419.6
Gaza	---	---	---	23,975	23.0	---	---	---
West Bank	---	---	---	54,357	16.0	---	---	---
TOTAL/AVG.	791,589	---	0.26	15,096,013	17.0	25,418	0.003	60,493.1
U.K.	354,315	100	1.45	22,031,000	2.6	37,868	0.16	10,252.0
Spain	318,022	56	0.63	12,807,332	3.0	12,563^c	0.02	6,461.4

^{a}National roads only. ^{b}Data more than five years old. ^{c}Route length (other railway lengths are for total track length). Column 3 is the ratio between the length of roads and the area of each country. Column 7 is the same for railways. Number of vehicles in Column 4 includes automobiles, buses, and trucks. Column 8 is the total of merchant marine ships in thousands of deadweight tons for 1989. Otherwise, data are latest available in early 1992. Source of basic data: *Britannica World Data 1991*. (With permission)

m above sea level. Similarly, the highway from Mecca to Taif offers spectacular views as it leaves the heat of the coastal plain and ascends into the cooler heights of Saudi Arabia's summer capital. The highway from Beirut over the mountains and across the Bekaa toward Damascus is famed for its landscapes. Less dramatic because of the lower elevations, but also interesting, is the drive from Tel Aviv and Jaffa on the Mediterranean coast to Jerusalem (2,500 ft./762 m) and down the eastern slopes to Jericho and the Jordan (1,200 ft./365 m below sea level).

The drive along the Mediterranean coast of southern Turkey has some of the scenic beauty of that along the French and Italian rivieras as well as sites of major archaeological interest. Another dramatic mountain drive is that from Tehran over the Elburz Mountains at 9,000 ft./2,745 m, to Chalus on the Caspian Sea shore, 80 ft./24 m below sea level. Spectacular scenery also characterizes two roads into northeastern Iraq, into the Rawanduz Gorge from Irbil and into the Sulaymaniyah area from Kirkuk. With almost no change in elevation, the drive between Cairo and Alexandria on the Delta Road, through the villages and the green landscape of the irrigated Nile Delta, provides an interesting contrast to the other Cairo-Alexandria link, the Desert Road.

The Middle East road net is rapidly achieving maturity of pattern. All major cities and towns are now connected, and the need in the 1990s is to integrate more of the villages, to construct shorter routes between some major cities, to make dual highways of standard roads in some

Figure 9-4. *Railway station in Tanta, located in the central Nile Delta. Railways are heavily utilized in Egypt, especially by passengers, in a country with a limited number of vehicles per 100 inhabitants.*

high-traffic areas, and to continue to densify the net.

Railways

The Middle East economic situation did not justify the construction of extensive rail nets during the heyday of railway building in other parts of the world, and the region's development from the 1960s onward took advantage of the more flexible facilities of highways and airways. As in many other areas with numerous long-distance travelers, passenger traffic in the Middle East is mostly by air, and since most cargo can be more easily shipped by truck, cargo aircraft, ships, or—in the case of petroleum and petroleum products—via pipelines and tankers, any appreciable expansion of Middle East rail nets seems unlikely in the foreseeable future.

The total length of railway lines in the Middle East is 15,794 miles/25,418 km, less than 5 percent of the total mileage of paved roads. The region's average 0.003 km of rail line per square kilometer of area compares with Australia's 0.005 km per km^2 in roughly the same amount of territory. By contrast, the United Kingdom, somewhat smaller than Oman, has a total 23,531 miles/ 37,868 km of rails, one-third more than that of the entire Middle East, and 0.16 km per km^2.

As is shown on Map 9-2, the densest rail net among the Middle East states is in Turkey, which has one-third of the region's rail total. The nets of Egypt and Iran are more open than the Turkish rail net, but they are nevertheless heavily traveled (Fig. 9-4) and are reasonably adequate in length, particularly in view of the two countries' extensive and virtually uninhabited desert areas. The entire Arabian Peninsula, with more than 1.3 million miles^2/3.17 million km^2, has only 555 miles/893 km of railway in Saudi Arabia. None of the six peripheral states of the Arabian Peninsula has any railways, nor does the Mediterranean island state of Cyprus.

Certain rail lines in the Middle East are renowned: the Orient Express from Calais, France, which technically terminated in Istanbul but actually continued to Konya and Aleppo on a reduced scale; the line from Cairo to Luxor and then to Aswan, part of the never-completed Cape-to-Cairo railway; the line built in Palestine in 1892 to transport pilgrims from Jaffa on the Mediterranean coast to Jerusalem; the Hijaz Railway from Damascus to Medina, which was built by the Ottomans at the beginning of the twentieth century for Muslim pilgrims traveling to the holy city of Mecca but which was wrecked south of Maan by the Arab Revolt in 1916–1917; and the line through the scenic Dez River gorge through the Zagros Mountains in southwestern Iran.

Airways and Airfields

The Middle East's location, astride the land, sea, and air routes across the tricontinental hub, led to establishment of a few transit airports prior to World War II. Rapid petroleum development stimulated demand for air service and airports after the early 1950s, and by the early 1990s, the Middle East possessed an excellent network of airports (see Map 9-2), including not only the world's largest but some of the world's technologically best equipped. Terminals such as Cairo, Jiddah, Riyadh, Tehran, Istanbul, and Lod (Tel Aviv) rank (in that order) between 26th and 50th on the list of international airports outside the United States in numbers of passengers embarked and disembarked.[2] Passenger traffic at all three Saudi airports decreased sharply after 1983–1984, although Jiddah, with 7.3 million arrivals and departures annually, ranks high because of the flow of pilgrims to nearby Mecca. Beirut is a bustling central airport in normal years but has even shut down completely at times in recent years. The number of airports with regularly scheduled service varies from 24 in Iran, 23 in Saudi Arabia, and 14 in Turkey to only 1 in Bahrain and Qatar.

Except that Bahrain, Qatar, Abu Dhabi, and Oman jointly operate one regional airline, Gulf Air, every country in the Middle East has its own national airline. Even tiny Dubai now operates Emirates Air, with a fleet of nine airbuses. Saudia, the airline of Saudi Arabia, is the largest and flies more than 100 major jet aircraft. Egypt Air and Iran Air fly 43 and 42 major aircraft, respectively. Most of the other national airlines have 20–30 major aircraft each, although Cyprus Airways registers only 9 jets. All of the major airports of the Middle East dispatch regular flights to Western European capitals, but most connections are intraregional, with the exception of those involving Israel's Ben Gurion Airport at Lod.

Water Transportation and Ports

A glance at Map 9-2 will serve as a reminder that land-water relationships in the Middle East offer easy human use of the interpenetrating seas. Only the heart of the Arabian Peninsula lies more than 200 miles/322 km from a seacoast. The seas have been sailed for at least 5,000 years, and numerous ruins of ports from earlier days are found in the Gulf and the eastern Mediterranean. Sailing the region's seas reached a golden age during the Abbasid Empire, especially during the eighth to twelfth centuries. The basic seagoing craft has long been some version of the ship popularly known as the dhow, and as they have been for more than 2,000 years, dhows are still equipped with the lateen sail, a triangular fore-and-aft sail hung from a very long yard. This rigging permits the ship to keep very close to the wind.

Following tradition, dhows still sail around the shores of the Gulf, along the coasts of Oman and Yemen, along the east African coast, and on the age-old routes to the mouths of the Indus and to the Malabar coast and Ceylon. Small modern ships are increasingly replacing the picturesque dhows; nevertheless, the latter serve a unique function and are still to be seen by the score anchored in "the Creek" in Dubai and in other Gulf ports, and they are still constructed in the traditional way in Kuwait, Bahrain, most of the coastal towns of the UAE, and in Oman.

Despite construction of the Suez Canal in the 1860s, the Middle East did not enter the mainstream of modern shipping until the mid-twentieth century. Turkey was most active in sailing, having regained its maritime lead after its World War I defeat; and as oil production mounted in the Gulf, the leading petroleum states entered the tanker market so as to be able to ship their own exports. Iran, Saudi Arabia, and Kuwait developed national tanker fleets, and Iraq and the UAE have also attempted to achieve a modest tonnage in tankers (see Table 9-2). Offering both a neutral flag of convenience and a long shipping tradition, Cyprus ranks first in the Middle East and fourth in the world in registered tonnage.

With the notable exceptions of the Nile, Tigris, and Euphrates, inland waterways, and therefore inland water transportation, are negligible in the region. Until the last few decades, shipping on the Nile had constituted the main method of movement of persons and goods up and down the linear axis of Egypt for more than 5,000 years. Construction of modern rail lines and highways has scarcely diminished either the number of picturesque but practical *faluqas,* the typical Nile sailboat, or the tonnage of cargo they transport. Modern motorized ships also transport hundreds of passengers up and down the river daily, many of them foreign tourists.

Shallower and more irregular than the Nile, the Tigris and the Euphrates are little used for navigation, and they can accommodate only boats of smaller size and draft. The picturesque circular rafts (*balams*), which were waterproofed with bitumen and used to float small loads downstream on the Tigris, have given way to modern transportation. By contrast, on the Shatt al-Arab, below the confluence of the Tigris and Euphrates, and on the Karun, which joins the Shatt al-Arab at Khorramshahr, there is normally a fair number of medium-large ships of considerable draft. Basrah, Khorramshahr, and Abadan, all fronting on the Shatt al-Arab, are normally three of the major ports, not only of the Gulf but of the Middle East. However, the Iran-Iraq war heavily damaged these port facilities and reduced navigation on the waterways to a minimum between 1980 and 1989. In early 1989, studies indicated clearing sunken ships and other debris from the Shatt al-Arab would cost about $2.5 billion. Damage was heaped on damage in early 1991 when coalition aircraft attacked the Basrah-area facilities.

The Marsh Arabs (Madan) along the regularly flooded lower Euphrates have been entirely dependent upon boat transportation for centuries, and their especially designed and locally built *mushhuf* is a variety of canoe ideally suited to transporting people and goods, especially loads of the local reeds, in the shallow but ever-present water. School children of the marshes use the *mushhuf* to go back and forth to school in the same way that children in some countries use bicycles.

Many modern Middle East coastal cities have served port functions for hundreds or even thousands of years—Istanbul (Byzantium or Con-stantinople), Beirut (Berytus), Jaffa, Alexandria, Aden, Muscat, and several Gulf ports. Some ports famed in antiquity now lack sufficient harborage or depth for modern shipping, such as Sidon and Tyre; other ports have silted up and now lie well inland, as is true of Miletus, Ephesus, and Ur, for example.

By virtue of the tonnage represented by the millions of barrels of oil pumped through an export terminal, large oil-shipping ports exceed even the most major dry-cargo ports in tonnage handled. (An average barrel of petroleum weighs about 300 lb./136 kg, so that only 7.35 bbl weigh 1 mt.) Petroleum shipments pushed Saudi Arabia to first rank and Iran to third rank in export tonnage among all countries of the world in 1982, before the drop in the oil export market. Thus, the relative ranking of Middle East general-cargo ports differs from the ranking of ports that include oil handling.

By the early 1990s, major modern ports were well distributed among the Middle East states, with four ports handling more than 10 million tons of dry cargo annually: Jiddah, Saudi Arabia's Red Sea port, important both for goods and for the pilgrims to Mecca who arrive by sea; Alexandria, Egypt's Mediterranean port at the western mouth of the Nile; Shuwaykh, the port of Kuwait (prior to the Iraqi invasion, although its tonnage was rapidly increasing again in 1992); and Dammam, the Saudi Gulf port. (For comparison, the port of Los Angeles, California, handled 13.4 million tons of international cargo during a comparable period.)

Seven Middle East ports handle 5–7 million tons of general cargo annually: Iskenderun (Alexandretta), a complex of facilities in the northeastern corner of the Mediterranean serving partly as a transit port for Turkey's neighbors; Bandar-e Khomeyni (formerly Bandar-e Shahpur), one of Iran's two main ports in the northern Gulf; Haifa, the principal general-cargo port of Israel; Aqabah, on Jordan's single stretch of coastline; Dubai, where Port Rashid is one of the largest in area in the Middle East; Ashdod, Israel's southern port on the Mediterranean; and (in normal times) Basrah, on the Shatt al-Arab, Iraq's main port but inactive during the Iran-Iraq war and again after early 1991.

TABLE 9-3: FOREIGN TRADE: EXPORTS AND IMPORTS (Values and selected products)

COUNTRY	1	2	3	4	5	6	7	8	9	10
	TOTAL VALUE, (MILLIONS $US)		RAW MATERIALS (%)				MANFCTRD GOODS (%)			
			AGRIC, ETC.		FUEL/ENR		TOTAL		% MACH/TE	
	EXPORTS	IMPORTS	EXP	IMP	EXP	IMP	EXP	IMP	EXP	IMP
Bahrain (1988)	2,273.7	2,362.1	0.4	11.4	80.5	45.9	18.9	42.2	0.6	15.7
Cyprus (1987)	619.9	1,479.9	33.2	15.2	5.2	12.3	59.6	61.7	9.8	24.5
Egypt (1988)	5,706.3	23,297.9	18.4	32.8	33.2	2.6	48.0	63.5	0.3	26.8
Iran (1985)	13,328.0	11,635.0	?	20.9	98.0	2.1	?	77.1	?	37.6
Iraq (1986)	9,007.0	10,190.0	0.4	17.6	99.6	0.3	?	81.9	?	39.8
Israel (1989)	10,720.2	13,166.4	10.4	11.4	0.6	8.5	58.1	56.3	26.5	23.4
Jordan (1988)	1,035.7	2,786.1	9.7	20.9	0.1	15.5	50.8	62.1	5.8	22.6
Kuwait (1986)	9,052.0	5,691.2	1.3	18.6	84.4	0.5	14.1	80.3	6.6	38.9
Lebanon (1988)	863.0	2,705.0	14.4	17.3	?	3.6	85.6	79.1	18.2	29.3
Oman (1988)	2,992.0	2,200.4	3.0	20.4	86.6	1.5	10.3	77.4	6.0	33.4
Qatar (1987)	1,984.6	1,134.0	?	20.4	93.9	0.8	14.6	76.9	6.2	31.5
Saudi Arabia ('88)	23,737.2	21,784.2	1.5	16.7	85.1	0.3	12.9	82.3	0.1	34.4
Syria (1987)	2,476.8	4,260.2	12.8	17.5	51.8	19.8	31.3	61.7	0.5	25.1
Turkey (1988)	11,662.0	14,335.4	27.7	9.4	2.9	21.3	66.0	65.1	6.4	29.4
UAE (1986)	15,837.4	6,776.8	2.0	18.8	89.9	4.8	8.0	75.4	2.5	30.7
Yemen (1986-1987)										
North	47.5	1,027.3	46.3	36.0	35.7	2.4	18.1	61.2	?	18.9
South	290.1	483.2	?	38.6	95.9	15.3	?	46.2	?	20.5
Gaza (1987)	157.1	412.1	---	—	—	---	---	---	---	—
West Bank (1987)	228.2	639.1	---	—	—	---	---	---	---	—
TOTAL	112,018.7	126,366.3	---	—	—	`---	---	---	---	—
U. K. (1989)	152,900.6	198,055.6	8.4	13.2	6.2	5.2	82.0	78.3	40.4	38.0
Spain (1988)	40,466.6	60,556.5	20.0	15.5	4.7	11.4	74.1	70.2	33.5	39.1

Columns 3 and 4 include animal and vegetable foods, beverages, and industrial agricultural products (tobacco, cotton. etc.). Columns 5 and 6 (Fuels and Energy materials) include mineral fuels (petroleum, natural gas, coal, lignite), lubricants, and related products. Manufactured goods includes all classes of manufactured products, including machinery. "% Mach/TE" indicates the percentage of machinery and transportation equipment included in the percentage total of manufactures. Source: *Britannica World Data 1991.* (With permission)

Trade

Intraregional trade in the Middle East (Table 9-3) has expanded greatly since the 1950s. Non-oil producers import petroleum from their oil-exporting neighbors, and several such importers exchange food products in return. Quantitatively, only the oil-deficient industrialized countries can absorb the enormous petroleum exports of the Gulf states, and the developing petroleum-exporting countries turn to their industrialized-country customers for the advanced technology items that constitute the bulk of their nonfood imports (Table 9-4).

Half of the states in the region include at least one other Middle East country as one of their three leading customers according to percentage of value of commodities traded. (All rankings of countries and commodities in this discussion are based on value percentages.) Three of Jordan's and Lebanon's top five customers are Middle East states. Isolated as it has been from its neighbors, Israel had no overt trade with its neighbors until the Camp David accords, which provided that Israel could purchase its petroleum supplies from Egypt. One result was that Israel became Egypt's second-largest customer for several years. Prior to 1967, Israel received most of its petro-

TABLE 9-4:   DIRECTIONS OF FOREIGN TRADE (Export and import percentages)

COUNTRY	1 YEAR	2 3 4 5 PERCENTAGE OF EXPORTS TO				6 7 8 9 PERCENTAGE OF IMPORTS FROM			
		EEC	USA	JAPAN	SU/EE	EEC	USA	JAPAN	SU/EE
Bahrain	1988	5.9	3.4	9.5	---	18.9	10.3	4.4	---
Cyprus	1987	41.0	1.8	0.5	5.0	56.9	4.5	10.2	5.9
Egypt	1988	37.1	6.3	4.7	17.8	40.8	11.9	5.0	10.0
Iran	1985	35.5	5.2	17.2	5.2	38.5	0.7	12.9	7.2
Iraq	1986	37.4	5.7	11.7	0.2	31.4	5.7	20.4	3.4
Israel	1989	31.7	31.0	7.1	0.7	50.6	17.9	2.7	0.4
Jordan	1988	9.7	1.0	1.9	3.8	29.3	12.6	5.3	5.9
Kuwait	1986	26.6	3.6	13.8	0.2	31.3	12.3	23.6	1.0
Lebanon	1988	14.1	4.4	0.3	5.4	41.0	5.0	3.2	12.2
Oman	1988	10.4	3.0	51.3	---	31.6	8.8	16.8	0.1
Qatar	1987	12.0	0.2	38.5	---	39.3	11.9	16.3	0.4
Saudi Arabia	1988	21.4	8.4	7.8	0.1	33.5	16.2	16.0	1.0
Syria	1987	47.4	0.6	0.1	36.2	35.3	5.3	3.0	17.0
Turkey	1988	43.7	6.5	1.8	4.7	41.1	10.6	3.9	6.1
UAE	1986	5.8	3.2	49.3	---	34.9	9.2	17.5	0.4
Yemen	1986	27.2	6.9	13.8	2.4	72.1	12.6	13.4	23.3

EEC=the twelve members (as of the years covered) of the European Economic Community (Common Market). USA=United States. SU/EE=pre-1991 Soviet Union and its seven East European satellites ("Soviet Bloc"). Many of the figures are estimates based on data from trading partners. Figures for the two Yemens are combined in this table. Source: *Britannica World Data 1991.* (With permission)

leum from Iran, and Iran continued to supply a high percentage of Israel's petroleum needs until 1979 and again in the late 1980s.

It should be noted that of the relatively limited exports from the non-oil Middle East states, the exports to neighboring states normally form a high percentage. For example, Jordan produces only modest amounts of vegetables, pharmaceuticals, and machinery, but its sales of such items to Iraq and Saudi Arabia constituted more than half of its total exports before 1991. Iraq was particularly important in Jordan's foreign trade, since it was Jordan's main customer and virtually its main supplier prior to August 1990. The Gulf crisis adversely affected Jordan's trade with both its main partners. Similarly, Lebanon exports primarily fruits and vegetables, but also modest amounts of paint, machinery, and small manufactures, and sales of such items to Saudi Arabia were formerly one-third its total foreign sales. As Lebanon's output diminished during the fighting of the late 1980s, exports were distributed more evenly among several customers. By contrast,

purchases of these relatively low-value and low-technology items make up an almost negligible percentage of all purchases by Saudi Arabia or Iraq. An overall significant aspect of the exports from Lebanon, Bahrain, and the UAE is that many of the exports are, in fact, reexports. Such trade has made Dubai and Sharjah major commercial centers.

From the general perspective of Middle East trade, the overwhelmingly main export of the area to the rest of the world is petroleum, with petroleum and petroleum products constituting at least 85 percent of the primary exports of all the major oil producers and normally up to 99 percent of the exports of Iraq. Petroleum even constitutes one-third of the exports of Egypt and one-half of those of Syria (see Table 9-3).

Among the top two or three non-oil exports of several states are, by percentage, fruits and vegetables (Cyprus, Turkey, Lebanon, Jordan, Syria, Israel, Yemen, Egypt); chemicals (Israel, Saudi Arabia, Qatar, Syria, Turkey, Jordan); cotton (Egypt, Yemen); textiles (Turkey, Syria, Egypt, Israel); and clothing (Cyprus, Turkey, Israel). A few of the region's specialty exports include aluminum (Bahrain, Egypt, UAE), footwear (Cyprus), and phosphates (Jordan, Israel, Syria, Egypt, and Iraq). A unique export from the region is cut diamonds from Israel, with the gems forming 29 percent of the state's exports. Armaments from Israel constitute more than 25 percent of its exports and are another unusual export item from the regional perspective.

As they are around the world, oil and petroleum products are the main imports of the nonoil states of the Middle East (see Table 9-3). They constitute around 20 percent of Turkey's and 16 percent of Jordan's imports but only 4 percent of Lebanon's. Although almost 46 percent of Bahrain's imports is crude petroleum, through a direct pipeline from Saudi Arabia, that crude is refined in the island's Sitra refinery and is reexported as product.

Food ranks among the three leading imports into virtually all Middle East countries with the notable exception of Turkey. Nearly one-fourth of Egypt's imports is foodstuffs, a major shift from the early 1960s. Again with the exception of Turkey, Israel's food import percentage is the lowest among the Middle East countries. Excluding food, the region's leading three or four imports by percentage are usually machinery, motor vehicles, chemicals, and iron and steel. Until the worst years of Lebanon's civil war, that country's second leading import was gold bullion. In Israel, the leading import (23 percent by value) is rough diamonds, which are cut and reexported.[3]

10

Where People
Congregate

Settlers and Settlements

Variety of Patterns

The Middle East has a wide range of settlement types, forms, and functions within its great variety of environments, historical traditions, and state systems. In size, settlements range from hamlets sheltering a dozen families to one of the largest cities in the world (Cairo). Villages by the scores of thousands dot the agricultural landscape, from Turkey's bridgehead in Europe to the cultivated mountain valleys of northeastern Iran (Figs. 10-1 and 10-2), and more than 155 cities have passed the 100,000 population mark. In morphology, Middle East settlements have traditionally exhibited a wide variety of forms, from very compact to widely dispersed, depending on topography, water supply, and other influences.[1]

Settlements in intensively irrigated areas, such as the Nile Valley and Delta, are compact to conserve valuable farmland (Chap. 20), whereas villages on the steppes of Syria and Iran show a more dispersed pattern (Fig. 10-1). Settlements that were—or still are—walled exhibit the usual crowding of enclosed places; but urban expansion since World War II has tended to open the settlement texture on the fringes, and newly established suburbs are more dispersed than are settlements that evolved in earlier centuries (Map 10-1). The typical Middle East urban structure has certain characteristic features, which have traditionally been designated as "Islamic."

The agricultural-settlement landscapes of the Middle East differ markedly from the rural landscapes of humid Western Europe and eastern North America. From house design and construction materials to street patterns and connecting roads, the settlements express their regional context—and are somewhat comparable to settlements in northern Mexico and the southwestern United States. The irregular patterns of fields around the agricultural villages on the Jordanian steppe contrast sharply with the geometric grid of the U.S. Corn Belt, and the pattern of wheat and barley fields on the steppes of the inner Fertile Crescent bears little resemblance to the field pattern in the intensively irrigated Nile Valley and Delta. Similarly, the agricultural villages and their surrounding fields in the basins and valleys of Iran, which are irrigated by qanats, contrast with villages perched on terraced mountain slopes in Lebanon and Yemen.

Five Types of Patterns

Five settlement patterns have evolved: (1) the house and its elements (courtyard, storage facilities, adjacent garden, and perhaps even its construction materials); (2) houses and other structures within the settlement; (3) distribution of settlements and their related fields over the landscape; (4) interdependent relationships among the settlements (central places); and (5) links (roads and paths) between settlements. Although settlement patterns have become immensely more complex since the 1950s, these fundamental categories are the same.

However managed, the five settlement patterns interact and are interrelated in a regional spatial system. Nomads or scattered peasants are interdependent with nearby villages and cities, villages with their central city, cities with their hinterland villages, and so on up and down the

Figure 10-1. *Typical agricultural village on the Iranian Plateau: Mud houses with flat roofs, small wall-enclosed courtyards, animal-manure patties drying in the sun for fuel, hay stacked on the corners of roofs to protect it from wandering animals, no systematic street pattern, few modern facilities.*

Figure 10-2. *Typical Kurdish village, northeastern Iraq, characteristic of such settlements extending from the lower Euphrates Valley in southeastern Turkey to well into Iran. Thousands of such villages were destroyed by the Iraqi government and their inhabitants resettled in government-controlled towns during the 1980s.*

hierarchy. Since no one element is an isolate, each can be fully understood only in its regional context.[2]

Many factors influence patterns of distribution, density, and dispersion of human groupings and their structures. Water supply is always a basic consideration, but other ecological factors are also significant: topography, vegetation, climate, soils. Cultural factors are often equally influential: transportation facilities, government support, regional function, defense, aesthetics, traditions, and industrial relationships. Such considerations condition a settlement's size, shape, morphology, function, and position within the regional hierarchy of places; and as Middle East settlements have vividly demonstrated since World War II, the historical-technological context is a compelling factor.

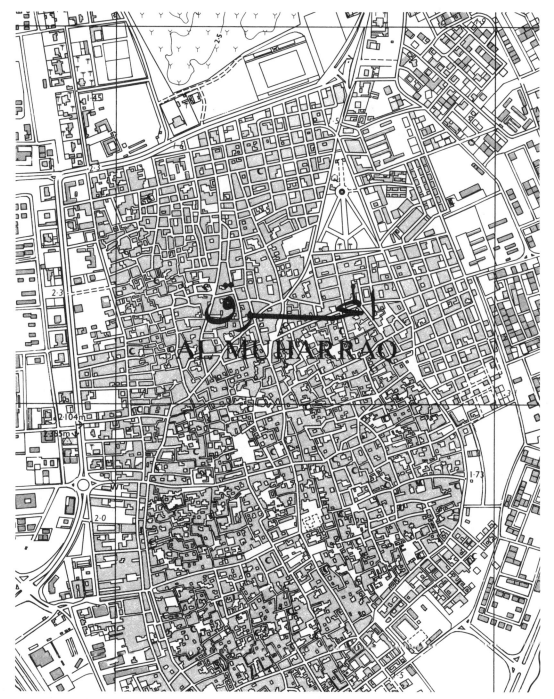

Map 10-1. *Muharraq, Bahrain: Traditional street pattern in an Islamic city—unplanned, narrow, winding. On the edges of the old core are planned, right-angle streets with larger blocks of post-1960 period. Area shown is same as that in Figure 10-3. (Courtesy Survey Directorate, Bahrain)*

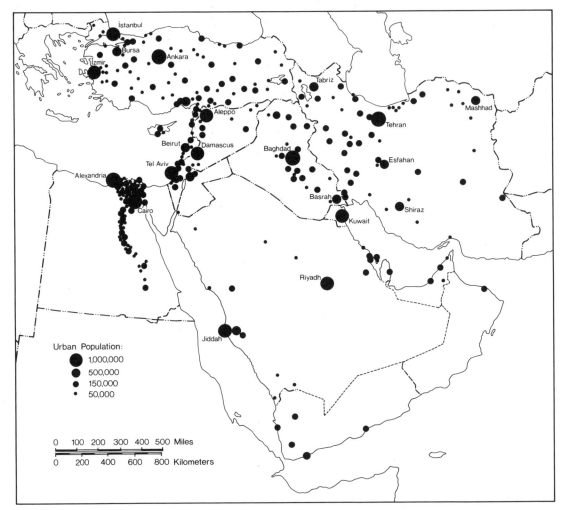

Map 10-2. *Pattern of distribution of urban populations. Note concentration of cities in the northern half of the region, in the Levant, and especially in the Nile Valley and Delta.*

Obviously, then, the ways in which people group themselves and their structures are a major expression of people's management of the space in which they live. Countryside, village, and city make up a spatial system, an ensemble of interacting subsystems that combine in a dynamic whole. None is a discrete realm unto itself.[3]

Overall Settlement Pattern

The distribution of population has already been examined (see Chap. 6). Map 10-2 shows that the principal concentrations of population, and therefore settlements, are in the Nile Valley and

Delta, Asia Minor, western Iran, and the Levant, with secondary concentrations along the Tigris and Euphrates rivers. Map 6-2 indicates the virtually uninhabited areas of the region and emphasizes the repelling influence of extreme aridity on permanent human settlement.

Until the mid-twentieth century, the overwhelming majority of Middle Easterners resided in villages. With the exception of nomads, whose mode of "settlement" is a special case, the isolated rural resident was rare in the Middle East and was restricted to special environments in Asia Minor and northwestern Iran. Although cities had long been important in the socioeconomic pattern of the region, they had declined in number, size, and importance after the sixteenth century. Modernization of the region, especially in the newly wealthy petroleum-exporting states, reversed the rural-urban percentages and gave impetus to a steady urbanization of the Middle East.

Urbanization

By the late 1980s, more than 50 percent of the population of the Middle East lived in cities. The urban trend was primarily the result of internal migrations from the villages to the cities and, in the Gulf, also of immigration from neighboring areas such as Yemen, Pakistan, and Jordan.

Unusual circumstances have created extraordinary percentages of urbanization in certain areas. Petroleum development attracted concentrations of population in virtual city-states on the western desert coastal fringe of the Gulf, areas that formerly supported only fishing hamlets on the coast and nomads in the hinterland. Today, virtually the entire population along this fringe is technically urban. Kuwait, for example, exploded from approximately 50,000 people in 1940 to 2.1 million in 1990, prior to the Iraqi invasion, nearly all of whom lived in Kuwait City and its immediate suburbs. Similar urbanization is found in Bahrain, Qatar, and the UAE.

For different reasons, urbanization is also high in Israel, despite the existence of scores of small settlements of several types. The high degree of urbanization in Iraq and Lebanon is a direct result of the movement of villagers into two or three major cities prior to warfare in both countries—Baghdad, Basrah (which was greatly reduced in population during the wars of 1980–1988 and 1990–1991), and Mosul in Iraq and Beirut and Tripoli in Lebanon. Even Egypt, the agricultural country par excellence, is approaching 45 percent urbanization. Surplus agricultural workers from the villages have migrated into Cairo especially, as well as Alexandria and other cities exceeding 200,000 population. A similar inpouring of villagers into Tehran has prompted its population to surge to more than 6 million, with Mashhad near 1.5 million and Esfahan and Tabriz near 1 million each. Across the Gulf, Saudi Arabia experienced remarkable urbanization during the 1970s and early 1980s. Riyadh, a desert town of 30,000 before World War II, exploded during the kingdom's oil boom and by unofficial estimate exceeded 2 million in the early 1990s.

Similarly, the urbanization that has characterized population movements in much of the world since midcentury has resulted in special permutations in the Middle East (see Chap. 6). Not only have millions of expatriates swelled the populations of the Gulf cities (Kuwait [until the Iraqi invasion precipitated a reverse flow of expatriates], Dammam, al-Khobar, Manama, Doha, Abu Dhabi, Dubai, Ahvaz, Bandar-e Abbas, and others), but also hundreds of thousands of nomads in much of the Middle East have abandoned their wandering life-style to become city dwellers. This process of sedentarization has been one of the major socioeconomic phenomena of the Middle East during the last several decades.

Internal Structures of Cities

The internal morphological and structural patterns of settlements reflect interaction between urban development and historical-geographical influences. These patterns include the street pattern, placement of central squares and other open areas, location and shape of commercial activities, presence and character of ethnic concentrations, and other aspects of settlements. Identification and analysis of such characteristics aid in understanding the initial role intended for a settlement in its regional system, as well as understanding subsequent accretions to its functions, successive modifications of the urban morphology, and the interrelations between the settlement and its several neighbors.

For many centuries past, the traditional Middle East settlement, whether village or city, has had a highly irregular pattern of narrow streets, with house blocks uneven in size and "cellular" because of the usual open courtyard in each house (Fig. 10-3). Such an appearance identifies the older core of virtually every Middle East city that developed before 1800 and also typifies villages in the region that predate the nineteenth century. The fundamental compactness of settlements in areas of aridity and heat minimized the length of water conduits and also reduced heat from the direct sun. Streets were pathways or

Figure 10-3. *Traditional pattern of houses and streets in a small Islamic city. Air view in the mid-1960s, looking southwest along causeway connecting Muharraq (foreground) with Manama, capital of Bahrain. Compare patterns in this photograph with map of the area (Map 10-1).*

lanes among the houses, and since wheeled vehicles were rarely used during the periods of morphological evolution of most of the towns, the narrow lanes were sufficient for pedestrians, porters, and animals.

Urban Core Elements

Except in Israel, Cyprus, and parts of Lebanon, virtually every older town and city has a core area comprising six elements: (1) a large mosque—the Friday Mosque (*Masjid al-Jami*); (2) the city's principal educational facilities, the *madrassah,* typically operated in conjunction with the mosque; (3) the main public water-based facilities—drinking fountains, latrines, and baths (*hammams*); (4) courts and other institutions of justice along with other related administrative institutions, depending upon the role of the particular city; (5) the citadel (*al-qalah*), often large and well fortified in most older cities; and (6) most extensive of all in area, the commercial district.

The last element—the very characteristic Middle Eastern *suq* (Arabic), *bazaar* (Persian), or *çarsı* (Turkish)—sometimes surrounds the other core elements and sometimes radiates along one

main axis in an alignment conditioned by environmental factors. Any major *suq* includes numerous craft shops in which artisans produce such items as copper and brass wares, leather goods, textiles, jewelry, and perhaps such specialty goods as inlaid woods. Formerly, inns (caravanserais and khans), which provided housing for travelers and their animal trains, were also included in or were adjacent to the *suq* area. Offices for levying customs (*gumruk*), banking facilities—especially for currency exchange—and related financial offices were usually included in the commercial core, and some still are.

Urban Quarters

Although the system is declining, the Middle East city has traditionally been divided into "quarters" (*harat, rayyat, mahallat, akhtat*). Many such quarters were closely knit and homogeneous communities in which people sought safety and protection among others of their own kind. Such group protection was the main or only recourse during many lengthy periods, and identity factors included religion, ethnicity, and village origin. There were commonly quarters, among religions, for Christians, Jews, Armenians, and Muslims; among Muslims, for Kurds, Turkmen, Persians, and Turks; among Arab Muslims, for Sunni, Shii, Druzes, or for respective villagers.

The contemporary quarters in most older Middle East cities had their genesis during the tenth century, the second or third century after the entrenchment of Islam in most of the region. It was during this time that the concept of "clients" (*mawali*) and "people of the book" (*ahl al-kitab*) became a firm tradition (see Chap. 6). There were as many as 37 quarters in medieval Cairo, 40 in Jerusalem (but only 9 major ones), 50 in Aleppo, and an impressive 70 in Damascus. Sectors for Europeans were set aside in the Galatea section of Constantinople for many centuries by both the Byzantines and the Ottomans, and similar European quarters evolved in several other cities after 1900 and especially after World War II—in Beirut, Damascus, Cairo, Baghdad, Tehran, and Gulf cities.

The expansion of diplomatic communities in burgeoning Middle East capitals added to the "foreign" quarters and in some cases created predominantly *corps diplomatique* enclaves, although the developments in Beirut and Tehran during the 1980s disrupted this development. When the Saudi government permitted the shift of foreign embassies from Jiddah to Riyadh in the early 1980s, it set aside a spacious new area in Riyadh for development of a splendid, exclusive diplomatic quarter. The Omani government has likewise established a diplomatic quarter in the new suburb of al-Khuwair, west of Muscat, where both Omani government ministries and foreign embassies are concentrated.

In most cities in the region, each major urban quarter replicated the city core on a reduced scale. During the centuries that most major Middle East cities evolved, a neighborhood mosque was required every few blocks to permit the muazzin (muezzin) giving the call to prayer to be heard from the mosque minaret. A hierarchy of mosques often developed, with the main mosque in a quarter becoming the hub for reduced versions of the institutions and facilities found in the city core. Facilities necessary for a subsection's social life were a *suq,* including bakeries, fruit and vegetable sellers, spice and ghee merchants, and public kitchen and restaurant;

hammam; and khan. Spacing among mosques increased after World War II when electronic amplifiers and loudspeaker systems greatly increased the distance over which the muazzin could be heard. Indeed, the call to prayer and Quranic readings have increasingly been tape recorded and, in many places, televised.

In several Islamic cities, as in certain well-known cities in Christendom, the nucleus is a religious monument or shrine dedicated to a religious leader or saint. The shrine attracts the usual array of ancillary facilities and institutions, particularly service facilities for the visiting pilgrims. Mecca is the prime city of pilgrimage in Islam, although it had an important shrine and served a significant commercial function prior to the time of Muhammad. Other major shrine cities are Medina, with the tomb of the Prophet Muhammad; Karbala and al-Najaf, just west of the Euphrates in Iraq, the two main Shii shrines; Mashhad and Qom in Iran, both tomb shrines of Shii imams; and such multifunctional cities as Jerusalem, Damascus, Konya, Istanbul, and others with major shrines that attract thousands of pilgrims annually.

Significant as the mosque and related core elements may be in Middle East cities, residential sections obviously occupy most of the built-up areas. Here the texture is finer and more uniform than in the grosser pattern of the city core. The traditional house, although not necessarily the contemporary dwelling, in the Middle East city is modest in size, with walls built to the edge of the property line, an open courtyard in the center or to one side, and different living quarters for males and females. Male members of the family have more open quarters as opposed to women's quarters, which have shuttered windows and generally greater privacy. Typically, the house is one or two stories high, and the staircase to the second story, if any, is in the courtyard. The flat roof is often surrounded by a low parapet and is regularly used by the family as a sleeping area during the warm season, which is also the dry season for most of the Middle East. The overall pattern of such houses, built wall against wall in small blocks and divided by narrow zigzagging streets, is one of cellular regularity (see Fig. 10-3).

These traditional characteristics have been appreciably modified with the expansion and mod-

Figure 10-4. *Hayil, village in the Yemen Central Highlands, about 50 miles/80 km south of Sana. Typical small fortress village built during the unsafe times 200–300 years ago when the central government was unable to provide security to the countryside.*

ernization of settlements virtually everywhere in the Middle East since 1950. New and old have come face to face. Although the traditional has yielded to the advantages of modern technology, the heritage of the past in many cities, but not in all parts and not in all cities, is often still perceptible in both architecture and city planning. Villages especially retain the character of fortified compounds and protected sites in certain areas (Fig. 10-4). Air-conditioning permits flexibility in house design, especially in window arrangement, and in many respects, middle-class and upper middle-class residences in many cities of the region would be acclaimed by Westerners of comparable income levels. Nevertheless, the traditional construction of walls along the property lines, preference for courtyards, and limited yard or garden area are readily identifiable.

A more striking departure from tradition is seen in the post-1960 urban street design. With very high automobile ownership per family in much of the region (see Table 9-2), especially in the Gulf area and in Cyprus and Israel, many new streets have been designed with generous widths. Newly planned cities such as Kuwait, Doha, Baghdad, Riyadh, Dammam, and Dubai had adequate areas of desert over which to ex-

pand, and planners took advantage of the space to provide wide main boulevards and wide secondary and tertiary streets in the new quarters, in contrast to the traditional lanes in older quarters.

Blending of traditional and modern also characterizes the market sections of many Middle East cities. The basic principle of the *suq*, with its rows of small shops, is too deeply ingrained in Middle East tradition and has served the purpose too well and too long to be discarded entirely in preference to European or American mercantile fashions. The old vaulted underground aisles lined with shops, or the palm-frond-covered lines of shops aboveground, still exist in less affluent areas or in carefully preserved places.

However, many old *suqs* have been replaced in the most extensively modernized cities with attractive air-conditioned commercial centers that combine the best features of the traditional *suq* and the American shopping mall—itself an adaptation of the oriental *suq* (Fig. 10-5 and Chap. 18). The range of goods traditionally offered for sale has also been enormously expanded since the 1950s, so that the *suqs* in Cairo, Riyadh, and Abu Dhabi; the bazaars in Esfahan, Tabriz, and Tehran; and the *çarsıs* in Istanbul, Konya, and Er-

Figure 10-5. *The huge Jamjoom shopping and business center, Jiddah, Saudi Arabia. Such centers have come full circle, having been modeled after U.S. shopping malls, which in turn were modeled after Middle Eastern* suqs *and bazaars.*

zurum now also offer transistor radios, stereo systems, Japanese and Swiss watches, pocket calculators, tape recorders, and a full range of household electric appliances. Indeed, the huge Shakiyah shopping center in Riyadh, Jamjoom Center in Jiddah, Suq al-Majariah in Sharjah, and similar centers in Kuwait are crammed with electronic and photographic items, jewelry, apparel, toys, and similar items to match the desires of the most avid consumer.

Urban areas planned and constructed since 1960 display a markedly different morphology from the older sectors, and dramatic changes in structural and textural patterns designate the lines beyond which the new planning has been carried out (Map 10-1). Such changes are obvious in Damascus, Jerusalem, Ankara, and Abu Dhabi; the urban morphology of the West is especially evident in cities along the western Gulf, from Kuwait to Dubai, but also in Istanbul, Cairo, Beirut, and Tel Aviv. High-rise office and apartment buildings, extensive suburbs, the coalescence of cities into conurbations, divided freeways (dual carriageways), and futuristic airports have become commonplace in only two decades.

Urban Problems and Prospects

In many cities where expansion was extreme, whether in Ankara, Baghdad, Amman, Abu Dhabi, or a score of other explosively growing metropolitan areas, newcomers poured into the urban fringe and erected spontaneous (squatter) settlements faster than adequate housing could be planned and constructed. Fortunately, in much of the Gulf area, central government funds from petroleum exports were available for adequate public housing to replace the squatter huts, although construction inevitably lagged behind the influx of new population. Lacking great oil income, Turkey, Jordan, and Egypt have found it difficult to fund housing in expanding areas. Jordan, Lebanon, and Syria faced the unique problem of having both unofficial and official Palestinian refugee camps spring up around Jericho, Amman, Irbid, Sidon, Beirut, and Dara. Improved housing for the refugees was financially and politically difficult to provide, even over a period of more than four decades. Israel is a special case in that foreign aid from both private and government sources supplied reasonably adequate amounts for housing—after some delay—the flood of immigrants in the late 1940s and the 1950s. Even with the 1991–1992 controversy over a U.S. loan guarantee to defray the cost of absorbing the hundreds of thousands of Jews from the former Soviet Union, Israel continued for several months to build impressive houses for the newcomers (see Chap. 15).

Spontaneous settlements in Turkey, *gecekondus,* were first built when surplus agricultural families began migrating into main urban centers—Istanbul, Izmir, Ankara—after World War II. These migrants erected simple huts on the urban fringes, and under Turkish law, a house built and roofed before government authorities can prohibit further construction must be allowed to stand where and as built. Most of the huts were constructed between dusk and dawn to avoid observation by authorities, hence the name *gecekondu* ("built overnight"), and the government generally did not attempt to prohibit the *gecekondu* settlements.

Under similar circumstances in Iraq, when villagers and Bedouins poured into Baghdad in search of employment and improved living standards during the 1950s, authorities were overwhelmed in their limited efforts to provide planning, space, and quarters for the hundreds of thousands of migrants. The settlers themselves built the same type of mud huts that lower economic group members had built in Mesopotamia for thousands of years—solid mud walls with palm fronds and reed mats forming a pitched roof. Spaced only a few feet apart and lacking basic amenities, these *sarifah* huts multiplied into sprawling settlements until they were replaced by public housing as Iraqi oil income increased.

Despite the problems of numbers in many instances, town planning in the Middle East has been on a scale unprecedented in the region's history and perhaps unmatched anywhere else in the world. The reconstruction of war-devastated cities in Europe during the 1950s demanded extraordinary town-planning efforts, and expertise developed at that time was later applied to the unparalleled urban expansion in the Gulf area. Urban planners had to be imported by most of

the rapidly expanding Middle East countries, since their own experts were few in number and were relatively inexperienced in such large-scale planning.

Most of the Gulf states turned to the British for expertise, since most of these countries had been under British tutelage prior to gaining independence in the 1960s and early 1970s. One consequence is that major Gulf cities bear the unmistakable stamp of British town-planning concepts, for example, the traffic "roundabout," known as a rotary or traffic circle in the United States, where it is rarely used. Local technicians were rapidly trained in town planning, and Middle East governments soon took over the enormous task of planning their own cities and villages. Some of the designs are striking, having been facilitated by the fact that cost of execution was often no object.

Planning in Israel after 1948 is unique in that a high degree of expertise had been developed during the mandate years and also a large number of expert planners immigrated to the Jewish state. As the new state expanded, they participated in a highly coordinated and well-financed program for planning at every level. The site of each settlement was carefully selected, whether as an adjunct to a former Arab village, a restoration of a known or supposed biblical site, or a completely new settlement. Once the site was determined, the internal design of the settlement was drawn up, and a selection of house types was supplied by the planners. Such planning assured balanced distribution of immigrants, efficient use of water, economic activity for the new inhabitants, and a systematic security pattern in the expanding state.[4] The category of settlement for a given site was also determined by the central planners—kibbutz, moshav, *nahal,* or multifunction town (see Chap. 15).

Despite planning efforts, virtually every Middle East city—and especially those with a population of more than 500,000—has found itself faced with the same urban problems that have caused difficulties in similar cities elsewhere and particularly those in the Third World. Traffic problems are near the top of the list, as increasing affluence doubles and triples the number of automobiles crowding onto the space allotted to them, which is expanding only slowly. Crowded streets, inexperienced drivers, lack of parking facilities, lack of adequate traffic policing, narrow streets in the older sections that often house the commercial core, problems with traffic lights, and, in some cities (Cairo, as a prime example), admixtures of animals and carts—all combine to create a traffic nightmare in many of the region's larger cities. Tehran, Beirut, Cairo, and Istanbul rank high on a world traveler's list of cities with the worst traffic congestion.

Along with traffic problems, some major cities of the region also struggle with serious shortages of water, gas, electricity, sewerage facilities, telephones, and similar utilities and services. Even cities in the more humid areas—Istanbul, Beirut, Haifa—suffer water shortages during the long, dry summers because their water distribution systems are inadequate. Likewise, Cairo, with a plentiful source of water in the Nile, may have water shortages during the hot summer as a result of an incapacity to distribute supplies at a sufficient rate. For many years municipal water was supplied in Ankara for only brief periods two or three times a day, and in Beirut, apartment houses even in normal times are, by design, supplied with water through such small pipes that it must be stored during the night in roof tanks, one for each apartment.

Coastal plain cities in Israel recycle their treated sewage in order to sustain a water supply, pumping the treated waste back into the aquifers under the coastal plain from which the basic water supply is obtained. Continuous recycling without plentiful recharging by natural runoff in dry years affects the taste of the drinking water in the Tel Aviv metropolitan area and worries some Israeli planners, but the procedure is basically a conservational success. Occasional wet years, such as the winter of 1991–1992, help counteract some of the problems.

Kuwait City is unique in having originally developed with virtually no natural surface or underground water supply. During earlier centuries, the small village on Kuwait Bay brought most of its fresh water in goatskins and other similar containers by boat from the Shatt al-

Arab, south of Basrah. With the beginning of its petroleum age, Kuwait took advantage of the availability of large supplies of fuel (and funds) to distill seawater in order to obtain its water supplies. In the mid-1950s, the price of a gallon of water delivered by tanker truck in Kuwait equaled the price of a gallon of gasoline. As the city's population doubled and redoubled, Kuwait installed additional and more efficient distillation facilities, along with exploiting newly discovered, limited groundwater supplies north of the bay. Distillation of seawater has been practiced on an increasing scale by other cities along the Gulf coast and on the Red Sea coast since 1970. By the early 1990s, Saudi Arabia alone had installed 23 large desalination plants, and it is probable that at least 40 such plants will be in operation in the region by the mid-1990s.

Partly because of a failure to modernize for either financial or technical reasons, partly because of problems with distribution systems, many Middle East cities and a substantially higher percentage of towns and villages utilize water that cannot be relied upon to be safe to drink as it comes from the tap. Since many residents nevertheless drink the water, intestinal parasitic diseases are endemic. Whereas Istanbul, Nicosia, Baghdad, Cairo, Damascus, and Tel Aviv supply safe potable water, Ankara, Beirut, and Amman, among other capitals, do not.

Nearly all Middle East cities have developed the capacity to supply reasonably reliable electrical power to their citizens. The electricity age has thoroughly pervaded the Middle East region and, indeed, has swept the Levant and the Gulf as much as it has most areas of Western Europe and North America. Seemingly inexhaustible supplies of energy in the Gulf have permitted the servicing of virtually every urban household with electricity, and air-conditioning, refrigeration, and a full range of household appliances have become as common as in American cities.

The typical settlement morphology in the Middle East since the 1950s has evolved under unique conditions. Explosive development accompanying the oil boom has had profound effects on settlements in the region, especially in the Gulf area. There the impact of Western technological influences on Middle Eastern traditional cities created a certain dichotomy of urban planning and execution: A major dilemma has been how to modernize and provide the desired conveniences without destroying or detracting from the charm and historical values of a Jerusalem, Cairo, Istanbul, or similar traditional city. Charm and tradition have too often yielded to technology, economic demands, and the urge to modernize, and historic structures and quarters have been razed to make room for stark, modular high-rise office and apartment blocks.

Hardly a city has escaped an unfortunate overuse of the bulldozer blade—Jiddah, Kuwait, Baghdad, Tehran, Beirut, and Jerusalem. Sharp debate has accompanied the razing of older quarters in some of these cities, particularly Jerusalem, which is sacred to three great world religions. Plans to rebuild the war-damaged old core of Beirut, the *burj* or Martyrs' Square, were fiercely disputed in late 1992.

The dilemma had no simple solution: Central business districts either had to be modernized or be overwhelmed with automobile traffic. Vigorous efforts of conservationists have rather successfully preserved most of the picturesque charm of the old cores of Sana, Istanbul, Esfahan, and Damascus. The entire town of Shibam, in the Wadi Hadramawt of eastern Yemen, has been declared a world historic site by the United Nations Educational, Scientific, and Cultural Organization (UNESCO) (see Chap. 19).

11

The Earth and
the State: Geopolitics

The Middle East has functioned as a tricontinental hub for thousands of years. During that time, peoples, armies, merchants, and ideas have flowed to, from, and across the region. Political ideas and political processes included in the flow were sometimes adapted and sometimes rejected but were often influential in the evolving pattern of the present sixteen states. Beyond each state, the complex political and other relationships established among the states, with neighboring areas, and with distant lands have been profoundly influenced by the patterns already examined. The reciprocal influence between these patterns and political behavior, that is, geopolitics, is the theme of this chapter.

In this book, geopolitics pertains to the spatial interaction between geographical area and political phenomena. It is conceptually equivalent to political geography, and the terms will be used almost interchangeably. Although the focus of this chapter is on the state as a political-geographical phenomenon, it also covers internal and external geopolitical relations of the Middle East.

Hub and Heartland

Early geopolitical concepts of "Heartland" and "World-Island" emerged in Sir Halford J. Mackinder's paper of 1904[1] and his conceptual modifications in 1919 and 1943. Mackinder defined the Heartland bastion as the general area of Siberia, which he conceived of as partially ringed by an Inner Crescent extending from northwestern Europe through southern Asia to northeastern Asia. Beyond the Inner Crescent he viewed an Outer

Crescent, comprising the Americas, southern Africa, and Australia. He labeled Europe, Asia, and Africa the "World-Island" and proposed in 1919 that:

> Who rules East Europe commands
>   the Heartland;
> Who rules the Heartland commands
>   the World-Island;
> Who rules the World-Island commands
>   the World.

Although the Mackinder dictum has received its just share of criticism, the idea of a World-Island emphasizes the links among Europe, Asia, and Africa. In emphasizing those links, it coincidentally spotlights the pivotal location of the Middle East in the World-Island.

Mackinder's Heartland concept was challenged by the theory of the "Rimland" proposed by Professor Nicholas John Spykman during World War II. To Spykman, control of the Heartland is only a strong defensive position; it is control of western and southern Europe, the Middle East, southern Asia, southeastern Asia, China, and Japan that is crucial. Spykman thus gave the key significance to Mackinder's Inner Crescent, which Spykman called the Rimland. He further theorized that domination of both the Heartland and the Rimland by one superpower or power group would create an unmatched power base. On the other hand, control of the Rimland, or most of it, by one power would offset domination of the Heartland by another power.

Viewed from the Mackinder, Spykman, or other world geopolitical perspective, the Middle

East location alone is of enormous global strategic importance. The region's geostrategic value thus enhances its human resources, oil wealth, and commercial role. The Middle East has repeatedly proved its significance under a variety of circumstances.

Although the Middle East was a secondary theater of operations in both world wars, the powers fought for control of the region in both conflicts, and dominance over the area or parts of it has been an even greater geostrategic aim since the 1950s. In World War I, Ottoman Turks, Germans, Russians, British, French, and even Greeks and Italians contended for Middle East territory. The British and French emerged dominant and became the main imperialist powers in the region between the wars. France held sway in Syria and Lebanon and also in part of the Horn of Africa; Britain held not only the three mandates of Palestine, Transjordan, and (until 1932) Iraq but also the Gulf shaykhdoms and Aden.

In World War II, Germany sought to control the Suez Canal and other lines of regional communications as well as the Middle East oil fields. Nazi plans called for a three-pronged attack through North Africa, the Balkans, and, as part of the assault on the Soviet Union, the Ukraine and Caucasus. British and Commonwealth forces, with U.S. assistance, resisted the attacks across North Africa, and they cooperated with the United States in transferring lend-lease war matériel through western Iran to the Soviet Union. Axis forces failed to gain a foothold in the Middle East, although troops from Vichy France (the French government during German occupation) held Syria and Lebanon for a brief time. Contemporary maneuvering for dominance in the area is examined later in this chapter.

The State in the Middle East

A Recent Political Mosaic

Of the sixteen contemporary Middle East countries, only seven were independent states before 1943—Egypt, Turkey, Iraq, Iran, Saudi Arabia, Oman, and the Imamate of Yemen; and British influence limited the sovereignty of Oman, Iraq,

and even Egypt. The area has, therefore, ancient cultures in new states—old wine in new bottles.

Much of the recent history of the Middle East emanates from the political adolescence, inexperience, and insecurity of the recently emerged states of the region. The middle and lower Gulf states achieved sovereignty only in 1971 (Kuwait in 1961) after decades as British protectorates or protected states. After several months of uncertain status, the crown colony of Aden and adjoining protectorate of the Hadramawt merged into an independent unity of the People's Democratic Republic of Yemen (PDRY) in 1967; and the PDRY, in turn, merged with the Yemen Arab Republic as recently as May 1990. Cyprus shed its British crown colony status and achieved independence in 1960, only to experience an invasion by Turkey in 1974 and creation of a de facto Turkish republic in the north of the island. The four Levant states emerged from mandate status and achieved independence between 1943 and 1948, with the fifth mandate (Iraq) having already realized nominal sovereignty in 1932. Even Saudi Arabia declared itself a united kingdom as late as 1932, and Egypt emerged from its British protectorate status in 1922. Both Turkey and Iran are centuries-old sovereign countries, although both declared republican status after centuries of monarchical rule only in 1923 and 1979, respectively. Egypt, Iraq, and North Yemen (YAR) also replaced their monarchies with republican governments between the early 1950s and early 1960s.

Not only have most of the contemporary states emerged from an imperialist context institutionally, they also owe their general political-geographical configurations to British-French boundary delineations. Only one or two boundary alignments in the entire Middle East were negotiated entirely by indigenous states on the two sides of a line. Boundary determinations from the outside sometimes ignored local tribal or traditional elements and in many cases created resentment of imperialist dictates. Iraqi bitterness over British definition of the boundary between Iraq and the then British protectorate of Kuwait has repeatedly manifested itself, as late as 1990. In other instances, imposition of borders from the outside has settled territorial and boundary disputes of long standing.

World War I Territorial Agreements

Among several such accords, three contradictory World War I agreements, plus others after the war, profoundly influenced future Middle East developments and contemporary political-geographical boundaries. Current patterns, crises, and conflicts can be understood only through a comprehension of these agreements.

Two incompatible agreements were made by the British in 1915 and 1916 with regard to the disposition of Ottoman territories in the Middle East after the war. The first was reached in 1915 in an exchange of official correspondence between Sir Henry McMahon, British high commissioner in Cairo, and Sharif Husayn of Mecca, governor of the Ottoman province of the Hijaz. In the exchange, the correspondents agreed that the sharif's Arab followers would revolt against the Ottoman Turks in Arabia and Syria and that Britain, in return, would support the creation of an independent Arab state in former Ottoman lands after the end of the war.

In spite of thus having committed His Majesty's Government to supporting Arab independence in most of the Fertile Crescent, Britain signed the Sykes-Picot Agreement with France and Russia in May 1916. This second agreement specified areas in the Fertile Crescent to be divided between British and French control and influence in the partition of the Ottoman Empire after the Allied victory (Map 11-1). Much of the same area was involved in both agreements.

The third agreement was the Balfour Declaration of November 1917, in which Britain unilaterally promised support for a Jewish homeland in Palestine (see the section "The Arab-Israeli Problem" later in this chapter). This statement provided for a third disposition of certain Fertile Crescent territory.

The Arab Revolt

In accordance with the Husayn-McMahon correspondence, and with British support, the Arab Revolt against the Ottomans began in June 1916. Coordinating the Arab attacks with British operations in Palestine was the legendary Lawrence of Arabia (Col. T. E. Lawrence), who chronicled the fighting from the Hijaz to Damascus in his *Seven Pillars of Wisdom*.[2] The principal Arab leader in

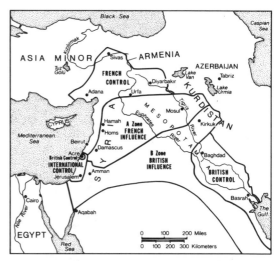

Map 11-1. *Sykes-Picot Agreement territorial allotments that, although later disavowed, became the basis for the post–World War I mandate system.*

the field was Amir Faysal, third son of Sharif Husayn of Mecca.

The Arabs, having upheld their commitment under the Husayn-McMahon correspondence, were later dismayed to learn of the Sykes-Picot Agreement and the Balfour Declaration, both of which effectively negated Britain's promises to Arab leaders. The Arabs were encouraged by President Woodrow Wilson's Fourteen Points, the twelfth of which specifically supported the principle of self-determination of peoples formerly under Ottoman control. However, the Arabs later became distrustful of Britain, France, and the United States as the Allies repeatedly reneged on promises to Arab groups; by contrast, Jewish groups succeeded in gaining support for their proposed homeland in the Middle East.

Peace Treaties and Mandates

In the postwar peace conferences, Britain and France dominated discussions, including the decisions on the future of the former Ottoman areas of the Middle East (Map 11-2). Unable to reconcile the agreements made in 1915–1917, they adhered generally to the Sykes-Picot Agreement and specifically to the Balfour Declaration. At U.S. insistence, a commission of inquiry, the

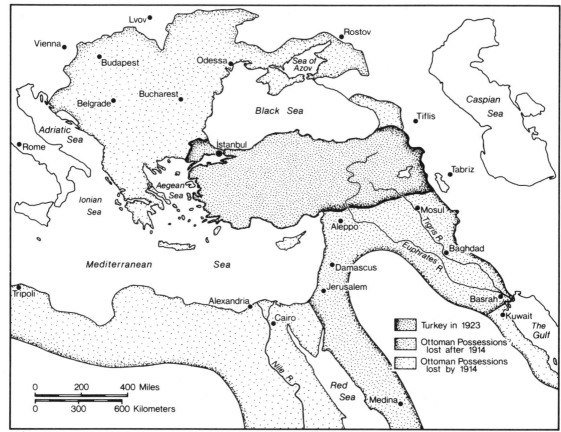

Map 11-2. *Ottoman Empire at its maximum, showing territorial losses by 1914 and after World War I. Losses after 1914 are of especial interest in this book.*

King-Crane Commission, went to the Levant from the Paris peace meetings to test Arab opinion. However, the commission lacked British or French support, and its report—warning against French control in Syria and against application of Zionist goals in Palestine—was ignored and was not even published for more than three years.[3]

A system of Middle East mandates under the proposed League of Nations emerged from talks among the Allied powers at the San Remo Conference in April 1920. Territorially, the suggested mandates followed the outlines of the Sykes-Picot Agreement (see Map 11-1). The agreements divided traditional Greater Syria so that the north passed to French control and the south to British control, and Mesopotamia became an ad-

ditional British mandate (Iraq). Other mandates were set up in Africa and the western Pacific.

Mandatory controls were to be temporary, to observe the principles of self-determination, and to lead to early independence of the polities involved. Unique among all the mandates, the Palestine mandate document included provisions that were incompatible with the purported intent of the mandate system. These provisions were the essential points of the Balfour Declaration, the basic commitment by Great Britain to support a Jewish homeland in Palestine. Their inclusion was a distinct victory for the Zionists but angered and alienated the indigenous Arabs of Palestine, who constituted more than 90 percent of the population of the mandate. After complex territorial trades and divisions, the mandates became official and de jure in 1923. By that time, Transjordan had been clearly excluded from the Palestine mandate, and Greater Lebanon had been constituted as a separate French mandate.

Present Basic Patterns

The State and Its Location

A major thesis of political geography is that *where* a state is located is the most important single factor in its evolution. Whether the location is a matter of latitude, coastal versus landlocked, island versus mainland, astride a mountain range as opposed to being in an intermontane basin—each aspect influences the state's geopolitical development.

Lebanon's à cheval position (literally, "on horseback") astride a linear mountain range imposes a problem of uniting people and communications on opposite sides of the mountains. Egypt's extension up the Nile Valley to just beyond the first cataract and its union of the valley and the delta is a classic case of a riverine state maintaining a linear unity, although the entire Nile Basin has never been united. Iraq, as modern heir to the Tigris-Euphrates Basin, is another classic example of a riverine state. Turkey and Iran illustrate mountain bastions holding long-lasting, independent polities.

Every Middle East state possesses some seacoast, although only Oman and Yemen face the open ocean (Indian Ocean), with the UAE also having coastal outlets on the Indian Ocean. Deep indentations of seas and gulfs into the region facilitate access to the seas, and most states are well endowed with coastlines. Jordan and Iraq, however, are exceptions, as Jordan has only a 16-mile/26-km corner of the Gulf of Aqabah for its single port of Aqabah; and Iraq, with a narrow 36-mile/58-km corridor to the marshy head of the Gulf, suffered serious disadvantages from a lack of adequate harbor and port facilities as it developed its independent economy as a mandate. The lack became critical in the late 1970s and even more so during the Iran-Iraq war. Iraq alleged that the problem was one factor in its attack on Kuwait in 1990. Saudi Arabia, Israel, Egypt, and Iran have two-sea locations, and Tur-key has the longest seacoast of all states in the region, opening onto the Mediterranean, Aegean, Marmara, and Black seas.

In an area as strategic as the Middle East, the location of virtually every state involves some strategic aspect. Bahrain's situation midway in the Gulf has historically been a strategic asset and still affords the island state advantages as an entrepôt and meeting point—now enhanced by the causeway link with the mainland. Similarly, the island state of Cyprus benefits from its eastern Mediterranean situation, which permits it to serve as neutral ground for Arabs and Israelis, Lebanese factions, Europeans and Middle Easterners, and, in better times, Greeks and Turks. On land, Turkey's "bridge" location has brought advantages and disadvantages from Hittite times to the present; and Syria's central location has provided commercial advantages, now reduced by political circumstances. These aspects are discussed in the respective country chapters in Part 2.

The State and Its Population

Both demographically and geopolitically, a state's population is of significance in terms of number, distribution, density, and composition (see Maps 6-1 and 6-2; Tables 6-1 and 6-3). Each major ethnic group has strong sentiments of nationalism.

Every Middle East state has minorities, and some states have ten or twelve sizable ethnic groups. Even the existence of minorities within a population is important, but the geopolitical significance of minorities increases with the degree of antinational sentiment or separatism manifested by such groups. Militant minorities in Lebanon and Cyprus have fractured the basic integrity of those states; Israel considers its Arab minority, increasingly militant over being transformed from a 9-1 majority in 1920, a threat; in Iraq, Iran, and Turkey, the central governments have periodically faced major rebellions by Kurdish minorities. Egypt, with the Copts; Saudi Arabia, with the Persian-descended Shii; Iran, with the Azeris, Arabs, Baluch, and a dozen other groups have all experienced ethnic conflicts.[4]

The State and Its Institutions

Most of the polities of the Middle East entered the second half of the twentieth century with traditional societies and traditional monarchies as governments. However, those societies have been forced to adjust to the contemporary technological, economic, and political influences brought by post–World War II developments. Such adjustment has involved replacement of monarchies in Egypt, Iraq, and Yemen by republics, yet the Iranian monarchy was overthrown as a reaction against modernization and for the restoration of religious traditionalism.

Although the more leftist revolutionary pressures have declined since the 1970s, traditional regimes were for several years under pressure from neighboring revolutionary regimes and from revolutionary groups within their territories. Increasingly in the early 1990s, many of the Middle East governments were most threatened by extremist religious fundamentalist movements both from within and, partly, from without. Monarchies in Saudi Arabia and Oman, and especially in Jordan, have adapted through gradualism; the individual rulers of Kuwait, Bahrain, Qatar, and the constituent amirates of the UAE have practiced economic liberalism while maintaining political traditionalism. The Gulf states upon occasion stabilize political trends with the expulsion or threat of expulsion of troublesome noncitizens. As of 1992, nine Middle East states are republics, six are basically monarchies, and one—the UAE—is a combination.

The degree of citizen participation in government in the nine or ten republics is highly variable, and the search for legitimacy is characteristic of several republican governments in the region. Democratic processes are best represented in Israel (excluding the occupied territories), Turkey, and Cyprus, the only states in the region that generally conduct open elections with freedom for most opposition parties (but see the Epilogue). Prior to its civil war, Lebanon conducted open parliamentary elections and exhibited many aspects of a laissez-faire democracy, but Lebanon had no effective central government between 1975 and 1991. Party membership or participation is limited in the other republics, although Yemen is moving toward an open democracy. Iran has had relatively open elections since 1979, but governments have been oppressive. Among the monarchies, Jordan has adopted the most progressive measures, having had probably the freest election in the Arab world when it elected its parliament in 1989. Firm pressure, although not an open revolutionary threat, moved all other monarchies to demonstrate a more liberal stance after the Gulf crisis of 1990–1991, but meaningful progress has come slowly. In the 1960s and 1970s, advisory councils were elected by popular vote in Kuwait and Bahrain but were dismissed or threatened with dismissal by the rulers for exceeding their mandates. The ruler of Kuwait promised several broad steps toward democratization of his amirate during and soon after the Iraqi occupation in 1990–1991. However, reforms were slow and modest, although the parliamentary elections scheduled for October 1992 took place on schedule, were open, and seated a substantial majority of opposition candidates (31 of 50 members of the National Assembly). No elections have ever been held in Saudi Arabia or Qatar, although in early 1992, King Fahd of Saudi Arabia announced the creation of a consultative council, as well as a formal constitution, including a bill of rights. Progress toward the reforms was limited by early 1993, with the king certain to be roundly condemned either way he moved.

Such steps may appear to be small advances in the Western lexicon, but they are progress in a broader context, if they are made effective. Western democracies did not spring full-blown from their Greek model, and Middle East states similarly require time to achieve self-identity, social balance, and political maturity (see the next section). They too will periodically slip backward before they resume forward momentum. It must be noted that civil rights or human rights are denied one group or another in every country in the Middle East—even in Israel, Turkey, and Cyprus.

Raison d'Être

The state idea, or its raison d'être (reason for being), is a state's basic centripetal force—the unique, distinctive idea manifested in the emergence and maintenance of a particular piece of territory and segment of humanity in a unit state.[5] As developed by Richard Hartshorne[6] and later applied by the author of this book,[7] the raison d'être reflects the dominance of unifying factors over divisive factors in a state, therefore the dominance of centripetal over centrifugal forces. The impact of an abstract idea on state evolution was further examined by Stephen B. Jones,[8] who traced the motivating political idea through four subsequent links: decision, movement, field, and political area (the state). Both the examination of the raison d'être and the tracing of the progress of Jones's unified field idea aid in understanding Middle East state patterns.

Many of the Middle East states were created by and delineated by outside powers in contradiction to pre-1919 Arab aspirations and expectations in the area. These states have thus faced problems in evolving successfully within their respective contexts without an indigenous initial idea or a consensus regarding their raison d'être. Developments after 1920 brought frustrations in the mandates of Syria, Iraq, and Palestine as well as to large segments of the populations in Lebanon and Transjordan. Later independence for the mandates found them still lacking consensus on a state idea.

Formerly independent areas, on the other hand, had a traditional reason for being, which could be adapted and followed. Turkey, under Mustafa Kemal Atatürk, was clearly motivated by "Turkey for the Turks, and the Turks for Turkey!" Iran under Reza Shah had centuries of Persian culture as a core state concept. Egypt had a long history as a polity and had a rather firm sense of direction. In the south of the region, although both were ruled by benighted monarchs, Oman and Yemen also had a centuries-long sense of polity. To their north, after 1932, the tribal leader in the Arabian Peninsula, Abd al-Aziz Al Saud, developed a raison d'être for Saudi Arabia. The Middle East state with the most explicit reason for being is the region's only settler state, Israel, which extended "a national home for the Jewish people" in the Palestine mandate into an independent Jewish state. By contrast, Cyprus has not found a commonality of purpose and modality between its Greek-Cypriot majority and its Turkish-Cypriot minority. Cyprus the island consists of two de facto Cypruses as polities, although the northern "republic" has received no international recognition.

Regional Linkages

Bases for Links

A region as large and diverse as the Middle East is inevitably faced with several centrifugal forces, but it also possesses some regional centripetal forces, with Islam being the strongest unifying link. Only Israel and South Cyprus lie outside the Islamic realm (*Dar al-Islam*), with Lebanon divided. In times past, Islam has held all of the Middle East area—and more—in one Muslim empire (see Map 2-5).

Nevertheless, as in times past, localism, ethnic separatism, nationalism, religious zealotry and militancy, and the ambition of leaders disrupt unity. Turkey and Iran sharply distinguish themselves from the rest of the Muslim Middle East, but all other states also have local concerns that counterbalance regional unity. Israel does not participate in regional political institutions—indeed, it is excluded from them. Arab nationalism and Arab unity often yield to national interests and competition among state leaders, to the extent that Arab unity appears to be observed as much in the breach as in the honoring.

Regional Organizations

Nevertheless, regional cooperation, coordination, and joint action can be underestimated because of the more obvious and more publicized regional differences. Six regional agencies exemplify both the efforts to coordinate action and the difficulties in achieving effective action.

OIC. The regional organization that embraces the largest number of Middle East states—fourteen of the sixteen, excluding only Israel and Cyprus—is the Organization of the Islamic Conference (OIC) with headquarters in Jiddah. The OIC also includes 29 other predominantly Muslim states, from Morocco and Gabon in western Africa to Brunei on Borneo, plus the Palestine Liberation Organization (PLO). Formally established in May 1971, the OIC has held six summit conferences, the latest in Senegal in 1991. Primarily intended to promote Islamic solidarity among member states, the organization sponsors economic, cultural, and political cooperation and serves as an umbrella for several agencies serving Islamic states.

Arab League. The twelve Arab states of the sixteen countries of the region constitute the core members of the League of Arab States. Although Egypt's membership was suspended when it signed the peace treaty with Israel in 1979, it was revalidated in 1990, and league headquarters were moved back to Cairo from Tunis, where they had been located for eleven years. Usually referred to as the Arab League, the organization also includes eight North African states—Mauritania, Morocco, Algeria, Tunisia, Libya, Sudan, Somalia, and Djibouti—plus Palestine. The Middle East Arab states initiated the league in 1945, with its center in Cairo.

The Arab League is institutionally the most unifying of the agencies in which most Middle East countries are members, even though it includes members from well beyond the Middle East core. Despite the fact that it regularly exhibits sharp disagreement and disharmony over major issues, as it did conspicuously regarding the Gulf crisis in 1990, it is the region's best sounding board. The league maintains offices and information centers internationally and carries out many of the same activities and has many of the same difficulties as similar regional organizations. Many of the league's most important statements and actions pertain to the Arab-Israeli problem.

OPEC and OAPEC. Scores of specialized organizations deal with specific aspects of inter-Arab coordination and with Arab participation in wider organizations. Two of the best known are the Organization of Petroleum Exporting Countries (OPEC) and the Organization of Arab Petroleum Exporting Countries (OAPEC), discussed in Chapter 8. Although most of the other agencies are economic (many under the aegis of the Council of Arab Economic Unity) and deal with everything from olives to tourism, some agencies unite, for example, Arab historians, jurists, and sports activities. Other organizations have a wider membership, as does, for example, the Afro-Asian Peoples' Solidarity Organization, founded in 1957 and headquartered in Cairo.

GCC. Created in 1981, a key subregional organization is the Gulf Cooperation Council (GCC), which coordinates economic, cultural, and political operations among its six member states: Saudi Arabia, Kuwait, Bahrain, Qatar, the UAE, and Oman. Their main concerted interests include management of their huge oil income, common problems of development, social problems (including expatriate labor flow), Gulf trade, and—as quickly became apparent—security. Membership comprises only conservative monarchies that to some extent sought security for their regimes as well as for their respective states. The revolutionary republican neighbors of Iraq and Iran, which were at war when the GCC was formed, could be justifiably excluded; and events later—especially in 1990–1991—confirmed the policy of exclusion. A unified defense against threats from Iran and Iraq was, after all, a prime impetus for establishment of the organization. The GCC gave its members some assurance during the 1980–1988 Iran-Iraq war and played a useful role in the 1990–1991 Gulf crisis. Members established a $15 billion fund in December 1990, in the midst of the Gulf crisis, to aid friendly countries. They also agreed in April 1991 to create a lending fund of $5 billion to aid development in the private sector of Arab countries.

ECO. In 1964, Turkey, Iran, and Pakistan—key members in the pre-1979 Central Treaty Organization (CENTO) (see discussion in the next section)—sought common nonmilitary economic benefits in a new organization, the Regional Cooperation for Development (RCD). Financial underwriting came primarily from increasingly oil-wealthy Iran, whose shah was continuing a historic quest for Iranian hegemony in the Northern Tier and the Gulf. The RCD achieved modest success in coordinating transportation connections and practices, tourism, postal arrangements, frontier formalities, and similar affairs. It phased down after the 1979 Iranian revolution but was revived in 1985; it was renamed the Economic Cooperation Organization (ECO), and its goals were expanded. Swinging into action in 1992 to take advantage of the disintegration of the Soviet Union, it signed agreements in November incorporating the six new Muslim republics that broke away from the USSR (Azerbaijan, Kazakhstan, Kyrghyzstan, Tajikistan, Turkmenistan, and Uzbekistan) as well as Afghanistan. The ECO thus had ten members, making it the largest economic bloc after the European Economic Community (EEC).

Unions: Attempts and Failures

Although post–World War I Arab aspirations for unity in the Fertile Crescent were frustrated by Britain and France and partly by inter-Arab rivalry, Arab states attempted several subregional political mergers between the late 1950s and 1980. A major effort toward Arab unity was the United Arab Republic (UAR), in which Syria and Egypt joined in 1958 and from which Syria withdrew in 1961, although Egypt called itself the UAR for another decade. The Yemen of that time also nominally federated with the UAR in 1958, but this alliance collapsed in 1961 after Syria withdrew.

Jordan and Iraq, ruled at the time by related Hashimite monarchs, merged in the Arab Federation in 1958, but this was dissolved after the overthrow of the king of Iraq the same year. The new Iraqi leader proposed a union of Iraq, Syria, and Jordan, but this plan was not accepted. Other unity efforts have been proposed but shortly failed: the re-creation of the United Arab Republic with Egypt, Syria, and Iraq in 1963; plans for a Federation of Arab Republics with Egypt, Syria, and Libya in 1971; and a merger of Egypt and Libya in 1972.

In preparation for its withdrawal from east of Suez, Great Britain created the Federation of Arab Amirates of the South in 1959 in the Aden Protectorate, which then, with some expansion, became the Federation of South Arabia. Militant leftist actions in 1967 forced the creation of the Marxist People's Democratic Republic of Yemen, which in turn merged with North Yemen in 1990 to form the Republic of Yemen (see Chap. 19). Different though the two parts are, the union promises to be a lasting one, since it was achieved after years of love-hate deliberations, and mutual benefits are obvious.

As Britain planned its withdrawal from the Gulf, the seven Trucial States of the time discussed with Bahrain and Qatar in 1968 the for-

mation of a Federation of Arab Amirates. However, by mid-1971, Bahrain and Qatar had each opted for independence, and the seven Trucial shaykhdoms confederated in the United Arab Emirates (UAE). Prompted by Egyptian President Sadat's dramatic visit to Jerusalem in 1977 and the ensuing moves toward Egyptian-Israeli détente, intensive talks between Syria and Iraq during the period October 1978–June 1979 almost produced agreement for a historic union between the two Fertile Crescent states. However, the talks broke down over several points, including leadership of the resulting united state—which is often the obstacle in such negotiations.

Alliances: Baghdad Pact

In addition to the informal alliance implied in the Arab League, regional military alliances—which sometimes involve little more than placement of military forces under one command—are formed during emergencies and then disbanded when they are over. The major impetus for such pacts has usually been a crisis between the Arab frontline states and Israel, and temporary alliances preceded the four major Arab-Israeli wars. The inclusion of some Arab states in the 1990–1991 coalition against Iraq was unusual because it mixed Arab states with outside, non-Arab states and also because it created frictions between the participating states and the rejectionist states.

The Baghdad Pact, a long-range pact involving Middle East states, was formed, with U.S.-British encouragement, in 1955 as a *cordon sanitaire* of the Northern Tier of states against Soviet expansionism. Formally termed the Middle East Treaty Organization, it initially included only Turkey and Iraq; but Britain, Pakistan, and Iran later joined. Following the overthrow of the monarchy in Iraq in 1958, that country withdrew from the pact. Renamed the Central Treaty Organization, the pact was headquartered in Ankara for two decades until it disintegrated in 1979 when revolutionary Iran and then Pakistan withdrew.

Regional Conflicts

The Middle East has had its share of conflicts over borders, access to scarce resources, competing ideologies, leadership, and self-determination since the establishment of numerous newly independent states. Geographically, the conflicts may be across frontiers, subregional, regional, or between the region and extraregional forces.

Not all major clashes have been between sovereign governments. Some of the conflicts have been and are between nonstate organizations and states, between paramilitary forces of subnational groups, or between leaders as personalities contending for regional supremacy. Lebanon was fragmented for more than fifteen years by fighting between the PLO and Kataib, the PLO and Shiis, Druzes and Kataib, and other intergroup conflicts (see Chap. 13). The PLO also fought Jordanian forces in 1970 and has periodically battled Israeli troops and conducted guerrilla raids in Israel. Militant Islamic fundamentalists have created internal and transnational movements in the region, and extremist elements have raised grave concerns in Egypt, Saudi Arabia, Lebanon, and other states, especially Israel. The Muslim Brotherhood, originally an Egyptian opposition group, has been active not only in Egypt but also in Jordan and especially in Syria (see the next section). The Baath (Arab Renaissance Party) has been influential in the Fertile Crescent states, and opposing factions of the Baath govern in Syria and Iraq.

Boundary and Territorial Disputes

Most Middle East countries have disputed with at least one neighbor over territory along part of their common boundary. Usually limited to diplomatic exchanges, some disputes have provoked skirmishes, and three have provoked devastating wars.

Early Disputes. Three territorial disputes in the preindependence Fertile Crescent involved (1) inclusion of the Mosul area in the British mandate of Iraq; (2) delineation of the southern Transjordan-Arabia border; and (3) transfer of Alexandretta (Turkish, Iskenderun), located before 1938 in northwestern Syria. The first two were readily resolved, but the third echoed for several years. A 1921 accord provided that the Sanjak (subprovince) of Alexandretta, which had a large Turkish minority and port facilities desired by both Turkey and Syria, would have a special regime in France's Syrian mandate. A League of Nations compromise created a separate Republic of Hatay in 1938, and in 1939 France ceded Hatay to Turkey, in violation of mandate provisions. Syria has not entirely accepted the loss of Alexandretta, and many Syrian-made maps show both the 1936 and 1939 boundaries with Turkey.

Arabian Peninsula Boundaries. Saudi Arabia, with the largest number of immediate land neighbors in the region (seven), sought to rationalize most of its boundaries through quiet negotiations during the 1960s and 1970s, although border tensions continue with Yemen and Qatar. An agreement with Jordan in 1965 gave Jordan an extra 10-mile/16-km coastal strip for the expansion of its port of Aqabah in exchange for a linear inland strip of desert, one with Iraq in 1975 divided the Arabia-Iraq Neutral Zone and straightened the boundary extending westward, and another with Kuwait in 1969 divided the Arabia-Kuwait Neutral Zone. An agreement with Qatar in 1965 defined their common boundary, and one with the UAE in 1974 defined a disputed boundary, including a prolonged problem regarding the Buraymi Oasis. Settlement of these two boundaries was especially remarkable, since they had a long and tortured history of friction not only between the indigenous governments concerned but also between Saudi Arabia and the pre-1971 British protectors of the two amirates. A Saudi agreement with Oman in 1982 deferred territorial questions, but in March 1991 agreement was reached for delimitation of their common border of more than 400 miles/645 km through the eastern part of the barren Rub al-Khali. Saudi Arabia has, however, reached no agreement with Yemen about their common but undefined and undelimited border along the edge of the Rub al-Khali. The Yemen government of the time and Saudi Arabia agreed in 1934 on part of the boundary between Yemen and the Asir region of Saudi Arabia but came to no agreement on the rest of their common frontier. Recent oil discoveries in the eastern part of Yemen lend greater urgency to a resolution of this problem. At least one long-standing boundary problem in Arabia Felix—over the border between the two former Yemens—was solved coincidentally with the creation of a united Yemen republic in 1990. Several other conflicts over boundaries actually involve territorial claims and are discussed in the next section.

Other Boundary and Territorial Problems. Of the problems over two other defined but undelimited boundaries on the Arabian Peninsula, one, involving the Iraq-Kuwait boundary, was at the core of the Gulf war of 1990–1991, discussed later in this chapter; and the other, concerning the Oman-Yemen border, was in the process of being resolved in the early 1990s.

Three disputes involving irredentist territories on the Arabian Peninsula and in offshore areas became acute during the period 1961–1991.

1. Iraq bitterly denounced the British boundary delineations and territorial allotments at the head of the Gulf as soon as the political-geographical patterns were made public in 1923. The fledgling mandate had two related complaints: that its access to the Gulf was incompatibly narrow compared with the state's breadth farther north, and that the territory used to create the shaykhdom of Kuwait should have been allotted to Iraq. Iraq emphasized that this territory had officially been included in the former Ottoman province of Basrah, most of which had otherwise been allotted to the mandate of Iraq. Although Iraq declared its acceptance of the status of Kuwait when Iraq became independent in 1932, it reasserted its irredentist claims periodically, especially during the late 1930s, sometimes including threats of military action. When Kuwait became independent in 1961 and was officially no longer a British protectorate, Iraq (by then a revolutionary republic) announced plans to annex Kuwait by force; but when both Britain and the Arab League firmly resisted Iraqi claims, Iraq reiterated its acceptance of the status quo in 1963. Nevertheless, in 1973–1974, Iraq attempted once again to take a part of Kuwait, at least the two islands of Warba and Bubiyan, in order to expand its outlet to the Gulf; but, as before, it dropped its claims and withdrew its forces.[9] Therefore, Saddam Husayn's military threat to invade Kuwait in August 1990 did not at that time appear to pose the imminent grave danger that in retrospect might have seemed obvious. Relevant aspects of the Gulf war of 1990–1991 are covered later in this chapter.

2. In 1968, with the approach of Britain's withdrawal from the lower Gulf states, Iran moved to fill the impending vacuum and definitively to affirm Iranian dominance in the Gulf, reasserting its old claims to Bahrain as Iran's "fourteenth province," as well as to several small islands in the southern Gulf. However, in 1970 the shah accepted the finding of the United Nations that Bahrainis preferred independence, and he renounced further claims to Bahrain.

3. Iranian claims in the south were successful. On November 30, 1971, the day before Britain withdrew from the Gulf, Iran occupied three islands in the lower Gulf that had long been understood to belong to Sharjah and Ras al-Khaymah, asserting that it required the islands in order to protect the Strait of Hormuz. Accords regarding one of the islands, Abu Musa—well away from the strait and appreciably closer to Sharjah than to Iran—included agreement that income from oil production on or around Abu Musa would be divided between Iran and Sharjah. Iranian speedboats used the island in the "tanker war" in the late 1980s for attacks on Gulf shipping. In 1992, Iran tightened its control of Abu Musa by restricting access to the island. The other two islands, Greater Tunb and Lesser Tunb, at the Gulf end of the Strait of Hormuz, had normally been considered to be under Ras al-Khaymah's sovereignty, but Iran occupied them as well prior to the independence of the proposed United Arab Emirates.[10]

The Gulf has also presented problems regarding maritime boundaries on the continental shelf of this semienclosed sea. As offshore oil discoveries pushed farther into the mid-Gulf from both sides, definition of maritime boundaries became essential. International discussions on the Law of the Sea at that time supplied possible solutions, and several median lines in the central Gulf, as opposed to the north and south, were agreed upon and surveyed in the late 1950s and the 1960s. Complexities regarding the lines among Iran, Iraq, Kuwait, and the now-divided Neutral Zone have delayed final agreement in the north, as have similar problems among the amirates and Iran in the south. Considering the amounts of oil beneath the Gulf and the potential for confrontation, agreements have been reached relatively promptly, and nonagreed-upon lines have caused few difficulties.

Another continental shelf dispute is under way in the northwestern corner of the Middle East, where the question concerns location of a median line in the Aegean Sea between Turkey and Greece. Since Greece exercises sovereignty over the large islands just off the western coast of Asia Minor, a basic median line would seem to belong between the islands and the mainland. However, such a division would extend Greek Exclusive Economic Zone rights over the entire Aegean Sea, including all potential offshore petroleum resources—a division that Turkey has declared it cannot accept.

The conflict over the Aegean partition is heightened by the Greek-Turkish split over Cyprus (see Chap. 13). Since both Turkey and Greece are members of the North Atlantic Treaty Organization and must otherwise be encouraged to be peaceful neighbors, the prospect of military action between them over the Aegean or Cyprus is of grave concern to the Atlantic community. Talks under UN auspices were under way in 1992 and offered hope that both the Cyprus conflict and the Aegean friction might be slowly advancing toward reduction in tension.

Finally, the median line/thalweg river boundary down the Shatt al-Arab between Iraq and Iran has been a matter of dispute and then of warfare between these two riparian states, as is discussed in detail later in this chapter.

Hydro-Geopolitics

We have seen that the natural resource of petroleum, a physical-geographical element, has been a major factor in the shaping of internal and external political relations of countries of the Middle East. Similarly, the availability, management, and sharing of the natural resource of water are, and increasingly will be, factors in the political geography of the area that will eventually surpass petroleum in import.

With great population increases in many countries of the Middle East, maximal use of water resources has become epidemic. Rivers, because of their transnational character, automatically become subjects of international concern. Egypt, with its explosive population growth, has seen the water in the Nile—with its sources in Ethiopia and the Sudan—decrease in recent decades. Exploitation of Tigris and Euphrates water by these three riparian states has dramatically increased since the 1960s. Such exploitation has been on an especially grand scale in Turkey's Southeast Anatolia Project (GAP), including the great Atatürk Dam on the Euphrates, for generation of electric power and for planned irrigation of millions of acres of land in southeastern Turkey (see Chap. 21). This large-scale utilization of Euphrates and Tigris water by Turkey obviously diminishes the downstream flow in both Syria and Iraq. Syria's Jazirah Project, with its core facility of the Euphrates (al-Thawrah) Dam, calls for irrigation of hundreds of thousands of acres in the Euphrates Valley and Jazirah and has also decreased the Euphrates flow downstream for Iraq.

The use of groundwater in Saudi Arabia to provide self-sufficiency in wheat has lowered the water table by 7 or 8 ft./2.1 or 2.4 m. Control over access to the Jordan, Yarmuk, and Litani rivers and to underground aquifers plays a significant role in the Israeli policy of control of the Golan Heights, southern Lebanon, and the occupied West Bank and Gaza.

Multilateral talks that began in Moscow at the end of January 1992 as part of the Arab-Israeli peace process designated water-sharing agreements as one of the central issues, but by late 1992, such water negotiations had made little progress. In other disputes, Turkey, Iraq, and Syria met in Ankara in June 1990 to discuss arrangements for sharing Euphrates and Tigris water, but no agreements were reached. The nine states of the Nile Basin discussed regional cooperation in Cairo, also in June 1990, and the United Nations Economic Commission for Africa and the UN Development Program are providing auspices for group water projects. Thus, initial steps have been taken toward water-sharing protocols, but the real problems have yet to be addressed.

Two international conventions apply in these discussions, but they are contrary to prevailing international law. According to the Helsinki Rules of 1966 and a UN 1972 convention, water rights are to be shared according to population and need, with historical allocations to be kept in mind; however, international law acknowledges the absolute sovereignty of states over the resources they control. Unless meaningful regional and international agreements can be reached regarding fair allocations of these river waters among the riparians, the national ambitions for development and the growing demands for water by the steadily increasing populations will inevitably lead to more rancor over water use in the Middle East. Details of the several national projects and the problems involved are discussed in relevant country chapters in Part 2.

Religious and Ideological Conflicts

The Role of Religion. Religious movements have periodically had strong impacts on part or all of the Middle East, and they remain important in the geopolitical equation of the Middle East today. Islam originally emerged as a theocracy, and religion and politics—"church and state"—are congenitally linked in the Muslim concepts. The extreme politicization of Islam is divisive among Muslims and creates some of the sharpest cleavages in the region. As is true in many so-called religious conflicts, the real discord often arises from national political hostilities, economic competition, ethnolinguistic and cultural dissensions, territorial disputes, and outside interference, which are then exacerbated by religious cleavages.

Such merging of religious and other discords may be seen in several of the current struggles between different religious groups in the Middle East. A closer look at the conflict "between Jews and Muslims" quickly reveals the territorial, political, and cultural bases for the hostility, plus showing that the fundamental hostility is between Zionists and their opponents, including many Christians. The fifteen-year civil war in Lebanon, "between Christians and Muslims," was driven as much by dominant-group economic-cultural discrimination and competition as by religion. The religious component in the revolutionary activities of the Shiis in Lebanon and elsewhere is overridden by economic disadvantages and partly by Iranian nationalism.

Modernization in most of the Middle East since about 1960 has caused social stresses that call attention to the inadequacies of modern industrialized culture, and major groups of Middle Easterners have opted for their own religious-po-

litical framework, Islam—a choice that has had an impact on Israel and Cyprus as well as on the Islamic states. In some Arab states, organizations such as the Muslim Brotherhood (Ikhwan al-Muslimun), established in Egypt in 1929 to urge a return to conservative Islam, have received new impetus. Numerous other "fraternities" (*jamaats*) emphasizing various lines of action have appeared in Egypt and Fertile Crescent countries, and many of these organizations advocate revolutionary and antigovernment positions. In advocating the rejection of modern trends and a return to traditional Islam, most fundamentalists in Arab states also reject the Arab socialism (but not the pan-Arabism) that was advocated by Nasser of Egypt and other Arab leaders of the 1950s and 1960s.

Called to the world's attention by the Iranian revolution of 1978–1979, the Islamic fundamentalist movement was a major regional dynamic in the late 1970s and after. Although it embodies a strong religious element, the movement is also a religion/ideology that combines expressions of the regional mood. This mood includes rejection of Western secular influences and of Western political modalities and reassertion of traditional Islamic values and religious-political relationships. Islamic fundamentalism became both cause and effect in radical political developments in the Middle East after the early 1970s. Extremists such as the late Ayatollah Khomeini have used it as banner and weapon, frightening less radical neighbors and opponents. Such rejection of Western influences is countered by "demonization" of Islamic influences in the West—making Islamic fundamentalism a target and a scapegoat for anti-Arab and anti-Islamic sentiment. Religious conservatism has also found expression in Israel, where religious differences within the Jewish population have become increasingly divisive. No less than radical Muslim fundamentalists have manipulated their religion, extremist Jews have exploited various aspects of Judaism to justify self-serving actions against both the Israeli government and Arabs, especially in the occupied territories (see Chap. 15).

Arabism in the Region. "Arabism" is partly an outgrowth of the regional identification of Arabism with Islam and partly a product of anticolonial nationalism and self-determination in the decades preceding World War II. Various unifying movements developing from Arabism have been the ideological dynamics that have matched those of religion. The linguistic and cultural homogeneity among the peoples of the Arab Middle East has generated strong emotional linkages among the Arab societies of the region and among Arab political systems. However, these emotional links have not translated into meaningful or sustained congruity or solidarity and certainly not into a unified polity, despite verbal expressions of Islamic and Arab unity.

Successful or not, the ties display slightly different emphases but are categorized under such names as Arabism, Arab nationalism, Arab solidarity, Arab unity, and, earlier, Arab socialism. Under some circumstances, the sense of Arab identity transcends nationalism of individual states and actuates joint stances on the basis of Arab kinship.[11] Under other circumstances, differing interpretations of Arab identity have engendered intense conflict among Arab states. Consensus is of almost mystical significance to Arabs, but in political crises consensus among Arab states is often little more than a noncommittal gesture. Even so, by the early 1990s, relations among Middle East Arab states had become more pragmatic, particularly after the Gulf crisis of 1990–1991, with national interests often being given precedence over ideology.

From outside the "Arab system," the impact of Iranian Shii fundamentalism has stimulated self-examination. Also outside the Arab system, Turkey has faced a similar sequence of developments, with internal ideological conflicts between secular and Islamic orientations. Nationalism, clashing ideological positions, and religious divisions have also caused internal conflict in Israel.

The Arab-Israeli Problem

Among the problems in global geopolitical relations of the post–World War II era, the conflict between Arabs and Israelis is exceptionally intractable (Map 11-3). It is unique in its profound regional impact, its worldwide ramifications, its great-power involvement, and its emotional associations. It has many facets: ethnic confronta-

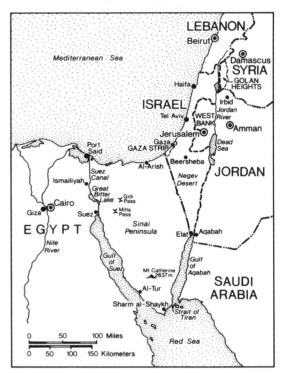

Map 11-3. *Political-geographical setting of the Arab-Israeli problem, showing all the territories directly involved in the conflict.*

tion, conflicting historical-territorial claims, religious implications, ethical dilemmas, and political and geopolitical impacts. It also has many perspectives, with the two main contenders fragmented into many subperspectives. From any perspective, the problem and its ramifications have caused a tragic number of casualties, prolonged human suffering, extensive physical destruction, and explosive divisiveness as well as retardation of development and a waste of human and other resources in the area. Hence the profound significance of the first steps taken directly by the Palestinians and Israelis in signing their joint Declaration of Principles on September 13, 1993.

The modern conflict began with the increasing spirit of nationalism among many groups of the late nineteenth century, including Jews in Europe and Arabs in the Middle East. Jewish nationalism evolved especially after 1880 as Zionism, indicating the aspiration to establish a Jewish polity in "Zion," named after a hill in Jerusalem but extended to the area of Palestine. Zionism expanded in area and influence until, with support from several sources, it achieved a Jewish state in Palestine in 1948. By contrast, Arab nationalism developed in regional isolation, focused on local problems—of which Palestine was only one—and was weakened by colonial influences that fragmented its aims and methods. Some aspects of the background to the problem are included in Chapters 2, 6, and 15; a few highlights and twentieth-century developments are discussed in this section.

As Jews in late nineteenth-century Europe achieved equality in European society, many of them began seeking a national identity similar to that of the Germans, French, and British. They joined in common efforts to achieve self-determination and group liberation, all according to the concepts of the Enlightenment. Jewish nationalism combined with secularism to direct Jewish attention to the Land of Israel (Eretz Yisrael) as a territorial base for a revived Jewish nation. Leaders emphasized links between Jews in the Diaspora (dispersion) and the Land of Israel and also focused on the perception of Jews as a minority "in exile," not just a religious group. The leaders encouraged the revival of Hebrew, which, having served for centuries as a liturgical language, was to be the literary and colloquial medium of Jewish-Hebrew nationalism.

Evolution of Zionism

In the early 1880s, pogroms against Jews in eastern Europe resulted in a movement, Hovevei Tzion (Lovers of Zion), which called for the migration of Jews to Palestine. The movement was institutionalized by Theodor Herzl, a Hungarian Jewish journalist, who came to believe, after covering the Dreyfus affair in France,[12] that Jews must achieve self-determination by having their own state. In 1896 he published *Der Judenstaat* [The Jews State], which called for an independent state for Jews; in 1897 he organized the First Zionist Congress.

At a meeting of the congress in Basel, Switzerland, Herzl founded the World Zionist Organization (WZO), which became the instrument of Jewish nationalism and is still the focal organization for support for the state of Israel. Herzl directed Jewish and world attention to Zionism, and still other movements evolved as vehicles to channel Jewish efforts and people to Palestine. A leading Zionist encouraged his co-workers to "make Jewish Palestine the mother country of world Jewry, with Jewish communities in the Diaspora as the colonies—and not the reverse."[13]

The WZO and subsidiary organizations attracted Jewish settlers to the Ottoman provincial area of Palestine and enlisted the support of world Jewry for Jewish nationalist aims. In Jones's "Unified Field Theory," mentioned earlier, Zionism is the idea that led through decision and movement over a world field to the Palestine area. One Zionist writer encouraged immigration for "a people without a land for a land without people"[14] in 1901—when more than 400,000 Palestinian Arabs lived in Palestine. Nevertheless, even against Ottoman opposition, the settler effort proceeded, and immigrants outnumbered the indigenous Arabs within three decades after the initiation of the serious drive for a Jewish national home. Colonists immigrated for various reasons, but the predominant objective was to establish a modern, secular, socialist state to serve as a national territorial base for Jews, not as practitioners of Judaism but as a people.

The Balfour Declaration

World War I offered opportunities for Zionist leaders to lay the practical groundwork for a Jewish state. Of the World War I British pronouncements already mentioned, the Balfour Declaration deserves a closer look because of its crucial role.

With change of territorial control in the Middle East imminent by 1917, British Zionists pressed the British government to announce official support for the establishment of a Jewish state in Palestine. Zionists emphasized that such a statement would attract the support of Jews in Germany and would rally Jews in the United States to urge that country to join the Allies against Germany. After intensive lobbying on both sides of the Atlantic, Britain issued the one-sentence Balfour Declaration on November 2, 1917:

> His Majesty's Government view with favour the establishment in Palestine of a national home for the Jewish people, and will use their best endeavours to facilitate the achievement of this object, it being

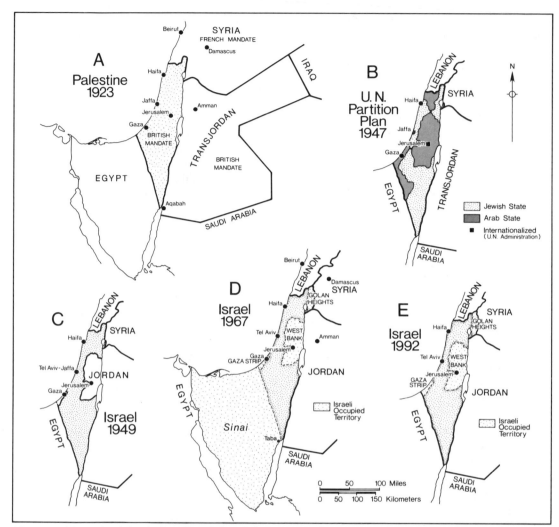

Map 11-4. *The territorial evolution of Israel, from Palestinian mandate to contemporary state with occupied territories.*

clearly understood that nothing shall be done which may prejudice the civil and religious rights of existing non-Jewish communities in Palestine, or the rights and political status enjoyed by Jews in any other country.

This sentence, with its two conflicting parts, was as internally contradictory as were Britain's several wartime pronouncements. Its first phrase changed the course of the history of the Middle East.[15]

World War I Through World War II

A 1922 British White Paper significantly clarified British intentions regarding the Balfour Declaration. The paper stated that the declaration, al-

though it was a basic factor in the establishment of the Palestine mandate (Map 11-4A), did not intend that Palestine as a whole should be converted into a Jewish national home, nor that Palestine was to become a wholly Jewish polity, nor that the declaration contemplated the "disappearance or subordination" of the indigenous Arab population or its culture. It also repeated that Britain regarded Palestine as excluded from the area of Arab independence contemplated in the Husayn-McMahon correspondence.

The organization and momentum of the Zionists, inflow of Jewish settlers (especially refugees from Nazi Germany), purchase of prime agricultural land by the Jewish National Fund

(JNF), and increasing support of Zionism by world Jewry combined to create favorable conditions for the emergence of the Jewish state called for by Herzl in 1896 and 1897. Expanding influence in Palestine of the Jewish Agency and related organizations gave emphasis to Zionist goals and de-emphasis to protection of the rights of the indigenous population mentioned in the Balfour Declaration.

Assurances by the British and French in November 1918 that they would establish in Greater Syria and Mesopotamia "national governments that drew their authority from the initiative and free choice of the native populations" were ignored by the British mandate government, as were declarations in Wilson's Fourteen Points and in the Covenant of the League of Nations. The Palestinian Arabs and their neighboring Arab supporters found that Zionist influence in London and Jerusalem outweighed Arab influence and that only the first half of the Balfour Declaration was being applied. Arab violence followed.

As early as 1919 and 1920, Palestinian Arabs attacked Jewish settlers in attempts to forestall further Zionist colonization. Periodic Arab forays evoked Jewish counterattacks and the formation of Zionist defense forces, since settlers claimed that the protection given them by British forces and mandate police was inadequate. Whereas Jewish efforts were highly organized, Arab efforts were fragmented and disorganized, partly because the Arab leaders were divided.

Progressive land purchases by the Jewish National Fund not only increased Jewish landholdings at the expense of the Arab owners but also displaced increasing numbers of Palestinian fellahin (farmers). The worst Arab-Jewish fighting of the first fifteen mandate years occurred in 1929, when an Arab attack killed 59 Jews in Hebron, causing the Jews to abandon that city until 1967. General strikes and virtual rebellion by the Arabs against both British and Jews broke out in 1936. Partly in response to British consideration of the partition of Palestine and partly because of events in neighboring areas, the violence upsurged periodically until the outbreak of World War II in 1939. Zionist leaders were able to exert greater pressure against both the Arabs and the British administrators as the Jewish population

increased and as the Zionists gained support because of the brutality of the Hitler regime.

Even before the end of World War II, Jewish extremists conducted terrorist campaigns to seize control of Palestine from the British mandatory authorities. At the end of the war, Zionist recruiters in war-torn Europe facilitated the movement of Jewish refugees into Palestine to become both fighters for the emergence of a Jewish state and settlers in that state. Efforts by the British mandatory officials to maintain some control over the immigration into Palestine were unsuccessful and exacerbated attacks by Jewish extremists. A climactic terrorist attack on the British on July 22, 1946, blew up government offices in the King David Hotel in Jerusalem. Conducted by the Jewish terrorist group Irgun Zvai Leumi, under the command of Menachem Begin (prime minister of Israel 1977–1983), the blast killed 91 British, Jews, and Arabs.

The Emergence of Israel

War weary and frustrated, Britain announced in 1947 that it intended to relinquish the mandate and leave the future of Palestine to the United Nations, successor to the League of Nations. Not only fatigued after their years of engagement in World War II, the British were also tired of the 30-year quandary they had been in because of their obligations to various parties in the Palestine problem. They clashed with both Jews and Arabs. Zionist pressure came from every direction, including the United States, with President Truman demanding that 100,000 Jews be admitted immediately to Palestine. Arabs demanded that the British keep their promises to the indigenous Palestinians.

As the British prepared to depart, the United Nations Special Committee on Palestine (UNSCOP) drew up a proposed plan for the partition of Palestine. The United Nations voted for the plan in November 1947, with U.S. pressure making a crucial difference in the vote. Although the plan was not put into effective operation, its provisions still have a certain juridical force and still retain importance.

The UN Partition Plan called for three entities: A Jewish state was to have 56 percent of mandate Palestine; an Arab state was to have 43 percent; and a small enclave comprising Jerusalem was to be a UN-administered, internationalized zone (Map 11-4B). It is of signal importance that Jerusalem and its environs were, therefore, to be a *corpus separatum* ("separate entity"), accessible to all faiths and peoples but belonging to neither Arabs nor Jews. Theoretically based on ethnic distribution, the proposed political-geographical jigsaw reflected the difficulties of equitably partitioning the mandate territory. Zionists resented not receiving endorsement for a Jewish state in the whole of Palestine in accordance with their interpretation of the Balfour Declaration. Other critics of the plan pointed to its partiality for the suggested Jewish state, which received 56 percent of mandate Palestine although Jews made up only one-third of the population and owned only about 7 percent of the land. The proposed boundaries would have included 407,000 Arabs in the Jewish state and 10,000 Jews in the Arab state, as well as 142,000 Jews and 68,000 Arabs in the internationalized district of Jerusalem.

The Arabs, relying on the principle that a mandate territory could not legally be alienated from the indigenous population, rejected the proposed surrender of over half of their Palestinian homeland to a settler people. Besides, they felt sure that they could, by force if necessary, prevent actual establishment of the Jewish state. The Zionists accepted the territorial proposal. Not only was it generous in its award of territory to the Jews, it also implied UN recognition of legitimacy for the Zionist assumption of sovereignty over half of Palestine. Jews and Arabs engaged in preliminary fighting, sometimes sweeping British forces into the conflict.

The Zionist leadership in Palestine proclaimed the new independent state of Israel, without mention of boundaries, immediately upon British relinquishment of the mandate and withdrawal of troops on May 14, 1948. At the same time, contiguous Arab states and Iraq sent military units into Palestine to aid their fellow Arabs, the Palestinians. Only the British-trained Jordanians and Iraqis held their ground in the highlands. After several months of alternating fighting and cease-fires, other Arab troops were defeated by the better armed, motivated, and organized Israelis.

Israel then controlled all of the area allotted the Jewish state in the Partition Plan, plus half of the territory allotted the Arab state. The Jordan Arab Legion, with Iraqi troops on its right flank, held the highlands to the north, south, and east of Jerusalem, and the Egyptians held the short, narrow strip northeast of the Sinai that came to be known as the Gaza Strip. Jerusalem was divided between Jordan and Israel, with Jordan holding the Old City and most of the holy sites along with the rest of the West Bank.

Territorial Phases

Theoretically, Israel became an independent state in May 1948 within the borders defined in the UN Partition Plan (Map 11-4B). However, more long-lasting borders resulted from the fact that the battlefronts at the end of the 1948–1949 fighting became the "cease-fire lines," negotiated by a UN mediator. These lines, which expanded Israel's original area by 50 percent, became and still are the de facto boundaries of Israel (Map 11-4C). Even with Jordan holding the eastern sector of Jerusalem, including the Old City, Israel unilaterally declared Jerusalem as its national capital in 1950. The declaration was pronounced invalid by the United Nations, on the basis that the original Partition Plan had designated Jerusalem as a *corpus separatum* under UN administration. Israel also seized the Sinai during the Israeli-British-French assault on Suez in 1956, creating a short-lived third territorial phase. The young state occupied the Sinai for several months but later evacuated it under international pressure.

The fourth phase of Israel's territorial evolution began after the Six-Day War (or June War) in 1967, which resulted in Israeli occupation of the Sinai, Gaza Strip, West Bank, and the southwestern corner of Syria, the Golan Heights (Map 11-4D). Seizure of the West Bank reunited the city of Jerusalem, a major Israeli goal, and Israel also extended the metropolitan boundaries of East Jerusalem and unilaterally annexed the entire area to the state of Israel. On the basis of a 1980 declaration by the Israeli parliament, the Knesset, Israel still insists that Jerusalem is its capital, never to be surrendered or divided, but only a few small states have recognized that claim, and all major embassies are located in Tel Aviv.

Israel's fourth territorial phase continued from mid-1967 until the beginning of Israel's step-by-step withdrawal from the western part of the Sinai under agreements reached through mediation by U.S. Secretary of State Henry Kissinger. The Kissinger mediation was conducted after Egypt and Syria attacked Israelis in occupied Sinai and occupied Golan in 1973, a conflict called by Israel the Yom Kippur War and by Arabs the Ramadan War. Israel's withdrawal from the Sinai continued under new accords reached in the 1978 Camp David negotiations and after the Egyptian-Israeli peace treaty of 1979. Completion of the evacuation of the Sinai, except for the Taba enclave, took place in 1982 (Map 11-4E). Taba remained in dispute between Egypt and Israel until it was awarded to Egypt in late 1988 by binding arbitration.

A debatable fifth phase began in 1981 when Israel declared its annexation of the Golan Heights, a unilateral annexation not recognized by any other country. A possible sixth phase might be identified as a consequence of the Israeli invasion of Lebanon in June 1982. Although most Israeli forces were withdrawn during 1983 and 1984, Israel still maintains control of a 440-mile^2/1,140-km^2 buffer zone with the South Lebanese Army (SLA), a 3,000-man proxy military force of mixed Lebanese that is organized, trained, armed, paid, and supplied by the Israelis. The SLA mission is to patrol and hold Israel's self-proclaimed "security zone," 9 miles/14.4 km wide, just north of the Israeli border with Lebanon. The zone has been used to match Israel's control from the air with control of southern Lebanon from the ground and to attempt to prevent rocket attacks and infiltration of northern Israel from the area.

First called by the Israelis "occupied territories," then "administered territories," then simply "territories," four areas—the West Bank, Gaza Strip, Golan Heights, and Sinai—were under Israeli military government from 1967 until the Sinai was evacuated and the Golan Heights annexed.

The West Bank and East Jerusalem remain the territorial core—but not the only territorial aspect—of the Arab-Israeli conflict, globally as well as locally. Palestinian Arabs declare their determination to remain in this area of Palestine;

Israelis show their equal determination to control the land and settle it as they did on the plains of Palestine. One of the most controversial aspects of the Arab-Israeli problem has been the program of Jewish settlement and displacement of Arab inhabitants in the remaining occupied territories (see Chap. 15). Clashes occurred periodically, until young Palestinians rose up in a citizens' rebellion in the West Bank and Gaza beginning in December 1987. The *intifadah* ("uprising") involved frequent confrontations between Israeli soldiers and rock-throwing Palestinian youths demonstrating against 26 years of military occupation and increasing Israeli settlements. By early 1993, the *intifadah* had become a different movement from that of earlier years as a reciprocal consequence of Palestinian resistance to continued Israeli occupation, opposing attitudes toward the ongoing peace talks, emergence of extremist groups of which Hamas (see Glossary) became the best known, and escalation of violence on the Palestinian side as a particular response to the Israeli deportation of 415 West Bank and Gaza Palestinians to southern Lebanon in December 1992. In early 1993, reliable figures indicated that since the beginning of the *intifadah*, 1,119 Palestinians had been killed by Israeli soldiers or civilians; 708 had been killed, allegedly by other Palestinians, for collaboration with Israeli authorities; more than 100,000 had been wounded or injured; more than 15,000 had been subjected to administrative detention; and more than 1,225 houses had been destroyed in collective punishment. Also indicative of the heightened violence is the figure of 124 Israeli soldiers and civilians killed, a sharply higher figure than that of a year earlier.[16] In taking such actions, Israeli officials emphasized their determination to preserve order in the occupied territories and to protect the security of the state of Israel. However, they were criticized both domestically and externally for the severity of their repression of the demonstrations. It was such mutually deadly relations that contributed to the Israeli-Palestinian accord on Gaza in September 1993.

The Palestinians

Although Palestinians are primarily refugees, they may be grouped geographically into six categories: those who stayed in the areas taken over by Israel in 1948–1949; those who stayed in the West Bank and Gaza; those who fled the areas incorporated into Israel in 1948–1949 and became refugees in adjoining districts (West Bank and Gaza) that were later occupied by Israel; those who fled to the East Bank between 1947 and the present (Jordan conferred citizenship on them); those who fled into adjoining countries and have remained there; and those who immigrated to other countries.

Even before the outbreak of full-scale fighting on May 15, 1948, Palestinian Arabs had lost the initiative to the better organized, motivated, and equipped Zionist fighters, and thousands of Palestinians had fled from areas in which Arabs and Jews were fighting for land and military advantage. They had been especially terrified by the massacre of 254 villagers in Deir Yassin, near Jerusalem, by Jewish forces on April 9, 1948, that was widely reported in order to panic the Arabs.[17] After mid-May, the thousands of refugees became hundreds of thousands as Israeli military units gained momentum.

By the time the 1948–1949 fighting had subsided, approximately 800,000 (official estimates vary from 720,000 to 960,000) Palestinians had fled from their homes and lands in the areas taken over by Israeli forces. The largest numbers sought refuge in the hill country of central Palestine, and many continued across the Jordan River into the Kingdom (former mandate) of Transjordan. Others crowded into the southwestern corner of Palestine that later became the Gaza Strip, and still others fled to Lebanon and Syria. About 160,000 Arabs, most of them in Galilee, refused to evacuate their lands and homes and stayed in the new Jewish state.

The refugees assumed that they would return home in a few days or weeks when the fighting ceased. As it became clear after the 1949 ceasefire that the Israelis would not allow the Palestinians to return to their homes, the United Nations created the United Nations Relief and Works Agency (UNRWA) to administer emergency care to the refugees. UNRWA set up more than 50 camps in and around the concentrations of homeless Palestinians: Gaza, the West Bank, East Bank Jordan (especially around Amman), southern and central Lebanon (especially around Bei-

rut), and Syria. Although UNRWA aid permitted only a marginal existence, it sustained—and continues to sustain—thousands of refugees. Not all refugees, of course, have been forced to call the camps home. Those with professional skills or sufficient funds generally neither registered with UNRWA nor resided in camps.

The status of the refugees within their host countries is varied: Only Jordan has extended citizenship to the refugees; Syria has extended equal rights but maintained strict control; and Lebanon, while accepting the Palestinians originally, feared the impact on the country's internal balance between Christians and Muslims and held most of the refugees at arm's length. Some Arab countries received only limited numbers of Palestinians. Many refugees have rejected integration into their host country's economy and society, deliberately maintaining their refugee status as a symbol of determination to return to their homeland and regain their patrimony.

After Israel seized the Golan Heights, West Bank, Gaza Strip, and the Sinai in 1967 (Map 11-5), more than 116,000 original Palestinian refugees were again uprooted, mostly from the West Bank. As 100,000 new refugees (referred to as "displaced persons" by UNRWA) fled across the Jordan River to the East Bank, 99,000 Syrians from the Golan Heights fled deeper into Syria and 35,000 Bedouins and villagers in the Sinai fled across the Suez Canal. (As with the earlier figures, these are estimates.) Thousands of the original Palestinian refugees who had gone to southern Lebanon fled again from their camps and villages as a result of Israeli incursions into southern Lebanon after 1969, especially after the Israeli invasion of 1982.

Whereas unskilled Palestinian refugees could find only menial jobs or no employment outside the UNRWA camps, large numbers of educated Palestinians have done well in their host countries, and many were significantly involved in the development of the Gulf states. Beirut became a center of Palestinian intellectual activity, Amman a demographic center, and Kuwait a center of Palestinian commercial activity. However, the role of Palestinians in Beirut diminished as the fighting in Lebanon continued into the late 1980s; and, more notably, of the approximately 350,000 Palestinians in Kuwait before the Iraqi

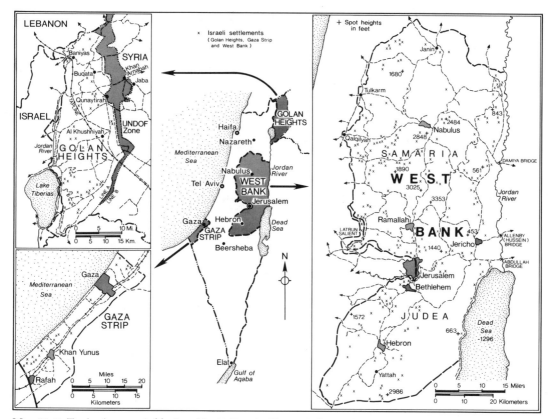

Map 11-5. *Territories occupied by Israel in 1967 and still occupied in early 1993.*

invasion, fewer than 20,000 remained in early 1993. Partly because of changing economic conditions but also because of altered political and social environments, the geographical distribution of Palestinian populations throughout the Middle East began changing appreciably after about 1987, and it changed dramatically virtually everywhere in the Middle East during and after the Iraqi occupation of Kuwait. The Institute for Palestine Studies gave the accompanying figures for Palestinian populations in various places in the fall of 1991; however, by late 1992, in addition to the change in the figure for Kuwait, there may well have been a greater number of Palestinians in Jordan, for instance, and a smaller number in the Gulf states.

Jordan	1.7 million
West Bank	1.1 million
Gaza Strip	620,000
Israel	690,000
Lebanon	330,000
Syria	300,000
Kuwait	100,000
Other Gulf states	293,000
United States	150,000
Other Arab states	102,000
Other	175,000
TOTAL	5.560 million

As the years dragged on and the Palestinians saw little evidence that they or their problems were receiving significant attention in the world councils, they sought some organized approaches to their problems. One group that emerged in the early 1960s, Fatah (the name is the reverse acronym for *Harakat al-Tahrir al-Filastiniyah,* Palestinian Liberation Movement), conducted guerrilla raids by fedayeen (literally "sacrificers") into Israel from neighboring countries. Not until 1964 did a broad-based Palestinian organization emerge that had as its goal the recovery of the Palestinian homeland.

This was the Palestine Liberation Organization (PLO), which gradually gained a major but highly controversial role in Palestinian and Middle East affairs, especially after Yasser Arafat became its chairman in 1969. After the late 1960s, the PLO evolved into an extensive and complex institution with a broad range of units that included not only guerrilla groups—some of whose terrorist activities have given the PLO its often unfavorable image—but also several welfare agencies serving Palestinian refugees. Its periodically well-financed activities were centered in Lebanon until Israeli military pressure on the PLO forces and other activities of the organization in 1982 forced PLO military withdrawal from Beirut to several other Arab countries. A new headquarters was established in Tunis, and although it was bombed by Israeli warplanes in 1985, it has been rebuilt and expanded on the same site.

A series of developments in late 1988 had an important impact on the Palestinian problem and the overall Arab-Israeli conflict. After a year of the *intifadah,* the 480-member Palestine National Council (PNC) met in Algiers and on November 15 proclaimed an independent State of Palestine in the West Bank and Gaza, with its capital as Jerusalem. The Palestinian state was to fulfill the establishment of the Arab state envisioned, along with the Jewish state, in the United Nations General Assembly Partition Resolution in 1947 (which also gave Jerusalem the status of *corpus separatum*). More than 80 governments had recognized the projected Palestinian state within one year.

In 1974, Arab governments recognized the PLO as the sole official representative of the Palestinian people. Despite the vicissitudes attending its evolution, for more than two decades the PLO operated in that capacity for the increasing numbers of Palestinians both inside the occupied territories and elsewhere. Israel rejected and bitterly condemned the PLO until late 1992, when the Rabin government decided to negotiate a dramatic agreement with its old enemy (see details in the Epilogue).

The Peace Conferences

In the aftermath of the 1991 Gulf war, members of the coalition that had worked together to liberate Kuwait determined to take definitive action on the most persistent source of conflict in the Middle East, the Arab-Israeli problem. With this determination providing an impetus, the United States and the then Soviet Union, acting as cohosts, convened a peace conference at the Royal Palace in Madrid on October 30, 1991. The involved parties that attended were a Jordanian-Palestinian team, Lebanon, Syria, and Israel. Also attending were Egypt and representatives of the twelve members of the European Community, as well as observer delegations from the United Nations, the Gulf Cooperation Council, and the five-member North African Maghrib-Arab Union.

The peace talks continued in Washington, D.C., in December and in February and August 1992. Among the concerns of the Arab delegations was the return of lands seized by the Israelis in the 1967 war (East Jerusalem, the West Bank, the Gaza Strip, and the Golan Heights) and, after the invasion of Lebanon in 1982, part of southern Lebanon. Specific Palestinian concerns (supported by other Arab delegations) included cessation of Israeli settlement in the occupied territories of the West Bank and Gaza, an interim period of limited self-rule leading to a Palestinian state (with international protection under the Fourth Geneva Convention for people living under occupation), and a Palestinian diaspora right to repatriation or compensation under United Nations Resolution 195. Of special interest to the Israeli delegation were recognition by other countries in the Middle East and trade and commercial opportunities within the region, as well as interests common to all the parties that were under discussion in the multilateral talks.

Multilateral talks on regional issues in the Middle East were held in Moscow on January 28, 1992, with more than 30 nations in attendance. Security issues/arms control, economic development, water resources and use, environmental problems, and refugees were among topics for continued discussion and negotiation at meetings at other locations between the end of April and mid-May 1992.

Progress toward the achievement of peace and agreements on negotiated elements was labored and slow early in the peace conferences. However, first-time meetings took place, and, after the change in government in Israel, negotiations were at least less rancorous and more meaningful. Despite some progress during the talks in 1992, the deportation of more than 400 Palestinians to southern Lebanon in December and the subsequent escalation of violence in the occupied territories threatened—at least for the time being—continuation of fruitful dialogue.

The Israeli Knesset took a significant step in January 1993 when it lifted a 1986 ban on contacts between Israeli citizens and the PLO. Only later did the reason for repeal of the law become clear. Beginning in that month, the new Labor government started secret negotiations with the PLO for a joint Declaration of Principles. The talks could and did move much more rapidly and decisively than the ongoing public rounds. The accord, which provided for interim autonomy for the Palestinians in the occupied territories, was signed in Washington on September 13, 1993. More details are given in the Epilogue.

The Iran-Iraq War, 1980–1988

Following the Khomeini revolution in Iran in 1978–1979, the centuries-long enmity along the Zagros piedmont, between "Mesopotamians" and others to the west and "Iranians" to the east, once again flamed into open conflict. For hundreds of years, the Sunni Ottomans were the power to the west of the piedmont and the Shii Persians and other Iranians were the power in the Zagros and the Iranian plateau. Post–World War I Iraq and Iran inherited the animosity and periodically clashed along the Zagros piedmont ridges and, more acutely, along the Shatt al-Arab. The new revolutionary Islamic republic's militancy and apparent instability in 1979–1980 led Iraq to deem that the time was right to force Iran to accede to several long-standing Iraqi demands. Following initial clashes in August and early September 1980, Iraq invaded Iran across the Shatt al-Arab on September 17. By late September Iraq held several positions inside Iran and called upon Iran to return the Tunbs and

Abu Musa islands occupied in 1971. Thus, the immediate Iran-Iraq conflict commenced.

One of the Baathist Iraqi aims was to force the reinstatement of the Iran-Iraq boundary along the lower Shatt al-Arab that had existed prior to 1975. Difficult to delineate equitably, the Shatt al-Arab boundary of modern times was first determined in 1847 and was slightly modified in 1913–1914. In 1937, another change ran the boundary line around Abadan to follow the *thalweg* (the deepest channel of the river). The remainder of the border continued to follow the low-water mark of the east (Iranian) bank (Map 11-6a), in accordance with the 1913–1914 agreement.

Tensions rose in 1969, when the shah of Iran abrogated the 1937 treaty. By 1975, Iran was clearly more powerful than Iraq, which had been weakened by an Iranian-backed Kurdish rebellion and was also isolated from other Arab countries; so Iraq agreed, in Algiers on March 6, 1975, to the Shatt al-Arab boundary claimed by Iran. The new boundary followed the *thalweg* along the entire Shatt al-Arab border (Map 11-6b). In exchange, Iran stopped supporting the Kurdish rebellion, which then abated.

War operations during the years 1980–1988 disabled some of the most productive facilities in the northern and northwestern Gulf, including Basrah and all of Iraq's most important ports. Air raids and missile attacks damaged major cities on both sides. Oil production decreased sharply in both countries during the first several months of the fighting. Casualties were tragically high, especially among young Iranians, and were reliably believed to exceed 1.2 million.[18]

All of the Gulf states incurred economic losses because of the Iran-Iraq war. In addition to the socioeconomic consequences of the enormous human casualties, the war is estimated to have cost $200 billion directly and more than $1,000 billion indirectly. The impact of the war on exports of Gulf oil was especially serious because of attacks by both sides on oil tankers calling at export terminals as the "tanker war" intensified in late 1987. All of the oil-producing Gulf amirates and Saudi Arabia combined to extend about $50 billion in aid to Iraq, partly because Iraq was a sister Arab country and partly because it was deflecting Iranian revolutionary danger from them. Kuwait and Saudi Arabia sold some of their oil

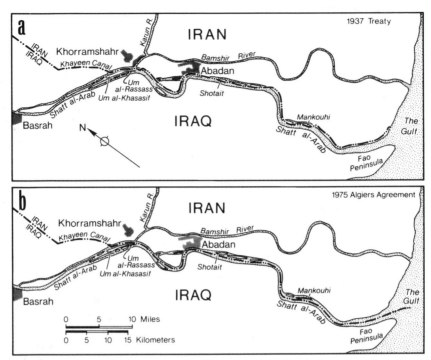

Map 11-6. *Iran-Iraq boundary along the Shatt al-Arab. Shift of the boundary from the east bank of the Shatt to the deepest part of the channel in 1975 was one reason for the Iran-Iraq war. (Redrawn from Tareq Y. Ismael,* Iraq and Iran: Roots of Conflict *[Syracuse, N.Y.: Syracuse University Press, 1982], p. 23. Names as on original. Used with permission.)*

for Iraq's account, and Saudi Arabia permitted construction of a "back-door" pipeline from Iraq to the Saudi East-West line. Contradictorily, the Gulf states also continued certain relations with Iraq's opponent, since they were reluctant to cut their long trade contacts with Iran. The United States continued its commitment to Gulf access by furnishing naval escorts to U.S.-registered tankers in the Gulf, most of them reflagged Kuwaiti ships. Before the convoying became regularized, the frigate USS *Stark* was mistakenly damaged by an Iraqi air-to-ship Exocet missile in a night attack on May 17, 1987, killing 37 of its crew; and the cruiser USS *Vincennes* mistakenly shot down an Iranian civilian aircraft with a ship-to-air missile on July 3, 1988, with a loss of all 290 people aboard. Both Iraq and the United States later agreed to pay damages for their errors.

Both Iran and Iraq were exhausted by mid-1988, but on July 18, Iran surprisingly accepted UN Security Council Resolution 598 calling for an immediate cease-fire between the two combatants. One reason for the Ayatollah Khomeini's turnabout may have been his fear of further chemical warfare attacks by Iraq. In March 1988, Iraqi military forces killed several thousand people in the Kurdish village of Halabja, near the Iranian border, with poison gas as reprisal for the Kurds' having joined Iranian forces in a recent attack. Iraq also used chemical warfare on several other occasions. A UN Iran-Iraq Military Observer Group (UNIIMOG) oversaw the cease-fire, and a UN-sponsored armistice took effect on August 20. (As surprising as Iran's initiation of the cease-fire was Iraq's acceptance of Iran's demands for a peace settlement two years later when Iraq needed Iranian neutrality in the Gulf crisis.)

Alignments in the Iran-Iraq war engendered some curious transnational relationships, as well as arms sales, in the Middle East. Both the People's Republic of China and the Republic of China on Taiwan supplied equipment to Iran. Syria, Iraq's Arab neighbor, refused to reopen Iraq's major pipelines across Syria to the Mediterranean and otherwise aided Iran. Despite public condemnation of Israel by the Republic of Iran, Israel regularly supplied spare parts and arms to Iran under its foreign policy principle of supporting enemies of Arab countries. A U.S.-Israel collusion was also exposed in October 1986, the Iran-Contra scandal, revealing that the United States and Israel were secretly supplying arms to Iran for complex and contradictory reasons, including seeking freedom for U.S. hostages in Lebanon. Ironically, it was two of Iraq's chief supporters, financially and logistically— that became Iraq's main victims two years later.

The Gulf Crisis, 1990–1991

A review of some relevant aspects of the seven-month-long Gulf crisis, including "Desert Shield" and its military successor "Desert Storm," affords insights into military/strategic facets of the Middle East—especially the Gulf area—and into some of the ramifications of the crisis. The review does not include details of the events, which have been covered in many sources.[19]

Emboldened by the outcome of the Iran-Iraq war, Saddam Husayn, the Baathist president of Iraq, reiterated the long-standing Iraqi claim to Kuwait and emphasized his intention to make Iraq the dominant power in the Gulf. At a May 1990 Arab summit meeting in Baghdad, the Iraqi leader denounced Kuwait and the UAE for exceeding their OPEC production quotas and thereby weakening the Iraqi economy. Iraq also demanded that Kuwait forgive the multibillion-dollar loans made to Iraq during the Iran-Iraq war, a war Iraq claimed it had fought on behalf of all the Arab Gulf countries, and that Kuwait cede the extension of the rich Rumaila oil field into Kuwait. Kuwait rejected these demands. While giving assurances that Iraq would not attack a sister Arab country, on August 2, 1990, President Saddam ordered the 100,000 troops that had massed on Kuwait's border in late July—which he had announced were on maneuvers—to advance into Kuwait.

Regional and world reaction to Iraq's assault on Kuwait varied in kind and degree. Since both Kuwait and Iraq were members of the Arab League, the Organization of the Islamic Conference, OPEC, OAPEC, and the UN, and Kuwait was also a member of the GCC, some members of these agencies reacted with ambivalence. Members of the GCC and the OIC condemned the action but could not confront Iraq militarily. The Arab League condemned the invasion, although with disabling internal disagreement, and discussed a military response.

Iraq sought support of the more oppressed and militant Arabs by proclaiming that it was championing Arabism, Islam, the Palestinian cause, the overthrow of wealthy monarchies, anti-imperialism, and other popular causes. One Iraqi proposal linked Iraqi withdrawal from Kuwait with Israeli withdrawal from the occupied territories and with Syrian withdrawal from Lebanon. Frustrated, embittered Palestinians—including those in Jordan, which had close economic ties with Iraq—embraced the Iraqi declarations, and the PLO leadership expressed support for Iraq. Yemen also expressed some pro-Iraq sentiments, as did the Sudan, Libya, Algeria, and Tunisia (headquarters of the PLO). Iran, after eight years of warfare with Iraq, echoed Iraq's denunciation of the United States and other Western governments, especially for sending forces to the Gulf, although it condemned Iraq's annexation of Kuwait. Iraq then assured Iran's neutrality by informing the new government that Iraq would accept the Iranian terms for a peace treaty ending the Iran-Iraq war.

Coalition Response

Acting under the 1980 Carter Doctrine, the United States sought and received prompt Saudi endorsement for the dispatch of U.S. troops to northeastern Saudi Arabia within days after Iraq invaded Kuwait. Otherwise, most of the Western reaction to the invasion of Kuwait was channeled through the UN Security Council (UNSC). The dozen little-opposed UNSC resolutions focused on the one aim of freeing Kuwait and did not authorize the invasion of Iraq or the overthrow of its government. Under the UN resolutions, 28 states joined in the U.S./U.K.-led coalition and cooperated, in some form, in the liberation of

Kuwait. Germany and Japan sent no troops but contributed large amounts of funding.

Having announced that Kuwait had been annexed as the "rightful nineteenth province" of Iraq, Iraqi authorities disavowed the legitimacy of the various embassies in Kuwait and demanded their closure. The American and British embassies withstood Iraqi intimidations and remained in limited operation—although under extremely difficult circumstances—until mid-December 1990. During its occupation of Kuwait, Iraq committed executions, widespread mistreatment of hundreds of Kuwaitis, hostage-taking, and large-scale looting. The systematic looting included not only motor vehicles, technical equipment, store inventories, and other consumer goods but also museum collections and $3–4 billion in gold bullion as well as cash in the banks. Later UN resolutions obtained the return of the museum collections and gold bullion.

Iraqi actions set in motion a human tide of more than 3 million refugees of many nationalities. Tens of thousands—Pakistanis, Indians, Sri Lankans, Thais, Filipinos, and others—as well as Kuwaitis, Palestinians, and other Arabs fled Kuwait, many of them through Iraq to Jordan, which bore much of the burden of aid to the refugees. Hundreds of thousands of Egyptian laborers left Iraq. Hundreds of Europeans and Americans were held hostage in Baghdad. Later, at the end of the fighting, Iraqi troops turned against hundreds of thousands of Shii and others from southern Iraq, many of whom sought refuge in Iran, and against the Kurds in the north, thousands of whom sought refuge in eastern Turkey and Iran.

The UN Security Council gave Iran a deadline of January 15, 1991, to leave Kuwait or face a full-scale military attack in both Kuwait and Iraq. When Iraq did not withdraw, on the night of January 16–17 the most intensive target-specific air strikes in history were directed at Baghdad and other major cities in Iraq. Iraq refused to capitulate, and the coalition ground attack began on February 24, 1991, overwhelming the Iraqi forces in Kuwait and adjacent areas.

Regional biophysical and cultural elements strongly influenced the coalition timetable. It was axiomatic that Iraq had to be held in place immediately upon its occupation of Kuwait, although it is unknown whether Iraq intended to proceed into Saudi Arabia. Military strikes to dislodge Iraq had to await a buildup of coalition forces, which was estimated to take until mid-January. Commanders wanted to avoid the heat of summer, the worst cold of winter, and especially the heavier rain of late winter and the succession of strong north winds—the *shamal* (see the section on winds in Chap. 4)—of the late winter. It was essential, if at all possible, to avoid military activity in a Muslim area during the month-long Ramadan fasting period, to begin in mid-March. All of these factors led to the timing of mid-January to begin hostilities.

Destruction and Eco-Terrorism

Iraq inflicted damage and caused casualties in two noteworthy respects in addition to its occupation of Kuwait. Thirty-two ground-to-ground Scud missiles were launched at targets in Saudi Arabia and 39 at targets in Israel. Some Scuds were destroyed by Patriot antimissile missiles, but others caused damage to buildings in both Saudi Arabia and Israel, and one caused 27 fatalities among U.S. military personnel in Dammam, Saudi Arabia.

Second, after the beginning of hostilities in mid-January, one tactic used by Iraqi forces was a quantitatively new tactic in environmental destruction, well labeled as "environmental terrorism" or "eco-terrorism"—dumping and setting fire to oil, thus making a weapon of the one commodity available in abundance. During the period January 19–23, to deter expected coalition operations along the Kuwaiti coast, Iraqis opened valves on oil storage facilities on Kuwait's Sea Island terminal off Mina al-Ahmadi and also dumped oil from tankers in the area and from the Iraqi terminal of Mina al-Bakr. They thereby deliberately created the greatest oil spill in history, 4–6 million barrels (the Valdez, Alaska, spill was 258,000 barrels). The spill gradually worked its way down the coast of Saudi Arabia, destroying enormous quantities of plant and animal life, especially sea grasses, fish, shellfish, and birds. Intakes for desalination plants were threatened, and pristine beaches were covered with thick hydrocarbons.

As the Iraqis evacuated Kuwait, they blew up and set fire to most of the oil wells in the amirate. About 611 wells were set ablaze, and another 60 spewed crude petroleum under high pressure; still others were damaged in various ways (see space image in Chap. 18). By early summer of 1991, about 5.5 million barrels of oil and enormous quantities of natural gas were lost each day—approximately twice the normal average daily production of Kuwait (also of Iraq)—with a value at that time of $75 million. Upon the liberation of Kuwait, the best oil-well fire-fighting teams in the world were immediately assembled to extinguish the blazes and cap the flowing wells, which, despite dangers and difficulties, they accomplished by early November 1991. Meanwhile, oil from the gushing wells had collected into "oil lakes" in low places, with the surface pools holding a rough estimate of more than 25 million barrels.[20]

The response to the Iraqi invasion of Kuwait involved enormous sums of money. Authoritative estimates in 1993 indicated that the war costs to Arab states totaled $676 billion, including $160 billion in damages in Kuwait and $256 billion in Iraq. U.S. officials estimated a cost to the coalition of about $61 billion, all of which was reimbursed by Saudi Arabia, Kuwait, the UAE, Japan, and Germany.

The stance of Yemen, Jordan, Sudan, and the PLO regarding Iraq's actions resulted in the loss of financial aid from Saudi Arabia and other former donors and in the expulsion of many of their citizens from Saudi Arabia and the Gulf states. More than 800,000 Yemenis were forced to return home, surrendering their jobs and depriving their families of millions of dollars annually in remittances. More than 300,000 Palestinians were forced to leave Kuwait without their property or funds.

Strategic Straits

Five sea passages, four major and one minor, in the Middle East are of geostrategic significance: the Suez Canal, the Turkish Straits (Dardanelles and Bosporus), Strait of Hormuz, Bab el-Mandeb, and Strait of Tiran. Some are familiar historically, and all have figured prominently in the news in recent decades.

Suez Canal

The man-made Suez Canal was excavated between 1859 and 1869 through the Isthmus of Suez, which formerly linked Africa and Asia. It is 110 miles/177 km long, including approach channels at Port Said and Suez, and has been enlarged at least nine times, the latest in 1980, when it was given a navigational width of 590 ft./180 m and a depth of 52 ft./16 m. Current dimensions permit passage of ships of 150,000 dwt fully loaded, 250,000 dwt partly loaded, and 375,000 dwt empty. Additional expansion under way in the early 1990s will increase the canal width to 1,360 ft./415 m and its depth to 72 ft./22 m.

The opening of the Suez Canal permitted shortening of the sea trip between Britain and India by 5,000 miles/8,000 km, so that during the 1870s most world shipping shifted from the route around the Cape of Good Hope, in southern Africa, to the Mediterranean-Suez–Red Sea route. Closures of the Suez Canal, for six months in 1956 and for eight years prior to June 1975, helped stimulate increased use of supertankers for shipment of petroleum from the Gulf exporting countries around southern Africa to Western Europe and the Americas. When the canal reopened, and even after it was enlarged in 1980, oil shipments tended to continue in the supertankers around the Cape, but most general-cargo freighters returned to the canal route. Revenue from the canal was almost $1.9 billion in 1991.

Straits

Turkish Straits. These straits, the Dardanelles to the southwest and the Bosporus to the northeast, are linked up by the Sea of Marmara (Map 11-7) and have been of crucial importance since the Bronze Age. The legend of the Trojan War tells of fighting over the beautiful Helen, a charming romanticization of the struggle during the twelfth century BC for control of the entrance to the Black Sea and its rich coastlands. The World War I Gallipoli campaign in 1915 is the most recent

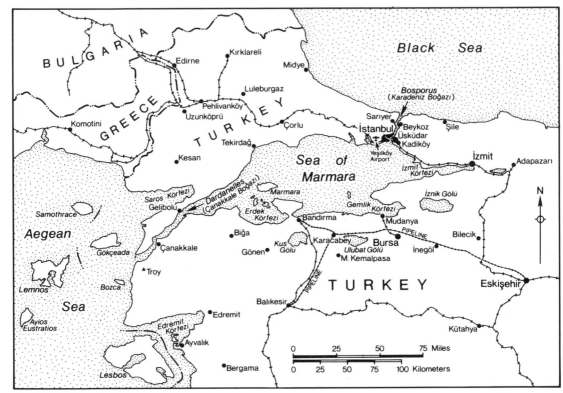

Map 11-7. *The Turkish straits (Dardanelles and Bosporus) and their geographical setting—a major world maritime connection.*

clash over control of the straits. International need for access to the straits was spelled out in the Lausanne Convention of 1923 and again in the Montreux Convention of 1936, which still governs international use of the waterways.[21] Of the average number of 60 ships a day that transited the straits in the late 1980s, about one-third at that time were of Soviet registry, many of them warships sailing between the Black Sea and the eastern Mediterranean. User ships in the early 1990s were increasingly cargo ships and tankers.

The Dardanelles (Turkish name, Çanakkale Boğazı), the ancient Hellespont, connects the Aegean Sea and the Sea of Marmara and lies between the Gallipoli Peninsula on the northwest and Asia Minor to the south. It is about 36 miles/57 km long, 4,000 ft./1,200 m wide at its narrowest and 4 miles/6.4 km at its widest, and is 150–300 ft./45–90 m deep.

The Bosporus (Greek for "ox-ford"; Turkish name, Karadeniz Boğazı) is shorter, narrower, and shallower than the Dardanelles—about 17 miles/28 km long, 3,000 ft./915 m at its narrowest, and 100 ft./30 m at its minimum depth. Since the Sea of Marmara is as deep as, and much wider than, the two straits, any ship afloat can make the passage between the Aegean and the Black seas. Although the three water bodies separate Europe from Asia Minor, the Bosporus was bridged in 1973 and again in 1988.

Traffic through the straits has increased enormously since World War I—international traffic by more than ten times. Shipping passing the straits in the late 1970s carried more than 70 million tons annually; 20,755 merchant ships transited the straits in 1980—approximately the number going through the Suez Canal. More than one-third of the Bosporus ships in the early 1990s flew the new flags of the successor states of the former Soviet Union—Russia, Ukraine, Georgia, and others.

Strait of Hormuz. Connecting the Gulf and the Indian Ocean, the Strait of Hormuz is squeezed

Figure 11-1. *Strait of Hormuz, one of the world's most important choke points, with Iran to the left, Oman and the UAE to the right. (Space view, looking southeast. NASA photograph)*

between Iran on the north and an exclave of Oman at the tip of the Musandam Peninsula on the south (Fig. 11-1). It is still one of the most vital channels of trade in the world, and although it no longer carries the 90 percent of the Middle East's petroleum exports that it did in the mid-1980s, it carries more than 13 million bpd. It has lost some of its oil traffic to the Red Sea and the Mediterranean but will regain some of it when Iraq and Kuwait reach normal production. The number of tankers and the quantity of petroleum transiting this strait daily vary with the world petroleum market and the political climate in the Gulf, as well as the size of the tankers. In 1980, about 19 million bbl of oil in 80 to 90 smaller tankers passed through Hormuz each day—one tanker every fifteen minutes.

With a depth of 290 ft./88 m and widths of 28–59 miles/45–95 km, Hormuz is the widest of the significant straits in the Middle East. Neverthe-

less, it is vulnerable to several kinds of weaponry and sabotage, and its defense is vital to both the Gulf petroleum exporters and the petroleum-consuming countries. Despite the indispensability of the strait for so many industrialized countries, the security of the Gulf and the strait came under serious threat from Iran and Iraq between 1980 and 1991.

Bab el-Mandeb. At the opposite corner of the Arabian Peninsula, the Bab el Mandeb (Gate of Lamentation) connects the Red Sea and Gulf of Aden. The strait is divided into two channels by the small but strategically located island of Perim, which belongs to Yemen. The main channel, with a width of 10 miles/16 km and a depth of 1,056 ft./322 m, is to the west of Perim on the African side, next to Djibouti. Three states are involved in the territorial waters in the straits—Yemen, Ethiopia, and Djibouti.

The relatively minor role of the Bab el-Mandeb changed significantly when the Suez Canal was opened in 1869, since virtually all of the ships transiting the canal also passed through the Bab el-Mandeb. With development of more Red Sea ports because of the canal traffic, the strait continued to carry heavy traffic even when the canal was closed, in order that Jiddah and other Red Sea ports normally served from the Mediterranean could be reached from the south. Development of the Saudi export port of Yanbu has enhanced the importance of both the strait and the Suez Canal. The port of Aden, lying a few miles east of the Bab el-Mandeb, achieved much of its modern importance as a result of the rise in importance of Suez and Red Sea traffic. An average of about 60 ships a day transit the strait.

Strait of Tiran. Connecting the Red Sea and the Gulf of Aqabah at the southeastern tip of the Sinai Peninsula, with Egypt on the west and Saudi Arabia on the east, the Strait of Tiran is of relatively minor importance in comparison with the Suez Canal and the straits already described. Nevertheless, its closure was considered as a major justification for the Israeli preemptive attack on Egypt in June 1967. The debate over the precise international principles relating to Tiran has not yet resolved the exact status of the strait. Saudi Arabia and Egypt were reported in 1992 to be seriously discussing the possibility of spanning the strait with a causeway similar to that constructed between Saudi Arabia and Bahrain during the 1980s.

Great-Power Rivalry

Britain and Russia long contended for spheres of influence in the zone from the Balkans to the Himalayas. Although traditional Russian pressure on the Northern Tier diminished during the 1920s and 1930s, the then Soviet Union resumed the Russian push into southwestern Asia after World War II. With Britain unable to counter the pressure as in the past, the United States joined the British as protectors of the Northern Tier states—Turkey and Iran, sometimes Iraq—against potential Russian expansion into an area of increasingly vital concern to the West. Rivalry between the United States and the USSR in the

Middle East became a major dynamic in the region's relations and geopolitics for nearly 45 years. Much of this "Great Game in the Middle East" was made obsolete by the collapse of the Soviet Union in 1991 and the subsequent cooperation between the United States and former Soviet republics. However, highlights of the rivalry are worth a historical review.

The policy of "containment" advocated in a watershed 1947 article by "X" (Ambassador George Kennan),[22] was formalized in the Truman Doctrine in March 1947. The declaration signaled a commitment on the part of the United States to maintain the balance of power in the Middle East while Britain made its phased withdrawals from Greece, Turkey, India, and the Palestine mandate. Later, Britain lost its influence in Iran, withdrew from Suez in 1956, and withdrew from the Gulf and the periphery of the Arabian Peninsula in 1971–1972. However, the British continue to have a vital interest in the Middle East and periodically coordinate political and military operations with the United States, as they did on a major scale in 1990–1991 during the Gulf crisis.

The Eisenhower administration sought to unify the region's resistance to the Soviet Union. With U.S. and British encouragement, the Baghdad Pact was formed in 1955, eventually including Turkey, Iraq, Iran, Pakistan, and Britain. The United States was a full member of the economic committee and the major source of funding for the pact. Consequent to the Suez affair of October–November 1956 (the joint Israeli-British-French invasion), the Eisenhower Doctrine was announced in January 1957, committing the United States to counter communist actions in the Middle East. This commitment, in one doctrine or another, was maintained through successive administrations, although it was applied in contradictory ways. On the one hand, the U.S. government tried to negate or minimize Soviet influence in the region until the USSR disintegrated in 1991; on the other hand, it followed regional policies that affronted key Arab countries and made some of them more receptive to Soviet influence.

The Nixon Doctrine encouraged the region's states to be responsible for their own defense and focused on the United States' reliance on Iran and, secondarily, Saudi Arabia. In the eastern Mediterranean, Turkey and Greece continued to be the southeastern flank of NATO, with the British providing support in southern Cyprus. Among states in the Fertile Crescent, Israel became increasingly involved in the so-called special relationship with the United States.

The Carter Doctrine was announced in early 1980, following the Iranian revolution, collapse of the Central Treaty Organization (CENTO— the former Baghdad Pact), and the Soviet invasion of Afghanistan in December 1979. This doctrine emphasized U.S. interest in the Gulf and in laying the groundwork for a Rapid Deployment Force, subsequently known as the Central Command. The Reagan administration exhibited its resolve to sustain U.S. power in the area by sending U.S. naval forces to the Gulf in 1987 and 1988. As we saw earlier, the dispatch of U.S. troops to Saudi Arabia in 1990–1991 by the Bush administration was based on the Carter Doctrine and was an extension of the Reagan support of Kuwait.

These successive doctrines are expressions of U.S. concern in an area in which other great powers have—and have long had—vital interests. Great Britain, France, Russia, and Japan join the United States as Great Powers with continuing interest in the Gulf area, with or without active hostilities to focus attention.

PART 2

Regional Geography

12

Syria: Middle East Heartland

Regional Keystone

Ancient Role, Modern Role

Historical-geographical Syria, lying between the Mediterranean and the middle Euphrates, has often functioned as the geographical keystone in the Middle East. Not only is its situation central, but also its location near the regional heart is enhanced by patterns of landforms, climates, and travel routes. Damascus and Aleppo have played outstanding roles as commercial and cultural centers for 3,500 years, and Syria's cereal belt has served as a granary for empires during many centuries. Two major corridors cross Syria: the main one south of the Turkish mountain wall and north of the desert, a second one through the Palmyra Oasis (Fig. 12-1). The routes were for thousands of years—indeed, until after World War I—the major east-west passageways through the region for the movement of people and goods. Western Syria has also long served as a segment of the north-south land route between Yemen and the northeastern Mediterranean and beyond into Asia Minor.

With such a location, Syria has for millennia experienced migrating peoples, marching armies, and political influences. Syrians have thereby at different times absorbed several ethnic and cultural groups and have sustained challenges to their capacity for unity and even survival. Periodically during its long history, the Syrian realm has served as a major power base, reaching its apogee during the Damascus-centered Umayyad Empire, 661–750. Later it was a focus of Islamic-Arab aspirations and potentially a modern political-spiritual center of the Arab world. The Syria of the last quarter of the twentieth century, with only moderate size, moderate population, and limited resources, has a major role in the region despite the serious problems it faces and its shifting relationships with its neighbors and with the Great Powers. Some of Syria's economic difficulties may be traced to its policy planning and relations; other problems stem partly from a mutual failure by Syria and the West to establish meaningful rapport. It is Syria's capabilities and role that this chapter will examine.[1]

The Three Syrias

The term *Syria* as used in this chapter will usually refer to the Syrian Arab Republic, so named in 1961. The republic is generally coextensive, except for the Iskenderun (Alexandretta) area, with the League of Nations mandate to France (1923–1946). However, a "historical Syria" existed for more than 2,000 years, and it comprised the general area that is now distributed among Syria, Lebanon, Jordan, western Iraq, Israel, and Israeli-occupied parts of Palestine. References to "Syria" in some writings imply this "Greater Syria."

The Physical Challenge

Regions of Syria

Syria has six rather well-differentiated natural regions, indicated on Map 12-1 by encircled numbers. [1] The Mediterranean coastal plain extends the full length of the country's seacoast, widest in the north behind Latakia and in the south near Lebanon. The plain is agriculturally productive

SYRIA

Long-form official name, anglicized: Syrian Arab Republic
Official name, transliterated: al-Jumhuriyah al-Arabiyah al-Suriyah
Form of government: unitary multiparty republic with one legislative house (People's Council)
Area: 71,498 miles^2/185,180 km^2
Population, 1991: 12,524,000. Literacy (latest): 64.5%
Ethnic composition (%): Arab 88.8, Kurdish 6.0, Armenian 2.5, Turkmen 1.7, other (including Circassian, Assyrian) 1.0
Religions (%): Sunni Muslim 74.0; Alawi, Druze, and other Muslim subsects 16.0; Christian (various sects) 8.9; other 1.1
GNP, 1989: $12.44 billion; per capita: $1,020
Petroleum reserves: 1.7 billion barrels
Main exports (% of total value, 1988): crude petroleum and petroleum products 43.9; textiles, wearing apparel, and leather 15.9; chemicals and chemical products 12.9; food, beverages, and tobacco 8.2
Main imports (% of total value, 1988): machinery and equipment 25.7; food, beverages, and tobacco 17.5; chemicals and chemical products 13.9; basic metals industries 9.0; textiles 6.0; paper and paper products 1.7
Capital city: Damascus (al-Dimashq, often al-Sham) 1,361,000; other cities: Aleppo (Halab) 1,308,000; Homs (Hims) 464,000; Latakia (al-Ladhiqiyah) 258,000; Hamah 214,000

Figure 12-1. *The ruins of the colonnade of Palmyra, prosperous oasis trade center under Queen Zenobia in the late third century, as a key caravan station and briefly a military power.*

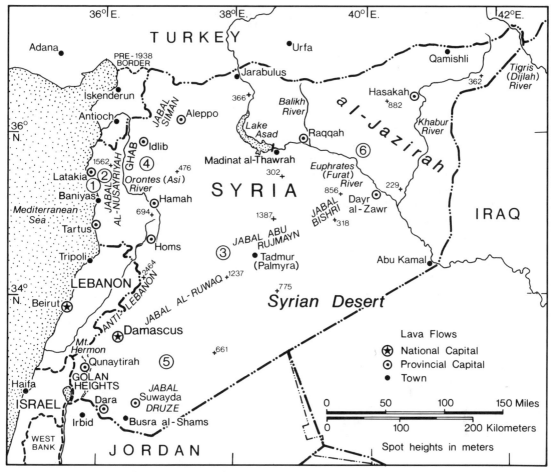

Map 12-1. *General map of Syria with major towns and physical features. Circled numbers identify Syrian regions.*

and is also the base for the main port of Latakia, for the oil-export port of Baniyas (formerly more active when it served as terminal for the Iraqi pipelines), and for the developing port and oil terminal of Tartus. [2] A succession of mountain groups lies east of the coastal plain: In the north is the continuous north-south range of the Jabal al-Nusayriyah, in the center are the southwest-northeast Anti-Lebanon Mountains dividing Syria and Lebanon, and in the south is the complex mass of Mt. Hermon. The uplifted Jurassic and Cretaceous limestone Jabal al-Nusayriyah is bounded on the east by an impressive fault with both vertical displacement and a strike slip of more than 12 miles/20 km. The fault is also the west side of the Ghab graben, the northern end of the Levant Rift System. East of the mountain frame is an extensive plateau divided by [3] a

southwest-northeast zone of complex folding and faulting associated with the Palmyra Folds (see Fig. 3-1). Several local names are applied to the successive sections of the splayed mountain ridges, including Jabal al-Ruwaq northeast of Damascus, Jabal Abu Rajmayn in the center, and Jabal Bishri toward the Euphrates River.

North of the Palmyra Folds and west of the Euphrates is [4] the level to rolling steppeland that supports extensive grain agriculture and Syria's second city of Aleppo as well as Hamah and Homs. South of the Palmyra Folds the plateau has a quite different character. Toward the west are [5] extensive basaltic lava flows of several ages, accompanied by numerous aligned cinder cones. Jabal al-Druze (Jebel Druze), which the Syrian government refers to officially as Jabal al-Arab, is a huge lava dome that reaches 3,300 ft./1,000 m above the plain and is flanked on the northeast by the extensive basalt plain of al-Safa and on the northwest by the thin, scabby, blistered lava flow of al-Laja. The plains area west of the Jabal al-Druze is the well-cultivated Hawran, its western edge a lava plateau that overlooks the Sea of Galilee and forms the Golan Heights. Well east of the lava belt, the Syrian Desert extends into Iraq, offering little except sparse grasses and bushes for the grazing animals of the Bedouins. In northeastern Syria is [6] the Jazirah, which lies east of the entrenched Euphrates River and continues the level to rolling landscape that lies west of the Euphrates. The Jazirah has been a focus of economic development since about 1970 following increased exploitation of the oil fields located there and following completion of the Euphrates Dam and its associated installations.

The Agricultural Base

Syria's share of the Fertile Crescent's climate, soil, landforms, and other beneficial characteristics endows the state with appreciable areas of relatively productive agricultural land. Making up about one-third of the country's total area, this agricultural land supplies the sustained economic base for the country. On the other hand, the problems of aridity and rough relief of the other two-thirds of the country present a major physical challenge. This challenge and the Syrian response are a major part of the saga of contemporary Syria.

By its very nature, the Fertile Crescent's inner boundary is a zone of marginal precipitation. Cyclical oscillation of the 12-in./300-mm isohyet (see Map 4-2) between wet and dry periods is a tensional element in Syrian agriculture. Consequently, it impinges on many aspects of Syrian economic and social life, including shifts between sedentarism and nomadism along the frontier. In its seasonal distribution, rainfall in this typical summer-dry Mediterranean climate area (Koeppen Csa) is concentrated in the cool months. Annual precipitation increases from 30 in./750 mm along the coast to 55 in./1,400 mm on the upper west-facing slopes of the Jabal al-Nusayriyah, then decreases sharply to the east, in the rain shadow of the mountains, to 22 in./550 mm in the Ghab Depression.

East of the mountains, the north-south subhumid agricultural belt with its steppe soils extends southward from Aleppo well into Jordan, and rainfall typically averages 12–20 in./300–500 mm along this southwestern horn of the Fertile Crescent. Eastward from Aleppo, the area averages 10–12 in./250–300 mm, with double those amounts in extreme northeastern Syria. Away from the more humid Fertile Crescent, the southeastern two-thirds of the country averages less than 8 in./200 mm, with the driest area, adjacent to the Jordan panhandle, receiving less than 4 in./100 mm. In this area and along the Euphrates in extreme southeastern Syria, mean July temperatures exceed 90°F/32°C. There the Syrian Desert is in full sway.

The Imprint of Time

Ancient Patterns

The western and northern parts of Syria were the sites of some of the earliest villages known, settlements dating well back into the ninth millennium BC (see Chap. 2). Some of the earliest pottery ever found was discovered in Syria on the banks of the Euphrates, and Damascus contends for the title of the oldest continuously inhabited city in the world. Ugarit just north of Latakia on the Mediterranean coast, Ebla 30 miles/50 km southwest of Aleppo, and Mari on the middle Euphrates were thriving city-states or imperial capitals early in the second millennium BC (see Map 2-1), and the earliest known alphabet, with 29 characters in cuneiform script and dating from the fifteenth century BC, was found during the excavation of Ugarit. Late in the second millennium, the Syrian region became and continued to be for almost 1,000 years a marchland, an area contested among successive great empires, including the Amorite and the Aramaean (the biblical Aram), which were rooted in Syria itself.

Alexander the Great's conquest of the Persians in 334–326 BC was followed by inclusion of the Syrian realm in the Seleucid Empire for more than 200 years. After Rome supplanted the Seleucids and made Syria a Roman province in 64 BC, the evolving Greco-Roman culture in Syria became infused with Christianity. The new sect gained its first major urban foothold in Antioch and flourished under the eastern Roman Empire and the successor Byzantine Empire. Ruins of churches and of entire abandoned towns from this period—Syria's several "dead cities"—can still be visited in the northwest and south, and impressive Greco-Roman buildings and cities are important tourist sites in Palmyra (see Fig. 12-1), Apamaea, Bosra, Dura Europos, and other areas. Beginning in AD 540, the century of warfare between the Byzantines and the Persian Sassanians inflicted great destruction on the Syrian countryside and cities. Ghassanians, Christian Arabs who lived chiefly in southern Syria, were the source of many powerful families in the Syrian society of the sixth and seventh centuries.

Arab Invasions and After

When the Arab Muslim onslaught came, the war-weakened Byzantines were unable to defend their Syrian possessions. As a result, in AD 636 Syria was the first area to fall to the Muslims after their eruption from the Hijaz. Just 25 years later, Syria entered its 90-year Golden Age when the Islamic Umayyad Empire, with Damascus as its capital, was established in the realms conquered by the Muslims. Arabic, the new official language, gradually displaced Aramaic and Greek; and Islam became dominant over Christianity, although it has never entirely displaced it. As it had before and as it did later, Syria demonstrated its ability to fuse cultures and evolve something "Syrian."

When the Abbasids supplanted the Umayyads in 750 and the Muslim power center shifted to Baghdad, Syria became a contested land for the next 800 years. Egyptians, Seljuks, Crusaders, Mongols, and the Abbasids vied for control. All held Syria, or parts of it, for varying lengths of time, leaving signs of their control in aqueducts, forts, and caravansaries. Ruins of spectacular Crusader castles in western Syria attract both tourists and serious students of medieval architecture. The Ottomans conquered Syria in 1516 and controlled it for most of the following 400 years until the breakup of the Ottoman Empire after 1918.

French Mandate

When the French assumed the mandate of Syria under the League of Nations in the early 1920s, their demarcation of the mandate's borders signaled the first time in history that a separate, quasi-independent polity of "Syria" had been formally defined. After part of the territory was detached in the creation of Lebanon, the mandate of Syria became the direct precursor of the contemporary state of Syria (see Chap. 11).

In order to inhibit Syrian nationalism and unity, French authorities divided the territory into internal "states": Aleppo, Damascus, and Alawite (called Latakia after 1930) created in 1920; Jabal al-Druze in 1921; and an autonomous Sanjak (subprovince) of Alexandretta (Turkish, Iskenderun) in 1923. In 1925, Damascus and Aleppo were united to form "Syria," and other shifts followed later. Revolts and instability typified the years of the mandate, but finally, after World War II, Syria became formally and officially an independent state on April 17, 1946.[2] Except for a revised boundary around the Alexandretta-Antioch (Iskenderun-Antakya) area, the frontiers of post-independence Syria embrace virtually the same territory as the mandate of Syria after separation of Greater Lebanon (see Map 12-1).

The United Arab Republic

Independent Syria shared with adjoining Lebanon and Jordan the impact of insecurity and instability consequent to World War II, the sudden assumption of independence, and the trauma of the emergence of a demonstrably powerful Israel on the territory of a putative "Greater Syria." On several occasions, Syria expressed interest in uniting—perhaps as a manifestation of the Greater Syria syndrome—with one or another of its Arab neighbors. Only once did an actual merger transpire, when between 1958 and 1961, Syria and Egypt were linked in the United Arab Republic (see Chap. 11). Whereas the union with Egypt served its original purpose of forestalling a communist coup in Syria, the aggressiveness of Nasserist Egypt offended Syria, which had long considered itself the standard-bearer of Arab nationalism. After three years of dominance by Egypt, rather than equal partnership, Syria withdrew from the UAR and has not acceded to any similar relationship since then. In 1978–1979 it did, however, discuss a possible merger with Iraq before resuming the usual confrontational stance over the question of leadership.

Figure 12-2. *The heart of the "new" downtown Damascus, telephoto view looking east from the top of Mount Qassiun. The multistory buildings date from the 1980s, the uniform-height buildings in the foreground from the French mandate prior to World War II. The Old City of Damascus is to the left. The rich, irrigated Ghutah is in the distance.*

The Syrian Mixture

Patterns of Population

In population, Syria ranks sixth among the sixteen states in the Middle East. Its population doubled between 1963 and 1987, and continuation of its present high birthrate would double its population again by about 2004. As in other Middle East countries, the raw population density figure for Syria is misleading, since the population is markedly concentrated in the more humid western area (see Map 6-2 and Table 6-1).

Syria has, from early times, had scattered cities of appreciable size and fame along the Euphrates and in the west. Damascus and Aleppo formerly alternated leadership in population, but since the 1960s Damascus has surpassed the northern center to become the primate city of Syria as well as its capital (Fig. 12-2). More than 50 percent of Syria's townspeople live in the two main cities.

The traditional population concentration axis along the humid steppe belt, Damascus-Homs-Hamah-Aleppo, has now expanded to include Latakia, Syria's main port. With development of the Euphrates Valley and the Jazirah east of the river, Dayr al-Zawr and Raqqah are in the 100,000 population range, and Hasakah and Qamishli are growing rapidly. In addition, scores of villages—some of them with populations of 10,000–20,000—are evolving in the broad, flat-floored river valley and adjacent plateaus in response to government development projects in the area. Suwayda, in the Jabal al-Druze, is the largest center in the south, with nearly 60,000 people. Syria's four universities are located in the four largest cities—Damascus, Aleppo, Homs, and Latakia.

Syrian Arabs and Their Religions

Among the several separate ethnolinguistic groups in the country, the dominant group has, for more than 1,000 years, been the Syrian Arabs, and they constitute nearly 90 percent of the population. The great majority of them (nearly three-fourths of the total population) are Sunni Muslim in religion. However, other Arab subgroups, especially religious sects, deserve mention in their Syrian context.

Other Muslim (or quasi-Muslim) sects besides the Sunni are mainly heretical Shii groups—Alawi, Druze, and Ismaili. Largest and, since the mid-1960s, most important of these sects is the Alawis, about 12 percent of the Syrian population and more than two-thirds of the inhabitants in and around the Jabal al-Nusayriyah in western Syria. Prior to the 1960s the Alawis were primarily agricultural workers, but they served in the army in numbers beyond their percentage of the population. The Baath party coup in 1963 enhanced the Alawi role, especially in the military, and when an Alawi, Hafiz al-Asad, became president in 1971 (and was still head of state in mid-1993), the role of the Alawis improved decisively.

The Druzes played a major political-military role during the mandate period. The Jabal al-Druze was one of the internal states created by France, and the periodic Druze revolts were a serious problem for the French mandatory authorities. However, the 424,000 Druzes (about 3.5 percent of the total population) play a subdued role in independent Syria. They are still concentrated in the rough lava dome of the Jabal al-Druze and in the Mount Hermon area in the south, composing more than 80 percent of the inhabitants in those areas. The Ismailis, less than half as numerous as the Druzes, are concentrated in the area of Salamiyah east of Hamah and in the mountains west of Hamah, where the Ismaili Assassins played an important role during the Crusades.[3]

Almost 9 percent of the Syrians are Christians, and except for the Armenians, a separate ethnolinguistic group, they are nearly all Arabs. Syrian Christians have a longer tradition than any other Christian group (they recall Paul's conversion near Damascus and the early role of Antioch), and their spiritual ancestors predated the Muslims in Syria by more than 500 years. The Christians tend to congregate in the larger cities of western Syria and are splintered into a dozen identifiable sects, the largest of which are the Greek Orthodox (nearly 5 percent of the Syrian population, but with several subsects), Armenian Orthodox (Gregorians), and Syrian Orthodox (Jacobites). Greek, Latin, Arabic, and Syriac (Aramaic) are employed as liturgical languages by the various sects, and Syriac is preserved as an everyday language among some of the Greek Catholics in the mountain village of Malula near Damascus.

Traditionally, Syrian Christians have affiliated with Arabism and were early leaders in Arab nationalism. Yet they have also felt an appreciable affinity with the West, having been a favored group during the Crusader occupation of the Levant and during the mandate period. The Nestorian Assyrians are some of the most recent arrivals in Syria. Having fled Iraq in 1933, they were settled in a score of villages on the upper Khabur River, west of Hasakah.

Ethnic Minorities

The largest ethnolinguistic minority in Syria is the Kurds, perhaps 800,000 in number—6.6 percent of the population. Speaking their own language, Kurds are primarily distributed across northern Syria, next to their ethnic homeland of Kurdistan, with concentrations in the mountains of the northwest and in the northeast. Some Kurds have occupied these mountains and foothills for centuries, but many of them, along with Armenians in the early years, fled from Turkey in the 1920s and early 1930s following a failed insurrection against Turkish authorities in eastern Anatolia. In addition to the main Kurdish belt in the north, where they are primarily agriculturalists but sometimes nomadic, several thousand Kurds live in the cities, especially in the Damascus Kurdish Quarter. Although most are Sunni Muslims, several thousand Kurds in the mountains west of Aleppo and around Lake Khatun east of Hasakah in the Jazirah are Yazidis, an extension of the religious community of Yazidis in northern Iraq.

The second-largest ethnolinguistic minority is the Armenians, who number roughly 519,000, about 4 percent of the Syrian population, and who are the least assimilated group in the country. Entirely Christian, they fled Turkish Armenia during several episodes, especially during the 1920s and 1930s. They settled particularly in Aleppo, where nearly 75 percent of the Armenians in Syria live, and also in Damascus. Educated and skilled, they work in trade, crafts (many of the jewelry artisans in Damascus are Armenians), small industry, and the professions.

Smaller minorities in Syria include Turkmen, Circassians, and Jews. Nearly all of these minorities speak some Arabic, but the Turkmen and Circassians, like the Kurds and Armenians, primarily use their own language. The roughly 110,000 Turkmen, who are Sunni Muslims and Turkic speakers, are chiefly semi-nomadic herdsmen in the Jazirah, but some are settled agriculturalists in the Aleppo area. The especially distinct Circassians occupy the Hawran in southern Syria, with Druzes east and west of them. Only half as numerous as the Turkmen, the Circassians play a more significant role in the Syrian economy and society.

Jews numbered more than 30,000 before World War II and had been present in the Syrian area for more than 2,000 years. Under the various Muslim empires, they were, like the Christians, people of the book. An urban group, like the Armenians, Jews lived mostly in Aleppo and Damascus. Israeli-Syrian hostility after 1948 put Syrian Jews in an ambivalent position. The status of the Jews remaining in Syria periodically becomes a topic of acute friction between Syria and Israel when Israel asserts and Syria denies that Jews are mistreated in Syria. In April 1992, under U.S. pressure, Syria declared that any of the 4,000 Syrian Jews who wished to emigrate were free to do so. By the end of 1992, 2,600 had received exit visas, and of the 1,400 who remained, about 400 indicated a desire to stay in Syria.[4]

Although decreasing, the ethnic and religious diversity among Syrians is apparent in the *suqs* of the cities, where mixtures of ethnic costumes and different languages add color to the crowds of shoppers and peddlers. Another indication of such diversity is the weekly schedule of various merchants: A Muslim furniture shop might well be closed on Friday, a Jewish copper and brass shop on Saturday, and an Armenian jewelry shop on Sunday. Differences in costumes may still be seen along city streets, but they are steadily disappearing, and most urban Syrians have long ago adopted Western clothing. Bedouins have been steadily decreasing in number and by the mid-1980s probably made up only 5 percent of the Syrian population.

Evolving Economic Patterns

The Syrian realm emerged economically moribund from four centuries of Ottoman control. Mandate Syria developed modestly during its years under French economic dominance, and it made the transition to independence in fairly good economic condition. Like many of the states of the area, Syria faced constraints in its efforts as a new state to enter the modern industrial world. Conflict with Israel in 1948–1949 also slowed development, and it was not until well into the 1950s that there began to be a significant rate of development and growth. As has been true of several Middle East states in recent decades, growth in productive sectors has been retarded by internal and regional instability, experimentation with political-economic ideologies, and concentration on military affairs and military buildup. In Syria, rigid government control increasingly dictated prices, wages, and what could be produced, imported, and sold. As long as the economy was propped up by foreign funding, the socialist management worked. However, when grants from outside dwindled, the centralized, inefficient, and bureaucratic system could not operate the economy at a reasonable level—as had been demonstrated in Nasserist Egypt and was later revealed in Baathist Iraq and, most dramatically, in the former USSR. For that and other more inherent reasons, Syrian development has not proceeded as well as might be expected. Even so, there has been appreciable growth in the economies of Syria and the other Fertile Crescent states.

Syrian economic evolution after 1961 exhibited three stages, each lasting a decade.

1. The 1960s were a time of buildup, with annual economic growth increasing from 2 and 3 percent to 6 and 7 percent later in the decade. Syria's traditional laissez-faire economy, formerly controlled by a small urban merchant-landowner class, experienced a turning point during Syria's union with socialist Egypt in the United Arab Republic, 1958–1961. A trend toward land redistribution and nationalization of private enterprises inaugurated under the UAR increased in pace into the mid-1960s and early 1970s. By that time, more than 100 of the largest enterprises had been nationalized, along with the mineral industries, including the petroleum industry. Railways, airline, and ports were also government owned (Map 12-2). Friction between private owners and the socialist government underscored the limited supply of capital.

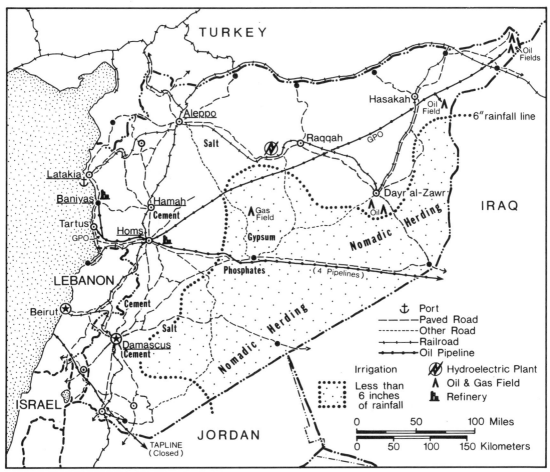

Map 12-2. *Economic map of Syria. Manufacturing centers are underlined.*

2. The second stage, from late 1973 until 1982, saw Syria's economy take off, with growth averaging an outstanding 10 percent annually. The determinative stimulus for such growth was the huge influx of foreign funding, primarily because income from Syria's four main sources of foreign exchange—foreign grant aid, foreign lending, foreign funding for major development projects, and remittances from Syrians working abroad, primarily in the Gulf—were at a sustained peak. Along with foreign capital came foreign technical expertise. Major donors were Gulf oil states, other OPEC countries, the USSR (which supplied funds, military equipment, military advisers, and technical support), the UN, the World Bank, West Germany, and others. The Baghdad Agreement of 1978 extended funding from the Gulf states for Syria (and Egypt) as a

"confrontation" state to receive $1.8 billion annually, and although the funding later broke down, it afforded Syria an opportunity to cap a decade of expansion. The crowning achievement of the decade, which came at the beginning of this stage of economic development and was a major stimulus of the boom, was completion of the Euphrates Dam, the second-largest dam (after Egypt's Aswan High Dam) in the Middle East when it was dedicated in 1973. Syria also developed expanded irrigation and land reclamation, an extended transportation system, more diversified manufacturing, and an extensive building program.

3. The third stage of economic evolution, 1982–1992, saw a marked downturn in the Syrian economy. The initial trigger was the sharp drop in oil prices, which halved the income of the Gulf

states and reduced employment of Syrians in the Gulf area. The lower oil price meant that Syria's oil exports earned less, even though the amount exported increased substantially. Foreign aid, including help from the then Soviet Union, steadily diminished to a nominal amount by the late 1980s. Soviet aid evaporated with the collapse of the USSR in 1991, and Syria found itself unable to utilize or best exploit some of its major projects. The value of Syrian currency dropped steadily during the middle and late 1980s to one-tenth its starting point in 1982; inflation reached 50, then 100 percent; lack of foreign exchange reduced imports, not only of consumer goods but even of important producer goods; and several factories were unable to continue operating. Military equipment and the occupation of parts of Lebanon by Syrian troops still required heavy expenditures. Syria lost credibility in the West because of its occupation of Lebanon, its continued ties with the USSR, and its apparent support of certain terrorist groups.

In 1986, when both the European Communities and the United States applied sanctions against Syria because of its evident ties with accused terrorists, the Syrian economy flattened still more. The government seemed unable to extricate itself from either the economic morass or the political labyrinth in which it was enveloped. However, with the Soviet Union collapsing economically and no longer being able to supply and support Syria militarily, the Syrians began to seek accommodation with the West. After Iraq invaded Kuwait, Syria promptly associated itself with the allied coalition and eventually sent 19,000 troops to join coalition forces. In return, the Gulf states renewed aid ($2.2 billion) to Syria, and the Syrian government finally undertook economic reforms to improve its situation: It accepted a realistic exchange rate for the pound; liberalized trade, investment, and tourism; improved telecommunications; and showed willingness to meet its creditors halfway. Meanwhile, the petroleum sector continued to be a bright spot in the economic spectrum.[5]

Agriculture

Agriculture has traditionally been a major element in the Syrian economy, and despite a percentage decrease in the farm population, agriculture continues to supply a major share of the GDP and export trade. A large share of the capital investment in economic development after the late 1960s went into land reclamation, land improvement, irrigation schemes, and agricultural programs. With Syria's appreciable agricultural base, these developments—although modest compared to those of Saudi Arabia or Israel—added stability to a significant economic sector. Land reform in 1958 and 1969 brought the average size of holding to 22 acres/8.9 ha (less in irrigated areas, more in dry-farming areas) with more than half the holdings averaging 12.4 acres/5 ha or less by 1988. Government actions have made Syrian farmers, typically small landholders or renters, now more independent and more productive, and the traditional conflict between urban landlord and rural peasant has diminished.

Cyclic variations in rainfall totals and seasonal distribution are a crucial factor in the western Fertile Crescent because of the enormous swings in grain production created by the variations. Between 1947 and 1960 about every third year was dry, and Syria's wheat crop in the dry year of 1973 was only one-fourth that in the very wet year of 1972. Since virtually all of the country's grain crop is subject to such variations, the average yield is low, as is the average income of grain-farming families; national and personal planning is therefore difficult. The new Mexican wheats are increasingly utilized, but they are expensive for the capital-short Syrian farmer to grow. The advantage of and need for expanded irrigation are obvious, and despite financial, technical, and geographical problems, Syria is working toward that goal (see Table 7-1).

As is true for the Middle East as a whole, wheat and barley are by far the dominant crops in Syria, occupying more than two-thirds of the cultivated area. The more humid agricultural lands produce cotton and sugar beets, with one government policy encouraging their production and another making sale of the crops unprofitable. Tomatoes and lentils grow widely, as do more than a score of other seasonal vegetables. Permanent tree and vine crops grow both in irrigated areas and on rainfed slopes: citrus on the coastal plain and in the Ghutah (the extensive oasis around Damascus) and olives, figs, and

Figure 12-3. *Euphrates Dam in eastern Syria, key element in the Syrian plan to develop the Jazirah (area east of the Euphrates), including the broad Euphrates Valley itself (Fig. 12-4). Lake Asad is to the left. Note eastern valley wall in distance.*

grapes on many slopes in the west, where they are well adapted to the Mediterranean regime. Rice is increasingly grown in the Ghab and in the Jazirah.

Ghab Project. The Ghab Project, which involved drainage, hydroelectric production, and irrigation and which was completed in 1965, reclaimed 61,780 acres/25,000 ha of former marshland in the Ghab Depression, east of and parallel to the Jabal al-Nusayriyah in northwestern Syria. Roughly 31 miles/50 km long by 9 miles/15 km wide, this northern end of the Levant Rift System was formerly flooded by the lower Orontes River. The basalt lava flow that dammed the Orontes at the Ghab Depression's northern outlet was cut through, and the marshland was made into a productive valley. Besides the marshland reclaimed, twice as much other land was improved as part of the Ghab Project, and the area now yields cotton, rice, sugar beets, wheat, and barley.

Euphrates Dam. The most important single development project in modern Syrian history is the Euphrates Dam system, which involves not only the huge dam itself but also a hydroelectric installation, a long-line electrical distribution

net, the lake behind the dam, an extensive irrigation system, a new town, and an agricultural development program in the Jazirah. Like the Aswan High Dam in Egypt, the project was made possible primarily by Soviet financial and technical assistance. Initiated in 1961 and dedicated in 1973, the dam is 197 ft./60 m high and 3 miles/4.5 km long (Fig. 12-3). The resulting reservoir, named Lake Asad in honor of Syria's president, extends for 50 miles/80 km upstream, covers 247 miles^2/640 km^2, and stores 12 billion m^3 of fresh water.[6]

The power station, inaugurated in 1978, has eight Soviet-made 100,000-kilowatt turbines, which generated more than 90 percent of Syria's electrical energy for several years; however, the percentage is decreasing as several new thermal power plants come on stream. Because water for irrigation must be pumped up to the plateau level from either Lake Asad or from the river downstream, a share of the electricity from the dam must be consumed locally; however, most of the energy is delivered to Aleppo and other consuming centers in western Syria to power many of Syria's new industries.

An equally significant long-range purpose of the Euphrates Dam is the irrigation of 1.58 million acres/640,000 ha of land along the Euphrates and its east-bank tributaries (Fig. 12-4). This undertaking will require the rest of the century and will, when complete, more than double the area under irrigation in Syria (however, see next paragraph). Tabaqah, the village at the original damsite, expanded into a town of 50,000 and was then renamed Madinat al-Thawrah (Revolution City). More than a dozen new villages have also been built to accommodate the 60,000–70,000 people brought into the Jazirah because of the new development there.

Nevertheless, several problems surround the project.[7] A basic one is that the Euphrates enters Syria from Turkey and leaves it for Iraq, so that the three states involved have contended sharply over the complex water rights (see Chap. 11). After the completion of the Euphrates Dam, a dispute between Syria and Iraq over division of the river's water brought the two states to the verge of war in 1975 before Saudi Arabia mediated a resolution. For its part, Turkey largely ignored Syrian complaints when it undertook a three-step damming of the Euphrates on its own territory and thus upset the Syrian timetable for irrigation projects in the Jazirah. More immediately serious was the revelation that large sections of the areas for which irrigation was planned are underlain by easily soluble gypsum. Since dissolution of the gypsum would both reduce soil quality and result in water loss, elevated concrete-trough channels must be used to carry water, and plans to irrigate large areas have had to be canceled. Thus, the actual irrigated area will probably be less than 50–60 percent of the area initially envisioned. Figures must also take into account the 77,170 acres/31,230 ha of irrigated land (and 18,532 acres/7,500 ha of other land) drowned by Lake Asad, whose waters also displaced nearly 60 villages.

Growth of Industry

Mineral Industries. A dearth of mineral resources hindered economic progress in Syria for centuries. Only in recent decades have modern technology and management combined to facilitate discovery of two moderately large and domestically important mineral resources, petroleum and phosphates. The mineral industry sector (including petroleum) accounts for less

Figure 12-4. *Well-developed, irrigated, flat-floored Euphrates Valley, looking east from western valley wall. Euphrates River is at bottom edge. Sugar and paper factories are in left and right distance.*

than 15 percent of the nation's output, but it is significant because of its capacity as a foreign currency earner, its marked increase between 1987 and 1992, and its further potential.

Petroleum. Intensive exploration by American companies and others led to discovery of oil in 1956 in the extreme northeastern corner of Syria, where several small, closely spaced fields show alignment with adjacent fields in Iraq and in Turkey farther north. Qaratshuk (Karatshuk), Syria's discovery field, was found in 1956, and Suwaydiyah was located in 1959. Major output began only in 1968 after a pipeline 404 miles/650 km long had been constructed to the Homs refinery and Tartus terminal. Increased production required a second line a few years later, and a third line for natural gas was opened in 1991.

Until 1986, virtually all of Syria's oil production was high-sulfur heavy crude that, for normal use, had to be blended with lighter crude, originally tapped at the Homs refinery from pipelines from Iraq. Following Syria's shutdown of those lines in the early 1980s (see Chap. 8), light crude brought by tanker from Iran to Tartus under a profitable barter agreement was blended with Syria's heavy oil. However, the new Tayyim field and a cluster of a score of small satellite fields discovered all around Dayr al-Zawr after 1984 have moderately large reserves of very light, sweet crude. Production from the Tayyim-Omar cluster is moving to refineries and export terminals in western Syria through the former Iraq Petroleum Company (IPC) pipelines. Thus,

Syria is now able to meet its own blending requirements. Average daily production rose from 27,000 bpd in 1968 to a high of 473,000 bpd in 1991, surpassing Qatar's daily average for the first time. With production continuing to rise in the early 1990s, petroleum and petroleum products totaled more than 60 percent of Syria's exports by value, an especially favorable development because they are, at least potentially, hard currency earners. Exploring for Syria's most valuable resource is also virtually cost free for the state, since foreign companies—U.S., French, British, Dutch—buy concession areas and then pay the costs of exploration. A half dozen small fields are being developed south of Lake Asad, and several gas fields in central Syria, near Palmyra, are supplying fuel for power plants and industry. By 1992, Syria possessed 1.7 billion barrels of oil reserves (see Table 8-1).

Syria's first refinery was built in Homs and originally used feedstock from Iraq Petroleum Company pipelines. It now has a throughput of 117,000 bpd, blending Syrian heavy and light crudes, as does the 120,000-bpd Baniyas refinery on the coast, built in 1980.

Phosphates. Rock strata comparable to those in which Israel, Jordan, and Iraq have enormous reserves of phosphate rock were traced into central Syria, and phosphorite production from moderate reserves rose from 600,000 mt in 1974 to 2.3 million mt in 1989 (Fig. 8-4). Reserves are great enough near Palmyra (Tadmur) that a railroad was built into the producing area in the late 1970s (see Map 12-2). Total reserves of 1 billion mt are sufficient for many years of production, but Syria's phosphates are of lower quality than those of neighboring states, and sales began to slow in 1990–1991. Production of other mineral industries commodities—salt, gypsum, sulfur from petroleum processing, cement (especially from two larger mills at Tartus and Hamah), and steel from a plant just north of Hamah—all unexceptional, is for domestic use only. All mineral resources in Syria were nationalized in 1964.

Manufacturing

For many centuries, Damascus and other cities enjoyed fame for their damascene metalwork, damask fabrics, muslins, linens, silk brocades, tapestries, carpets, tooled leather, carved and inlaid furniture, glassware, pottery, jewelry, mosaics, and similar craft work. Fortunately for Syria and the world, all of these crafts have survived to some degree to the present time; however, they are an inadequate basis for a national manufacturing complex in the modern technological world.

Limitations that became apparent in the late 1940s typified industrial development at that time. Management lacked modern expertise, and labor lacked technical skill. The controlling merchant families were unable or unwilling to invest the amounts needed for industrial expansion, and domestic instability discouraged outside investors, who were not encouraged to participate in any case. When the Baath government nationalized all the major industries, investment capital for certain industries became available through government channels. However, in general, all of Syria's political-economic deficiencies converged to inhibit rational and presumable industrial development.

Planning and development during the 1970s gave early emphasis to infrastructure and basic industries: highways, railroads, the Euphrates Dam, cement plants, iron and steel plants, and similar industries. No consideration could be given to production of precision goods or high-technology items. Production in the limited secondary industries, such as the production of machines and appliances, was chiefly the assembly of primarily imported parts. Still, the variety of manufactured products increased appreciably and included clothing, shoes, wet and dry batteries, cables, and pencils.

The new patterns of production reflected an attempt to decentralize industries. The dispersion of plants was not only to avoid an overconcentration in Damascus, and thus to encourage development in other centers, but also to move production away from potential threat of an Israeli attack. Virtually every Syrian city is benefiting from the industrial expansion, with Aleppo gaining tractor and other agricultural machinery plants as well as appliance factories, cement and food-processing plants; Hamah, iron and steel, textile, and cement plants; Homs, a fertilizer plant, using phosphates from near Palmyra; Tartus, Syria's largest cement plant;

Baniyas, a refinery larger than the older Homs facility; and smaller plants in Latakia, Dayr al-Zawr, Hasakah, and Raqqah.

Transportation and Trade

As a keystone in the Fertile Crescent, Syria has been the focus of route junctions and crossings for millennia, and to some extent contemporary Syria still fulfills that function. From the late Neolithic onward, the Damascus-Aleppo axis has been a junction for routes from the south—the Via Maris (Sea Route) from Egypt and the King's Highway from Arabia; east—along the Fertile Crescent from Persia and Mesopotamia; and north—through the Cilician Gates from Anatolia. Even with today's technologically advanced transportation systems, primary regional highway and air routes cross Syria both north-south and east-west.

Syria in the early 1990s possesses a modest road and rail network (see Table 9-2) that is approaching adequacy for current needs. The more densely settled areas naturally have the densest network of roads, and only through routes cross the sparsely inhabited desert areas of the southeast. The transportation net has expanded markedly since World War II, and highways have improved in alignment, surfacing, and width. All major cities are now connected by modern paved highways, with a four-lane divided throughway now extending from the Jordanian border along the full length of the main axis Damascus-Homs-Hamah-Aleppo. New railroads have facilitated the development of the northeast, especially the Jazirah, and the center of the country. The rail line from Latakia through Aleppo, Madinat al-Thawrah, Raqqah, Dayr al-Zawr, and Hasakah to Qamishli has been a major factor in agricultural development of the northeast, in Latakia port activity, and in stimulating the growth of all of the cities through which it passes.

Prior to World War II, Syria utilized four traditional Mediterranean ports—Beirut, Iskenderun (Alexandretta), and, to some extent, Haifa and Tripoli. By the late 1940s, Iskenderun and Haifa were, for all practical purposes, closed to Syria; Beirut was awkward to reach; and Tripoli was unsatisfactory. With no adequate general-cargo ports of its own, Syria continued to utilize

Beirut but meanwhile initiated a long-range development program for Latakia and, later, Tartus. Baniyas had long served as an oil export port as terminus for IPC lines from Iraq.

Although trade in and through Syria diminished during the later decades of Ottoman rule, exchange of goods has long been a lively activity in this centrally located area. The *suq* is a prominent feature of every Syrian town and city. The bustling Suq Hamidiyah in Damascus and the underground Aleppo *suq* have been famed for centuries throughout the region, with each *suq* containing hundreds of small shops selling a wide range of specialty and common items. One reminder of Syria's commercial traditions is the annual Damascus International Trade Fair, conducted in late July since 1954 and attracting hundreds of thousands of visitors. Trade continues to play a major role in the Syrian economy. However, the authoritarian government imposed restrictions on the free flow even of ordinary goods that appreciably reduced Syria's export and reexport trade. After the early 1980s, much of the country's trade shifted to commerce with the European Economic Community (EEC) and Eastern Europe rather than with the country's immediate neighbors. Syria's unstable political relations with each contiguous state have reduced its regional trade to a minimum.

Political Geography

Internal Relations

Like other Fertile Crescent states, Syria found its political and territorial aspirations redirected at the end of World War I and, as a mandate, had its potential state form imposed upon it. Thus, when Syria emerged as a newly independent state in 1946, its boundaries were pre-fixed, and Syrians were forced to achieve a state idea—raison d'être—within an imposed context. As one consequence, national memories of the Umayyad Empire and the long-persistent national consciousness of "Greater Syria" resurfaced in the new state. Although mandate Syria had been unable to prevent the dismemberment of Greater Syria, the independent state could express irredentist claims regarding detached territories. The most burning issue was the severance of

Lebanon, which Syria considered to be amputation of an inherent piece of Syrian land, a stance that was revived as a peripheral claim after 1976 when Syrian troops occupied part of Lebanon—and were still there in early 1993—originally as the main units in the Arab Deterrent Force. A secondary territorial issue was the detachment of the Sanjak of Alexandretta from mandate Syria in 1939.

With no specific historical boundaries to guide them, France and Britain delimited mandate Syria to accord with the rough outlines of the Sykes-Picot Agreement (see Map 11-1). Two interesting boundaries resulted: The unique northern boundary simply followed the southern rail of the Berlin-to-Baghdad railway from north of Aleppo to Nusaybin, a distance of 200 miles/322 km. The southeastern border is entirely geometrical, with one stretch from the Jabal al-Druze to the Euphrates a straight line of 275 miles/443 km extending across the Syrian Desert. Even though Bedouins continue their seasonal migrations across the southeastern line, and although tensions have waxed along the Turkish border on several occasions, both boundaries have proved to be reasonably satisfactory.

Three sections of the western land boundary have produced problems. The northwestern segment, around the Sanjak of Alexandretta, has already been discussed (see the section in Chap. 11 on "Boundary and Territorial Disputes"). The boundary with mandate Lebanon was objected to by Syria because some of the territory awarded Lebanon was a Muslim area whose inclusion in a Christian Lebanon mandate could not be justified. The segment along the southeastern shore of the Sea of Galilee ran several hundred meters back from the water's edge, thus giving the shore to the mandate of Palestine. The 1949 Armistice Line gave the entire shore to Israel, and after 1967 Israel occupied the whole of the Golan area.

Golan

Israel's military conquest of the strategic and heavily fortified Golan Heights in the 1967 June War, occupation of the heights after the war, and announcement of the integration of the area into Israel in December 1981 added to Syria's territorial losses. Syria has not accepted detachment of the Golan from the Syrian homeland. Syria's strong irredentist determination over the Golan was manifest in each of the rounds of the Arab-Israeli peace talks in 1991–1993, especially in Washington, D.C., in September 1992. (Details about the Golan Heights are given in Chapter 15 for statistical convenience, although Israel's claim to the Golan has not received international recognition.)

Centrifugal Forces

Not until the early 1970s could Syria achieve sufficient internal political stability to establish a national unity and a rational government structure. Prior to that time, Syria suffered coups d'état more frequently than any other Middle Eastern state. Even with political stabilization, the government has a double minority power structure. Ideologically, the party in power is the Baath (Arab Renaissance Party), which achieved power originally in a 1963 coup; ethnically, the man who has been president since 1970 is from the relatively small minority of the Alawis.

In addition, there is a running conflict between the Sunni urban oligarchy and the rural peasantry, now reinforced by the Baathist-Alawi political strength. Still another social competition that creates a centrifugal force within the country is the increasingly important conflict between conservative and liberal Islam, along with the opposition of both of these groups to the secularism represented by the Baath-Alawi combination. The best organized of the militant fundamentalist Islamic groups, the Muslim Brotherhood, instigated the two most serious challenges to President al-Asad's basically secular Baathist regime led by Alawis. Stimulated by Sunni opposition to the Alawis, the Muslim Brothers killed more than 60 Alawi military cadets in Aleppo in 1979. They then, as the key members of the Islamic Front, took over Hamah in February 1982, and government security forces killed several thousand of the city's inhabitants and destroyed much of Hamah in breaking the rebel hold. The Hamah assault is the blackest mark against the al-Asad regime, and the clash is indicative of a major centrifugal factor. Otherwise, the regime has not outwardly evinced massive brutal physical repression. Whereas large Palestinian refugee groups have formed a crucial centrifugal force in Lebanon and Jordan, the very large Palestinian refugee population in Syria—approximately 300,000—has been kept under strict control, although assured of Syrian sympathy for their cause.

Centripetal Forces

In the face of the potent divisive forces just reviewed, it is noteworthy that two related aspects of nationalism, Syrian nationalism and Arab nationalism, have remained sufficiently effective to offset the centrifugal forces and to bring the Syrians together into a viable national group. The regularity and frequency of coups d'état prior to 1963 seem to have been broken, and the national will to stand firm vis-à-vis Israel and against political criticism and opposition from Iraq and Western states, including the United States, was sufficient to maintain Syrian unity into 1990. By that time, Syria had experienced the trials of losing Soviet support, reversing aspects of its relationship with the West, and had received promises of outside aid. By 1992, the Baathist regime had yielded some of its most rigid controls, but political openness and the residual internal stresses have yet to be reconciled, and inherent stability is still more of an aspiration than an achievement.

Regional Relations

A leading role by Damascus in Arab nationalism was widely accepted in the Fertile Crescent at the end of World War I. The Arab leadership that backed the Arab Revolt of 1916–1917 had been centered in Damascus, and a short-lived kingdom was established in Syria under Faysal ibn Husayn in 1920. In assuming its mandate, France forced Faysal to abdicate, but Syria has never forgotten its moment of glory. However, attempts by the state of Syria to assert a leading role for itself after the early 1960s have been viewed with caution by its Arab neighbors. Observing the mistakes of Nasserist Egypt, Syria has chosen to balance its support of Arab nationalism with a focus on Syrian nationalism and Syrian development rather than to enter the overcrowded arena of Arab socialism and nationalism. Having shown its support of Palestine in three wars with Israel, Syria has taken in scores of thousands of Palestinian refugees. It was a charter member of the League of Arab States (Arab League) and has played a reasonably active role in that organization. The office for the Arab boycott of Israel is located in Damascus. While Syria considers itself part of the Islamic world and has participated in several Islamic world organizations, it advocates and practices a greater degree of secularism than do the more conservative Muslim states.

Syria's relations with virtually all of its neighbors for most of the years since World War II have been marked by tensions and, in the case of Israel, by hostilities. Syria's relations with Lebanon are of special significance but have already been discussed in Chapter 11 and are further examined in Chapter 13. Despite the Alexandretta dispute and occasional tension northeast of Aleppo during the 1950s and 1960s, Syria's relations with Turkey have been correct most of the time until recently. Relations with Jordan on the south have ranged from close ties to border closures on several occasions and even to at least two brief, abortive Syrian invasions of northwestern Jordan.

Syria and Iraq pursued their mutual economic interests until the mid-1960s. For many years, Iraq's only petroleum outlet was through pipelines across Syria, with terminals in Baniyas and in Tripoli, Lebanon (see Chap. 8). The pipelines and terminals were vital to Iraq, and they brought Syria royalties of more than $120 million annually, plus another $120 million annually in discounts to Syria on Iraqi crude for use in the Homs refinery. Nevertheless, because of disputes between Iraqi and Syrian Baathists, as well as disagreements over oil royalties, Syria closed the pipelines sporadically in the 1970s and definitively in 1982. In an indication of its intense rivalry with Iraq for leadership in the Fertile Crescent, Syria supported Iran during the Iran-Iraq war, despite its long and vigorous advocacy of Arab unity. Therefore, despite vigorous popular opposition in the street, in 1990 the Syrian government had little hesitation about joining, along with Egypt, the coalition that forced Iraq to withdraw from Kuwait. In addition to weakening an adversarial regime, Syria reaped substantial political benefits as well as economic rewards of well over $2.2 billion. It thus restimulated its domestic economy and entered the 1990s with some optimism.

Global Relations

On the world scale, Syria was bound to special relations with France as a result of France's administration of mandate Syria. Despite its resentment of that country, Syria inevitably adopted certain aspects of French culture, including the French language for special purposes, to varying degrees. Franco-Syrian relations after 1946 decreased to an ordinary commercial exchange.

As was true with Egypt after the mid-1950s and with Iraq after the late 1950s, Syria found its channels with the West increasingly constricted because of Western—especially U.S.—support of Israel. Syria therefore turned to the USSR and its East European satellites for arms, economic aid, and technical assistance. The Soviets furnished Syria not only enormous supplies of military equipment but also financial aid for such projects as the Euphrates Dam. Soviet military advisers and liaison personnel served in Syria for more than three decades. However, Syria kept communism in Syria firmly under control and, like Egypt, did not permit itself to become a Soviet satellite. The collapse of the Soviet economy and the disintegration of the USSR itself in 1991 suddenly deprived Syria of its politico-economic mainstay and compelled President al-Asad to pursue realignment with the West.

Syria's relations with the United States had an early foundation for a friendly interchange, and in 1919, the King-Crane Commission discovered a reservoir of goodwill toward the United States, partly because of the work of the Syrian Protestant College and partly because of the ideals of President Wilson's Fourteen Points. Relations cooled after publicity of the U.S. endorsement of the Balfour Declaration and after the United States supported Zionist colonization in Palestine. Relations warmed and cooled during the 1950s and early 1960s,[8] but the trend after the 1967 Arab-Israeli war was downward. Syria broke diplomatic relations with the United States after that war and agreed to restored relations only in 1974. The United States (and other Western countries) viewed Syria with suspicion after Syrian troops entered Lebanon in 1976, and the two countries came into open conflict in late 1983 in Lebanon. A pragmatic lessening of tensions between the United States and Syria followed the phasing out of Soviet-Syrian cooperation, Syria's disassociation from terrorism and its increasing moderation, its participation in the Gulf coalition, and its role in the 1991–1993 Arab-Israeli peace talks. Other factors being equal, Syria's geopolitical and historical role as the Middle East keystone can no longer be ignored or dismissed and appears to be increasingly recognized.

13

Lebanon and Cyprus: A Mountain and an Island

The Character of Lebanon

Lebanon differs strikingly both physically and culturally from other states of the Middle East. It is dominated by the rugged and well-watered range of Mount Lebanon, green on its western slopes, facing the blue Mediterranean, and brown from the steppes and deserts at its back. It is small enough to be traversed by car in a few hours even on its long axis. Yet it displays almost as much landscape diversity as does Turkey, with an area 76 times that of Lebanon. Culturally, it has been one of the most highly developed countries in the Middle East: It is one of the most Western, modernized, literate, and education-centered, with a laissez-faire, entrepreneurial society and economy. Lebanon is also the most multisectarian state in the region, and, because of interconfessional hostility, after 1975 it sank steadily into anarchy to become for sixteen years the area's most devastated and endangered country. Once called the Switzerland of the Middle East—and Beirut the Paris of the Middle East—Lebanon in the 1980s was fragmented, a nation in jeopardy, and a nation in the process of collapse. Not until late in 1990 did the internecine killings finally cease under determined pressure from other Arab League states. In mid-1993, Lebanon was starting the long process of recovery.

Rich Past, Complex Evolution

The advantages and resources of Lebanon attracted humanoids to the land more than 800,000 years ago, during the Mindel glaciation, as is revealed by artifact finds near Sidon and in the high intermontane Bekaa. Byblos and numerous other sites show evidence of occupancy before and during the Neolithic period, from the ninth to the fourth millennium BC. "Phoenicia," the name applied to the area after about 1200 BC, is the Greek translation of "Canaan," land of purple-red. The color probably referred to the important Phoenician export of textiles dyed "royal purple" with secretions from the murex shellfish found at Sidon and Tyre. The coastal city-states of Tyre, Sidon, Beirut, and Byblos used the famous Cedars of Lebanon for shipbuilding and for export from Byblos to Egypt before 2400 BC. By the thirteenth century BC, the Phoenicians had also developed, probably for use in their active maritime trade, an alphabet that was gradually adopted, adapted, and diffused throughout the ancient world. Despite repeated invasions and later control by the Seleucids, Romans, and Byzantines, the area thrived, as monuments and ruins in every part of modern Lebanon attest.

The strength of the Christianity that developed during the centuries of east Roman-Byzantine control plays a key role in contemporary Lebanon. The Muslim conquest after 636 slowly altered the confessional balance and, later, the linguistic pattern. Nevertheless, the dominance of Christianity in Mount Lebanon persisted through thirteen centuries under the Umayyads, Abbasids, Crusaders, Mamluks, and, after 1517, the Ottomans. Under the *millet* system of the Ottomans, Mount Lebanon enjoyed a high degree of autonomy from the sixteenth century onward. After fighting between Christians and Druzes in

LEBANON

Long-form official name, anglicized: Republic of Lebanon

Official name, transliterated: al-Jumhuriyah al-Lubnaniyah

Form of government: multiparty republic with one legislative house (National Assembly)

Area: 3,950 miles^2/10,230 km^2

Population, 1990 (rough estimate): 3,000,000. Literacy (latest): 76%

Ethnic composition (%): Lebanese 82.6, Palestinian 9.6, Armenian 4.9, Syrian, Kurd, and others 3.8

Religions (%, estimated): Shii Muslim 33.0, Sunni Muslim 20.0, Maronite Christian 20.0, Greek Orthodox 8.3, Druze 8.0, Greek Catholic 6.0, Armenian Christian 4.0, other 0.7

GNP, 1988: $1.8 billion; per capita: $690 (rough estimate; down sharply from 1975, beginning of civil war)

Petroleum reserves: none

Main exports (% of total value, 1985): jewelry 10.2; clothing 5.2; pharmaceutical products 4.9; metal products 4.8

Main imports (% of total value, 1982): consumer goods 40.0; machinery and transport equipment 35.0; petroleum and petroleum products 20.0

Capital city: Beirut 300,000 (rough estimate, 1992; 1,000,000 in 1975); other cities: Tripoli (Tarabulus) 500,000; Zahlah 200,000; Sidon (Sayda) 100,000; Nabatiyah 100,000

1860, Mount Lebanon had a special status that continued until World War I.

Lebanon emerged as a separate entity as a mandate of France under the League of Nations after World War I. Its territory was detached from the basic mandate Syria and was enlarged so as to create *Grand Liban,* "Greater Lebanon." This Greater Lebanon included not only the coastal plain and Mount Lebanon, but also the Bekaa paralleling Mount Lebanon on the east and the separate Anti-Lebanon mountain ridges beyond the Bekaa trough (Map 13-1). After two decades under French tutelage, Lebanon was declared independent by the Free French on November 26, 1941, although a reaffirmation of independence was required on November 22, 1943, the official independence day. As in Syria, French forces did not finally evacuate the country until 1946.

Lebanon and the Lebanese

Lebanon is synonymous with cultural diversity, as virtually every major ethnic or religious group in the Fertile Crescent is represented. However, the diversity among Lebanon's peoples that underlies the country's factionalism is not ethnolinguistic but sectarian. Moreover, emphasis on the conflict between Christians and Muslims ne-

Map 13-1. *Map of Lebanon. Circled numbers identify regions discussed in text.*

glects the serious antagonisms among more than a dozen Christian subgroups and half a dozen Muslim subgroups. Intercommunal tensions are so great that all sects have opposed a census since the 1932 numeration, which showed a Christian majority and, under the system arranged with French guidance, gave majority government and military power to the Christians. This political arrangement was not adjusted, in the absence of a new census, until 1990, even though there has been an obvious Muslim majority for years.

The estimated 1990 population of 3 million represents no increase in the 1975 estimate of 3 million, the only such population plateau in the Middle East during those years. Because of war-time destruction and dislocation, the percentage of the country's population located in Beirut has declined from about 40 percent in 1975 to about 10 percent in 1989 during the climactic artillery duels. Beirutis were gradually returning to their battered city in 1991–1992, but they probably still numbered only 30 percent of the pre-1975 number of 1.1 million.

Ethnolinguistic Groups

Ethnolinguistically, about 92 percent of the Lebanese are Arabs in that their mother tongue is Arabic. In spite of this similarity, however, the variations among Arabs seen in many parts of the Middle East are especially wide and critical in Lebanon. Some Maronite Christians, for example, even deny Arab heritage and claim descent from the Phoenicians or Byzantines. By contrast, Palestinian refugees in Lebanon find their identity, in addition to their Palestinian status, in their Arabism and in Islam, or as Palestinian Christians. Yet other Lebanese Arab Christians consider themselves Arab and advocate mutual Christian-Muslim tolerance.

Despite their low percentages, non-Arab minorities have high visibility in Beirut and other major cities. By far the most numerous are the Armenians, estimated to number more than 120,000, about 4 percent of the national population. The Kurds are the second-largest minority, constituting as much as 1 percent of the population. The formerly sizable Jewish minority—estimated to have numbered more than 20,000 at the turn of the century and more than 7,000 in the 1950s—was smaller than 100 by the early 1990s.

Although not a separate ethnolinguistic group in Lebanon, the Palestinians were at the focus of the fighting in Lebanon for much of the period 1975–1991 and therefore are a significant element in the complex pattern of the country. Of the 800,000 Arab refugees who fled Palestine or Israel during the 1947–1949 fighting, about 150,000 crossed into southern Lebanon, most of them expecting to return to their homes within a short time. Additional thousands came to Lebanon during the 1967 Arab-Israeli war and after the 1970 fighting in Jordan. Most of them crowded into seventeen refugee camps built with help from the United Nations Relief and Works Agency (UNRWA) near Tyre, Sidon, Tripoli, Beirut, and Baalbak in the Bekaa. By 1987, estimates of the number of Palestinians in Lebanon were as high as 350,000.[1] Some Palestinians, especially professionals, have obtained Lebanese citizenship, but many Palestinian refugees have remained stateless refugee camp dwellers, their numbers so large that their assimilation has been considered a threat to the delicate power balance in Lebanese politics. Many Palestinians and their leaders have also rejected assimilation, keeping open the option for a return to Palestine.

Confessional Groupings

Among the multidimensional, interactive factors in the matrix of Lebanon, religious affiliation is the single most vital identity among the Lebanese. Christian and Druze mountaineers enjoyed special status under the Ottomans, and Christians were the core sect around which France created mandate Lebanon. Distinct from the Sunni Muslim lands around it, Lebanon—first as a mandate and then as an independent state—evolved under a carefully constituted balance of confessional elements: The majority of Christians held key positions, but power sharing and confessional distribution of offices were designed to produce stability and effectiveness. The breakdown of the system can be better understood through an examination of the basic religious groupings. Map 13-2 shows the proportional distribution of the major confessional groups prior to the outbreak of the civil war in 1975, and although the information is old, it is still instructive.[2]

Muslims. Making up nearly one-third of the population, Shiis (Shiites) are now the largest single sect in Lebanon. Formerly and occasion-

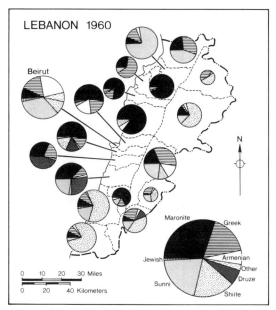

Map 13-2. *Patterns of religions for latest year with reliable data. Circles are in proportion to population involved, and pie graphs indicate percentages of adherents to the various sects. Figures have surely changed appreciably but are not available for recent years.*

ally still referred to as Mutawalis, the Shiis have traditionally been the most oppressed people in the area. Emerging from their passive role in the 1970s, the Shiis matched other groups in Lebanon with their own militias—first, Amal (Hope) in 1974 and then, in 1980, Hizballah (Hizb Allah, Party of God), the latter a more militant and extremist fundamentalist Islamic group than Amal. Hizballah (or Hezbollah, in transliteration from Farsi) is generously financed and otherwise supported by Iran and maintains liaison with the Iranian Revolutionary Guards in the Bekaa. It is ironic that after having been aided by Israel in the early 1980s, as was revealed in the 1986 Iran-Contra scandals, Iran should support the group that regularly attacks the Israelis and their surrogates in southern Lebanon. In return, Israel regularly attacks Hizballah centers and has kidnapped and even assassinated Hizballah leaders in southern Lebanon. By the mid-1980s the Shiis had three strongholds in Lebanon—the south, Beirut, and the northern Bekaa.

Sunnis (Sunnites), 20 percent of the population and formerly the largest and most influential Muslim group in Lebanon, are widely distributed in the country, with concentrations in Beirut, Tripoli and the Akkar, the southern Bekaa, and the Shuf (see Map 13-1). More than any other sect, the Sunnis resented being separated from Syria in 1920 when mandate Lebanon was detached from Greater Syria. The Sunnis did not affiliate with an overall paramilitary organization, and in many respects, the quiet sympathies of this conservative and mostly middle-class Muslim group lie more with some of the more moderate Christian groups than with militant fellow Muslim Shiis.

Druzes, despite their relatively limited share of the population (8 percent), have figured significantly in the sociopolitical dynamics of the Lebanon area for several centuries. Concentrated in the mountains southeast of Beirut (Druzistan) and especially in the Shuf, the Druzes played a key role in the fighting of both 1958 and 1975–1991 but also in the everyday political life of the state.

Alawis, who supported Syrian Alawi leaders when Syrian troops entered Tripoli in the early 1980s, number around 60,000 in Lebanon, most of them in Tripoli. A few thousand Ismailis round out the Muslim groupings in Lebanon.

Christians. Maronites, formerly the largest single sect in Lebanon, composed 30 percent of the population in the mid-1950s, but their proportion had diminished to 20 percent by the early 1990s. Even so, they were still the second-largest sect in Lebanon and by far the largest Christian sect. Of all the Christian groups, Maronites have been the most aggressive in insisting on Christian political supremacy, usually through the Phalange (Kataib). During the 1975–1991 war, the Phalangists, with broad Israeli support, formed the core of the militias opposing the Palestinians and associated Muslim groups. The Phalangist quasi-alliance with Israel heightens Muslim hostility toward the politically dominant minority Christians. A split among the Maronites in 1989–1990 over Syria's role, leadership of Christian militias, and the presidency of Lebanon led to internal Maronite warfare and additional tragic death and destruction in Beirut.

In addition to the Maronites, another dozen Christian sects claim separate identity and roles in the Lebanese political structure. Most of them appear in Table 6-2. The Greek Orthodox make up about 8 percent of the population and are widely distributed in Lebanon. They urge accommodation with other groups. None of the remaining groups play a major role in the state's politics.

Disrupted Economic Patterns

From Phoenician times, the major economic activities of Lebanon have taken advantage of locational and physiographic assets: (1) the country's central location on the eastern Mediterranean coast, which has permitted the Lebanese to serve as middlemen between the hinterland to the east and Mediterranean lands to the west; (2) its central location in the Middle East, making it an intraregional and interregional crossroad; (3) its well-watered coastal plain and somewhat indented coastline, facilitating development of port cities; (4) its likewise well-watered mountain background, which has passes that lead inland; and (5) its original forest cover and present agricultural development. Beirut's post–World War II development as a central place for much of the Fertile Crescent is a case in point.

It is a sad commentary, but the fact remains that for most of the fifteen years after 1975, the main business of Lebanon was literally inter-militia warfare. Millions of dollars poured into the coffers of the various political and military groups to cover costs of personnel and their dependents, arms and ammunition, medical supplies, transport, individual port development and operation, smuggling operations, and similar items. Naturally, none of these funds entered official channels or records, and they can scarcely be found in the national accounts. As a result of years of warfare, large amounts of cash flowed from sector to sector, having been supplied to surrogates, mercenaries, and allies by Israel, Iran, Iraq, Libya, and others. An ad hoc economic system evolved that became one of the obstacles to a return to peacetime and sanity.

In normal times, Lebanon is the most advanced of the Arab countries in economic performance and sociocultural development. The Lebanese economic infrastructure deteriorated after 1975 as a result of the civil war,[3] and the

sharp fall in oil prices in the 1980s further depressed the sectors of the economy that are tied to the oil-producing economies of the region. It is unlikely that Lebanon will recapture its economic peak of 1974, when the Gulf oil economy was expanding and wealthy Gulf petroleum producers competed for Lebanese expertise and services and invested heavily in the free-enterprise and then safe Lebanese real estate boom. Even so, Lebanon's geographical position, developed infrastructure, and international ties will contribute to an economic revival if Lebanon is permitted to continue to resolve its political and social conflicts. Although only limited information is available on post-1975 developments, traditional patterns and certain current trends can be meaningfully examined.[4]

Services

By 1975, Lebanon offered a full modern range of services, from personal services to banking operations to aircraft engine maintenance. It had excellent educational and medical facilities: In addition to the second-oldest university in the Arab world and one of the best, the American University of Beirut, there was the French Jesuit Université St. Joseph, Beirut Arab University, Lebanese University, Armenian Hagazian College, and Beirut University College (formerly Beirut College for Women) (Fig. 13-1). Medical facilities, especially the American University Hospital and the French Hotel Dieu, both connected with good medical schools, served patients from Lebanon and much of the Arab Middle East.

Lebanon's label of Switzerland of the Middle East also applied to the formerly extensive banking system, and 80 banking houses were operating in the country by 1974 (only one-tenth of them remained a few years later). Not only were deposits and trusts attracted from Saudi Arabia, Kuwait, and other Gulf oil states before the civil war but also flight capital came to Lebanon from the less stable economies of Syria, Egypt, Iraq, and Jordan. This capital helped fuel the remarkable development of Lebanon during the period 1955–1975. The Lebanese pound, 90 percent gold-backed and freely convertible, was one of the world's most stable currencies for three decades after World War II. However, the steady loss in

Figure 13-1. *High-rise apartment buildings in West Beirut. Some of these structures were later damaged in warfare.*

the value of the pound during the 1980s caused it to drop from 3.2 to the U.S. dollar to as low as 800–900 to the dollar before it rose to 300 in early 1988 and then plummeted to a disastrous 3,000 to the dollar in late 1992.

On the eve of the civil war, more than 1.5 million visitors annually were attracted to Lebanon, partly because of its wide variety of historical monuments and ruins, from prehistoric and Phoenician through Crusader to Ottoman times. The massive Roman ruins at Baalbak were a major tourist site. More than 300 hotels, numerous beach resorts, both summer and winter mountain resorts, the striking Casino du Liban, a wide range of goods, a varied night life in Beirut—in general, a palpable joie de vivre—and easy access by land, sea, or air contributed to the attractions of Lebanon as a center for tourism. The devastating loss of this source of foreign exchange will be difficult to overcome, since rebuilding the physical facilities for tourism and restoring tourist confidence will require several years. Neighbors competing for the tourist dollar have already shown that they will try to delay Lebanon's return to its former premier tourist role.

Prior to 1975, Lebanon served as a center for regional offices of many firms, both Middle Eastern and international, dealing with investments, insurance, and other economic activities. All the offices were closed by 1976–1977, and they cannot be expected to return to Lebanon until the recovery and reconstruction of Beirut are well under way—assuming that peace is preserved.

Trade and Transportation

Trade was formerly and probably will soon again be Lebanon's main economic activity. Significant from Phoenician times, Lebanon's trade started its modern growth after World War I and burgeoned after the region's oil industry began its rapid development in the later 1950s. The country's economic liberalism spurred a lively reexport trade and other commercial transactions, facilitating customs clearances and the operation of a free port (duty-free zone) in Beirut; and the stability and free convertibility of the Lebanese pound was an additional stimulus. The location of Beirut's port enabled it to become a break-in-bulk point and an entrepôt to warehouse products for later onward shipment. Large stores and small shops handled widely varied articles—European crystal, Persian rugs, German and Japanese optical goods, electronic equipment, Parisian apparel, automobiles of all types, gems and textiles from India and other countries, and Middle Eastern craft items. Lebanon's foreign trade picture underwent major alteration after 1975 and especially after the Israeli invasion in 1982. During the decade after 1975, a major import was weaponry and ammunition for the military forces and militias, with specific groups developing and using individual ports.

The increasing diversification of Lebanon's production sectors was reflected in the diversity of exports after the mid-1950s. Agriculture's share of exports had fallen by half by 1973, although fruits remained the largest single export item. During that same period, the proportion of manufactured products doubled: clothing, mechanical and electrical equipment, furniture, textiles, printed materials (including financial papers and postage stamps) and paper products, aluminum items, and iron and steel bars, as well as the reexport of such items as automobiles and aircraft. All of these exports are likely to appear among Lebanon's main trade items by the mid-1990s.

A sign of the economic distress and the demand for foreign exchange during the 1980s was that Lebanon produced large amounts of illegal hashish and opium in the Bekaa, which even in normal times produces some of these two drugs. During the war years, 12–15 tons of hashish was shipped annually—20 percent of the world consumption—and in 1991, narcotics from Lebanon had an estimated street value in the West of $6.5 billion. In 1992, both Syrian troops and Lebanese police were seriously enforcing rules that drug cultivation was *mamnua* (forbidden).

Because of the importation of quantities of consumer goods, the balance of Lebanon's trade in tangible goods has long been negative. However, the country's overall balance is normally well on the profit side because of services and other income that reflect the wide range of Lebanon's economic activities during normal times. Beirut's seaport and airport were ideally situated to serve as gateways to the Levant and beyond. Beirut International Airport formerly served as the Middle East aviation hub for both passengers and cargo and was the busiest civil airport in the region during the 1960s. Many airlines used Beirut's excellent catering services for their onward flights, and Middle East Airlines (MEA), headquartered in Beirut, became a main airline in the region. Although local fighting and hijackings

Map 13-3. *Economic map of Lebanon.*

associated with the civil war reduced traffic through Beirut International Airport (BIA) to a fraction of its normal level, both the airport and the city's port should rebound in peacetime because of Lebanon's geographic centrality. The first Western passenger plane to touch down at BIA since 1985 landed in June 1991, and Beirut's port opened in March 1991 after two years of suspended operations.

The cog railway over the mountains from Beirut to Damascus is antiquated, as is equipment on the other Lebanese rail lines, and most goods and passengers move by road. The road net is relatively dense, considering the rugged terrain in much of the country (Map 13-3). Although many mountain roads are narrow and steep, most are surfaced to withstand the winter rains and, at higher elevations, the deep snows. The Beirut-Damascus highway and the coast road are scenic routes but are inadequate for the heavy traffic of normal periods.

Manufacturing

Lebanon's modest production of specialized craft products and textiles developed and diversified after the early 1950s until manufacturing surpassed agriculture in the economic hierarchy. However, manufacturing, too, was disrupted, falling by more than 75 percent between 1976 and the mid-1980s. In normal times, most manufacturing establishments, like most shops and service institutions, are small—85 percent of such establishments employ fewer than 25 people. The main light industries cluster around Beirut, producing clothing, textiles, printed materials, cigarettes, paints, and furniture. Three cement plants and two steel plants normally operate near Tripoli. The oil refineries in Tripoli and Sidon originally used crude from the pipelines from Iraq and Saudi Arabia, respectively, but shifted to crude delivered by tanker, mostly from Saudi Arabia, when the pipelines were closed in the early 1980s. Both refineries have been heavily damaged, but they have normal capacities of 35,000 bpd (Tripoli) and 7,000 bpd (Sidon). The Tripoli plant is being restored to use crude from Syria delivered through the last segment of the old Iraq Petroleum Company (IPC) lines. The agriculturally productive Bekaa has several food-processing plants, including beet sugar mills and, in Ksara, wineries. In addition to furniture and metal products, Tripoli produces soaps from olive oil and other local raw materials.

Agriculture

Lebanon's combination of physical assets yields large harvests of fruits, nuts, and vegetables that are scarce in the Arab Middle East, certainly in the premium quality of the Lebanese products. Even though precipitation is concentrated in the cool season, hydrogeological conditions permit collection of the runoff, directly or indirectly through springs, for irrigation purposes well into the summer. Meltwater from heavy winter snows is particularly useful. Elaborate terracing both protects the slopes from erosion by the runoff from heavy rainfall (50–60 in./1,270–1,525 mm) at this elevation and also spreads water from the runoff and artificial irrigation to the crops in the terraced beds.[5]

The upslope of Mount Lebanon offers ecological conditions suitable for subtropical crops along the coast and for progressively cooler-environment crops at increasing elevations—a vertical zonation of crops on the principle that "altitude equals latitude." In the alluvial soils immediately along the coast, there are irrigated groves of bananas, lemons, oranges, grapefruit, and similar tender fruits. Slightly higher and on rocky soils, there are extensive olive groves and smaller almond groves that need little or no irrigation. Still higher, from 2,000 to 5,000 ft./610 to 1,525 m, there is a vertical succession of irrigated orchards of peaches, apricots, pears, plums, cherries, and similar soft fruits and vineyards, primarily producing table grapes, at several levels. At still higher elevations there are apple orchards, which were greatly expanded after World War II. Vineyards for wineries also thrive on the lower and drier eastern slopes of the Lebanon range, around Zahlah and Ksara, and spread into the central Bekaa (Fig. 13-2). Otherwise, crops in the Bekaa are normally of four types: nonirrigated wheat and barley; irrigated fruits; semi-irrigated sugar beets, onions, potatoes, and melons; and irrigated tomatoes and a wide range of other vegetables, especially in the Shtawrah (Chtoura) "oasis." A fifth type during much of the 1980s fighting was the hashish and opium poppy production.

A Subregional Perspective

Looking down at Lebanon from 10,000 ft./3,050 m, an air passenger flying from Beirut to Damascus can view the whole of the compact land of Lebanon. The same passenger can clearly see the four distinct parallel regions that extend south-southwest to north-northeast: a narrow coastal plain, the core area of the Lebanon Mountains, the linear flat-bottomed depression of the Bekaa, and the complex Anti-Lebanon Mountains on the border with Syria (see circled numbers on Map 13-1; also see Fig. 3-1).

[1] Coastal Plain

Extending the full length of the country's 140 mile/225-km Mediterranean shoreline, the narrow plain along the coast is partly wave-cut rock platform and partly alluvial, comprising fan deposits of streams debouching from their deep mountain valleys. Interrupted in five places by mountain ridges that reach the sea, the plain is only wide enough in some places to accommodate a highway and a parallel rail line. Between Tyre and Sidon it is carpeted by citrus groves for

Figure 13-2. *Famous Ksara vineyards, west side of central Bekaa, Lebanon. Snow-covered Mt. Sanine in distance. The vines had recently received their winter pruning.*

more than 1 mile/1.6 km back from shore; in the extreme north, it opens into the 20-mile-/32-km-wide triangular Plain of Akkar.

Urbanization has spread up and down the coastal plain, supplanting many of the fruit groves and market gardens that characterized the coast for so long. Greater Beirut extends more than 20 miles/32 km from Juniyah north of the capital to Damur to the south. Scenically located on a separate low structural peninsular plateau, one of the few significant protrusions from the eastern Mediterranean coast, Beirut has been occupied since the Neolithic. A Phoenician port and city-state, Beirut achieved greater stature as a Roman city, which, with its great law school, was destroyed in an earthquake and tidal wave in AD 551.

As both capital and primate city of Lebanon, Beirut developed rapidly after the early 1950s. By 1975 it contained more than 1.1 million people, one-third of all of Lebanon's population at the time. High-rise luxury hotels and apartment buildings, especially in Ras Beirut, part of West Beirut (see Fig. 13-1), contrasted with slum settlements on the fringes, particularly the Palestinian refugee camps and poor areas often occupied by

Shiis. Central Beirut was destroyed in the civil war, and by 1991, the city's population had decreased 70 percent and all public services were sporadic and limited. Elaborate plans have been formulated for the revival of Beirut under the coordination of the Council for Redevelopment and Reconstruction. Some of the plans for rebuilding Beirut provoked sharp debate among city leaders in 1992, with modernists and traditionalists taking opposing sides.[6] A serious problem will be the financing of the estimated $10 billion reconstruction project, particularly if fighting breaks out again.

Toward the north end of the coastal plain lies Lebanon's second city and second port, Tripoli (Arabic, Tarabulus),[7] which suffered less damage and dislocation during the civil war than Beirut. On the southern plain is the Phoenician port of Tyre (Arabic, Sur), and adjoining it are extensive Greco-Roman ruins. The Phoenician port of Sidon (Arabic, Sayda) lies north of Tyre, with a Crusader castle offshore. Both Sidon and Tyre, which served as headquarters for militias, were damaged in civil war fighting and were heavily bombed by Israeli planes in 1982. Also worth noting is the small northern port of Jubayl (better known as Byblos), with its renowned excavations showing a profile of civilizations from Neolithic times to the present.

[2] *Mount Lebanon*

The traditional core of Lebanon is Mount Lebanon (Arabic, Jabal Lubnan), technically called Jabal al-Gharbi (Western Mountains), and this range of mountains has played a profound role in the historical-cultural development of the area. Lying west of the great Yammunah Fault (see Chap. 3), the range's sedimentary strata were arched up by relatively gentle east-west compressional forces during the Miocene-Pliocene. The resulting arch is a rather open anticlinal structure aligned southwest-northeast and extending from the low Homs Gap at its northern end to the complex tectonic junction in southern Lebanon. The range is affected by several faults along its axis and by many cross faults. Highest elevations are toward the north, reaching 10,129 ft./3,088 m at Qurnat al-Sawda, east-southeast of Tripoli (snow-covered at upper left in Fig. 3-1); however, elevations around 6,500 ft./2,000 m continue southward along the ridgeline to east of Sidon.

A significant hydrogeological feature of Mount Lebanon results from the outcropping of permeable rocks on the upper slopes, which are subject to heavy winter precipitation. Underlying impermeable layers trap the water absorbed by the aquifers, forcing groundwater to the surface in lines of springs along the outcrops of the aquifers. Some of these springs are exceptionally large, contributing to short, swift rivers that erode and dissolve spectacular canyons in the western slopes (visible in Fig. 3-1) and thus add to the rugged relief. The springs also supply water for irrigation on the terraces and more gentle slopes, as well as pure drinking water, much of which is bottled for consumption in Beirut and for export to the Gulf states.

The western slopes were originally heavily forested with oak, pine, fir, cedar, and juniper, with the famous Cedars of Lebanon (*Cedrus libani*) forming a belt between 4,600 and 7,200 ft./1,400 and 2,200 m. Exploitation for at least 4,000 years has degraded the vegetation primarily to maquis, although a few small stands of Cedars of Lebanon are preserved. The main group is near the ski resort area of Bsharri. Plantations of stone pine (*Pinus pinea*) and Aleppo pine (*P. halepensis*) give small areas a wooded aspect (Fig. 13-3), and stone pine yields the edible piñon nut (Arabic, *snubar*).[8]

Maronites and Druzes gradually intensified and diversified agriculture on the western slopes, building thousands of terraces (Fig. 13-3). Villages developed on spectacular sites, some formerly occupied by Phoenician and Roman settlements. Particularly after World War II, many towns in the 2,000–4,500-ft./600–1,475-m zone evolved as summer resorts. Although almost abandoned in winter, in summer they are normally crowded not only with vacationers from the Gulf, Syria, and Egypt but also with Lebanese families from Beirut and Tripoli who move to summer mountain homes to escape the humid heat of the coast. At upper levels, around 6,500 ft./2,000 m, ski resorts such as the Cedars and Laqluq thrive between mid-December and late March.

[3] *The Bekaa*

The Bekaa ("the valley") is a young tectonic trough, a segment of the Levant Rift System. Along the western side of the Bekaa, the Yammunah fracture slices off Mount Lebanon on its eastern side and creates a vertical displacement of several thousand meters and a left-lateral horizontal displacement of about 4.4 miles/7 km, clearly visible in Figure 3-1. It is the most active of the many fractures in the Levant, and Ksara Observatory (virtually on the fault line, just south of Zahlah) records micro earth tremors almost daily. Perceptible earthquakes result from displacement along one or another of Lebanon's fault planes every few years. Severe tremors strike once every 100–150 years, with the most recent being in 1956, when 7,000 buildings were destroyed east of Sidon by slippage along the Roum Fault. Several fold ridges extend along the Bekaa floor as linear "islands" in the "sea" of alluvium that gives much of the Bekaa a flat floor.

The main drainage of the Bekaa, the Litani River flows southward from near Baalbak, with a flow of 700–900 million m³ a year at Qirawn (Qaraoun). It has been dammed to create a reservoir at Qirawn, and the water is diverted to produce a considerable amount of hydroelectric-

Figure 13-3. *Mount Lebanon's partly forested, partly terraced, and well-watered western slope. The village is Abadiyah, a few miles southeast of Beirut.*

ity and also to supply water for a limited amount of irrigation.[9] It is also important that Zionist water planners as early as 1919 sought access to the Litani as a water source for the proposed future Jewish state. Periodically, evidence suggests that Israel still wants to divert Litani water into the Jordan River basin.

A low, barely perceptible divide near Baalbak separates the watershed of the Litani from that of the Orontes (Asi) River to the north. Both rivers are fed by numerous springs on both sides of the Bekaa. These water sources attracted Paleolithic wanderers, and at least 30 Neolithic villages were established, their tells prominent features on the Bekaa floor.

Although the northern Bekaa lies in the rain shadow of the highest segment of Mount Lebanon and receives only 9 in./230 mm of rain a year, the central area around Shtawrah receives 24 in./610 mm, the south even more. Wheat and barley production, recorded from Roman times, has declined as more area is irrigated for fruit trees and market gardening. Seen from the adjacent heights, the Bekaa floor in spring is colorful with fruit blossoms, cultivated flowers, and green fields.

[4] Anti-Lebanon

Properly the Jabal al-Sharqi (Eastern Mountains), the Anti-Lebanon Mountains are linear highlands east of the Bekaa and along the frontier with Syria; indeed, only the western ridges lie within Lebanon. An anticlinal structure similar to Mount Lebanon, these eastern highlands have several ridges exceeding 6,500 ft./2,000 m, and the summit of Mount Hermon, a southerly extension of the eastern highlands, reaches 9,230 ft./2,813 m. They are the least exploited part of Lebanon and in the north, are virtually uninhabited.

Factions and Territories

State Idea and Its Failure

It can be said on the one hand that the Lebanese polity created in the early 1920s carried the formula for its own destruction. It can be said on the other hand that the system embodied vigorous self-sustaining, interacting, pluralistic checks and balances. Seventy years have revealed that, in fact, both statements are true.

When the French determined in 1920 that they would detach the formerly semiautonomous

Mount Lebanon from Greater Syria, their intention was to create a separate mandate around the Maronite Christians, the dominant sect in the mountains, with whom the French had maintained special relations since the Crusades and especially since 1860. The Maronites were pleased to have their traditional separateness continued and strengthened, but a portentous aspect of the French action was the addition to mainly Maronite Mount Lebanon of surrounding areas: the coastal plain, the Bekaa, and part of the Anti-Lebanon, with their Sunni Muslims, Shii Muslims, Druzes, and non-Maronite Christians. As was intended, the additional territory enhanced the new mandate's economic viability. However, it not only proportionally increased Syrian resentment of the detachment of Syrian territory but also engendered long-lasting animus among the Sunnis, Shiis, and Druzes who were separated from the mandate of "Muslim" Syria and included in the mandate of "Christian" Lebanon. Most critically, the territorial mold merged incompatible human elements.

With some help from the French, the several groups who found themselves in the Lebanese confessional confederation after 1920 evolved a unique political structure of pragmatic, representative government. Lebanon's raison d'être expanded to embrace its pluralistic society; and power sharing, checks and balances, and compromise were inherent guarantees of preservation of the state idea.

The role and identity of Lebanon have been debated from the beginning, and perspectives usually congeal along confessional lines. However, most groups accepted the Lebanon of the mandate years and even the early republican years—a neutral, separate state serving as a bridge between the West and the Arab Muslim lands of the Middle East.

The mechanics of the Lebanese system were codified less in the formal constitution than in the informal National Pact of 1943. This unwritten 1943 "gentlemen's agreement" specified the method of power sharing through the distribution of political offices among confessional groups. The system worked in cycles and might very well have succeeded over the long run. However, it was buffeted from within and especially from outside by forces it was not even designed to withstand. It stumbled in the 1958 civil war, again in 1968–1969, once more in 1973, and finally, it failed in 1975. The system could and did withstand stresses, but it could not endure superstresses.

The National Pact and other agreements recognized and partly reconciled the confessional pluralism of the state. They did not, however, ever come to grips with the territorial aspects of the confessional groups, each of whom possessed a fairly defined "turf" and core area (see Map 13-2). When the political equilibrium broke down, the territorial patterns solidified and evolved into a mosaic of ministates. Lebanese territorial sovereignty became as fragmented as its body politic.

Internally, the demographic balance after World War II shifted from a Christian majority to a Muslim majority. At the same time, Muslim groups increasingly challenged the Christian dominance of the Lebanese economy and political mechanism. The civil war of 1958 was a first armed test of relative strengths and even revealed the beginnings of infighting, not only among Christian groups but also among Maronite groups. As confessional dissensions continued and economic differentiation became even greater, the political system became increasingly fragile.[10]

The mortal catalyst was the rapidly growing strength and aggressiveness of the Palestinian refugee groups in the Levant and especially in Lebanon. Whereas Syria and Jordan kept strict control over the Palestinians within their borders, Lebanon lacked the strength to restrain the Palestinians on its territory. Although many Lebanese were sympathetic with Palestinian aspirations, they sought to preserve Lebanon's security and sovereignty against Palestinian pressures and also against Israeli reprisal raids for Palestinian actions against Israel and Israeli interests. Syria, Jordan, Egypt, and other Arab states supported the Palestinians' using Lebanon as a base of operations. Feeling isolated in the larger region, militant Maronites increasingly turned to Israel for support. Israel responded with massive assistance, and the Maronites and their allies felt strong enough to go on the offensive, even though they thus became the local surrogates for Israel against the Palestinians.

When neither the Maronites nor the Lebanese government was able to restrain the Palestinians, Israel either bombed Palestinian centers or sent forces across the border into Lebanon. Asked to supply the greater part of the 1976 Arab Deterrent Force, Syria sent large contingents into eastern Lebanon to maintain equilibrium and to discourage potential Israeli incursions into Syria through Lebanon. President al-Asad exploited the ambiguity of the situation to prolong Syrian occupation of Lebanon and apparently to test the possibility of reattaching *Grand Liban* to "Greater Syria." The idea of outright reattachment was eventually dismissed, but 35,000–40,000 troops remained in early 1993. Bitter local clashes during the period 1975–1981 were a prelude to the explosive battles of 1982.

The Israeli invasion of June 1982 (called by the Israelis Operation Peace in Galilee) was designed to (1) break the influence of the Palestine Liberation Organization (PLO) in the West Bank and uproot it completely from Lebanon so that Israel could then deal with more malleable Palestinian leaders, (2) evict the Syrians from the Bekaa and Beirut, and (3) impose a pro-Israel central regime in Beirut.[11] Inevitably, therefore, Lebanon became the battleground for a regional confrontation. Before the year was out, the array of forces in Lebanon included the several paramilitary forces that had been warring among themselves for seven years, Syrians, Israelis, Iranians, Americans, British, French, and Italians, as well as UN observers (United Nations Interim Force in Lebanon [UNIFIL]) who had been in Lebanon for many years.

Israel suffered three negative aftermaths to Operation Peace in Galilee. First, the loss of more than 600 Israeli troops in Lebanon contributed to the development of a majority opposition in Israel to the invasion. Second, world opinion hardened against Israel because of the invasion, especially after Israeli commanders' negligence facilitated the Sabra-Shatila refugee camp massacres, in which more than 1,000 Palestinians were murdered by Lebanese Phalangists.[12] Third, the operation failed in most of its goals.

Before the invasion and its immediate shock waves had dissipated, 10,000–12,000 Lebanese and Palestinians had been killed and tens of thousands wounded; 650 Israeli soldiers had been killed and more than 1,000 wounded; the American Embassy had been truck bombed on April 18, 1983, with 46 killed and 100 injured, then a substitute embassy building had been car bombed seventeen months later and 23 killed; a U.S. military barracks had been truck bombed on October 23, 1983, and 241 Marines killed—and hundreds of casualties were also being suffered by other nationalities. Rarely in such a small area have so many miscellaneous groups vented their rage on so many other groups in open warfare, car bombings, assassinations, conspiracies, and double deals.

Finally, under the aegis of the Arab League and with strong pressure from Syria inside Lebanon, a majority of the remaining members of the 1972 Lebanese Parliament met in Taif, Saudi Arabia, in October 1989 and agreed on the Document of National Understanding. The agreement still ratified the old 1943 National Pact (discussed above) but, significantly, made deconfessionalism an explicit—if long-range—goal. Implementation was delayed by internal fighting between Christian factions that was some of the most sanguinary of the entire fifteen-year civil war, but in late 1990, the warring factions finally sought compromise and reconciliation. A more complete Parliament amended the constitution to change the most basic provision in the Lebanese political system—the apportionment of parliamentary seats on the basis of five Christian seats for every four Muslim seats to a new 50–50 system. The former presidential powers were decreased, also to diminish Maronite influence, and the Council of Ministers gained powers.

While world attention was focused on the Gulf crisis, a government of national reconciliation—including leaders of major militias—was announced at year's end, and during 1991 it succeeded in initialing the Greater Beirut Security Plan. Again, backed by Syrian forces, a revived and newly empowered Lebanese Army disarmed the militias, returned the main ports to government jurisdiction, and gradually extended central government control to most of the country. Only in the fractious south, with the most militant and intractable remaining groups (Hizballah, PLO, Amal, Iranian Revolutionary Guards, and other smaller militias), as well as the Israeli proxy South Lebanese Army, has the government failed to assert sovereignty. Still determined to ensure its own precautions against rocket attacks and infiltration from south Lebanon, Israel has declared its intention to maintain its self-proclaimed security zone until regional peace has been achieved and south Lebanon is tranquil (Map 13-1).

Thus, in early 1993, Lebanon could feel some optimism that it has at last awakened from its fifteen-year nightmare of carnage and devastation, that the specter of partition has dissipated, and that remedy of some of the root causes of confessional conflict has finally been initiated. Although Lebanon recognized a "special relationship" with Syria in the Accord of Brotherhood, Cooperation, and Coordination signed in May 1991, Syria so far has exercised its hegemony with restraint. Lebanon joined in the 1991–1993 peace talks, regardless of whether it has its own voice in the negotiations. The Lebanese can only hope that they will be able to utilize their famous entrepreneurship and energy to reconstruct and redevelop their small state.

CYPRUS

Two geographical facts—that Cyprus is an island and that it is located in the eastern Mediterranean—are the most important aspects of Cyprus's existence. Occupied during the Neolithic period, nearly 8000 BC, it has been fought for and used as an intermediate base for more than 3,500 years, with its former mineral wealth and its agricultural resources valuable bonuses. A third current basic fact, primarily a consequence of location, is the contemporary conflict on the island between two ethnic groups and the unilaterally forced division of the island between them in 1974. The imposed division installed an ambivalent Turkish polity in the northern one-third of the island, while the recognized Republic of Cyprus continued in the south.[13]

Two Mountains, Three Plains

About the size of Puerto Rico, Cyprus is the third largest, after Sicily and Sardinia, of the Mediterranean islands. Its mountains are clearly visible across the 43 miles/69 km of water that separate it from Asia Minor, and it lies 65 miles/105 km from Syria and 475 miles/765 km from mainland Greece. Its coastline exhibits several semiprotected bays in which harbors have sheltered ships for millennia. Cyprus was formed during the Tertiary mountain-building period along the arcuate boundary between the African and Eurasian plates (see Map 3-2). Seismic repercussions from continuing plate convergence produce periodic earthquakes in Cyprus, some of them occasionally catastrophic.

The island has five regions: east-west mountain ranges to the north and south, a broad basin in between, and plains along both the north and the south coasts (Map 13-4). Toward the southwest are [1] the Troodos Mountains, the oval nucleus of the island and a true massif, with an intruded granite core now exposed by erosion and Mt. Olympus, the highest elevation on the island, reaching 6,407 ft./1,953 m. Extensive mineralization accompanied the intrusions, and breakdown of the Troodos rocks produced fertile soils. Stretching the full length of the northern edge of the island is [2] the Kyrenia Range, a narrow, steep mountain ridge primarily of Cretaceous limestone that attains 3,360 ft./1,025 m. Some igneous patches occur, and metamorphism has produced marble in places. Much of the range is porous because of solution cavities and is a source of springwater. Its ridges are rough and craggy, appropriately wild for the Crusader castle ruins that cling to its pinnacles.

Nestled between the Kyrenia Range and the Troodos is [3] the Mesaoria, the island's breadbasket, primarily an alluvial plain with fertile soils but with a platform of upturned sedimentaries between the Kyrenia ridge and the lower basin. Open at both its east and west ends, the Mesaoria slopes primarily eastward, from about 700 ft./215 m to sea level on the eastern coast. Nicosia, the primate city of the island and the capital of the Republic of Cyprus (and also designated as the capital of the self-proclaimed Turkish Republic of Northern Cyprus), nestles in the center of the Mesaoria. North of the Kyrenia Range, [4] a narrow coastal plain separates the steep northern slopes of the range from the shore, with citrus groves in irrigated areas and

Long-form official name, anglicized: Republic of Cyprus (ROC, south); (Turkish Republic of Northern Cyprus [TRNC] in the north not recognized except by Turkey)

Official name, transliterated: Kipriakií (Greek), Kıbrıs Cumhuriyeti (Turkish) in the south; (Kuzey Kıbrıs Turk Cumhuriyeti in the north)

Form of government: unitary multiparty republic with a unicameral legislature (House of Representatives) (south)

Area: 3,572 miles^2/9,251 km^2 (entire island); 2,277 miles^2/5,896 km^2 (south); 1,295 miles^2/3,355 km^2 (north)

Population, 1991: 747,900 (entire island); 574,300 south, 173,600 north. Literacy (latest): 95% (south)

Ethnic composition (%): Greek 99 (south), Turkish 99 (north)

Religions: predominantly Greek Orthodox (south), predominantly Sunni Muslim (north)

GNP, 1989: $4.89 billion (south); per capita: $7,050 (south)

Petroleum reserves: none

Main exports (% of total value, 1990): clothing 16.1; potatoes 6.7; citrus fruit 5.0; footwear 3.2 (south); food and live animals 56.1 (north)

Main imports (% of total value, 1990): consumer goods 14.9; transport equipment 12.6; petroleum and petroleum products 8.2 (south); machinery and transport equipment 26.1 (north)

Capital city: Nicosia (capital for both south and north) 205,400; other cities: Limassol 132,000; Larnaca 61,000; Paphos 27,800 (all in the south); Famagusta (Magosa) 19,428 (north)

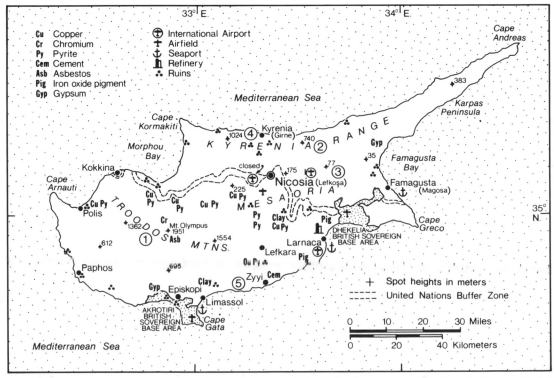

Map 13-4. *General and economic map of Cyprus, showing dividing line between north and south Cyprus. Circled numbers indicate the regions.*

rainfed crops in the remaining segments. [5] The coastal plain south of the Troodos is generally wider but more irregular. It is also more densely populated and more industrially developed, with two main centers, Limassol and Larnaca.

Mediterranean Climate, Mediterranean Crops

Cyprus has a typical Mediterranean climate, with hot, dry summers and mild, moist winters. The island receives 75 percent of the possible sunshine in an average year, and it attracts thousands of northern European tourists to its warmth and scenic sites. With 13 in./340 mm of rainfall at Nicosia on the open Mesaoria, crops other than the dominant grains must be irrigated. The upper slopes of the Troodos exert the typical orographic effect and wring up to 40 in./1,000 mm of moisture from the westerly winds in winter, much of it as snow, which is sufficient for a modest skiing season in most winters. Much of the runoff from the impermeable igneous rocks is captured in reservoirs or aquifers to be used for irrigation during the dry summer.

With assets of climate, relief, and soils, the island has had a good agricultural base for many centuries, and its farmers cultivate a high percentage of the total area (see Table 7-1). The island's agriculture includes several tree crops—olives, carobs (Cyprus leads the Middle East in carob bean exports), almonds, citrus and other fruits—and especially grapevines. Cyprus wine, although not of premium quality, is very good, and extensive vineyards occupy the southern midslopes of the Troodos (Fig. 13-4). Table grapes, raisins, and wines are major products and major exports, as are citrus fruits of all types. Potatoes rank with citrus and grapes in tons produced and are also a major export. Wheat and barley are major crops, but production is insufficient to meet local demand. More than half of the farms in Cyprus have some form of irrigation, although only 21 percent of the cultivated land is irrigated.

Nonagricultural Economy

Mineralization in the Troodos during the igneous intrusions and the accompanying metamor-

phism gave the island major resources of copper, iron pyrites, chrome, asbestos, and iron oxide pigments as well as lesser sources of gold, silver, and zinc. The deposits of copper, the main metal in bronze alloy, were exploited as early as the third millennium BC and became a major source of the metal during the Bronze Age. Indeed, the Greek and Latin words for copper are related to the island's name. In modern times, mining was second only to agriculture in Cyprus during the 1950s–1960s, but intensive mining methods had virtually exhausted the copper and chrome by the late 1970s. By the early 1990s, the island produced only modest tonnages of pyrite, iron oxide pigments (for paints), bentonite clays, celestite, and gypsum. Exploiting the large reserves of asbestos in the high Troodos, the Amiantos mine (Fig. 8-5) operated for many years before closing in 1989 because of decreased world demand. However, with shutdowns in production in Canada and the former Soviet Union, Cyprus hopes to resume asbestos mining. Recently, the island's once considerable income from mineral exports was nearing a negligible level ($1.4 million in 1989).

Diversification after independence in 1960 encouraged tourism and other services, light manufacturing, and transportation and trade. Even with grave political-economic difficulties between the Greek and Turkish Cypriot groups, Cyprus developed rapidly and solidly during the 1980s, achieving a well-rounded economy in the south, with a thriving tourist industry. The GDP of north Cyprus is only one-third that of the bustling south. Reinforcing its contention that it is part of Europe, Cyprus, with its part-Greek and part-British traditions, has turned increasingly to the European Communities for trade.

Before Division

Four crucial events in the long history of Cyprus are fundamental to the contemporary situation on the island. Because of the mining of copper and exploitation of the forests for shipbuilding during the Bronze Age, thriving ports and other cities were established by Minoans from Crete and Mycenaeans from Greece, a fact underscored by Greek Cypriots. Successive masters ruled Cyprus until the Greco-Roman period, during

Figure 13-4. *Olive groves and vineyards on the lower southern slopes of the Troodos Mountains of Cyprus.*

which the second important event occurred: conversion of the population of the island to Christianity by Paul and Barnabas (AD 45), as related in the New Testament. The third main event was the assertion of Ottoman control over the island in 1570–1571, after which several thousand Muslim Turks settled on the island. These developments set the stage for conflict between Cyprus's Greeks and Turks and their respective supporters. A fourth crucial development was the coming of the British in 1878 under agreements among the powers at the Congress of Berlin. For well or ill, Britain influenced Cyprus fortunes for nearly a century.

Annexed by Great Britain in 1914 and made a crown colony in 1925, Cyprus sought independence after World War II. Although they opened a paramilitary revolt against British colonial control, a majority of Greek Cypriots desired union with Greece (*enosis*) rather than actual independence for the island. After nearly five years of the revolt, the Zurich-London Agreements among all parties—Britain, Greek Cypriots, Turkish Cypriots, and the Greek and Turkish governments—led to the independence of the Republic of Cyprus on August 16, 1960.

The creation of a sovereign Cyprus entailed predictable dilemmas because of internal ethnic

division. Studies showed that of a total population of 550,000, 79 percent of the Cypriots were Greek speaking, practiced the Greek Orthodox religion, and, generally, strongly desired *enosis*. About 18 percent were Turkish speaking, adhered to Sunni Islam, and desired autonomy under some system of confederation or partition (*taksim*); and 3 percent were descendants of Armenian and Maronite refugees, all Christians, plus a few thousand British expatriates who had retired to the pleasant life of Cyprus. All these ethnic groups were scattered over the island, and although most villages tended to be either Greek or Turkish, some villages were mixed.

After independence, a power-sharing agreement prorated political positions at a ratio of 7 Greek Cypriots to 3 Turkish Cypriots (even 6 to 4 in the proposed army), although the population ratio was about 8 to 2. An indication of the island's strategic location is the United Kingdom's retention of two sovereign base areas on the south coast (see Map 13-4). (Augmenting forces already on Cyprus, British military components had occupied the areas when Britain evacuated the Suez Canal Zone during the period 1954–1956.)

The power-sharing compromise was not successful. In December 1963, conflict on Cyprus—

and resulting tensions between Greece and Turkey—became so serious that the UN Security Council established the UN Peacekeeping Force in Cyprus (UNFICYP) in 1964. For the next decade, the Greek Cypriots operated the government and economy primarily by themselves, with an increasing division between those who wanted *enosis* with Greece and those who were content with an independent Cyprus republic.

When the intra-Greek struggle culminated in an attempted coup in 1974 and a series of confused events, Turkey invaded northern Cyprus in July, declaring that it was protecting the Turkish Cypriot population. Backed by a strong military presence, the Turks drew the Attila Line, named after the Turkish commander, to divide their zone from the ROC. This division gave the Turkish zone 38 percent of the island territory and 18 percent of the population. Again, the Turks declared that they were offsetting the strength of the Greek Cypriots so as to protect their minority ethnic kin against continued oppression by the majority Greek Cypriots. During the Turkish invasion, 150,000–200,000 Greek Cypriots fled to the south, and about 45,000 Turkish Cypriots fled to the north—possibly 6,000–8,000 died during the fighting and the population exchange.

Divided Cyprus

The Autonomous Turkish Cypriot Administration established in late 1974 north of the Attila Line was replaced on February 13, 1975, with a unilaterally declared Turkish Federated State of Cyprus (TFSC). The name implied a future creation of the kind of island federation the Turkish Cypriots had demanded 20 years earlier. The TFSC became the Turkish Republic of Northern Cyprus (TRNC) on November 15, 1983, countering the southern zone's continued use of the original official name, Republic of Cyprus. Neither polity in the north has received recognition by any country other than Turkey.

The TRNC is, in certain respects, little more than an autonomous province of Turkey. It is tied to the mainland in various ways: It uses Turkish currency, depends upon Turkey for protection (including up to 30,000 Turkish soldiers), and receives a subsidy of several million dollars

annually from Turkey. In its 38 percent of the island are located the former main port (Famagusta—Turkish, Magosa), half of the capital city of Nicosia (Turkish, Lefkoşa), 40 percent of the cultivated land, most of the tobacco fields, 80 percent of the citrus groves, 60 percent of the tourist facilities, and 30 percent of the factories of 1974 Cyprus. Yet its economy is depressed and the output low. An estimated 30,000 Turks arrived as colonists (although 20,000 were later reported to have left), and an additional 30,000 Turkish citizens have settled in the TRNC since early 1985; more than one-third of the population in northern Cyprus is now estimated to be from Turkey.

The Republic of Cyprus in the south is still considered by the international community to be the legitimate government of the island. Having lost an enormous percentage of the island's productive capacity, the republic has, nevertheless, many more tourists, more industrial output, and more income from services than the pre-1974 state did with most of the island included in the economy. A significant stimulus to the development of southern Cyprus was the use of the area as a neutral adjunct of Lebanon during the Lebanon fighting in the period 1975–1991. Various factions used Cyprus as a rest and recreation area, staging area, arms transfer area, meeting ground, and supply center.

Attempts continued in the early 1990s to devise a political compromise acceptable to both the Greek and the Turkish Cypriots and also to Greece and Turkey. The United Nations has tried to mediate the conflict, but no plan has yet proved acceptable to all factions. A search for modalities continues and should eventually prove successful, since all parties desire a solution: Greek Cypriots want the advantages of a state that is coextensive with the entire island; Turkish Cypriots want a remedy for their isolation and economic ills; Greece wants a reduction in tensions and military spending but especially wants negotiations on conflicting claims to potential offshore oil fields in the Aegean; and Turkey wants entry into the EEC, continued and even increased aid from the United States, and resolution of the Aegean oil dispute. No one doubts the benefits of reunification or peaceful coexistence. The question is how to achieve it.

14

Jordan: The Land Beyond

During its long history, the area of the contemporary Kingdom of Jordan has undergone many changes in name, economic level, and political status. One result of these shifts, especially during the twentieth century, is confusion regarding Jordan's political geography, specifically its territorial base. Further uncertainty has been added in terminology because of the use of "Jordan" as the name of the famed river and valley and also as the name of the country.

The autonomous polity of Transjordan was created in the early 1920s, in former Ottoman Empire lands taken from the Turks during World War I, as a League of Nations mandate to Great Britain. The Amirate of Transjordan, as it was officially known for 25 years, became an independent kingdom on May 25, 1946, when Britain withdrew as mandatory power. Attachment of the West Bank, part of the former Palestine mandate, to the kingdom in 1948 (officially 1950) made "Transjordan" a misnomer (see below). A final change of name produced the Hashimite Kingdom of Jordan, commonly shortened to "Jordan." Occupation of the West Bank by Israel in 1967 placed both the West Bank and Jordan in an ambiguous situation that continued until Jordan announced its disengagement from the West Bank in August 1988.

For the sake of clarity, terms referring to the area east of the Jordan Valley may be distinguished in this way: The expression trans-Jordan basically indicates direction, "beyond the Jordan River," as opposed to cis-Jordan, "this side of the Jordan River"—both from the European perspective. The term Transjordan is a specific political designation referring only to the polity that occupied a specific area east of the Jordan River between 1923 and 1948/1950, first as a mandate and then as a kingdom. A third designation, trans-Jordania, revives an old regional name that has no political implications. It could be said that Transjordan was a trans-Jordan polity in trans-Jordania.

Four major general aspects of spatial relations regarding the Kingdom of Jordan are noteworthy. First, whatever the name or status of the area, its location "beyond the Jordan" has been a significant factor in its geography and history. The physical barriers of the deep Jordan trench to the west and the desert expanses to the east were once serious obstacles to the movement of peoples and goods, although camel caravans found some useful routes. Second, the rather narrow, better-watered highland zone squeezed between trench and desert in the trans-Jordan region nevertheless functioned as a north-south transit land, the eastern counterpart of the Trunk Road or Via Maris (Way of the Sea), which extended northward from Egypt through Gaza, Lydda, and Megiddo to Damascus. Caravans followed either of two ancient routes in trans-Jordania: the King's Highway through the hill country past Petra, Karak, Madaba, and Amman, then northward to Damascus; or the level Desert Road, 18 miles/29 km farther to the east out on the plateau (Map 14-1).

The transitional character of the area is the third major geographical aspect. It has never been a power center, nor has it served as a significant part of a power center. Conflict between "the desert and the sown," between nomads and settlements, has inhibited development east of the Jordan Valley. Although the area embraced petty kingdoms such as Rabboth-Ammon and Moab 3,000 years ago and although small areas had sustained regional identity (Gilead, for ex-

JORDAN

Long-form official name, anglicized: Hashimite Kingdom of Jordan
Official name, transliterated: al-Mamlakah al-Urdunniyah al-Hashimiyah
Form of government: constitutional monarchy with two legislative houses (Senate, House of Deputies)
Area: 34,342 miles^2/88,946 km^2
Population, 1991: 3,285,000. Literacy (latest): 80.1%
Ethnic composition (%): Arab 99.2, Circassian 0.5, Armenian 0.1, Turk 0.1, Kurd 0.1
Religions (%): Sunni Muslim 93.0, Christian 4.9, other 2.1
GNP, 1990: $3.41 billion; per capita: $1,076
Petroleum reserves: 20 million barrels
Main exports (% of total value, 1988): chemicals 28.2; phosphate fertilizers 23.5; basic manufactures 16.3; vegetables, fruits, and nuts 9.5; beverages and tobacco 0.5
Main imports (% of total value, 1988): machinery and transport equipment 22.9; basic manufactures 17.3; mineral fuels and lubricants 17.0 (of which crude petroleum 12.4); food and live animals 16.9; chemicals 9.8; miscellaneous manufactured articles 7.4
Capital city: Amman 936,000; other cities: al-Zarqa 318,000; Irbid 167,785; al-Rusayfah 72,580; al-Salt 47,585

---

ample), the general trans-Jordan area lacked a specific regional unity from earliest times until its establishment as an entity after World War I.

Confirming the lack of a core area and the transitional character of the realm, the *raison de création* of mandate Jordan, beyond the purely political goals mentioned in the next section, encumbered the amirate and the successor kingdom with the destiny of a buffer state. Designed to keep the French north of the Yarmuk, to hold back the Saudis from the Jordan Valley, and to keep the Iraqis focused on Mesopotamia, the mandate was designed, delineated, and operated by the British as a buffer. With the advent of the state of Israel, independent Transjordan— slightly smaller than the U.S. state of Indiana— became the archetypal buffer for all three of its adjacent neighbors, and its fate became inextricably linked to the vagaries of the conflict between Israel and the Palestinians and other Arabs. Contemporary Jordan not only has the longest border with Israel of all the Arab states, but it is in the unenviable position of being targeted by extremist Israelis as the preferred future homeland for all Arabs remaining in Israel and the occupied territories.

The fourth aspect concerns Jordan's territorial stability and integrity. During the mandate and its first few years as a kingdom, Jordan's territory lay entirely east of the Jordan River, as was suggested by its common Arabic name of that time, Sharq al-Urdunn (East of the Jordan). In 1950, incorporation of the central Palestine hill country (the West Bank) expanded Jordan's territorial base by a very important 2,270 miles^2/5,880 km^2, but for all practical purposes the West Bank was lost to Israeli conquest and occupation in the June War of 1967. After 21 years of uncertainty and crisis, Jordan renounced claims to the West Bank; therefore, description, data, and analysis of Jordan in this book pertain only to the East Bank—in effect, to virtually the same territory as that of the mandate.

Historical Evolution

From Early Times
to the Muslim Conquest

The history of the trans-Jordan area is sharply etched into the landscape of the western fourth of contemporary Jordan. In this settled part of the country, one is rarely out of sight of some reminder of Jordan's past—a dolmen, tell, ruined building, Roman milestone, or the partially excavated ruins of an entire city such as Jerash, Umm al-Jimal, or Petra.

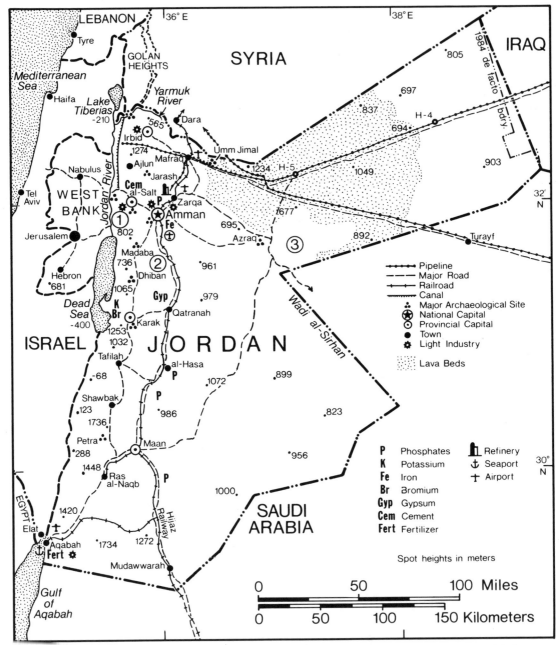

Map 14-1. *General and economic map of Jordan. The northeastern borders are shown in both de jure and de facto versions. Circled numbers identify regions discussed in text. Note concentration of settlement and development in western Jordan.*

Trans-Jordania's golden age began under the Seleucids of Syria and continued through the Roman era and into the Byzantine period (about 200 BC–AD 600), when the area was the setting for successful trade routes, trade centers, and caravan towns. Prime movers in the trade through Jordan were the Semitic Nabataeans, who operated from their extraordinary capital and caravan center of Petra.[1] The modern Jordanian capital of Amman was the Rabboth Ammon of the Old Testament and the Greco-Roman Philadelphia (Fig. 14-1). It and Jerash (see Fig. 2-4), north of Amman, were two principal members of the Decapolis, a ten-city league formed to resist nomadic attacks.

Mosaic floors from Byzantine Christian churches and other buildings of the fifth and sixth centuries are found in many sites. Outstanding are the numerous mosaic floors in the small highland town of Madaba, south-southwest of Amman. One such floor preserves the famous Madaba Map of the sixth century, which shows in intricate mosaic the Palestine area and adjacent parts of the Middle East, including a recognizable plan of Jerusalem.

From Muslim Conquest to the Present

The changed political and economic relationships of the greater region minimized trans-Jordania's role after the Muslim conquest. External contacts were also minimal until the early 1900s, when construction of the Hijaz Railway from Damascus to Medina, through Amman and Maan, in 1900–1908 stimulated some commercial development in the area.

World War I action in the Middle East and, a few years later, the memoirs of T. E. Lawrence, *Seven Pillars of Wisdom,* reintroduced trans-Jordania to the West. In the hasty territorial settlements following the war, the vagueness of the trans-Jordan area was revealed. It sprawled over a generally undefined and unattached expanse east of the Jordan trench, between the future Syria on the north, the future Iraq on the east, and desert areas to the south that were later consolidated into the Kingdom of Saudi Arabia.

Great Britain, as the mandatory power for both sides of the Jordan Valley, declared to East Bank shaykhs and notables at al-Salt in August 1920 that it favored self-government for them. At a meeting of British Middle East experts with Colonial Secretary Winston Churchill in Cairo in March 1921, conferees agreed on a somewhat tentative status for the inchoate trans-Jordan realm between the Jordan trench and the emerging mandate of Iraq. The decision demonstrated both a partial fulfillment of the British promises to the Arabs in the Husayn-McMahon corre-

spondence of 1915–1916 (see Chap. 11) and a desire to placate Amir Abdullah ibn Husayn, son of the sharif of Mecca and brother of Amir Faysal, who contemporaneously became king of Iraq. In part to block further southward expansion of French territorial control from Syria, the British created the separate Arab mandate of Transjordan to be ruled by the Amir Abdullah under supervision by Britain as League of Nations mandatory. Churchill personally met Abdullah in Jerusalem and informed him of the decision, which was regularized in mid-1923 in time for the official entry in force of all Middle East mandates in September 1923.[2] The amirate continued as a mandate until it became an independent kingdom on May 25, 1946, with Abdullah automatically becoming king.

The political-geographical, demographic, economic, and social character of Jordan altered dramatically with the advent of the State of Israel on May 14, 1948: Palestinian refugees crossed over the Jordan River to Transjordan, King Abdullah annexed the West Bank, and Jordan was pulled into the conflict vortex that characterizes Arab-Israeli relations. Abdullah was assassinated in al-Aqsa Mosque in Jerusalem in 1951 and was succeeded briefly by his son Talal, who was in turn succeeded in 1952 by his young son Husayn. Still on the throne in 1993, King Husayn is the longest-governing head of state in the Middle East. Israel's territorial conquests in the June War of 1967 and the territorial readjustments at that time severed all territory west of the Jordan from the East Bank. Jordan thereby lost more than a third of its most-educated population, much of its arable land, and its Holy Land sites. Territorially, the kingdom returned to its trans-Jordan status of pre-1948, a status confirmed by King Husayn when he renounced all legal ties with the West Bank in August 1988.

Turbulence has characterized Jordan's development from its independence to the present: The country has experienced the 1948–1949 wars with the new state of Israel, the disastrous 1967 ("Six-Day") war, periodic border clashes, and a series of internal coup attempts. The most serious of the clashes within Jordan was the showdown between the government and the PLO in September 1970 (called "Black September" by the

Figure 14-1. *Amman, capital of Jordan. Old heart of the city, with Grand Husayni Mosque, in foreground. Newer residential quarters climb the slopes of Jabal al-Ashrafiyah (upper left), Jabal al-Nadhif (upper right), and Jabal Amman (right center).*

Palestinian insurgents), when an estimated 3,300 were killed on both sides. In this civil war, the Jordan Arab Army definitively asserted control of the kingdom and forced the withdrawal of the PLO forces, mostly to Lebanon. King Husayn was later reconciled with PLO leaders, but political restrictions continued until 1988. In that year Jordan held free and open elections of a fully democratic parliament and joined the world's democracies.

Peoples: Arabs, Minorities, Refugees

The population of trans-Jordania is estimated to have been stable at approximately 300,000 for centuries prior to World War I. During those centuries, as now, the people were overwhelmingly Arab, Arab language speakers, and predominantly Sunni Muslim. When the people were incorporated into the new mandate, they were overwhelmingly villagers and Bedouins, but they gradually became appreciably urbanized and sedentarized. Even Amman, now the modern, well-developed capital, was a rank village of Roman ruins and squatter Circassians. Seven decades later, Jordanians are 60 percent urbanized, and the villagers—many of whom were formerly

only semisettled—now enjoy most modern amenities and often commute to nearby towns.

Most of the urbanized Jordanians live on one or another of the *jabals* ("hills") of Amman, the capital and primate city on the East Bank (Fig. 14-1). This group, many of whom are Palestinians, evolved after World War II along with the rapid growth and development of the Jordanian economy. Many of them have been educated abroad and speak English as a second language, and an appreciable number of them are Christian. Rusayfah and Zarqa to the east of Amman are actually large suburbs of the capital and lack the full development of a city. Irbid, Jordan's third-largest city, is the population node in the northwest, and steadily expanding Aqabah is the kingdom's single port in the southwest.

Before 1900, Bedouins made up the majority of the trans-Jordanian population and constituted a major segment of the Jordanian social structure. Bedouin codes and traditions were the heritage of all Arabs, especially trans-Jordanians. During the mandate years, tribal shaykhs wielded decisive political influence and regularly attended national council meetings with Amir Abdullah in Amman, and nomadic pastoralism contributed significantly to the amirate's economy. But after World War II, the Bedouins in Jordan became increasingly sedentarized, as did Bedouins in neighboring areas. By the early 1990s, Bedouin tribes comprised only 2–3 percent of the population, and detribalization and sedentarization were steadily continuing. Despite the diminution of the role of tribes and tribalism, a general sense of tribal identity and Bedouin heritage remains a significant pillar of both society and political culture.[3] The percentage of Bedouins in the army is predictably decreasing, but earlier, during internal crises in the 1960s and 1970s, they showed their traditional loyalty to their paramount chieftain, King Husayn, thereby helping to maintain the kingdom's political structure.

Of the score of Bedouin tribes in modern Jordan, by far the most important have been the Bani Sakhr and the Huwaytat. The Bani Atiyah, the Adwan, and the Bani Hasan are semisedentary and engage in only limited wandering. Much larger tribes, wandering over more extensive *dirahs* and thus not exclusively Jordanian, include the Rawalah, Anazah, and Shammar.

Both ethnic and religious minorities play noteworthy roles in the Jordanian political and social systems. About 30,000 Circassians (see Chap. 6) make up the majority in eight villages around Amman and are numerous in the capital itself. Several hundred Armenians sought refuge in Jordan between the 1880s and 1920s, and their descendants continue to be unassimilated in Jordanian society. The western expatriate community, almost entirely British before World War II, is growing steadily and now includes not only British but also Americans, Germans, Yugoslavs, and others.

Jordan's social fabric is not torn by intercommunal conflict, as is that of Lebanon, since relations between the Sunni Muslims (more than 90 percent of the population) and the Christians (about 5–8 percent, mostly Eastern Orthodox) have always been good. Amir Abdullah demonstrated cordial relations with Christian families and tribes from the time of his first entry into trans-Jordania, and King Husayn has followed suit. His second and fourth wives were Christians before converting to Islam upon their marriages. Distributed among several sects, Christians number approximately 170,000, a community that dates back to the earliest spread of Chris-

tianity in the second and third centuries. Almost two-thirds of the East Bank Christians are Greek Orthodox and about one-third Greek Catholic, but there are also a few hundred Roman Catholics, Armenian Orthodox, Armenian Catholics, and Protestants and a few Syrian Orthodox, Nestorians, and Chaldean Catholics. Certain towns are primarily Christian centers—Karak, Madaba, and al-Salt—and Amman has a high percentage of Christian inhabitants.

Ethnic and religious distinctions aside, it is the division between native "East Bankers" and "Palestinians" that is the crucial dynamic in all aspects of the Jordanian sociopolitical system. The cleavage is theoretically not ethnic: Both Palestinians and East Bankers are Arab, speak Arabic, are mostly Sunni Muslim, were under Ottoman control for 400 years, were in British mandates for a quarter-century, and have other characteristics in common. But the essential difference is that the Palestinians were dispossessed of their homeland, property, and national identity and have, therefore, profoundly different national sentiments and aspirations from those of the indigenous Jordanians.

Problems of Population

When the Transjordan mandate was sketched onto a map in 1921, roughly half of the estimated population of 300,000 was settled (or semi-settled) in the villages along the more humid western belt of highlands, whereas the eastern deserts were a Bedouin realm and had practically no settled population. Even by the time Jordan became an independent kingdom in 1946, the population was estimated at only 433,659.

This figure increased dramatically in 1948–1949 with the influx of Palestinian refugees. About 132,000 Palestinians fled to the East Bank, and another 365,000 took refuge among the 400,000 permanent Arab inhabitants of the West Bank, which was defended against Israeli attacks by the Jordan Arab Legion and its allies. In a matter of weeks, the East Bank population increased nearly one-third, and subsequent annexation of the West Bank area increased the population of the kingdom by 765,000. Jordan's population total thereby jumped during that brief period from about 435,000 to about

1,332,000, which obviously resulted in the original East Bankers' finding themselves suddenly outnumbered two to one by Palestinians. Furthermore, half of the West Bankers were also refugees, displaced by Israelis from their lands and livelihood, and both the refugees and the natives in the West Bank resented annexation by a neighboring polity.

Jordan's demographic—and territorial—status again altered radically with Israel's 1967 conquest of the West Bank, not only depriving Jordan of the territory, along with its tourist attractions and agricultural lands, but also reducing the population of the kingdom by half. More than 125,000 West Bank "old refugees" became twice-displaced as they fled invading Israeli military forces and joined their fellow Palestinian refugees on the East Bank, and an additional 100,000 West Bank residents and another 45,000 Palestinians from the Gaza Strip also fled eastward as "new refugees" or "displaced persons." These immigrants totaled 270,000 to be added to the 132,000 refugees of the late 1940s, their children, and casual immigrants during the period 1949–1967. A small population flow from West Bank to East Bank has continued since 1967, and Israeli extremists declare that all Arabs west of the Jordan must eventually be expelled to Jordan.

By early 1992, the estimated population of Jordan (i.e., East Bank only) had reached 3.5 million, including natural increase since 1990 (Table 6-1) and also the 300,000 returnees from the Gulf during 1990–1991. Ironically, many of these "returnees" are third-time refugees, having been expelled—this time by fellow Arabs—from Kuwait and other Gulf areas after the Gulf crisis. Thus, during the 44 years after 1948, the East Bank population increased 705 percent on a very limited resource base.

More than 1.5 million Palestinian refugees, displaced persons, and their descendants lived in the East Bank in the early 1990s. Of this total, more than 250,000—about 7 percent of the kingdom's population—still resided in the ten refugee camps located in and around Amman and Irbid, in the valley north of Amman, and on the plateau south of Irbid. Most of them have accepted citizenship in Jordan, the only country to offer citizenship to any Palestinian refugee applying for it.

Physical Resource Base

Jordan has exhibited remarkable flexibility during the changes in its territorial base and population, particularly in view of its limited physical resource base. A brief survey of this base and the state's exploitation of its resources will aid in understanding the challenges to this buffer kingdom.[4]

Regions of Jordan

An east-west cross section of Jordan shows a threefold physical division (see circled numbers on Map 14-1): [1] Along the western edge is the Jordan Valley, a major segment of the Levant Rift System, which contains the lowest continental elevations on earth along the shores of the Dead Sea. [2] Immediately east of the Jordan Valley is a north-south belt of highlands, with elevations of 4,100 ft./1,250 m in the north and the highest elevations in the Palestine–trans-Jordan area, 5,575 ft./1,700 m, in the south. [3] Extending eastward at a general level of 2,625–2,950 ft./800–900 m is the Eastern Desert, which occupies about 85 percent of the country and has a surface that is variously flat, rolling, or exhibiting erosional remnants.

[1] **Jordan Valley.** The Jordan Valley (Arabic, *al-Ghor*), 65 miles/104 km long, may be subdivided into four narrow parallel belts. (1) The Jordan River itself (see Fig. 3-4), winding in tight meanders in its narrow bed, descends from the confluence of the Yarmuk River just south of the Sea of Galilee (Lake Tiberias) to the river's mouth in the Dead Sea. (2) The river floodplain (Arabic, *zor*), with a mantle of rank vegetation called "thicket of the Jordan" in biblical passages, has a level surface that is just a few meters above the river level. (3) The upper terrace level (Arabic, *ghor*—the feature that gives the valley its general name in Arabic), is several hundred meters wide and is divided from the *zor* by a narrow eroded slope. The East Ghor Canal was constructed on the gently sloping upper terrace level (see "Water" section below), enabling development of the most productive farmland in Jordan (Fig. 14-2). The East Ghor is an archaeologist's paradise, with 224 sites having been identified between the Yarmuk River and the Dead Sea. One of the sites,

Figure 14-2. *Irrigated citrus groves south of Karamah on East Ghor, Jordan Valley, Jordan. White structures left of center are hothouses for producing early vegetables.*

Pella—just off the Ghor in a side wadi—is proving to be one of the most exciting sites in all of Jordan; it is the scene of human activity far back into the Paleolithic and has been almost continuously inhabited for the past 6,000 years.[5] (4) The high, ruggedly eroded escarpment—with a total rise of more than 4,265 ft./1,300 m within 1.2 miles/2 km—forms the eastern wall of the great rift that contains the Sea of Galilee, the Jordan River, and the Dead Sea (see Chap. 3 and Fig. 3-1).

[2] **Highland Belt.** Extending from the Yarmuk River on the north to the Gulf of Aqabah in the south, the highland belt receives the most precipitation of all the regions of Jordan and therefore has always served as the core of settlement, development, and culture east of the Jordan Valley. The hill zone varies markedly in width and relief, and there are fundamental differences in rocks and structure among its northern, central, and southern thirds. The principal subregions of the highland belt are, from north to south, (1) the Ajlun Highland (Gilead), (2) the Northern Balqa or Amman Highland (ancient Heshbon and Ammon), (3) the Southern Balqa or Karak Plateau (ancient Moab), (4) the Shara Mountains (ancient Edom), and (5) the Hisma.

(1) With an average 24–30 in./600–750 mm of precipitation, moderate slopes, productive soils, and a remarkable number of flowing springs, the Ajlun Highland is the best-watered and most naturally productive part of Jordan. It supports the densest population in the greatest number of villages of all the trans-Jordanian area outside the capital metropolitan area. Along with cultivated crops, natural woodland has been legendary since ancient times, when resin of trees on these hills yielded the celebrated "balm in Gilead."

On the plateau north of the Ajlun Dome lies Irbid (ancient Arbela), Jordan's third-largest city, whose population includes thousands of Palestinian refugees. East of Irbid is Ramtha (ancient Ramoth or Ramoth Gilead), an old caravan station and now the border crossing point between Syria and Jordan. Along the eastern flank of the dome, on the main highway, is the extensive ruined city of Jerash, with its well-preserved gate, colonnaded main street, forum, theaters, and temples from Hellenistic, Roman, and Byzantine times (see Fig. 2-4).

A convenient southern boundary of the Ajlun is the deep but broad valley of the Wadi Zarqa, the biblical River Jabbok. The stream has gouged its valley into the southern flank of the Ajlun

Dome, exposing a geological sequence of successively older rocks of the Cretaceous, Jurassic, and Triassic periods (Fig. 5-3). Rising in springs near Amman, the Zarqa joins the Jordan River after a descent of 3,580 ft./1,090 m. The King Talal Dam, Jordan's largest, was built across the lower Zarqa in 1977.

(2) South of the Wadi Zarqa is the Northern Balqa Highland, sometimes called the Amman Highland. In the western Balqa upland is al-Salt, the main center of trans-Jordania before the mandate. On the southeastern edge of the Balqa upland is Amman, the capital and also the administrative, economic, communications, industrial, and cultural center of Jordan. With buildings of limestone and chalk dimension stone covering the steep slopes of the several *jabals*, the city's morphology is dramatic (Fig. 14-1). From a population of about 6,000–7,000 in the 1920s, Amman has grown to absorb nearly one-third of the country's population and was edging toward 1 million inhabitants in mid-1992.

(3) The Southern Balqa lies south of the Northern Balqa/Amman Highland on a plateau, sometimes called the Karak Plateau, a realm of grain cultivation and seminomadic pastoralism. This is the biblical Land of Moab and the classical Peraea. Winding across the plateau is the scenic modern equivalent of the historic King's Highway, connecting the cities of Hisban (ancient Heshbon), Madaba, Dhiban (ancient Dibon), and Karak (ancient Kir Hareseth, chief city of the Moabites)—all mentioned in biblical accounts. Northwest of Madaba is the eminence of Mt. Nebo, from which Moses viewed the Promised Land.

(4) The most rugged part of Jordan, the Shara Mountains (from Seir, meaning "rock," of the biblical period) traverse the ancient land of Edom ("red"). The King's Highway continues along the crestline of the Shara to the Hisma, passing diminishing numbers of villages as aridity increases. The village of Wadi Musa adjoins the archaeological site of Petra, referred to by a British poet as the "rose-red city, half as old as time," hidden in the colorful mesas of Nubian sandstone on the western edge of the Shara (Fig. 14-3).

(5) The Hisma landscape includes the Hisma Depression itself, with broad sand corridors winding their way among vertical-sided mesas and buttes of red Nubian sandstone, the dramatic, silent land of the Wadi Ram—similar to Monument Valley in northern Arizona and southern Utah in North America. From the Wadi Ram, a rugged corridor for highway and railway reaches Jordan's only seaport at Aqabah. Aqabah has grown from a fishing village of fewer than 2,000 people in 1945 to 30,000 in 1989, expanding into a bustling modern port, especially for the export of phosphate rock. It also now has chemical fertilizer plants and a thriving tourist trade, with its own international airport. Aqabah is the anchor center for Jordan's short coastline, 16 miles/26 km.

[3] **Eastern Desert.** Stretching eastward from the highland belt is the Eastern Desert, a dry tableland that is the northwestern corner of the Arabian Desert. Except in one or two depressions, the tableland is everywhere over 2,000 ft./610 m. Lying nearly 1,000 ft./305 m below the general level of the highland belt, as well as in its rain shadow, the tableland receives only 2–8 in./50–200 mm of precipitation a year. The western belt of the dry realm is Jordan's phosphate belt, and the kingdom's small oil field and its new natural gas field are found in the Eastern Desert (see below). One notable cultural feature of increasing economic importance as a link to Aqabah is the Hijaz Railway, which was constructed by the Ottoman Turks in the early 1900s along the dividing line between the sown region on the west and the desert on the east.

Of the Eastern Desert's several subdivisions, two have served historic roles: The depression of the Wadi al-Sirhan, which extends southeastward along the Jordan–Saudi Arabia boundary, was a traditional route for caravans for many centuries and is still used for Bedouin migrations. Azraq Oasis is a complex of shallow pools and marshes that forms the only permanent body of water in the Jordan desert and provides sanctuary for enormous flocks of migrating birds during the spring and fall flights through the great Levant flyway. Much of the north-central desert is a barren lava plain (Map 14-1), a *hamadah*, in which angular lava boulders constitute the surface.

Figure 14-3. *Its original name and purpose unknown, this monument in Petra was carved out of a red sandstone cliff about 2,000 years ago.*

Water: The Vital Resource

As in all Middle East countries, the water balance in Jordan is the most important factor not only in the agricultural economy but also in the life of the country. With an average annual precipitation generally below 5 in./125 mm, Jordan calculates its average annual renewable surface and underground water resources as 1.2 billion m³. It also estimates that by 2000 its demand will be about 934 million m³, despite the limited and cautious use Jordanians habitually make of the scarce supplies. Thus, Jordan must make strenuous efforts to achieve optimum utilization of its water resources.

Large-scale planning and projects would yield more substantial benefits if regional cooperation could distribute fair shares of Jordan basin waters to the riparian states (see Chap. 11).[6] Cooperation between even Syria and Jordan would be advantageous. For more than 40 years, plans have called for a major dam to be constructed on the deeply entrenched Yarmuk River between northwest Jordan and southwest Syria. Construction of the dam, called the Maqarin Dam, was finally undertaken during the 1980s, but frictions between Jordan and Syria followed by Israeli resistance delayed work. Renamed al-Wahdah (Unity) to celebrate agreements between Syria and Jordan—which, unfortunately, were short lived—it is planned as a 328-ft.-/100-m-high structure to impound more than 250 million m³ of water for irrigation and urban supply to Irbid. Continued delay because of Israeli complaints over its share of the basin waters prompted Syria to construct small dams on Yarmuk tributaries, and Jordan continues to be without the benefit of the Unity Dam. Jordan did, however, add 33 ft./10 m to the height of the King Talal Dam to increase its storage capacity from 48 million m³ to 90 million m³.

Using water directly from the Yarmuk, the East Ghor Canal is the most important irrigation project in Jordan. Completed in 1964, primarily with financial aid from the United States, it diverts Yarmuk River water into a canal along the level *ghor* between the Jordan River floodplain and the eastern wall of the Jordan Valley. The canal takes Yarmuk water in order both to take advantage of the greater hydraulic head at the elevation at which the diversion takes place and to use Yarmuk water before it mixes with the much saltier Jordan River water. By the mid-1980s, the East Ghor Canal had been extended, in three stages, to reach a length of 72 miles/116 km to the Dead Sea, and the irrigated area was steadily increasing (see next section).

Agriculture

The independent Jordan that emerged after World War II and that was soon overwhelmed with refugees faced bleak prospects. Testimony to the low level of its mid-1940s economy is the fact that with only about 4 percent of its area cultivable, 75 percent of Jordan's population was dependent on agriculture (including grazing), half of its population was engaged in nomadic pastoralism, and 90 percent of its limited exports were agricultural products. Nevertheless, with large inflows of grants and other aid, but with great local effort, Jordan absorbed the refugees discussed earlier and achieved an expanded, modernized agriculture, along with a considerable manufac-

turing and service base.[7] By 1988, the share of agriculture in the GDP was down to 10 percent and that of manufacturing was up to 12 percent.

About 85 percent of the East Bank receives less than 8 in./200 mm of precipitation, and only 1.3 percent receives a mean annual precipitation of more than 24 in./600 mm, the amount necessary to assure good crops. One result is that of the state's total area, only 4 percent is cultivated. Since the limited amounts of precipitation are also highly variable from year to year (see Chap. 4), nearly half of Jordan's cultivated acres suffer crop failures in most years. Of the cultivated area, only 15 percent is fully or partly irrigated, which represents a significant increase during the 1980s.

Of the irrigated area, more than half is in the Jordan Valley, which composes only 0.6 percent of the country's land area but produces half of the kingdom's fruits and vegetables and 90 percent of its export crops. Increasing use of temporary plastic greenhouses (Figs. 5-3 and 14-2) not only raises crop yield but permits an earlier harvest of spring vegetables and therefore earlier marketing, ahead of competing producers.

Economic Geography

Mining. Phosphate-bearing horizons underlie extensive areas of Jordan, generally along the alignment of the Hijaz Railway, and are believed to total 1.5–2 billion tons of high-grade phosphate rock. Since beginning open-cast mining of phosphates in 1934, Jordan has increased its exports of phosphate fertilizers in response to growing world demand—and steadily higher prices—until it is now third in world exports, shipping 5–6 million tons annually to 30 countries, especially India. The kingdom raised its share of the world phosphate export market to nearly 14 percent by 1988, when it earned more than $200 million. Mining from the original pits in Rusayfah, east of Amman (farthest from Aqabah), was suspended in 1985, but new operations were undertaken at the huge newly discovered site al-Shadiyah, north of Aqabah, in 1989. Large-scale production continues at al-Hasa and Wadi al-Abyad, midway between Rusayfah and Aqabah.

Although Israel set up a huge processing operation to recover chemicals from brines in the southwestern corner of the Dead Sea in the early 1950s, Jordan began another processing operation only in October 1982, with a $425-million plant on the southeastern shore of the Dead Sea. The plant produces about 1.3 million tons of potash and associated bromine and magnesium annually from evaporated Dead Sea brines. Exports of these chemicals and of phosphates and chemicals from them comprise more than half of Jordan's exports by value.

Years of exploration for hydrocarbons and drilling of about 50 wells have resulted in the discovery of few fuel resources. The small Hamzah oil field, near Azraq, yields only 300 bpd, which is trucked to the Zarqa refinery. Limited natural gas found recently in the Rishah area, near the Iraq border, is being used to fuel two on-site gas turbine generators that were installed in early 1989 and supplied 15 percent of Jordan's energy needs. After having received all of its crude petroleum requirements for the Zarqa refinery for most of 35 years via the Saudi Tapline, Jordan had to search for another dependable supply during the 1980s when Tapline was phased down and Saudi-Jordanian relations eroded. During the Iran-Iraq war, when Jordan became an important outlet for Iraq's exports—including petroleum and its product—the kingdom obtained some of its crude needs from its eastern neighbor, which supplied 85 percent of those needs as of mid-1991. Jordan would like to continue this symbiosis under normal political-economic conditions.

Manufacturing. When Jordan emerged from isolation and found itself host to hundreds of thousands of refugees in the late 1940s, it was forced to shift from a preindustrial agricultural economy to an expanded and diversified economic base. Only then could it hope both to give employment to the greatly increased work force and to supply the needs of a larger and more sophisticated population. The initial plants were relatively small and simple and were mostly in and around Amman. Later industries reached appreciable size and technical advancement; they were still concentrated in the Amman-Zarqa area but were also located in the Irbid area and in Aqabah. Products include the usual cement and refined petroleum products and also chemicals,

processed foods, steel, detergents, paper and cardboard, footwear, cigarettes, batteries, textiles, beer, and similar items. The labor force is well educated and motivated, but insecurity and limited investment capital have slowed Jordan's attempts to reach its industrial potential.

Transportation. Jordan was geographically fortunate to inherit the Hijaz ("Pilgrim") Railway, which ran right past the phosphate fields and could be refurbished and extended to transport the bulky rock shipments to the kingdom's only port. Prior to 1965, Aqabah lacked sufficient coastline to handle its port functions, but a territorial exchange with Saudi Arabia in that year gave Jordan several kilometers of extra coastline south of Aqabah that permitted the necessary expansion of port facilities and the construction of a railhead and chemical plants using both phosphates and Dead Sea chemicals.

Jordan's highway system is very satisfactory and is being improved along the main north-south axis. To handle the important trade with Iraq prior to 1990, a cross-desert shortcut highway, which avoids the railway crossings and heavy traffic of the main Desert Road, was undertaken between Maan and Azraq (see Map 14-1). The national air carrier, Royal Jordanian Airlines (RJA), is headquartered at Queen Alia International Airport south of Amman and operates a score of modern aircraft with worldwide routes. RJA is an important factor in Jordan's considerable tourist industry, built around the country's major archaeological sites—especially Petra and Jerash, the Aqabah beaches, and the Dead Sea.

Finances and Aid. From the earliest years of the mandate, domestic sources for funding Jordan's national budget have been inadequate, and foreign transfers have supplied 50 percent and more of the budgetary funding. The United Kingdom provided the modest budgetary support required between the early 1920s and the mid-1950s. The United States replaced Britain as Jordan's financial supporter for the decade 1957–1967, and Arab petroleum-producing countries have provided large transfer payments in most years since 1967. Saudi Arabia, Kuwait, the United Arab Emirates, and Iraq have been the major supporters, especially Saudi Arabia, on the premise that Jordan—along with Egypt and Syria—is an important "front-line state" in the Arab-Israel conflict and therefore deserves support by wealthy Arab governments. Aid from the Gulf states surpassed $1.2 billion in some years, and such transfers permitted Jordan to achieve astonishing relative development during the 1970s and early 1980s; however, Arab aid fell to zero after Jordan declined to support the UN action against Iraq in 1990–1991, and Jordan's economic problems mounted in 1991.

Jordan lost not only the financial aid from its former supporters but also more than $2.5 billion in trade and services as a direct result of the Gulf crisis, because of sanctions against Iraq and because of loss of markets in the Gulf and elsewhere. Even more serious in the longer run was the influx of about 300,000 Jordanians (including Palestinian refugees and their families) who were expelled from Kuwait and elsewhere in the Gulf, whose return imposed multiple strains on the economy. Jordan's economic balance suffered a devastating blow as unemployment rose to 32 percent—83 percent among returnees. The government is the kingdom's largest employer, but it cannot absorb unlimited numbers of workers.

International Relations

Jordan as a League of Nations mandate to Great Britain had close ties with the West, and it has continued to maintain those ties. British support, both political and financial, gave the penurious amirate and later the kingdom its viability, and British-Jordanian relations remained close until the king's dismissal of Glubb Pasha as commander of the Arab Legion in 1956. Indeed, friendly relations continue. After 1956, U.S. aid and support of both civilian and military operations became Jordan's main prop as a large aid staff assisted Jordan in a variety of projects and programs, including the important East Ghor Canal and highway program. U.S. support may well have preserved the kingdom during the short, sharp civil war between PLO insurgents and Jordanian forces in September 1970. U.S.-Jordanian relations cooled in the late 1970s as the perception mounted that the United States—especially the U.S. Congress—gave Jordan only

minimum support to keep it viable but pliable in the Arab-Israeli problem. Relations deteriorated suddenly and sharply when Jordan appeared to side with Iraq after the 1990 Iraqi invasion of Kuwait. Two vital economic facts were that Jordan and Iraq had developed an almost symbiotic relationship during the Iran-Iraq war and that the UN coalition sanctions and military actions impacted severely on Jordan's fragile economy. A more emotional political issue was, as the king explained, that although Jordan condemned the invasion of Kuwait, it also condemned the arraying of non-Arab forces against an Arab state that—even if it invaded a sister Arab state—also claimed to defend Arab interests against imperialist-colonialist Western powers, to fight for the rights of Palestinians, and to stand against Israeli actions. U.S.-Jordanian relations improved somewhat after King Husayn visited Washington in March 1992. They warmed appreciably after Jordan signed the "Agenda for Peace" with Israel on September 14, 1993, and after it moved to cooperate with Israel on mutual interests.

Important as the country's relations with Britain and the United States may be, Jordan is in and of the Middle East and in and of the Arab and Islamic world. It has not been a prime mover in the Arab world, but it was one of the seven charter members of the League of Arab States in 1945, and its political and economic policies must be relatively consonant with those of its Arab neighbors—without jeopardizing the security of its powerful Jewish neighbor. As the last two nominal kingdoms remaining in the Middle East—aside from the Gulf amirates—Saudi Arabia and Jordan normally felt a certain empathy and perceived a commonality of interest, especially in their moderate political and economic stances. Nevertheless, Jordanians, exercising their newly acquired democratic freedoms in late 1990, considered that their rapport with Iraq took precedence over relations with and even dependence on their Saudi neighbors. Jordan sacrificed its friendly relations with Egypt on the same basis. Syria and Jordan continue a cautious, on-and-off relationship that has its roots in the early 1920s.

Jordan's favorable central location in the Middle East has not resulted in any decisive traditional role for the country to play in the region's long, eventful history. However, its long border with Israel and its 70 years of being enmeshed in the Palestinian problem have escalated Jordan's importance in more recent years.

Personifying his vulnerable realm and treading carefully on his geopolitical tightrope, King Husayn has repeatedly played the role of mediator and regional statesman. He has often sought diplomatic solutions in explosive situations, as he did during the Gulf crisis of 1990–1991 when he first sought an "Arab" solution to Iraq's occupation of Kuwait and, failing that, pursued an "Islamic" solution. The kingdom finds itself pulled by moderate Arab states, Palestinians within and outside the kingdom, the United States (as it acts both as mediator and as surrogate for Israel), and Israel itself. This ambivalent role was demonstrated once again in the peace talks initiated in 1991 to bring Israel and its Arab neighbors face to face, for which the Jordanian delegation served as the host for Palestinian representatives. The essential political-geographical question is whether or not Jordan can maintain the delicate balance necessary between Western pressures and the crosscurrents of regional crises—above all, the crosscurrents of juxtaposition with Israel. Still further questions arise from the momentous reorientation of the regional geopolitical relationships as one consequence of the September 1993 Israeli-Palestinian Declaration of Principles and Israeli-Jordanian Agenda for Peace (see the Epilogue).

15

Israel and Occupied Territories: "Palestine" or "Eretz Yisrael"?

Of the world's 117 or so newly independent states (since 1943) and the Middle East's 10 new states, Israel has stimulated an unprecedented level of international involvement, both in support and in opposition. Chapter 11 examines the Arab-Israeli problem, the geopolitical aspects of the Jewish state and of the territories Israel has occupied since 1967, and the problem of the use of names regarding these areas. This chapter focuses on Israel itself, with sections on the local aspects of the occupied territories.

One of Israel's leaders once commented that Israel is in but not of the Middle East. The state is, indeed, distinct from its neighbors, in both cultural attributes and statistical measures. Because of interacting circumstances of its advent and evolution, it is not only distinct but also virtually isolated from its neighbors. Relations with Egypt since the Egyptian-Israeli peace treaty of 1979 fluctuate, and relations with other neighboring countries are strained or nonexistent.

Historical Background: A Brief Summary

The long history of Palestine[1] holds a special significance for Christians and Muslims as well as for Jews because of biblical and Quranic associations with the land. For many Jews, the Old Testament accounts buttress modern Zionist claims to the land, whereas more recent history underlies the often conflicting claims of Muslims and Christians (see Chap. 2).

Defeat of Turkish forces in the Middle East in 1917 was followed by British occupation of Palestine and the Transjordan area and later by establishment of the British mandate over Palestine in the early 1920s. After absorbing scores of thousands of Jewish immigrants, the mandate was theoretically partitioned by the United Nations in 1947 (see Chap. 11). However, when the new State of Israel was proclaimed on May 14, 1948, fighting between Jews and Arabs erupted, and Israel—the Jewish-controlled area of Palestine—expanded 50 percent after the Arabs were defeated (see Map 11-4). Israel occupied Sinai briefly in October 1956, in coordination with the British and French attack on the Suez Canal. Eleven years later, when President Nasser of Egypt closed the Strait of Tiran to Israeli shipping and mobilized troops, Israel responded with an attack on Egypt in the June War (or Six-Day War) of 1967; and after defeating Egypt and its allies Jordan and Syria, Israel controlled Sinai, Gaza Strip, West Bank, and Golan Heights. The Sinai was returned in 1982, but Israel still occupies the other three territories; therefore, the West Bank, Gaza Strip, and Golan Heights are included within the area discussed in this chapter.

Varied Landscapes

Regions and Climate

Long latitudinally and narrow longitudinally, Palestine is 265 miles/425 km long and 47 miles/ 76 km wide (Map 15-1). Although the area is relatively small, it is located over such critical latitudes that it lies astride varied climate zones; and with the addition of contrasting landforms, it

Long-form official name, anglicized: State of Israel
Official name, transliterated: Medinat Yisrael (Hebrew); Israil (Arabic)
Form of government: multiparty republic with one legislative house (Knesset)
Area: 7,992 miles^2/20,700 km^2
Population, 1991: 4,821,000. Literacy (latest): 95%
Ethnic composition (%): Jewish 81.8, Arab and others 18.2
Religions (%): Jewish 81.5, Muslim (mostly Sunni) 14.4, Christian 2.3, Druze 1.6, other 0.2
GNP, 1989: $44.13 billion; per capita: $9,750
Petroleum reserves: 1.4 million barrels
Main exports (% of total value, 1990): machinery 28.8; diamonds 26.4; chemicals 12.5; textiles 6.8; food, beverages, and tobacco 5.6; rubber and plastic 3.2; ores and minerals 2.5
Main imports (% of total value, 1990): diamonds 19.2; investment goods 14.8; consumer goods 10.6; fuel and lubricants 10.2
Capital city: Jerusalem (seat of government) 504,100; other cities: Tel Aviv-Yafo 321,700; Haifa 223,600; Holon 148,400; Petach-Tikva 135,400; Bat Yam 133,200; Rishon le-Ziyyon 129,400; Netanya 120,300; Ramat-Gan 116,100; Beer Sheva (Beersheba) 113,800

---

displays a great range of environments in relation to its size.[2]

The area exhibits a basically simple regional pattern, with three parallel linear belts extending along most of the north-south axis (see circled numbers on Map 15-1): [1] a moderately broad coastal plain along the Mediterranean, [2] a broad arch of limestone hills down the center, and [3] the deep Jordan–Dead Sea–Arabah trench on the east. In addition, [4] the desertic Negev in the southern triangle is a complex area of cross-folds and basins, with a summit elevation of 3,390 ft./1,035 m on the highest anticline. In the north, from sea level at the coast, the hills rise to 3,963 ft./1,208 m in Upper Galilee (highest summit in Palestine) and to 2,500 ft./762 m at Jerusalem. Eastern slopes descend to the Jordan trench and Dead Sea, with the Sea of Galilee surface at 692 ft./211 m below sea level and the Dead Sea surface at 1,310 ft./400 m below sea level, although both surfaces vary in level.

The latitude and resulting climate of Palestine are similar to those of southern California and Baja California, with a Mediterranean climate (Koeppen Csa) phasing southward into low-latitude steppe (BSh) and desert (BWh). Although summers are hot and dry, with literally no rainfall, the coast around Tel Aviv is uncomfortably humid in late summer. Higher elevations are hot during the clear, cloudless days of summer, but they have low humidity and are cool at night. January is comfortably cool in the lowlands but can be raw in the hills, and snow falls nearly every winter in the Jerusalem area and especially in Upper Galilee. In occasional years, colder and wetter winters dump heavy snows in the highlands, as in 1991–1992, when four snowstorms paralyzed Jerusalem. At one time, 3 ft./1 m of snow blanketed the area, and heavy rains flooded some lower elevations. The coastal plain has a long season for crops, and frosts are rare.

As in Syria and Lebanon, rainfall decreases from north to south and from the coast inland: Acre receives 26 in./650 mm, Tel Aviv 20.8 in./529 mm, Gaza 10.5 in./263 mm, and Elat 1 in./26 mm. A locality halfway up the western slopes of the Samarian Hills receives twice the rainfall that a station at the same elevation and latitude records on the eastern slopes, in the rain shadow. An unusual element and bonus for agriculture are the 200 dew nights in coastal areas that contribute an additional average 1.2 in./30 mm of moisture.[3] Thus, much of the area suitable for agriculture receives moderate to appreciable rainfall, with only the southern Negev and the southern Jordan Valley having an actual desert climate.

Map 15-1. *General and economic map of Israel, without transportation. Major archaeological sites are indicated because of their historical significance. Circled numbers indicate regions mentioned in the text.*

Soils and Vegetation

Patterns of soils and vegetation in Israel and in all of Palestine are, because of the area's varied environments, notably complex.[4] Characteristic *terra rossa* soils developed on most of the hard carbonates (limestone and dolomite) in the hills, but many soils have long ago been eroded away. Similarly, rendzinas that formed on the softer carbonate outcrops (marls and chalks) east and west of the main *terra rossas* have also been seriously eroded. Loss of these hill soils has exposed the bare rock, often exhibiting lapies (fluting and grooving by solution processes), the common landscape in the hills of the Holy Land.

Alluvial soils dominate in the Huleh Valley, Jezreel Valley, and much of the coastal plain, with *hamra* ("red") clayey-sandy soils alternating with alluvials on the coastal plain. Many basins in the uplands, especially in the Galilee and Samarian hills, contain alluvial soils derived from *terra rossas* and rendzinas eroded from the slopes above. Productive loessal soils (loess is fine windblown material) occupy the Beer Sheva (Beersheba) Basin and adjoin a belt of moderately fertile but dry steppe soil; however, most of the remaining soils of the Negev are sandy or stony desert soils, including *hamadahs*. Dark soils on basaltic lava occupy small areas north and southwest of the Sea of Galilee. Partly owing to reclamation work since World War I, the best agricultural areas are in the coastal plain and other plains areas, including the northern Negev, the plains and valleys of Jezreel and the Huleh, and the major basins.

The maquis, garigue, and *batha* vegetation (see Chap. 5) of the Palestine hills is the Mediterranean vegetative landscape most familiar to tourists. However, Palestine as the meeting ground of three major phytogeographical zones—Mediterranean in the more humid areas, desertic Saharo-Sindian in the southern Negev and in the southern rift valley, and transitional Irano-Turanian in between—displays an exceptional variety of plants. About 2,500 plant species are known in Israel, compared with, for example, 1,700 in Great Britain. The vegetative landscape has been greatly modified in the twentieth century by the planting of pine trees in the humid north and center and of eucalyptus trees on the lower slopes and plains, including the northern Negev. However, the realm of the true desert remains generally barren, with widely scattered bean caper bushes, broom, and, where more moisture is available at depth, acacia trees.

Water

As we have seen, water is a crucial element throughout the Middle East (see Chap. 11). Because Israel has keyed its planning and development to a high level of water consumption, its water supply is of particular significance, involving not only major technical challenges but also serious political encounters.[5]

In discussing the future Palestine mandate with British officials in 1919, Zionist leaders solicited possession or control of maximum water resources for the mandate and its successor Jewish state. In partial response, the boundaries of the mandate were extended well to the north to encompass the Sea of Galilee, Lake Huleh, and some of the Jordan headwaters. However, the border delineation apportioned some headwaters among the new mandates concerned and excluded the upper headwaters of the Jordan as well as the lower Litani, which the Zionists had sought but which was left undivided along with the upper Litani in Lebanon. However, with the conquest of the Golan in 1967 (and unilateral annexation in 1981), the occupation of the West Bank and Gaza also in 1967, and control of southern Lebanon after 1978 (tightened after 1982), Israel gained command of virtually all the water it had originally sought in 1919. Achieving such water control was, indeed, a major objective of taking and holding these four areas, under the general rubric of ensuring greater security for the state.[6]

Nevertheless, so heavy are Israel's water demands that even with efficient utilization of all the water of the state and of the occupied areas, Israel's annual water use is exceeding average supply by 15 percent. An increasing population, especially with the influx of former Soviet Jews, and ever-increasing water use inexorably signify that unless proper action is taken promptly, "Israel is on the threshold of a catastrophe."[7] Some planners urge that the state abandon its emphasis on agriculture, which uses more than 75 percent of the water. Industrial applications—now accounting for only about 5 percent of water use—yield a higher return per unit of water consumed, and manufacturing produces export items to exchange for food at a good profit. Desalination is another option, but it requires energy supplies that Israel already lacks.

Furthermore, since the coastal plain aquifers are extensions of strata underlying the West Bank, where they receive most of their water charge, the apportionment of underground water in the hill country is increasingly a critical issue of contention between West Bank Arabs and the Israeli authorities, who apportion water, as well as Jewish settlers. In both the West Bank and Gaza, Jewish settlers are allotted and use substantially more water per capita than the indigenous Arabs, who claim that they are at least systematically deprived of their rightful share of water—or of all water—and are often being forced out of their lands and villages. The claim is denied by some Israeli officials but confirmed by some extremist Jewish settlers.

Among a number of major water projects, the state's greatest undertaking has been the National Water Carrier. Partly a canal but primarily a massive underground concrete pipeline 8.86 ft./2.7 m in diameter, it conducts water from Tabagha at the northwestern corner of the Sea of Galilee down the coastal plain to the northwestern Negev (see Maps 15-1 and 15-2). Opened in 1964, the project spans 140 miles/225 km and delivers an average of nearly 400 million m^3 per year, most of it during the summer months, from the water-surplus north to the water-deficient south. Drought years and overuse can reduce delivery to only 160 million m^3, as in the summer of 1986 when the level of the Sea of Galilee was 20 in./0.5 m below the acceptable minimum. However, the following wet winter refilled Galilee to its maximum. The same cycle was repeated in the drought years of 1987–1990, when the Sea of Galilee was at its lowest level in 30 years but refilled during the extraordinarily wet winter of 1991–1992. The cycles are another reminder that climatic conditions in these marginal areas swing widely from period to period.

On the coastal plain, groundwater is pumped from shallow aquifers that are fed by the area's moderate rainfall and runoff from the slopes to the east (see Map 15-2). These substantial groundwater supplies augment water piped from Galilee and the Yarqon River for the intensive irrigation agriculture on the plain and for urban consumption. Potential dangers in the delicate balance were emphasized in 1986 when a decade of overpumping had lowered the water table more

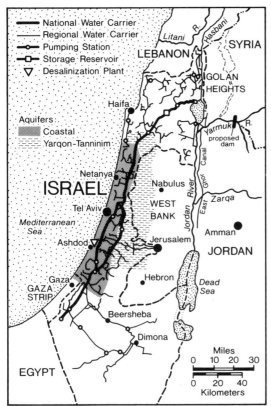

Map 15-2. *Water situation in Israel, the occupied territories, and adjacent areas. (Adapted from map in* Geographic Notes, *no. 13, U.S. Department of State)*

than 8 ft./2.5 m below any previous level. The drop occurred despite increasingly efficient use of irrigation water and despite a vigorous program of recycling urban wastewater for storage in the underground aquifers. However, the natural cycle temporarily remedied much of the problem with unusually heavy rains in the winter of 1986–1987. As with the Sea of Galilee, the underground aquifers experienced the same cycle of four dry years and one wet year in the years 1987–1992.

Population and Peoples

Immigration

The goal of Zionism, the creation of a Jewish state in the territory of Palestine, required a rapid increase in the *yishuv* ("settlement," the Jewish community in Palestine) in order to create a Jewish majority by the end of the mandate period.

The First Aliyah (ascent, in this case to Palestine) in 1880–1904; the second, until 1919; and the third, until 1923 brought several tens of thousands of *olim* ("ascenders"), but the numbers were much larger in the Fourth (1924–1928) and Fifth Aliyahs (1929–1939, which brought more than 250,000 *olim*). Unrestricted Jewish immigration, an essential in the Zionist program, was a serious problem for British mandatory authorities, who were as obligated under the Balfour Declaration to protect the rights of the indigenous Arabs as they were to permit specified Jewish immigration. The inflow was regarded by the Palestinian Arabs as an invasion and displacement by European outsiders.

"Ingathering" After Independence. After May 15, 1948, when Israel became independent, Jews around the world were zealously encouraged to immigrate to the new state to fulfill the basic Zionist ideological goal of "the ingathering of the exiles." The resulting influx had long been anticipated, and exceptional organization and preparations permitted the flood of 686,748 arrivals by the end of 1951 to be processed, housed, and fed. Special operations were undertaken to fly in virtually entire Jewish communities by chartered aircraft or aircraft lent by friendly governments. More than 121,000 of the 130,000 Jews in Iraq, descended from an ancient community including those who stayed behind after the Babylonian Captivity, were flown to Israel, as were 44,000 of the 45,000 Jews in Yemen. Thousands more flooded in from all continents, until more than 60 countries had supplied immigrants—an additional 810,000 during the two decades between 1952 and 1972.[8] Until the mid-1970s, immigrants constituted more than half of the population, but a decade later they represented less than 40 percent.

Immigration to Emigration. Inevitably, the huge influx of immigrants during the early years of the independent Israel diminished as the supply of would-be Israelis dried up and as word spread about the difficulty of life in Israel. The total of *olim* fell from 239,076 in 1949 to 10,347 in 1953 and rose to another peak of 71,100 in 1957 before averaging 25,000–35,000 annually for the next several years. Even before the 1973 war, not only were Jews outside Israel no longer seeking aliyah but Jews in Israel—even "Sabras," native-born Jewish Israelis—were emigrating in calamitous proportions. By 1981, no fewer than 2,000 Israelis were leaving monthly, and at least 500,000 Israelis—many of them young and well educated—had left for greater opportunities abroad. More than 300,000 had settled in the United States alone by 1975.[9] Additional thousands are believed to have emigrated during the 1980s, and in many months, outflow exceeded inflow.

Jews from the Former USSR. Thus, it was of compelling importance for Israel to arrange for the immigration of large numbers of Soviet Jews, whose inflow could help offset the outflow. Their free emigration had been demanded of the USSR for more than 25 years, with the United States pressed to include the topic on the agenda of virtually every negotiating session with the Soviets. Once the restrictions were lifted, Jews poured out of the USSR area and into Israel by the scores of thousands, totaling about 350,000 between late 1989 and early 1992 and peaking at 35,000 in December 1990. Israeli authorities voiced tentative expectations that 1 million Jews from the area might well seek settlement in Israel within three or four years. However, the immigrants soon found that Israel's absorptive capacity had been strained by mid-1991, and with 40 percent of the Soviet Jewish work force in Israel unemployed, the pull of aliyah sharply diminished. Moreover, the push from the area of origin likewise abated when the Soviet economy (and then the Soviet Union itself) disintegrated and perestroika permitted greater economic flexibility and opportunity.[10] By February 1992, immigration from the former USSR was down to 4,000, and more than 7,000 of the recent immigrants had returned to the then USSR during 1991. Even if the eventual total number of immigrants is less than half the expected 1 million, the social, economic, and political impact on Israel would be enormous in both the immediate future and the long range. In its determination to accommodate the newcomers, Israel turned to its longtime supporter, the United States, for a $10 billion loan guarantee, which was granted in October 1992 after the new

Labor government reversed the Shamir-Sharon policy of expanding Jewish settlement on the West Bank.

Present Population Structure

Immigration of Jews to Israel from numerous and varied countries has generated a rich and complex social structure and vigorous, not always amicable, sociopolitical relationships.[11] The six countries that have supplied the greatest number of immigrants are, in order, the former Soviet Union, Romania, Morocco, Poland, Iraq, and Iran. However, many more languages persist in Israel, reflecting both the national origins of earlier immigrants and the perseverance of mother tongues: Russian (along with Ukrainian and other Slavic languages), Romanian, Western and Eastern Arabic, German, French, Spanish, Ladino (the basic language of Sephardic Jews), and, of course, Yiddish and English are all found. This accounts for the large number of periodicals in various languages displayed on Israeli newsstands. In addition to language and sometimes costume, the wide range of physical characteristics—the Ethiopian features of the Falashas, the southern Arabian appearance of the Yemeni Jews, and the blond hair and blue eyes of the German Jews (nicknamed *yeckis* because of their characteristically formal male jacket attire)—attests to the varied origins of Israelis.

Multi-Cultures: Who Is a Jew?

In 1950 the state passed a Law of Return, which authorized immediate Israeli citizenship for any Jew settling in Israel. However, internal conflicts arose over the criteria for citizenship, and debate on the so-called Who is a Jew? question continues officially and informally in Israel. Landmark court cases have narrowed the issue but have not resolved it. Professed Jews with Jewish mothers or those who have converted to Judaism in accordance with religious law satisfy the criteria. However, some converted Jews, especially those converted by nonorthodox rabbis, face barriers, as do those who have converted from Judaism to another religion. The practice of Judaism as a religion is not a criterion for citizenship—Israeli studies show that more than half of the country's Jews are "nonobservant" (secular)—and it is significant that family descent has become the primary standard, reinforcing the ethnicity of Jewishness.

Inter-Group Conflicts. European Jews—the Ashkenazim (from the Hebrew for "Germany")—founded Zionism to establish a secular, socialist, European-style state. As immigration into Israel increased, however, oriental Jews from North Africa, the Middle East, and southern Asia came to outnumber the Ashkenazim. Sometimes grouped under the term *Sephardim* (from the Hebrew for "Spain"), oriental Jews failed for almost three decades to achieve a meaningful role in the political and economic life of Israel. After 1948, many incoming oriental Jews were assigned to frontier settlements, either in the Negev or in vulnerable border towns. By the late 1980s, they composed 54 percent of the population but were represented far below their proportion in upper ranks of employment and education. Increasingly referred to as "the second Israel" or "the other Israel," they protested their second-class citizenship not only by demonstrating in the 1970s but also by right-wing bloc voting against the traditional, liberal Ashkenazi establishment (Labor party). By the election period in 1992, Sephardi leaders were also at odds with the Likud leadership. Although the incipient rift has been somewhat repaired, Sephardi alienation and frustration remain serious problems, and Ashkenazi apprehensions remain that the higher Sephardi birthrates will combine with the still-higher Arab birthrates to relegate the European–North American Jews to an increasingly minor role.[12] Mindful of the necessity to amalgamate immigrant groups from diverse cultural backgrounds, the Israeli government relies on compulsory military service for immigrant absorption and national integration, along with intensive training in Hebrew as a national language for all *olim* and general education to "Israelize" the newcomers.

The primary interethnic conflict within Israel is that between the majority Jews and the minority Palestinian Arabs.[13] Although most of the Palestinians fled in 1947–1949 (see Chap. 11), about 160,000 remained, with major concentrations in Galilee. With a higher birthrate than that of the Jews, the Arabs within Israel numbered about 860,000 in 1991, about 17 percent of the population.

Mutual distrust and resentment, as well as mutual preference for segregation, generally characterize contemporary Jewish-Arab attitudes, although there are individual exceptions on both sides. Most remaining Arab population centers have been surrounded by "mirror" government-planned Jewish housing. Thus, following the Sephardim as the "second Israel," the Arabs inside the pre-1967 borders, including one in every six Israeli citizens, comprise the "third Israel." Inequities in budget allocations (five times higher for Jewish communities than for Arab communities) and government grants to municipalities (three times higher for Jewish municipalities) have resulted in consequent inequities in housing, economic development, employment, welfare, and general services. Although about 14,000 Arab university graduates live in Israel, they find suitable employment difficult to obtain: Of 1,310 senior civil servants in 1989, only 17 were Arabs or Druzes; only 10 of the approximately 5,000 academic positions in Israeli universities are held by Arabs; and among the thousands of physicians within the Histadrut organization, only 2 percent are Arabs.[14] Some Israeli Jews call for equal treatment of Israeli Arabs and mutual tolerance. However, some Jewish extremists, such as the Kach party followers of the former U.S. rabbi Meyer Kahane, express a candid determination to "cleanse" Israel of all Arabs.[15]

Religions and Religious Frictions. In 1991, in a total population of 5 million, Israel proper had 4.1 million Jews (82 percent), 700,000 Muslims (13.9 percent), 120,000 Christians of all denominations (2.4 percent), and 85,000 Druzes (1.7 percent). Frictions between Jews and Muslims (and Christians) are manageable since the Jews hold the balance of power, but frictions among Jewish groups are much more serious and sensitive. Somewhat as in Lebanon, religious communities, sects, and subsects are critical per se and are also critical in the governmental structure. Especially fragile is the relationship between religious groups that are pro-Zionist and those that are anti-Zionist. The unusual Samaritans are discussed in Chapter 6.

Figure 15-1. *Heart of Haifa from Mt. Carmel. Bahai Center in domed structure, foreground; Israel's main port in the distance; huge Dagon grain silos to the right.*

Conflict between religious conservatives and liberals, evident in diverse religious groups throughout the region, also intensified in Israel in the 1980s. Within the national government, the debate is between proponents of a theocracy and proponents of a secular democracy.

Public confrontations occasionally occur in major cities between ultrareligious Israelis (*haredim*) and secular Israelis. Some *haredim* attempt to impose traditional Jewish religious law (*halakah*) on all phases of life in Israel while secular citizens demand freedom of choice, including secularism. One small group of ultra-Orthodox Jews, the Neturei Karta (Guardians of the City) of the section of Jerusalem known as Mea Shearim, emphasize spiritual redemption and oppose Zionism and the existence of a political state of Israel. They also reserve the use of Hebrew, language of the Bible, for religious purposes only. Yet leaders of another ultra-Orthodox group, the Hasidim, believe that the Torah (the Pentateuch) provides the Jewish claim to the land of Israel.

Religions of Non-Jews. Of the non-Jews in Israel, most are Arabs, of whom three-fourths are Muslims, primarily Sunni. Recognized as a separate religious group since 1957, the 85,000 Druzes stand out because they remained through the hostilities in both 1948 and 1967 (especially in Golan), and they are allowed to serve in the Israeli Defense Forces. A few thousand Shiis who came from Lebanon several decades ago inhabit the northern hills, along with a few hundred Alawis. About 3,000 Circassians, speaking their own Circassian language and practicing Islam, live primarily in two Galilee villages, Kafr Kamma and Rihaniya, and also serve in the army. The eclectic Bahais, originally quasi-Shiis, have their world center on Mt. Carmel, overlooking Haifa (see Fig. 15-1), but number only a few hundred members of varied ethnic backgrounds within Israel.

Because of the close ties between Christianity and the Holy Land, at least 30 different Christian sects, representing several nationalities, are found in Israel. They congregate especially in Jerusalem, where thousands of them maintain centuries-old churches, monasteries, hostelries, and schools (see Fig. 6-4). The approximately 120,000 Christians, 13 percent of the non-Jewish population, are predominantly Arabs, although the Christian category also includes most of the non-Arab, non-Jewish population of Israel. Perhaps 25,000 longtime resident Europeans and Americans, most of them connected with ecclesiastical or charitable institutions, reside in Israel. Many, however, are actually in East Jerusalem, not a de jure part of the state of Israel.

Nearly three-fourths of the Christians are Greek Orthodox and Greek Catholics (Melkites). Roman Catholics (Latins), third in number, have a patriarch in Jerusalem and supervise many of the Christian holy sites through several orders. A bewildering variety of other Christian churches maintain at least small congregations in the Holy Land. Major Protestant groups include Anglicans and Lutherans; several other Protestant groups, from Baptist to Mormon, have "missions" or small offices in Jerusalem. Proselytizing efforts among Israeli Jews by Christian groups is punishable under Israeli law.

Settlements

Patterns of settlement are particularly relevant in Israel because of the quintessential role of settlement of the land in Zionist ideology. They are also significant in the rapid transformation of the landscape and because of the unique aspects of settlement preplanning, design, functions, and interrelations with inhabitants. The societal organization foreseen by Zionist planners called for collective and cooperative rural settlement types. Groups of similar cultural background could be assigned to one settlement, producing a maximum group effort, and the land, title to which was held by the Jewish National Fund (JNF), could be leased to groups rather than to individuals.

Three Rural Types

Three rural settlement types evolved: the kibbutz, moshav, and *moshav shittufi* ("collective moshav"). The kibbutz, the first of which was established in 1921 as an outgrowth of the twelve-year-old *kvutza* settlement concept, is a commune based on agriculture but with the potential to become an industrial collective. Eventually numbering more than 300 but now reduced to 270 with a total population of 126,100, kibbutzim have become one of the two main forms of Jewish rural settlement in Israel. The kibbutz leases land in common, serves meals in a common mess hall, and cares for children in a common nursery. At present, nonagricultural kibbutzim

might specialize in diamond polishing, cement block manufacture, souvenir production, or hostel operation.

The moshav is a smallholders' cooperative agricultural settlement on JNF or government land, in which a member family has an individual home and a plot of ground worked by the family (Fig. 15-2). Marketing of produce, however, is done cooperatively. Moshavim became the main rural settlement type, reaching 424 in number in the early 1970s but declining to 409 in 1988 with a total population of 146,500. Economic difficulties in the early 1980s forced many to disband, and a larger number of others are still in financial trouble.

In the *moshav shittufi*, combining features of the moshav and the kibbutz, members have individual homesteads but conduct agriculture and economy as a collective unit. Two other agricultural settlement types, the *moshava* and *moshav ovdim*, are found in limited numbers.

Urban Planning

Of more than 650 Arab villages before and during the mandate years, 394 were destroyed by the Israelis in 1948, and only a modest number remain in Israel within the pre-1967 boundaries. Many had few residents after the flight and expulsion of Palestinian refugees in 1947–1949, and an uncertain number of occupied villages were sequestered by Israeli military authorities after independence. Since the older settlement sites usually had a locational asset—water supply, good soil, defensibility, transportation—new Jewish settlements were usually built adjacent to an older site (Fig. 15-2).

Although early Zionist planning emphasized rural settlement, the flow of immigrants to towns made urban planning also necessary. Zionists established separate quarters for Jews outside the older sections of existing towns in the late 1800s, and in 1909 they founded the new town of Tel Aviv, the planned modern hub of the state of Israel, north of Jaffa. New and planned extensions of Haifa and Jerusalem followed. Major institutions and monuments were planned for hilltop sites in Jerusalem: Hebrew University, Knesset (the Parliament), other government buildings, memorials, and similar structures. The government built mass high-rise apartments in strate-

Figure 15-2. *Margaliyot, 1958 and 1990. A moshav founded in 1954 on a dramatic site on the Galilee Heights overlooking the Huleh Valley, Margaliyot replaced the older Arab village of Hunin, seen in the background of the photograph on the left. By 1990, the moshav had been largely rebuilt two or three times, and Hunin had virtually disappeared (right).*

gic locations around East Jerusalem after Israel took the West Bank in 1967 and extended the municipality boundaries of the city.

The Jewish Quarter inside the walls of the Old City of Jerusalem was, after 1967, also largely cleared of the centuries-old houses and rebuilt; one large block of ancient houses was bulldozed to make the Wailing Wall plaza. As in many historical cities worldwide, new construction often occurs at the expense of traditional older architecture, and the disproportionate demolition of Arab buildings and homes aggravates interethnic hostility. In Haifa, several sites on Mt. Carmel have been built up with Jewish residential areas, resorts, and institutions, including two universities.

Economic Patterns

A General Economic Perspective

Israel's economic distinctiveness is as marked as its political and religious differentiations in the region. Initial economic plans predate the Zionist immigration begun at the turn of the century. The basic institution was the World Zionist Organization (WZO), founded in 1897 by the First Zionist Congress. The Jewish National Fund (Hebrew, Keren Kayemeth Leisrael) was founded in 1901 to purchase land for Zionist colonies in Palestine. The Keren Hayesod was founded in 1920 as the main Zionist international fund-raising agency, although the United Jewish Appeal serves this function in the United States. The

Jewish Agency, founded in 1919, served as an informal government for Jews under the British mandate in Palestine, and it continues to act, along with WZO, as a basic Zionist institution, working hand in hand with the government of Israel.

In modern Israel, specialized planning and research agencies direct or coordinate virtually every phase of the economy. Similar planning addresses defense, science, education, and the arts. Such centralized planning rests on participation of interlocking national institutions (government, JNF, Jewish Agency) and the central labor organization (Histadrut), which controls industries and other economic establishments. This diverse expertise has contributed to an economic development in Israel that, even without a petroleum sector, yields a high standard of living.

In spite of many advantages, advanced development, and central planning, Israel lacks an independent, viable political-economic base to sustain itself at the level it considers appropriate. Israel's economic isolation from the other states in the region supports the observation that Israel is in but not of the Middle East. However, this regional isolation is expected to diminish as Israel presses for economic advantages pursuant to the accords it has negotiated with Egypt, the PLO, Jordan, and others. Despite its remarkable development and elaborate interlocking with international companies, Israel is heavily dependent on the billions of dollars in annual aid supplied by the United States and other governments, Jewish organizations, and individual donors. Israeli officials claim that the country can sustain itself well without foreign aid, but cessation of aid would reduce the country to a standard of living far below that it now enjoys. Even with large annual grants, Israel has severe economic problems, partly because of the high military budget, ambitious technological undertakings (nuclear energy and weapons, space rocketry, aircraft), wide-ranging diplomatic and intelligence programs, massive welfare payments, subsidies on many foods and materials, and the extensive bureaucracy.[16]

Agriculture

Agriculture in the original Zionist plan to colonize Palestine was not just a routine economic activity nor just a necessary process to provide employment and food to the immigrants. Above and beyond these, it represented an ideological and mystical bonding of the Jewish people to the Land of Israel, as we have seen in the discussion of settlements. Nevertheless, the practical aspects of farming were not neglected.

Israel's agriculture has become the most scientifically planned, organized, systematized, modernized, and mechanized in the Middle East (see Chap. 7) and ranks among the most productive in the world.

The basic range of crops, however, differs little from that in other Mediterranean areas. As in Lebanon, citrus fruits are outstanding: Jaffa oranges, famous for centuries on the irrigated coastal plain, supply one of Israel's major exports, and grapefruit production is second only to that of the United States. Market-oriented horticulture is especially highly developed, systematized by area, growing techniques, and exact dates so that specialty crops, including flowers, can be rushed to European markets earlier than those from other producing areas. In the relentless quest for maximum yield from each unit of land, Israeli agricultural researchers have urged adoption of new varieties of plants, use of best patterns of planting (such as growing tender crops on gentle slopes for cold air drainage), and, above all, maximum extension of irrigation and most effective use of water, as in drip irrigation (see Chap. 7).

As in crop growing, the state's dairying, fishing, and forestry are also scientifically planned and conducted. For example, the milk yield of Israeli dairy cows is twice that of any other Middle East country and ten times that of Iran. In forestry, more than 100 million trees have been planted in forest and woodland as well as along roads, in windbreaks, and along frontiers and in other security areas.

Whereas virtually all Jewish agriculture is institutionalized and cooperative, Arab farms, located primarily in Galilee, are generally individual and traditional. Lacking the funding given the Zionist rural communities and without access to Jewish marketing cooperatives, Arab farms remain less mechanized, more conservative, and less prosperous. Several thousand nomadic Arab pastoralists in the Negev have gradually been forced to settle and have surrendered their *dirahs* for use as airfields, settlements, and mining areas.

Mining

Mining is not a major activity in the Israeli economy, although two aspects contribute appreciably to the country's GDP: phosphate mining and Dead Sea water evaporation. A third aspect, technically a mineral industry, is diamond polishing, which forms the basis for a leading export. Petroleum production now plays a negligible role (see Chap. 8), although exploration efforts continue. The state's only known significant hydrocarbon deposit is lean oil shale in the Negev, where there are an estimated 12 billion mt. One power plant using enriched shale operates in the area. Meanwhile, Israel imports 99 percent of its petroleum consumption of about 148,000 bpd, an amount that has held rather steady since 1981 by a shift to imported coal in formerly all-oil electricity-generating plants. The use of coal (about 3.5 million mt per year) is, in turn, raising questions about pollution of the normally clean, crisp air in the area.

Israel's major subsurface resource is phosphorite (phosphate-bearing rock), part of the great regional belt of late Cretaceous phosphates. Extensive open-pit mining of high-grade phosphorites is concentrated in the northern Negev, where Oron is the main center (see Map 15-1). Phosphate production of 3.5 million mt in 1990, eighth-largest in the world, was shipped by rail to Ashdod for export.

Evaporation of Dead Sea water in extensive ponds at Sedom at the southern end of the lake yields large quantities of bromine, potash, and magnesium chloride as well as smaller amounts of related chemicals. Bromine output is about 28 percent of the world total, potash about 4 percent, and the chemicals are significant export items. Continued evaporation of the lake's water, combined with a curtailed inflow of the Jordan River, is drying up the southern third of the lake (Map 15-2).

Manufacturing

Even more than agriculture, manufacturing differentiates Israel from its neighbors in its organization, scope, technical level, and markets. In spite of a limited resource base and an import dependence for energy, Israel's industrial development is by far the most diversified and most technologically advanced in the Middle East. Expertise brought by European Jewish immigrants, along with subsequent Israeli research and engineering advances, yielded rapid development. Initial industries produced basic items: processed food and beverages (notably wine), textiles, clothing, and similar light articles. Increased population, with its notable brain gain, and transfers of both capital and technology led to far more complex production than Israel's age as a state, population, size, geographical area, and resource base would suggest. Institutional research in the universities—especially research carried on by Technion, the Weizmann Institute, Soreq nuclear reactor, Dimona nuclear facility, and similar agencies—carried scientific and industrial technology well beyond that learned from immigrant researchers and outside sources.[17]

Israeli industry is now producing not only the predictable household appliances, vehicle tires, plastics, and similar routine items but also medical equipment, advanced optical and other precision goods, and high-technology electronic equipment—with emphasis on computer hardware and software. Israel's special industry of diamond cutting gives the country its most important single export item. On a much greater scale, and increasingly controversial, is the state's production and export of large quantities of some of the world's most sophisticated armaments and

military support equipment. Although it failed to fulfill Israel's commitment in a mid-1980s project to produce the Lavi fighter aircraft, in which the United States invested nearly $1.5 billion, the Israeli Aircraft Industries (IAI), with South Africa, produced a Lavi-type aircraft and reportedly sold the Lavi electronics system to China.[18] The IAI does produce combat and civil aircraft, as well as armored cars, missiles, patrol boats, and similar military items. Israel has become one of the world's half-dozen main exporters of armaments, including the Uzi submachine gun, missiles, artillery shells, armored vehicles, and naval craft.

Israel's most famous weapons facility is the Dimona nuclear establishment, built secretly in the mid-1950s in the northern Negev with French assistance. The uranium found in the phosphorite rocks near Dimona is extended with ore imported from South Africa, with which Israel cooperated in weapons development. Israel's nuclear capability and its possession of a considerable number of nuclear devices were revealed in 1986 when an Israeli who was a former technician at Dimona handed photographs and details of the underground operations to a London newspaper.[19] As a member of the exclusive nuclear club—although it refuses to sign the Nuclear Nonproliferation Treaty—Israel is recognized as being far more technically advanced and militarily powerful than had been thought in the early 1980s.

Israel's main concentration of industry lies on the coastal plain from the Haifa area south to Ashdod, with outliers in Ashqelon and the Negev centers of Beer Sheva, Dimona, Arad, Sedom, and Elat. Haifa has the greatest single concentration in Israel: oil refining, production of chemicals (including fertilizers), shipbuilding, and many other industries. Tel Aviv has a variety of lighter industries, and Israel Aircraft Industries, the largest single employer in Israel, operates near Ben Gurion Airport.

The bulk of the country's domestic production comes from large manufacturing enterprises, most of which are either state owned or owned by a combine of government and quasi-government agencies. However, a significant proportion comes from small establishments. Many of the small industries develop in kibbutzim that turn from agriculture to light industrial activities. Manufacturing is increasingly being dispersed, for reasons of both security and local employment, into and around small settlements literally from Dan to Beer Sheva.

Transportation

Palestine functioned as a land bridge from early times; by contrast, independent Israel is largely isolated along its land boundaries. Normal, open intercourse is still not conducted with any of its four neighbors, although limited legal movement takes place between Israel and Egypt. The Negev corridor to the head of the Gulf of Aqabah gives Israel an outlet to the Red Sea, and thence to the Indian Ocean, and also a land link between the Gulf of Aqabah and the Mediterranean (Map 15-3). That link has been used since 1969 for a 42-in./107-cm oil pipeline (see Map 15-1), and Israel plans to use it for a rail line as well. Conversely, the Negev corridor divides the Arab states of the Fertile Crescent–Arabian realm from those of North Africa, a matter of great economic and strategic significance.

Highways. North of Beer Sheva, Israel maintains an extraordinarily dense road net that is entirely paved, and heavily traveled sections east and north of Tel Aviv are divided throughways. The main north-south trunk route extends southward from the Ladder of Tyre, north of Akko in the northwest, along the coastal plain through Haifa, Tel Aviv, and Ashqelon to Gaza, then cuts southeastward across the Negev to Elat. A parallel north-south route 30 miles/48 km to the east runs from Metullah at Israel's northern tip down the west side of the Jordan rift to Elat. Similarly, a main crest road runs the length of the occupied West Bank hill country, whose roads are integrated into the highway net of Israel.

Railways. Rail lines are used primarily for transporting heavy, bulky freight—phosphates and other minerals, grains, fuel, and citrus. Building on the modest rail net of mandate Palestine, Israel has constructed new standard gauge lines— from Hadera (south of Haifa) to Tel Aviv in 1953, to Beer Sheva in 1956, on to Dimona in 1965, then to Oron and Arad. A final extension from Sedom to Elat was under construction in the early 1990s.

Map 15-3. *Israeli transportation facilities.*

Ports and Shipping. Supplanting Jaffa (Yafo), which had served as a major harbor since the Bronze Age, the Bay of Haifa became the dominant port after 1900 and has evolved into one of the busiest general-cargo ports in the Middle East. Ashdod, 20 miles/32 km south of Tel Aviv and formerly of negligible importance, has been developed by Israel as a second major Mediterranean deep-water port to handle exports of phosphates and Dead Sea chemicals and imports for south-central Israel. Elat, the country's third major port, serves the Indian Ocean trade and handles petroleum imports—originally from Iran but later from Egypt, after 1979. Ashqelon is an oil tanker port at the terminus of the large pipeline from Elat.

Airlines. Air service is of particular importance for Israel because of the state's relative isolation from its landside neighbors. A commercial airport built at Lydda (Lod) on the coastal plain southeast of Tel Aviv in 1936 became Lod Airport, later renamed Ben Gurion International Airport. The installation handles all of Israel's international air traffic and ranks sixth in the region in the number of passengers processed. El Al is the Israeli national airline for international flights, and ARKIA is a primarily internal airline.

Commerce and Services

Israel has become one of the most trade-dependent countries in the world and has evolved a remarkable ensemble of trade agreements and export-import procedures. It receives preferential treatment for its exports to the United States, the EEC, and many other countries, and Israel has agreed to remove customs duties on imports from these countries by the mid-1990s. Most of its merchandise trade—$30.3 billion in 1991—is with the EEC, but the United States is Israel's leading single trade partner. The increasing deficit in the overall goods and services account—up to $7 billion in 1991—is a matter of concern, although Israel has enjoyed a moderately positive balance of payments in recent years. Exports and imports are listed in the country summary early in this chapter, but it is noteworthy that in 1989, Israel imported 7.88 million carats of rough diamonds and exported 3.96 million carats of cut and polished diamonds worth $3.114 billion. Value of diamond exports dropped to $2.48 billion in 1991.

A full range of services has been developed, with banking and tourism as major segments after public services. The state's banking system has worldwide connections, and two of the banks are in the world's top 100 banking institutions. Branches of such Israeli banks as Bank Leumi Le-Israel are located in the United States and Western European countries.

With some of the world's most important religious, historical, and scientific sites (Fig. 15-3), Israel has developed a vigorous tourist industry. From 4,000 in 1948, the number of tourists rose to a total of 1.5 million in the peak year of 1985 and to 1.13 million in 1990, despite the Gulf crisis. Tourism income in 1990 was $1.38 billion. Both the hotel system and the tour bus transportation system are highly organized. Although the restaurants serve a variety of national foods, most practice *kasrut,* religious dietary practices for observant Jews.

Reflecting traditional Jewish emphasis on education and medical care, Israel has built major universities and hospitals. Supported both by the government and by contributions from abroad, there are seven universities with 65,000 students in Israel (excluding occupied territories), the largest in Tel Aviv and Jerusalem. Hebrew University of Jerusalem is best known and is one of the finest universities in the Middle East. Israel Institute of Technology (Technion) in Haifa was founded in 1924, a year before the Hebrew University. Hadassah Hospital, on a hilltop in West Jerusalem, is the major medical facility.

Relations

Because of hostilities between Israel and its neighbors over the circumstances of Israel's establishment and expansion, relations between the Jewish state and its neighbors continued to be antagonistic for more than four decades (see Chap. 11). Only after the U.S.-mediated Israeli-Egyptian peace treaty in 1979 did Israel have diplomatic relations with any adjacent state. No member of the Arab League other than Egypt maintained relations with Israel until September 1993, and among other Middle East states, only Cyprus and Turkey recognized Israel.

However, Israel has steadily developed diplomatic relations with many other countries, a total of 120 in early 1993, including such longtime holdouts as China, India, and the USSR before it disintegrated. Pursuing every opportunity to ensure its security, Israel seeks to maintain patterns of relations that not only strengthen its own national well-being but also weaken its foes and po-

Figure 15-3. *Jerusalem, looking west from the Mount of Olives. Eastern wall of the Old City at the bottom, Dome of the Rock and other buildings of the Old City in the middle ground, and new buildings of the burgeoning West Jerusalem in the distance (1990).*

tential foes, particularly neighboring opponents. With Egypt neutralized, Syria and Iraq especially are considered to be menacing, but even moderate Arab states are subjected to Israeli proscriptions. Relations with Lebanon have posed a frustrating problem, as was shown in Chapter 13. For many years, Israel categorically refused to have relations with the Palestine Liberation Organization (PLO), and in 1986 the Knesset passed legislation that made dealing with members of the PLO even by private individual Israeli citizens a criminal offense. However, the act was repealed in January 1993 in the context of the ongoing peace talks and in recognition of the more moderate stance of the PLO vis-à-vis that of Hamas. In September 1993 Israel and the PLO exchanged mutual recognition, as is explained in the Epilogue. Inter alia, Israel maintained—and still maintains—off-the-record relations with some states with which it is publicly antagonistic. Iran, which supplied petroleum to Israel for many years, is one example. Even after the Khomeini revolution, Israel not only assisted Iran in its war against Iraq but also persuaded the United States to join it in the Iran-Contra affair, which received intense attention in 1987.[20] After having assisted Iran for many years, Israel cooled its support after Iran assisted Shii Hizballah extrem-

ists in southern Lebanon who attacked Israelis and the Israeli-backed SLA.

Great Britain. Among European states, the United Kingdom was formerly the most involved with Zionist agencies and independent Israel. The British government issued the Balfour Declaration in 1917 (see Chap. 11), and Britain was the mandatory authority in Palestine from the early 1920s to 1948. In 1956, the British, French, and Israelis cooperated in the Suez invasion. Since that time, because of its varied interests in the Gulf, petroleum affairs, and other economic sectors in the Middle East, Britain has maintained a balanced policy in Middle East affairs and has been wary of identification with U.S. support of Israel.

Germany. The enormous loss of life by Jews in Nazi World War II concentration camps remains an overwhelming political, ethnic, and even religious event affecting Israel's policies. Postwar West German authorities not only expressed guilt and regret but also gave more than $4 billion in reparations to Israel as the center of the Jewish people, restitution to individual Israelis who suffered under the Nazis, and development loans. Germany donated $163 million to Israel in

1991 to help compensate Israel for damage it suffered from Scud missiles and economic dislocation during the Gulf crisis.

France and Others. The French Jewish banking family of Rothschild gave the first large-scale financial support to Jewish colonization in Palestine (early 1880s). After World War II, the French government assisted the Israelis in construction of their Dimona nuclear facility and sold fighter aircraft and other military equipment to Israel. More recent French-Israeli relations have been temperate. The Netherlands is often bracketed with the United States as Israel's strongest supporter on the world scene, and Belgium has major trade ties through the diamond industry. The diamond and arms industries are the economic bases for ties between Israel and South Africa. In part, the two countries were drawn together because each had a crucial antinational ethnic problem that had led to its ostracism as a pariah state in its respective region. However, the relationship was criticized in both directions, especially because of UN sanctions against South Africa at that time. When liberalization in South Africa permitted a lifting of sanctions, the Israeli–South African ties were restrengthened.

The USSR and Successor States. In 1948, the Soviet Union quickly recognized and then supported the new Jewish state, possibly because it realized that the regional impact of such a state would make the Middle East more unstable and easier for communism to penetrate. The Soviets soon emphasized their relations with several Arab states and in 1967, broke diplomatic relations with Israel. In the absence of relations with the USSR, Israel depended on the United States to communicate with the Soviets, especially regarding emigration of Jews. The USSR and Israel restored relations in late 1990, after which all the former Soviet satellites of Eastern Europe followed suit. After dissolution of the Soviet Union, the Russian Republic and the Ukraine reaffirmed relations, and Israel sought confirmation of recognition with other former Soviet republics, including Azerbaijan and the Muslim Central Asiatic states.

The United States. Although no formal alliance between the United States and Israel has ever been signed, the so-called special relationship between them has been far closer than any long-term alliance with which the United States has been associated. Zionist aspirations received U.S. support as early as 1917, when the U.S. government responded to Zionist lobbying and endorsed the Balfour Declaration. President Truman extended U.S. recognition of the State of Israel eleven minutes after Israel was declared independent. During the 45 years since U.S. recognition of Israel, U.S. support has rarely faltered and, overtly and covertly, has escalated quantitatively and qualitatively. The United States extended direct loans and grants totaling more than $47.6 billion between 1949 and 1990 and transferred all funds as free grants after 1984. These transfers were made "up front," in cash at the beginning of the fiscal year. In 1990, one-fifth of all U.S. direct foreign aid went to Israel and more than one-sixth to Egypt as a continuing reward for maintaining peace with Israel.[21] In addition, various grants and subsidies to Israel from U.S. government agencies for research and development—such as that on the Lavi fighter—are estimated to exceed $18 billion. In some years, U.S. grants have funded more than 80 percent of all research activity in Israel; similarly, the United States has underwritten intelligence activities conducted by Israel, sometimes as U.S. surrogate, especially during the cold war.[22] Moreover, tax-deductible private donations to Israel by individual Americans and by organizations such as the United Jewish Appeal, along with sales of Bonds for Israel, are estimated to have totaled $15 billion during the period 1949–1990.

The United States differs with Israel on several policy issues. First, it maintains its embassy in Tel Aviv, opposing Israel's unilateral declaration of Jerusalem as its capital. Second, the United States rejects Israel's unilateral annexation of the Golan Heights. Third, it has warned Israel about annexing the West Bank and Gaza Strip, which would be a violation of several declarations by the United States and of the Fourth Geneva Convention. Fourth, the United States believes that Israel should surrender occupied territory to facilitate peace agreements.

After the 1990–1991 crisis in the Gulf, both the United States and the United Nations as an institution were morally and logically obligated after 25 years of waiting for progress on UN Resolution 242 to press for the definitive initiation of regional peace talks. The United States was also obligated to evince a firm position on Jewish settlements in the occupied territories in order to substantiate its long-term but formerly subdued policy of opposing such settlements. The Arab-Israeli peace process is discussed in Chapter 11.

OCCUPIED TERRITORIES

As was shown in Chapter 11, Israel took three separate pieces of land, one from each of its foes, in the 1967 Six-Day War: Sinai with the Gaza Strip from Egypt, the West Bank from Jordan, and the Golan from Syria. Neither Sinai nor Golan had ever been part of mandate Palestine; hence, they were not involved in the 1947 UN partition of Palestine. However, both the West Bank and the Gaza Strip had been integral parts of Palestine, and both had been included in the half of the mandate allotted to the potential Arab state in the 1947 partition. As part of the philosophy of "exchanging a piece of land for a land of peace" urged upon Israel from several sides, Israel withdrew in stages from the largest area, Sinai—which is two-thirds larger than Israel itself—pursuant to the peace treaty with Egypt.

However, after 26 years, Israel continues to occupy all three of the remaining areas, although it signed an agreement with the PLO in September 1993 for later Palestinian autonomy in Gaza and the West Bank. Syrian-Israeli talks on the Golan were also under discussion. The Golan area, taken from Syria, was an integral part of Syria from the original French mandate delineation and was never part of the Palestine mandate, however, Israel strengthened its hold on Golan by unilaterally extending Israeli sovereignty over it in 1981, citing security requirements. The West Bank and the Gaza Strip, which were recognized as solidly Arab in the 1947 partition plan, have become a microcosm of the Arab-Israeli problem and the focus of the Palestinian uprising, the *intifadah*. They thus underscore the fundamental fact that not only the Arab-Israeli problem but

also many other regional problems are essentially geopolitical. West Bank and Gaza have emerged as the geographical and human symbols of the struggle between Arabs and Israelis for the land itself, with Israeli extremists claiming the areas as part of Eretz Israel and asserting that Jews have a right to settle in any part of Eretz Israel. Hardliners thus insisted on "creating facts" so that by creeping annexation, Israel would achieve permanent control without having to declare outright annexation. These hardliners rejected the applicability of the Fourth Geneva Convention of 1949 to Israeli settlement, but the United States and others adhere to the convention's relevance.[23]

West Bank

Definition and Significance

The West Bank received its name in 1948–1949 when its area was defended by Arab forces against Israeli capture and was annexed by Transjordan (the East Bank), officially in 1950. Its shape is deeply indented on the west by the Jerusalem salient; the area's northern half includes the Samarian Hills, with Nabulus as a center, and the southern half embraces the Judean Hills, with Hebron as center (Fig. 15-4). The kidney-shaped 2,270-miles^2/5,879-km^2 area (see Map 11-5) was militarily occupied and generally administered by Israel after 1967, but it is neither de jure nor de facto under Israeli sovereignty. The boundary of the West Bank with Israel is the Armistice Line agreed to by Israel and Jordan after the 1948–1949 fighting.

Severed by the 1949 Armistice from the rest of Palestine, the West Bank was annexed by King Abdullah of Transjordan reportedly to be kept in trust for the Palestinian people pending an eventual treaty disposition of the area. When Israel took the area in the 1967 war, it referred to the West Bank as Judea and Samaria and placed it under firm military occupation. Jordan continued to claim the territory until August 1988, when King Husayn renounced all claims to it.

Demography

The 1947 population of the area, estimated to be 400,000, was increased in 1948 by the influx of 365,000 refugees from the area occupied by Israel.

Figure 15-4. *Part of the old* suq *of Hebron on the West Bank, with ancient limestone block buildings surmounted by TV antennas.*

A May 1967 estimate gave the area a population of 845,000, despite an outmigration, primarily to the East Bank, of more than 400,000. The census of September 1967 showed a drop to 596,000, mostly reflecting the flight of refugees across the Jordan River to the East Bank as Israeli forces approached in June. In 1990, the Arab population was officially estimated at 1.1 million,[24] inhabiting more than 450 settlements. About 10 percent of the population lives in eight UNRWA refugee camps, and about 25 percent live in 25 towns, the largest of which are Ramallah, al-Birah, Nabulus, Janin, Hebron (al-Khalil), Bethlehem, Jericho, Tulkarm, and Halhul. More than 140,000 Arabs live in East Jerusalem.

Two demographic trends are significant. First, the West Bank Arab population is impacted by two opposing factors—outmigration, which continues despite the declared determination by West Bank Arabs to remain, and a high birthrate. An estimated 300,000 Palestinians have left the West Bank and Gaza since 1967, including a high percentage of Christians. The second trend is that the Jewish settler population is increasing, having reached about 27,500 in 1983, 60,000 in 1987, and 205,000 in 1992, including 110,000 in East Jerusalem (see Fig. 15-5). The number of Jewish settlements is stated to have been 173 in 1990, with more than 110 of them holding fewer than 100 families.[25] Many settlements have been

Figure 15-5. *One of the several Jewish settlements around Jerusalem, this one extending East Jerusalem. Such settlements became the subject of sharp debates between the United States and the former Shamir-led Likud government of Israel.*

established by Amana, the settlement arm of the extremist Gush Emunim. Especially after the onset of the *intifadah*, West Bank Palestinians have retaliated with violence against some settlers and some Israeli soldiers, who have responded in kind in the seemingly unending cycle of reciprocal violence in the occupied territories (see Chap. 11).

Water and Land

In addition to land itself, water is the basis for many of the conflicts between immigrant Jewish settlers and indigenous Arabs in the West Bank. Although much of the soil has been eroded from the limestone slopes of the West Bank highlands, some alluvial soils have collected in structural basins and erosional valleys, affording agricultural possibilities in scattered, moderately large areas. Slopes that appear to be denuded often support olive groves and other fruit trees, making the hills unexpectedly productive in selected crops and thereby supporting a relatively dense agricultural population. Runoff from the considerable winter rainfall accumulates in underground aquifers, some yielding water in springs where they outcrop, others retaining underground water for wells. Modern techniques have discovered and traced large supplies of groundwater.

Controlling the technical hydrogeological information, the technology, and the government, Israel and Israeli settlers increasingly control the water resources, leaving many of the original Arab farmers with little or no water for farming or even for domestic use.[26] Concomitantly, increasing amounts of land are being taken by Israelis, through various techniques. Large blocks of state-owned land have been requisitioned or declared security areas or nature reserves, with the result that Israel has gradually acquired 40 percent of the land in the West Bank.

Without sufficient water for farm and family use, encircled by Israeli settlements, and living under a military government that gives preference to Jewish settlers, some Arab farmers eventually sell their family lands to Israeli purchasing agents. Land is also taken over by Jewish settlers on the basis that some Arab farmers have no legal proof of their long landownership, because of the failure of past governments—Turkish, British, Jordanian—to establish complete and accurate cadastres (official landownership registers). A former Israeli official in the West Bank wrote:

> Redemption of the land (*geulat haqarqa*) is a fundamental Zionist concept. ... The history of the Zionist enterprise is an account of physical *faits accomplis* through land acquisitions and settlement, created to achieve national, political, and military objectives. ... The Palestinians, attaching the same macronational and symbolic value to the land, resist Israeli land acquisition efforts with whatever means they can muster. The unequal strength of the conflicting parties, however, dictates the results.[27]

The Economy

Outwardly, the West Bank economy before the *intifadah* appeared strong, since farmers and manufacturers could sell to both Israeli and Jordanian markets. Arab laborers were in demand for construction work, farm work, or similar unskilled jobs in Israeli towns. Ironically, with no other employment available, Palestinians were building the Jewish settlements that were consuming scarce land and water. Many jobs inside Israel formerly filled by day workers from the West Bank are now taken by immigrants from the former Soviet Union, leaving only reduced amounts of the most menial employment for the Palestinians. Civil disobedience aspects of the *intifadah*—demonstrations, merchant strikes, actions against movement of workers into Israel, and selective boycott of Israeli goods—reduced the Palestinian GNP by one-third. Economic constraints to repress the uprising included disruption of marketing of West Bank produce and punitive confiscation or destruction of property of accused offenders. If the West Bank is able to exercise the autonomy envisioned in the Israeli-Palestinian accord of 1993, it will require billions of dollars in outside aid to become even basically viable.

The Future

The overall prospect for the West Bank as a remnant of Arab Palestine will remain uncertain until the provisions of the 1993 agreements can be assessed in practice and implemented in fact. Successful application of the autonomy envisioned for both the West Bank and Gaza would create an atmosphere of hope for the Palestinians and relief for both the Palestinians and Israelis. Under Israeli occupation, even if the Arab inhabitants resist displacement, their political freedom, economic welfare, and very livelihood would be increasingly abridged. Although more-moderate Israeli leaders are cautious about settlement on the West Bank, many Israelis' goals continue to include expanded Jewish settlement. The continuation of the *intifadah* and the proclamation by the Palestine National Council on November 11, 1988, of an independent State of Palestine in the West Bank and Gaza greatly altered prospects for the occupied territories (see Chap. 11).

For Israelis, the West Bank represents a dilemma. The area's projection into the core of Israel had reduced the east-west width of the state at its "waist" just north of Tel Aviv to 9 miles/14.5 km, and the long 185-mile/300-km land border around the West Bank has been reduced to about 50 miles/80 km along the Jordan River line. However, as either an occupied territory or a Palestinian polity, the area is itself a security problem. Israeli withdrawal from the West Bank would create several alternative possibilities: autonomy under Israeli oversight, autonomy in federation with Jordan, independence as a sovereign Palestinian state, or some variation or combination of these, including some arrangement for demilitarization.

Gaza

The Gaza Strip is a small area along the Mediterranean coast, sandwiched between Egypt and Israel, that Egyptian military forces were able to hold until after the armistice that ended the 1948–1949 fighting. Separated from settled Egypt by the full width of Sinai, it remained under Egyptian military occupation until it was captured by Israeli forces in the abortive tripartite Suez invasion in 1956. It reverted to Egyptian military occupation after Israel was forced to withdraw from Sinai and Gaza in early 1957, but it was again taken by Israel in the 1967 assault on Sinai and has remained under Israeli military occupation for the ensuing 26 years.

Because of its small size and isolated location, the Gaza Strip (see Map 11-5) and its human and political importance were often overlooked until clashes between Gaza Palestinians and Israeli troops in late 1987 provoked the outbreak of the widely publicized *intifadah*. The Gaza Strip is only 25 miles/40 km long and 5.6 miles/9 km wide—about twice the size of the U.S. District of Columbia—yet it shelters a large population of 700,000, giving it the markedly high density of 5,000 people per mile^2/1,928 per km^2. Such densities usually characterize urban areas or extraordinarily rich agricultural lands, whereas Gaza conforms to neither category.

The Gaza Strip is part of the Sinai-Palestine coastal plain, with high sand dunes along the shore backed by areas of good soils of sandy clay, silt, and loess. Marginal annual rainfall of 12 in./300 mm is supplemented in extensive areas by irrigation from wells tapping the appreciable groundwater supplies. With the need to support the overcrowded population, intensified irrigation agriculture has overpumped the aquifers, endangering both the amount and the quality of the groundwater. Lowering of the water table near the seacoast reduces aquifer resistance to seawater intrusion, raising the groundwater's salinity level.

The Gaza area has been agriculturally productive for centuries. Citrus is a primary crop; other tree products include dates, almonds, grapes, and olives; and there are also vegetable and other field crops. With 45 percent of the area under crops, agriculture is still a major sector of the economy. It has, however, been surpassed as employer and contributor to the GNP by public and other services and by construction. Much of the GNP is supplied by remittances from workers employed abroad, UNRWA minimal support of refugees, private charities, and wages earned by 30,000–35,000 Gaza day laborers in Israel, mostly in construction and agriculture.[28] Tensions consequent to the *intifadah* provoked periodic Israeli curfews and periodic prohibition against Gaza workers' entry into Israel. Unemployment rose to 40 and 50 percent even during normal circumstances. The UNRWA program has saved Gazans from starvation: More than two-thirds of the inhabitants are registered with UNRWA as refugees, and half of these live in eight UNRWA refugee camps in Gaza, thus eking out a living. No visitor to this concentration of human misery can disagree with one writer's characterization of Gaza as "a pressure-cooker ready to explode"—which indeed it did in initiating the *intifadah*—with "overcrowding, poverty, hatred, violence, oppression, poor sanitation, anger, frustration, drugs, and crime."[29] As in the West Bank, many Gaza Palestinians are strong supporters of the PLO, which funnels appreciable charitable funds into Gaza. Full of despair and feeling dispossessed, Gazans turn to radical fundamentalist Islam, the Islamic Resistance Movement (Hamas), and the Islamic Jihad, which in turn generate Israeli suppression. All of these trends were overtaken by the signing of the Israeli-PLO Declaration of Principles in September 1993. The accords especially involved the Gaza Strip, with its teeming hundreds of thousands of refugees from other areas of Palestine, which the Israelis were relieved to agree to turn over to the PLO.

Whereas the West Bank was integrated into its contiguous Arab neighbor, Jordan, in 1948, the Gaza Strip was placed under Egyptian military occupation and experienced little economic development during its eighteen years of Egyptian occupation. Gazans were not accorded any of the privileges of Egyptian citizenship, nor were they allowed into Egypt itself. Seizure by Israel in 1967 led to the Israeli military occupation that continued with increasing bitterness on both sides until the 1993 accords called for Gazan autonomy. Economic development since 1967 has been greater than during the Egyptian occupation, but it has been negligible compared with that in adjacent parts of Israel. As in the West Bank, and despite serious overcrowding, Jewish settlements have been established in the Gaza Strip, with a total of approximately 2,500 settlers in eighteen communities by 1990,[30] with 34 percent of the Gaza area appropriated for the 0.4 percent of the Gaza Strip population in the Jewish settlements.

The future for Gaza is usually considered to be linked with that of the West Bank, but its economic prospects are far bleaker. Gaza faces the additional complication of its separation from the West Bank by 24 miles/38 km of Israeli territory. Thus, the problem arises of how to achieve geographical linkage of Gaza with the West Bank in any autonomous or independent Palestinian entity. Certainly Israeli occupation had reached an impasse. It remains to be seen if under the promised autonomy Gaza can attract the huge economic support required to counter the poverty and past frustrations of the Gazans.

Golan

Of the three territories in addition to Jerusalem that are still occupied by Israel, Golan is the only one that was and is indisputably a de jure segment of another existing sovereign state, Syria (see Chaps. 11 and 12). Yet Golan is the only one of the three territories captured in 1967 that Israel has annexed to its state territory, by announcing in December 1981 that Israeli law is applicable to the Golan. This unilateral declaration, like the declaration of annexation of East Jerusalem and of its detachment from the West Bank, has not been accorded international recognition and has been internationally condemned. Often overlooked in the more dramatic attention to the West Bank and Gaza, the Golan problem was also under bilateral discussion in the fall of 1993.

Israel's annexation and settlement of the Golan occurred after the flight of more than 90 percent of the area's 93,000 Syrian inhabitants from the fighting in the 1967 war, leaving only 5,875 Druzes, 385 Alawis, and a few hundred others, mostly Circassians in Qunaytirah. In 1992, the non-Jewish population totaled about 15,000.

The present eastern border of the Golan Heights was determined in the 1974 disengagement agreements between Israel and Syria after the 1973 war. The border is actually a variable-width buffer zone, up to 5.5 miles/9 km wide and as narrow as 0.2 mile/0.32 km, between lines A and B (see Map 11-5). The agreement also called for Israeli evacuation of Qunaytirah, which lay within the buffer zone and which the Israeli forces demolished prior to their pullback.

Extending about 40 miles/64 km north-south and 8–16 miles/13–26 km east-west, the Golan covers about 445 miles^2/1,150 km^2. Mainly a basaltic plateau rising from 985 ft./300 m to 3,935 ft./1,200 m, highest in the north, the Golan Heights is a tilted tableland sloping toward Israel. A high escarpment, 1,310–2,625 ft./400–800 m—again, highest in the north—overlooks Israel on the west, matched by the Galilee escarpment across the Huleh Basin and the Sea of Galilee.

The Golan Heights thus possesses a strategic advantage. The Syrians installed fortifications, including both gun emplacements and bunkers, on the brow of the heights in anticipation of an eventual conflict, but the fortifications did little to impede the Israeli advance when Israeli-Syrian fighting broke out in June 1967. Israeli control of the area after 1967 has denied Syria the elevation advantage and, in contrast, has given Israel the benefit of a *glacis,* a territorial cushion. Such control emplaces Israel on the shoulder of Mt. Hermon and gives it command of the whole tristate junction—southeastern Lebanon, southwestern Syria, and, of course, northeastern Israel.

Jewish settlements began in the Golan almost immediately after the 1967 fighting ceased, especially since few inhabitants remained from the former Arab population. An intensive program of water and road development has accompanied the settlement effort, along with numerous military installations. Paramilitary *nahal* settlements held the main points, although all settlements had to be evacuated when fighting broke out in 1973. By 1992, the Jewish population of the Golan was approximately 12,500 in 35 settlements of various sizes (see Fig. 15-6). The future of the settlements will be decided in future agreements on the Golan reached between Israel and Syria.

Figure 15-6. *Two of the new Jewish settlements on the Golan Heights. The Golan was taken from Syria in 1967 and was unilaterally attached to Israel by the Begin government in December 1981.*

16

Iraq: Modern Mesopotamia

Iraq and Its Antecedents

Modern Iraq emerged as an independent kingdom in 1932, its boundaries and major institutions having been defined while it was a League of Nations mandate under British tutelage. As constituted in the early 1920s in accordance with the 1920 San Remo talks and the 1923 Treaty of Lausanne, mandate Iraq generally incorporated the three former Ottoman *vilayets* ("provinces") of Mosul, Baghdad, and (partially) Basrah. With the possible exceptions of the western panhandle and the northeastern mountains, the mandate was generally coextensive with the traditional geographical region of Mesopotamia ("between the rivers"). The Arabic name *al-Iraq* ("the cliff") had sometimes been applied as a geographical term to lower Mesopotamia but had not previously designated a state occupying the Mesopotamian Basin.

Whether traditional Mesopotamia or the modern state, Iraq is the land of two rivers, the Tigris and Euphrates, two of the three great rivers of the Middle East (Map 16-1). This eastern limb of the Fertile Crescent was the cradle of the earliest known civilizations and served as the culture hearth from which the first ideas of sedentary agriculture, domestication of animals, the wheel, writing, and urban development are believed to have diffused westward to the Nile Valley and eastward to the Indus Valley. Evidence of the Neolithic agricultural revolution is scattered along the Zagros piedmont east of the lower Tigris Valley, and ruins of the world's first cities have been uncovered on the interfluve south of Baghdad (see Chap. 2). Sumer, Akkad, Babylo-

nia, and Assyria are part of the historical and cultural heritage of Iraq, and their material remains constitute a major element in the Mesopotamian landscape, attracting modern scientists and tourists alike.

Mesopotamia has periodically functioned as one of the major political and military power bases of the Middle East (see discussion of power foci in Chap. 2). For 2,000 years after Cyrus the Great, the Tigris-Euphrates Basin was usually linked with the adjacent power on the plateau to the east, from the Persian Achaemenids to the Arab Muslims in AD 633. Twice in the five decades after 633, the Euphrates Valley served as the locus for conflicts over the Islamic caliphate (see Chap. 6), which resulted in the martyrdoms of Ali and his son Husayn.

Reduced to a province of the Umayyad Empire in 661, Mesopotamia reasserted itself in 750 to supplant Syria as the Muslim imperial center. As the center of the Abbasid Empire, it became the nucleus of a cultural efflorescence under Caliph Harun al-Rashid (r. 786–809) of *Arabian Nights* fame. However, decline following the Islamic golden age eventuated in the sacking of Baghdad by the Mongols. Mesopotamia was first overrun in 1258 by Hulagu, grandson of Genghis Khan, then in 1393 by Tamerlane, who killed or enslaved most of the intellectual cadre of savants, artisans, writers, and engineers. Both conquerors destroyed Mesopotamia's extensive irrigation systems, developed over millennia, as well as its cities, craft shops, and trade routes. The ravaged basin then was subjected to Ottoman and Persian contention, in which the Ottomans finally triumphed in 1638. Their control of the basin

IRAQ

Long-form official name, anglicized: Republic of Iraq
Official name, transliterated: al-Jumhuriyah al-Iraqiyah
Form of government: unitary single-party republic with one legislative house (National Assembly)
Area: 167,975 miles^2/435,052 km^2
Population, 1991: 18,317,000. Literacy (latest): 59.7%
Ethnic composition (%): Arab 77.1, Kurd 19.0, Turkmen 1.4, Persian 0.8, Assyrian 0.8, Armenian and other 0.9
Religions (%): Muslim 95.8 (Shii 60.0, Sunni 35.8), Christian 3.5, other 0.7
GNP, 1989: $35 billion; per capita: $1,940
Petroleum reserves: 100 billion barrels (second-largest in Middle East and world)
Main exports (% of total value, 1989): fuels and other energy 99.5; food and agricultural raw materials 0.5
Main imports (% of total value, 1986): machinery and transport equipment 39.8; manufactured goods 27.1; food and agricultural raw materials 15.5; chemical and pharmaceutical products 7.5
Capital city: Baghdad 5,348,117; other cities: Basrah 616,700; Mosul 570,926; Irbil 333,903; Sulaymaniyah 279,424 (all population data predate the 1991 Gulf war)

continued until World War I, when British and Indian forces drove the Ottomans back into Anatolia, and Great Britain was given the mandate over the newly created Kingdom of Iraq in the early 1920s.[1] Iraq was the first mandate to become an independent state (1932).

The independent kingdom of Iraq became a republic through a military coup d'état led by General Abd al-Karim Qasim (Kassem) in July 1958, when the young King Faysal II and his closest advisers were murdered. The Qasim revolutionary government fell in turn to a coup in 1963 that first brought to power the Baath (Arab Renaissance Party), although the Baath was soon ousted. Coup attempts in 1965 and 1966 failed before a decisive Baath coup succeeded in July 1968. The Baathists have since retained political power under a one-party government in Iraq, maintaining leadership under strongman Saddam Husayn (Hussein) after 1979.[2]

From its creation as a mandate, Iraq has felt deprived of its proper place in the Middle East and Arab sun. It resented its mandate status and demanded independence until receiving it in 1932. Iraq objected to continued British influence in its affairs until the overthrow of the monarchy in 1958, when it finally felt independent.

Iraq has pursued many avenues to demonstrate its political potency. As Chapter 11 explained,

from the first, Iraq has repeatedly asserted its claim to Kuwait. The government accused oil companies in Iraq of discrimination against Iraqi interests—not a groundless charge—and later led in the successful organization of OPEC. When Britain withdrew from the Gulf in 1971, Iraq competed against Iran in declaring its claim as the rightful leader of the Gulf. It yielded leadership to Iran, which was under the rule of the shah and supported by the United States at that time, but the claims served notice of Iraqi ambitions—which, indeed, were reexhibited in the war against Iran and in the invasion of Kuwait.

Iraq during the 1970s benefited from a period of maximum oil prices and rapid development in the Gulf, and it achieved marked progress during the decade. When the Baath leadership selected Saddam Husayn as president in 1979, Iraq became personified in the most ambitious leader of the country since its creation in the early 1920s. Within a year Iraq was at war with Iran as a result of miscalculation by President Saddam, and before it could extricate itself in 1988, it suffered not only hundreds of thousands of casualties among its young men but also the destruction of many of its new industrial plants, transport facilities, and buildings. Much of southern Iraq lay in ruins. Iraq received billions of dollars in aid from Gulf oil states during the war, and the country

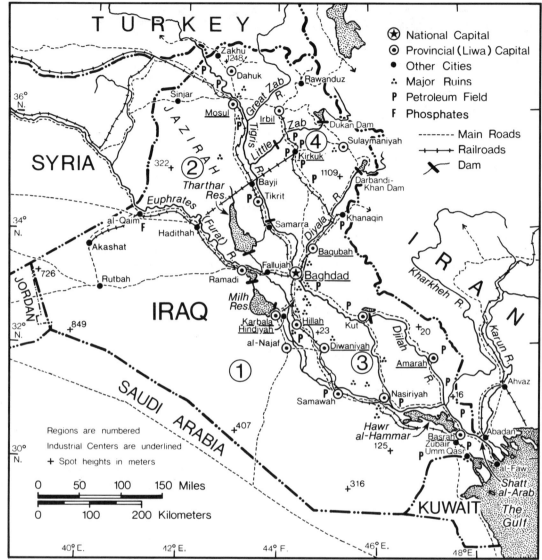

Map 16-1. *Iraq: Main cities, economic aspects, and antiquity sites. Circled numbers designate regions. Note 32nd and 36th parallels, which marked UN "no-fly zones" after the 1990–1991 Gulf war.*

continued development during the 1980s. After the cease-fire with Iran, Iraq undertook an aggressive rebuilding and redevelopment program, using oil production as collateral for major projects and otherwise contracting for goods and services from countries and companies that provided generous long-term financing.

In August 1990, the leadership once again miscalculated and invaded Kuwait (see Chap. 11). When Iraq refused to withdraw and coalition aircraft attacked Iraqi targets in mid-January 1991, the damage inflicted on Iraq's main cities and in-

frastructure was so great that UN inspectors visiting Baghdad and other Iraqi cities in March 1991 reported enormous damage to the economic infrastructure and destruction of most means of modern life support.[3]

Refusing to accept the UN conditions for lifting sanctions against it, Iraq in mid-1993 was in a general state of bitter frustration but surprisingly steady infrastructural recovery, even though it was unable to export its petroleum production or to import raw materials and machinery. Living at their lowest level in decades, Iraqis sought survival in a dilemma—they exhibited determination to outlast the sanctions they declared to be unjust on one hand and unwillingness or inability to oust a leader whose control signifies continuation of the sanctions on the other hand. Much of the discussion in this chapter must be considered within the context of Iraq's wounded yet defiant status in mid-1993.

Regional Patterns

Cradled in the land segment of the great tectonic trough downfolded between the Arabian Platform to the southwest and the Zagros ridges to the northeast, Iraq embraces four distinct natural regions, each of which plays and has historically played identifiable roles in Mesopotamian political and economic life: [1] western and southwestern desert plateau, [2] Jazirah or northern Mesopotamian upland, [3] southern Mesopotamian alluvial plain, and [4] northeastern uplands and Zagros Mountains (see circled numbers on Map 16-1).

[1] Western and Southwestern Deserts

This extension of the Syrian and Arabian deserts lies west of the Euphrates Valley and composes the barren western third of Iraq. It is the realm of Iraq's few thousand remaining Bedouins and is the least populated and least developed part of the country. In the far west is a continuation of the Jordanian desert platform and the Arabian area of al-Widyan, furrowed with numerous east-west wadis and traversed along its northern edge by the major highway from Baghdad to Amman and Damascus. Rutbah as a way station has developed from a dusty village in the 1970s into a bustling highway junction and trading center. The highway became a vital link for Iraq during the Iran-Iraq war and during the aftermath of the 1991 Gulf war. Farther east is al-Hajarah, a limestone platform strewn with flint and chert, crossed by the old caravan trail of the Darb Zubaydah for pilgrims to Mecca. Farther southeast is the sandy, gravelly plain of Dibdibah, cut by the prominent Wadi al-Batin, which forms the western boundary of Kuwait (see Map 18-1; the other subregions are named on Map 17-1). The open desert west of the Wadi al-Batin was utilized by coalition ground forces in late February 1991 to outflank and encircle Iraqi forces in Kuwait. The far west panhandle of Iraq gained a place in history when it was used by the Iraqi military as the launch area for nearly 80 Scud missiles into Saudi Arabia and Israel during the Gulf war.

[2] Jazirah: Northern Mesopotamian Upland

Most of the Jazirah upland, extending from Syria into central Iraq, is a desert plateau descending from 1,475 ft./450 m in the northeast to 260 ft./79 m at Baghdad. Except for the river floodplains and for the segment northwest of Mosul, population is sparse and development relatively limited. In the extreme north a prominent outlying ridge of the Zagros–Anti-Taurus folds, the Jabal Sinjar, extends westward from Mosul.

The region is drained from north to south by the steep-banked Wadi Tharthar, which empties into the extensive Tharthar Depression midway between the Tigris and Euphrates. A major project in the 1950s developed an artificial lake in the depression into which Tigris floodwaters can be diverted by the Samarra Barrage and from which overflow can be spilled southward into the Euphrates. North of Jabal Sinjar, the undulating plateau is devoted to rainfed cultivation of wheat and barley and is bisected by the main rail line from Europe to Basrah. Iraqi development plans envision later development of the Jazirah, including appreciable irrigation, comparable to that undertaken by Syria in the extension of that same region into the neighboring state. Mosul, located in the heart of ancient Assyria—and, indeed, partly developed on the site of ancient Nineveh—has now overtaken Basrah as the second-largest city in Iraq. It lies on the northeast periphery of the Jazirah but serves as the main center for the northern third of the country.

[3] Southern Mesopotamian Alluvial Plain

Extending southeastward from near Ramadi on the Euphrates and from just south of Samarra on the Tigris is the flat alluvial plain that has in recent geological time been built Gulfward by the accumulated silt in the coalesced deltas of four rivers: Tigris, Euphrates, Karkheh, and Karun.

The original shoreline is marked by a sinuous cliff, probably the feature for which Iraq is named, which extends from Ramadi to near Samarra. Along and between these lower courses of the Tigris and Euphrates, where ancient empires thrived and the ruins of the most ancient cities of the world still stand, the cultural and economic core of modern Iraq has evolved. On the area's western periphery lie the two most sacred shrines of Shii Islam, in Karbala and al-Najaf, the former the tomb of the martyred Husayn and the latter the tomb of Ali, Husayn's father and the fourth caliph and first Shii imam. Despite their sanctity, both Karbala and al-Najaf were heavily damaged during the Shii insurrection against the Iraqi government in March 1991, when Samawah and Nasiriyah—farther down the Euphrates—were also damaged.

Temperatures during the dry summers average 95°F/35°C for July and soar to daytime highs of more than 122°F/50°C. Winter rainfall averages only 5.5 in./140 mm. Elevations and relief are low. Heights range from 80 ft./25 m in the north to sea level in the south, but some areas beyond the rivers' natural levees are actually below sea level upstream from the Shatt al-Arab.

The northern end of the alluvial plain, where the Tigris and Euphrates make their closest approach to each other, constitutes one of the historically most strategic sites in the Fertile Crescent. Its importance is manifested by the transit of the narrow interfluve by a major trade route since Neolithic times; by the location of successive capitals and primate cities in the immediate vicinity—Akkad (although its exact site is uncertain), Babylon, Seleucia, Ctesiphon, and Baghdad; by its development for irrigation agriculture for many centuries; and, of greatest current significance, by its multiple advantages and attractions for the development of modern industry, including production of weapons and other armaments.

Southeast of the Baghdad area, the central interfluve is mostly wasteland or marshes that become desiccated in the dry, hot summers. A high water table and inadequate drainage on some of these deltaic silt lands combine to raise soil salinity to levels that prevent cultivation of otherwise good soils that could be irrigated if adequate drainage could be maintained.

In part to facilitate such drainage, during 1992 the Iraqi government undertook the rush construction of a 350-mile/563-km canal that extends from Baghdad to Basrah along the axis of the central interfluve. Often called "the Third River," the canal has several purposes and is intended not only to aid in soil reclamation in southern Mesopotamia but also to provide an outlet for drainage of the extensive southern marshes. Both the canal and the drainage project are major undertakings. Some observers expressed reservations about drainage of the marshes, both about technical feasibility and advisability and about its depriving the marsh dwellers of their protected environment. Construction of the canal, which continued night and day for most of 1992 and employed 4,500 workers, was in part an indication of the Iraqi government's determination to persevere under the discouraging circumstances imposed by the UN sanctions at the time.[4] Multiple traces of abandoned channels of the Tigris and Euphrates indicate radical course changes by the rivers, as do the present locations of ancient cities—Kish, Nippur, Uruk, Ur, and others—now far from the riverbanks along which they originally lay. Such a former Tigris course is followed by the Shatt al-Gharraf, fed by water diverted from the Tigris by the Kut Barrage to the Euphrates near Nasiriyah. Between this former channel and the present course of the Tigris are large marsh areas and little cultivation, reflecting serious soil salination.

Both settlement and cultivation tend to exhibit a ribbon pattern, since they are concentrated along the banks of rivers and canals, including the Shatt al-Gharraf. Such concentration of cultivation is due both to the proximity of irrigation water and, more important, to the better drainage on the broad natural levees built up on both banks during regular river overflow. Where the stream has bifurcated, as the Euphrates has in several places below Hit, both naturally and artificially, irrigated agriculture and settlement have become especially intensive. Such patterns are dense between Ramadi and Nasiriyah.

Between Nasiriyah and the confluence of the Euphrates with the Tigris at Qurnah there is an area of unusual ecological relationships, the lower Euphrates marshes occupied by the Marsh Arabs, the Madan. For thousands of years, these

Figure 16-1. *Reed houses and islands in the marshes of the lower Euphrates east of Nasiriyah.*

marshland dwellers have utilized the local reeds (*qasab*) growing in the marshes to build their shelters on artificial reed-mat islands and to construct their council houses (*mudhifs*). They have caught the plentiful fish in the surrounding waters; raised water buffalo for milk, yogurt, and hides; and moved between houses and villages by the typical local boats, the high-prowed *mashhuf*, which they pole through the shallow water (Fig. 16-1). Shii fugitives from Iraqi military persecution took refuge in these marshes in 1991–1992.

East of the marshes and the Hawr al-Hammar, the confluence of the Tigris and Euphrates creates the Shatt al-Arab, through which the combined rivers flow 100 miles/160 km to the Gulf. For much of the Shatt's length, a broad belt of date palm groves parallels both riverbanks, naturally irrigated by an intricate network of canals in which the fresh water rises and falls with the daily tidal backup of the river water. Midway up the Shatt and on its west bank lies Basrah, normally Iraq's main port and second city. This historic trade center has long been a Shii stronghold, and older quarters and buildings attest to the strong influence of India on the city's development over the centuries. Basrah was heavily damaged in repeated battles during the Iran-Iraq war, was again devastated in military operations in 1990–1991, and suffered still further destruction during the Shii insurrection in March and

April 1991 after the end of Desert Storm operations. Although it is again rebuilding and will retain a major role, Basrah has been replaced by Mosul, at least temporarily, as Iraq's second city. In the desert west of the Shatt is one of Iraq's main groups of oil fields, notably Rumaila and Zubair. West of the mouth of the Shatt al-Arab is Iraq's "window" on the Gulf, 36 miles/58 km of Gulf coastline at this lower end of the Iraq "funnel." In this strategic outlet of Iraq's corridor to the sea is an increasing concentration of oil activity, heavier industries, and multiple port development (discussed later in this chapter under "Economic Patterns and Problems"). Also in this strategic corridor is focused Iraq's historic grievance against Britain's allocation of territory and delineation of boundaries in the early 1920s. The strip is thus the focus of Iraq's complaints and claims against Kuwait and Iran, and it is from here that Iraq lashed out in 1980 and 1990. The details of Iraq's claims regarding the Shatt al-Arab boundary are given in Chapter 11 (see Map 11-6). A precise new boundary between Kuwait and Iraq, delineated in 1992 by the United Nations, deprives Iraq of port facilities and a section of its short coastline.

The physical geography of extreme southeastern Iraq is as much influenced by the southwestward-building deltas of the Karun and Karkheh rivers as by the southeastward-building deltas of the Tigris and Euphrates and their common outlet, the Shatt al-Arab. The building of the Karun-Karkheh deltas has had three geomorphic effects: It has aided in filling in the head of the Gulf, it has forced the Tigris and Euphrates together into the Shatt al-Arab, and it has simultaneously blocked some of the combined drainage and thus contributed to the formation of the lakes, intermittent lakes, and marshes that sprawl over much of the landscape of the combined deltas of the four rivers.[5]

[4] Northeastern Uplands and Zagros Mountains

Uplands, piedmont, and rugged mountains rising northeastward from the upper Tigris in Iraq exhibit a sharp contrast to the desert plains areas that cover most of the rest of the country and that typify perceptions of Mesopotamia and Iraq. Except for a few prominent ridges near the Tigris (Jabal Hamrin, for example) the major highlands lie northeast of a line connecting Zakhu, Mosul, Irbil, Kirkuk, and Khanaqin. Elevations rise from 655 ft./200 m on the lower piedmont just east of the Tigris to 3,000 ft./915 m in the foothills, then reach 5,900 ft./1,800 m on the typical ridge tops and 11,808 ft./3,600 m in a summit elevation on the Iranian border east of Rawanduz. Lying at 36° N Lat, only 6° farther north than Iraq's torrid desert Gulf coast, these elevations are blanketed with snow half the year and can be cool at night in summer. In the lower elevations, Mosul and Kirkuk are still hot in summer, but they receive 15 in./385 mm of winter precipitation compared to Basrah's 6.5 in./164 mm.

Ridges in the far north extend east-west, following the trend of folding in the Taurus and Anti-Taurus mountains, whereas tectonic trends south of Rawanduz turn southeast and thence combine with the dominant Zagros folds. Several streams follow deep gorges that are parallel to the folds in their upper courses and then cross the grain of the folded ridges to join the Tigris: the Khabur, Great Zab, Little Zab, Udhaym, and Diyala. The highest ridges contain Iraq's only forests, some of them quite extensive, preserved by the isolation and ruggedness of the area. Most of the mountain slopes permit only grazing, lower and more gentle slopes support fruit and

Figure 16-2. *Typical landscape in the foothills of Iraqi Kurdistan, east of Kirkuk. Photograph taken from one upfolded ridge, looking across an intervening valley to the next upfolded ridge.*

nut trees, and the broad lower valley bottoms are intensively cultivated (Fig. 16-2). Access to the higher areas is limited, and passes through the rugged Zagros summit ridges into Iran are few. Most famous of these routes is the Rawanduz River gorge, with the spectacular Spilak Pass and Ali Beg Gorge west of Rawanduz and the Shinak Pass near the Iranian border.

Some of Iraq's earliest and largest hydraulic projects were developed in the late 1950s in these well-watered, rugged mountain areas, where deep gorges and solid rock offered ideal sites for dam construction. The Dukan Dam and accompanying large reservoir were built on the upper Little Zab, the Darbandikhan Dam and reservoir on the upper Diyala, and, later, the Dibs Dam on the Little Zab. The Great Zab's potential was finally under exploitation in the late 1980s with the construction of a large dam in its upper course.

Apart from its landforms, northeastern Iraq is also noteworthy for its role as a human minority refuge, a political-cultural buffer and frontier, and an underground reservoir of hydrocarbons. It is the Iraqi segment of Greater Kurdistan, in which Kurdish tribesmen normally move freely among Iraq and Iran and even Turkey. Kurds are overwhelmingly the dominant group, using the ruggedness and isolation of the elevated Zagros as their fortress and refuge in their successive wars for autonomy against the Arab central government—including the widely publicized fighting of 1991–1992. In the lower hills are many Turkmen, smaller numbers of Assyrians, and small groups of Sarliyyas, Yazidis, and other groups. The same tectonic forces that created the folded hills and mountains produced the subsurface structures in which petroleum and gas accumulated.

Population and Peoples

Population Patterns

Iraq's estimated population of 18.5 million in 1991 marked a 285 percent increase over 1947. This growth has occurred primarily through natural increase, unlike the growths of 2,600 percent in Gulf states such as the UAE, which have resulted primarily from immigration. Map 6-2 shows that Iraq's population is concentrated in linear patterns along the banks of rivers and canals on the plains but is more generally distributed in the villages and towns of the northeastern uplands and mountains.

The greatest single concentration of population, about half of the total for the country, begins north and west of Baghdad, sprawls westward and southward across the mid-Iraq interfluve, and then follows the Euphrates and its various branches along the west side of the alluvial plain to Samawah. Metropolitan Baghdad alone has one-third of Iraq's population. Other major nuclei in the concentration include the shrine city of al-Najaf; Hillah, one of the main date-producing centers in Iraq; Diwaniyah; Karbala, with the shrine to Husayn; and Fallujah. The middle Euphrates concentration has a well-balanced economy, based on agriculture, industry, trade, tourism, and catering to pilgrims visiting Karbala and al-Najaf.

Secondary concentrations of population are found in the south, normally along the Shatt al-Arab and with a focus on Basrah, whose population fluctuated wildly during the decade prior to 1992; in the north around Mosul; and in the northeast piedmont, around the oil developments of Kirkuk and the ancient city of Irbil. The Kurdish "capital city" of Sulaymaniyah, in the heart of the Iraqi Zagros east of Kirkuk, is probably Iraq's fifth-largest city.

Ethnolinguistic Groups

Some groups within Iraq's borders have maintained their separateness for many centuries, to the extent that their group identities compete with Iraqi nationalism. Although the primary ethnic conflict is between Arab and Kurd, also significant is the religious rift between Sunni Muslim and Shii Muslim, discussed below. Smaller ethnic minorities—Turkmen, Assyrian, Armenian, Yazidi, Lur and smaller Persian-speaking groups, Mandaean, and others—remain distinctive but, except for the Assyrians between the world wars and some of the Persians in the 1980s, are not actively separatist or antinational.

Arabs. Composing more than 77 percent of the population, Arabs have been the dominant group numerically and politically for 1,000 years. During most of that period, they have considered themselves the eastern bulwark against non-Arab influences (Fig. 16-3). The Iraqi Arabs represent a biological mixture of many peoples over thousands of years, since repeated assimilations have undoubtedly merged ancient populations as well as more modern groups such as Persians, Turks, and Mongols.

Although only about 20 percent of the Arabs in Iraq are Sunni, they have been the dominant economic and political group for many centuries. Since Shiis have long been associated with Iran and Iranians, Sunnis have considered themselves the Mesopotamian "loyalists," with a reciprocal affinity for the predominantly Sunni Arab neighboring countries. During the centuries of Sunni Ottoman control of the basin, Shiis became alienated, isolated through endogamy, and suffered decreased cultural and economic opportunities. Virtually all of the Kurds are also Sunni, so that the combined Sunni groups make up approximately 36 percent of the total population.

Shiism, the original partisanship for Ali, emerged in southern Iraq during the seventh century. Shii strength in southern Iraq has continued to the present time, although the greater concentration of the sect evolved in neighboring Iran during the sixteenth century. The proportion of Shiis in the Iraqi population exceeds 60 percent, with their major strength in the areas in which population is most concentrated.

Kurds.[6] The approximately 3.8 million Kurds in Iraq live primarily in the northeast uplands and

Figure 16-3. *New tomb and monument for an unknown soldier, Baghdad. The monument was built by the Saddam Husayn government to replace a more modest one built 25 years earlier. It is one of several large monuments in Baghdad glorifying Iraqi armed forces.*

Zagros Mountains, the Iraqi sector of Kurdistan. They speak a different language and have their own distinctive cultural system, actively maintaining a strong sense of Kurdish group identity opposed to that of the Iraqi Arabs. Tenaciously holding their compact rugged mountain homeland, the Kurds in centuries past were isolated in their mountain area, raising livestock and cultivating the lower slopes, living as a tightly knit tribal society and resisting outside interference. After 1927, petroleum development around Kirkuk, on the periphery of traditional Kurdish territory, prompted a new interaction between plain and mountain. However, the inability of the central government and Kurdish leaders to achieve mutual accommodation has led to a series of internecine conflicts between the two groups, from the mandate period at least intermittently through such periods as 1919–1930, 1943–1946, 1961–1970, 1974–1975, during much of the Iran-Iraq war, the late 1980s (a crucial period), and, most recently, the months in 1991–1992 following the Gulf war when more than 1 million Kurds fled Iraqi military attacks. The normal cycle is that the Kurds make demands for regional autonomy, sometimes even for independence; the national government rejects such demands, fearing that autonomy might lead to sep-

aratism, which might in turn involve loss of the area oil fields; and fighting breaks out that ends indecisively and sets the stage for the next cycle.

Each of the two cycles in the late 1980s and in 1991–1992 was unique. The first was a climax to bitter fighting along the border with Iran east of Darbandikhan Reservoir in early 1988, when local Kurdish *peshmergas* (guerrillas) supported an Iranian attack inside Iraq. As they had on previous occasions when they were seriously threatened, according to UN charges during the early 1980s, Iraqi forces used poison gas both in the battle and against civilians in the neighboring Kurdish town of Halabjah, where several thousand died.

The Iraqi government then undertook a wide-ranging program of razing Kurdish villages and resettling populations from several villages together in cement-block "towns" erected by the Baghdad government. In stark contrast to the picturesque Kurdish villages on mountain slopes (see Fig. 10-2), 4,000 of which were demolished by explosives and bulldozers, the new towns were built in a grid pattern on strictly controlled plains or basin floors, away from the protective ruggedness of the mountains.[7] Scores of thousands of Kurds reportedly disappeared during this process. The central government expected the resettlement program to solve definitively the Kurdish rebellion problem.

At the end of Desert Storm operations, Iraqi forces once again vented their frustration on the Kurds, more than 1 million of whom temporarily fled to Iran and Turkey to escape the oppression. Coalition forces attempted to protect and reassure the refugees, most of whom eventually returned to Iraq, and some returnees took advantage of the absence of Iraqi troops to rebuild hundreds of villages that had been razed by Iraqi authorities several years earlier. Kurdish leaders reopened negotiations with the central government for the creation of an autonomous Kurdistan in northeastern Iraq, but the two parties achieved little more progress than the Kurds and Baghdad authorities had in past negotiations. Controlled by coalition aircraft from Turkish airfields, the United Nations established and maintained a security zone above the 36th parallel, which was still in effect in early 1993. The May 19, 1992, election for Kurdish leadership was indecisive, resulting in a power-sharing arrangement between the two major parties.

Turkmen. Making up about 1.4 percent of the Iraqi population, Turkmen live in the piedmont and foothills of the northeast. They form an ethnic transition between the Arabs of Mesopotamia and the Kurds of the Zagros and are numerous in both Kirkuk and Irbil as well as in villages on the piedmont. Turkmen are Sunni and middle class, and many have become integrated and serve as government employees.

Other Ethnic Minorities. Smaller ethnic minorities include Persian-speaking Shiis with strong ties to Iran, about 1.5 percent of the Iraqi population prior to expulsions of thousands who voiced anti-Iraqi sentiments in the early years of the Iran-Iraq war. Their strongholds were Karbala, al-Najaf, and al-Kazimiyah (near Baghdad) as well as Basrah. Another Persian-speaking group, the Lur, are concentrated in tribally organized villages near the Iranian frontier.

Jews numbered 118,000 in the 1947 census but were undoubtedly more numerous, since in 1951 about 121,000 emigrated to Israel and several thousand went to Iran. Before 1951, Iraqi Jews generally lived in urban areas, often as merchants, professionals, and government officials in Baghdad. A few thousand remained in Iraq in the mid-1980s, but most of them had emigrated by mid-1992.

The Christian Armenians are estimated to number 20,000 and are usually urban. The small group of Mandaeans—also called Sabians, Subba, or John the Baptist Christians—are an interesting ancient people of uncertain origin who are differentiated primarily by religion but who are also physically distinct. Their stress on ablutions keeps them close to rivers and streams, with centers in Baghdad and the south. Many are skilled silversmiths in Baghdad, and in Suq al-Shuyukh, in the lower Euphrates marshes, they are expert boatbuilders. The Yazidis, an extension of the Yazidis in Syria, live in villages along the Jabal Sinjar west of Mosul.

Christian Minorities. In addition to the Christian Armenians, several other distinctive Christian groups are significant in Iraq. Most of them are in the north, particularly in the Mosul area, but there are others in the Baghdad area. The largest group is the Chaldeans, in Mosul and villages on the surrounding plain but also numerous in Baghdad, seat of their patriarch. Assyrians, sharing a common origin with the Chaldeans, are concentrated mainly in the extreme north around Zakhu and Dahuk, in Kirkuk, and in Baghdad. Originally from eastern Turkey, they moved into northern Iraq at the end of World War I, where many of them fought with the British mandate military forces against Iraqi insurgents, and were oppressed and expelled in 1933 after Iraq became independent.

Economic Patterns and Problems

Economic Interrelations

Mandate Iraq emerged in the early 1920s with an economy based on agriculture, its practice well below the high standard developed under the Abbasids nearly 1,000 years earlier. Agricultural practice failed to meet Iraq's great potential, with the country's abundant supply of river water and cultivable soils on level lands; and even after petroleum development offered increasing capital and diversification of the economy, agriculture often lagged. A shortage of trained managers and skilled labor slowed all sectors of the economy. Moreover, investments often failed to produce commensurate increases in real economic growth, as was particularly evident in agriculture.

Thus, despite wealth in oil resources and agricultural potential, Iraq's economic development proceeded slowly even after independence in 1932, first requiring infrastructural expansion—roads, railways, ports, dams, schools, and other structures. Uneven emphasis on industrial development created an overcapacity in some sectors and strained labor resources. Equally uneven oil development combined with political instability, especially during the decade after 1958, to limit expansion. However, significant gains did occur during and after the 1950s, often under turnkey arrangements. Most major industries were transferred to the public sector (later called the "socialist sector") in 1964, and nationalization of the petroleum sector began in 1972. After 1980, as was explained earlier in this chapter, the Iran-Iraq war consumed capital and labor, diverted energies to the war effort, and destroyed some of Iraq's most important new infrastructural and industrial developments.

Iraq's geographical vulnerability was exposed after 1977, as neighboring states on both sides pursued confrontational policies, Syria economically and politically and Iran militarily after 1980. Syria shut down Iraq's export pipelines to the Mediterranean in the late 1960s, late 1970s, and in 1982, necessitating Iraq's increasing use of export terminals off the Shatt al-Arab. Yet, after 1980, all ports on Iraq's window on the Gulf were subject to Iranian ground and air strikes, interdicting oil exports and imports of arms and consumer goods through the country's Gulf ports. Access to routes across territories of neighboring states became essential: pipelines across southeastern Turkey and northeastern Saudi Arabia, as well as roads across Jordan to Aqabah and other roads down the Gulf coast across Kuwait and Saudi Arabia. After having been afforded access to such routes—through Turkey and Jordan for mutual benefit and through Saudi Arabia as a goodwill gesture—Iraq destroyed its links by its 1990 invasion of Kuwait.

Agriculture

From the country's major economic activity in the 1920s, agriculture dropped to 18 percent of the GDP in 1990. Even so, 13 percent of the labor force continues to be engaged in agriculture, more than in any other sector except services. The figures for agricultural workers in the late 1980s were skewed by the fact that most of the 2 million expatriate workers—1.5 million Egyptians, 300,000 Sudanese, and 200,000 South and East Asians—were farm laborers. Moreover, after March 1991, the percentage of workers in agriculture probably doubled as Iraq tried desperately to feed its population and to employ workers unable to pursue their jobs in the near-dormant industrial sector. Thus, Iraq was forced to emphasize agriculture to a greater extent than it had done for several decades.

Of the country's total area, about 13 percent is arable. A surprising 53 percent of the arable land is rainfed, nearly all of it in the north and northeast, although most of the agricultural production is from the more intensively cultivated areas of the irrigated plains.

Iraq's major crops are grown in both the irrigated plains and the rainfed northern uplands—barley, wheat, rice, cotton, potatoes, tobacco, millet, and sorghum. Wheat and barley are winter crops, utilizing the winter rainfall of the Mediterranean climate, whereas the other plants are summer grown, with some irrigation in the north. Other crops, especially dates, are restricted to the southern irrigated areas along the rivers and canals, with citrus often grown in the shade of date palms. Thousands of date palms, which formerly supplied an important export, were destroyed during Iraq's two wars, 1980–1988 and 1991–1992. A complete range of temperate and subtropical fruits and vegetables is produced in Iraq.

During recent decades Iraq has shifted from net food exporter to food importer. This shift was prompted by several factors, including population increase, a rising standard of living, increased industrialization, migration of farm workers to the cities, and a loss of soil productivity in poorly drained irrigated areas of the south. Ambitious land reclamation and irrigation projects were accelerated after 1988, especially in the

Jazirah along the East Euphrates channel and in the Third River Project in the southern interfluve. Irrigated area was greatly increased in the late 1980s, and agricultural efficiency has improved as collectivized farms have been privatized and a minimum size has been established for individual farms (62.5 acres/100 dunums). Further development may at last permit Iraq to approach its great agricultural potential.

Petroleum

The first well drilled in Iraq, by the Turkish Petroleum Company or TPC (later renamed the Iraq Petroleum Company or IPC), struck a major reservoir with enormous gas pressure at Baba Gur, north of Kirkuk, in 1927. However, shipment of Kirkuk's output was delayed for seven years pending completion of export pipelines. The government of Iraq believed that IPC sacrificed oil developments in Iraq for British political-economic interests, and Iraq-IPC relations remained discordant until Iraq nationalized its oil operations in 1975. Iraq had already joined OPEC as a charter member in 1960, passed Law 80 in 1961 reclaiming all concession area not in production, and created the Iraq National Oil Company (INOC) in 1964. These frictions in the country's oil operations, which continued even after nationalization of the industry, and the resultant retarded economic development in Iraq contrast with the smooth relations that exist in Saudi Arabia and Kuwait and the resulting unparalleled development there.

Long ranking among the regional "big four" in reserves and production—Saudi Arabia, Iran, and Kuwait are the other three—Iraq finally achieved a peak production of 3.4 million bpd in 1979, only to fall sharply the next several years during the price collapse and the war with Iran. It approached the 3-million-bpd level in 1989, only to decrease again in 1990 when it invaded Kuwait. Prohibited from exporting by UN sanctions, Iraq saw its 1991 output plummet to the level of 40 years earlier.

One refinery, now with a 71,000-bpd throughput, was built in the 1950s at Dawrah, near Baghdad. Basrah's refinery has a comparable capacity but has had limited output after experiencing especially heavy damage in both recent wars. A new refinery in Bayji, on the Tigris midway between Baghdad and Mosul, is the country's largest (150,000 bpd); and it has brought Iraq's refining capacity to 320,000 bpd, counting the output of four small refineries in central Iraq. However, all were bombing targets in early 1991 and were under repair a year later. Even so, with no export market, Iraq adequately supplied its domestic needs for products from its own refineries, using plentiful crude production. It similarly filled other energy needs from its great supplies of natural gas.

Details of the several complex Iraqi pipeline projects are given in the "Pipelines" section of Chapter 8: The projects include lines through Jordan and Palestine to Haifa, shut down and abandoned in 1948; multiple lines across Syria to the Mediterranean coasts of both Syria and Lebanon, shut down in 1982; dual lines through southeastern Turkey to Yumurtalık built over the decade 1977–1987 and at least temporarily closed in 1990; and the huge IPSA line through Saudi Arabia, also closed in 1990. Entirely within Iraq are the two large internal strategic two-way north-south pipelines, one opened in 1975 and the second—a 400-mile/645-km, 42-inch/107-cm line—opened in 1988. The parallel lines connect Hadithah, the major pipeline junction on the upper Euphrates, and Rumaila field to Iraq's Gulf terminals, permitting pumping in either direction. The country's oil export terminals on the Gulf include al-Faw on the Shatt al-Arab and the two artificial trestle ports of Mina al-Bakr and Khawr al-Amayah, all three of which were out of operation after the Iran-Iraq war.

Thus, Iraq has all the essentials for a highly productive and profitable petroleum industry: 100 billion barrels of proved reserves—second-largest in the world (after Saudi Arabia); a well-distributed pattern of more than 70 fields, from the Turkish border to the Gulf coast; a normal producing capacity of 5 million bpd, expandable to 6 million bpd; an export capacity of 5.3 million bpd if all pipelines and terminals are operating; and an institutional system (which needs improving) to oversee operations. A major problem for the country is how to spread its oil income over even its priority obligations, which now include reparations to Kuwait, payment for rebuilding the country, and continued disposition of debts or at least debt servicing. It is vital for

Iraq to shift from a confrontational mode to one of at least pragmatic cooperation in order to benefit fully at long last from its great potential, not only in oil but also in other economic and political spheres.

Other Minerals

Nonfuel mineral resources of Iraq have so far proved to be relatively limited, compared with those of neighboring Turkey and Iran; and only sulfur, phosphates, and modest iron ore outputs are noteworthy. In addition to by-product sulfur from its refineries, Iraq also mines mineral sulfur at Mishraq from one of the world's largest deposits—130 million mt, located south of Mosul—and derives a range of acids and other products from it in nearby plants. Phosphate mining at Akashat (near al-Qaim, on the Euphrates near the Syrian border) was expanded several times to exploit these 7.5 billion mt of reserves after the late 1970s, and an enlarged plant at al-Qaim processes some of the phosphates for acids and enhanced fertilizers. Both the sulfur and phosphates, along with products derived from processing them, supply important exports.

Manufacturing

Most of Iraq's industrial development has occurred since 1960. Inevitably, as was suggested earlier, concentrations of industries evolved around Baghdad, because of its market and labor supply, and around Basrah, because of its import-export advantages and the availability of oil and gas for energy and raw materials. Increased production of oil and gas in the north stimulated growth of population and industry in the Mosul-Irbil-Kirkuk triangle, giving Iraq its third manufacturing belt (see Map 9-1). Otherwise, fabricating plants have been distributed among the different settled parts of the state, partly for strategic dispersion and partly to stimulate more widespread economic development. The more important manufacturing centers are underlined on Map 16-1, although many smaller towns pursue traditional crafts.

Food and beverage processing is a leading activity and is well distributed around the country. Textiles, a product of Mesopotamia for centuries, have increased in importance since the mid-1950s. Mosul, which gave its name to muslin, has regained its status as a textile center. Central Iraq has many small to medium plants producing paper products, plastic items, pharmaceuticals, and similar light manufactures; and large plants produce assembled automobiles and trucks, household appliances, television assemblies, and, prior to 1991, a wide range of military weapons and support systems. The armaments industries both quantitatively and qualitatively surprised UN inspectors who inventoried and monitored such plants after the end of hostilities in early 1991. Although research on and production of nuclear materials were strategically dispersed, they were focused on the mid-Iraq interfluve. It was in this area that Iraq developed its Osiran nuclear reactor, bombed by Israel in 1981, and conducted advanced work on fissionable material at Tuwaytha, southeast of Baghdad. The strategic southern corridor is being developed as a center for heavy industry and petrochemicals. Along the Zubair oil field—Khawr al-Zubair—Umm Qasr axis, plans call for an iron and steel works, salt works, pipe plant, and similar works basic for further development of Iraq.

Despite the impressive growth of manufacturing, its contribution to the GDP was still only 12 percent in 1990, and it undoubtedly dropped to 6–8 percent in 1991. In any case, the role of large state-owned firms must be emphasized. Once industry was heavily socialized, private investors were wary about entering the sector, although the Iraqi government actively encouraged Arab participation in industry, tourism, and retailing (non-Arab investment was forbidden). After two wars and world ostracism of Iraq in 1990–1991, few private investors were interested in such risky use of their funds. The government reapplied the policies of seeking offshore contractor financing on long-term credit and of offering oil as payment—although the oil has often been obligated on earlier debts and debt servicing.

Transportation and Trade

Roads. Iraq's physical geography and early development—mostly along the two northwest-southeast axes of the Tigris and Euphrates—imposed an early pattern on road and railroad development. Road traffic flows primarily along the Tigris axis between Mosul and Baghdad, but alongside the Euphrates south of Baghdad, a route also followed by the country's main line railway. Lighter traffic follows the Tigris from Baghdad southward through Kut and Amarah to Basrah and also follows the Euphrates northward from al-Musayyib to the Syrian border. Major links continue southward to Kuwait and onward to Saudi Arabia, westward across the desert to Jordan, up both rivers to Syria, northward from Mosul to Turkey, and to Iran in the north, center, and extreme south. The links to north, west, and south brought in essential food and military matériel during the Iran-Iraq war, especially the route from Jordan's port at Aqabah through Rutbah and Ramadi to Baghdad. It was the nearest single link to function as a lifesaver and has since been reconstructed as a first-class divided freeway. Again during the Gulf crisis in 1990–1991, this highway was Iraq's one ground link with the outside world, and it continued to serve as a vital artery during the lengthy period of Iraq's relative isolation after the crisis.

Railways. A railway from Berlin to Baghdad was a goal of the Germans and other Europeans during the heyday of railroad building, and the southern segment of the realized line enters Iraq northwest of Mosul, parallels the Tigris to Baghdad, then follows the Euphrates to Basrah and the Gulf. It was the country's only railway until development of the phosphate deposits near al-Qaim prompted construction of a 318-mile/512-km railway, completed in 1984, down the Euphrates and across to Baghdad. A second new line, 156 miles/252 km long, parallels the major pipelines from Kirkuk to Hadithah on the Euphrates, where it joins the line from al-Qaim to Baghdad. The greatest railway project is construction of a 416-mile/670-km double-track system connecting Baghdad and Basrah, the line with the heaviest traffic in Iraq. On all its railways, the country had an enormous reconstruction task after the Gulf war, particularly with regard to bridges.

Ports. The narrowness of Iraq's window on the Gulf restricts the country's ports to a small area. Despite the geographical constraint, several ports are normally essential because of the scale and variety of Iraq's imports and exports. Basrah long served as Mesopotamia's only port. Its location on the relatively shallow Shatt al-Arab, however, limited growth and led to congestion. Oil development and Iraq's economic expansion after the 1950s occasioned construction of an oil terminal at al-Faw, down the Shatt al-Arab from Basrah; two general-cargo ports, Khawr al-Zubair and Umm Qasr, on the Khawr al-Zubair drowned estuary near the Kuwait border, with Umm Qasr also serving as a naval base; and two oil export terminals—Mina al-Bakr and Khawr al-Amayah—on causeways into the deeper water at the head of the Gulf. Even before the Iran-Iraq war, Iraqi ports were overloaded, and Iraq imported through Aqabah and Kuwait as well as other Gulf ports. Virtual destruction of Iraq's ports in the early 1980s necessitated greater reliance on Kuwait and especially Aqabah, neither of which was accessible to Iraq during the 1990–1991 Gulf war. All Iraqi ports required rebuilding in the early 1990s.

Trade. For many years, crude petroleum has constituted 98–99 percent of Iraq's exports. The remainder has been primarily processed dates and fertilizers. Like other aspects of the Iraqi economy, foreign trade was profoundly affected by the war with Iran and much more so by the aftermath of the Gulf crisis of 1990–1991. UN resolutions prohibited trade with Iraq by any member of the United Nations, and movement of virtually all goods into and out of Iraq was interdicted. Later, after hostilities had ceased, food and medicines were allowed in, but Iraq was not permitted to export oil or other goods in any appreciable quantity until it reached agreement with the United Nations regarding parameters of trade. Iraq's trading partners were appreciably shuffled after the Iran-Iraq war, when the Soviet Union ceased being a leading supplier (of armaments), and the United States became the leading partner in exports and imports. However, countries ranging from Jordan and Turkey to Brazil and Japan ranked among the ten leading partners. Iraq was a difficult partner to trade with, since it sold its petroleum and fertilizers for hard currency cash only but bought almost entirely on long-term credit, a policy that dictated who its trading partners would be. The once-strong Iraqi dinar steadily lost value after the mid-1980s until its offshore exchange rate in 1990 was one-tenth the internal rate strictly enforced by the Iraqi government. After the Gulf crisis, the dinar had little offshore value and minimal domestic value.

Relations

Iraq's external political and economic relations have fluctuated widely since 1958, both because of internal politics and because of regional changes. In early 1993, Iraq, under President Saddam Husayn, was a pariah state with only very tenuous relations with its neighbors, its former trading partners, its former supporter in Russia, and certainly North America and Western Europe.

Iraq's long political and economic relationship with Britain, steered for many years by the pro-Western Nuri al-Said, linked Iraq with Europe internationally until 1958. One consequence of this link was that Iraq became the sole Arab country to join the Baghdad Pact. However, the revolutionary republican government reversed the trend, withdrew from the pact in 1959, and accepted a breach with the West.[8]

Iraq since 1958 has made its primary foreign policy concern the reaffirming and strengthening of its links with the Arab world but also the assertion of a leadership role in the region. Iraq had supplied troops in the 1948–1949 war between Arabs and the new state of Israel, and it did so again in 1967. It has consistently supported the Palestinian Arab cause within the context of Arab unity and has periodically given sanctuary to individual terrorists. It, like Egypt, has accepted a minimum number of Palestinian refugees. However, Iraqi government leaders—particularly President Saddam Husayn—have issued calls for a remedy of the Palestinian problem, usually involving confrontation with Israel. Thus, as implacable opponents and genuine threats to each other's security, Iraq and Israel view each other as mutual major foes. For its part, Israel bombed Iraq's Osiran nuclear reactor in June 1981, gave military assistance to Iran during the Iran-Iraq war, undercuts Iraq's economic development, and wages an effective war of words against Iraq.

Since World War II, and especially since the 1958 revolution, Iraq has emphasized its historical role in Islam (Fig. 16-4) and has considered itself the eastern anchor of the Arab world and the natural eastern flank of the Mashriq, the Arab Middle East, of which Egypt is the western flank. As a member of the Arab League, it is regularly militant, often advocating more vigorous stands than do the majority of the members. It is a "rejectionist" state on many political points. Its direct relations with Egypt have blown hot and cold since 1958 but reached their nadir in 1990 when Egypt, greatly moderated since the radical years of Gamal Abd al-Nasser, joined the coalition to force Iraq to withdraw from Kuwait. Other Arab states of the Mashriq are ambivalent toward Iraq: They condemn its aggression against Kuwait and its firing Scud missiles into Saudi Arabia, as well as other acts by Saddam Husayn; but they still appreciate its role in attesting to Arabism, its stand against Iran, its defiance of vestiges of imperialism, and its opposition to Israel. Yemen has voiced support for Iraq for these reasons. Because of rifts between Syrian Baathists and Iraqi Baathists, relations with Syria deteriorated after that country's 1963 Baath coup. Iraq, Syria, and Egypt have contended for leadership of the Mashriq.

Iraq's relations with Jordan historically rested on the fraternal relationship of the Hashimite kings of the two countries. Although meaningful implementation of the proposed Arab Federation between the two kingdoms was prevented by the 1958 revolution, mutual interests restored relations. The link has proved critical to Iraq, as well as economically beneficial to Jordan, as has been shown in Chapter 14 and earlier in this chapter. Close Jordanian-Iraqi relations are certain to be resumed when UN sanctions are removed because of the compellingly reciprocal advantages that cooperation between these neighbors provides.

It is with its Arab neighbors of the Gulf region that Iraq's relations become the most critical and sometimes contradictory. Those relations became prickly after the overthrow of the monarchy in the 1958 revolution in Iraq, and each Iraqi reassertion of claim to Kuwait and of dominance over the Gulf region heightened the tensions, as occurred in 1971. When the Gulf states, including

Figure 16-4. *Spiral minaret, Samarra, Iraq. Built in the ninth century when Samarra was the capital of the Abbasid Empire. Figures at base give scale of this unusual minaret, 171 ft./52 m high, which served the Friday Mosque glimpsed at lower left.*

Saudi Arabia, organized the Gulf Cooperation Council, they discouraged Iraq's inclusion. Yet when Iraq desperately required assistance after its invasion of Iran in 1980, proclaiming itself the bastion of Arabism against Persian designs, all the Gulf states came to its aid with billions of dollars and other assistance. Monetary, material, moral, and political support flowed into Iraq from all its Arab neighbors except Syria. Kuwait and Saudi Arabia were especially helpful. In addition to their financial aid, they helped with proxy shipments of oil on Iraq's OPEC quota and

account, and Saudi Arabia agreed to the construction of the IPSA pipeline to the Red Sea. Iraq's about-face invasion of Kuwait and attacks on Saudi Arabia during the Gulf war were, therefore, all the more inexplicable. The timing of a resumption of moderate relations between Iraq and the Gulf states was difficult to forecast in early 1993.

Following its alienation from the West after 1958, Iraq turned to the USSR, accepting USSR military supplies denied by the West. Iraq intermittently retreated from other relations with the

Soviets. Iraqi-Soviet relations were strained by the Soviet Union's support of Syria and even Iran, and cautious relations between Iraq and the West were resumed after 1980, affording Iraq a more balanced support system during its life-or-death struggle with Iran. Iraq also thus positioned itself to receive assistance from the West in the late 1980s just as the Soviet Union disintegrated.

Although relations with Turkey had been passive for decades, they were reinvigorated in the mid-1970s by the agreement on the pipeline from Kirkuk to Yumurtalık. Further agreements regarding the pipelines and Turkey's receiving oil supplies through the system afforded increasingly close relations and greater trade between Iraq and Turkey. However, this mutually beneficial rapport collapsed overnight in August 1990 when Turkey reluctantly agreed to abide by the UN sanctions against Iraq.

The historical antagonism between the people of the Mesopotamian Basin and those of the Iranian Plateau intensified and finally broke out in open warfare between Iran and Iraq in September 1980 (see Chap. 11). After the eight years of fighting, it was ironic that in 1990, President Saddam Husayn should renounce in Iran's favor all that Iraq gained by its Pyrrhic victory in order to keep Iran neutral and thus avert the danger of having to fight on two fronts. Curiously, Iraq's relations with non-Arab Iran in mid-1992 were warmer than those with its Arab neighbors.

U.S.-Iraqi relations following the 1958 revolution in Baghdad were little more than "correct," and Iraq broke relations with the United States after the 1967 Arab-Israeli war on the basis that the United States had assisted Israel during that conflict. Quiet improvements in contacts during the late 1970s finally led, in December 1984, to a resumption of full diplomatic relations. The détente survived both the revelation of the U.S.-Israeli arms sales to Iran and also the May 1987 Iraqi nighttime Exocet missile strike on the U.S. Navy frigate *Stark* while it patrolled Gulf waters. The United States made many gestures toward Iraq in the late 1980s in an effort to "build bridges"; it provided food shipments and badly needed machinery and other goods on favorable credit terms, then bought 100,000 bpd of Iraqi crude oil for cash. Opponents in both countries minimized the attempts at rapprochement, and U.S. efforts were heavily criticized, especially after Iraq invaded Kuwait; however, such efforts are standard approaches and have been used with considerable success with other countries. The policy did fail in Iraq, and U.S.-Iraqi relations sank to an all-time low during the Gulf war, in which the United States took the lead in policy and in operations against Iraq. For more than a year after the war—including leading in establishing the 32nd parallel as a "no-fly" zone in southern Iraq in mid-1992—the United States took the hardest line of any country against Iraq and seemed likely to maintain it until an appreciable modification of the Iraqi government occurs.

Iraq continues to be a country with many assets but beset by major problems and challenges. It cannot afford morally or economically to resume the internecine struggle that has absorbed its energies, humanity, and treasure for so many years. Iraq faces difficulties that will test its resolution and capabilities, including the crucial problem of a new Iraq-Kuwait boundary delineated in May 1992 by UN surveyors.

17

Saudi Arabia: Development in the Desert

The Arabian Peninsula (Arabic, *Jazirat al-Arab*— Island of the Arabs) has played a significant role through 7,000 years of Middle East history and into the present. Three especially important roles should be emphasized. One, it served as the source area for Semitic peoples who migrated into the Fertile Crescent as Akkadians, Amorites, Assyrians, Aramaeans, and Chaldeans; as smaller groups that included Canaanites, Hebrews, Edomites, and Nabataeans; and, of particular interest, as Arabs in the seventh century. Two, it is the cradle of Islam, the religion of more than 935 million people, and the destination of more than 2 million pilgrims to Mecca every year. Also, hundreds of millions of Muslims face toward Mecca for prayers five times daily. Three, under its eastern margins lie 47 percent of the world's known petroleum reserves. Seven states occupy the Arabian Peninsula: Saudi Arabia, the four Gulf states (see Chap. 18), and Oman and Yemen (see Chap. 19).

Saudi Arabia: A Preview

Saudi Arabia figures prominently in international rankings for both geographical and economic reasons. It is the largest country in the Middle East as delineated in this book (Sudan is a larger Arab country) and ranks twelfth in size in the world. Among the countries of the world, it possesses the largest reserves of petroleum, largest single oil reservoir, largest-capacity oil export terminal, one of the two or three largest-capacity petroleum refineries, largest oil storage tanks, longest natural gas liquids pipeline, larg-

est-capacity seawater desalination plant, and largest airport.

Saudi Arabia possesses significant contemporary characteristics other than those related to petroleum and to the religion of Islam. Although politically conservative and internationally oriented toward the West, the country's economic power reinforces its independence and the development of its distinctive assets. It possesses the longest Red Sea coast of all the littoral states; its Gulf coast is second longest after that of Iran. It adjoins every state on the peninsula plus Jordan and Iraq. Although it maintains a comparatively low profile politically and militarily, it has worked toward internal stability and a modest defense capability.

Funded with petrodollars, Saudi Arabian development proceeded rapidly after about 1960, requiring millions of foreign consultants, managers, and laborers, yet the kingdom preserved most of the indigenous traditional social values. The Saudis demonstrated a socioeconomic resilience in their adaptation to both two decades of affluence and the years of recession after 1982, the disturbing years of the eight-year Iran-Iraq war, and the traumatic Gulf war of 1990–1991. Current planning focuses on the development of human services and resources—planners, managers, and workers—to replace at least some of the expatriate technicians by a new generation of educated Saudis who are trained in the skills needed in the country's economy.

Saudi Arabia is a young nation—dating from only 1932, although it was developing for 30 years prior. It was born of a special combination of cir-

SAUDI ARABIA

Long-form official name, anglicized: Kingdom of Saudi Arabia
Official name, transliterated: al-Mamlakah al-Arabiyah al-Saudiyah
Form of government: traditional monarchy; Consultative Council planned
Area: 865,000 miles^2/2,240,000 km^2 (area imprecise, since some land boundaries undelimited)
Population, 1991: 14,691,000 (rough estimate; includes many expatriates). Literacy (latest): 62.4%
Ethnic composition (%): Saudi 84.0, Yemeni 7.6, other Arab 3.0, other (Indian, Pakistani, Filipino, American, British, other expatriates) 5.4
Religions (%): Muslim (mostly Sunni) 98.8, Christian 0.8, other 0.4
GNP, 1989: $89.99 billion; per capita: $6.230
Petroleum reserves: 257,504 billion barrels (world's largest)
Main exports (% of total value, 1989): crude petroleum 54.0; refined petroleum 18.9; other 27.1
Main imports (% of total value, 1989): transport equipment 18.5; machinery and appliances 18.4; foodstuffs and tobacco 15.9; textiles and clothing 9.9; metals and metal articles 8.2; chemicals 6.7
Capital city: al-Riyadh 1,308,000; other cities: Jiddah 1,500,000; Mecca 666,940; al-Taif (summer capital) 514,410; Medina 360,353

cumstances and has adhered to many of the traditions that were and are an integral part of its raison d'être. Such conservatism has strengthened the Saudi social fabric and, conversely, has both weakened the nation's social evolution and attracted foreign criticism. This contradiction received widespread attention when Saudi Arabia played host to several hundred thousand foreign troops, support groups, and media personnel from 33 countries, along with thousands of planes, tanks, and vehicles, during the Gulf crisis and war in late 1990 and early 1991. Although the Saudis were well aware that the forces were present in a protective role and were not on vacation in the kingdom, they were also apprehensive that most of the forces represented many social mores and values to which the conservative Saudis had long been antipathetic. For the first time in the kingdom's history, huge numbers of people and matériel were in the country without specific invitations and were not under Saudi control. Strict Saudi rules, regulations, and customs—which were considerably exaggerated in early media reports—were soon adapted and adjusted, and goodwill on all sides permitted a reasonably smooth operation for the six months of the crisis.

Historical-Political Geography

Limited archaeological exploration of the peninsula before the mid-1970s found evidence of widespread ancient occupation, settlement sites, and burial mounds. Dramatic discoveries in the mid-1980s confirmed that bands of *homo erectus* had brought their Developed Oldowan tool culture from the Olduvai Gorge area in East Africa to western Arabia more than one million years ago (see Chap. 2). Late Paleolithic and Neolithic tools found in the now-barren Rub al-Khali were left by hunters or settlers along old lakeshores more than 17,000 years ago and again 10,000–5,000 years ago.[1] Finds along the northeastern coast and on Tarut Island reveal ties with Mesopotamian civilizations of 2500 BC and earlier (see Map 2-1).

A retracing of old trade routes has shown that many towns depended economically on serving one of the several main caravan tracks. The major ancient route from Aden led northward through Asir and the Hijaz to the caravansary and watering point of Mecca before continuing northward. Traffic along this route in the early seventh century influenced the emergence of Islam.

When the focus of political and military power of Islam passed from Mecca and Medina to Damascus in the seventh century and later to Baghdad, the role of the Hijaz and of Arabia diminished for several centuries. Most of Arabia remained a frontier zone, isolated and tribally fragmented. With the breakdown of the Abbasid caliphate (1258), Mamluk Egyptian control extended to the Hijaz holy places. Mamluk control passed in turn to the Ottomans when the Turks conquered Egypt in 1517. The peninsula's interior evolved separately, leading to the emergence in the eighteenth century of the family of Al Saud. Battling other tribes and clans, the Sauds achieved a leading role in Najd, the central plateau core of the Arabian Peninsula. Najd has continued to be the Saudi power nucleus.

In the mid-eighteenth century, Al Saud leader Muhammad ibn Saud allied the family with a religious reformer, Muhammad ibn Abd al-Wahhab, linking Saudi political-military power and Muslim puritanism. The resulting religious belief is sometimes called "unitarian" and sometimes, inappropriately, Wahhabi. From their center in al-Diriyah near Riyadh, the two leaders had expanded Saudi control of most of the peninsula by the early 1800s. Wary of the growing Saudi strength, the Ottomans ordered Muhammad Ali of Egypt to overthrow the Sauds and to reestablish Ottoman authority over the holy Hijaz. The Egyptians captured the Saudi capital of al-Diriyah in 1818, destroyed its forts, and interrupted Al Saud dominance but failed to eradicate Saudi power. A few years later, the Sauds regained their lost territories, except in the Hijaz, and established a new capital in Riyadh, where it has remained.

With Saudi leadership weakened by family disputes, the Ottomans occupied al-Hasa in the eastern part of the peninsula; and the Rashids, a family contending against the Sauds, asserted control over much of the Najd. Al Saud leaders took refuge in Kuwait, from which a young Saud, Abd al-Aziz ibn Abd al-Rahman, regained control of Riyadh and Najd in 1902. As the new family leader, Abd al-Aziz organized many of the Bedouins into groups of *ikhwan* ("brethren") and gradually reclaimed control over most of the peninsula. He annexed the last major area in 1924–1925 when his *ikhwan* warriors conquered the Hijaz—the western highlands and coast of the peninsula. This former Ottoman province, governed by the Hashimite family of the Sharif Husayn of Arab Revolt fame, included the holy cities of Mecca and Medina; and control of them gave Abd al-Aziz the distinction of being Servitor of the Two Sanctuaries.

In January 1927, Abd al-Aziz was officially proclaimed King of the Hijaz and Najd and Its Dependencies, with Mecca and Riyadh as his capitals. In the Treaty of Jiddah (1927), Great Britain recognized the status quo in Arabia. On September 22, 1932, Abd al-Aziz, who became known in the West as Ibn Saud, renamed the country the Kingdom of Saudi Arabia, still the official designation.[2]

Abd al-Aziz accepted the concept of modernization of the country and persuaded the ultra-conservative religious leaders to accept new technologies: automobiles, radio, telephone, aircraft, and television. After 50 years of rule, Abd al-Aziz died in 1953 and was followed by a succession of sons—Saud ibn Abd al-Aziz, Faysal ibn Abd al-Aziz, Khalid ibn Abd al-Aziz, and since 1982, Fahd ibn Abd al-Aziz.

Reflecting the joint power structure, Saudi Arabia is controlled by the Saud family, specifically represented by the Al Saud member serving as king, and by the religious leaders of the country, the ulama. The ulama influence the choice of the Saud family member to be named as the next king, and they intervene if the king departs from conservative Islam. The king thus faces constraints on policies and actions, with respect to modernization, for example. Yet the escalating pressure and need for liberalization in the late 1980s and especially in the early 1990s prompted the government to respond. As in the past, the Sauds sought the delicate balance between modernism and conservatism—in this case, between the demands of the young, educated, and more progressive Saudis and the traditional influence of the older, more religious conservatives. In March 1992, the government announced a new constitution that provides for a 60-member consultative council (*majlis al-shura*) that can initiate laws and review policies, a bill of rights, and a generally more liberal approach to political relationships. The ultimate power of the monarchy appears to be undiminished, and the king later stated that free elections, however well suited they might be in European-style democracies, were not appropriate in the traditional societies of the Arabian Peninsula. There was also no indication of a change in the kingdom's customary status of women.

Thus, the steps taken were limited and cautious and were consistent with the Saudi practice of pursuing evolution rather than revolution, which the Sauds consider to have been so disruptive in Iraq, Iran, and the former South Yemen. Caught between strong opposing pressures from progressives and Western influences on the one hand and traditionalists (who are in turn pushed by fundamentalist extremists) on the other hand, King Fahd had achieved little outward liberalization a year after the announcement of the new reforms. Predictably, the more liberal Saudis were disappointed in how little was gained and the more conservative in how much was granted.[3] Time will tell whether gains in the sociopolitical realm during the 1990s will resemble the patently remarkable economic and material development in Saudi Arabia during the past 30 years.

Physical Patterns

Diversity in the Desert

Despite the preponderance of desert in the country, Saudi Arabia's landforms exhibit great diversity, even in the sizes, shapes, and colors of dunes in the extensive sand deserts.[4] The relatively green mountains of Asir in the southwest are especially differentiated from the rest of the country. Scarped sedimentary Najd in the center, crystalline shield Najd farther west, lava-covered areas in the north and the west, and immense sand seas in north, south, and east contrast with one another in both geomorphology and cultural character.

The gross geomorphological characteristics of the peninsula are influenced by its formation as a separate tectonic plate that split from northeastern Africa along the Red Sea rift during the Tertiary period (see Chap. 3). The west-central third is a massive crystalline block of Precambrian igneous and metamorphic rocks, with young basalts on the west. Eastward, sedimentary layers cover the rest of the peninsula, except in al-Hajar in Oman, with strata dipping generally eastward and with successively younger outcrops toward the Gulf. Sand seas and sand dunes blanket more than one-third of the peninsula, including the Nafud in the north, the Rub al-Khali in the south, and the arc of the Dahna dunes connecting the two.

Regions

[1] **Tihamah.** Starting on the west, the first natural region (see circled numbers on Map 17-1) consists of a sandy-gravelly coastal plain, Tihamah, which extends virtually the full length of the Red Sea coast. Squeezed between the coast and the rugged Hijaz range, Tihamah varies in width from only a few meters at the Gulf of Aqabah to more than 25 miles/40 km near Jaizan in the south. The plain is referred to in the north as Tihamat al-Sham, in the center as Tihamat al-Hijaz, and in the south as Tihamat Asir. Although it is naturally barren and forbidding, almost waterless between infrequent rains, and lacking significant harbor indentations, Tihamah has been a major route of passage for centuries. Small ports—Wajh, Yanbu, Jiddah, Jaizan—somehow persevered, supported by fishing and limited trade, with Jiddah serving as a passenger port for Mecca pilgrims after the seventh century. Modern development has produced a first-class highway running the entire length of the coast, with Jiddah—one of Saudi Arabia's two largest cities—extending for several miles along the central Tihamah shoreline. Almost unlimited funds permitted construction of the kingdom's largest port at Jiddah, with excellent facilities also at the recently expanded Yanbu and the old city of Jaizan.

[2] **Hijaz-Asir Mountains.** To the east of the coastal plain is a mountain belt ranging in width from 25 to 87 miles/40 to 140 km. It is generally low in the north but increases in elevation toward the south, with crest elevations reaching 6,987 ft./2,130 m northwest of Medina and 9,840 ft./3,000 m near Abha. A gap in the mountain belt near Mecca has been used for a travel route for centuries. It is from this formidable uplifted

Map 17-1. *Reference map of Saudi Arabia. Circled numbers correspond to regions discussed in text.*

crystalline mountain block that the name for the western region—al-Hijaz ("the barrier")—is derived. The elevated southern segment constitutes Asir, the best-watered area of Saudi Arabia, receiving 12–20 in./300–500 mm of precipitation annually, much of it during the summer monsoon. In addition to the Asir rainfall, the Hijaz crestline receives the most winter rainfall of any part of the kingdom. Nestled in barren volcanic basins in the central Hijaz are the two most sacred cities in Islam, Mecca and Medina, and also the summer capital city, al-Taif. In Asir are found the rapidly expanding agricultural and resort area around Abha, the military area of Khamis

Mushayt, and the pleasant Najran district. National parks west of Abha attract thousands of visitors, with spectacular views down the great seaward-facing escarpment and hundreds of hamadryas baboons scampering through the wooded uplands.

[3] **Najd.** Continuing eastward from the central segment of the uplifted Hijaz-Asir highland and extending to the middle of the peninsula is the main crystalline block of the Arabian Shield. It comprises granites, gabbros, gneisses, schists, marbles, and related rocks. Like most shield areas, the Arabian Shield has mineralized areas,

with deposits of copper, gold, silver, lead, zinc, and other metals. However, unlike most other such areas, these mineral occurrences are limited, although numerous ancient gold and silver workings have been found through intensive searches by U.S., French, and Saudi geologists. Only a few of the many discoveries, including one major gold deposit, have proved to be worth exploiting on a modern large-scale commercial basis.

Along the western edge are six major lava fields, 390–7,720 miles²/1,000–20,000 km² in extent, which are dotted with numerous lava cones and cinder cones in north-south alignments. One of these relatively young basalt flows near Medina dates from as recently as AD 1250. As Map 6-2 shows, extensive areas of the crystalline shield between the Hijaz Mountains and central Najd are virtually uninhabited.

East of the shield and distinctly contrasting with it is sedimentary Najd, a part of the central plateau with outcropping sedimentary rocks in a great curved belt around the eastern edge of the crystalline basement. Escarpments, ridges, and buttes, each with a resistant cap, are characteristic features around this Central Arabian Arch. One particular escarpment, an Upper Jurassic limestone cuesta extending along a 1,000-mile/1,600-km crescent, forms Jabal Tuwayq, the most prominent physiographic feature of central Arabia. All of these outcropping strata dip eastward and are found at depths several thousand feet below the surface in the oil fields of eastern Arabia. The outcropping layers of sedimentary rocks in eastern Najd both serve as catchment rocks for aquifers that are tapped in the Eastern Province and also provide conditions for many local contact springs. These springs gave rise to numerous ancient and still persisting Najd settlements, and their presence prompted the drilling of water wells in modern times.

Groups of villages around several central places and coordination of agricultural activity have resulted in the evolution of a subregional consciousness along the Jabal Tuwayq. The main subregion in the north is al-Qasim, located west of the Tuwayq cuesta and centered on the large towns of Buraydah and Unayzah, southeast of Hayil.[5] South-southeast of al-Qasim and still west of Jabal Tuwayq is the Washm subregion,

embracing several small towns and a vastly expanded agricultural economy. East of al-Qasim, on the backslope of the Tuwayq escarpment, is the Sudayr, centered on Majmaah and less populated than al-Qasim. All three districts experienced remarkable development of irrigation agriculture during the 1980s. Southeast of Riyadh is the subregion of al-Kharj, which has significant solution springs and has long been one of the largest oases in the peninsula. Modern techniques were introduced in al-Kharj by U.S. irrigation specialists in the early 1950s. Extending southward from al-Kharj along a secondary cuesta are two well-defined subregions: al-Hawtah, with the villages of al-Hillah and al-Hilway, and, farther south, al-Aflaj, centered on Layla. Al-Aflaj refers to the irrigation system that formerly supported extensive gardens around Layla. The Hawtah subregion was launched into a local oil boom in the period 1989–1991 with the discovery of completely new petroleum fields extending 47 miles/75 km from the southern Hawtah to al-Dilam, south of al-Kharj.

[4] **Dahna, Summan, Coastal Plain.** Between Najd and the Gulf coast lie three belts that generally parallel the arcuate Jabal Tuwayq. All are generally considered to be in the Eastern Province, and they contain most of the Saudi Arabian oil fields: the Dahna, a great arc of rust-colored sand dunes 30 miles/48 km wide and extending from the Nafud in the north to the Rub al-Khali in the south; al-Summan plateau, with escarpments and buttes on its eastern margins; and near the Gulf coast, an irregular plain terminating in a ragged coastline of *sabkhahs*, sand spits, and offshore sandbars.

Under the plateau and coastal plain, as well as offshore, are the world's greatest petroleum reservoirs, now well delineated and intensively exploited. Except for the Hofuf Oasis and two or three small coastal villages, this vast realm was the haunt of the Bedouins and their camels prior to World War II. Now it throbs with hundreds of oil wells flowing under high pressure, gas-oil separator plants, flow lines, pump stations, heavy traffic on a dense road net, oil-related industries, sprawling cities, bustling ports, and a still-expanding general economy. The nerve center of the vast operation is the oil-company headquarters in Dhahran, near which lie the University for Petroleum and Minerals, the older international airport and the huge new airport, and, on the coast, the growing cities of Dammam (the provincial capital) and al-Khobar and its residential suburb of Thuqbah. North of Dammam is the great oil-export terminal and refinery of Ras Tanura.

[5] **Rub al-Khali.** Vast seas of sand in the north and south of the country constitute two of the most distinctive physical features on the peninsula. The largest single dune field in the world, the Rub al-Khali (Empty Quarter) covers more than 230,000 miles²/600,000 km². Referred to simply as al-Riml ("the Sands") by Bedouins, the Rub al-Khali comprises almost entirely loose, dry sand shaped into dunes that vary from one sector of the desert to another depending upon the wind. Three types of dune predominate: numerous linear or longitudinal dunes (*uruq;* singular, *irq*), some of them 60 miles/100 km long, in the western half (see Fig. 1-1); barchans or crescentic dunes in the northeast; and giant dunes, the remarkable Sand Mountains, along the eastern and southern margins. Formless "sand seas" fill other areas. Although limited areas exhibit some vegetation, the Rub al-Khali's loose sands are relatively barren, and because so few wells exist in the area, even Bedouins generally avoid the vast desert. Al Murrah and occasional other tribesmen move along the edges and infrequently cross it.[6]

[6] **The Nafud.** In the northwest is the great Nafud, called by the Bedouins simply *al-Nafud,* the northern term for "sandy desert." Characterized by complex dune forms including deep pits, the reddish sands of the Nafud cover 45,000 miles²/116,550 km². The sediment source for the sand is an extensive area of poorly cemented Paleozoic sandstones that lie upwind from the Nafud. The Nafud is sparsely inhabited but constitutes an important seasonal grazing area.

[7] **Northern Regions.** To the northwest, north, and east is a sequence of varied landscapes, each with its own identification. In the extreme northwest, at the northern end of the Red Sea, is the rugged area of Midyan (biblical land of Midian),

which drops eastward to the plain around the steadily developing military cantonment town of Tabuk. Farther east is the mountain mass of al-Tubayq, which sinks northeastward to the Wadi al-Sirhan, the great depression extending from al-Azraq in Jordan to the oasis of al-Jawf in Saudi Arabia. The depression is more than 200 miles/322 km long, about 25 miles/40 km wide, and 1,000 ft./305 m below the level of the plateau. The Wadi al-Sirhan gives way on the northeast to the extensive lava fields and cinder cones of al-Harrah, southeast of which extend al-Hamad, al-Widyan, and al-Hajarah, stony plains traversed by the Trans-Arabian Pipe Line (Tapline). Southwest of Kuwait is the well-marked Wadi al-Batin and the great gravel plain of the Dibdibah.

Most of these vast northern regions had virtually no permanent inhabitants prior to 1950, when the great Trans-Arabian Pipe Line (Tapline) spanned the desert wastes and gradually opened the sandy-gravelly plains to development. Towns grew up around the pump stations, and international travelers followed the pipeline track, which was later blacktopped and then upgraded to a major highway. Each of the pump-station towns now exceeds 25,000 in population and functions as a service center for traffic along the long stretches of the highway. The military cantonment of Hafar al-Batin built near Qaysumah has attracted special development and served as a key center for ground forces during the buildup and operations in the Gulf war in 1990–1991.

Population and Peoples

Census-taking in Saudi Arabia is both a complicated procedure and a sensitive matter: It is complicated because the population is widely scattered over a large area, Bedouins move frequently and dislike government attention, urban populations shift rapidly, and expatriates present special problems of enumeration; it is sensitive because Saudis are reluctant to recognize that millions of foreign professionals and workers have been brought in to help develop the kingdom. Also, this land of the cradle of Islam is averse to acknowledging that perhaps 8–10 percent of the population—however temporary—is non-Muslim. A 1963 sampling displaced the Saudi gov-

Figure 17-1. *New Ministry of Interior building, Riyadh. The structure was not quite completed when photographed in 1990. Many of the government and office buildings in the Saudi capital exhibit unusual architectural design.*

ernment, and a census in 1974 gave uncertain and puzzling results. Population in the early 1990s is variously estimated to be between 9 million and 14.5 million. A new census planned for 1993 should help to clarify the problem.

Saudi Arabia has three principal population nuclei and a few outlying foci, all separated by relatively empty or sparsely settled desert. Most populous of the three population nuclei is Najd, with its node in greater Riyadh, which now has about 1.5 million inhabitants (Fig. 17-1). Relatively concentrated Najd settlements extend from Hayil and Buraydah in the north southeastward to al-Kharj in the south, and there are a score of towns of small to medium size in the irrigated depressions on the plateau and along the escarpments, as was mentioned in the paragraph on Region 3, Najd.

In the west, the Hijaz-Asir nucleus is aligned on the Jiddah-Mecca-Taif (al-Taif) axis, and it contains about 2.8 million people. The extended area reaches from Yanbu and Medina in the north to Jaizan and Najran in the south and includes Abha and Khamis Mushayt in the rapidly developing resort and agricultural Asir. Across the peninsula, the Eastern Province population is more compact than that of the other two cores. It centers on Dammam Municipality (which includes Qatif, Dammam, Dhahran, al-Khobar, and al-Thuqbah) and has a population of 800,000. The extended concentration extends from the new industrial port city of Jubayl on the north to Hofuf in al-Hasa Oasis on the south and

includes Qatif Oasis, the oil terminals of Juaymah and Ras Tanura, the coalesced populations of al-Khobar, al-Thuqbah, and Dhahran, and the oil-producing center of Abqaiq.

Outlying centers with sizable populations include Tabuk, in the northwestern corner of the kingdom, with more than 100,000 population; the Hayil Oasis, south of the Nafud, with about 80,000; al-Jawf Oasis, north of the Nafud; settlements along Tapline; and the smaller settlements of al-Khamasin and al-Sulayyil toward the southern end of the Jabal Tuwayq.

Prior to the petroleum age in Saudi Arabia, an estimated 60 percent of the population was nomadic; by the early 1990s, the number of Bedouins was estimated at less than 4 percent. To some extent, the decrease was due to the demand for labor in the eastern oil fields and in major urban centers after the mid-1960s, but most of these workers were not Bedouins. The rural population, which supplied most of the labor, has dropped from more than 80 percent in the prepetroleum age to less than 25 percent in 1992. Although the indigenous Saudi population is relatively uniform ethnically, it includes diverse tribal affiliations. The number and ethnic variety of expatriate workers and managers also diversify the population. Having avoided the migrations and invasions experienced by the Fertile Crescent countries, and lacking habitable mountain masses for places of refuge for migrant groups, Saudi Arabia does not have the pockets of ethnic minorities that are typical of Syria and Iraq. On the other hand, during the thirteen centuries of annual pilgrimage seasons in Mecca, some pilgrims have remained, adding to the Saudi ethnic mixture such cultures as those from the East Indies, Bengal, Punjab, Iran, Morocco, and other Muslim areas. Such diversity is evident in the Hijaz.

In coastal Asir, the inhabitants display some African traits, combined with characteristics that are neither typically Arab nor African. In the Qatif and Hofuf oases of the Eastern Province, some inhabitants are descendants of Iranians who settled on the Arabian Peninsula several centuries ago, bringing Shii Islam to the predominantly Sunni peninsula.

Clothing is also traditional. Males wear the loose-fitting, ankle-length white *thawb* (see Fig. 6-1), similar to the *dishdashah* worn in the Gulf area. In cool weather and on more formal occasions, the flowing cloak (*bisht* or *mishlah*) is worn over the *thawb*. The head covering for both outdoors and indoors is the ubiquitous *ghutrah* and *igal,* the headcloth and double ring of black cord to hold the *ghutrah* (called a *kufiyah* in the Levant) in place. Workers in the oil industry and other industrial plants commonly wear Western-style work pants and shirts during the day. A female in public wears the loose, floor-length *abayah* over her head and body. The *abayah* may cover a dress similar to the male *thawb,* except that it is usually colorful, or it may cover the latest Paris fashion. Any of several types of veil or partial face covering may be added to the *abayah.*

The marginal economy and lack of population unity and security in past centuries prompted many kinship groups to seek localized order in tribalism. Although modernization since the 1950s has weakened this tribalism, a diminished tribal identity retains its validity among many Saudis, especially Bedouins. In this highly traditional society, village organization and tribal affiliation remain basic social factors among both settled and nomadic populations.

Foreign workers were drawn to the oil fields and cities of Saudi Arabia as early as the 1940s but arrived in large numbers after the early 1970s. They have become a significant proportion of the population and are estimated to number 3–4 million, about one-fourth to one-third of the population. More than half of the foreign (or ex-patriate) workers are Asians. Yemenis have traditionally been the largest single national group and may have numbered 1–1.5 million or more during the 1980s. Because of the Yemen government's opposition to the military action against Iraq after the Iraqi invasion of Kuwait, at least 800,000 Yemeni workers were forced by the Saudi government to return home in late 1990. The size of the expatriate community is meticulously controlled and varies sharply with the country's oil revenues and development budget. No one is given a visa to enter the country unless the person is sponsored by the Saudi government or by a company or institution that the government can hold responsible. No casual salesmen, fortune seekers, or tourists are permitted to enter. Hence the uneasiness of the Saudis over the presence of nearly half a million foreign troops in the kingdom in 1990–1991.

Settlements

Although traditions of nomadism are strong in the Arabian Peninsula, sedentarism preceded nomadism. Until after World War II, the typical pattern of settlement consisted of widely scattered oasis villages and occasional towns in a symbiotic relationship with nomadic Bedouins living in their long rectangular tents. Nor were the two life-styles mutually exclusive: During severe droughts, Bedouins moved into villages; conversely, villagers—especially former nomads—sometimes moved into the desert. Settlement of the Bedouins has been a deliberate policy of the government of Saudi Arabia since the time of King Abd al-Aziz. The petroleum age also stimulated sedentarization of the nomads, contributing to urbanization. Permanently settled nomads consider themselves *hadar,* that is, no longer Bedouins.

Since World War II, urbanization has accelerated in Saudi Arabia as elsewhere, with increased growth of cities after the development of the petroleum industry. No extensive preindustrial cities had developed in Arabia, and even the largest settlements—Mecca and Medina, for example—were moderate-sized towns of 30,000 population each in the 1930s. Nevertheless, few towns or cities in Saudi Arabia of the 1990s exist on completely new sites; even the "new towns" of Jubayl

Figure 17-2. *University of Petroleum and Minerals in Dhahran. Built in the 1960s on a stretch of sand and rock south of Aramco headquarters, it was the first of several new universities built in Saudi Arabia with some of the rising oil income and represents the plans for a modernized and technological segment in Saudi society.*

and Yanbu are extensions of earlier villages. The country's urban areas have completely reconstructed centers, and historic structures have often been replaced with international-style high-rise buildings. Similarly, the traditional architecture of picturesque walls and fortress towers has given way to ring roads and office buildings.

Building styles and internal urban structure in Arabia draw on Islamic traditions, with some additional Arabian architectural features (Fig. 17-2). In the mountain villages of Asir, exterior house walls typically show alternating courses of mud and projecting rock, with the rock ledges deflecting rain to prevent erosion of the primarily mud walls. Typical building walls in Najd are topped by decorative battlements, vestiges of military architectural features. In Najd, but also in other parts of the country, the wooden doors of many houses are decorated with elaborate geometric designs. Traditional architectural features are rapidly giving way to modern convenience and efficiency, and travelers into interior Arabia in the late 1900s could only lament the

disappearance of these regional features of folk art.

Economic Patterns

Economic patterns in Arabia had remained stable for centuries when discovery of petroleum in 1938 initiated a literally fabulous transformation. Prior to 1938, the remote and generally poor Arabian realm survived on limited pastoralism and oasis agriculture, profits from the Mecca pilgrimage, and meager trade. With modest but increasing oil production after 1945, during the 1950s and 1960s the kingdom caught a glimpse of things to come, then exploded with development during the 1970s. National income from oil sales alone exceeded $300 million per day between 1977 and 1981, supplying billions of dollars for perhaps the most complete transformation of a large country on a grand scale and in a short time in history. Drawing on urban and systems planners, design engineers, architects, contractors, educators, and workers from Western Europe, North America, the Middle East, and South Asia, Saudi Arabia virtually built an entire country from infrastructure to complete university campuses to U.S.-style fast-food shops. Private financing and investment contributed the retail centers, many of the industries, and much of the agricultural expansion.

Much of the development has taken place under a series of five-year plans, with a peak during the $195-billion second plan, 1975–1980, when 28 dams, 4 ports, 175,000 new homes, 15,000 miles/24,000 km of roads, and Jiddah airport (the world's largest until the opening of the Riyadh airport) were completed. Before and after this period, water projects, industrial developments, petroleum operations, infrastructure, the billion-dollar causeway to Bahrain, and other operations were constructed or greatly expanded. The fourth plan, 1985–1990, had to be curtailed because of the recession that followed the sharp drop in the world oil market in 1982. Saudi oil sales dropped from 9.6 million bpd in 1980 to 3.3 million bpd in 1985, and the price per barrel plummeted from $35–40 per barrel in 1980 to $10–12 per barrel in 1985—both occurring at a time when the value of the U.S. dollar was shrinking. This triple impact reduced gross income from oil by almost 90 percent, and even though the economy had become much more diversified, total revenue fell by more than 75 percent between 1981 and 1988. The fifth five-year plan, 1990–1995, calls for less than $100 billion in development spending, but that amount may be increased as oil production continues to increase.[7]

Each development plan programmed economic diversification so that the kingdom would not be at the mercy of oil prices and, in the longer range, so it would develop viability for the time following the depletion of oil resources. Early planning emphasized energy-intensive and capital-intensive operations, since Saudi Arabia had enormous supplies of oil and gas and petrodollars but a critical lack of labor at all levels. Thus, the kingdom had a population smaller than London's occupying an area one-fourth that of the United States executing huge development programs that were dependent primarily on imported labor, services, and materials. In recent years, development has emphasized

Figure 17-3. *Terraces in the relatively well-watered mountains of the Asir Province, southwestern Saudi Arabia.*

expansion and diversification of industry, especially nonpetroleum industry and import-substitution manufactures; expansion and diversification of agriculture; accelerated Saudization of labor in all sectors through education, training, and position substitution; and general emphasis on human resource development in education, health care, and human services.

Agriculture

The share of agriculture in the economy of Saudi Arabia decreased sharply after 1960, until its percentage contribution to the GDP was only 3 percent in the mid-1970s. The percentage then increased to 13 percent a decade later under encouragement of subsidies but fell to 7 percent in 1990. The number of workers engaged in agriculture, pastoralism, and fishing is increasing and is now 14.3 percent of the labor force. The Saudi government seeks greater self-reliance in agriculture, aiming for a long-range agricultural sufficiency. Crop production in Saudi Arabia relies overwhelmingly on irrigation, although rainfed agriculture dominates in Asir, where highlands intercept summer monsoon rains and the water is efficiently utilized on terraced plots (Fig. 17-3). Since 1973, the main emphasis has been expansion of the area under cultivation, mostly irrigated, and especially of the area planted to subsidized wheat. The amount of cultivated area increased from 704,000 acres/285,000 ha in 1973 to 3 million acres/1.2 million ha in 1990, with much of the expansion coming in wheat acreage. With the government offering many times the world market price for wheat produced domestically, wheat acreage rocketed from 370,650 acres/150,000 ha to 1.6 million acres/0.65 million ha in the decade after the mid-1970s. In 1981, wheat production was only 4,000 mt, but in 1989, it was 3.1 million mt. Since only 800,000 mt was needed domestically, the excess was exported or donated. The Najd landscape was completely transformed in the 1980s as hundreds of startlingly green circles of wheat irrigated by self-propelled center-pivot sprinkler systems appeared against the tawny desert as the Saudis made the desert produce grain.

Of the many oases in the kingdom, the two largest—both in the Eastern Province—are classic examples. Hofuf (al-Hasa) Oasis,[8] the largest on the peninsula and considered to be the largest groundwater-fed oasis in the world, is watered by 159 springs, including 8 major artesian springs (*ayns*) that flow a total of more than 1,900 gal./7,190 l per second. The largest single spring has a flow of 475 gal./1,800 l per second. A major project in the early 1970s modernized and systematized the oasis irrigation and drainage, replacing ditches with concrete conduits. Qatif (or al-Qatif) Oasis, a few miles north of Dammam, required much of the same modernization achieved in al-Hasa. Like most of the peninsula's oases, these two grow large amounts of date palms and other crops.

Although their number is decreasing, many thousands of Bedouins still pursue a nomadic life-style and continue to supply animals and animal products to the Saudi economy. Increasing numbers of Bedouin families divide their time between desert nomadism and crop raising or other economic pursuits in villages on the perimeters of their tribal *dirahs*.

Water resource studies have yielded approximations of the water balance, permitting systematic efforts for more effective use of renewable water resources. Hydrogeological studies reveal that much of the deep aquifer water in the Najd is "fossil water," stored as long ago as 40,000 years, and that water in the relatively shallow aquifers of the Eastern Province is 18,000–28,000 years old. Thus, withdrawing water from such aquifers amounts to "mining" nonrenewable resources, and systematic efforts must be made to substitute renewable water for fossil water, in the production of heavily subsidized wheat, for example.

Fundamental to the agricultural development program has been a series of water development projects that peaked in the late 1970s and added 170 dams, several hundred deep wells, and many miles of irrigation conduits. Most of the dams were constructed in the regions of Asir and Najd.

Domestic supplies and irrigation systems rely also on the desalination of seawater. Availability of large amounts of fuel prompted the initiation in 1965 of a massive construction program of large-scale desalination plants, of which there were 26 by the end of 1991 (20 on the Red Sea and 6 on the Gulf) with a capacity of 732 million m^3 per year—about 2 million m^3 per day. By 1992, desalted water, blended with brackish groundwater, supplied about 60 percent of home use in major cities. On the Gulf coast, desalination plants are operating in Khafji, Jubayl, al-Khobar, and Uqayr. The Jubayl plant is the biggest in the world and pumps millions of gallons per day of distilled water to Riyadh. As of the early 1990s, Saudi Arabia leads the world in the production of potable water by desalting seawater.

Fishing

Important on both coasts, fishing has been especially developed on the east coast. Traditional fishing methods have been replaced by modernized techniques and equipment, with ships operating primarily out of Dammam, and there are processing and freezing plants in Dammam and al-Khobar. Additional facilities are opening in the new port and industrial city of Jubayl. With all of the Gulf littoral states intensifying fishing efforts, over-fishing has occurred, and the total Gulf catch peaked in 1967–1968. Fish population and other marine life off the eastern coast suffered serious deterioration as one result of the deliberate massive pollution of the upper Gulf by the Iraqis in early 1991.

Petroleum Industry

Beneath the deserts of eastern Arabia, the world's largest petroleum reserves lay unrecognized until the 1930s. King Abd al-Aziz granted a concession for oil exploration to a British financial syndicate in 1923, but the syndicate did not pursue exploration and lost the concession. In 1933, the king granted Standard Oil of California (Socal) the exclusive right to prospect for and produce oil in eastern Arabia, along with preferential rights in other parts of the kingdom, for a period of 60 years—later extended for an additional six years. A new subsidiary, California Arabian Standard Oil Company (Casoc), was assigned the concession in 1934 and was converted to 50-50 ownership by Socal (which later became Chevron) and the Texas Company in 1937. In 1944 Casoc was renamed Arabian American Oil Company, with the now world-famous acronym Aramco, which is still used even for the Saudi-owned company. In 1948, the Standard Oil Company of New Jersey (later renamed Esso and still later Exxon) and the Socony-Vacuum Oil Company (later named Mobil) joined in the Aramco ownership. The four owner companies remained the all-U.S. capital and technical forces behind oil development in mainland Saudi Arabia until 1973.

Drilling started in April 1935 in Dammam Dome, near the Gulf coast, and production began in March 1938. The first oil was loaded in May 1939 at Ras Tanura, which was later developed into one of the world's great oil export terminals. Exploration for new fields—which continues 55 years later—soon showed that the Eastern Province contained the leading fields in the world. The first segment of Ghawar, the world's largest oil field, was found in 1948; Safaniya, the largest offshore field in the world, in 1951. By 1991, 60 commercial fields had been discovered (see Map 8-2), five in 1990 alone, making a total of seven new fields of especially valuable sweet, light crude found in two years south of Riyadh completely outside the formerly assumed oil areas; more than 60 billion barrels had been produced just by Aramco since 1938, yet reserves were 257.5 billion barrels and were expected to increase as the southern Najd fields are delineated; reserves of nonassociated natural gas exceeded 180.4 trillion ft.^{3}; and expansion programs were under way to increase production to 10 million bpd.

In 1973, Saudi Arabia assumed 25 percent ownership of Aramco's rights and facilities. Government participation increased to 60 percent in 1974 and to 100 percent in 1980. Officially designated the Saudi Arabian Oil Company, or Saudi Aramco, in 1988, Aramco continues to be known in the industry by its familiar 48-year-old acronym. Aramco continues as operator for Saudi production and as intermediate contractor for a range of engineering and construction projects. The company served such a function as early as 1949, overseeing construction of the Saudi government Dammam-Riyadh railway, and more recently by overseeing implementation of the Master Gas Plan. Aramco also expanded into overseas downstream operations in 1988 through a joint venture with Texaco for refining, distributing, and marketing petroleum products in the eastern and Gulf Coast regions of the United States.

Although Aramco manages 95 percent of the production for Saudi Arabia, two other companies operate in the Saudi half of the Divided Zone, the former Kuwait-Saudi Neutral Zone. The U.S.-owned Getty Oil Company holds the concession for the land area, and the Japanese-owned Arabian Oil Company (AOC) holds the offshore concession. The territory of the zone, which was partitioned in 1965 and demarcated in 1970, was divided roughly equally between Kuwait and Saudi Arabia. On a similar basis, the two countries agreed to share equally the oil reserves of the zone and to divide proceeds from oil produced there. Proved reserves of the entire zone totaled 5 billion barrels in 1991, and production averaged 359,000 bpd in 1985–1989, the Saudi half of which constituted from 2 to 4 percent of all the Saudi production.

As sole operator in the Eastern Province, Aramco needed to drill and produce only the optimum number of wells; even after half a century, none of the wells requires pumping. One reason for maintenance of reservoir pressure is the use of a water injection system, in which nonpotable brackish groundwater is pumped into major reservoirs as oil is withdrawn. Only about 850 wells are utilized to produce up to 9 million bpd in Saudi Arabia, thus averaging approximately 10,588 bpd each.

Handling, transporting, and processing the petroleum require a complex of facilities distributed across eastern Arabia—strung together with more than 13,050 miles/21,000 km of pipelines. Each of more than 60 gas-oil separator plants (GOSPs) serves several wells in a considerable radius via flowlines, each showing its fiery flare—

now reduced to conserve natural gas—against the sky. Stabilizers in Abqaiq and Juaymah "sweeten" sour crude, and natural gas liquids (NGL) plants produce propane, butane, and natural gasoline. A major downstream facility is the Ras Tanura refinery, opened in 1941 and expanded many times. It is located on the sand spit that gave the refinery its name, and it has a capacity that has been gradually enlarged to more than 530,000 bpd. There are also numerous large petroleum-related industrial plants along the Gulf coast, especially in the new industrially specialized city of Jubayl, and huge oil-export terminals operate at Ras Tanura and Juaymah (as well as at Yanbu on the Red Sea).

Large refineries have also been opened in Jubayl (280,000 bpd) and Yanbu (250,000 bpd for the export refinery and 170,000 bpd for the domestic refinery). Refineries in Riyadh (134,000 bpd), Jiddah (95,000 bpd), Rabigh (332,000 bpd), and Khafji (30,000 bpd) bring to eight the refineries onstream in Saudi Arabia in 1992, with a total capacity of 1.82 million bpd.

As Chapter 8 explained, the great Trans-Arabian Pipe Line (Tapline) that opened in 1951 was beset by problems and became unprofitable during the 1970s and was shut in—but not abandoned—by 1990. However, the Saudis had revived the concept of an outlet to the west, not for normal exports but for strategic insurance against the potential dangers of Gulf shipping and the Hormuz choke point. This led to billion-dollar spanning of the peninsula, from the eastern fields to Yanbu, with three pipelines during the 1980s: The East-West natural gas liquids (NGL) pipeline, 726 miles/1,170 km long and 26–30 in./66–76 cm in diameter, was commissioned in March 1981; and the East-West crude oil pipelines, one 48 in./122 cm in diameter, was commissioned in July 1981, and a "loop" of this line that is 56 in./142 cm in diameter was commissioned in 1987—both are 745 miles/1,200 km long. (The IPSA pipeline is a separate Iraqi project; see Chap. 16.) The addition of pumps and the expansion of facilities at each end of this East-West crude oil system in 1991 raised its capacity to nearly 5 million bpd—ten times Tapline's capacity and half of Aramco's production capacity. The parallel NGL line carries 270,000 bpd of ethane and natural gas liquids.

These transpeninsula systems afford the Saudis an entirely domestic, secure route that reduces the threat of a cutoff of Saudi exports. The Saudis are, however, still subject to an interdiction of their exports from Yanbu at either end of the Red Sea.

In the late 1970s, Saudi Arabia undertook the ambitious Master Gas System. Gas that was formerly flared after being separated from oil in gas-oil separator plants (GOSPs) now drives power generating stations, water desalination plants, a glass factory, and cement, fertilizer, and lime plants. Gas is also piped to the new industrial cities of Jubayl and Yanbu as fuel and feedstock for oil refineries, petrochemical and fertilizer plants, steel plants, and rolling mills, and other industries, as well as for large-scale exports. Designed to process 3.5 billion ft.^{3}/99 million m^3 of gas a day, the Master Gas System can add the equivalent of about 750,000 barrels of crude oil a day to the world's supply of energy.

Saudi Arabia was a charter member of both OPEC and OAPEC (see Chap. 8), and has played a particularly major role in OPEC since its founding. As Saudi production constituted an increasingly greater share of the OPEC and world totals, the country played a "swing role" in influencing the world price of petroleum by varying its output for several years.

Other Industries

In the 1950s, manufacturing expanded after four key developments: expansion and diversification of oil operations and the industry work force; rapid increase in population and consumer demand; growing availability of private and government capital; and increasing foreign company joint ventures with Saudi partners—including the Saudi government. Successive decades saw a marked increase in the number, size, and diversity of producing establishments. At first they turned out processed foods, paper and plastic items, clothing, and basic furniture. After the early 1970s, they added items such as paints, air-conditioners, aluminum prefabricated buildings, steel rods, and an increasing number of products using oil and gas as feedstocks and fuel. These latter items include fertilizers, petrochemicals and other chemicals, and by-product sulfur. The country still lacks sophisticated industries in such fields as electronics, optics, and other precision goods.

Saudi Arabia, with a shortage of indigenous technological experience and trained labor, has relied on overseas contractors for technology, equipment, services, and labor for construction and industrialization projects—often on a turnkey basis (see Chap. 9). For many major projects, the contracts extended beyond construction to operation and maintenance. However, educational and vocational programs by contractors have provided more trained local workers, and "Saudization" of establishments is raising the percentage of Saudis in companies, especially with the business retrenchment after 1982. The president of Aramco is a Saudi Arab, as is the chairman of the board of directors.

Investing the high petrodollar income of the 1970s, Saudi Arabia constructed the two model industrial and port cities mentioned earlier, Jubayl on the Gulf coast and Yanbu on the Red Sea coast. Focusing on industries based on oil and gas, both cities have oil refineries and plants producing petrochemicals and other chemicals, fertilizers, plastics, steel, and plastic and metal goods. Facilities at Jubayl and Yanbu now include ports and airports, huge dual-purpose systems that combine seawater desalination and power generation, and satellite industrial and consumer goods plants. Integrated planning and construction included both service and residential sectors in contemporary architectural designs.

By the early 1990s, manufacturing contributed more than 9 percent to the GDP. Many incentives attracted both local capital and joint ventures by foreign companies. A government agency, the Saudi Arabian Basic Industries Corporation (SABIC), was established in 1976 to develop large petrochemical and steel plants; it has achieved major goals.

Transportation

Highways. With sparse population and a preindustrial economy, Arabia before the mid-twentieth century had no road network to move people and goods over the deserts. The camel continued to be the common mode of transport, especially of goods, until after World War II. A limited number of automobiles drove across the open deserts, following old caravan routes, but they often foundered in deep sand before the development of four-wheel drive and sand tires.

Increasing petroleum development called for an expanded road net, and the first surfaced roads linked the main towns and oil facilities in the Eastern Province. Highway construction reached a peak during the early 1980s; by the early 1990s highways extended to every town, and remote villages were tied into the network by branch rural roads (see Map 9-2). A four-lane divided highway connects the Red Sea and Gulf (Jiddah-Mecca-Riyadh-Dammam), with a spur to Medina in the west and another to Unayzah and Buraydah in the northern Najd. At the Gulf end, the highway crosses a 15.5-mile/25-km causeway from al-Khobar to Bahrain that was opened in 1986 (see Fig. 9-3). The causeway carries unbroken lines of cars on Thursdays and Fridays, the Saudi weekend. It has been so successful that planning is under way for a 9.2-mile/14.9-km causeway across the Strait of Tiran to connect Saudi Arabia and the Sinai Peninsula of Egypt. Tiran Island would serve as the midway connection.

Air Facilities. Population concentrations widely separated by barren deserts encouraged the use of air transportation in preference to railways and roads in the early years of the country's development. Saudia, the national airline, founded in 1945 and evolved originally under a management contract with the U.S. airline TWA, has expanded to become the largest airline in the Middle East. A ten-year airport building program has supplied all cities and major towns in the country with modern airports, their runways accommodating at least medium-sized jet aircraft. By the early 1990s, more than 40 airports, 18 with regular commercial service, served Saudi cities and towns.

Between 1981 and 1984, Saudi Arabia opened two new international airports, the first in Jiddah, the second in Riyadh. They are the two largest airports in the world: Jiddah's covers 40 miles^2/103 km^2 and includes a separate facility for the hundreds of thousands of pilgrims who arrive by air for the annual ten-day religious pilgrimage to nearby Mecca. Nearly three times the size of the Jiddah airport, the opulent Riyadh air-

Figure 17-4. *One of the several whimsical monuments built during the 1980s in Jiddah, Saudi Arabia. Unexpected in the conservative country, the amusing monuments are popular sights in the Red Sea port city.*

port was opened in 1984. They are the two busiest air hubs in the Middle East after Cairo.

Railways. The Saudi Government Railroad, opened in 1951, links the port of Dammam with Riyadh and is the sole operating rail line in the country, although a shortened alignment was constructed in the early 1980s. A second line was under consideration in the early 1990s, a 62-mile/100-km link between Dammam and the new industrial port city of Jubayl. The Hijaz Railway tracks in Saudi Arabia are disused (see Chap. 9).

Ports and Shipping. Development required a manifold expansion of the port of Jiddah (Fig. 17-4), the major pre–World War II commercial port, and the construction of an east-coast general cargo port in Dammam—a functional extension of the railroad to Riyadh. Most recently, the drive for industrialization and implementation of the Master Gas System have required construction of the all-new integrated ports of Jubayl in the east and Yanbu in the west. The kingdom's fifth main port is at Jaizan, in the extreme southwest, serving the steadily developing and expanding Asir and the surrounding southern region.

Trade

Formerly limited by the sparse and low-income population, domestic trade in Saudi Arabia has become a significant segment of a large economy involving an affluent population of more than 12 million. The growing domestic economy reflects both the size of the national income and its widespread (although unequal) distribution both geographically and vertically through the social classes.

The traditional *suq*, with multiple small, specialized shops, characterized Saudi Arabian marketing into the late 1950s. As consumer spending multiplied, stimulated by Western retailing practices, outlets also changed; shops became larger and now carry a great variety of imports from Western Europe, the United States, and Japan. The huge multistory Shakiyah shopping center in Riyadh and Jamjoom Center in Jiddah (see Fig. 9-5) are the equals in facilities and inventory of almost any shopping center in North America. However, Westerners find it disconcerting for the shops—including restaurants—to close for about 20 minutes during evening prayer time. Large, well-stocked supermarkets operate in every city, offering most brands of products on the international market. Fresh fruits and vegetables arrive by road and air from horticultural centers as far as 1,500 miles/2,410 km away.

As in the Gulf area, large automobile dealerships offer major makes of cars, primarily Japanese and German. With a national ratio of 2.7 people per car, one of the lowest such ratios in the world, Saudi Arabia has automotive service and repair establishments in all towns and cities.

Saudi Arabia's imports are diversified by both type and source. Imports range from heavy equipment used by oil companies and contractors to large amounts of armaments and military support equipment to a wide variety of consumer products including automobiles, electronic equipment, and food. Saudi exports were formerly 99 percent petroleum and petroleum products but are becoming increasingly diversified (see country summary). Saudi Arabia now ranks as both the world's leading producer and the world's leading exporter of petroleum. The United States imports more than 1.8 million bpd from Saudi Arabia, more than from any other supplier. Oil exports, which are only slightly less than production figures (see Chap. 8), rose from about 2 million bpd in the early 1960s to an average of more than 9 million bpd in 1979–1981, fell to less than half that total in 1988, then rose again to well above 8 million bpd in 1991. Major export destinations were the United States, Japan, Singapore, France, and others. Major suppliers are the United States, Japan, and Britain.

Relations

The Kingdom of Saudi Arabia has, since its inception in 1932, maintained generally good relations with its eight neighbors, although not uniformly so. Prior to the 1990–1991 Gulf crisis, the most notable exceptions were a short war with Yemen in 1934, a dispute with Abu Dhabi and Oman over the Buraymi Oasis during the 1940s and 1950s, and tensions over Saudi support of the imam of Inner Oman against the sultan of Oman during the late 1950s and 1960s. Relations with all three of these neighbors have since been uneven, although co-membership in the Gulf Cooperation Council (GCC) and other shared developments have warmed Saudi relations with Abu Dhabi/UAE and Oman. A border dispute with Qatar flares periodically, as in late 1992, but was

smoothed over in early 1993. Relations with republican North Yemen after 1970 were strained because of Saudi Arabia's having supported the royalists during the civil war, but they gradually eased and were maintained briefly even after the unification of the two Yemens. However, Yemen's refusal to condemn Iraq's invasion of Kuwait (Yemen was a rotating member of the UN Security Council at the time) caused Saudi ire, and hundreds of thousands of Yemeni workers in Saudi Arabia were forced to return home. The tension was exacerbated by the renewal of the long-standing dispute over the Saudi-Yemeni border. Similarly, Jordan's ambivalent stance regarding Saddam Husayn derailed the rapport that had evolved between the two moderate monarchies. Saudi Arabia ceased large-scale financial support of Jordan, major purchases from Jordan, and the hiring of thousands of Jordanians.

Saudi Arabia is an active participant in and headquarters for the GCC. Saudi support for Iraq in its war against Iran beginning in 1980 was both financial and political, including the agreement for the IPSA pipeline from southern Iraq to extend across the kingdom to the Red Sea just south of Yanbu. Saudi Arabia turned bitterly against Iraq after Iraq invaded Kuwait in 1990, and it closed the IPSA line, supplied bases for the coalition forces against Iraq, and joined in the coalition. Conversely, Saudi Arabia has had good relations with Kuwait, sharing the Divided Zone and coming to Kuwait's rescue when it was invaded by Iraq in 1990. Good Saudi-Bahraini relations are evident in the fact that modest amounts of Saudi crude oil have been pumped to Bahrain for refining from the early years, as well as the facts of a 1960 agreement to divide the income from the offshore Abu Safah field near their median line and the agreement on a causeway, financed by Saudi Arabia and completed in 1986, linking Bahrain to the mainland.

Financial support from Saudi Arabia and the other Gulf states had for several years been the Palestine Liberation Organization's main source of income, although some of the actions conducted under the PLO umbrella contrasted with Saudi Arabia's basically nonviolent political philosophy and moderate stance. However, the PLO lost that support when PLO Chairman Yasir

Arafat chose to support Iraq's invasion of Kuwait in 1990.

Saudi Arabia plays a low-key leadership role in the Middle East, based on religious, economic, and political influence. In addition to its role of protecting the holy cities of Mecca and Medina and administering the annual pilgrimage, Saudi Arabia provides funding for Islamic institutions, including a new Islamic University in Asyut, Egypt. The country also contributes from its oil income to less wealthy countries of the region, and the rapid development in Saudi Arabia provides employment and worker remittances for other economies.

Overall, British-Saudi relations have remained good, with Britain filling multibillion-dollar Saudi arms contracts after U.S. sales to Saudi Arabia halted because of pressure by pro-Israeli groups. British-Saudi relations were further demonstrated by the scale of Saudi tourism and seasonal residence in London during the peak years of Saudi oil affluence. Increasing numbers of British are serving in a wide range of professional, managerial, and technical capacities, especially as more British military equipment is utilized in the kingdom. British are also steadily replacing Americans in many such positions. In addition, Saudi Arabia through the GCC is drawing closer to the EEC in general.

Saudi Arabia's close relations with the United States began with Aramco's exploration for and production of petroleum after the late 1930s. Thousands of U.S. employees and their dependents have lived in Aramco camps for decades, devoting their entire working lives to the ongoing project. Aramco's continuing role as an operating company for Saudi Arabia's petroleum production and for much of its petroleum processing, as well as its role as intermediary contractor on other major projects, assists in maintaining ties between the two countries.

The United States and Saudi Arabia also cooperate in other technical areas: The United States Geological Survey (USGS) conducted geological and mineral studies in the western shield area for many years and cooperated in the production of geographical and geological maps of the shield. In 1974, a U.S.–Saudi Arabia Joint Commission for Economic Cooperation, funded by the Saudi Arabian government and still operating, was established for research into economic issues of mutual interest and for technical economic assistance. The United States depends on Saudi Arabia for an increasing percentage of its oil imports, averaging 24 percent in early 1993 and growing because of the Aramco-Texaco joint venture mentioned under "Petroleum Industry" above. As many as 65,000 U.S. citizens lived and worked in the kingdom in the early 1980s, but the number fell to half that in the late 1980s before rising again to perhaps 40,000 after the Gulf war.

In 1942, King Abd al-Aziz agreed to the construction of a U.S. air base south of Dhahran, which became a combined military-civilian airfield and one of the kingdom's three largest airports. In 1953, the United States Military Training Mission (USMTM) began training elements of the Saudi air force, army, and navy, and that program continues. The United States has also been the kingdom's major supplier of military equipment and services—amounting to more than $40 billion by the mid-1980s—including consultant and supervisory services by the U.S. Army Corps of Engineers for military construction in Tabuk, Hafar al-Batin, Riyadh, and Khamis Mushayt. Thus, there was no hesitation, when the Gulf crisis erupted in August 1990, in the United States' offering protection to Saudi Arabia or in Saudi Arabia's accepting the offer. Military airfields, command centers, and cantonments were ready for the main elements of the coalition. As is mentioned elsewhere, the Saudi government compensated the U.S. government $16.8 billion in war costs, in addition to supplying airfields, facilities, and millions of gallons of drinking water without charge. After the end of the Gulf war, some U.S. units remained in the kingdom, although hosting permanent base operations is a delicate step for Saudi Arabia.

The military relationship between the United States and Saudi Arabia has encountered difficulties on both sides because of the relationship between the United States and Israel. Pro-Israeli forces in the United States have consistently attempted to constrain military sales and services to Saudi Arabia[9] (the Airborne Warning and Control System [AWACS], for example), and the Saudi Arabian leadership has for this reason diversified its military suppliers to include other Western nations.

Saudi Arabia's intentions to broaden its contacts in the world were demonstrated in the early 1990s when the kingdom established diplomatic relations with the long-shunned former Soviet Union and China; reestablished relations with Iran, which had been broken off in 1988; and indicated plans to exchange diplomats with East European countries. Saudi Arabia was also a charter member of the United Nations, and it is particularly active in some of that organization's specialized affiliated agencies such as the International Monetary Fund and the World Bank.

18

The Gulf
and Its Oil States

The body of water almost enclosed between the Arabian Peninsula and the Iranian coast is variously designated as the Persian Gulf, Arabian Gulf, Persian/Arabian Gulf, or increasingly, simply the Gulf. By whatever name, it has become well known because of its regional oil resources and because of its place in news headlines during the tanker war of 1987–1988 and the Gulf crisis of 1990–1991. Whatever else may be said of them, Desert Shield and Desert Storm left no doubt about the explosive significance of the geopolitics of the Gulf region. However, prior to the 1930s, the Gulf region was little recognized in the Western world other than by a few British officials and adventurers. Remote and poor, the area was characterized in 1928 by one British official: "The amenities of life are few and far between. Nature is in her fiercest humour and man has done little to improve upon her handiwork."[1]

Nevertheless, between 1960 and 1985, the span of one generation, the coast of the Arabian Peninsula from Kuwait to Muscat underwent a dramatic transformation. Former villages mushroomed into cities with populations 50, 100, and 150 times those of 1928, including Kuwait, Dammam, al-Khobar, Doha, Abu Dhabi, Dubai, Sharjah, and Muscat-Matrah. Per capita income of all of the countries along the western Gulf coast now ranks among the highest in the world.

Although "nature is in her fiercest humour" even yet, "man" has done a great deal to improve upon nature's handiwork. Billions of petrodollars have covered the huge costs of finding and transporting water for urban domestic supplies and for irrigating parks and gardens. With enormous amounts of energy available from local gas and oil supplies, air-conditioning makes the temperature inside virtually any dwelling comfortable. Albeit most of the commodities and much of the labor are imported, few of the conveniences and comforts of contemporary living are lacking along the Gulf littoral.[2]

Earlier chapters covered several functional aspects of the Gulf: its physical characteristics, influence on climate, role in the petroleum industry, strategic aspects, organization in the GCC, and maritime function. Now it is time to examine the regional characteristics of the smaller states along the western coast of the Gulf: Kuwait, Bahrain, Qatar, and the United Arab Emirates (UAE).[3]

A Glance at History

Neolithic sites have been found in several locations around the Gulf, including a number of presently barren desert areas of the Qatar Peninsula, and artifacts from rather intensive archaeological explorations conducted since the 1950s are now on exhibit in handsome museums in all the Gulf littoral states. Archaeological finds substantiate an established sea traffic through the Gulf and eastward to the Indus Valley from about 2300 BC, with another peak during Babylonian times. With its gushing artesian springs, Bahrain was an important way station in ancient times for Gulf mariners sailing between the Indus Valley and Mesopotamia. A famous transit of this same sea-lane was made by Nearchus, Alexander the Great's military commander, as he returned from Alexander's expedition to the Indus Valley in 325 BC. Romans mastered the difficulties of sailing with the monsoons to and from India but utilized the Red Sea rather than the Gulf.

Islamic civilization and its maritime trade reinvigorated the economic significance of the Gulf after the eighth century. From this period came the tales of Sinbad the Sailor, woven around voyages that began and ended in the Gulf. The basin's economic importance relapsed in the thirteenth century but revived with the arrival of Portuguese ships in the Gulf in 1514, after the opening of the route around southern Africa. Drawn by the wealth of Persia under the Safavid shah, Abbas the Great, Dutch and British ships supplanted those of the Portuguese. Expanding Ottoman power coalesced with the Dutch and British bridgeheads in the Gulf, and Basrah, Bushehr (Bushire), Bahrain, Bandar-e Abbas, Hormuz, and other Gulf ports were thriving trade centers and entrepôts during most periods after the early 1600s. By the early 1800s, British economic, military, and political dominance extended along almost the entire Gulf littoral, with the exception of the stretch of coast from Kuwait Bay south to the Qatar Peninsula.

By the end of the 1920s, southwestern Iran was a British "sphere of influence"; Iraq was a British mandate; and Kuwait, Bahrain, Qatar, the Trucial States, and Muscat and Oman were all either official British protectorates or under British influence. The British installed navigational aids (Persian Gulf Lighting Service) and undertook surveying, charting, and mapping of both the Gulf and its coasts and the Tigris and Karun rivers. The later British role and withdrawal from the Gulf, as well as the emergence of independent Gulf states, are discussed in Chapter 11 and in following sections.

A Glance at Gulf Oil

In 1992, oil reserves in the eight producers facing the Gulf totaled 657 billion barrels, 66 percent of the world's reserves; and average daily output of the eight during the decade 1976–1985 totaled 16.48 million bbl, which decreased to 13.94 million bpd during the lower production years 1986–1990. Of these totals, the four smaller Gulf states covered in this chapter show reserves of 200 billion bbl, an average 1976–1985 output of 3.56 million bpd, and an average 1986–1990 output of 3.46 million bpd. The numerous producing oil and gas fields in and around the Gulf are shown in Map 8-2, which in addition indicates the large number of fields that are completely or partially offshore. Map 8-2 also shows the numerous Gulf oil terminals, several of which rank among the world's largest: Ras Tanura, Juaymah, and—before the Iran-Iraq war and again after 1992—Kharg Island. A general discussion of the Gulf petroleum industry is included in Chapter 8, and additional details are given under the individual countries below.[4]

A Geopolitical Perspective

Intra-Gulf Relations

Regionally, the Gulf has long served both as an arena of contention and conflict and as a theater of peaceful trade and regional intercourse. For most of the past 150 years, partly under the aegis of the *Pax Britannica,* the littoral states have usually been willing to seek nonmilitary resolutions to discord in the Gulf. Most of the clashes that have taken place have occurred in the hinterland—over water sources, grazing rights, dynastic disputes, or territorial consolidation—rather than over the Gulf as such. However, Gulf states have periodically disputed control of offshore islands, access to pearl beds, and freedom of navigation. Rulers of the city-states of the southern Gulf shore have clashed over access to and control of wells and springs in the desert, and Bahrain and Qatar have contended for two centuries over dynastic and territorial questions. The Buraymi Oasis dispute is one of the classic conflicts among the modern Gulf states.

The extensive petroleum fields of the Gulf trough frequently lie astride political boundaries, onshore and offshore, but conflicting claims regarding land and maritime boundaries affecting parts or all of certain fields have been settled amicably. Britain has sometimes served as arbiter, and the United States conducted a cross-Gulf survey in the mid-1960s for peaceful delineation of a median line in the central Gulf. One unsettled offshore boundary problem—affecting Kuwait, Iraq, and Iran—involves the equitable division of offshore oil resources at the head of the Gulf. In a second such conflict, Bahrain and

Qatar dispute ownership of islands and waters between them, a problem that the Gulf Cooperation Council requested the king of Saudi Arabia to mediate in December 1988.

By far the most serious conflicts in the Gulf region since World War II have been the protracted Iran-Iraq war, 1980–1988, and the Gulf crisis of 1990–1991, both sparked by Iraqi aggression that backfired (see Chap. 11). The beginnings of the Iran-Iraq war continued the historical land conflict along the line of disjunction between the Zagros Mountain belt and the Mesopotamian Basin, two major power foci of the Middle East. The Iraqi invasion of Kuwait was more complicated, but, inter alia, it was one of a series of events that manifested a resurgence of the Mesopotamian power focus.

Global Perspective

However, because the Gulf Basin countries possess 66 percent of the world's petroleum resources and produce between one-fourth and one-third of the world's daily oil output to energize much of the world's industry and transportation, the Gulf's geopolitical interactions extend to virtually every part of the inhabited world. Such extension was clearly demonstrated when nearly 30 governments joined the coalition to liberate Kuwait and restore stability in the upper Gulf in 1990–1991. The troubled waters of the Gulf are an unstable chessboard on which every energy-dependent country must try for at least checkmate. This subject has been examined in Chapters 8 and 11 and will be touched on again in this chapter.[5]

KUWAIT

Kuwait Fort and Port

Originally a small port and trade center, the town of Kuwait historically took advantage of its geographical location on a deep coastal indentation that facilitated maritime activities and a modest land trade (Map 18-1). Its name is from the Arabic *kuwayt* ("little fort," from *kut*, "fort"). Landward, overland trade and pastoralism supported 10,000–15,000 townspeople and several thousand Bedouins.[6] More important was its maritime economy of pearling, fishing, boatbuilding, and sea trade with India and upper Gulf coastal towns. Its excellent harbor on Kuwait Bay gave it the greatest port potential in the northern Gulf, which, however, was never realized because of its lack of fresh water. Basrah, on the Shatt al-Arab, had better links with its hinterland and had plentiful fresh water. In view of its water shortage, Kuwait's population of 100,000 after World War I was surprisingly large. However, the world depression of the 1930s and competition from Japanese cultured pearls combined with changing technology and trade patterns to undermine Kuwait's traditional livelihood. By 1936–1937, the shaykhdom's economic future looked bleak, as the 700 pearling boats of 1921 decreased to 320 in 1933, 125 in 1939, and 40 in the 1940s.[7] Many pearling dhows shifted to transporting fresh water from the Shatt al-Arab to Kuwait, which reduced profits per trip but speeded up cash return. The depressed economy recovered and expanded dramatically when the discovery of petroleum in 1938 led to increasing oil exports after World War II, which brought immense wealth and rapid development in little more than a decade.[8] By 1961, Kuwait had achieved economic and political viability; and it gained independence from Great Britain, its protector since 1899, reaffirmed in 1914.

Sovereignty for the amirate, including withdrawal of British protection, brought its own problems, as Kuwaitis quickly discovered. Extremely wealthy but small and weak, and long coveted by a strong neighbor to the north, independent Kuwait was immediately claimed once again by Iraq, now a three-year-old revolutionary republic. However, Britain promptly revived its protection policy—later assumed by Arab League forces—and Iraq withdrew its threat and its border troops. The Iraqi claim and threat were periodically renewed, provoking several border incidents, some of the most serious in 1973.

For three decades Kuwait enjoyed almost unparalleled economic development and redevelopment. Billions of dollars of income from oil exports and investments permitted the hiring of expertise and labor for development, as well as the purchase of goods and equipment. As has

KUWAIT

Long-form official name, anglicized: State of Kuwait
Official name, transliterated: Dawlat al-Kuwayt
Form of government: constitutional monarchy
Area: 6,880 miles^2/17,818 km^2
Population, 1990: 2,143,000 (rough estimate of 1,250,000 in early 1992). Literacy (latest): 73%
Ethnic composition (%), prior to Iraqi occupation: Kuwaiti Arab 40.1, non-Kuwaiti Arab 37.9, Asian
(mostly Pakistani and Indian but also Sri Lankan and Filipino) 21.0, European 0.7, other 0.3 (non-Kuwaiti percentages decreased markedly after the Gulf war)
Religions (%, 1990): Muslim 90.0 (Sunni 63.0, Shii 27.0), Christian 8.0, Hindu 2.0
GNP, 1989: $33.08 billion; per capita: $16,380
Petroleum reserves: 94.525 billion barrels
Main exports (% of total value, 1989): crude petroleum and petroleum products 92.2
Main imports (% of total value, 1987): machinery and transport equipment 31.1; miscellaneous manufactured articles 24.7; manufactured goods 24.0; food and live animals 17.7; fuels 1.4
Capital city: Kuwait City 44,224; other cities: al-Salimiyah 153,220; Hawalli 145,215; al-Jahra 111,165; al-Farwaniyah 68,665 (virtually all are part of greater Kuwait City) (all population data predate the 1991 Gulf war and were substantially lower in 1992)

been explained elsewhere, the Iran-Iraq war created eight years of problems and fears for the Kuwaitis, who negotiated for and bought what they needed, including security. Then, on August 2, 1990, Kuwait's complacency was shattered when Iraq invaded the coveted territory. The little-known, even though very wealthy, small amirate suddenly dominated world television screens, radio, and headlines.

Although the Gulf crisis is discussed in Chapter 11, the impact inside the amirate may be examined briefly here. Significantly, at the time of the invasion (early August), as is true every year, scores of thousands of Kuwaiti residents were on vacation—wealthy citizens in the cooler lands of Western Europe or elsewhere and expatriates in their homelands. The absence of so many residents made the invasion easier for the Iraqis and complicated the situation for the Kuwaitis both during and after the occupation.

Destruction in Kuwait City and environs was extensive, but most buildings remained structurally sound and were reparable. The greatest damage inflicted on the country resulted from Iraqi looting of transportable items and sabotaging of fixed facilities. The value of looted materials can be only approximated but has been roughly estimated to be between $70 and $100 billion.[9] For-

tunately, some of the most valuable items were later returned by Iraq under UN cease-fire resolutions. Nearly 17,000 items stolen from the Kuwait National Museum were returned, as were 3,216 gold bricks weighing 27.56 pounds/12.5 kilograms each.[10]

More obvious was the sabotage of Kuwait's oil wells, tank farms, oil-export terminals, pipelines, and refineries, which not only caused direct losses of billions of dollars in resources and facilities but also despoiled many aspects of the local and regional environment. In an act sometimes called environmental terrorism and ecocide, Iraq blew up 749 wellheads of Kuwait's 935 wells, leaving more than 750 wells afire or blowing wild (Fig. 18-1), causing millions of barrels of oil to flow out onto the desert around wells and tanks, and burning other millions, at the rate of 4.6 million bpd (twice Kuwait's normal daily production) in the late spring of 1991. In addition, in late January 1991, Iraq dumped 150,000 bpd of oil from Kuwaiti storage tanks into the upper Gulf, a spill that exceeded 4 million bbl before it was staunched. This amount may be compared with the 258,000 bbl spilled by the Exxon *Valdez* in Alaska in 1989. While smoke particles from the burning wells polluted the air over Kuwait and areas to the south, lakes of oil from wild wells

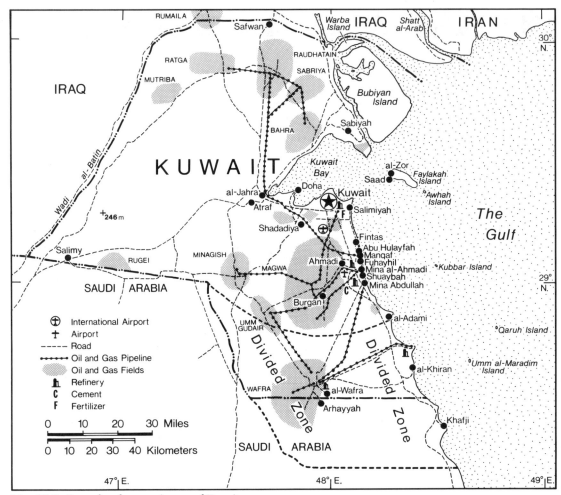

Map 18-1. *General and economic map of Kuwait.*

fouled the desert, and oil spills in the Gulf polluted beaches and water in a large area between Kuwait and Qatar, especially along the Saudi coastline north of Ras Tanura.

Time has shown that the environmental impact has not proved to be as apocalyptic as was originally feared, but the surface and marine pollution has nevertheless been devastating. Kuwait's landscape will be despoiled for decades by the black blight of the oil flows. Even more serious, the sabotaging of the wells will result in lost reserves (perhaps 3 billion bbl, about 3 percent of the known total), lost reservoir drive mechanism, and lost well productivity. The Kuwait Oil Company (KOC) decided to plug and abandon 10 percent of the damaged wells. Nearly half of them require a workover in any case, and more than 100 new wells are being drilled to make up

for those lost.[11] Kuwait exported its first post-occupation oil in late July 1991 and has steadily increased production and exports each month. Its goals are a capacity of 2.5 million bpd and an output of the preinvasion 1.25–1.5 million bpd, a level it had even exceeded in early 1993.

By the time the last burning well was extinguished on November 6, 1991, most basic public services had also been restored; and by mid-1992, Kuwait was physically well along in outward reconstruction, although much remained to be done. But a great deal more needed to be remedied in the social and political spheres, which will take much longer than physical reconstruction.

In the aftermath of the Gulf war, UN surveyors, acting under UN Security Council Resolution 687, have redrawn and demarcated the Ku-

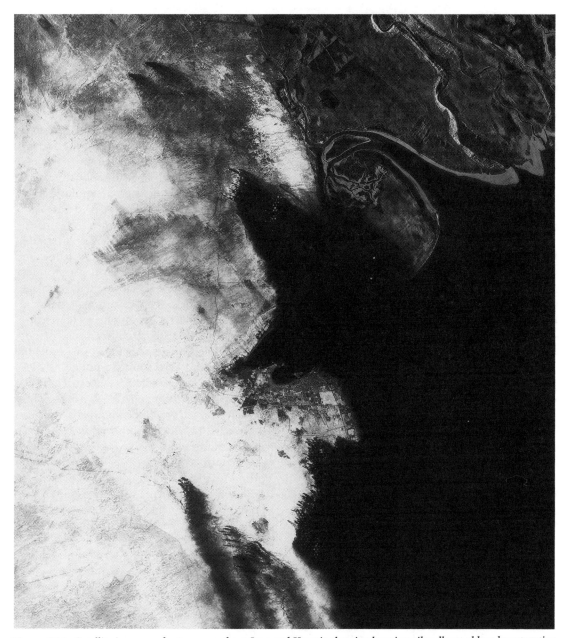

Figure 18-1. *Satellite imagery of extreme southern Iraq and Kuwait, showing burning oil wells set ablaze by retreating Iraqis in February 1991. Note sharp contrast between the irrigated, damp soil area of Iraq and the desert soils of Kuwait. Black smoke covers southern Bubiyan Island, eastern Kuwait City, and the built-up area along the southern Kuwait coast. (Courtesy NASA)*

wait-Iraq border, moving it 570 yards/521 m to the north along one sector. In addition to more territory, the change also gives Kuwait ten more oil wells in the Rumaila field, which it shares with Iraq, and part of the Iraqi naval base of Umm Qasr (see Chap. 11).[12]

Oil and Oil Industry

A surface showing of asphalt spurred the first interest in Kuwait's oil potential in 1911, and the first geological survey, conducted in 1914, yielded encouraging results. Without its promise of oil production, Kuwait would probably not have been maintained as a separate polity by the British after World War I and would likely have been incorporated into the mandate of Iraq. Certainly, petroleum has been the axis around which the amirate has revolved since the initial discovery. After World War I, the Anglo-Persian Oil Company and the Gulf Oil Corporation[13] of the United States combined to create a jointly owned local subsidiary, Kuwait Oil Company (KOC), and in 1934 that company obtained an oil concession from the government of Kuwait. After a dry hole in the north, KOC struck a gusher in the Burgan Dome south of Kuwait Bay in 1938 and later proved that Burgan, with oil in several relatively shallow horizons, was the world's greatest field of its time. It is still the world's richest field for its size. Delayed by World War II, the first commercial exports of crude from the Burgan Dome were lifted in 1946.

The Kuwait government awarded concessions to the U.S. Aminoil group for the Kuwaiti half of the Kuwaiti-Saudi Neutral Zone in June 1945, and four years later it extended the concession to include several offshore islands. In 1958, Kuwait followed the lead of Saudi Arabia and awarded a concession for its offshore half of the Neutral Zone to the Japanese group, Arabian Oil Company. Later, concessionary exploration was conducted by the Spanish at Raudhatain, in northern Kuwait, where both more oil and the amirate's only sweet groundwater were found in the late 1950s.

As oil production mounted rapidly, Kuwait became increasingly cognizant of its dependence on a single depletable resource. Upon the advice of a young group of "technocrats," the Kuwait government moved toward conservation of the country's source of wealth by reducing petroleum output. It also moved to reduce the wasteful flaring (because no economic market was available) of gas separated from the crude prior to further handling. After increasing its production each year to a peak output of 3 million bpd in 1972, Kuwait reduced output sharply to less than 2 million bpd during the late 1970s. By this time, the amirate had amassed such enormous wealth for its small size and population and had been so intensively developed economically that conserving its oil resources was more logical

than accumulating additional millions of dollars. The world petroleum oversupply required a further cutback to a minimum of 675,000 bpd in 1982. Although urging an OPEC quota of not less than 1.25 million bpd in late 1986, Kuwait has moved to balance production with conservation objectives. Ironically, Kuwait's allegedly exceeding its OPEC production quota was claimed by Iraq as one basis for its invasion of the amirate. In early 1993, during OPEC quota discussions, Kuwait demanded the right to produce at maximum levels because of its desperate need to recoup its financial losses from the 1990–1991 fighting and during the war's aftermath.

Like other OPEC countries, Kuwait sought participation in its concessionary companies and by 1975 controlled KOC, which it placed under the newly formed Kuwait National Petroleum Company (KNPC). The government nationalized Aminoil and its operations in the Neutral Zone (by that time the Divided Zone) in 1977. KNPC and related companies were put under the umbrella Kuwait Petroleum Corporation (KPC) in 1980, and its subsidiaries have become the largest petroleum-centered industry in the Third World. It competes with the multinationals, having purchased Gulf Oil Corporation facilities in Benelux and Scandinavia in 1983 and in Italy in 1984. It controls refineries in Western Europe and North America and holds 24.9 percent of Hoechst, the West German chemical giant. Other KPC subsidiaries include the Kuwait Oil Tanker Company and Petrochemicals Industries Company.

With its economy dominated by the petroleum industry, Kuwait has expanded beyond the production and shipping of crude petroleum to domestic downstream processing: refining, petrochemical production (including ammonia and fertilizers), and manufacturing of natural gas liquids (NGL), including liquefied petroleum gas (LPG). Three main KNPC refineries at Mina al-Ahmadi, Mina Abdullah, and Shuaybah, with a total throughput capacity of 750,000 bpd, were damaged to varying degrees. Mina al-Ahmadi was the least damaged, since the Iraqis used it to produce gasoline for their military operations. However, all three facilities were restored to nearly normal operations by mid-1992. Other processing plants are located near the refineries.

Other Industry and Trade

Government goals for industrial development focus on capital-intensive and energy-intensive industries, as opposed to labor-intensive manufacturing, in the fields of petroleum, petroleum by-products, construction materials, consumer goods, and electronics. Diversification of industry and the shift to domestic production of basic commodities that have been traditionally imported are deterred by the small size of the consuming population, regardless of the high per capita income. The relatively few nonpetroleum Kuwaiti industries currently include cement, pharmaceuticals, nonalcoholic beverages, processed and frozen fish, building materials, plastics, paper products, furniture, and milled flour.

Kuwait's main non-oil product is "manufactured water," sweet water produced by desalination of seawater through several processes, including distillation and flash distillation. All of the processes are energy intensive. Kuwait is fortunate that it has an environmental trade-off: A serious deficiency (natural supplies of sweet water) is offset by a valuable excess (enormous amounts of fuel). With this trade-off, Kuwait has developed the world's greatest concentration of desalination facilities (although Saudi Arabia's total capacity is greater) and satisfies most of its need for sweet water, producing 215 million gallons/0.813 million m^3 daily.

With one of the highest per capita incomes in the world, Kuwait has developed a consumer-oriented economy to match the oil export sector. From a tradition of trading, shipping, fishing, and pearling, the knowledgeable Kuwaiti merchants moved rapidly into importing, retailing, appliance service, electronic products, furniture and other household furnishings, and automobiles. The shops in the quaint old town *suqs* have long since been replaced by modern Western-style shopping centers and individual merchandising outlets. Virtually all the retail stores were plundered by the Iraqis during their 1990–1991 occupation. Increasing numbers of banks at one time ranked among the leading independent financial houses, as investors sought to place surplus funds. However, four events during the decade after 1981 seriously impacted Kuwait

economically—and politically: (1) a scandalous collapse in 1982 in the extraofficial Suq al-Manakh "stock market" that resulted in more than 500 bankruptcies; (2) the 50 percent drop in oil prices during the early 1980s that necessitated a sharp retrenchment in development, especially in construction; (3) the Iran-Iraq war, which further depressed economic activity in Kuwait and brought its considerable entrepôt trade to a halt; and (4) most traumatic of all, the devastating Iraqi occupation between August 2, 1990, and February 27, 1991. Kuwait's total financial wartime costs—cash outlays, losses to looting and in destruction of resources, and damage to buildings, industries, and oil facilities—have never been authoritatively determined but can be estimated at nearly $200 billion.

In addition to Kuwait's income from oil and trade, its return on investments, although affected by Gulf war costs, is a major source of income. About $90 billion is invested abroad—about half in the United States and half in Europe and Japan—in two main funds. The General Reserve Fund is a portfolio of normal investments, whereas the Reserve Fund for Future Generations has been accumulated since 1976 by allocating 10 percent of ordinary revenues each year as assets for the twenty-first century, not to be drawn on until after the year 2000.

The Kuwait Fund for Arab Economic Development (KFAED), created in 1961, had lent or granted $5.5 billion to Arab neighbors by 1989. Separate grants of huge sums were made to the Front Line States of Egypt, Syria, and Jordan, as well as to the PLO; and, ironically, Kuwait supported Iraq in its war against Iran with loans (never repaid) of $4–5 billion. The amirate has also contributed heavily to multilateral aid funds.

From the time of its initial settlement, Kuwait has had minimal agricultural development and even today imports 95 percent of its food. The 12,000–15,000 Bedouins of a century ago supplied appreciable meat, but their number has dwindled to only a few hundred, who contribute little to the food supply. Small date groves persist around some of the brackish wells, and new dairy and chicken farms, along with limited hydroponic vegetable production, add to the fresh food supply. By contrast, public administration and the extensive and varied service sector in this affluent ministate employ more than half of the labor force.

Society and Settlements

Kuwait town was settled in the early eighteenth century by Arabs from the Najd (central Arabia). Although the environment was niggardly, especially because of its shortage of water, benefits of the excellent harbor sustained the tenacious population. Gradually, numbers of Arabs from Mesopotamia, the peninsula, and Oman, as well as Iranians, joined the small settlement, which was ruled by Al Sabah shaykhs. By the early 1900s, the population was estimated at 35,000 and was double that size in 1946, when the first commercial oil was exported from the shaykhdom. Increasing oil production attracted immigrants by the thousands, until the population reached 206,473 in the first census, taken in 1957, and 2.1 million—ten times that of the first census—in mid-1990.

By 1965, the aliens ("non-Kuwaitis," or immigrants or expatriates) outnumbered the native Kuwaitis, and firm nationality criteria were stipulated to restrict citizenship to those who had been inhabitants prior to 1920 and their offspring. Stringent conditions for naturalization effectively precluded attainment of Kuwaiti nationality by immigrants except for about 50 per year. Of the 2.1 million inhabitants in mid-1990, fewer than 600,000 were citizens, and only they were entitled to the full range of extraordinary welfare benefits extended by the government. Only adult males who lived in Kuwait before 1920 and their male descendants, totaling about 140,000, are politically franchised.

Kuwait's population fell precipitously after the Iraqi invasion as expatriates especially, but also Kuwaitis, fled the terror and hardships of the occupation. Many thousands of residents already on vacation in August when the invasion occurred extended their visits abroad. The number remaining in Kuwait may have been as low as 500,000 by early January 1991. After liberation of the amirate in late February 1991, scores of thousands of citizens and expatriates sought reentry, but many lifelong resident expatriates were dis-

mayed to find themselves turned away. Further, many expatriates who had remained during the occupation were expelled. For much of March and April 1991, self-appointed militiamen forced some noncitizen residents to evacuate their homes and leave the amirate. Seizing the opportunity to achieve a social and political restructuring, government authorities then embarked on a firm restoration of Kuwait for the Kuwaitis, announcing a postwar population goal of about 1.2 million.

The symbiotic relationship between Kuwait and its expatriates, somewhat similar to that of the other Gulf amirates, is complex; and Kuwait's 1991–1992 policies of population reduction were mutually traumatic. As merchants, traders, and sailors, the Kuwaitis of 1938 and following years imported the necessary employees—technicians and managers, primarily from the West, and clerks, service men, laborers, and domestics, primarily from the East—to develop their oil industry and most of the country. After oil production began, the few British and Americans were soon submerged by Iranians, Iraqis, Jordanians, Lebanese, Omanis and other Gulf Arabs, and South Asians.

Especially numerous were the Palestinian refugees, who came by the thousands in search of livelihood and home following their loss of both to Israelis during and after 1948–1949. Arabs and mostly Muslims, educated and motivated, the Palestinians became available just as Kuwait had a critical need for the skills and characteristics they possessed; and by the late 1980s, they and their descendants numbered nearly 400,000, contributing their skills as civil servants, engineers, technicians, middle managers, and teachers. However, when some Palestinians became politically and journalistically activist, the entire group became suspect to the authorities, and Palestinians were no longer welcome as newcomers. During the Iraqi occupation, the support for President Saddam Husayn—or at least for his expressed ideals—demonstrated by many Palestinians in Jordan and by some in Kuwait created bitter resentment among many Kuwaitis (and other peninsula and Gulf Arabs) against the longtime Palestinian resident aliens. Such was the stimulus for the expulsion by Kuwait of hundreds of thousands of Palestinians—with other expatriate inhabitants—until fewer than 20,000 Palestinians remained.

A serious consequence was the loss of scores of thousands of the amirate's most effective workers on several levels, thus prolonging the area's recovery. Kuwaiti authorities were also systematically selective in permitting the return of several other expatriate groups, reducing non-Kuwaiti Arab groups in favor of Asian groups, who are less politically active and more manageable. Thus, the structure and texture of the Kuwaiti population and society were fundamentally altered in a period of months.[14]

Basic in the amirate's social structure and its development is the historical evolution of a capable and group-conscious society in which a core of energetic merchant families complemented a skilled ruling family, Al Sabah. Merchants and shaykhs experimented with consultative councils and assemblies, and into the 1990s, political participation by Kuwaiti residents continues to exceed that by residents of other Gulf states. Even so, the elected National Assembly has been dissolved at least twice when it impinged on rulers' powers, and the amirate's political structure is certain to be problematic during the 1990s. An election for members of the National Assembly held on October 5, 1992, resulted in 31 seats in the 50-member parliament being held by candidates of the diverse opposition, including Arab nationalists, tribal leaders, Islamic fundamentalists, and businessmen. One unifying demand was for disclosure of and accountability for use of oil revenues, since revelations after the 1990–1991 crisis showed that graft and other irregularities had defrauded the state out of billions of dollars.

The ruling Al Sabah family, which now numbers almost 1,000, supplies the amir, who acts as head of state, and also key members of the cabinet. The Al Sabah family gained a high degree of independence from tax and customs receipts as recipients of early oil payments, but the Kuwaiti elite are still able to influence the shaykhs. They comprise the notable old families from generations back—Sunni Muslim, conservative, and wealthy—who have the confidence and ear of the

ruler. The 30 percent of the native Kuwaitis who are Shii are less influential, although some of them are descendants of Iranian families who settled in Kuwait 100–200 years ago. The Islamic Revolution in Iran inspired radicalism among some of the Shiis in Kuwait, especially among more recent immigrants, some of whom were involved in terrorist attacks in 1983 and 1985. Several thousand Shiis and other alleged radical aliens were deported in 1985 and again in 1991, underlining the uncertain status of nonindigenous residents.

Kuwaiti citizens have profited especially from the rapidly expanding political and economic systems of the oil-rich state. However, alien residents have also enjoyed great benefits from the obviously wide distribution of wealth among the general population, although they are not entitled to some of the welfare privileges. Free public education, free medical treatment and hospitalization, and public welfare receive high priority, and the schools reflect this emphasis. Thousands of Kuwaitis, mostly men, have been sent to Britain and the United States for free university educations, although most Kuwaiti university students now attend the well-equipped University of Kuwait, opened in 1967. In a significant break with local tradition, increasing numbers of Kuwaiti women also attend the university, where they have outnumbered men since the early 1980s.

Kuwait City, once a small port on the southeastern coast of Kuwait Bay, now is an elaborately planned metropolis covering much of the center of the state. Some of its ultramodern buildings echo traditional Islamic architecture, and each of the carefully planned sectors suggests the traditional Islamic urban "quarter" and includes a mosque and shopping area reminiscent of the traditional *suq;* otherwise, few features reflect the typical Islamic city. Serving as a city symbol, the three unique Kuwait Towers on the tip of Ras Ajuzah are a dominant feature of the landscape (Fig. 18-2). The southwest-northeast axis of the built-up area and most streets follows the trend of coastline that forms the northwestern boundary of the city. The historic mud wall was dismantled during the expansion of the city in the

Figure 18-2. *Kuwait water towers, the Kuwaiti capital's hallmark, serving an identifying function similar to that of the Eiffel Tower in Paris. The highly colored and decorated spheres store municipal water, and the tower on the left includes a luxury restaurant. Palm trees indicate scale.*

late 1950s, but two of the old gates have been preserved. The central business district covers most of the old *madinah*, the pre-1945 walled town. Three harbors retain features of the old Kuwait along the bay, and traditional dhows still anchor inside the breakwaters. Concentric ring roads centered on the old town carry residential sectors southeastward and industrial sectors southwestward. Kuwait's main general-cargo port is at Shuwaykh on the western side of the city.

Relations

Like the shaking of a kaleidoscope, the disarray caused by the Gulf crisis forced Kuwait into certain new patterns of regional and world relations. Connections with such traditional friends as Saudi Arabia and other GCC neighbors, Britain, the United States, Japan, and others were greatly strengthened. Indeed, Kuwait owes its rescue primarily to them. Bonds with Iraq fell to an absolute nadir, as they did with Jordan and Yemen. Ironically, relations with Iran improved from the low level of 1980–1988. Relations with the United States became extraordinarily close, building on the U.S. Navy's convoying of Kuwaiti tankers in 1987–1988. Both internal and external relations in the late 1992 remained primarily reactive, with new patterns to be established only dimly discernible.

BAHRAIN

An Overview

Bahrain (Arabic for "two seas") is the main island of a group of 33 small low-lying islands, also called Bahrain, which is the smallest of the sixteen Middle East states.[15] It is located 15 miles/24 km off the east coast of Saudi Arabia, with which it is connected by a causeway, and 18 miles/29 km from the Qatar Peninsula (Map 18-2). Only five of the islands are inhabited. Of the archipelago's total area, the main Bahrain Island covers 221 miles^2/572 km^2; second-most important is Muharraq, with the state's second-largest city (also called Muharraq), international airport, and dry dock. A causeway 1.5 miles/2.5 km long, built in 1929, connects Muharraq with Bahrain. Other islands include Sitra, site of the state's oil export terminal, linked to Bahrain by bridge and more recently by a causeway to Manama; Nabih Salih, its date palm groves fed by artesian springs; Umm Nasan, private island of the ruler and a link in the new Arabia-Bahrain causeway; and Jiddah, with the state prison. The Hawar group of islands off the southwestern coast of Qatar is disputed between Bahrain and Qatar. The dispute evoked a diplomatic crisis and alleged gunboat fire in the fall of 1991, when Qatar took its claim to the World Court, and King Fahd of Saudi Arabia attempted mediation. Most urban development has taken place on the *sabkhahs* in northeastern Bahrain and southern Muharraq, and these areas are surrounded by oases, which give way southward to rocky and gravelly barren desert.[16]

Despite its island situation, Bahrain is very hot in summer, with regular afternoon temperatures exceeding 106°F/41°C. Consistently high humidity makes the high temperature especially uncomfortable. November to March is a milder period, the season when Bahrain receives its average annual 3 in./76 mm of rainfall.

The main island of Bahrain is fringed by a shallow rock platform and by extensive coral reefs. The island is a surface expression of a breached asymmetrical anticline with a north-south axis in which oil and gas have been trapped at several depths. Erosional breaching of the anticline has produced a shallow basin in the center of the island that is surrounded by a low, oval-shaped, inward-facing escarpment of resistant limestone. Several erosional remnant hills that mark the former crest of the arch rise 100–200 ft./30–60 m above the inner basin. Most prominent of the hills is Jabal Dukhan, near the center of Bahrain's oil field, the highest elevation on the island at 440 ft./134 m. Oil company headquarters are at Awali, in the northern part of the basin and north of the field itself.

Important as oil became after 1932, another liquid resource attracted visitors and settlers as early as the Neolithic and especially during the Bronze Age: the plentiful supply of sweet artesian water from numerous *ayns* in the northern part of Bahrain Island and on adjacent islands. Other freshwater springs that erupt from the floor of the Gulf between Bahrain and Saudi Arabia have supplied mariners with drinking water for centuries. Bahrain's central location on the Gulf's long axis and the fact that it is the largest and best-watered of the Gulf islands south of Kuwait made it a transit point for Sumerians sailing between Mesopotamia and the Indus Valley. The same ba-

BAHRAIN

Long-form official name, anglicized: State of Bahrain
Official name, transliterated: Dawlat al-Bahrayn
Form of government: Monarchy (amirate), with a cabinet appointed by the amir
Area: 267 miles^2/692 km^2
Population, 1991: 516,000. Literacy (latest): 77.4%
Ethnic composition (%): Bahraini Arab 68.0, Asian (mostly Indian, Pakistani) 14.0, other Arab 4.1, Iranian 8.0, European 2.5, other 3.4
Religions (%): Muslim 92.0 (Shii 65.0, Sunni 35.0), Christian 7.3, other 0.7
GNP, 1988: $3.01 billion; per capita: $6,360 ($9,500 in 1981)
Petroleum reserves: 97.46 million barrels
Main exports (% of total value, 1990): petroleum products 79.0; aluminum products 5.6
Main imports (% of total value, 1990): crude petroleum products 54.3; nonpetroleum products 45.7
Capital city: Manama 151,500; other cities: al-Muharraq 78,000; Jidd Hafs 48,000; al-Rifa 45,000; Isa Town (Madinat Isa) 40,000

sic advantages, plus the oil industry, pertain today.

Excavations near the ruins of Bahrain Fort on the northern coast of Bahrain Island uncovered an ancient temple complex where artifacts were found that link Bahrain with Sumer and the Indus Valley. Archaeologists conclude that Bahrain is the Dilmun mentioned in Sumerian inscriptions[17] and that it also had ancient cultural links with Faylakah Island off Kuwait Bay and with settlements in Abu Dhabi. Grave mounds estimated to number more than 100,000 in a huge necropolis in northwestern Bahrain date from as early as 2400 BC and from every period after that through the Sassanian. Such prominent landscape features have caught the attention of visitors and writers for 2,300 years. Unfortunately, thousands of the tumuli have been bulldozed to clear ground for highways and new and expanding settlements.

Transit trade, dhow building, fishing, and pearling underpinned the island's economy for centuries as Bahrain was occupied or controlled by Sassanians, Umayyads, Abbasids, Hormuzis, Portuguese, Persians, mainland Najdis, and Ottomans. The leading shaykhs, Al Khalifah—who had tribal affiliations with the Al Sabah in Kuwait—came to be accepted as rulers in the eighteenth century and threw off Iranian control in 1783. Soon after, they were included under the umbrella of British Gulf protection, which con-

tinued for 150 years. The decline of pearling during the 1930s coincided, fortuitously, with the discovery of oil. Bahrain emerged from British protection in 1971, 40 years after it became the first oil producer on the west side of the Gulf, just in time to enjoy an economic boom as a sovereign state.

A new constitution in 1973 afforded more political participation by the inhabitants through the creation of an experimental National Assembly, but the fledgling parliament was disbanded by the ruler in 1975. With escalating oil prices and explosive development in the Gulf during the first decade of the independence of the Gulf amirates, Bahrain profited in many ways from its geographical location, relative stability, diplomatic finesse, and able work force. As its economic development expanded, its traditional strategic importance also increased. Its balancing act during the Iran-Iraq war preserved its links with all sides, and during the Gulf war in 1990–1991, the main island played a significant role as an insular aircraft carrier for British and U.S. warplanes. Indeed, Bahraini pilots also flew strike missions in Iraq.

People and Population

During Bahrain's long history as a center for traders and seafarers, many ethnic groups settled on the islands, producing a characteristic indige-

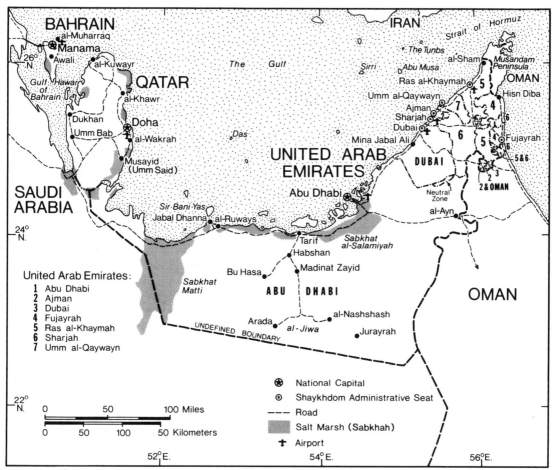

Map 18-2. *States of the lower Gulf: Bahrain, Qatar, and the United Arab Emirates. Numbers in the UAE refer to exclaves belonging to the respective amirates. Several islands in the Bahrain Archipelago are too small to be shown at this scale.*

nous mixture. Earlier Iranian influence induced the present 65 percent adherence of Bahrainis to Shii Islam, although the ruling family of al Khalifah and most members of the power structure are Sunni. Although the distinctions are becoming less important, three main social groups among the Shii include the Baharna, descendants of the original inhabitants of the island; the Hassawi, descendants of settlers from oases in the Eastern Province of modern Saudi Arabia; and the Ajami, whose families migrated from Iran in more recent times. Sunni Arabs originally from Arabia who migrated to Iran and then back to Bahrain are called Hawala. The ethnically complex population also includes large numbers of Indians and Pakistanis, other Gulf Arabs, some Europeans, a few Jews, and a few black Af-

ricans. Although not socioeconomically stratified, the groups tend to concentrate in certain areas of Bahrain or in certain quarters of Manama and Muharraq. By the early 1990s, one-third of the population was non-Bahraini.

Population increase in Bahrain has been steady since World War II, rising from 90,000 in 1941 to 516,000 in 1991, somewhat larger than that of Qatar, which has the Middle East's smallest population. The main concentration of population is around the capital and primate city of Manama and its suburbs, with a secondary node on the island of Muharraq (see Fig. 10-3). Manama displays an interesting mixture of old and new, its Indian-style bazaars contrasting with surrounding new high-rise office buildings and luxury hotels. A few miles southwest of Manama is a completely new settlement, Isa Town, begun in 1968 as a model town for the growing population. Hamad Town, in western Bahrain, was added in 1982 and has expanded rapidly.

Economic Patterns

The petroleum industry and related activities have dominated Bahrain's economic patterns since the 1930s, but such traditional activities as trade, shipping and servicing Gulf shipping (including entrepôt services), dhow building, fishing, and agriculture are still important sectors. Only pearling, in which Bahrain led the world in the early 1900s, has virtually disappeared, although trade in pearls is still important in the Manama *suq*. Major activities added since mid-century are banking, tourism and recreation, air transport servicing, and specialized manufacturing.

Oil

The first oil well in Bahrain, and the first in the Gulf proper, was drilled by Bahrain Petroleum Company (Bapco) in 1931–1932 at Jabal Dukhan and produced 9,600 bpd from 2,008 ft./612 m. It is still producing. Using mostly Saudi crude, received through undersea pipelines, as feedstock, a small refinery opened in 1936 and expanded to handle a 255,000-bpd throughput, producing more than 80 products, most of them exported from Sitra. Oil from Saudi Arabia still supplies 50 percent of Bahrain's imports.

Steady at only 30,000 bpd for many years, Bahrain's oil production then rose steadily to a peak of 76,600 bpd in 1970 before declining to 42,000 in 1988. By that time, half of Bahrain's oil income came from its half-share of the production from the Abu Safah offshore field near the median line between Saudi Arabia and Bahrain. Bahrain's onshore oil reserves are expected to be exhausted by the year 2000; however, depending on production, gas reserves in the deep Khuff formation (about 10,000 ft./3,048 m) should last several decades beyond that time. New industries were developed to make use of the considerable supply of Khuff gas.

Bapco, which held the Bahrain concession for more than four decades, was incorporated in Canada but was originally a wholly owned subsidiary of Standard Oil of California (Socal), now Chevron. In 1936, Texaco bought 50 percent of Bapco and joined Socal in the California-Texas Oil Corporation, which became Caltex Petroleum Corporation in 1968 and which owned Bapco as a subsidiary. The company was for many years the main employer and income earner in the islands, and, enjoying an amicable partnership with the government, played a long, vital role in the development of the country. In 1975, Bahrain, which considered itself too minor a producer to join OPEC, assumed 60 percent participation in Bapco and took over the other 40 percent in 1980, administering control through Banoco (Bahrain National Oil Company), founded in 1976. Bapco as an integrated oil company was dissolved in 1981 and was replaced by Bapco BSC(c); 60 percent was owned by the government and 40 percent by Caltex Bahrain, which only operates the refinery and a few other facilities.[18]

A decade-long program of drilling new exploratory wells has found no additional oil, either onshore or offshore. This confirms the 50-year-old concern that the shaykhdom's reserves were originally modest, and, indeed, they proved to be the smallest of all those of the Middle East producers. The realization prompted Bahrain to utilize intensive conservation techniques and to develop new economic enterprises. In addition to the large 55-year-old refinery, oil-based industries include a liquefaction plant (built in 1979) and a petrochemical plant (built in 1980).

Other Industry

Using the island's large gas resources, a joint venture opened a large aluminum refinery (ALBA) in 1971. Alumina is imported from Australia as raw material, and the 180,000-mt output is exported mainly to Japan, with some used locally in the Bahrain aluminum extruding plant and the rolling mill. A second large installation is the Arab Ship Repair Yard (ASRY), completed in 1977 on an artificial island linked to Muharraq. Owned jointly by Bahrain and six OPEC states, ASRY's huge facility services supertankers up to 500,000 dwt. Smaller vessels are serviced in an older yard and slipway. The facilities proved to be of great value during the tanker war in the 1980s and during the 1990–1991 Gulf crisis. The large industrial area behind the main port of Mina Sulman and the naval base of Jufayr, in northeast Bahrain, embraces a score of smaller plants. Elsewhere on the island there are food-processing plants, clothing factories, potteries, and similar light industries. Dhows are still constructed for both utilitarian and recreational use.

Other Economy

Several additional sectors are also significant: banking, trade, tourism, shipping, air transportation, agriculture, and fishing. As the Gulf economy expanded in the early 1970s, Bahrain encouraged offshore banking houses to open branches on the island, several assuming financial functions displaced by the civil war in Lebanon. More than 40 banks operated profitably until the regional recession of the early 1980s, when several closed. After the recession, more than 50 banking units were attracted by Bahrain's financial advantages and excellent communication facilities. The state has continued its traditional Gulfwide trade as the regional economy has grown, increasingly serving as a regional distributional center with a strong retail trade.

Muharraq International Airport served as a major stopover point for British civil aircraft during the early years of aviation links between the United Kingdom and British holdings of South and Southeast Asia, and it is still a major transit point between Europe and the Far East. More than 25 major airlines serve Muharraq, and Bahrain is the headquarters for Gulf Air, jointly owned by the lower Gulf states. The billion-dollar new causeway that links more liberal Bahrain with conservative Saudi Arabia has already had a major influence on Bahrain's socioeconomic life since it was opened in 1986. Hundreds of automobiles from Saudi Arabia transit the 15.5 mile/25 km causeway on the Thursday-Friday weekend.

Relations

Despite its small size and small population, Bahrain has multidirectional foreign relations. Its intimate connections with its larger Gulf neighbors are counterbalanced by its close relations with Britain and the United States. Bahrain must obviously maintain good rapport with Saudi Arabia, with which it has long had many close ties. For many years from the mainland has come 75

percent of the feedstock for the Bapco refinery; Saudi Arabian money paid for the new causeway and fuels much of Bahrain's industrial development, banking operations, retail trade and entrepôt operations, tourism, and even its basic budget, since much of the island's income derives from Saudi-produced oil from the offshore Abu Safah field shared between Bahrain and Saudi Arabia. With many Persian families among its mainly Shii population and with past ties to Iran, Bahrain maintains correct relations with revolutionary Iran and hopes that Iran will continue to honor the late shah's repudiation of Iran's long-standing claim to the archipelago. The state is cautious about involvement with Arab and Islamic issues and maintains strict control over militant groups on the islands, whether pro-Palestinian, pro-Arab nationalist, or pro-Iranian. The shaykhdom carefully maintains good relations with the other Gulf amirates except for Qatar, with which it contends over ownership of the Hawar Islands. Currently, Bahrain focuses on Gulf affairs through the Gulf Cooperation Council (GCC).

Ties with Britain during the decades when Bahrain was a British protected state have continued as a basic aspect of the state's political, commercial, and cultural relations. Relations with the United States have been numerous and extensive, beginning with the fact that Bapco was first a U.S. company, even though it operated under British (Canadian) charter and had mainly a British managerial staff. Bahraini-U.S. military ties increased during the 1960s and later, as Bahrain served as the low-profile home port of the U.S. Navy's Middle East Forces (MIDEASTFOR) until the mid-1970s. Bahrain also gave quiet but significant assistance to the U.S. and European convoys during the 1987–1988 tanker war in the Gulf, and it actively participated in the coalition fighting Iraq in 1990–1991.

QATAR

Peninsula State

The State of Qatar lies on a mitten-shaped peninsula midway down the east coast of the Ara-

QATAR

Long-form official name, anglicized: State of Qatar
Official name, transliterated: Dawlat Qatar
Form of government: traditional monarchy, with unicameral Advisory Council
Area: 4,412 miles^2/11,427 km^2
Population, 1991: 456,000. Literacy: estimates vary from 40% to 76%
Ethnic composition (%): Qatari Arab 20.0, other Arab (Palestinian, Lebanese, Omani, Syrian, Egyptian) 25.0, Pakistani 18.0, Indian 18.0, Iranian 16.0, European and other 3.0
Religions (%): Muslim (mostly Sunni) 92.8, Christian 5.9, Hindu 1.1, Bahai 0.2
GNP, 1988: $4.08 billion; per capita: $9,707
Petroleum reserves: 4.5 billion barrels
Main exports (% of total value, 1989): crude petroleum, petroleum products, and liquefied gas 82.0; chemicals 12.4; manufactures 5.1
Main imports (% of total value, 1989): machinery and transport equipment 37.0; manufactured goods 23.9; food and live animals 15.1; chemicals and chemical products 6.0; beverages and tobacco 1.6
Capital city: Doha (Dawhah) 217,294; other cities: al-Rayyan 41,603; al-Wakrah 13,159; Umm Said (Musayid) 6,094

---

bian Peninsula. Formed by a broad, gentle anticlinal upfold, the peninsula is a generally flat, low-lying area of mostly barren Tertiary carbonate rocks (primarily Middle Eocene limestones, dolomites, and marls), with much of the surface overlain by aeolian sheet and dune sands and *hamadah* (gravel-like desert pavement). Elevations in most of the peninsula are less than 130 ft./40 m, with limestone ridges in the west and Miocene-Pliocene mesas in the south, one of which was Qatar's highest point of 338 ft./103 m. The main western ridge is Jabal Dukhan, the surface expression of a tight north-south anticlinal fold that lies parallel to the main peninsula upwarp and to the similar Bahrain and Dammam folds to the northwest. The ridge also reflects the subsurface structure that contains Qatar's Dukhan oil and gas field, the amirate's only onshore producer. Sterile sand dunes and *sabkhahs* characterize the base of the peninsula. The remarkable northwest-southeast lineation of aeolian sand ridges in all parts of the peninsula connotes the prevailing northwest wind, the *shamal*.[19] Of the several islands included in the state, Halul, to the east of the peninsula, is of particular importance in oil operations. The Hawar Islands off the west coast of Qatar are disputed with Bahrain.

The desert climate is reflected in the widely spaced and stunted flora, and temperatures and precipitation are similar to those in Bahrain. Qatar has no streams or springs, and only in recent years has well drilling found modestly productive underground aquifers. The groundwater is pumped to irrigate scattered small agricultural plots that utilize about 250 of the 850 generally circular surface depressions located mainly in the northern half of the peninsula. Varying in depth from about 6.5 ft./2 m to 65 ft./20 m and in diameter from approximately 700 ft./213 m to 1.2 miles/2 km, the depressions (*rawdahs;* often *rodas*) are surface expressions of underground collapse of solution structures in limestone and evaporites. The *rawdahs* collect water after rains and support denser vegetation; thus, they are nature-provided plots for agriculture. Irrigation of the *rawdahs* by groundwater has led to dangerous over-pumping from the shallow aquifers, diminishing the water supply for Doha and necessitating desalination of seawater at a plant near Doha.[20]

Shallow Gulf waters in the bay west of the peninsula prevent maritime approaches; thus, despite the location of the Dukhan field just inland from the west coast, port and urban development has taken place on the eastern shore. Land has also been reclaimed along the eastern shore north and south of the capital city, Doha (Dawhah), which takes its name from the same Arabic word for a small crescent bay. In addition to several other *dawhahs,* the coast of Qatar exhibits a score of *khawrs,* more elongated and deeper indentations than *dawhahs,* and several *sabkhahs* (see Glossary and Fig. 5-2).

Several Neolithic sites have been found in northern Qatar, but later occupation appears to have been limited, presumably because of increasing desiccation of the climate. By the eighteenth century, Qatar was controlled by the family of Al Khalifah in the west and Al Thani clan, originally Bedouins from Najd, in the east. When the Al Khalifah family moved to Bahrain, the Al Thani assumed control in Qatar, and it is still the ruling family. Qatar became a British protectorate in 1916 and achieved sovereignty in September 1971, when the British withdrew from the Gulf.[21]

From Poverty to Prosperity

Qatar was isolated, sparsely populated, and poor before the late 1930s. Prior to that time, limited fishing and pearling, with bits of irrigation agriculture, supported fewer than 20,000 people. Petroleum Development (Qatar), renamed the Qatar Petroleum Company (QPC) in 1963, an Iraq Petroleum Company subsidiary, received a petroleum concession in 1935, found oil in the Dukhan fold in 1940, and began exporting in 1949. Shell received the concession for Qatar's offshore areas in 1952 and discovered the Idd al-Shargi field in 1960, Maydan-Mahzam in 1963, and Bu al-Hanin in 1970. By the early 1990s, Qatar's proved reserves exceeded 4.5 billion barrels. In 1971, Shell drilled into the Khuff zone in Qatari waters 165 ft./50 m deep and 44 miles/70 km north of the peninsula and discovered the North Field gas reservoir, its 150 trillion ft.^{3} in proved reserves making it the world's largest known single nonassociated gas reservoir. The North Field gives Qatar the sixth-largest proved gas reserves in the world, and the probable reserves of 350 trillion ft.^{3} would rank Qatar third.

Qatar assumed ownership of QPC in stages and held 100 percent by 1976, added 100 percent of Shell operations in 1977, and consolidated both in the Qatar General Petroleum Company. Qatar and Abu Dhabi share production from the offshore Bunduq field, located astride their median line. Qatar's oil output rose to more than 500,000 bpd in the late 1970s and then stabilized at about 390,000 bpd in the early 1990s. Thus, the substantial production continues to afford the small population of Qatar a very high per capita income.

In modernizing and industrializing, Qatar faced shortages in most factors except energy. In order to gain access to technical and managerial skills, it arranged joint ventures with the Norwegians, Japanese, French, and others for a fertilizer plant; a direct-reduction iron and steel plant, using imported ores and exporting three-fourths of the output; and a petrochemical complex that is one of the largest in the Middle East. All were installed in a heavy-industry park at Musayid (Umm Said), 25 miles/40 km south of Doha. The concentration also has a 62,000-bpd throughput refinery, twin natural gas liquids (NGL) plants that are planned to be among the world's largest, and several support activities.

After many years of study and three years of construction, actual production of 800 million ft.^{3}/day in Phase I, which cost $1 billion, began in 1990. Gas and condensates are pumped to Musayid initially to be used to produce NGL for export. Phase II will utilize dry gas domestically for liquefaction and possibly for long-distance export by pipeline. Phase III will expand NGL production. The North Field could produce 2 billion ft.^{3}/day for at least 200 years and probably for 400 years. Qatar's already hydrocarbon-dedicated industry is thus gearing up for great expansion to make maximum use of North Field Khuff gas. A light-industrial zone near Doha supplies processed foods and small manufactured items for Qatar's limited number of inhabitants.

Qatar's small population has increased by more than eighteen times since the 1930s, rising to slightly more than 444,000 by 1991 as the economy attracted thousands of Iranians, Omanis, Indians, Pakistanis, Baluch, and Arabs from North Yemen, Egypt, Lebanon, and Palestine. As one consequence of the influx of immigrants, only one-fifth of the population is now indigenous Qatari. More than two-thirds of the state's

Figure 18-3. *Royal palace, Doha, Qatar.*

population live in Doha and its immediate sub-urbs, with a secondary concentration in the oil export terminal and industrial town of Musayid. The interior of the peninsula is very sparsely in-habited but supports a varying number of small *rawdah* farms and a few hundred Bedouin fami-lies, whose numbers decrease yearly.

Intensive city planning began in Doha after the discovery of oil. The original town has been completely redeveloped, with new areas added along successive ring roads, as in Kuwait City. A series of palaces to house the ruler and his ad-ministrative offices was climaxed by construc-tion in the late 1980s of a grand marble palace on the shore of Doha Bay (Fig. 18-3). A former pal-ace now houses Qatar's national museum, and other palaces are integrated into the design of the city. It is fortunate that Qatar and other Gulf states have seriously undertaken to preserve arti-facts of their interesting but rapidly changing cultures.

UNITED ARAB EMIRATES (UAE)

A Survey

Youngest of the Middle East states, the United Arab Emirates[22] comprises seven desert compo-nent polities: Abu Dhabi, Dubai, Sharjah, Ajman, Umm al-Qaywayn, Ras al-Khaymah, and, the only amirate not facing the Gulf, Fujayrah (see Map 18-2). Thus, the UAE occupies coasts on both sides of the Musandam Peninsula in the eastern corner of the Arabian Peninsula. Formerly an aggregation of British-protected

tribal shaykhdoms known as the Trucial States, the amirates moved abruptly from isolation and poverty in the 1950s to oil wealth and dramatic development in the 1970s and 1980s.[23]

Neolithic and Bronze Age settlements and tombs, found especially in Abu Dhabi and Du-bai, reveal ties with the Dilmun and Sumerian cultures in the northern Gulf and Mesopotamia. The coastal area became familiar to Europeans—the Portuguese in the early 1500s and then the British in the 1700s. The sequence of coastal is-lands and indentations, offering shelter to Gulf fishing and pearling dhows, were dotted with coastal villages that, through a series of treaties, were placed under British protection. After sev-eral British naval operations in the southern Gulf, the British imposed the first coastwide maritime truce in 1820 and followed it with other treaties and imposed agreements in 1835, 1839, and 1847.[24] The Treaty of Maritime Peace in Per-petuity (1853) gave the British navy supervision over maritime relations in the lower Gulf, leaving land relations to the shaykhdoms. From this 1853 truce evolved the official designation of the coastal settlements as the Trucial States (some-times Trucial Shaykhdoms, Trucial Coast, or even Trucial Oman), a designation that lasted for more than a century. Out of these "village states," whose patterns of independence shifted as ruling families altered relationships and domains, de-veloped the post-1971 United Arab Emirates.

In 1951, the British persuaded the rulers of the shaykhdoms to create a Council of Trucial State Rulers, and in the same year the Trucial Oman Levies were organized to suppress slave traffic and maintain law and order. These forces later

UNITED ARAB EMIRATES

Long-form official name, anglicized: United Arab Emirates

Official name, transliterated: Ittihad al-Imarat al-Arabiyah al-Muttahidah

Form of government: federation of seven monarchies (amirates or shaykhdoms)—Abu Dhabi, Dubay, Sharjah, Ajman, Umm al-Qawayn, Ras al-Khaymah, and Fujayrah—with specified powers to the central government and remaining powers to the individual rulers

Area: 30,000 miles^2/77,700 km^2 (area imprecise, since some land boundaries undelimited)

Population, 1991: 1,945,000. Literacy (latest): 73%

Ethnic composition (%): Emirian 19.0, other Arab (Egyptian, Lebanese, Palestinian, Sudanese, Omani) 23.0, South Asian (Baluchi and other Pakistani, Indian, Sri Lankan, Bangladeshi) 48.0, Iranian 5.0, African 0.8, European and other expatriates 4.2

Religions (%): Muslim 95.0 (Shii 20.0), Christian 4.0, other 1.0

GNP, 1989: $28.45 billion; per capita: $18,430

Petroleum reserves: 98.1 billion barrels (third-largest in Middle East and world)

Main exports (% of total value, 1989): crude petroleum 65.6; reexports, fish, dates 25.0

Main imports (% of total value, 1986): machinery and transport equipment 31.0; basic manufactures 21.1; food and live animals 16.0; chemicals 6.7; mineral fuels 4.9; crude minerals 1.8

Capital city (populations as of 1989): Abu Dhabi 510,000; other cities: Dubai 475,000; Sharjah (al-Shariqah) 200,000; al-Ayn 195,000; Ras al-Khaymah 105,000

---

became the storybook Trucial Oman Scouts (TOS), who, under a handful of British officers seconded to them, were responsible for security in the area. Disbanded after independence, the TOS supplied cadres to the new military units of the UAE.

The landscape along the UAE coast has been transformed in one generation. Formerly, cross-country tracks and wadi bottoms served as roads until the mid-1960s (see Fig. 9-2), and a few small generators supplied electricity only part of the time in the towns. After the decline of pearling, fishing was the leading economic activity, although there was some dhow trade. In the early 1960s, the oil boom began in Abu Dhabi, later in Dubai, and then in the other amirates. Within a few years after independence, the UAE achieved a level of economic development that could be described only as spectacular, its people enjoying the world's highest per capita income.

Preliminary to their withdrawal from the Gulf, the British delineated shaykhdom boundaries for the first time, partly to inhibit later boundary conflicts and partly to prevent dissension over oil and gas exploration. With British warnings against political fragmentation, the Trucial States explored confederation with Bahrain and Qatar but finally remained separate, becoming inde-

pendent under a provisional constitution on December 2, 1971. Ras al-Khaymah originally held back but relented and joined the federation in February 1972.

Despite British efforts, boundary disputes among several shaykhdoms jeopardized the success of federal integration in the early months; however, Dubai and Abu Dhabi resolved their boundary problem by agreeing to a Neutral Zone, and Dubai and Sharjah settled their dispute in 1976. Although the federation envisioned in the provisional constitution encountered certain difficulties, especially the reluctance of local rulers to surrender their traditional powers to a central government, the UAE has evolved into a viable political unit. To the relief of the people, other Gulf states, and the British, centripetal forces were stronger than centrifugal forces; and the UAE emerged as a political-geographical oddity, a republic in which the federal units are monarchies.

Population

Development in the amirates stimulated growth of the population from about 95,000 in 1960 to about 230,000 in 1970, followed by an explosive sixfold increase between 1970 and 1991, when the

Figure 18-4. *Inner court (foreground) and wall and tower of the old fort, contrasting with new high-rise office buildings in distance, Abu Dhabi, UAE. When I called on the ruler of Abu Dhabi (Shaykh Shakhbut) for the first time in 1964, the fort was one of only half a dozen permanent structures in the town. All others were* barastis—*built of palm fronds.*

Figure 18-5. *Fabled Dubai Creek (Khawr Dubay), 1964 and 1979, from same hotel roof. Note filled land in foreground and new buildings along boulevard to right. The inlet long served as the city's port and helped make Dubai the main commercial center of the lower Gulf.*

total exceeded 1.9 million. By far most of the population is concentrated in the UAE provisional capital city of Abu Dhabi and in the coalescing cities of Dubai and Sharjah (Figs. 18-4 and 18-5). Additional nodes of population mark the other amirate capitals, several scattered oasis towns, and especially the merging villages and towns in al-Ayn, the UAE section of the Buraymi Oasis. The ethnic composition of the population is noteworthy, not only because it is the most complex of the varied population mixtures of the Gulf states but also because only 19 percent of the UAE population is indigenous Emirian.

The sparse local population of the early 1960s could not meet the demand for labor, either in numbers or in technical skills, that erupted in the early boom years. The rate of migration created housing shortages, forcing many workers, some with families, into *barasti* ("palm frond") huts, tents, and other spontaneous housing until the wealthier amirates erected extensive block after block of houses. By the early 1980s, the construction boom had ended, even before declining oil prices depressed the UAE economy. The two trends reduced the demand for expatriate workers, especially unskilled laborers, and the UAE is attempting to reduce its huge expatriate (noncitizen aliens) population, which comprises more than 80 percent of the work force. If it succeeds, the total UAE population will decrease appreciably by the late 1990s. However, some of the demand for professionals and technicians remains.

Economic Development

Oil and related industries dominate the economy of the UAE as they do in Qatar and Kuwait. For example, crude oil exports supply 77 percent of export earnings, and 70 percent of government revenues are from oil. It is noteworthy that Abu Dhabi produces nearly three-fourths of the UAE's oil and contributes more than three-fourths of the federal government's income. As in the other Gulf oil producers, especially Bahrain, the UAE has followed a vigorous program of diversifying industries that are energy-related and several that are only indirectly related. Although most of the plants are export-oriented, some of them cater to the affluent population distributed over the union area.

However, as important as the oil industry is, the several amirates have expanded their traditional economic activities: trade and transit trade, shipping, and modest but increasingly important agriculture that includes animal raising and fishing. Even more significant is the great role of services, including government and banking, which supply 25 percent of the GDP, compared with 34 percent supplied by oil, 12 percent by trade, and 9 percent each by manufacturing and construction. The rapid influx of banks brought, among others, the Bank of Credit and Commerce International (BCCI), founded by a Pakistani national but with headquarters in Luxembourg. Various directors and managers included persons of several nationalities, and the ruler of Abu Dhabi and president of the UAE was sold major shareholdings. Accused of fraudulent operations on a grand scale, the BCCI was closed down in the United Kingdom and the United States in mid-1991, although the ruler offered to make good the major shortages.[25] The scandal was still reverberating a year later. Thus, the diversified and vigorous economy in a larger territory gives the UAE an outward and genuine air of energy and a lively bustle. Different centers have developed specializations and characteristics: Abu Dhabi is an oil, financial, industrial, recreational, and shipping center (Fig. 18-5); Sharjah complements Dubai as a diversified shipping, manufacturing, and business center; and Fujayrah is a beach resort. Al-Ayn is a productive agricultural oasis, as are Sharjah's Dhayd and Ras al-Khaymah's Diqdaqah (Digdagga) Oasis.

Oil and Oil Industries

Ranking second or third in both the Middle East and the world in proved petroleum reserves, along with Iraq and after Saudi Arabia, the UAE possesses a known 98.1 billion barrels. New discoveries tripled the reserves between 1987 and 1988. The UAE thus modestly surpassed Kuwait and Iran (see Table 8-1) and has far more reserves than any of the next three oil giants—Venezuela, the former Soviet lands combined, and Mexico—with 50–60 billion barrels each. It has nearly four times the oil of the United States and could produce 2 million bpd for 135 years. In addition, as a result of the new discoveries in 1986–1988, the UAE has the second-largest nonassociated gas reserves in the Middle East (after Iran) and third-largest in the world (the former Soviet Union area leads all others). Abu Dhabi alone has 94 percent of the federation's oil reserves and 91 percent of the gas (see Table 8-1). Each member amirate in the federation retains full rights to its individual oil and gas resources, sharing with other states only that income unanimously agreed upon.

Petroleum Development (Trucial States), an Iraq Petroleum Company subsidiary that became Abu Dhabi Petroleum Company in 1962, conducted initial exploration in southwestern Abu Dhabi in 1939, found oil in 1958, but exported only in 1963. Produced in the great Bab field (originally Murban), the oil was lifted from a major new terminal at Jabal Dhanna in extreme western Abu Dhabi. Meanwhile, oil had been found by Abu Dhabi Marine Areas in the offshore Umm Shaif field, which began production in 1962. A second offshore field, Zakum, went on stream in 1967, with production pumped to the Das Island terminal, along with output from Umm Shaif and from Bunduq, jointly owned with Qatar. By the early 1990s, more than a score of offshore fields had been found in Abu Dhabi's waters (only half of which have been put on stream), along with ten major onshore fields and a huge gas field, on the border with Saudi Arabia. The Abu Dhabi National Oil Company (ADNOC), operating mainly onshore, and Abu Dhabi Marine Areas (ADMA), mainly offshore, are the principal operating and service companies in Abu Dhabi. Together they are substantially increasing production capacity, especially from Bab onshore and Zakum offshore.

Although exploration was begun by Petroleum Development (Trucial Coast) in Dubai in 1937, it was unsuccessful. Not until 1966 did Dubai Marine Areas (DUMA, a consortium of U.S. and European companies) find the moderately large field of Fateh, 56 miles/90 km offshore (see Fig. 8-2). Associated fields were found a few years later, and Dubai's total production rose to 469,000 bpd in 1990.

Sharjah and Ras al-Khaymah found oil still later. After onshore wildcat wells in Sharjah proved dry, a new concessionaire (Crescent Petroleum Company, with Buttes Gas and Oil of the United States as operator) found the small Mubarak field near Abu Musa Island, 45 miles/72 km offshore, in 1972. Oil from this field was first exported in 1974, and revenues were shared with Iran as a result of accords regarding Iran's claim to Abu Musa and therefore to its territorial waters. Mubarak production rapidly declined from 38,300 bpd to less than 5,000 bpd in 1990. However, an onshore gas condensate field found (by Amoco and Sharjah Petroleum Department) in 1980 at Saja, 5 miles/9 km inland, yielded more than 65,000 bpd in 1989, an important source of revenue for Sharjah. However, like Mubarak, the Saja field output fell rapidly and yielded only 22,500 bpd in 1990. Ras al-Khaymah also produces a gas condensate from its offshore Saleh field, opened in 1983–1984 and lying 26 miles/42 km into the Gulf. Saleh is operated by Gulf Offshore Ras al-Khaymah, which drilled in 320 feet/97 m of water, an unusually great depth for Gulf offshore drilling operations, and production is from 13,000–15,000 ft./3,960–4,570 m, also unusually deep. Petroleum explorations in Ajman, Umm al-Qaywayn, and Fujayrah have been commercially unsuccessful, but some gas has been found in Umm al-Qaywayn.

For its large reserves and considerable production, the UAE has been slow to develop an oil-processing industry. A 72,500-bpd-capacity refinery went on stream in 1984 near Abu Dhabi City to supplement the 120,000-bpd refinery opened in 1982 (its capacity was doubled in the early 1990s) in the Abu Dhabi industrial zone at al-Ruways, near Jabal Dhanna. That zone also has plants producing fertilizers, petrochemicals, and NGL. Similar NGL plants operate in Sharjah and Ras al-Khaymah. A combined LNG/LPG plant began operating on Das Island in 1977 and was greatly expanded in the late 1980s. Dubai has a large oil-field-equipment fabricating facility serving offshore operations in the entire lower Gulf, a service in which Sharjah also joined in recent years. The future for UAE oil and associated industry is certain to be bright.

Other Industries

In addition to the petroleum-processing plants, the al-Ruways industrial zone contains other plants, including a steel mill producing iron bars for construction. However, a much greater industrial development along Dubai's desert coast has overtaken al-Ruways. Dubai opened its considerable industrial zone in the mid-1970s at Jabal Ali, 17 miles/27 km southwest of the city of Dubai. With a large deep-dredged port, complete with modern container facilities, the complex has had explosive development under Dubai's aggressive and progressive free-enterprise business policies. With a large aluminum smelter—expanded to 235,000 tons per year in the early 1990s—as an initial feature, Jabal Ali added a huge free zone and has attracted 300 manufacturing, shipping, and trade enterprises employing 13,000 workers. Raw materials can be brought in, processed, and reexported as manufactures without customs levies. Plentiful cheap electric energy from a continually expanding dual power station and desalination plant powers the industrial park and serves as a strong attraction. An aluminum extrusion mill, a cement plant, a steel plant using sponge iron from India, petrochemical plants, heavy maintenance shops, paint factories, food-processing establishments, clothing factories, and many other enterprises operate in the sprawling Jabal Ali complex. Modest but impressive industrial parks have also been developed in Sharjah

Figure 18-6. *Sharjah City's old* suq *(left, 1964), with palm frond roof for shade, and one of Sharjah's new* suqs *(right, 1979). In the background are high-rise buildings of the city's new central business district. In 1990 an ornate "new new* suq," *al-Majarrah, opened in Sharjah.*

and tiny Ajman. As in other energy-rich Gulf states, desalination is a major and still expanding industry. More than 32 plants generate large amounts of electricity plus 250 million gallons per day (MGPD) of desalted water. Abu Dhabi, Dubai, and Sharjah alone invested $1.5 billion in plant expansion in the early 1990s.

Trade and Transportation

Crude petroleum and refined products constitute the bulk of the UAE's exports, most of which go to Western Europe, Japan, and the United States. However, reexports and UAE-fabricated products such as aluminum are becoming increasingly important and constitute more than one-fourth of exports. The highly varied imports include decreasing percentages of food as the UAE expands its own agricultural output. Machinery, much of it for oil operations, and many consumer goods together constitute more than half of imports. A centuries-long tradition continues in regional maritime trade and in extensive commerce with India. The picturesque dhow operations from the Creek in Dubai smuggle gold and consumer goods to the subcontinent and to Iran. A wealthy upper class and an affluent middle class create a lively demand for consumer goods. Most impressive is the continual influx of travelers from Eastern Europe who take "shopping vacations" in Sharjah and Dubai, with their low-duty or duty-free shops. The shoppers fly in specifically to buy electronic items, watches, jewelry, photographic equipment, and other low-bulk,

high-value goods to take back to their home countries and sell at handsome profits. The trade is highly organized, from shopping flights to discount hotel rates to shopping buses to the huge new magnificent *suqs* of Sharjah, Dubai, and Ajman. These extraordinary shopping malls feature world-class architecture (Fig. 18-6) and are brimming with inventories of goods from Japan, India and Pakistan, Iran, Europe, the United States, and the Arabian Peninsula. The Abu Dhabi–Dubai–Sharjah triad is approaching the world trade level of Hong Kong and Singapore.

Large, planned ports in Dubai, Abu Dhabi, and Sharjah contrast with their tiny predecessors, which were used only by dhows for Gulf and Indian trade, fishing, and pearling. Port Rashid in Dubai is one of the largest ports in the Middle East, enclosing more than 500 acres/200 ha within its breakwater. The Jabal Ali port in southern Dubai has steadily increased its cargo handling. In a manner typical of the competitiveness among member amirates, Abu Dhabi has expanded its Port Zayyid, especially its container facilities; Sharjah has vigorously pushed its smaller Port Khalid in Sharjah town and its container port of Khawr (Khor) Fakkan on the east coast, facing the Indian Ocean; and Ajman and Ras al-Khaymah promote their small ports.

Of the federation's four larger airports (Abu Dhabi, Dubai, Sharjah, and Ras al-Khaymah), Abu Dhabi is the busiest, but Sharjah's more central location and its promotion of "shopper vacations" (along with its aesthetically remarkable terminal) gave it first place in passenger arrivals in the late 1980s. Again, competitiveness led Ajman and Fujayrah each to open its own airport. Thus, the UAE is oversupplied with both seaports and airports. All towns and villages in the UAE are now integrated into an excellent national highway network (see Fig. 9-2b).

Agriculture and Fishing

Although their relative contribution to the economy is now minor, fishing (including pearling) and agriculture (including nomadic herding) were the main bases of the Trucial States economy prior to World War II. Agriculture in this desert environment was then confined to small oases and date palm groves around the coastal villages, and the limited water resources were minimally developed. After the mid-1960s, the greatly increased availability of capital and the greater demand for fresh foods stimulated development of the few potentially productive agricultural areas.

Increased production has come especially from the two extensive oases of al-Ayn, located in eastern Abu Dhabi (see Map 18-2), and Diqdaqah in Ras al-Khaymah. Both lie at the western foot of the Oman Mountains and both tap aquifers fed by runoff from the mountain slopes. Diqdaqah, south of the town of Ras al-Khaymah, contains an agricultural experimental station established in the oasis in 1956; fruits and vegetables from Diqdaqah supply many of the needs of the cities to the south. The formerly small but well-watered oasis of Dhayd, east of Sharjah, has burgeoned into an extensive groundwater-irrigated farming area producing varied crops from strawberries to lemons. Al-Ayn, Diqdaqah, and Dhayd exemplify the marvels that can be wrought with huge inputs of capital and technology. Large dairy farms also operate in all the large oases, as do air-conditioned chicken farms marketing several million chickens each year. More than 50 small groves of date palms extend along an arc of tiny oases in al-Jiwa (or al-Liwa) in southwestern Abu Dhabi.

Relations

With some of the world's largest petroleum and gas reserves in a crucial location, yet with a small population and negligible military strength, the vulnerable UAE must walk a strategic tightrope. It follows a pragmatic but skillfully diplomatic balancing act by maintaining, for example, mutually beneficial "correct" relations with Iran on one side and Saudi Arabia on the other. It ensures that, as a former British protectorate, it can rely on British assistance in a crisis; and, for double insurance, it has since independence in 1971 maintained good relations with the United States—close private commercial ties and friendly government-to-government relations, including U.S. security assistance. Relations with the United States became much closer after the Iraqi invasion of Kuwait, and the UAE contributed more than $4 billion to the coalition fighting Iraq. Locally, the UAE places much of its diplomatic emphasis on the GCC and regionally on the Arab League.

Sketches of Individual Amirates

Abu Dhabi

Largest (86 percent of the total UAE area), most populous (about 775,000 people), and by far the wealthiest (with 94 percent of the federation's oil) of the seven component amirates, Abu Dhabi is the dominant member of the UAE. Located on a low near-shore island of *sabkhah* and sand, Abu Dhabi City, the population core, grew from a small village of *barasti* huts and a fort in the 1950s to a wealthy, bustling, planned city of 510,000 in the early 1990s, with high-rise office buildings, luxury hotels and palaces, divided boulevards, mosques and schools, housing estates, and irrigated plantings bordering and dividing boulevards and ornamenting large traffic circles. It also serves as the provisional capital of the UAE. A secondary core is in the oasis of al-Ayn, and other clusters are in the al-Ruways–Jabal Dhanna oil and industrial area and in the arc of al-Jiwa (al-Liwa) oases.

Dubai

Next-largest polity and next in location to the north of Abu Dhabi is the amirate of Dubai, population 540,000, with about 45 miles/72 km of sand and *sabkhah* coastline. The commercial and shipping center of Dubai (population

475,000) developed on both sides of Dubai Creek, which affords an ideal and picturesque harbor for dhows engaged in fishing, pearling, smuggling, and other maritime trade (see Fig. 18-5). Dubai proper, more of an administrative center, lies south of the creek and has a carefully preserved group of older structures topped by *badgirs,* Persian wind towers (see Fig. 4-1); Dayrah, with more of the commercial functions, developed north of the inlet. With a laissez-faire commercial philosophy, this amirate predominates as the commercial center of the coast, with a lively nightlife.

Sharjah

Third-largest amirate and adjacent to Dubai on the north is Sharjah (al-Shariqah), and the cities of Sharjah and Dubai virtually coalesce. The amirate's 10-mile/16-km coastline formerly included a small dhow harbor, which developed into a modest modern port after 1970. Sharjah's territory, with a population of 295,000, is the most fragmented of all the amirates (see Map 18-2). With three exclaves on the Batinah coast of the Gulf of Oman (Diba, Khawr Fakkan, and Kalba), Sharjah thus has a common border with all six of the other polities in the federation. Dhayd Oasis and irrigated plots along the Batinah coast combine to give Sharjah a plentiful supply of fruits and vegetables. With only limited resources in hydrocarbons, Sharjah pursued a vigorous program of tourism and tour-shopping, and the city has an extraordinary number of four-star and five-star hotels and retail shops. Two Gulf islands, Abu Musa and Sir Abu Nuayr, are claimed by Sharjah, but Iran also claims Abu Musa, maintains troops there, and shares revenues from the offshore field in the island's territorial waters. Sharjah, with 200,000 people, was the site of the coast's first airfield and also hosted a Royal Air Force detachment and, after the mid-1950s, the headquarters of the Trucial Oman Scouts.

Ajman

Next up the coast is the amirate of Ajman, the smallest unit in the UAE, with 75,000 people. It includes the town of Ajman, population 71,000, a strip of desert behind the town, and two tiny exclaves in the interior. In competition with Sharjah, Ajman has developed a small but lively industrial park in its port area and in 1990 opened a large, gleaming white shopping mall, Suq al-Ajman. It retains seafaring traditions in a large dhow-building yard and in a fish-trap fabricating facility.

Umm al-Qaywayn

North of Ajman is the second-smallest and the least populated (35,000 people) of the amirates, Umm al-Qaywayn. With a population of 33,000, the town occupies a site on the tip of a narrow peninsula, reached by a spur from the coastal highway. With no energy resources until recently, and only limited gas fields found so far, Umm al-Qaywayn has lagged behind the other members in the federation in developmental growth, although it has attracted a few clothing-manufacturing and printing establishments.

Ras al-Khaymah

Northernmost of the polities and occupying a triangular area west of the mountain spur that reaches the sea at the village of Sham, Ras al-Khaymah, population 126,000, exhibits appreciable diversity. The town itself, with 105,000 people, lies on a peninsula and has a long seafaring tradition. The Diqdaqah agricultural station and half a dozen other towns and villages are distributed around the amirate. In the mountains at the northern tip of Ras al-Khaymah lives a small but interesting non-Arab ethnic group, the Shihuh. The two offshore islands of Little Tunbs and Great Tunbs were long claimed by Ras al-Khaymah but were seized by Iran in 1971. Ras al-Khaymah's only known oil comes from its offshore field of Saleh.

Fujayrah

The only federation member located on the eastern, or Gulf of Oman, side of the peninsula, Fujayrah, now with 68,000 people, was isolated until federal highways made it easily accessible and encouraged a beach-resort development. Having only a limited fishing economy and a few date palms until the 1960s, Fujayrah's resort facilities include stretches of clean, sandy, and still uncrowded beaches. Huge chicken farms with air-conditioned hen houses and a major dairy have also been developed inland from the resort.

19

Oman and Yemen: The Southern Fringe

Extending from the Strait of Hormuz to the Bab el-Mandeb along the southern fringe of the Arabian Peninsula are Oman and Yemen, the two largest of the six peripheral states of the peninsula. Since 1971 Oman has developed increasingly close relations with the Gulf states (with which it is often grouped because of its exclave on the Strait of Hormuz) and with neighboring Saudi Arabia. In 1990, the long-separated North Yemen and South Yemen merged to create a unified Republic of Yemen.[1]

Oman and the two formerly separate parts of Yemen maintain individually distinct characters physically, culturally, economically, and politically. Oman is a sultanate, the formerly almost absolute monarch now (since 1981) advised by an appointed consultative council. Conservative and stable, it maintains cautious links with the West and has had a decade of well-planned development, financed by its moderately large oil income. Pre-1990 South Yemen, the People's Democratic Republic of Yemen (PDRY), was a Marxist republic with links with the USSR, North Korea, and China. A pariah state in the region, it was, outside the Aden urban area, the least developed country in the Middle East, the most unstable state on the peninsula, and the country with the poorest prospects, brightened somewhat by modest oil finds in the mid-1980s. The former North Yemen, the Yemen Arab Republic (YAR), the most populous of the peripheral states of the peninsula, was a republic with relations with both East and West. Recent oil discoveries gave this heavily populated, long-poor region justified expectations of a much brighter future. The unified Republic of Yemen merges the respective characteristics of the formerly separate states, so far to their mutual benefit.

OMAN

Termed Muscat and Oman prior to 1970, the Sultanate of Oman was also sometimes confused with Trucial Oman, an alternate name for the Trucial States, now the UAE. Among other things, the several names reflect the regionalization of Oman into two basic parts: Inner Oman, west of the mountains, and the Batinah coast along the Gulf of Oman (Map 19-1).

The only sultanate in the Middle East, Oman exhibits many of the same types of development and modernization seen in the other oil states of the Gulf region. However, Oman has evolved in its own distinctive way, modernizing while maintaining much of its traditional culture. Caution and conservatism, therefore, characterize the Omani approach to development, and the sultanate deliberately maintains modest growth rather than allowing the explosive expansion of Kuwait, Abu Dhabi, and Dubai. For example, the population is estimated to have grown less than 220 percent between 1960 and 1992, compared with an increase of more than 1,900 percent in the UAE during the same period.

Oman lies on the Tropic of Cancer; it is exceptionally hot in summer and is warm even during the low-sun season. It is a desert land except in a few higher elevations and in the highlands of southern Dhufar. Muscat, the capital city, lies virtually on the Tropic of Cancer, has an average

OMAN

Long-form official name, anglicized: Sultanate of Oman
Official name, transliterated: Saltanat Uman
Form of government: monarchy with a consultative council appointed by the sultan
Area: 120,000 miles^2/300,000 km^2 (area imprecise, since land boundaries undelimited; other estimates are as low as 81,850 miles^2/212,000 km^2
Population, 1991: 1,559,000 (rough estimate; no census ever taken). Literacy (latest): 41%
Ethnic composition (%): Omani Arab 73.5, Indian and Pakistani (mostly Baluch) 21.0, Bengali 2.5, other 3.0
Religions (%): Ibadhi Muslim 75.0, other Muslim 11.0, Hindu 13.0, other 1.0
GNP, 1989: $7.76 billion; per capita: $5,220
Petroleum reserves: 4.3 billion barrels
Main exports (% of total value, 1990): crude petroleum and gas 91.7; reexports 5.1; food and live animals (including fish) 1.1; copper cathodes 1.7; fruits and vegetables 0.4
Main imports (% of total value, 1990): machinery and transport equipment 36.1; manufactured goods 18.4; food and live animals 16.0; miscellaneous manufactured articles 10.4; chemicals 5.8; minerals, fuels, lubricants, and related materials 4.0
Capital city: Muscat (Greater Capital Area) 400,000; other cities: Nazwa 62,880; Samail 44,721; Salalah 35,000

---

annual temperature of 84°F/29°C, and receives less than 4 in./100 mm of rainfall annually. Along with the Yemen Mountains, highland Oman receives appreciable amounts of summer monsoon rain, particularly in the mountains around Salalah in the extreme south, as well as orographically enhanced winter cyclonic storm rain, exceeding 18 in./457 mm in parts of the northern ranges. Runoff from such rains in the northern mountains supplies the irrigation water for crops along the Batinah coast and in the interior oases.

Physical Regions

Oman comprises five distinct physical regions, each of which possesses its individual cultural character: [1] the Batinah coast, [2] al-Hajar (or Oman Mountains), [3] Inner Oman, [4] Central Oman, and [5] Dhufar (see circled numbers on Map 19-1).

[1] Batinah Coast

The Batinah coast is a coastal plain 6–18 miles/10–30 km wide that extends for 168 miles/270 km along the arc of the Gulf of Oman coast. Composed primarily of coalesced alluvial fandeltas of gravel, sand, and silt, the plain is

Oman's primary agricultural area, cultivated for thousands of years. Crops are irrigated in a strip about 1.8 miles/3 km wide, using the appreciable groundwater stored in the sandy gravels of the alluvial fans that have been built at the mouths of the streams after descending the mountain slopes. Unfortunately, modern pumps installed after 1976 have overdrawn the numerous but limited aquifers, and seawater is increasingly intruding the coarse aquifers. Several irrigated plots had to be abandoned before Ministry of Water controls reduced the drawdown. Towns and villages, several of considerable antiquity, are strung along the coast at the mouths of larger wadis, with Suhar probably being the best-known town.

[2] Al-Hajar

Often referred to as the Oman Mountains, al-Hajar ("the Rock") is a high, rugged, almost unbroken chain of mountains that parallel the Batinah coast in a 435-mile/700-km arc from the northern tip of the Musandam Peninsula to Ras al-Hadd. The northern end of the mountains overlooks the Strait of Hormuz and constitutes Ras Musandam, a striking desert fjord-type land that forms a maze of isthmuses and islands with

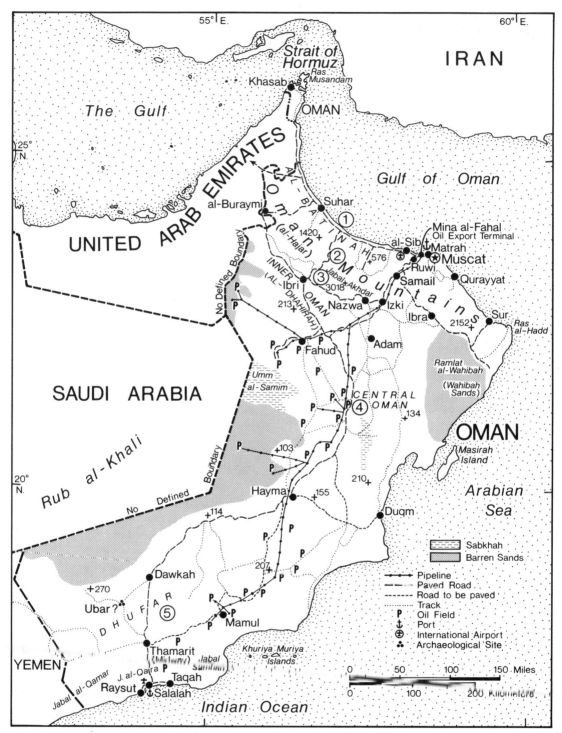

Map 19-1. *General and economic map of Oman, with circled numbers indicating regions mentioned in text. Note the widespread occurrence of petroleum fields. The political boundaries between Oman and its neighbors are in the process of gradually being officially defined.*

coastal cliffs dropping sharply to sea-filled valleys. Politically, this tip of the Musandam Peninsula is an Omani exclave, separated from the rest of the sultanate territory by a wedge of the UAE. Much of the mountain chain exceeds 4,800 ft./1,463 m. Peak elevations reach nearly 10,000 ft./3,048 m in the central block, the very rugged Jabal al-Akhdar (Green Mountain), a name sometimes mistakenly applied to the entire Hajar range. The one major pass through the chain is Samail Gap, just east of Jabal al-Akhdar, which is traversed by the main route connecting the Muscat area to Inner Oman. Oman's lifelines—large oil and gas pipelines—parallel the highway and carry the sultanate's entire production to the export terminal west of Matrah. The gap divides the Hajar range into the larger, scenically rugged Western Hajar (Hajar al-Gharbi) and the smaller Eastern Hajar (Hajar al-Sharqi).

[3] Inner Oman

Inner Oman (al-Dhahirah) is an amorphous area extending southwestward from al-Hajar to the sands of the Rub al-Khali. The pattern of long-settled villages—Izki, Nazwa, Bahlah, Ibri, Dank, and others, as well as the oasis town of Buraymi—along the internal piedmont and belt of alluvial fans resembles the string of Batinah settlements on the eastern side of al-Hajar. However, the interior settlements are less endowed with water resources and have traditionally been isolated because of their remote location, wedged between the rugged mountains to the east and the barren sands to the west. Even so, Inner Oman has long had ties with the Gulf shaykhdoms, especially through the Buraymi Oasis, as well as with Muscat and the Batinah. Subregional designations reflect a certain variety even in this seemingly uniform area: The northern extension of Inner Oman toward the large Buraymi–al-Ayn oasis is al-Jaw; and the subregion of the piedmont of Jabal Akhdar is al-Juf, supporting the major oases of al-Hamra, Bahlah, Nazwa, and Izki. East of the Samail Gap, the piedmont of the Eastern Hajar is usually referred to as al-Sharqiya (the East) and has its string of oasis towns in Ibra, al-Mudayrib, al-Mintirib, and al-Kamil. Modern highways and excellent telecommunications now facilitate closer relations in both directions, integrate the interior

economically, and strengthen political ties with the sultanate core around Muscat. This interior area is associated with the special Islamic group in Oman, the Ibadhis, who enjoyed a militant autonomy under their own imam for several decades prior to 1959. It is also the location of Oman's first and main producing oil fields.

[4] Central Oman

Central Oman extends from Inner Oman southward as a large, virtually barren area that for centuries has been little more than the realm of less than a dozen small Bedouin tribes. In the east, wedged between the Arabian Sea coast and the eastern Oman Mountains is an unusual dune field, the Wahibah Sands. The Wahibah contains a range of dune formations, including fossil sand seas, of such interest that it was the object of an intensive multidisciplinary investigation by the Royal Geographical Society (London) and Omani counterparts in 1985–1987. Otherwise, Central Oman is a monotonous land of sand and gravel, and it had little to offer until more than a score of oil fields were discovered beneath its surface (see Map 19-1). Continued exploration found another 60 small pocket fields, some of which are actually in Dhufar. A high-speed highway completed in 1986 traverses the region, connecting Muscat and Salalah.

[5] Dhufar

Dhufar is an ill-defined area that merges imperceptibly with Central Oman to the northeast and with Yemen to the west. Primarily a rough, barren, sparsely inhabited desert area inland, it has mountains just back of the south coast with green slopes and monsoon forests, some producing frankincense, that contrast spectacularly with the inland desert. Like the southern Asir in Saudi Arabia, the mountains have become a resort area and are now attracting increasing numbers of visitors seeking the monsoonal mists and the delightful autumn weather and brilliant green of the mountains after the summer rains. Dhufar was poorly known until intensive exploration opened more than a dozen producing oil fields centered 100 miles/160 km northeast of Salalah, the provincial capital. Southern Dhufar was contested between Dhufar rebels and Oman in the early 1970s (see next section). Mountain areas and some coastal villages are inhabited by several ethnolinguistic groups that are believed to pre-date Arab occupation of the area. Lying offshore are the Khuriya Muriya Islands. In November 1991, amateur archaeologists guided by satellite imagery discovered and test-excavated the ruins of an ancient city 93 miles/150 km north-north-east of Salalah that is believed to be Ubar, famed center of frankincense trade from 2000 BC to late Roman times. The ruins are located near al-Shisur wells, which tap water in gravels of a wadi draining the Jabal al-Qamar.[2]

A Historical Sketch

Although incompletely studied, the antiquity of human occupation in the region has long been recognized in sites along the coast, in Inner Oman, and in Dhufar. Artifacts and other mate-rial evidence of Phoenician settlement have sug-gested identification of the name of the ancient Omani port of Sur with that of the Phoenician Mediterranean city-state Sur (Tyre), and some scholars are persuaded that there were Omani-Phoenician maritime connections about 1500 BC. Dhufar was a major source of frankincense and engaged in a significant trade for millennia.

Like the rest of the peninsula, Oman adopted Islam in the seventh century, but the theologi-cally distinctive sect of Ibadhism, neither Sunni nor Shii, evolved in Oman in the eighth and ninth centuries and continues to be dominant. Ibadhis are the spiritual descendants of the Kharijis ("seceders"), a group that first sup-ported Ali in his claim to be caliph but then sep-arated from Ali during his conflict with the Umayyads. Oman has the only concentration of Ibadhis in the Middle East, although there are other Ibadhi communities in Zanzibar and North Africa.

Even more than in the Gulf amirates, Portu-guese control for 142 years after 1508 left its mark in the forts and towers that are still prominent along the coast, especially around Matrah and Muscat, and on hilltops elsewhere in the sultan-ate. With increasing British regional control after the Portuguese and Dutch were supplanted in the region, British influence in Oman remained strong for the next 300 years. However, the sul-tanate was technically independent after 1650,

and Britain formally recognized Omani inde-pendence in 1951. Omani seafarers ranged the In-dian Ocean and even established political control in Zanzibar and neighboring areas of East Africa and in the exclave of Gwadar on the Baluchi coast, near the present Iran-Pakistan border. Oman held Gwadar until 1958 and Zanzibar, at least indirectly, until 1964.

The Al Bu Said line, an Ibadhi dynasty, be-came the ruling power in 1744 and has retained the sultanate ever since. Inner Oman and the coast have been periodically disunited, suffering a particularly sharp division during the late nine-teenth and early twentieth centuries, when the interior Ibadhis chose to have a theocracy ruled by their religious leader, the imam of Oman. The struggle was temporarily resolved by the Treaty of Sib, signed in 1920, which granted the imam autonomy in Inner Oman but recognized the nominal sovereignty of the sultan in the interior. However, when the latest imam, Ghalib ibn Ali, was elected in 1954, conflict erupted anew; the Imam Ghalib's rebellion against the sultan's con-trol of the interior was defeated, with British help, only in 1959. The sultan of that period, Said bin Taimur Al Bu Said, prohibited use of private motor vehicles, refused expansion of the small electricity and telephone net in the capital area, and maintained a nighttime curfew in Muscat, having the city gates locked soon after dark. Oman at that time was the most backward and isolated area in the Middle East.

Four developments have dominated Oman's history since 1960. First, Oman's petroleum re-sources were discovered and have been devel-oped into an appreciable industry providing a national income of billions of dollars each year. Second, a separatist revolt by the communist-backed rebels of the Dhufar Liberation Front broke out against the sultanate in 1964. Third, the old sultan was forced to abdicate in favor of his son, the present ruler, Sultan Qabus ibn Said, in 1970. Fourth, Sultan Qabus soon abolished many of his father's antiquated restrictions, urged educated Omanis to return home to a new regime, oversaw the defeat of the Dhufar rebel-lion, launched a major development program, and united Oman.

Success of the Dhufar rebellion would not only have meant the overthrow of the sultanate and the spread of the Aden communist regime into Oman, it would probably have also threatened other conservative regimes in the Gulf. The original Dhufar Liberation Front later merged with the Marxist-dominated Popular Front for the Liberation of Oman and the Arab Gulf (PFLOAG), which proclaimed its goal of overthrowing all traditional regimes in the Gulf region. In mid-1974, PFLOAG, renamed the Popular Front for the Liberation of Oman (PFLO), was defeated and was finally driven out of Dhufar by the combined efforts of the Omanis, British officers, an Iranian task force, military forces from Jordan, and others.

The Omanis

Possibly one-fourth of the estimated total population of 1.56 million[3] is concentrated in the Muscat-Matrah-Ruwi core. Much of the rest lives in the belt of Batinah towns and the string of inner villages paralleling the southwestern piedmont of al-Hajar. Major population outliers are Salalah and surrounding villages on the southern Dhufar coast and Sur at the eastern corner of the country.

Oman's basic Arab population differs perceptibly from that of neighboring Saudi Arabia and the UAE. The distinction arises partly because influences from southern Asia and East Africa entered along the Indian Ocean coast and partly because Arab influences from the interior diminished as they diffused into this most easterly projection of the Arabian Peninsula. Furthermore, fragmented by mountain ranges, highland masses, and desert belts, Oman embraces many different ethnolinguistic and religious minorities, some still surviving in isolated mountain refuges. Strong tribal affiliations in the interior further diversify the Omani people.

Oman's maritime connections with southern Asia and East Africa and the sultanate's earlier political control of Gwadar and Zanzibar attracted immigrants from those areas. Indians, Baluch, Iranians, and Somalis and other East Africans settled in Oman, with many of the Africans being brought as slaves. The Shii Muslim Khojas (Arabic, Lawatias), a prominent minority, are members of a close-knit community of Hindu converts to Islam originally from India

but resident in Oman as merchants for more than two centuries. The Khojas occupy a separate walled quarter in Matrah but also constitute communities along the Batinah. Other Shii Muslims include the Baharinah and the Ajam, of Persian background. A considerable Hindu community, the Binya (Arabic, Banyan), similar to the Khojas in their occupations in areas of residence, came from Gujarat in India and have resided in Oman for several centuries. Several minor ethnic groups, including some unassimilated pre-Arab peoples, occupy remote mountain areas.

Indigenous Omanis are divided into two basic tribal lines. The Hinawi, the older of the two, migrated from the Yemen highlands more than 1,800 years ago, and the Ghafiri arrived later from northern Arabia. This basic division, although less significant now than a few decades ago, cuts across socioeconomic groupings and is accepted as a fundamental fact of Omani society.

Although Islam is the predominant religion in Oman, the sultanate's major sector, the Ibadhi, is distinct from all other Islamic sects in the Middle East. Oman was established as an Ibadhi state and has evolved an Ibadhi particularity. Whereas Inner Oman has long been the main concentration and theological stronghold of Ibadhism, the Al Bu Said ruling dynasty, while Ibadhi, has its power base in the southern Batinah. Conservative, fundamentalist, and simple in their principles, without being extremist, Ibadhi norms have strongly shaped Omani culture. Sunnis constitute the largest non-Ibadhi sect in Oman and are dominant in Salalah, distinguishable by their dialect. Shiis form the third-largest religious group, concentrated in the Batinah and especially in Muscat-Matrah, where the Khojas form a significant Shii community. The main non-Muslim group is the Indian Hindu community on the coast, with the only Hindu temple in the Gulf. Among the small number of Christians are Goanese, British, and Americans, the last including medical missionaries. As in the UAE, Christians have freedom of worship and have their own churches.

Most Omanis of both sexes can be immediately differentiated from other Middle Easterners by their national costumes. The standard male attire is the white, calf-long *dishdasha,* comparable to the ankle-length *thawb* in Saudi Arabia. The headgear is of one of two types: Dominant is the *kumma,* a fitted, brimless, round cap that is typically colorfully embroidered and usually expensive (see Fig. 6-3). It is unique to Oman. More formal is the elaborate modified turban, the *amamma,* a large square of light Kashmir wool artfully wound around the head. Traditionally, the well-dressed Omani male also wore a *khanjar,* a curved dagger with a highly decorated scabbard, frequently worn in the southern peninsula. Omani women also dress distinctively, with articles from both Arabia and India. Under a colorful *dishdasha* they wear ankle-length trousers, the *surawal,* and usually add one or more decorated filmy scarves or shawls. Specific items, colors, patterns, and methods of draping vary from region to region and from group to group.

Economy

Oman's preindustrial economy of seafaring, fishing, and irrigation agriculture rested on a broader base and supported a larger population than did similar economies in the Gulf shaykhdoms. For example, Oman has nearly twice the cropland of all the other four Gulf states combined, with most of its agricultural areas divided between the Batinah coast and the inner piedmont of the Hajar. Two-thirds of the agricultural area is in permanent crops, primarily dates, bananas, and limes. Fishing remains a significant economic activity, much of it still traditional, although an increasing percentage is being modernized and systematized to take advantage of the rich fisheries in the upwelling waters along the coast. Much of the catch is dried and used for animal feed and fertilizer, but about one-third is for human consumption; and dried fish, along with Oman's regionally famous dried limes, constitutes an appreciable export.

As elsewhere in the general Gulf region, Oman's economy has been revolutionized by oil developments, although Oman was the last of the Gulf region countries to discover petroleum. After several years of unsuccessful exploration in the late 1950s, the Iraq Petroleum Company (IPC) surrendered its concession, later taken up by Petroleum Development (Oman) (PDO). PDO, with Shell as its major partner, made its initial strikes at Natih, Fahud, and Yibal, 140–185 miles/225–300 km southwest of Muscat, in 1962–1964. A pipeline from the discovery area was laid through the Samail Pass to an export terminal at Mina al-Fahal, just west of Matrah, and all subsequent producing areas have been linked to this same terminal. Oman's single refinery is also at the terminal (see Table 8-2). By the early 1990s, intensive exploration by PDO and several other companies had discovered more than 80 fields, many of which are too small to tie into the system. Main output is still from a half dozen fields in the original discovery area, but appreciable production comes from fields in Central Oman and Dhufar (see Maps 8-1 and 19-1). As is shown in Table 8-2, Oman requires as many producing wells as Saudi Arabia to yield about 12 percent as much oil. Petroleum revenue is 83 percent of the total government revenue, 91 percent of the value of exports, and 45 percent of the GDP. By 1992, Oman's reserves were a moderate 4.3 billion barrels, comparable to those of Egypt, Qatar, and Yemen; and production was about 705,000 bpd. Since it is not an OPEC (or OAPEC) member, Oman is not subject to OPEC quotas or restrictions.

Few of the many minerals found in the complex rocks of al-Hajar are worth commercial exploitation; however, ancient copper workings near Suhar, in the northern Batinah, have been reopened and are open-pit mined. The processed copper has been exported as cathodes since 1983, but reserves are expected to be exhausted by 2000. Also recently exploited are deposits of chromite, manganese, asbestos, and marble.

Starting its development after the 1970 coup as the most backward country in the region, Oman under the new sultan moved deliberately, with guidance from competent, experienced consultants. Advisers and contractors were mostly British, since Britain had supplied protection and advice to Oman for many decades. Following a series of well-designed five-year plans that began in 1976, Oman first installed its basic infrastructure. For example, in 1970 only 6 miles/10 km of surfaced roads existed in the sultanate, since private vehicles were prohibited, and there was minimal electric and telephone service only in Muscat and Matrah. Oman then improved its agriculture and fishing, initiated education and

Figure 19-1. *Old and new in Oman: Ruins of the splendid old mud fort in Bahlah, in Inner Oman (left), and the magnificent al-Bustan Palace Hotel, near Muscat (right). The fort dates from the eighteenth century, the hotel from the mid-1980s.*

other social programs, and finally undertook a modest import-substitution industrial program. By the early 1990s, more than 226,000 vehicles of all types utilized thousands of miles of well-surfaced roads and a total of 13,000 miles/21,000 km of maintained roads.

West of Matrah, on the main highway to Inner Oman, is the expanding industrial estate of Rusayl, where more than 40 modest, privately owned plants manufacture a wide range of basic products for the local market: textiles, car batteries, plastic pipe, tiles, air-conditioning units, radiators, cement, aluminum products, nonalcoholic beverages, and others.

Because of the small size of the picturesque old harbor of Muscat, the new and modern port of Mina Qabus was constructed in the larger harbor at Matrah, a few miles west of Muscat, in the early 1970s. With development of southern Oman, a new port was also opened at Raysut, a few miles west of Salalah. In 1974, a large new airport was opened at Sib, west of Matrah, which is now serviced by 21 scheduled airlines. Oman's only other airport with scheduled service is at Salalah.

While pushing aggressively ahead with modernization, Oman has taken remarkable care to preserve important archaeological and cultural monuments. Most noteworthy are the picturesque sixteenth-century Portuguese forts overlooking Muscat and Matrah, the fine old mansions inside the former Muscat wall, the splendid fort of Rustaq (old capital of Oman) north of Jabal Akhdar, and the Nazwa fort. The grand mud fort of Bahlah (Fig. 19-1, left) is in restora-

tion. Worthy in themselves, these conservation measures are also intended to serve the recently launched tourism program—a remarkable contrast to the pre-1970 period when virtually no outsiders were permitted to visit the sultanate. Excellent new hotels also cater to tourists, with al-Bustan Palace Hotel, in a spacious setting east of Muscat, one of the most sumptuous hostelries in the region (Fig. 19-1, right). The Capital Area has greatly expanded west of Matrah toward the Sib airport, with a commercial and banking center in Greater Matrah–Ruwi, residences in Qurum and Madinat Qabus, and ministries and embassies in al-Khuwair.

Relations

During the many decades that the sultanate was a British protected state, most of Oman's relations were handled by His Majesty's Government. After the abdication of the reactionary former sultan in 1970, and British withdrawal from the Gulf region in 1971, Oman broadened its relations. In the West, it retained friendship with Britain but turned especially to the United States, with which it has maintained a moderately close relationship. It was quietly but firmly supportive of the coalition against Iraq in 1990–1991, a continuation of its cooperation with the Gulf states, Britain, and the United States during the Iran-Iraq war. Omani cooperation includes permitting Britain and the United States to use Masirah Island as a military base. Oman, already friendly with the UAE, has drawn increasingly close to Saudi Arabia, and in March 1990 the two neighbors agreed to survey and define their common boundary. Détente between Oman and Yemen was sharply set back by Yemen's stance on the Gulf crisis. Oman has not become intimately involved in Arab nationalist movements.

YEMEN

The newest state in the Middle East, contemporary Yemen emerged on May 22, 1990, from the fusion of the two formerly separate states of the Yemen Arab Republic (YAR, often informally referred to as North Yemen) and the People's Democratic Republic of Yemen (PDRY, often South Yemen). The united Yemen is the second-largest state and has the second-largest population on the Arabian Peninsula. Indeed, the next censuses may reveal that Yemen has an even larger population than Saudi Arabia.

The country occupies the area of the classical Arabia Felix (Fortunate Arabia), the southwest corner of the vast Arabian Peninsula. The former PDRY was the poorest Middle East country and, as a radical client of the former Soviet Union, was virtually a pariah state in the region and in the world. The former YAR was the second-poorest Middle East country and was ambivalent in its East-West relations. United Yemen is still the poorest state in the region, certainly in terms of development and productive capacity, although Egypt's GNP per capita is apparently equivalent to that of Yemen. Both Egypt and Yemen face intractable problems in the ratio between their populations and their limited employment opportunities. Indeed, unification leaves many problems unsolved and has created certain new ones; however, it was of great mutual benefit and instantly reduced many redundant expenses, numerous points of inter-Yemeni conflict (such as control over Karaman Island north of Hudaydah and Perim Island in the Bab el-Mandeb), and obstacles to economic and social development. Yemen started at a low developmental level, and it still has a long way to go—with limited capital—to reach the regional average.[4] Moderately promising petroleum production raises optimism for the future, and unification facilitates rational exploitation of shared oil and gas fields. However, Yemen's support of Iraq during the Gulf crisis has cost the new state politically and financially. The impact of these developments is examined later, following a review of the country's regions.

Five Regions

Yemen extends from the border with Oman on the east along half of the southern peninsula coast and around the corner at the strategic Bab el-Mandeb and northward along the Red Sea coast to the border with Saudi Arabia. With greatly contrasting rocks and rock structures, as well as sharp variations in relief, its dramatically rugged volcanic landscapes, including actual craters of extinct volcanoes (as in Aden), have quite different aspects from the flat-lying limestones of the Hadramawt Plateau and from the coastal plains. Most spectacular is the steep but highly dissected escarpment towering over the Red Sea Tihamah coast. Circled numbers on Map 19-2 indicate Yemen's five geographic regions.

[1] Tihamah

The Red Sea coastal plain, al-Tihamah, is a segment of the coastal fringe that reaches the full length of the western edge of the Arabian Peninsula. Averaging approximately 40 miles/65 km in width and sandy-gravelly along most of its length, it extends 325 miles/523 km from the Saudi border to the Bab el-Mandeb. Although climatically a desert, the extremely hot, humid Tihamah is traversed at intervals by large wadis that carry heavy runoff after spring and fall monsoon rains on the high escarpment above. The broad bottoms of the wadis crossing their own alluvial fans are cultivated for cotton, melons, bananas, papayas, and similar crops; and the underground water in the wadi gravels is tapped by shallow wells for domestic use, as well as for irrigation. Smaller settlements have a distinct African appearance and an appreciable population percentage of Ethiopians and Sudanese from across the Red Sea. Hudaydah, fourth-largest city in the republic, has replaced Mocha as Yemen's main Red Sea port.

[2] Central Highlands

From the Tihamah's inner margin, an escarpment rises abruptly and steeply through block-

Long-form official name, anglicized: Republic of Yemen (new name of the now-merged pre-1990 two Yemens)

Official name, transliterated: al-Jumhuriyah al-Yamaniyah

Form of government: unitary multiparty republic with one legislative house (House of Representatives)

Area: 205,356 miles^2/531,869 km^2 (area imprecise, since some land boundaries undefined)

Population, 1991: 11,843,000. Literacy (latest): 38.5% (south has twice the percentage literate of the north)

Ethnic composition (%): Arab 90.0, Indian, Somali, Afro-Arab mix, European, other 10.0

Religions (%): Muslim 99.9 (Sunni 53.0, Shii 46.9), other 0.1

GNP, 1989 (YAR and PDRY combined): $7.2 billion (PDRY: $1.0 billion); per capita: $650 in YAR, $430 in PDRY

Petroleum reserves: 4 billion barrels

Main exports (% of merged Yemens' exports not available): coffee, cotton, fish, cigarettes, biscuits, leather, grapes, sesame seeds

Main imports (% of merged Yemens' imports not available): food and live animals, basic manufactured goods, machinery and transport equipment, chemical products, beverages and tobacco

Capital city: Sana (political capital) 427,000; Aden (economic capital) 318,000; other cities: Taizz 178,043; al-Hudaydah 155,110; al-Mukalla 59,100; Saywun 25,400

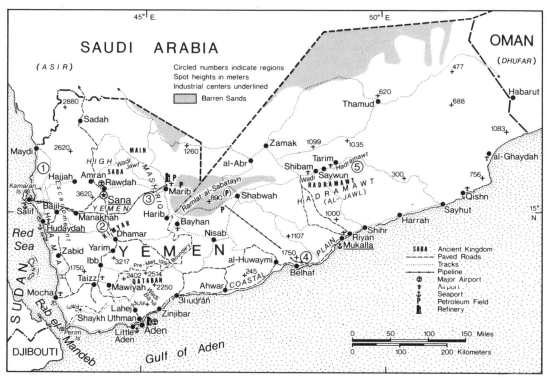

Map 19-2. *Republic of Yemen, comprising the pre-1990 Yemen Arab Republic (North Yemen) and the People's Democratic Republic of Yemen (South Yemen). Circled numbers indicate regions discussed in the text.*

Figure 19-2. *Typical terraced mountainside on west-facing escarpment in northern Yemen.*

faulted and ruggedly eroded topography to the plateaus and shallow basins of the Central Highlands. Elevations commonly exceed 7,000 ft./ 2,135 m, with one summit elevation of 11,877 ft./3,620 m, located southwest of Sana and only 80 miles/130 km from the Red Sea coast. Facing west-southwest, the upper slopes of the escarpment intercept the monsoon winds in April-May and August and wring from them 20–35 in./500–900 mm of orographically enhanced rainfall, with more than 40 in./1,000 mm falling on the southern highlands around Ibb. The escarpment is almost vertical in places but in many other places has slopes that permit terraced agriculture (see Fig. 19-2), making this scenic subregion the most productive part of Yemen and one of surprisingly high population density.

Farther east is the backbone of Yemen, the Central Highlands or High Yemen. With a width varying from 40 to 75 miles/65 to 120 km, this subregion extends as an elevated plateau with several flat-floored basins from the northern border of Yemen to the former boundary between the pre-1990 Yemens. The plateau aspect is broken toward its northern and southern ends, and irregular mountain masses rise above it near and south of Sana. The relatively dense population of the upper western escarpment laps onto the high plateau and concentrates in and around Sana, the

capital and primate city of the former YAR and now the political capital and still the largest city of unified Yemen. With the highest elevation of any Middle East capital, Sana lies at 7,250 ft./2,210 m, so that at this latitude it has moderate temperatures with a large diurnal range and cool nights all year round. More accessible and better known than the distinctive architecture of the Wadi Hadramawt (see [5] below) is the building and ornamental style of the High Yemen, well preserved in the old walled core of Sana (Fig. 19-3). The practice of whitewashing the surrounds of windows and doors gives a unique character to the multistoried houses of basalt dimension stone or mud in the urban landscape.

Noteworthy towns serve as population nodes along the plateau backbone, all of them with the distinctive Yemeni architectural styles and most with picturesque old walls, towers, forts, and mosques (see, for example, Fig. 19-3). From north to south, they include Sadah, the central place for extreme northern Yemen and focus of road traffic with Saudi Arabia; Amran; Sana, anchoring the center; Dhamar, old Himyaric city and agricultural center; Yarim; Ibb, an especially picturesque old city that has become a major development center; and, former capital of Yemen and central place of the southern plateau, Taizz, clinging to a rugged volcanic slope. Indeed, the evidence of

Figure 19-3. *Old houses and part of western wall of the Old City of Sana, capital of Yemen. The whitewashed surrounds of the windows are typical decorations of traditional houses in highland Yemen.*

volcanism is rarely out of sight anywhere on the plateau. Much of the highland itself is built up of successive lava flows, and extending northward from Sana is a striking series of cinder cones.

From the plateau summit, the eastern escarpment descends to the interior less steeply and with much less relief than does the western escarpment. By wadis and spurs it steps down from more than 7,000 ft./2,135 m to the eastern desert general level of 3,300 ft./1,000 m. Lying in the rain shadow of the Central Highlands, the escarpment contrasts climatically with the west and is dry and sunny. It also contrasts lithologically and primarily displays dissected Jurassic and Cretaceous sedimentary strata—mostly limestones—as opposed to predominantly lava flows on the west. Like the vegetation, population is sparse.

[3] Mashriq

Toward the bottom of the escarpment, volcanic forms reappear, then both the sedimentary layers and the lavas lose themselves under the sands of the southwestern Rub al-Khali, where locally the dune fields are known as the Ramlat al-Sabatayn. This eastern region, the Mashriq (not to be confused with the same term used for the entire eastern Arab world), was well developed 3,000–1,500

years ago when Marib was a main station on the Incense Trail during a more pluvial period and when the Sabaeans maintained the famed Marib Dam. The dam (actually, a system of dams) retained floodwaters in a large wadi and permitted intensive irrigation downstream during several centuries. Shifts in trade patterns, final collapse of the main dam, and diminution of Sabaean vigor ended the local civilization in the sixth century, and the area was isolated and little known during the last millennium. Excavations in the early 1950s revealed temples of the Marib heyday, but it was exploration for and discovery of substantial oil fields in the early 1980s that opened the Mashriq once again (see Fig. 8-1). A new Marib Dam impounds floodwaters once more, and extensive irrigation has created a green oasis in the otherwise barren landscape. The future of Marib, the Mashriq, and—if oil and gas finds continue—all of Yemen is more promising than could have been imagined by the ancient Sabaeans.

[4] Indian Ocean Coastal Plain

The south coastal plain along the Gulf of Aden and the open Indian Ocean is separated from the Tihamah by the volcanic masses at Aden and by the right-angle intersection of two sets of ocean-spreading rifts (see Chap. 3, especially Map 3-2). It is a generally flat, sandy coastal strip varying from 5 to 10 miles/8 to 16 km in width. Reddish-black volcanic hills and other ragged, barren masses of lava frequently rise above and interrupt the plain, overlooking numerous fishing villages that fringe the shore. Occasional wadis cross the plain, bringing runoff from the inland hills, with irrigated cultivated plots along the wadis. The entire coast exhibits only two appreciable port cities, Aden and, farther east, picturesque Mukalla in the center.

With its complex of harbors created by its location on one side of an old volcanic crater, Aden has been used as a port and an entrepôt for millennia. As a modern city, its several sections—Crater, Maala, Khormaksar, Steamer Point, Tawahi, Little Aden with its refinery—play hide-and-seek with one another behind dark, barren, pockmarked volcanic masses. Nearly 300 miles/480 km to the east, Mukalla, seat of the former sultanate of Quaiti, has also functioned as an important port. It has served the eastern areas for centuries, specifically the Wadi Hadramawt, with which it is connected by a well-surfaced road up and over the intervening plateau. Its port facilities were improved and expanded during the 1989–1991 period. Its airport is at Riyan, on the coast a few miles east of Mukalla. The coastal village of Bir Ali, west of Mukalla, became the storage area and oil-export terminal for southern Yemen's Shabwah fields when a new pipeline was completed in 1991. The large, strategic island of Socotra, 215 miles/346 km off the coast of eastern Yemen (not included on Map 19-2, but see Map 3-1), was used extensively by the Soviets during the 1970s and 1980s.

[5] Hadramawt

Stretching over most of the eastern reaches of Yemen and inland from the coastal plain is the extensive Hadramawt, which includes several plateaus and the great flat-floored valley famed as the Wadi Hadramawt. The plateau proper that lies between the wadi and the coastal plain is the Jawl, an extensive tableland of flat-lying reddish-brown limestones, moderately dissected by wadis a few feet to 200–500 ft./60–150 m deep. All of the wadis were eroded primarily during earlier pluvial periods and now appear oversized for the

amount of water presently draining down the system. The Jawl flats lie at 3,300 ft./1,000 m and, on the south, fall abruptly to the coastal plain 10–12 miles/16–20 km back from the shore and, on the north, drop by vertical cliffs into the Wadi Hadramawt. After the valley was initially eroded, silt, sand, and gravel later partially filled the bottom of the wadi, giving it a flat floor that has been irrigated and cultivated along much of the wadi course for thousands of years. The irrigated agriculture supports scores of small villages and several towns—particularly neighboring Shibam, Saywun (locally Sayoun), and Tarim—that are remarkable settlements with architectural treasures constructed of mud bricks by local builders (see Saywun palace, Fig. 19-4). Centuries-old "skyscraper" mud-brick houses in Shibam were added to the UNESCO World Heritage list in 1982 (Fig. 19-5). Although rare, devastating floods can play havoc with the mud structures, as happened during the May monsoonal rains in 1989.

The Wadi Hadramawt was little known even when it was accessible under British control, and it was virtually a closed area during the PDRY period. One result of this inaccessibility is that it retained its special character, its unique architecture, its distinctive ethnic mix, and its social and religious conservatism, although tourism and other modernization will probably change it in many ways after the early 1990s. An especially unusual custom among the Hadramis was the practice of sending young men to Malaysia and Indonesia to work for and with fellow Hadramis who had been established in these countries before them. A smaller number went to East Africa for the same purpose. Virtually all of these men returned to the wadi to retire, many of them exceedingly wealthy, and built mansions in a mixed Hadrami-Malay-Javanese style. Many such handsome homes contribute to the special character of the town of Tarim.

Historical Sketch

During the first millennium BC and until the sixth century after Christ, southwestern Arabia gave rise to several kingdoms: Saba (Sheba), with the famous dam at its capital of Marib; Main (Minaea) farther north; Himyar, still flourishing

Figure 19-4. *Palace of the former sultan of Qathiri, in Saywun (Sayoun), in the Wadi Hadramawt. The palace is made entirely of mud, which has been painted white, and is a fine example of the Hadramawti architectural skill and the art of mud construction.*

Figure 19-5. *Western facade of the all-mud city of Shibam, Wadi Hadramawt. These remarkable mud "skyscrapers" earned Shibam inclusion on the UNESCO World Heritage list in 1982.*

as late as the sixth century, south of Saba; Qataban southeast of Himyar; and Hadramawt well to the east. All of these kingdoms (shown on Map 19-2) thrived on the flourishing and long-lived transit trade.

Islam swept southwestern Arabia during the time of Muhammad and remains virtually the exclusive religion of the area. Local rulers, Abyssinians (Ethiopians), Persians, Muslim empires, Egyptians, Portuguese, and Ottoman Turks controlled part or all of the area politically before the British took Aden in 1839 and gradually extended control in the south up the wadis and across the plateaus. From that time until 1990, the High Yemen and the southern coast and plateaus experienced separate historical development. In the south, the fragmented pattern of local control by paramount shaykhs in the west and by sultans in the east was maintained by the British, although they declared the immediate area of Aden a British crown colony in 1937. The southern hinterland was divided into a Western Aden Protectorate, with nineteen sultanates, and an Eastern Aden Protectorate of Hadramawt and other states, sultanates, and shaykhdoms. This three-way pattern continued until the late 1950s, when Britain prepared to withdraw from the area.

What later became the PDRY, 20 years before it merged with the YAR, evolved through a complicated series of political and name changes. Preparatory to withdrawal from the region, Britain sponsored the creation of a Federation of Arab Amirates of the South in 1959, which, after some expansion, became the Federation of South Arabia. However, radical groups caused the disintegration of the fledgling federation. Rival nationalist groups seeking domination of South Yemen after independence in 1967 engaged in a costly civil war and in terrorist attacks against the British prior to their departure in 1968. Renamed the People's Republic of South Yemen, the new state became more radical and assumed the name People's Democratic Republic of Yemen in 1970. Old enmities emerged in successive coup attempts—1978, 1980, and 1986. Having thrown off British imperialism, the state embraced communist ideology under appreciable Soviet and Chinese influence, adopting regionally incongruous radical centralized control of political and social structures.

In the north, however, the historical evolution during most of the past two millennia has followed quite different routes. Although both north and south grew wealthy from early trade between Aden and the Levant, particularly in frankincense and myrrh, northern Yemen enjoyed better climate and soil and hence more developed agriculture and a larger population.

Highland Yemenis embraced Islam in the mid-seventh century and served with distinction in Muslim armies from North Africa to central Asia. Having been under Muslim control, from the Hijaz, Damascus, and Baghdad, in 897 the High Yemen came under the rule of a descendant of Zayd, great-grandson of Ali. For most of the next 1,100 years, until 1962, the Shii Zaydi dynasty continued to rule all or part of the area as imams, with periodic interruptions. During much of the Middle Ages, the Highlands and Tihamah were fragmented into scores of small shaykhdoms, sultanates, and kingdoms perched on mountainsides or mountain peaks. Elevated and protected sites of many contemporary villages, though picturesque and even spectacular in today's landscape, reflect this period of disorder and insecurity (see Fig. 10-4). More serious is the persistence of tribal feuds and disputes over lands, water, and political influence. Ottoman Turks exercised varying degrees of suzerainty in the Highlands and Tihamah until the last full Turkish occupation in the period 1872–1918.

Two very conservative Zaydi imams, Yahya (1904–1948) and his son Ahmad (1948–1962), ruled independent Yemen until the country became a republic, with both imams unsuccessfully seeking to extend their rule over British-controlled Aden and the protectorates. Increasing Nasserist influence persuaded Ahmad in 1958 to lead Yemen into a loose association with Egypt and Syria (the UAR, 1958–1961) in the virtually meaningless United Arab States.

When Imam Ahmad died in 1962, the army opposed the succession of his son Badr and, with support from Nasserist Egypt, staged a coup and declared a republic under strongman Colonel Abdullah al-Sallal. Revolutionary republican forces, mainly from the Sunni Shafii population south of Sana, were joined by scores of thousands of Egyptian troops in a civil war against royalist forces supporting Imam Badr. Royalists were primarily tribesmen and other primarily Zaydi groups north of Sana, who were in turn aided by Saudi Arabia and Jordan. More than 200,000 were killed, and, with the Egyptians utilizing chemical warfare on several occasions, the civil war dragged on until 1969, although Egyptian forces were withdrawn in 1967. Significantly, in the mid-1960s the political capital was shifted back from Taizz, in the southern plateau, to Sana, in the more neutral center, where the capital had been before 1948.

In 1971, North Yemen's first nationwide elections marked a reconciliation between republican and royalist forces that has remained in effect despite various underlying tensions. During the following 20 years, the north walked tight-ropes internally, externally, and with the "other Yemen." With moderately large capital transfers and technical assistance from many countries— Saudi Arabia, the United States, China, Britain, the former USSR, Kuwait, and others—Yemen installed a basic infrastructure, especially a high-way net, that moved it beyond the level of South Yemen and that stood it in good stead when de-velopment accelerated in the 1980s.

Republic of Yemen

Highland Yemen to the north and Aden and the Hadramawt to the south and east have each op-posed the other and resisted control by the other for centuries. After the north declared itself a re-public in 1962 and the British left an independent south in 1967, the two areas outwardly declared a desire for unity but in reality sparred for domi-nance. They engaged in brief but savage bilateral warfare in 1972 and 1976, further wasting both human and financial resources already depleted by a decade of fighting in both areas.

The Marxist-Leninist ideology of the south promoted secularization, especially in Greater Aden; and "progressivism" altered the traditional status of religion, social classes, women (less so in the Hadramawt), education, and, of course, government. Influence of the USSR, China, and North Korea increased as Western influence de-creased. Revolution and progress in the north were sharp departures from imamate days, but Highland Yemen retained many conservative customs and resisted communism. It sought po-litical nonalignment and profited by accepting aid from all quarters. A higher percentage of the women remained veiled there than in the south, and although women attended the University of Sana along with men in the 1980s, the reason given for this by some academics was the greater economy of coeducation.

Thus, along with the unmistakable desire for and trend toward unity, the ability of the two societies to merge such incompatible politico-economic-social systems was moot. After a pro-cess of lengthy discussions, preparation of a draft constitution, and votes in each parliament, the two Yemens united on May 22, 1990, and in 1993

remained firmly committed to their chosen course. The following topics examine the post-1990 Republic of Yemen and reveal basic aspects of its likely future.

The Yemenis

The population of the Yemen Republic is esti-mated to be 11,843,000, about 83 percent of whom are in the former YAR area, with growth rate traditionally high throughout Yemen. The Sana area has by far the greatest concentration of people, the Aden area the second largest, and Taizz and Hudaydah the third and fourth largest, respectively. Basic ethnic uniformity is high: The overwhelming majority of the people are "Yemeni Arabs," although biological differences and descent characteristics differ appreciably among regions. For example, an upper-class in-habitant of Sana is shorter and has lighter skin than an upper-class Hadrami. Many Hadramis are descended from dark-skinned migrants from the subcontinent, probably Dravidians, and are mixed with both Malay-Indonesians and East Af-ricans. Many villagers along the Tihamah are of African descent. Accents and dialects may vary, but nearly all Yemenis speak Arabic as a mother tongue. Tribal affiliations are paramount in the north and east, even in towns and villages, al-though the remaining actual Bedouins are found primarily in the Mashriq and the Jawl. The Bed-ouin tradition is not a significant influence in the republic, and, as elsewhere, the numbers of no-mads are decreasing.

Ethnic relative uniformity is partly offset by persistent tribal distinctions and conflicts (which, however, are slowly diminishing), by the sectarian division of the former YAR area into a Shii Zaydi northern two-thirds and a Sunni Shafii south of Dhamar, and by sharp political groupings in the Adeni south. The greater power in the highlands region has traditionally been wielded by the tribally conscious Zaydis, from whom came the ruling imams; but Shafiis, with some ties to the south, have gained strength un-der the republics. Another social question has been how to deal with the influence of the *say-yids,* honored male descendants of the Prophet Muhammad through Fatimah, who are identi-fied by special headdress and who for centuries have enjoyed special privileges in north and south. They have been steadily deprived of their special status and are approaching egalitarian treatment in both areas. Outwardly, these various distinctions are becoming less relevant and will continue to do so as long as democratic republicanism prevails.

The western escarpment and the Central Highlands especially exhibit a surprisingly dense pattern of villages distributed over landscapes that would appear to limit human settlement. Although only about 8 percent of the Yemenis continue to be nomadic, a low 12 percent of the population is urban. The half dozen cities are growing rapidly as urban pull attracts job seekers from the more impoverished rural areas. Another 70 towns have more than 2,000 inhabitants each. Yemen as a country of villagers is confirmed by data on the former YAR, which are also applicable to the south: 11,000 villages have 100–500 inhabitants, and an astonishing 41,000 hamlets have fewer than 100 residents. This pattern of settlement is consistent with most of Yemen's topographic and climatic environments, which offer few sites for extensive settlement possessing adjacent cultivable area for supporting agriculture. Further limiting settlement size was the traditional siting in medieval times of fortress-type villages on peaks and ridges for protection during the frequent local wars (see Fig. 10-4).

A sizable minority of Jews lived in the cities—especially Sana, Sadah, and Aden—for 1,800 years, the earliest arrivals probably having come when Jews were expelled from Roman Palestine in AD 70. In 1949–1950, about 50,000 Yemeni Jews were airlifted to Israel on special flights, and only a few hundred remained in the country.

As with their landforms and historical evolution, the Yemenis' costumes are also distinctive. Unlike virtually all other Arabs, males in all parts of Yemen wear a calf-length, patterned wrap around skirt (*lungi* or *futah* or, in the Wadi Hadramawt, where Malay-Indonesian influence is considerable, *sarong*); a colorful turban headdress similar to the Omanis' but wrapped differently; and, often, a folded shoulder shawl, especially in the higher elevations where temperatures can suddenly drop below the comfort level. More than anywhere else in Arabia, men also tra-

ditionally wear a *janbiyah,* a curved dagger in a decorated scabbard, comparable to the Omani *khanjar.* Western wear is steadily becoming more common in Yemen, as it is in most of the Middle East. Female attire is more similar to that in southwestern Saudi Arabia.

A particularly detrimental social problem common among highland Yemenis especially is the daily pastime of chewing qat (*Catha edulis*), a mild stimulant. About 60 percent of the men—and 20 percent of the women—of all social classes participate in the old, deeply rooted ritual that is a socially accepted custom. The consumer packs several *qat* leaves inside one cheek in the early afternoon and maintains them as a prominent wad for two or three hours, much as some people chew tobacco. Long-term effects are not clearly understood, but the reduction in productivity among millions of Yemenis during the daily *qat*-chewing period slows economic progress and is a matter of grave concern to many responsible Yemenis. If nothing else, the leaves must be picked fresh daily and rushed to the nearest *suq*, where they are quite expensive, especially those of premium quality. A daily supply can absorb one-third of a low-income worker's earnings. The *qat*-chewing routine, never as ingrained in the south as in the highlands, was abolished under the PDRY.

Merged Emerging Economy

As with their historical development, the economic evolution of the two parts of unified Yemen was appreciably different, as are the bases for their economies. The former PDRY, with less agricultural potential, had a more balanced economy. Aden, the overwhelming focus of economic activity in the south, has benefited for centuries—indeed, for millennia—from its location at the junction of sea and land routes to and from the eastern Mediterranean, southern and eastern Asia, and eastern Africa. From early times, ships called at Aden's excellent harbor for both trading purposes and servicing. Although somewhat depressed during the eighteenth century, Aden regained primacy after 1839 when Britain took control and made it the regional coaling station for the increasing number of steamships plying the Indian Ocean. Its importance was greatly enhanced with the opening of the Suez Canal in 1869, when Aden became the midway port of call for ships sailing between the Mediterranean and India and points east. That importance was further augmented when fuel oil replaced coal in steamships and Aden, declared a British colony in 1937, served as a key oil-bunkering port. Increasing production of petroleum in the Middle East after World War II added to the importance of routes passing Aden and encouraged the British to construct a major refinery in 1954 on the western arm of the harbor, in Little Aden. Feedstock was imported from the Gulf, and product was exported to several customer states until the trade broke down under the PDRY.

In the late 1950s, Aden was one of the world's busiest ports, with as many as 250,000 passengers debarking annually from ships waiting to be bunkered. Local merchants revived the ancient transit trade, established a free port, and enjoyed a booming retail trade for a decade. Closure of the Suez Canal in 1967 combined with civil war in Aden to depress trade, which has never recovered. Ownership of the refinery was transferred to the PDRY in 1979, and it was refurbished in the early 1990s to resume its former throughput (161,000-bpd capacity), using the increasing Yemen crude oil production. With the merger of north and south, Aden was designated the "economic capital" of Yemen, and it is likely to be reinvigorated and redirected on the road to lively activity.

More rural and with less European influence before 1970, northern Yemen desperately needed and sought large-scale aid abroad, and it received substantial help from its neighbors and from both the West and the communist world. The Central Planning Organization coordinated the foreign aid, focusing first on infrastructure, then on social services, public administration, and agriculture. With relations between Yemen and Saudi Arabia variable, aid from the Saudis was sometimes uncertain but in some years exceeded $100 million. U.S. assistance was modest but effective and was responsible for Yemen's first modern highway up the escarpment. Chinese, British, Dutch, German, Swiss, Soviet, and especially UN technical assistance combined to endow northern Yemen with a basic network of paved highways, planned urban expansion, a number of small industries, and fair educational and health systems. The largest industry in highland Yemen is a cotton textile mill north of Sana that was built in 1967 by the People's Republic of China (PRC). The PRC also constructed, with its own Chinese labor force, the scenic highway from Hudaydah up the escarpment to Sana, as well as roads in southern Yemen.

Much of the economic growth after 1975, especially in the north, was fueled by remittances from the more than one million Yemenis working abroad, mainly in Saudi Arabia. Employment, salaries, and therefore remittances diminished after the drop in oil prices in 1982–1983. Aid from Saudi Arabia and other oil producers likewise decreased, slowing development. With union of the north and south approaching, several contributing states raised their level of aid to encourage an obviously beneficial step forward. However, just after the merger, Yemen's financial supporters were alienated by the country's failure to join in the condemnation of Iraq, and they withdrew aid and otherwise penalized the new united Yemen. Simultaneously, Saudi Arabia canceled the special status long enjoyed by Yemenis as expatriate workers free to seek employment without Saudi sponsors, and in late 1990 and early 1991, it expelled several hundred thousand Yemenis without allowing them to settle their affairs. Financial losses for individuals and for the state of Yemen were great, and a likely 800,000 formerly well-paid workers returned home to swell the ranks of the unemployed, who were approaching 40 percent of the potential work force.

Two sectors of the economy deserve special attention: the traditional mainstay of agriculture and the new promise of petroleum. Highland Yemen and Tihamah have been overwhelmingly agricultural: Well into the 1950s, agriculture engaged 90 percent of the economically active population, and it still engaged more than 56 percent in the late 1980s, the highest level among Middle East states (Table 9-1). In the former PDRY, 46 percent of the labor force worked in agriculture, still a high number. Once self-sufficient in food, Yemen now imports significant percentages of its wheat, rice, animal feed, and other foodstuffs. Extensive rainfed agriculture is practiced in the highlands by virtue of the centuries-long practice of terracing the slopes and thus conserving soil (virtually creating it in some ways) and making maximum use of runoff from the seasonal rains (see Fig. 19-2). The degree of slope that has been terraced and the extent of the terracing are astonishing in parts of the escarpment. The terrace walls must, of course, be carefully maintained, especially after heavy rains; and the exodus of so many young men from the terraced farms to more lucrative work in Saudi Arabia and the Gulf has been a cause of concern. Some terraces are eroding and breaking down, endangering other farms downslope. More active irrigation is necessary on Tihamah, in the south, and in the Wadi Hadramawt.

In addition to the expected crops of wheat, barley, maize, grapes, several fruits, and various vegetables, Yemen produces cotton and dates on the coastal plains and in the Wadi Hadramawt; and three other crops are unusual among Middle East countries: sorghum (*durrah*), coffee, and *qat*. *Durrah* is especially well adapted to the double-monsoon rainfall regime and occupies up to three-fourths of the cultivated land. Yemen held a virtual world monopoly on coffee during the period 1500–1775, giving it appreciable local wealth. Because for many decades most of the coffee beans were exported from Yemen's Red Sea port of Mocha, one name for coffee has long been *mocha*, as another name, *java*, was adopted after production shifted to Indonesia. Later, Aden became a main export port for coffee beans and gave its name to a blend that is still standard in the trade. Although Yemeni coffee continues to be a premium product, the output of less than 3,000 mt is negligible on the world market, and production continues to decline.

Unfortunately, coffee and *qat* plants have the same ecological demands, and coffee trees are steadily being uprooted from the high terraces of the western escarpment and being replaced by *qat* bushes. Coffee trees require several years to reach optimum bearing age, and they then yield only one crop a year. *Qat* bushes begin producing marketable leaves after only a few months, and they yield a high-value crop every day, averaging 20 times the annual income of coffee. Thus, Yemen loses the value of an export commodity while sustaining the social and economic losses associated with *qat* chewing. In addition, major food crops are being replaced in some areas by *qat*, so that Yemen is becoming less and less able to feed itself.

With decreasing remittances and foreign aid reducing Yemen's GNP, oil finds in the Mashriq and the adjacent Shabwah area of the south came at a particularly auspicious period. In the former YAR, the first strike came on July 4, 1984, in the Alif field in the Marib–al-Jawf Basin 37 miles/60 km east-northeast of the town of Marib in the Mashriq. Discovery was made by the Hunt Oil Company, a U.S. firm, which later, as Yemen Hunt Oil Company, became the operator of a production-sharing agreement with participation by Exxon and a Korean consortium. During the same period, exploration on the PDRY side of the border was under way by Soviet technicians, who were later joined by other companies and then replaced by an Arab group. Agreement between the YAR and PDRY in 1989, even before their union, called for joint exploration and exploitation on both sides of the border by several national groups.

Marib production quickly reached 175,000 bpd, by which time a small 10,000-bpd refinery was in operation near the Alif field and a 24–26-in./61–64-cm pipeline had been completed up the eastern escarpment, across the Central Highlands, and down the western escarpment to Salif on the Red Sea: a total of 257 miles/414 km (see Map 19-2). Maintaining consistent pressure in the line along such great changes in elevation (up 4,000 ft./1,220 m and down 7,000 ft./2,135 m in short horizontal distances) requires complex engineering and equipment. Further exploration has led to the discovery of several new fields, some with nonassociated gas, but additional facilities and pipelines will be required to exploit additional reserves.

Farther southeast, in the Ayad and Amal fields near Shabwah in the former PDRY, production was limited for the first few years by the necessity to truck output to the Aden refinery. However, a 20-in./51-cm pipeline was completed in 1991 from the Ayad-Amal fields to the small port of Bir Ali on the Gulf of Aden, a distance of 130 miles/210 km. Production exceeded 30,000 bpd in 1991, giving Yemen a total from both producing areas of over 200,000 bpd. Total reserves are estimated at 4 billion bbls, and reserves of nonassociated gas are increasing substantially. Thus, this poorest corner of the Middle East can view its foreseeable future with greater optimism than it could have had reason to hope would be the case in the early 1980s. One possible difficulty is the warning issued by Saudi Arabia in mid-1992 to companies operating or exploring in the Mashriq, cautioning them to ensure that they stay back from the uncertain boundaries in their area.

Finally, regarding economic activity, it can be noted that fishing is an important source of food and income. The upwelling of cool waters along the south coast of the peninsula was mentioned in the section on Oman, and for that same reason, fisheries are significant along the Indian Ocean coast of Yemen. Fishing along the Red Sea coast has long been a major activity, and Hudaydah has appreciable fish-processing facilities. In another economic sector, air transportation has opened Yemen's links with the world more than anything else has done. International airports operate in Sana, Taizz, Hudaydah, and Aden, and local flights use Riyan (Mukalla), Saywun, and Marib. Limited traffic uses Qadub (on Socotra Island) and al-Ghaydah and Qishn in the east. North and south have merged their airlines into Yemen Airways, which, by associating with Saudia, has proved to be very successful.

Relations

Unification eliminated one of the most persistent problems in relations faced by each of the Yemens, and the collapse of Soviet influence and of the standing of communism provided a more salutary climate for the merger. It is unfortunate that the new merged Yemen provoked the rancor that was directed toward it in late 1990 and early 1991 because of its stance on Iraq, and some major fence-mending will be in order as the mid-1990s approach. Saudi Arabia continues to play a critical role in the relations complex and can revive or depress Yemen by the amount of aid it grants or withholds and by its dealings with expatriate Yemeni workers. Border questions all along the interior of both parts of Yemen seriously need addressing by the Saudis and Yemenis in an atmosphere of goodwill, since even the defined and demarcated northern boundary of Yemen can be called into question in the mid-1990s. Basic rapport had been reestablished between Oman and the PDRY, and that can be renewed after Yemen recovers from the tensions of the Gulf crisis and its aftermath. Yemen remains in critical need of foreign assistance from any quarter, a need that further demands détente between Yemen and its many former supporters. Having been reestablished in 1972 after Yemen broke them in 1967, relations with the United States, which had been steadily warming—especially after the U.S. success in finding oil in the Mashriq—were set back in the 1990–1991 crisis.

20

Egypt: A River and a People

A View of Egypt

"Egypt is the gift of the Nile," wrote Herodotus 2,500 years ago. Kipling, in turn, described the Nile as "that little damp trickle of life." Both comments emphasize the role of a single river as a fundamental element in the existence of this ancient land.

In few countries are the basic geographical factors and their direct influences as plainly imprinted as in Egypt. The Nile Valley is unique in its singular symbiosis of people and environment and in its remarkable history and contemporary development. Flanked by desert ramparts, the Nile Valley kingdoms flourished for millennia, with only occasional major disruptions. Egypt's location on the link between Africa and Eurasia gives it a pivotal position in the World-Island.

Inscriptions, carvings, bas-reliefs, statues, and monuments—all well-preserved for millennia in the dry climate but now under stress from contemporary pollution—provide detailed documentation of everyday life and beliefs in Pharaonic and Ptolemaic Egypt. Both tourism and archaeological scholarship focus on such ancient works as well as on the numerous pyramids, temples, tombs, and colossi, with their hieroglyphics and distinctive arts. History is an essential ingredient of everyday life in Egypt (see Figs. 2-1 and 20-1).

Although the imperial domains of ancient Egypt were less extensive than those of Persia or Assyria, they periodically extended well into the Levant, and the Nile Valley has persisted as one of the four major power foci of the Middle East (see Chaps. 2 and 11). Ensconced behind its desert glacis (buffer zone) and well supplied with military resources, it has suffered fewer conquests than the Fertile Crescent states. Domestic stability and protected location contributed to a historical continuum that, although several times disturbed, was not devastated as was the development of the Hittites, Assyrians, Israelites, and Byzantines, for example. Similarly, evolution along a riverine ribbon has made Egypt a linear geographical unity that, once integrated about 3000 BC, has rarely been seriously ruptured. The city-states that were so adapted to the environments of mainland Greece, western Asia Minor, and Phoenicia contrast with the integrated polities of the Nile Valley and Delta. The productive agricultural economy that developed along the river has always supported a relatively large population, and Egypt now has one of the three largest national populations in the region (see Table 6-1 and Graph 6-1).

Located near the center of the Islamic and Arab worlds, Egypt has long played an influential role in both realms, partly because of the influence of Cairo's al-Azhar University on religious affairs and partly because of the country's long intellectual tradition. Similarly, Egypt has exercised a dominant influence in the Arab world, particularly since World War II, sometimes contending with Syria and Iraq (and occasionally with Saudi Arabia) for leadership. Egypt's cultural output—motion picture films, television productions, radio programs, and publications—has long exceeded that of all other Arab

Long-form official name, anglicized: Arab Republic of Egypt
Official name, transliterated: Jumhuriyat Misr al-Arabiyah
Form of government: republic with one legislative house (People's Assembly)
Area: 385,229 miles^2/997,739 km^2
Population, 1991: 54,609,000. Literacy (latest): 48.4%
Ethnic composition (%): Egyptian 99.8 (including some Nubian, Berber, Beja), other (Greek, Italian, Syro-Lebanese) 0.2
Religions (%): Sunni Muslim 90.0, Christian (mostly Coptic) 10.0
GNP, 1989: $32.5 billion; per capita: $630
Petroleum reserves: 4.5 billion barrels
Main exports (% of total value, 1990): cotton yarn, textiles, and fabrics 26.1; petroleum and petroleum products 23.6; raw cotton 3.3
Main imports (% of total value, 1990): machinery and transport equipment 22.6; foodstuffs 21.8; chemical products 11.1; base metals 9.2
Capital city: Cairo (al-Qahirah) 6,452,000 (Greater Cairo exceeds 14,000,000); other cities: Alexandria (al-Iskandariyah) 3,170,000; Giza (al-Jizah) 2,156,000; Shubra al-Khaymah 811,000; al-Mahallah al-Kubra 385,300

---

countries combined. In late 1988 an Egyptian novelist received the first Nobel prize for literature awarded to an Arab writer.

Egypt has moved from persistent power core to colonial possession to political leader of the Arab world to regional pariah for several years after 1979. These changing roles have accompanied variations in Egypt's own stability and in the regional environment. In adapting to its changing roles, Egypt has sought security and economic viability—survival—within new relationships and new patterns.

A Rich History

Historic Continuity

Over the centuries, Egyptian civilization developed a stability that enabled it to survive, if not always to repel, incursions by foreign forces. Although defeated militarily upon occasion, Egypt not only preserved its population and sustained its culture but also absorbed the conquerors, sometimes adapting part of their religious or political concepts.

Once Upper Egypt (i.e., up the Nile River Valley, to the south) merged with Lower Egypt (the delta) about 3000 BC, the two physically different but interdependent parts of Egypt remained integrated most of the following centuries. The unifying of Upper and Lower Egypt after a major cleavage in the seventeenth century BC was celebrated in numerous contemporary symbols, including the form of the royal crown, and in thousands of hieroglyphic inscriptions, even though the river civilization could not entirely overcome the incompatibility between valley and delta with their cultural and environmental differences. The centripetal-centrifugal relationships between Upper and Lower Egypt remain meaningful, although modern communications and increased interregional dependence have emphasized the sense of unity.

The shifting of royal capitals and religious centers between north and south in ancient times reflected shifts in the political center of gravity. Memphis, the first capital of the united kingdom of Upper and Lower Egypt, was established at an intermediate location, at the apex of the delta, a location to which the capital returned periodically after shifts to Thebes (opposite Luxor), other valley cities, and delta cities (see Map 2-3). Significantly, the political center of Egypt for the past 1,300 years—Cairo—is located, as was Memphis, at the precise junction of delta (Lower Egypt) and valley (Upper Egypt).

Figure 20-1. *Ancient and contemporary in the Nile Valley: Ruins of Saqqara from the third millennium BC in foreground, with 1980s high-rise apartment buildings of Maadi in distance.*

Despite incursions over many centuries by Hyksos, Libyans, Nubians, Ethiopians, Assyrians, Persians, and others, Egypt has maintained an unmistakable Egyptian character and unity. The Persian conquest in 525 BC began a series of conquests by more distant powers: Greeks under Alexander the Great, 332–323 BC; successor Greek Ptolemies, 304–30 BC; Romans 30 BC–AD 476; and Byzantine successors to the Romans, AD 476–640. A major modification of the ancient Egyptian culture was introduced during the east Roman–Byzantine hegemony, when Christianity became the dominant religion (see Chap. 6). It persists today among the minority Copts.

Arab-Islamic Transformation

In AD 642, the Muslim Arab conquest brought a momentous and permanent transformation of Egypt. The Arabs not only overwhelmed Egypt militarily but also immigrated into Egypt by the thousands, intermarrying with the indigenous population. Their intangible contributions included a proselytizing religion (Islam), a new language (Arabic), and a concept of strong ties between religion and government. Islam supplanted Christianity, and by 706 Arabic had been decreed the language of official transactions.

Once ingrained, Islam has never been challenged. Sunnism, however, was displaced for two centuries under the Shii Fatimid state, 909–1171, which supplanted Abbasid control in most of North Africa. Sunnism returned permanently with the Ayyubids, 1171–1250, whose dynasty included Salah al-Din (Saladin), a Kurd who became one of the most honored heroes of the Ar-abs. Under the succeeding Mamluk ("slave") sultans, who ruled Egypt for more than 250 years, Cairo gained architectural treasures, underwritten mainly by income from the rich Red Sea–Mediterranean trade. Mamluk buildings, especially mosques with characteristic minarets and fluted domes, are some of the contemporary city's most interesting monuments. Loss of the profitable Red Sea–Mediterranean trade routes to Portuguese merchantmen sailing around the Cape of Good Hope deprived Mamluk Egypt of its main revenues, and Egypt fell to the Ottoman Turks in 1517. Although Ottoman control was tenuous after the late 1700s, it technically continued until 1914. After 1805, Egypt was locally ruled by the Muhammad Ali dynasty under Ottoman suzerainty, but in fact British control prevailed after 1882.

Contemporary Republic

Contemporary Egypt was born in a bloodless military coup on July 23, 1952. King Faruq (Farouk), last of the Muhammad Ali line, was sent into exile, and the present republic emerged, led by members of a revolutionary junta. The following two decades brought a sequence of historic events that shook the Middle East and, in some cases, the world. Many of the events were orchestrated until 1970 by Gamal Abd al-Nasser, the charismatic coup leader who became president in 1954.

Among his more memorable actions, Nasser forced the withdrawal of Britain from Egypt 1954–1956, negotiated a Czech-Soviet arms deal in September 1955, nationalized the Suez Canal

Figure 20-2. *Anwar al-Sadat memorial monument, Cairo. Erected in the mid-1980s near the site of the assassination of Egypt's second president.*

in July 1956, preached and promoted aggressive pan-Arabism and Arab nationalism, oversaw the merger of Egypt and Syria in the United Arab Republic (UAR) in February 1958, and escalated tensions that encouraged Israel's invasion of Egypt in June 1967. He was attempting to reconcile the Palestine Liberation Organization and the government of Jordan in September 1970 when he suffered a fatal heart attack.

Nasser's successor, Anwar al-Sadat, brought increased pragmatism to and a changed direction in Egyptian policies. After he initiated a joint Egyptian-Syrian surprise attack on Israeli lines at the Suez Canal and in the Golan Heights in 1973, he downgraded relations with the Soviets and established close relations with the United States. As one step to remedy the country's growing economic malaise, he minimized the Nasserist socialism and declared an economic "open door" policy (*infitah*). To escape continued entanglement in military adventures and with U.S. promises of support, he made a dramatic visit to Jerusalem in November 1977 to address the Israeli Knesset and signed the Camp David accords with Israel in September 1978 and the Egyptian-Israeli peace treaty on March 16, 1979. President Sadat was assassinated by disaffected Egyptian fundamentalists in October 1981 (Fig. 20-2). His successor, President Husni Mubarak, has taken a low-key approach and has tried to balance foreign and domestic issues.[1]

River, Delta, and Deserts

Egypt comprises five regional elements: [1] Nile River Valley, [2] Nile Delta, [3] Western Desert, [4] Eastern Desert, and [5] Sinai Peninsula (see circled numbers on Map 20-1). It is worth noting that whereas Egypt has long been considered a seismically stable region, a 5.9 earthquake centered 20 miles/12 km southwest of Cairo occurred on October 12, 1992, causing more than 400 deaths and 3,000 injuries. Not having been built according to earthquake-resistant codes, many buildings collapsed; however, major ancient monuments seem to have escaped serious damage.[2]

[1] Nile River and the Aswan Project

Egypt is the Nile, and the Nile is Egypt. The headwaters of the Nile rise far to the south, fed by runoff from heavy summer rains in the East African lake district and the Ethiopian highlands. These headwaters form the White Nile and Blue Nile rivers, which in turn join at Khartoum in the Sudan, whence the single Nile flows to enter Egypt through Lake Nubia/Lake Nasser. It then flows 938 miles/1,510 km across the entire length of Egypt, including Lake Nasser, before debouching into the Mediterranean.[3]

Nile Valley: Upper Egypt. Below the first cataract at Aswan, the Nile flows in a relatively nar-

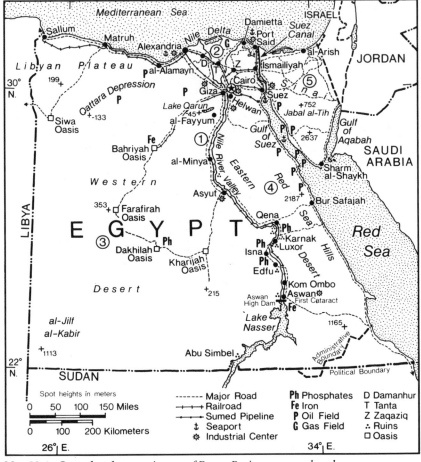

Map 20-1. *General and economic map of Egypt. Regions are numbered.*

row, flat-floored valley, eroded as much as 1,000 ft./300 m below the flanking plateau near Qena (Qina). The valley floor continues to be flat but broadens downstream below the Qena bend, until it is 6–11 miles/10–18 km wide as it approaches Cairo. The valley walls are reduced to less than 165 ft./50 m high at Giza before they disappear entirely as the river flows out onto its delta. It is the lush ribbon of irrigated, cultivated fields on the flat floodplain along the Nile Valley that is the quintessence of traditional Egypt.

Just upstream of the delta, a prominent feature west of the valley is the Fayyum, a circular depression in the limestone plateau of the Western Desert. Nile waters formerly poured into the Fayyum, at least during flood, through the Hawara channel, which used to feed a large lake (Moeris). However, later diversion of the river from the basin reduced Lake Moeris to a rem-

nant, now called Lake Qarun, with a present surface 147 ft./45 m below sea level. Most of the bed of old Lake Moeris is now intensively cultivated and supports a dense population in a significant subregion of the country.[4]

The evolution of the Nile Valley is extremely complex. Stream flow, valley erosion, and deposition of sediment both within the valley and in the delta have varied greatly with alternating periods of pluvial and arid conditions in the Nile watershed. On top of thousands of feet of earlier valley fill, an average of 30 ft./9 m of silt has been deposited in the valley since beneficial silt deposition began approximately 10,000 years ago.[5]

Although some important archaeological sites are found in the delta and in the desert, the vast majority of the great monuments are located along the valley (see Map 20-1). Few stretches of the river between Aswan and Cairo exhibit no ruins of some period or other, and remarkable new finds have recently emerged in Luxor and on the Giza Plateau. Modern cities, some with large populations, have developed around some of the monuments: They include Aswan, Luxor, Qena, Asyut, al-Mina, Helwan, and Giza.

Aswan High Dam. Inaugurated in 1971, the Aswan High Dam (Sadd al-Aali) has had the greatest physical and symbolic impact of any construction project in Egypt in modern times.[6] In its technical transformation of the country's vital resource, the dam altered the equilibrium of the Nile below Aswan, changed the rhythm of valley life, and had significant impact on crucial aspects of the valley's ecology. One example is the effect of Lake Nasser on the Nile's silt load: Now that the upper Nile empties into Lake Nubia (the Sudanese segment of Lake Nasser), the 50 million mt of silt formerly spread annually along the valley and dumped into the Mediterranean is deposited in a new delta that is building northward in the lake.

The constricted valley of the Nile at Aswan, where it crosses resistant granites and other basement rocks, had long been considered as a site for a high dam. The original low Aswan Dam, constructed in 1902 and raised in 1912 and 1934, had demonstrated the benefits of control of the river, and its usefulness stimulated discussion of a higher structure. Work began on the multipurpose high dam in 1960, and teams of environmental impact specialists studied the potential effects of the project during the decade it was under construction.

The completed dam, power station, and impounded lake are among the world's largest. A few statistics indicate the impressive scale of the project: The dam is 365 ft./111 m high, 2.36 miles/3.8 km long at the top, and 0.62 miles/1 km thick at the base, and it contains 17 times the volume of the Great Pyramid of Giza. The impounded reservoir is 297 miles/478 km long and an average of 6 miles/10 km wide. The power station doubled Egypt's generating capacity in 1970 but supplies 25 percent now.

On the positive side, the dam permits flood control and, by regulating river flow for optimum benefit to downstream agriculture, permits perennial irrigation, and thus multiple cropping.

In addition, the dam allows for economical hydrogeneration of enormous amounts of electricity. The lake supports both commercial and sport fishing, and the lake and the dam are major tourist attractions.

Negative impacts, many of which were projected in the feasibility studies, are of serious concern to Egyptian authorities and others. The water table under the cultivated fields in the floodplain has risen, and resulting poor drainage threatens salination of productive valley and delta soils, a risk that can be minimized by the installation of underground drains. Fields formerly naturally fertilized during the annual Nile flood must now be treated with chemical fertilizers, which are changing the chemical balance of much of the valley. The number of acres reclaimed as a result of the Aswan project has, disappointingly, been one-third less than the projected total.

Cessation of sedimentation at the outer limit of the delta by the now-clear river has caused the delta coast to be eroded back as much as a mile, and the related loss of nutrient-rich materials in the southeastern Mediterranean has reduced fish life, especially sardines, by as much as 90 percent. In the exceptionally dry climate of southern Egypt, evaporation from the extensive surface of Lake Nasser is enormous, totaling several hundred billion cubic meters each year. More alarming during the 1980s was the drought that received worldwide attention because of starvation among the Ethiopians. The diminished rainfall reduced the runoff into the Nile headwaters, and the decreased Nile flow caused a drop of more than 75 ft./23 m in the level of Lake Nasser in 1988 compared with a decade earlier. Periodic droughts have, of course, beset the Nile watershed throughout history, but the balance is now so delicate that the potential scale of catastrophe is very much greater.[7]

[2] Nile Delta: Lower Egypt

The Nile Delta encompasses a total area of about 8,495 miles^2/22,000 km^2 and includes more than half of the cultivated area of the country (Fig. 20-3). A classic delta deposit, it was built up by continued sedimentation of Nile silt in a former embayment in the northeast African coast. (The earlier coastline reached to present-day Cairo.)

Figure 20-3. *Nile Delta and the Sinai. The Suez Canal crosses the center of the photograph; sand-choked wadis crisscross the central Sinai. View from space looking southeast. (NASA photograph)*

Although distributaries of the river have varied in number and in their courses during the past several thousand years, two main branches of the Nile traverse the delta at present: the Rosetta on the west and the Damietta on the east.

As is typical of deltas, the alluvial area is very flat, with a low gradient to the distributaries as they cross the plain. Many of the low mounds scattered over the surface are tells (archaeological mounds) marking the sites of ancient settlements. The delta is one of the most intensively cultivated areas in the world, and it also contains thousands of agricultural villages and several of Egypt's larger cities: Alexandria, an ancient city at the northwest corner of the delta, Egypt's second-largest city and most important port; the large central-delta textile-manufacturing cities of Mahalla and Tanta; and other cities such as Zagazig, Rashid (Rosetta), and Damietta. With rural population densities of 3,500–4,000 per mile^2/1,350–1,545 per km^2, the delta has one of the highest agricultural population densities in the world. The thousands of small settlements show as gray dots in the space photograph in Figure 20-3.

[3] Western Desert

The huge Western Desert region covers 263,000 miles²/681,000 km², an area slightly smaller than the state of Texas and more than two-thirds the total area of Egypt. Reaching from the western edge of the delta and valley to Libya, it is an extension of the Libyan Desert, itself part of the Sahara. Although the Western Desert is basically a low plateau with a cover of generally horizontal sedimentary rocks, landforms vary moderately from section to section in response to changes in rock types, wind erosion, and occasional faulting. Nubian sandstones prevail in the south but are overlain by Tertiary limestones to the north, with an extensive Great Sand Sea in the west blanketing nearly half of the Western Desert region. Several strata of the Nubian Formation that underlie much of the northern Sahara serve as aquifers and have large amounts of artesian water, most of it fossil water. Egypt plans to exploit these "water deposits," as Libya does in its Kufrah Oasis, but only limited progress has been achieved because of budgetary constraints. Nevertheless, the potential water supply is believed to be great.

Overlying the Nubian sandstone, Tertiary limestones form a barren plateau tableland that extends eastward to the Nile Valley and slopes gently northward to the Mediterranean. Along their southern edges, the limestones form prominent ragged escarpments 985–1,640 ft./300–500 m high.

Embayments along the escarpments embrace several large semienclosed depressions watered by contact springs. In the depressions lie five historic oases: Siwa, al-Bahriyah, al-Farafirah, al-Dakhilah, and Kharijah (see Map 20-1). In anticipation of tapping Nubian aquifers and rejuvenating the southern oases, the government has grouped the oases in the New Valley Project (al-Wadi al-Jadid), which, however, has not made great progress. Geomorphically, the Fayyum Depression mentioned above may be considered in this same group.

In the northwest is the largest of the Western Desert depressions, the forbidding and uninhabited Qattara Depression, about the size of the state of Delaware. With an irregular floor 436 ft./133 m below sea level in its lowest part, the depression is projected to play a key role in an ambitious but risky project to generate hydroelectricity. The plan, now in abeyance, calls for Mediterranean Sea water to be piped to the depression's edge and then down through penstocks to drive turbines halfway down into the basin. In addition to the Qattara Depression, towns along the northern coast became internationally known during World War II because of their roles in North African campaigns—Sallum, Sidi Barrani, Matruh, and al-Alamayn (el-Alamein). Modest oil and gas fields are exploited south of Matruh and al-Alamayn.

[4] Eastern Desert

The two deserts divided by the Nile Valley are markedly different in character. In contrast to the Western Desert just described, the Eastern Desert consists essentially of a backbone of elevated and mostly rugged mountains running parallel to and just inland from the Red Sea coast. These Red Sea Hills are an elevated and faulted edge of the Nubian Shield composed of igneous and metamorphic rocks of the basement complex (see Chap. 3). Overlapping the western and northern portions of the hills is a relatively low, maturely dissected, extensive Eocene limestone plateau; the resistant crystalline hills farther to the south reach 7,175 ft./2,187 m.[8]

More elevated and slightly better watered than the Western Desert, the Eastern Desert is less inhospitable and is traversed by several routes between the Nile and the Red Sea. The crystalline rocks of the Red Sea Hills contain numerous mineral occurrences, but few are commercially exploitable. The Red Sea coast—partly fringed by white sand beaches—has a number of small ports, some dating from ancient times. Bur Safajah, among others, is being developed as a resort. Along the coastal plain of the Gulf of Suez, as well as offshore and across the gulf, are Egypt's largest and most productive oil and gas fields.

[5] Sinai

The large triangular Sinai Peninsula, 23,590 miles²/61,100 km² in area, belongs geomorphically to the Red Sea Hills but has been separated by vigorous faulting along both sides of and beneath the Gulf of Suez (see Fig. 3-3). Such tectonics have in some stretches created structural conditions for moderate accumulations of petroleum. The southern extent of Sinai is composed of uptilted igneous and crystalline rocks that reach 8,650 ft./2,637 m in Jabal Katherina, highest elevation in Egypt, and 7,495 ft./2,285 m in nearby Mount Sinai. Nestled in these rugged highlands is the famous St. Catherine Monastery, which has a unique collection of ancient manuscripts.

Sinai's landforms are easily seen in Figure 3-3: The northern two-thirds of the peninsula is a great northward-draining limestone plateau that rises from the Mediterranean coast and terminates southward in a high escarpment, Jabal al-Tih, on the northern flanks of the igneous core of Sinai. The backslope of the limestone is relatively open country that drains to the Mediterranean through numerous tributaries that merge into the Wadi al-Arish, the River of Egypt of the Old Testament (some Israeli writers question this traditional identification). The northern reaches of the plateau have been traversed through the centuries by armies and migrating peoples, including Egyptian and Israeli armies in 1948–1949, 1956, 1967, and 1973. The peninsula is connected with Africa by the sandy Isthmus of Suez, through which the Suez Canal was cut by 1869 (see discussion under "Waterways" below). Anchoring the northern end of the canal is Port Said, on the Mediterranean, and at the southern end is Suez. The midway city is Ismailiyah.

The Egyptians

Population

With a 1992 population of 55 million, Egypt adds 1 million people every 9 months, an increase that will double the population in 28 years. With an Egyptian baby born every 26 seconds, the population will exceed 70 million by the year 2000 even if the birthrate declines moderately. The large population and high rate of increase involve several significant geographical relationships. That a population of 55 million could evolve and mostly be supported until recently on

such a limited amount of cultivated land is a tribute to the productivity of this great river oasis. However, the increasing population is shrinking the amount of available cultivable land per capita and, under foreseeable financial conditions, threatens to overwhelm the national capacity to supply basic services and even food and water. Increasing percentages of the food consumed are being imported each year.

Peoples

The dominant group in the Egyptian population, Egyptian Arabs, represents a mixture of the already mixed indigenous Egyptians and the immigrant Arabs who entered the area during the seventh to ninth centuries. Egyptians long considered Bedouins as "the Arabs" and viewed the majority of the population as "the real Egyptians." Fellahin (literally, "tillers of the soil") in many isolated Nile Valley villages have maintained features and many customs of ancient Egyptians, as those are shown in ancient representations. By the late 1800s, Egypt identified increasingly with the Arab world and stimulated some of the main currents of Arab nationalism; and after the mid-1950s, Arabism was a driving factor in the political life of Nasserist Egypt and its regional relationships.

Egypt does not exhibit the complexity of distinct ethnolinguistic groupings of Iraq or Iran. Most of the ethnic groups that immigrated into Egypt in the past have been absorbed into the population, although some small groups have emigrated en masse. Significant minorities, including Greeks and Jews for millennia and Europeans for shorter periods, lived in Egypt for many centuries, but many left during the Nasser period.

Copts, by far the largest minority, preserve an ancient Egyptian lineage. Although most Copts are strongly differentiated physically from other Egyptians, their major distinction is that they are Christians, remnant of a community that included most Egyptians prior to the Arab Muslim invasion (see Chap. 6). Estimates of their number vary, but Copts apparently make up less than 10 percent of the total population; they are concentrated in Luxor and the Asyut and Minya provinces of Upper Egypt and in Cairo and Alexandria. They formerly held many influential positions in the government and in business, but thousands have emigrated to escape discrimination since the mid-1950s.[9]

The second-largest minority is that of the Nubians, numbering possibly 200,000, now concentrated around Kom Ombo, north of Aswan. Formerly living in villages along the Upper Nile Valley southward into the Sudan, the Nubians were resettled in the early 1960s because their villages were to be submerged under Lake Nasser after completion of the Aswan High Dam. Although compensated for their lost property and given new lands and new homes, the Nubians have found the dislocation and loss of their traditional houses culturally disruptive.

The Bedouins in Egypt have been moving away from nomadism and toward sedentarization for more than a century.[10] However, several thousand nomadic Beja people (non-Arabs) migrate into and out of southeastern Egypt from and into northeastern Sudan. A small Bedouin tribe, the Maaza, with probably 1,000 members, wanders the hills and wadis of the Eastern Desert.[11] A few other small groups are also elements in the mixture of peoples in Egypt. Berbers are the main group in several villages in the Western Desert, especially in the Siwa Oasis in the northwest of the country, having inhabited the area for many centuries. Several thousand Armenians live mostly in Cairo and Alexandria.

Although Old Testament sources recount that Hebrews lived in Egypt in serfdom as Bnai Yisrael (Children of Israel) about the thirteenth century BC, that group left in the emigration described in the book of Exodus. In Ptolemaic times, Jews settled in Alexandria and started a Jewish community in Egypt that still exists, expanded by Spanish and central European Jews until World War I. Growing Zionism, the later emergence of the State of Israel, and periodic wars between Israel and Egypt created a backlash against Egyptian Jews, most of whom gradually emigrated to Israel and elsewhere. Of about 80,000 Jews in 1947, only a few hundred remain in Egypt. The number of Western European expatriates decreased during the Nasser years, but the expatriate community was again expanding by the late 1980s.

The pluralistic coexistence in Egyptian society broke down during the Nasser period and was further pressured by growing Islamic fundamentalism beginning in the late 1960s. Between 1975 and 1985, religious militancy diffused among many groups and associations in Egypt, including extremist Islamic fraternities (*jamaats*)—more militant outgrowths of the Muslim Brotherhood (Ikhwan al-Muslimun) movement—and Coptic students. As elsewhere, conservative Islam has increasingly entered the political system. In response, the Coptic church after 1971 declared its determination to protect the rights of the Coptic community.[12] Despite guarantees of religious freedoms in the constitution, intercommunal conflict remained a serious social problem during the 1980s and the early 1990s. Members of an extremist Muslim fraternity, Tanzim al-Jihad, assassinated President Sadat in October 1981. The Jihad group became extremist and violent in the early 1990s and announced its goal of imposing a fundamentalist Islamic government on Egypt similar to that in Iran. The group's members or other like-minded fundamentalist zealots clashed with Copts in late 1991 and early 1992, assassinated a moderate critic of fundamentalism in June 1992, and launched violent attacks on selected tourist groups in late 1992 and early 1993 in an announced effort to destroy the $3.3-billion tourism industry and thereby break the government. As tourist arrivals dropped sharply, the government struck back and captured and executed many of the zealots in 1993.

Settlements

Traditionally, Egypt has been predominantly a land of small agricultural villages. Despite steadily increasing urbanization, that tradition remains, and thousands of villages are scattered the length of the valley and in the delta. Valley villages are usually sited just beyond the edge of irrigation, in order to conserve irrigable land, and are located for most of the length of the Nile on the western edge of the floodplain. Most of these valley villages are linear in morphology. Until recently, houses have been constructed of mud from the clay-silt that is in plentiful supply along the Nile or from a nearby canal (Fig. 20-4). Two or three villages can be seen from any given point along the river, and a periodic town functions as a service center for several villages. Villages in the delta, on the other hand, display a

Figure 20-4. *Village under date palms in the Fayyum Depression, Egypt. Typical of villages and towns in the Nile Valley and Delta, this village has older houses of mud bricks and newer structures of red fired bricks. Mud construction has been banned in Egypt because of the toll on agricultural soils taken by digging for mud.*

nucleated morphology and, in the absence of the stone that is available on the valley fringes, were formerly even more likely to have houses constructed of mud. Obviously, as the rapidly increasing population necessitated greatly increased numbers of houses, continued use of mud from nearby fields turned former productive plots into useless pits. A farmer could earn more from the sale of the top 3.3 ft./1 m of his land for making mud bricks than he could earn from the sale of the land. So much arable land was being lost that in 1982, a law was passed prohibiting use of mud for building construction. The change entirely altered the appearance of Egyptian villages, where all new construction is of generally reddish fired brick. The brick is appreciably more difficult to prepare and is therefore more expensive.

The dominance of the village has been diminishing since the early 1950s, and the percentage of urban population increased from about one-third in the 1950s to 44 percent in 1987 (see Table 6-1). Despite the marked growth of several cities, especially Cairo, Egyptian social structure retains village roots more than the urban migration would indicate. Increasing hundreds of thou-

sands of landless and displaced fellahin have flooded into the cities since the 1950s, often grouping themselves by place of origin and thus preserving their village identity.

Cairo has for many years been the largest city in Africa and the Middle East.[13] By the mid-1980s it had tripled its population of 1960, and the greater Cairo metropolitan area includes 25 percent of the total population of Egypt. The explosive growth has outrun the capacity to service the population. Faced with mounting budget deficits, Egypt could not expand the water supply, educational facilities, necessary services, and housing in proportion to the population increase in Cairo and other cities after 1967. Of the more than 1 million shortfall in housing units in Egypt in recent years, half were needed in the capital. An estimated 1.4 million Cairo homeless—about 10 percent of the population—have taken refuge in the tombs and monuments in the City of the Dead, the extensive Cairo cemeteries east of the capital. New suburbs have been built around Cairo, which are criticized as urban encroachment on valuable irrigable land, but inflow from the villages continues to exceed the city's housing capacity. Traffic in the central business district was becoming virtually immobile until the initial segments of a new subway system were opened in 1987.

With nearly half of its population urbanized, Egypt has 26 cities with populations exceeding 100,000 and more than twice as many with 50,000–100,000 inhabitants. Growth far outruns the census taker. Most of the larger cities are in the delta, where urban sprawl consumes vital agricultural land. Thus, the overurbanization problem also reflects Egypt's population-economy imbalance. Overpopulation combines with a housing shortage, unemployment, and a low per capita income to create acute socioeconomic pressures.

Changing Economic Patterns

An Economic Perspective

The riches of Egypt are proverbial—the productivity of the irrigated soil, the creativity of the Egyptian artisans, the gold from the Pharaonic and Ptolemaic tombs, the trade between Red Sea entrepôts and Mediterranean coastal states. It was such richness that attracted the Romans, Byzantines, Umayyads, Ottomans, and British. However, the ever-increasing population of modern times presses on the maximum limits of even Egypt's fabled resources. The agricultural productivity is several times greater today than in centuries past, but demands on that productivity have increased even more. Once a net food exporter, then at least self-sufficient, Egypt now imports growing percentages of its food consumption—more than 60 percent in the early 1990s.

The political revolution of 1952 brought a correlative economic revolution. Economic efforts of the revolutionary junta included land reform, controls over agriculture, nationalization of industries and institutions (notably the nationalization of the Suez Canal in 1956), sequestration of foreign businesses and agencies, an inflow of bilateral and multilateral loans and grants, and construction of the Aswan High Dam system. Progress toward these well-intentioned goals was impeded by administrative problems, by bureaucratic inefficiency, and by Egypt's military buildup and three wars with Israel. President Nasser's insistence on a socialist approach to state management repelled both foreign and domestic investment.

President Sadat reversed the last trend when he opened Egypt's economic doors by means of his moderate *infitah* policy of 1974, which reduced earlier restrictiveness. However, conditions in Egypt and in the Middle East as a whole have countered some of the goals of *infitah*.[14] Thus, the policy in its early years resulted in a certain amount of deindustrialization and increased indebtedness. Falling incomes and government austerity measures produced riots in Aswan and Alexandria and reinforced Sadat's move to seek peace with Israel. More balanced policies evolved during the early 1980s to produce an improving economy based on diversification and pragmatism. *Infitah* began to yield benefits, but it has not been able to overcome the deep-seated economic problems that characterize the Egyptian scene and that are certain to do so for the foreseeable future.[15]

The defects of the Nasser-instituted statist-paternalistic approach in the mid-1950s soon became apparent and later proved to be a near disaster. Originally, the land reform, nationalization, and imposition of tight control over the economy had popular appeal, as the power of the large landowners, foreign capitalists, and wealthy Egyptians was greatly reduced. Nasser's "social contract" guaranteed provision of basic human needs—food, housing, health care—at subsidized prices, free education through university level, employment for all university graduates, and virtual prohibition of dismissal of employees. These policies were embodied in the constitution of 1971 and are still basically applicable. With government ownership of most large industries, control over much of the major private-sector activity, and price controls over most rents and agricultural produce, the government loaded its own bureaucracy and the public manufacturing sector with redundant employees simply to give them jobs, from which they could not be dismissed.

The situation discouraged private investment and guaranteed a downward spiral until, in the late 1980s and early 1990s, the government finally acceded to reforms urged by the World Bank, the United States, and friendly Arab states. The delicate economic balance required caution in handling, and progress has been modest. However, steady privatization of industry, increased taxation, decreased subsidies, improved efficiency, and a uniform exchange rate are improving the economic forecast for Egypt. Nevertheless, a large foreign debt (even after U.S. forgiveness of $7 billion and Gulf states' forgiveness of $6.7 billion in 1991), continuing large annual budgetary deficits, large annual trade deficits, and inflation are indicators that Egypt has many problems yet to solve before it can begin to feel economically comfortable.

In 1989, Egypt's national accounts showed that its principal source of earnings was remittances from Egyptians working abroad ($3.5 billion), with the next three sources being exports ($2.55 billion—down from $3.93 billion in 1985), Suez Canal dues ($1.3 billion), and tourism ($920 million). In the same year, U.S. aid totaled $2.47 billion. After the Gulf crisis of 1990–1991, remittances decreased as perhaps 1 million workers returned to Egypt from Iraq, Kuwait, and other states. Tourism continues to be a leading source of income, contributing more than $2 billion directly and indirectly in 1988. Canal income will also increase after the increase in tolls in 1991.

Agriculture

The Nile Valley has supported a flourishing agriculture for more than 8,500 years, and much of the valley and delta was under cultivation soon after the union of Upper and Lower Egypt about 3000 BC. Once the cultivable area had been cleared of forest and brush, increasing portions of the area that is now cropland were farmed under the natural flood-irrigation system that was dominant in Egypt until after AD 1800.

The irrigation system so long practiced was basically simple. It utilized the runoff from the heavy summer rains in the East African highlands that poured down the Nile channel and raised the water level 20–25 ft./6–8 m, covering the entire floodplain with several feet of silt-laden floodwaters. When the floodwaters receded after several weeks, the silt loam soils, built up by past floods, were water soaked and were also covered with a fresh few centimeters of nutrient-rich new silt. Thus the valley soils were watered, fertilized, and renewed annually by natural means,

without human intervention. Crops were then planted to mature before the soil dried out some months later. Perennial tree and vine crops, carefully sited as to elevation, could also be maintained; otherwise, only one crop in a flood season could be harvested. In later centuries, water was retained in basins to prolong irrigation; still later, canals were installed by Pharaonic engineers. As experience was passed from generation to generation, the fellahin of the Nile Valley became expert hydraulic farmers, and their traditional culture was as immutable as the annual Nile flood.

The area available for cultivation is restricted by the topographic relationships of the valley floodplain and the fringing deserts on the higher plateaus. Since use of plateau land necessitates pumping water to the higher level, land reclamation is thus a difficult and expensive process, even if water is available to irrigate reclaimed areas. Despite vigorous efforts, reclamation of such areas as the Tahrir (Liberation) Project west of the delta in the 1950s has failed to meet expectations. Plans continue for reclamation in other areas, such as the New Valley Project in the western oases mentioned above. In fact, however, UN data show an actual decline of more than 741,000 acres/300,000 ha of cultivated area in Egypt between the early 1970s and the early 1980s. Much of the loss was the result of urban encroachment. The trend was reversed between 1984 and 1988, when some large projects and many small-scale individual reclamation efforts added a net of 271,810 acres/110,000 ha.

Overly zealous land reform measures from the 1960s had reduced some farms below the size for profitability, and recent government actions have readjusted landholdings. Policies cannot escape the fundamental fact that not only is the proportion of agricultural workers to units of arable land steadily rising, but also the proportion of arable land per capita of total population is steadily decreasing.

Cereals occupy 40–50 percent of the total cropped area. Whereas wheat was the dominant cereal and the dominant crop in the past, maize has surpassed it in both acreage and tonnage produced, since it outproduces wheat and can be used for both human consumption and animal feed. Production of both crops has expanded in

Figure 20-5. *Families of agricultural workers sorting tangerines in a citrus grove in the southern Nile Delta. The grove owner is to the right in a dark robe* (bisht).

recent years in response to liberalization of government controls and high free-market prices. With the increased planting of high-yield varieties of wheat, farmers achieved a 40 percent higher yield in 1989 than in 1985, although more than two-thirds of wheat consumption must still be imported. Millet continues to be an important cereal, but barley has declined because it can be more cheaply produced on the steppelands of neighboring countries, as is also true of wheat.

Noncereals occupy less acreage but produce considerable tonnage, and several are of major economic importance. Egyptian long-staple cotton has been the preferred cotton fiber on world markets since its development by a French agronomist in the 1820s. Although long-staple cotton is increasingly produced elsewhere, Egypt still produces more than one-third of the world crop. The main cotton area is in the central delta, where long expertise and government extension work and control ensure quality. The cotton produced is increasingly being used in the important domestic textile industry, and cotton textiles and yarns now constitute Egypt's leading export by value, surpassing petroleum, which led in the early 1980s. Raw cotton is of only minor importance as an export. One continuing problem in cotton production is the low mandatory price paid to farmers by the government purchasing

agency. Sugarcane is also a significant crop. Well suited to conditions in Upper Egypt, it furnishes most of Egypt's sugar requirements and supplies numerous sugar mills. However, the planting of sugarcane—as well as rice—is being discouraged because both are water-intensive crops.

The range of fruits and vegetables extends from mangoes and bananas through melons and strawberries to apples and potatoes. As in several other Middle East countries already discussed, Egypt is making increasing use of greenhouses for growing vegetables (for example, tomatoes, green peppers, beans) for the early market. Egypt leads the Middle East in orange production in quantity if not in quality and is a major producer of other citrus fruits and grapes (see Fig. 20-5). Along with Saudi Arabia, it is a world leader in date production (see Table 7-3).

Animals have been an integral element in the activities of virtually every Egyptian farm since ancient times. Tomb paintings depict the role of cattle and other animals in early Egyptian agriculture, and the cow and the bull were venerated in the ancient Egyptian pantheon. Sheep, goats, and ducks have also been of prime importance for more than 4,500 years, as has the donkey. Cattle, buffalo, and donkeys are multipurpose farm animals, pulling plows and carts, carrying loads (the donkey serving also for individual transportation), supplying manure for fields and fuel, and furnishing milk. The useful camel came later and is still common. The Indian buffalo (*gamus* or *gamush*) was imported in the Middle Ages and is now the most numerous farm animal. It is well adapted along the river and canals, yielding milk, meat, manure, and hides and serving as a plow animal.[16]

Fishery production in Egypt was 250,000 mt in 1988, only 40 percent that of Turkey, the Middle East leader. The fish catch has increased in recent years, with Lake Nasser replacing the Mediterranean as the main source.

Industry

Oil and Oil Processing. The first oil well in Egypt was drilled in 1886, although commercial production came only in 1913. After World War II, several foreign companies, most of them American, conducted oil explorations, primarily under concession agreements. Oil operations in Egypt expanded in the 1960s, and production averaged 850,300 bpd in 1986–1990, reaching an all-time high of 899,000 bpd in 1987. Although Egypt is a member of the Organization of Arab Petroleum Exporting Countries (OAPEC), it is not a member of OPEC and is, therefore, not subject to OPEC production quotas. On the other hand, official Egyptian output for more than a decade after 1967 was affected by Israel's exploitation of the fields along the Sinai coast during that country's occupation of the area.

Egypt's increasing petroleum production and its growing oil exports have had a major impact on the national export economy. In 1974, a low-production year for Egypt, oil sales constituted only 4 percent of the country's revenues from commodity exports. By 1981–1982, with the price between $29 and $34 per barrel, oil was Egypt's leading export, but it is now slightly surpassed by cotton manufactures.

The most important oil field developments have been in and along both coasts of the Gulf of Suez (see Map 20-1). Intensive exploration in the Western Desert has found several fields in the northern sector, although output has been low. However, the possibility remains that oil fields in Libya extend into western Egypt. Modest gas fields have been found in the northern delta, off-shore near Alexandria, and in the Western Desert.

Egypt is credited in 1992 with having oil reserves of 4.5 billion barrels, roughly comparable to the reserves in Qatar and Oman. Main production is by the Gulf of Suez Petroleum Company, originally a joint venture between the Egyptian General Petroleum Corporation and Amoco of the United States. Fourteen other companies, several involving government participation, also operate in Egypt.

Two Egyptian pipelines are noteworthy: The Sumed (Suez-Mediterranean) line, from Ayn Sukhnah on the Gulf of Suez to Sidi Krir just west of Alexandria, is a dual 42-in./107-cm line with a capacity of 1.6 million bpd. Its capacity is being increased to 2.4 million bpd in the early 1990s. Egypt owns it jointly with Saudi Arabia, Kuwait, Qatar, and Abu Dhabi. Sumed was opened in 1977 to bypass the Suez Canal, both because the largest tankers exceeded the capacity of the canal and also because the canal had been shut down between 1967 and 1975 after the June War with Israel. Intended to complement the canal, Sumed has not been utilized to the extent anticipated. The second line, opened in 1981, extends from Ras Shuqayr on the Gulf of Suez to refineries at Suez and Cairo. Ras Shuqayr is the export terminal for the adjacent offshore fields.

Of the eight refineries in operation in 1992, the largest is at Mostorod near Cairo, with a throughput of 156,750 bpd. The total capacity of the eight is 523,153 bpd. Principal petrochemical plants are near Alexandria and Suez.[17]

Other Mineral Industry. Contemporary commercial solid-mineral mining is extensive and involves a considerable range of minerals, but it is not a major contributor to the Egyptian national economy. Iron ore from Aswan was used in the Helwan iron and steel mill from its opening in 1958 until the mid-1970s; however, somewhat better and more plentiful sedimentary ore from al-Bahriyah Oasis now feeds the Helwan mill via a railway newly constructed for this purpose. The new Alexandria National Iron and Steel plant is the newest and most efficient steel plant in the Middle East, producing 932,000 mt in 1989, two-thirds of Egypt's total output.

Phosphate rock is mined near Isna (south of Luxor), near Bur Safajah, and in neighboring areas. Production averaged 1.15 million mt in the late 1980s, about the same as Iraq's. Other nonmetallic minerals produced were of relatively low value and included large tonnages of gypsum, fire clay, kaolin, and salt, as well as all varieties of dimension stone. Aswan granite is noteworthy and is in increasing demand. As is true elsewhere in the Middle East, cement production is a major minerals industry.[18]

Other Manufacturing. Egypt experienced delayed industrial development before World War II and suffered uneven development after the 1952 revolution. The unskilled labor supply was more than adequate, and skilled labor was moderately available; however, large supplies of capital were limited, as were planning and management skills, thereby constraining industrial growth in Egypt during the 1950s and 1960s. Petroleum development, benefits of the High Dam, and *infitah* policies finally stimulated a significant growth of the manufacturing sector.

Approximately 75 percent of the manufacturing sector is government owned, and virtually all of the larger and medium-sized establishments (approximately 375 in number) are in the public sector. A program of privatization is achieving only a modest pace of implementation but is moving forward. Geographically, half of Egypt's manufacturing is concentrated in the Shubra al-Khaymah area north of Cairo and Helwan south of the capital. Increasing industrialization of the capital area during the 1980s has produced an incongruous pollution of the formerly crisp, clear desert air at the junction of valley and delta.

The 375 public sector plants provide two-thirds of the value added in manufacturing and mining and half of the industrial employment. They include such plants as the Helwan iron and steel plant; an aluminum plant at Naj Hammadi, opened in 1975 to use surplus electricity from the High Dam to process Australian and Guinean bauxite; textile mills in the major delta textile cities of Tanta and al-Mahallah al-Kubra; engineering industries, with the largest, El-Nasr Automotive Manufacturing Company, established in 1959 near Cairo; shipyards in Alexandria; and medium-sized armaments industries in Lower Egypt, including assembly of tanks, helicopters, and jeeps. Egypt is also attempting to develop an aircraft assembly plant.

The private sector establishments are small, usually with fewer than ten and often with fewer than three employees, and are generally artisan in character. They are located primarily in and around Cairo, especially in the old *suqs* of the Muski and Khan al-Khalili; but they also operate in Alexandria, Asyut, Luxor, Aswan, and other main cities and towns. Their output includes food products, textiles, leather goods, jewelry, artistic glass objects, copper and brass ornamental and utilitarian items, and furniture and other wood products, including intricately inlaid boxes and other household items.

Transportation and Trade

Roads. With settlement highly concentrated in the Nile Valley and Delta, transportation by river, road, and railroad is equally concentrated (see Map 20-1). A medium-speed paved highway extends the full length of the Nile Valley between Cairo and Aswan and also extends from Cairo to Alexandria and other terminal points along the northern delta. At right angles to the valley-delta routes is the Mediterranean coastal highway between the Libyan border on the west and the Israeli border on the east. Successive military operations in Sinai and increasing development of the area have prompted the construction of other transpeninsular and circumpeninsular roads in Sinai, opening an area that was isolated as late as the mid-1950s.

A recently completed north-south Red Sea coastal highway connects Suez and the Sudan border, opening a new area for beach resorts and secondary ports and relieving traffic on the Nile route. The Suez Canal is paralleled on both sides by roads that are linked by the 1-mile/1.6-km Ahmad Hamdi Tunnel, which passes under Bitter Lake. The two main north-south routes, Nile Valley and Red Sea coast, are connected by several east-west roads. The Delta Road between Cairo and Alexandria and the Desert Road between the same two cities reveal a marked and interesting contrast in Egyptian landscapes.

Railroads. Unlike many national rail systems, Egyptian lines are heavily used by passengers, giving Egypt half of the total passenger-kilometers for the Middle East. Indicative of the pressure of population on facilities, trains into and out of Cairo are so overloaded that hundreds of passengers must either stand inside or cling precariously to the outside of trains. This hazard is being addressed by a new mass transit system between al-Marg, a northern suburb of Cairo, and Helwan to the south.

Waterways. In addition to the Suez Canal, Egypt has 2,175 miles/3,500 km of inland waterways, half along the Nile River itself and half along several major canals, especially in the delta. Sailing on the Nile was the only north-south method of travel in Egypt until completion of the railway to Aswan and the later construction of a motorable road. The Nile between Aswan and the Mediterranean is still used by hundreds of the typical Nile sailing boats, *faluqas* (feluccas), as well as by rapidly increasing numbers of motor-powered tourist boats. *Faluqas* are a practical and inexpensive means of north-south shipment of heavy and nonperishable goods such as cement, ballast, ceramic items, and grain, which are picked up and delivered at many points along the river. Egypt is expanding its river transport system in order to relieve the burden on land and air facilities.

Since its opening in 1869, the Suez Canal has been both a significant symbol and an integral economic element for Egypt (see Chap. 11). Operated by an Anglo-French company until it was dramatically nationalized by President Nasser in 1956, the canal quickly became Egypt's leading foreign exchange earner. It was closed by the 1967 Arab-Israeli war but was reopened in 1975 and enlarged in 1980 to a draft of 52 ft./16 m to permit transit of larger tankers, up to 150,000 deadweight tons (dwt). (See additional details under "Suez Canal," Chap. 11.) Earnings from canal tolls reached a record $1.3 billion in 1988–1989.

Ports. Alexandria, Egypt's most important port, was founded by Alexander the Great, and for much of 23 centuries it has functioned as one of the largest and busiest general-cargo ports in the eastern Mediterranean and the Middle East. It fills so many functions—port, resort, industrial center, commercial center—that a new port, to be one-third larger than that of Alexandria, is under construction at Dikhaylah just west of the city. Along the Suez Canal, the three port cities of Port Said, Ismailiyah, and Suez, all damaged in the three wars fought along the canal, are being reconstructed and expanded to handle increased activity. They are not only reviving but are flourishing with the growing industrial development and population in the area.

Air Transportation. The government-owned airline, Egypt Air, was founded in 1932 and operated for many years as Misr Air (Arabic *Misr* = Egypt). Egypt Air operates the second-largest civil aviation fleet in the Middle East (after Saudia) and flies an extensive network from Western Europe to the Far East and into Africa. Along with its civil fleet, Egypt has a large air force and also maintains a significant number of medium-sized combined civil and military airports. Cairo's new airport is the busiest in the Middle East and sends frequent flights to the country's main tourist centers in Upper Egypt, Aswan and Luxor.

Trade. Still almost entirely in the private sector, most domestic retail trade follows the Arab commercial tradition, in which outlets tend to be small, often operated only by the owner and perhaps one or two family members. Central Cairo and Alexandria have relatively large Western-style "department" stores. Countrywide, food shops predominate, but other retail stores offer clothing, textiles, small household items, and jewelry and other items handcrafted in Egypt for the tourist and internal trade. Such items include a wide range of inlaid wood pieces, hand-engraved brass and copper, turned and carved alabaster, jewelry and costume jewelry, tooled leather, traditional screens of turned wood (*mashrabiyah*), and paintings on Egyptian-grown handmade papyrus.

Cairo preserves the traditional *suq* in addition to its modern, Western-style central business district. The Khan al-Khalili, located in a fourteenth-century Mamluk caravansary or khan, has been famous for centuries throughout the Middle East. Traditional Egyptian goods and certain types of specialty goods from around the world are on sale in the primarily small stalls.

The adjacent Muski sells similar items but also has sections for utilitarian and lower-value items. Both bazaars are a paradise for leisurely shopping for the curious and the unusual, especially if the shopper is a skilled bargainer.

Still largely under government control, foreign trade has long been a major factor in the Egyptian economy. Exchange between Lebanon and Egypt, for example, flourished before 2400 BC. Shifts in commodities traded and in directions of trade both historically and recently reflect significant changes within Egypt and in its foreign relations. For example, exports of long-staple cotton during the American Civil War brought Egypt instant but short-lived prosperity, petroleum exports during the early 1980s offset increasing trade deficits until the world oil price collapsed, and Egypt's trading partners shifted in accordance with its political orientation between 1970 and 1980.

For many years, Egyptian exports were overwhelmingly agricultural raw materials, chiefly food products and cotton. The share of agricultural products is now less than 20 percent of value of exports. Other exports and imports are given in the country summary at the beginning of this chapter.

Relations

Egypt's relations both with its neighbors and with the major powers have been of crucial importance since 1947.[19] Under Nasser, relations were confrontational and erratic. Under Sadat, they involved complete reversals in policies with Israel, the USSR, and the United States. They then stabilized and followed a relatively consistent policy during the 1980s. Egypt met the Gulf crisis with major readjustments in 1990 and 1991.

A watershed in Egyptian relations was President Sadat's turning away from the USSR in the early 1970s, establishing close ties with the United States, and signing a peace treaty with Israel in 1979. His making peace with Israel precipitated the expulsion of Egypt from the Arab League, which Egypt had led since the league's inception in 1945, and the transfer of the league's headquarters to Tunis. The peace treaty also prompted most Arab countries to break diplomatic relations with Egypt. The Organization of the Islamic Conference (OIC) reinstated Egypt in 1984, and after the 1987 Arab Summit meeting in Amman, most Arab states that had broken with Egypt in 1979 reestablished diplomatic relations. By 1989, Egypt's return to the Arab League fold was a foregone conclusion, and league headquarters were reestablished in Cairo in October 1990. Also in 1989, President Mubarak took the chair of the Organization of African Unity (OAU). Thus, Egypt has been restored to both Arabism and Africa and has retained its position within Islamic world affairs. In February 1989, Egypt, Iraq, Jordan, and the then Yemen Arab Republic joined to form the Arab Cooperative Council (ACC), a regional grouping similar to the GCC with aims comparable to those of the European Common Market. Egypt sharply opposed the Iraqi invasion of Kuwait in 1990, and the fledgling ACC collapsed, as has every union Egypt has attempted.

Egypt's relations with its upstream neighbor, the Sudan, have been important since the dawn of history. During the period of Britain's de facto hegemony over Egypt, the Sudan was an Anglo-Egyptian condominium. These long relations found expression in a friendly 1982 agreement, a ten-year Charter of Integration, calling for close cooperation in foreign policy, security, and development. However, the relations deteriorated in the late 1980s as a consequence of three developments: increasing threats by the Sudan to dam the Nile; assumption of power in the Sudan in June 1989 by a new government that was more fundamentalist and anti-Egypt; and the Sudan's siding with Iraq after the invasion of Kuwait. Relations with President Qadhdhafi (Qaddafi) of Libya have been spasmodic. Tentative plans for political unity in 1971 were abrogated in 1984, giving way to conflict and brief border warfare. After more years of tension, Egypt and Libya were reconciled in mid-1989, although proof of détente in the resumption of full diplomatic relations was slow in coming.

Relations between Egypt and Israel have been the mainspring of the post–World War II geopolitical evolution of the Levant and northeastern Africa (see Chap. 11 and other country chapters). In late 1992, diplomatically correct relations continue between the two neighbors, aided by the peaceful settlement—in Egypt's favor—by arbitration of the Israeli claim on the small Taba en-clave (late 1988); however, frictions remain over such issues as the status of the Palestinians, the West Bank and Gaza, and Jerusalem. Both Egypt and Israel are participants in the ongoing talks in the Middle East peace process initiated in 1991. Thousands of Israeli tourists visit Egypt annu-ally, the only neighboring Arab country they may legally enter, but few Egyptians visit Israel.

Relations with the United States after 1974 be-came a key factor in Egypt's political-economic position. Cut off by Nasser after Israel's attack on Egypt in 1967, U.S.-Egyptian relations resumed in 1974 after the United States brokered the Sinai disengagement agreements. In other efforts to foster détente between Egypt and Israel, the United States established the Sinai Support and Field Missions after 1976 and sponsored the Camp David accords and the Egyptian-Israeli peace treaty.[20] Financially, the United States first supplanted then supplemented Arab aid with U.S. aid, committing nearly $30 billion in eco-nomic and military grants, credits, military training, economic support, and food aid be-tween 1974 and 1990. Egypt continues to be the second-largest recipient (after Israel) of U.S. aid. Egypt, in turn, maintains peace with Israel and has provided facilities for use by U.S. forces in Lebanon and the Gulf and for joint military exer-cises.[21] Of signal importance was Egypt's role in persuading the majority of Arab League mem-bers to support the coalition against Iraq in the Gulf crisis. Also important was Egypt's military contribution to the coalition effort—35,000 men and equipment, third largest after the United States and Saudi Arabia. U.S.-Egyptian relations became particularly close during 1991–1992, when the United States forgave $7 billion of Egypt's debt.

Relations between the former Soviet Union and Egypt are primarily of historical interest. Af-ter seventeen years of close Soviet-Egyptian rela-tions on a basis of mutual advantage, those rela-tions deteriorated. In July 1972, President Sadat expelled 15,000–20,000 Soviet advisers and repu-diated the 1971 friendship treaty with the Soviet Union. In September 1981, the Soviet ambassador and several aides were expelled on charges of es-pionage, but relations were restored in July 1984.[22] Soviet-Egyptian relations remained cor-rect after the reestablishment of U.S.-Egyptian ties. After the breakup of the USSR, Egypt pur-sued good relations not only with Russia but also with the new Muslim republics—Azerbaijan and the five republics in central Asia.

Despite having exercised imperialist control over Egypt after 1882 and having participated in the 1956 tripartite invasion of the Suez, Britain retains good relations with Egypt. France also had imperialist interests in the area and assumed an especially important role in the construction and operation of the Suez Canal. Because of the involvement of Britain and France in the 1956 Suez affair, Nasser sequestered British and French properties in Egypt. European cultural influence carries over, however, and both English and French are second languages for many edu-cated Egyptians.

Thus restored to a pivotal role in Arab and Is-lamic world affairs, and once again demonstrat-ing the continuing advantages of its major power focus location, Egypt strives to pursue a moder-ate course between its ties with both the West and the Arab world. Nasser directed Egypt away from its European links and propounded Arabism but was confrontational in both direc-tions. In a grand pragmatic gamble, Sadat turned Egypt inexorably Westward, and Mubarak has maintained that orientation while also reaching out to his Middle East neighbors. He restored diplomatic ties with Syria in December 1989 after more than a decade of tension, and he encour-aged the Damascus Declaration of March 1991 (among Egypt, Syria, and the GCC)—which, however, proved to be another Middle East polit-ical phantom. President Mubarak also restored relations with Iran in 1991 after four years of mu-tual distrust. With Naguib Mahfouz winning the Nobel Prize for Literature in 1988 and the former Egyptian foreign minister Boutros Boutros-Ghali being chosen secretary-general of the United Nations, Egypt has achieved positive rec-ognition on the world stage.

21

Turkey:
Bridgeland in Anatolia

Between Europe and Middle East

With its geopolitically strategic bridgeland location, Asia Minor has functioned as a transit land and transition between Europe and southwest Asia for more than 3,000 years. Traversing that bridgeland millennia ago, Europeans worked their way down the valleys and over the passes of the Balkans and into the Anatolian basins and beyond. Similarly, other peoples from the Caucasus and the Iranian Plateau traversed the rugged mountains of eastern Anatolia and mingled with Europeans in the central basins. Later empires were centered in Constantinople and ruled lands from central Europe in one direction to the Arabian Peninsula coastlands in the other. Post–World War I republican Turkey has retained its tenacious foothold in Europe and, now connected to the continent by actual bridges over the Bosporus, links Europe with the eastern reaches of Asia Minor. The only Middle East state adjoining Europe, contemporary Turkey is also the only Middle East Muslim state that openly pursues Europeanization, that uses the European (Roman) alphabet, and that belongs to the North Atlantic Treaty Organization (NATO). In the early 1990s it was still actively seeking full membership in the European Common Market.

Turkey's geographical assets include not only its location in the strategically major Anatolian power center but also its control over the straits of the Bosporus and the Dardanelles. Facing imperial Russian lands then later the Soviet constituent republics and now the successor republics across the Black Sea and in the Caucasus Mountains, Turkey has been involved in more wars with Russia than any other nation. One reflection of Asia Minor's strategic location is Turkey's function as an anchor on the southeastern flank of NATO; evidence of its transitional function was shown in its simultaneous membership in NATO and CENTO (Central Treaty Organization) before CENTO collapsed in 1979. The disintegration of the USSR diminished the importance both of NATO and of Turkey's role in NATO, but Turkey's intermediate location thrust it once again into a geopolitical vortex vis-à-vis the former Soviet satellites and successor republics in the trans-Caucasus and in central Asia. Moreover, Turkey is the only country that bordered both contestants in the 1980–1988 Iran-Iraq war, and it was one of the six immediate neighbors of Iraq in the 1990–1991 Gulf crisis.

Fourth-largest state in the Middle East, Turkey also has the largest population. It leads the region in a wide range of agricultural products and, with the major exception of petroleum, a range of both mineral resources and production. Turkey's development has focused on human, agricultural, mineral, and industrial resources; and after several decades of lagging progress, it showed evidence after the mid-1980s of a growing realization of its national potential. Serious problems remain, but the country has advanced significantly toward modernization, democratization, and Westernization.

Physical reminders of Asia Minor's rich history are found not only in Istanbul and other cities but also along the coastlands and in the remote valleys of Turkey. Sites of the numerous

TURKEY

Long-form official name, anglicized: Republic of Turkey
Official name, transliterated: Türkiye Cumhuriyeti
Form of government: multiparty republic with one legislative house (Grand National Assembly)
Area: 300,948 miles²/779,452 km²
Population, 1991: 58,376,000. Literacy (latest): 76%
Ethnic composition (%): Turk 85.7, Kurd 10.6, Arab 1.6, other (Laz, Georgian, Circassian, Jewish, Armenian, Greek) 2.1
Religions (%): Muslim (mostly Sunni) 98.0, other (mostly Christian and Jewish) 2.0
GNP, 1989: $74.7 billion; per capita: $1,360
Petroleum reserves: 650 million barrels
Main exports (% of total value, 1990): textiles 31.3; agricultural products 18.8; iron and nonferrous metals 14.4; food 6.3; leather and hides 5.8; chemical products 4.8; machinery 1.7
Main imports (% of total value, 1990): fuels 17.1; machinery and transport equipment 16.8; chemicals 11.0; iron and steel 8.7; electrical equipment 7.1
Capital city: Ankara 2,559,471; other cities: Istanbul 6,620,241; Izmir 1,757,414; Adana 916,150; Bursa 834,576

---

successive civilizations in the diverse environments of the peninsula are becoming increasingly accessible and well known.

For clarity in nomenclature, it should be noted that "Turkey" refers to the contemporary state, the Republic of Turkey, which includes the 3 percent of its territory that lies on the southeastern tip of Europe (eastern Thrace). "Asia Minor" refers to the broad peninsula of southwest Asia that lies between the Black Sea and the northeastern Mediterranean and east of the Aegean. "Anatolia" (Turkish, Anadolu), although frequently considered as synonymous with Asia Minor, technically refers to the interior plateau and traditionally excludes the coastlands on three sides of Asia Minor. Both Asia Minor and Anatolia exclude Turkey-in-Europe, with Anatolia implying the antithesis of Europe. "Ottoman," of course, refers to the empire or aspects of that empire (dynasty, culture, territory) that centered in Constantinople and Asia Minor prior to 1918.

Complex Regional Patterns

A Physical Interlocation

The rugged and often picturesque landscapes of Turkey are the product of particularly complex and powerful earth forces that have shaped Ana-

tolia for millions of years and still manifest themselves in frequent and major earthquakes and related seismic events (see Map 3-3). Like Iran, ancestral Asia Minor lay in the former Tethyan geosyncline and has been literally squeezed between the African and Eurasian tectonic plates (see Chap. 3). It is one segment of the huge belt of Alpine folding during the Tertiary period that extends from the Atlantic to the eastern Himalayas. Anatolia and Iran are the two halves of the Mobile Belt Province (see Map 3-2), and both—Turkey more so than Iran—exhibit exceedingly complex geomorphology that has a strong impact on other patterns.[1]

The massive tectonism that shaped Asia Minor created a virtually continuous belt of folded mountains across northern Anatolia and a similar belt across the south. The compression enclosed resistant blocks in between, and accompanying forces raised and depressed masses in the east and west. In the west, the alternating raised blocks (horsts) and depressed basins (grabens) create the irregular coastline along the Aegean. In the east, the confused mountain mass comprises some of the most rugged topography in the Middle East (see Fig. 3-2), with lofty volcanoes including the well-known Mount Ararat. Other volcanic cones rise high above the central Anatolian plateau in symmetrical grandeur.

At least three blocks in southern Turkey are allochthonous terrains—segments of the earth's crust rafted in from some considerable distance and literally rammed into place in the process of compression between the African and Eurasian plates.[2] Thus, relatively recent folding, faulting, and volcanism have combined with interrelated soils, vegetation, and climates to endow Turkey with a wide variety of landscapes and environments. These, in turn, have been utilized and shaped by successive civilizations to produce modern Turkey.

A Mosaic of Regions

[1] **Pontus and Black Sea Coast.** The northern fold belt comprises principally the Pontic Mountains (or North Anatolian Mountains), which include a variety of sedimentary rocks, some igneous intrusions, and large areas of lava flows (Map 21-1). Topographically, the mountains embrace long, narrow chains and lengthy troughlike valleys and basins, followed by rivers for part of their courses toward the Black Sea. Some of the trenches mark the strike of the North Anatolian Transform Fault. Several ridges in the west and one toward the east form an almost unbroken wall between the Black Sea and the interior, with ridge elevations of 5,000–6,000 ft./1,525–1,830 m in the west and higher summit elevations in the east, 10,000–13,000 ft./3,050–3,960 m (see Fig. 1-2). The upper and steeper slopes, especially those facing northwest, support Turkey's densest forests, primarily hardwoods in the west and evergreen softwoods in the east.

Features with major historical, economic, and strategic significance include the down-faulted basins now flooded by the Sea of Marmara and its eastern extensions into the gulfs of Izmit and Gemlik. The eastern Marmara area has the greatest concentration of population in the country, including the historic city of Istanbul (formerly Constantinople) and its suburbs. Especially in European Turkey (Thrace), the countryside has orchards and market gardens near the cities, with fields of sunflowers beyond.

North of the Pontic Mountains, a narrow coastal plain extends most of the length of the Black Sea shore, with the Kızıl and Yeşil rivers forming prominent deltas west and east of Samsun. Except where mountain shoulders push against the shore, the plain is densely populated, with the major coal-mining and industrial town of Zonguldak toward the west and one of Turkey's two main tobacco areas toward the east, around Samsun. East of the tobacco belt lies a strip of citrus groves and, east and west of the ancient city of Trabzon, the world's leading area for the production of hazelnuts (filberts). Farthest east, beyond Rize, extensive tea plantations were developed after World War II, and the southeastern Black Sea is Turkey's highest-yielding fishery.

[2] **Taurus and Mediterranean Coast.** Embracing approximately the southern one-third of Asia minor, the Taurus Mountains (Toros Dağları) stretch from the southwestern corner of the peninsula eastward to the upper Seyhan River Basin to the north of Adana. From there, the Anti-Taurus Mountains extend to the region of Lake Van. The upper elevations of the broad mountain belt of the Taurus vary from 7,000 to 9,000 ft./2,135 to 2,745 m. Primarily limestone, the maquis-clad highland separates the Mediterranean coast and the Anatolian interior. The few rivers that cut through the limestone mass follow almost vertically walled canyons, and only three or four major routes connect coast and interior. The most famous of the routes passes northwestward from Adana through the Cilician Gates (Gülek Boğazı), at 3,444 ft./1,050 m.

Along the southern coastal bulge from Alanya to Mersin, mountain shoulders drop steeply into the sea, separating eastern settlements from those to the west around Antalya. Impressive karst features are common—collapsed caverns, sinkholes, and dolines and poljes (larger solution basins)—and several are spectacular tourist attractions. Many of the dolines and poljes are floored with alluvial soils on which wheat, barley, and sometimes grapes and figs are grown. Where a coastal plain exists, or on small deltas formed by rivers slicing through the Taurus, citrus and banana groves, early vegetables, and other tender plants are cultivated.

At the eastern end of the coast is the Çukurova (Çukur Plain), on the extensive coalesced deltas of the Seyhan and Ceyhan rivers. The Çukurova is the best-developed agricultural area in Turkey, with primarily irrigated cotton fields. Cotton gins, cottonseed mills, textile mills, and clothing

378

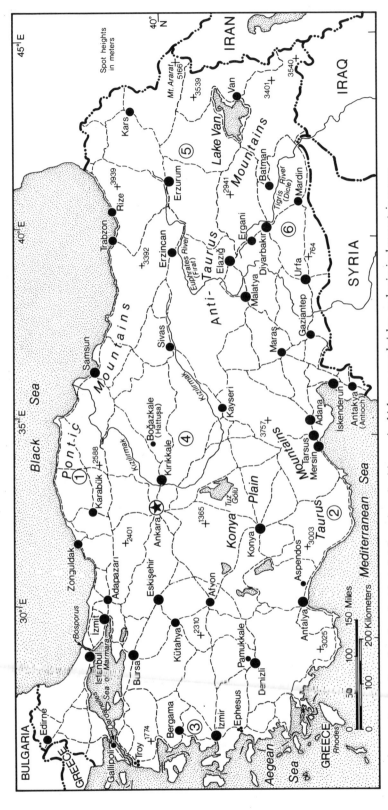

Map 21-1. *Turkey. Regions (numbered with circled figures), main cities, major highways, spot heights, and principal mountain ranges.*

factories employ part of the dense population of the plain. Adana, the central place, is Turkey's fourth-largest city, and near it is the huge NATO airbase of Incirlik. Strung along the coast from Antalya to Adana is a series of ruins of ancient settlements, most from Hellenistic and Roman times, indicating a dense, seaward-facing population during those periods. Aspendos has a well-preserved Roman theater, and Antalya, Perge, Sillyum, Side, Alanya, Anamur, and other sites attest the classical history of the area.[3] A first-class highway constructed along this Turkish "riviera" in the 1960s affords easy access to the scenery, ruins, and sandy beaches of the southern shore.

[3] **Aegean Area.** The Aegean area of Turkey resembles much of Greece in topography, climate, soils, and even the numerous ruins of classical cities along the coast. Until the early 1920s, much of the population of the area was Greek. The upthrust horsts and down-dropped grabens follow the predominant east-west structure of Asia Minor, offering easy access to climatic and cultural influences. Grabens afford deep eastward penetrations of valleys, some drowned by the sea, and horsts form extensions of the land westward as mountainous peninsulas. Rivers such as the Büyük Menderes drain the alluvium-filled grabens and have built deltas westward into the narrow bays. Some deltas advance several meters per year and in doing so, have silted up ancient harbors, leaving ruins of classical port cities such as Ephesus and Miletus several miles inland.

These and the ruins of other Greco-Roman cities combine with modern resorts and the scenery to give Turkey some of its most outstanding tourist attractions.[4] Major classical sites include Pergamum (modern Bergama), Izmir (formerly Smyrna), Sardis, Colophon, Ephesus, Priene, Miletus, Didyma, and Halicarnasus (modern Bodrum). The central place of the Aegean region is Izmir, Turkey's third-largest city, site of NATO's largest naval base in the eastern Mediterranean and of the annual Izmir International Trade Fair. Among the newly built coastal resorts, Kuşadası is one of the best developed. The alluvial-filled grabens are prime agricultural areas, planted in olive groves next to the coast (see Fig. 7-2), then fruit and nut trees (citrus to-

ward the south and almonds toward the north), and tobacco and cotton. Aegean tobacco complements Black Sea tobacco and helps supply one of Turkey's traditional exports. The broad grabens have long provided access between the Aegean and the productive interior.

[4] **Interior Anatolia.** Immured between the Pontic wall on the north and the Taurus barrier on the south is the inner Anatolian Plateau, technically the true Anatolia. Its surface, except in the heart of the region surrounding Tuz Gölü, displays a greater variety of relief than might be suggested by the term *plateau*.

Western Anatolia, which is hilly to mountainous, exhibits evidence of continuing tectonism, with numerous earthquakes, lava flows, and hot springs. The thermal springs indicate molten rock intrusions close to the surface. Hot springs near Denizli served as a spa for classical Hieropolis, and its calcium-carbonate travertine terraces at Pamukkale attract scientists and tourists. Still more volcanism can be seen in the city of Afyon, which has developed around a prominent mountain that peaks in a volcanic plug. Wheat and corn grow over large areas, and uncommon specialty crops are produced in selected localities—for example, opium poppies around Afyon (Turkish *afyon* = "opium"), tobacco in several areas, and roses near Isparta, north of Antalya. From roses is derived an essential oil for rose water, used both as an essence in desserts and for fragrant hand washing on special occasions throughout the Middle East.

This transitional area between the Aegean and central Anatolia was the major battleground for the Greek-Turkish fighting in the early 1920s. The same area, then underpopulated, later received many of the Turkish immigrants from the Balkans in the population exchange with Greece and Bulgaria in the 1920s. Industry has developed steadily in the area, bringing factories to Isparta, Kütahya, Eskişehir, Afyon, and elsewhere. A scenic lake district between Isparta and Konya includes twelve larger lakes that occupy grabens and solution basins and serve as local sumps. Most of the lakes have no outlet and are saline.

Farther east, in the central and eastern parts of the interior plateau, lies the quintessential Anatolia with its vast flat to rolling treeless steppes

Figure 21-1. *Two of Turkey's famous archaeological sites. Hollowed-out volcanic-ash stacks in the Göreme Valley (left) were used as dwellings and churches by early Christians. Huge stone heads from a Commagene monument on remote Nimrud Dagh (right) date from the second century* BC.

devoted to the region's characteristic wheat fields. Climatic stress typical of steppe conditions brings rain-deficient years that reduce the grain yield sharply, as in 1928, when the harvest was less than one-tenth the average yield. The semiarid core, with less than 12 in./300 mm of rainfall, produces primarily wheat and barley, whereas the more humid peripheral areas grow fruits, cotton, sugar beets, grapes, and tobacco.[5]

Formerly poorly developed, central Anatolia benefited economically from the focus of national attention on the area after the breakup of the Ottoman Empire following World War I. A particular stimulus was the shift of the political capital from Istanbul to Ankara in the 1920s and the subsequent development of infrastructure such as dams and paved highways in the region. Hirfanlı Dam was constructed on the Kızılırmak northeast of the Tuz Gölü in the mid-1950s. Scholars and tourists frequent Hattuşa, the ancient Hittite capital east of Ankara; Göreme, with unique early Christian churches and homes hollowed out of volcanic ash pinnacles west of Kayseri (Fig. 21-1); remarkable underground cities, excavated in the soft volcanic tuff and used by early Christians for refuge, at Derinkuyu and Kaymaklı; Konya, the Seljuk capital; and other sites. Tuz Gölü is a shallow salt lake at the bottom of the enclosed central Anatolian sump. With a surface slightly below 3,000 ft./900 m, the lake varies greatly in area, depending on local precipitation and runoff.

[5] Eastern Anatolia. The rugged eastern Anatolian mountains comprise the eastern end of the Anti-Taurus and also the complex folding and volcanism resulting from the junction of three tectonic units (see Map 3-2 and Fig. 3-2). Several extensive Tertiary lava flows and volcanic cones testify to vigorous volcanicity attending the interplate compression, with Mount Ararat towering to 16,948 ft./5,166 m. Several peaks reach 8,000–10,000 ft./2,440–3,050 m. Lake Van, the largest of Turkey's lakes, has a surface elevation of 5,400 ft./1,646 m and so completely blocks transit routes that the railway to Iran must cross the lake on a ferry from Tatvan to Van. The massive and frequent earthquakes in the area are the result of slippage along two fault systems that intersect west of Lake Van. Erzincan, located near the intersection of the North and East Anatolian faults, has suffered three earthquake disasters in the last 50 years—45,000 people died in the 1939 quake, 1,330 in the one in 1983, and 1,000 in the one in March 1992.

These rugged highlands have afforded refuge for several peoples, especially the Armenians (after whom the mountainous area of Armenia was named) and, south of the Armenian area, the Kurds. Covered with heavy snowfalls during the long winters, these mountains serve as a major hydrographic center, and their melting snows and some spring rains supply the headwaters of several rivers: both the Tigris and Euphrates, flowing southward to the Gulf; the Aras, flowing eastward to the Caspian; and several small streams that empty into the Black Sea or into the enclosed Lake Van basin.

Numerous villages lie among the valleys and on the steep slopes, but towns are widely separated; Erzurum is the major central place. To the northeast, Kars and Ardahan anchor territory long contested between Turks and Russians. Around Ergani in the southwestern part of eastern Anatolia is one of the most important mining and metallurgy areas of Turkey. In the Batman area east of Diyarbakir are Turkey's limited oil fields. The Elazığ and Malatya areas have become the flourishing foci of Turkey's most ambitious river development scheme (see "Statism and After" below).

[6] The Southeast: The Arabian Platform. Lying south of the Anti-Taurus and the Arabian Fold Belt is the Arabian Foreland, which extends far south into Syria. The broad plateau surface exhibits gentle relief and elevations between 1,640 ft./500 m and 2,625 ft./800 m. The main center is Urfa—awarded the honorific title "Şanlıurfa" in 1983 and now one of the fastest-growing cities in Turkey—once the capital of the Crusader kingdom of Edessa. Gaziantep, sixth-largest city in the republic, serves as a center west of the Euphrates, and Mardin serves the area toward the east. Toward the northern edge of the platform, on the upper Tigris, is the ancient basalt-walled Kurdish city of Diyarbakır. Traditionally a wheat and barley area, the region had achieved only limited development until recent major irrigation projects brought Euphrates water to farmlands in the western section. The region is experiencing an economic boom and a transformation of the landscape in response to development of the Southeast Anatolia Project. About 600,000 Arabs inhabit the area, along with Kurds who have moved from mountain villages in the north to the southeastern cities. Unfortunately, the Kurdish rebellion since 1984 has disturbed much of the area's stability.

A Historical Tapestry

Like Egypt and Iran, Asia Minor reflects a long history of cultures and empires (see Chap. 2), and recent intensified field research has pushed back both the beginnings and the scope of early Anatolian cultures. The increasingly rich physical evidences of this history may be seen in the thousands of tells (*hüyüks* or *tepes*), tumuli, towers, tombs, and ruins. National museums in Is-

tanbul and Ankara contain superb collections of prehistoric implements and later pottery, statuary, cuneiform tablets, jewelry, and other artifacts.

Caves near Antalya show evidence of Upper Paleolithic occupation. Hacılar, the earliest agricultural settlement in Asia Minor, has been dated to 7040 BC, and Çatal Hüyük with its remarkable artworks flourished 6500–5650 BC (see Map 2-1). The fabled city of Troy, guarding the entrance to the Dardanelles, has early layers predating 2500 BC, although the legendary Trojan War was associated with events of about 1200 BC. The Hittites evolved in central Anatolia and maintained a great capital at Hattuşa. A score of other peoples waxed and waned in the fastnesses of Anatolia and along the rugged coastlines. Lydians in the west had Sardis as their capital and Croesus (fl. 550 BC) as their most famous king. Aeolian, Ionian, and Dorian Greeks ensconced themselves along the Aegean coast. Among the many peoples in the interior were the Galatians (Gauls), of European descent, to whom the apostle Paul wrote epistles later included in the New Testament. Indeed, Asia Minor nurtured first-century Christianity, harboring the "Seven Churches of Asia"—Pergamum, Smyrna, Ephesus, Sardis, Laodicea, Philadelphia, and Thyatira—and emerging as the area in which Christianity was then strongest.

A watershed geopolitical event occurred in AD 330, when Emperor Constantine transferred the Roman capital from Rome to Byzantium, which was renamed Constantinople and later Istanbul. Constantinople served as the capital of the eastern Roman, Byzantine, and Ottoman empires for nearly 1,600 years. With the steady decline of the once-mighty and once-extensive Byzantine Empire, Arab Muslims from one direction and Seljuk Turkish Muslims from another carved away at Byzantine territories. Crusader efforts to help protect the Christian Byzantines delayed but hardly prevented Turkish inroads. The Seljuks established the central Anatolian Sultanate of Rum (Rum = Rome—i.e., Europe), which was soon joined by other Turkish and Turkmen principalities that rose and fell for two centuries. Finally, the Ottoman Turk principality achieved dominance and, after encounters with a second wave of invading Mongols, established control of

Asia Minor and extensive areas beyond (see Chap. 2).[6] The Ottomans seized Constantinople in 1453 and made it the Ottoman capital until the end of the Ottoman Empire after World War I.

Contemporary republican Turkey arose on the ruins of the Ottoman Empire, the "sick man of Europe," defeated in World War I.[7] Led by the charismatic Mustafa Kemal, later surnamed Atatürk ("Father Turk"), the young republic asserted a new Turkish viability in the early 1920s. It resisted partition of the Turkish Anatolian homeland and achieved substitution of the Treaty of Lausanne in 1923 for the onerous Treaty of Sèvres (1920). The aggressive Kemalist program for national resurgence called for republicanism, nationalism, populism, reformism, secularism, statism (state capitalism), and economic development. Atatürk insisted on Turkishness, the modernization of Turkey, and economic and cultural Europeanization. One fundamental and symbolic change, for example, was the abandonment of the Arabic alphabet for writing Turkish and the adoption of a modified Roman alphabet (1928). Also replaced were several items of traditional Turkish clothing, notably the fez (or tarbush) worn by Turkish men. Most men then adopted the visored cap, common in America and Europe during the 1920s, a headgear that still gives Turkish workingmen a characteristic appearance. The veil formerly worn by women was forbidden, a proscription that angered conservative families, especially in inner Anatolia, and that continues to rankle fundamentalist Muslim Turks.

The Turkish Population

Turkey has the largest population among all Middle East states (see Table 6-1), and Turks are, after Arabs, the second-largest ethnolinguistic group in the entire region (see Table 6-3 and Graph 6-1). Because of the percentage annual growth rate, the population has more than doubled since 1960. Population growth exceeds employment growth, and thousands of excess workers took temporary jobs in labor-short Western Europe during the 1960s. By 1985, about 1.1 million Turks were employed abroad, mostly in West Germany. However, when the European labor market became saturated, temporary immigration shifted to the Arab oil states. By the 1980s, many thousands of immigrant workers had returned to Turkey, and only a few thousand new workers were going abroad each year.

Among the larger of the states of the Middle East, Turkey has the most nearly evenly distributed population, indicating that most of the country's environments, although variable, are habitable. Lacking desert areas, Turkey shows reduced densities only in the more rugged mountains and on the central steppe. As Map 6-2 shows, the highest densities are in the Istanbul area and its surroundings, along the Black Sea coast, along and inland from the Aegean coast, around Ankara, and on the highly developed Çukurova around Adana.

A multiethnic empire in Ottoman times, Turkey sought greater ethnic homogeneity in the new republic. Under the Ottoman *millet* system, which permitted ethnic groups maximal autonomy, some groups developed separatist sentiments that evolved into anti-Turkish nationalism. Supported by European powers, various groups did gain independence. The republic renounced the multinational state and, downplaying ethnic differences, proclaimed "Turkey for the Turks and the Turks for Turkey."

Ethnic Turks are basically descendants of central Asiatic nomadic Turkish tribes who intermarried with more than a score of identifiable groups during the centuries. In the Ottoman golden age, the designation "Turk" was a term of disdain for Anatolian peasants as opposed to the cosmopolitan "Ottomans" of Constantinople. However, republican leaders acclaim Turkishness with national pride and have systematically "purified" the Turkish language of many of its Arabic and Persian loanwords.

Census reports minimize ethnolinguistic differences, grouping most citizens as Turks. As a result, the size of the several known minority groups can only be estimated. The obviously large Kurdish population may be as much as 20 percent (as claimed by Kurdish sources) or as little as 10 percent of the national total, and the Arab minority may be between 1.5 and 2 percent.

The 2.1 percentage of smaller minorities includes Circassians, Abkhaz (related to Circassians), Georgians, Laze, Armenians, Greeks, and Jews (including Dönme—see below). Turkmen and Tatars, like the Yoruk, are grouped with Turks.

Kurds, sometimes referred to as "mountain Turks," are firmly entrenched in the southeastern Turkey extension of their mountain homeland. Kurds, Armenians, Turks, and Russians were involved in fighting in eastern Anatolia in 1915, with Kurds and Armenians each fighting for independence from both Turks and Russians and Kurds and Armenians sometimes fighting each other. Once Turkey had achieved a certain stability in the mid-1920s, it specifically rejected Kurdish identity and ensured that Kurds made no progress toward separatism, as it had earlier done with Armenians. Southeastern Turkey was kept under martial law for many years, and use of the Kurdish language in schools, publications, broadcasting, and courts was made illegal—although some use of Kurdish was permitted after 1991. As Kurds in Iraq were increasingly suppressed under Saddam Husayn, the Marxist Kurdish Workers Party (PKK) in Turkey initiated open rebellion in southeastern Anatolia in 1984. By 1992, about 3,400 people had been killed in the fighting for Kurdish independence. (Additional details are given under Kurds in Chap. 6.)

The Kurdish-Turkish situation has created dilemmas for Turkey and contradictions for several interested parties. For example, while suppressing Kurdish separatism in Anatolia, Turkey both battled Iraqis in 1991 for their mistreatment of Kurds in Iraq and also took in tens of thousands of Iraqi Kurdish refugees. Conversely, Turkey has bombed Kurdish *peshmerga* (guerrilla) training camps inside northern Iraq, allegedly inflicting casualties on women and children in the camps. By late 1992, Iraqi Kurds were attacking PKK camps inside Iraq to force anti-Turkish rebels out of Iraqi Kurdish areas in order to maintain the goodwill of the Turkish government and eliminate the reason for Turkish bombing. (Other major training camps were located in the Bekaa of Lebanon.) As further incongruities, Turkey invaded Cyprus in 1974 to ensure the separatist rights of Turkish Cypriots; and it has also demanded that Bulgaria rescind a long-range program of forcing the one million or more ethnic Turks in Bulgaria to cease speaking and writing Turkish and otherwise to accept assimilation. One consequence is that the European Community is delaying action on Turkey's application for membership, partly because of Turkish suppression of Kurdish separatism.

Further exacerbating an already complex situation in southeastern Turkey is the presence of a religious minority, the Alevis, a heretical Shii group closely akin to the Alawis (the terms are linguistically the same) in northwest Syria. Some Kurds and Arabs are Alevis, but ethnic Turks constitute the greater percentage of the group of several million. Although they are most numerous in the southeast, many Alevis are found in most major cities.

Relatively small minorities of peoples from the Caucasus include Circassians and the related Abkhaz, with many of the Circassians living in the Adana area; Georgians, a group that actually embraces several different minorities; and the Laze, a small group of primarily fishermen in the southeastern Black Sea area (see Table 6-3).

Greeks and Armenians are the major Christian groups in Turkey. Both are heavily concentrated, primarily in the business sector, in the Istanbul area, and both are fractional remnants of much larger pre–World War I groups (see Chap. 6). Armenians were formerly dominant in the eastern Anatolian area, generally known as Armenia, but now are a small minority found only in the northwest. Details of the Armenian problem are given in Chapter 6.[8]

Of an estimated 90,000 Jews in Turkey at the end of World War II, fewer than 20,000 are believed to remain. About 30,000 emigrated to Israel in the late 1940s, and several thousand more have left Turkey since then—some of them also going to Israel. Most remaining Jews are in business in Istanbul or Izmir. Nonhomogeneous, they include Sephardim, who speak Ladino; Ashkenazim, who speak Yiddish; and some Karaites, viewed by other Jews as heretics, who speak Greek. All speak Turkish (and often French) as a second or equal language. Dönme are Jews who converted to Islam but are now merging with the general population and are considered neither Jews nor Muslims by most of their compatriots.

Village and City

Although Turkey is becoming more urbanized, it is still very much village oriented, with more than 40,000 villages well distributed over the country. The widespread pattern of humid climates and rainfed agriculture enables Turkish villages to be located on upper slopes and hilltops, thus presenting landscapes more typical of the humid Levant or Europe. Widely differing house construction and materials appear in different environments: wooden houses in forested areas, masonry houses on barren limestone slopes, and often houses of mud brick or with mud walls in river bottoms.

Mosque, public bathhouse, small fruit and vegetable market, and the village teahouse (*halkevi*—literally, "people's house") form the village center.[9] The *halkevi* continues to be ubiquitous in city and village, where the clientele is virtually all male, and village attitudes remain conservative regarding the role of women. Except where they have become urban enclaves of expanding cities, villages also remain politically conservative, religious, and stable. Shadow puppet shows provide a popular entertainment, revolving around a traditional hero, Karagöz, and dating at least from the seventeenth century. In villages near larger cities, television inevitably edges out the Karagöz shows. An important element in village life is the weekly market, conducted in centrally located larger villages.

The rapid growth of the rural population in the 1950s and 1960s drove hundreds of thousands of landless villagers to larger cities. Whereas the rural component of the total population was nearly 80 percent in the early 1950s, it had dropped to 46 percent by the early 1990s. Migrants to Istanbul, Ankara, Izmir, and other larger cities found shelter in the rapidly spreading *gecekondus* ("built overnight"), the squatter settlements that were made possible by a Turkish law that prohibits the forced removal of habitations having completed roofs (see Chap. 10). The Muslim tradition of urban "quarters" for respective groups carried over to the *gecekondus*, which

are clustered according to ethnic and sectarian affiliations.[10]

Turkey's cities exhibit great variety, especially those that were former capitals of kingdoms or principalities. Istanbul, as an imperial capital built on the peninsula overlooking the Bosporus, Sea of Marmara, and Golden Horn, has a unique architectural skyline because of its numerous domes and minarets. The old Seljuk capital of Konya, its ruins mixed with modern buildings rising from the plain in interior Anatolia, preserves a concentration of structures in the old Seljuk style. By contrast, Turkey's current capital city of Ankara has a core of primarily contemporary government buildings.[11]

Economic Development

Statism and After

Having lagged in its national economy during the declining years of the Ottoman Empire, Turkey encountered great difficulty in progressing toward a modern economy after World War I. To counterbalance the shortage of private capital and to protect against the dominance of foreign capital, Atatürk adopted statism (state capitalism) as the country's basic economic philosophy (Fig. 21-2). This emphasis on government participation in industry constrained development because of its bureaucratic approach carried over from the Ottomans, an approach that inhibited the rationalization of industry and other economic sectors. Nevertheless, persistence finally brought the country to a level of appreciable development and accelerated growth in the mid-1980s,[12] although by the late 1980s unemployment had risen to 20 percent and inflation had edged toward a runaway level. The Turkish economy clearly has its ups and downs. The State Planning Organization created in 1961 established a basis for progress in a series of five-year plans, the sixth, to cover 1990–1994, is expected to bring significant advances in the 1990s despite the faltering of the late 1980s and, more serious, the staggering blows consequent to the Gulf crisis of 1990–1991.

Two political changes accelerated development. One, embodied in the 1954 Law 6224, facilitated joint ventures between Turkish govern-

Figure 21-2. Anıt Kabir, *impressive mausoleum in Ankara of Mustafa Kemal Atatürk, founder and longtime leader of the post–World War I Republic of Turkey. The Grand Memorial reflects the reverence in which Atatürk is held.*

ment agencies and foreign firms. German, U.S., Swiss, French, Italian, and other European companies joined in establishing automobile assembly plants, chemical plants, tourism enterprises, and other undertakings. The second modification came only in 1980 and was reinforced in 1984, when economic reform under the progressive economist Prime Minister Turgut Özal (later president) revised the cumbersome commercial code that had retarded development for six decades.

With the exception of its lack of significant petroleum resources, Turkey approaches the most nearly balanced economy in the Middle East (Map 21-2).[13] As a corollary (and, again, excepting its deficiency in oil), Turkey enjoys a high degree of self-sufficiency, although it is far from the autarky sought by Atatürk and other leaders well into the 1970s. The percentage of the economically active population employed in the various sectors is shown in Table 9-1.

Within the Middle East, Turkey ranks near the top in production of most agricultural crops (see Chap. 7) and in transportation routes (see Chap. 9) but lags in most aspects of consumption. Its leadership in various aspects is impressive and is worth noting: Turkey leads in total area under cultivation (and in percentage of area cultivated), roundwood production (almost two-thirds of the total for the Middle East), fish

landed (40 percent of the Middle East total), coal production (95 percent of the Middle East total), total value added in nonpetroleum manufacturing, length of roads and of paved roads, and length of railways (one-third of the total for the Middle East).

Turkey is also credited with the highest potential for hydroelectric power among all European countries except Norway and Sweden. Lacking significant petroleum resources, Turkey looks to its hydropower potential to help solve its energy shortage.[14] Significant dams had already been constructed before 1970 in widely separated river basins—Hirfanlı Dam on the Kızılırmak, Almus on the Yeşil, Demirköprü on the upper Gediz, Sarıyar on the Sakarya, Seyhan on the Seyhan, and smaller dams elsewhere. However, it was the ambitious program of construction of the giant Euphrates dams after 1965 that established Turkey's major rank in hydropower and large-scale irrigation. The keystone of the huge program is the Southeast Anatolia Project (Turkish, Güneydoğu Anadolu Projesi—GAP).

Embracing thirteen interrelated subprojects distributed over 28,185 miles²/73,000 km², GAP is one of the largest projects of its kind ever attempted and is the largest in Turkey. It involves eventual construction of 22 dams and 19 hydroelectric installations, as well as irrigation of 4.2 million acres/1.7 million ha of land—two-thirds

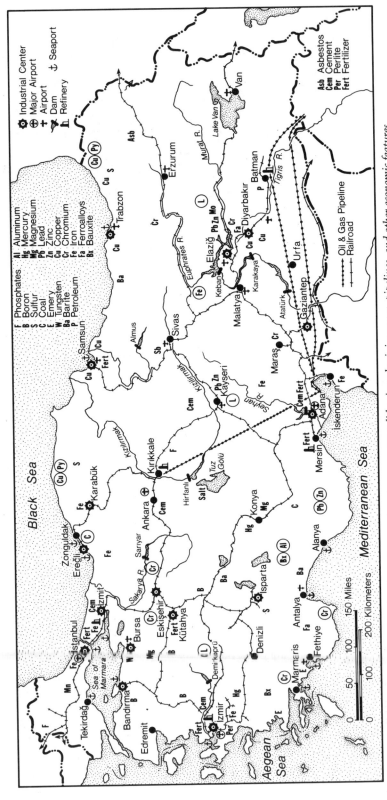

Map 21-2. *Economic map of Turkey, showing railways, airports, numerous solid-mineral mining areas, pipelines, and other economic features.*

Figure 21-3. *Atatürk Dam in final stages of construction. Giant spillway to right and eight penstocks of the power station far left. Each penstock is 24 ft./7.25 m in diameter. This dam, on the Euphrates River, is the centerpiece in Turkey's GAP.*

of the total irrigated area of Egypt. Both the Euphrates and Tigris rivers are being harnessed, with the Euphrates already dammed by three giant barrages, Keban (technically not included in GAP), Karakaya, and Atatürk (see Map 21-2). GAP's grand scale exploits the steep gradients of the rivers descending from the well-watered east Anatolian mountains and the several deep canyons they have cut along their courses—especially the Euphrates. The Euphrates profile permits the construction of the series of three high dams that form successive reservoirs in a stair-step configuration, with a difference in elevation of 495 ft./151 m from one reservoir to the next.

The first dam upstream is the Keban precursor to GAP, completed in 1974 for power purposes only. Behind its 670-ft.-/204-m-high embankment is a lake 70 miles/113 km long, covering 260 miles²/675 km², and below the dam is a power station with an installed capacity of 1,280 MW. Located 103 miles/166 km downstream from Keban is the Karakaya Dam, completed in 1987—as with Keban, for power generation only—which impounds a reservoir 115 miles²/298 km² in area, smallest of the three man-made lakes. Another 112 miles/180 km downstream is the showpiece of Turkish development and of GAP, the Atatürk Dam and its 2,400-MW power sta-

tion (see Fig. 21-3). In back of the dam is a ramifying reservoir 315 miles²/817 km² in area, largest in GAP and in Turkey. This dam, near the southern margin of the Anti-Taurus, is planned to supply water through canals, tunnels, and pipelines to irrigate about 1.8 million acres/730,000 ha of high-quality land in ten plains areas in the Arabian Foreland just north of the Syrian border. Specific areas are around Gaziantep, Birecik, Suruç, Urfa, Harran, Mardin, and, east of the reservoir, Siverek. Turkey's interference in the Euphrates flow and its consumption of the river's water on a major scale have raised deep concern in both downstream riparian states Syria and Iraq (see Chap. 11).

Although seven of the thirteen subprojects in GAP involve the Euphrates, six others involve the Tigris between Diyarbakır and the Syrian border. All are on a smaller scale than those in the Euphrates Basin, but they will nevertheless affect the Tigris flow and have raised concern in Iraq.

More than 35 percent of Turkey's electric power is hydrogenerated, 31 percent is from lignite, and 33 percent from petroleum. The country is attempting to expand its use of geothermal energy, now only 0.1 percent, generated from steam rising from subsurface molten intrusions in western Anatolia near Aydın and Çanakkale.

Agricultural Development

Varied climate and productive soil have sustained agriculture in Anatolia for more than 3,000 years. As during the Atatürk era, major emphasis is being given to agriculture in national planning, especially to extending modernization of agriculture into the more remote and less productive areas.

Such modernization has already achieved a marked improvement in many parts of Turkey. Chemical fertilizers, new varieties of wheat and other crops, mechanization (Turkey has two-thirds of all tractors in the Middle East), pest control, and irrigation have contributed to increased production. Industrial crops have been expanded, supplying both new exports and also raw materials for agro-industries—cotton, sugar beets, jute, flax, tea, and sunflowers along with such traditional crops as tobacco and olives. The government has improved and expanded irrigation and calls for still greater increase in the 1990s, particularly in conjunction with GAP. From 2.72 million acres/1.1 million ha in 1962, the irrigated area had been expanded to 5.5 million acres/2.22 million ha by 1989, and it is expected to approach 7.4 million acres/3 million ha by the end of the twentieth century.

Agricultural landholdings are small to medium. Peasants typically live in one of the thousands of agricultural villages distributed over Turkey, working in their own fields or, much less frequently, in fields rented from a landlord. To an increasing extent, farmers and their families use tractors for transport to their fields, although the distinctive two-wheeled Anatolian horsecarts are still seen on the roads of more rural areas.

Animal husbandry has always been an essential part of Anatolian agriculture, both as animal raising on farms and as herding of sheep, goats, and camels by nomadic pastoralists (see Fig. 7-4). As in crop cultivation, breeds of animals, breeding practices, feeds, meat processing, and marketing are all being improved. Cattle have received particular attention, and dairying is a major aspect of agriculture in the high pastures of the northern Anatolian mountains. Grazing is by far the dominant type of agriculture practiced in the mountainous eastern fourth of the country. As elsewhere in the Middle East, poultry raising has expanded markedly; and Turkey continues to be second, after the United States, in world production of mohair, sheared from the famous Angora goat.

In its great variety of environments, Turkey produces a remarkable range of crops: bananas, dates, citrus fruits, and cotton along the southern coast; olives, cotton, tobacco, citrus, and figs in the west; tobacco, tea, and hazelnuts along the Black Sea in the northeast; and, above all, wheat and barley in central Anatolia. Potatoes, sugar beets, pulses, oats, and other crops are widely distributed (see Fig. 7-1). Sunflowers, grown for their oilseeds, flourish in extensive fields in the open landscapes of Thrace (European Turkey). An unusual aspect of Turkish agriculture is the regulated growing of opium poppies in the west-central basins. Maize has proved to be well adapted to the more humid areas of Anatolia (see Fig. 1-2) and is increasingly produced for both food and feed. Turkey leads the Middle East in the production of a score of crops and for many of them produces from 40 to 70 percent of the total for the entire region (see Tables 7-2, 7-3, and 7-4).

Forestry and Fishing

Turkey and Iran are the only two countries in the Middle East with well-developed forest industries. Of the two, Turkey possesses more extensive forests (45 million acres/18 million ha of all types) and has developed its production to an output level of almost two-thirds of the total roundwood output of the Middle East. Forests cover the steeper slopes of the mountains rimming the central Anatolian plateau and basins, with particularly dense forests in the higher Pontic Mountains in northern Anatolia.

As the leading fishing country in the Middle East, Turkey increased its annual catch by eleven times from 1975 to 1989 to 627.9 mt of fish and similar aquatic animals of several kinds, about 40 percent of the Middle East fish total. More than $45 million worth of fish is exported annually, mostly to Western Europe, including such specialty items as shrimp, lobsters, snails, eels, sponges, tortoises, and frog legs. Half of the Turkish fish catch is taken in eastern Black Sea waters, but virtually every town and village along all three coasts engages in fishing.

Industrial Development

An Overview. As we have seen, Turkey's range of industrial establishments and their total non-oil output already lead those of all other countries in the region and are growing under the liberalized policies developed in the period 1983–1989 under Prime Minister Turgut Özal, who continued economic liberalization after he became president in late 1989. The variety and quantity of agricultural products support the food-processing and agrobusiness sector, and the country's minerals industry—the most varied and highly developed in the Middle East—further contributes to the diversification of manufacturing. As it has from the early years of industrial expansion, the deficiency of energy sources, particularly petroleum, has constrained the growth of manufacturing. However, Turkey's manufacturing sector steadily increases its contribution to the GNP, reaching 26 percent of the GNP in 1989.

The government owns more than 40 percent of Turkey's major industries, with state firms organized as wholly or partially owned State Economic Enterprises (SEEs) set up as corporations. Although this state capitalism is a holdover from the strong Kemalist tradition of the 1920s, it is decreasing progressively as SEEs demonstrate lower efficiency and profitability in comparison with private-sector firms, many of which are joint ventures between foreign and Turkish companies. Privatization of state-owned enterprises is thus accelerating, as, indeed, is the case in Egypt and elsewhere in the region. In the late 1980s and early 1990s, the government encouraged foreign firms to submit proposals on the "build, operate, and transfer" (BOT) model, which in effect transfers much of the risk to project sponsors. Therefore, the share of private ownership is increasing and is expected to mount under the recent liberalization of government policy.

As with agricultural production, mining operations, and population, which are unusually uniformly spread over the state territory, industrial concentrations are likewise well distributed over Turkey (see Map 21-2). The largest industrial complexes, especially those producing consumer goods, are in the main population centers. As a consequence, the half-dozen largest cities are also the leading industrial centers: Istanbul (which has more than half of the country's industries), Ankara, Izmir, Adana, Bursa, and Gaziantep. However, towns in specialty crop areas usually have industries to process foods, beverages, and industrial crops. Examples include Rize, tea packing; Trabzon, hazelnut shelling and packing; Tekirdağ, wine making; Afyon, opium processing; Isparta, rug making using local wool; and Adana, cotton milling and cotton textile manufacturing.

Benefiting from its intermediate location between Europe and the Middle East, Turkey has linked its industrial growth both northwestward and southeastward; more recent expansion has been especially stimulated by marketing goods and services in Saudi Arabia and the Gulf as well as in both Iran and Iraq.

Minerals Industries. The tectonic and structural conditions in the Mobile Belt, extending across the Anatolian and Iranian plateaus, give rise to several zones of extensive mineralization. The Turkish Mineral Research and Exploration Institute (TMA) has coordinated a minerals survey using some of the latest exploration methods, including that of space imagery, and it found numerous mineral occurrences, many of them in commercial quantities. Unfortunately, Turkey possesses a relatively large number of small deposits and few large ones. Reserves for most metallic commodities are not large by world standards, although those for bauxite (aluminum ore), chromite, copper, iron ore, and silver are appreciable. The most significant reserves are of such industrial minerals as boron, barite, magnesite, perlite, pumice, and dimension stone. The government-owned Etibank oversees commercial mineral production, and the minerals industry has evolved steadily under the republic, with steadily increasing privatization. Mineral utilization has a long tradition in Anatolia: Ironworking was a profitable activity of the Hittite Empire 3,700 years ago, the wealth of Croesus came from gold taken from the rivers of the Aegean region, and obsidian (volcanic glass) from the volcanic area of central Anatolia was traded in the Fertile Crescent during the Neolithic period.

Hydrocarbons. Turkey's mineral fuels include coal, lignite, and small amounts of petroleum. Although Turkish coal and lignite production is more than 96 percent of the total for the Middle East, the country's petroleum output is only 25 percent more than that of tiny Bahrain (see Table 8-1). Bituminous coal reserves, 1.4 billion mt, and lignite reserves, 8 billion mt, are sufficient for 200–300 years at the present rate of production. By contrast, known petroleum reserves of 650 million barrels indicate less than a 33-year supply, even at the low rate of production.[15] Recent natural gas discoveries, primarily in Thrace, improve the energy outlook modestly. Turkey must import more than 83 percent of its petroleum needs and 40 percent of its total energy requirements. As one of the benefits of allotting right-of-way for Iraqi pipelines in 1977 and 1987, Turkey shared oil from the pipelines from Iraq to Yumurtalık (see Chaps. 8 and 16) until it was obliged to shut down both lines under terms of the UN sanctions against Iraq in August 1990. The consequent shift to alternative supplies of oil was expensive and disruptive, and the lines were still closed in early 1993. In 1986–1987, Turkey began importing large amounts of natural gas by pipeline from the USSR through Bulgaria, and the imports continued and even increased after the political disintegration of the Soviet Union in late 1991.

Although lignite is mined in several areas (45–50 million mt in most years), especially in east-central Anatolia, coal is mined almost entirely in the Zonguldak area on the western Black Sea coast (7 million mt of anthracite in an average year). Because the coal veins are thin and contorted, extraction is increasingly difficult and costly, and coal is now imported for industrial use in the western and southern parts of the country.

Petroleum. The first encouraging oil strikes in Turkey, in the Batman area between Diyarbakır and Siirt in southeastern Anatolia, were not made until 1940. Shell and Mobil have been the most successful of the several cooperating companies, but the public-sector petroleum company, TPAO, produces about half of the crude oil and all of the marketed gas. Despite widespread exploration, discoveries have involved mostly heavy, high-sulfur crude and have been virtually limited to the Fold Belt. Fields are small, scattered, and often deep and are found in complex geological structures. Production averaged 40,000–45,000 bpd, about the same as Bahrain's, during the early 1980s but rose to 55,000 bpd in the late 1980s. The all-time peak of 86,700 bpd in 1991 was an emergency response to the shutting down of the supply from Iraq. Output from the Batman-area fields moves by pipeline to Dörtyol on the Gulf of Iskenderun.

Oil Processing. Turkey's downstream operations include five refineries (see Map 21-2). The recently opened refinery at Kırıkkale receives feedstock through a new pipeline from Yumurtalık, southeast of Adana, terminus of the pipeline from Iraq, shut in since August 1990. Petrochemical production has been relatively limited, since feedstock would have to be imported, and many finished products can be imported more cheaply at the present time than they could be produced domestically.

Metallurgy. Many of Turkey's mineral processing plants and manufacturing establishments that use mineral raw materials are mine oriented, so that mining areas and mineral industry concentrations are locationally related (see Map 21-2). Steel mills are located in three widely separated areas: around Zonguldak, with large plants at Karabük and Ereğli; Iskenderun; and around the eastern part of the Sea of Marmara, where three small plants utilize primarily scrap metal. A small plant in Izmir also uses scrap steel. Aluminum ore (bauxite) is mined and processed in a large new complex at Seydişehir, southwest of Konya.

More important on the world scale is Turkish production of several ferroalloys, none of which is plentiful on the world market. They include chromite (6 percent of the world total, from Kütahya, Ergani, and Muğla), antimony (northwest of Sivas), manganese (Thrace, Eskişehir, Ereğli, and Denizli), and tungsten (near Bursa). Also significant is the production of such nonferrous metals as copper, from several sources but especially from the major metallurgical centers of Ergani and Murgul, as well as lead and zinc from several mines, especially those around Kayseri and Elazığ. Turkey produces significant percentages of the world's emery (50 percent), boron (35), magnesite (4), perlite (2), and barite. Near Eskişehir is the world's only commercial deposit of meerschaum, which is machined and carved in cottage industries and small plants in and around the city. It is used primarily for making smoking-tobacco pipes.

Other Industries. In addition to the crop-related and mineral industries, Turkey has developed a wide range of other plants and factories. Their varied output includes metal products, electrical equipment, farm machinery, assembled vehicles, railway rolling stock, cement, machine tools, and similar items. In cooperation with European firms, factories in the Istanbul and Ankara areas produce electronic goods as well as such household appliances as refrigerators and electric irons. More than a dozen plants assemble automobiles, trucks, motorcycles, and motorbikes, utilizing an increasing percentage of domestically produced parts and accessories, including tires and batteries. Railway locomotives are produced in Eskişehir and railway cars in Adapazarı. Large numbers of tiles with Turkish designs are produced in the old tile center of Iznik; they are notable as are the pottery and other ceramic products from Kütahya.

Transportation

Turkey's large size, the country's well-distributed development, and planning have combined to produce Turkey's impressive transportation network. Although several links require improvement, the basic nets are the largest and best-balanced in the Middle East. Through rail and road nets, Turkey is well connected with all five of its neighbors, excluding former Soviet republics, and some traffic began moving between Turkey and the trans-Caucasus republics even before dissolution of the Soviet Union. Shipping and airlines also link Turkey with its neighbors and more distant states.

Railways. A trans-Anatolian rail line served Turkey as early as 1918, and an additional 2,052 miles/3,302 km of railway had been completed by the end of World War II. Major post–World War II additions have been made in the southeast and

east, along the steadily developing Malatya-Elazığ-Diyarbakır-Siirt axis and on the CENTO- and RCD-supported line to Iran, which crosses Lake Van by ferry. All the Turkish trackage is standard gauge (4.7 ft./1.435 m) and is operated by Turkish State Railways (TCDD), which has scheduled a badly needed overhaul of much of the system. By 1992, Turkey possessed one-third of the Middle East's rail lines and had provided all major sectors of the country with a heavy-duty transportation system especially adapted for shipping coal, other bulky minerals, and grain hundreds of miles to ports or internal markets.

Roads. Turkey entered the post–World War II era with a very limited road network, most of it poorly surfaced. Some of the financial aid supplied Turkey under the Truman Doctrine was devoted to road building, for economic and political purposes as well as for security reasons. Funding also came from CENTO, and planning for east-west links observed major aims of the RCD (later the ECO). By 1991, Turkey had 40 percent of the total length of all roads in the Middle East (see Table 9-2); and every town in Turkey had been integrated into a well-designed, well-constructed, and serviceable network. However, so successfully has the road system served to increase highway use by domestic and international traffic that in some heavily traveled links, two-lane roads are inadequate. Four-lane highways—several of which are already opened—are difficult and costly to construct through many mountain areas but are essential.

Despite an efficient and colorful ferry service across the Bosporus, heavy and rapidly increasing automobile and truck traffic in the late 1960s necessitated construction of a bridge across the strait. Spanning the narrowest part (about 0.6 mile/1 km) of the lower Bosporus a few miles up the waterway from old Istanbul and high above the water level, the suspension bridge links Europe and Asia and enables traffic to avoid long delays at ferry crossings. The bridge so facilitated the rapidly increasing through traffic across the Bosporus that a wider, second span was opened in 1988 to carry long-distance traffic, leaving the 1973 bridge to handle local traffic. Despite early

Figure 21-4. *Bosporus Strait, looking north toward the Black Sea. Rumeli Hisar, built in 1453 by Ottoman sultan Mehmet the Conqueror to facilitate his seizure of Constantinople, is to the left. The newer Bosporus Bridge, opened in 1984, spans the Bosporus in the distance.*

fears, the structures detract little from the beauty of the Bosporus (Fig. 21-4).

The new Trans-European Motorway (TEM) will enter Turkey at Edirne, cross the Bosporus by bridge, and extend eastward through Ankara and Erzurum to the Iranian border opposite Maku, a stretch of 1,120 miles/1,800 km. Branch highways will reach south to Adana (and beyond to Syria and Iraq) and north to the Black Sea at Trabzon, giving Turkey a total of 2,235 miles/3,600 km of the motorway. Having become an important transit land for vehicular traffic, especially tandem trailer trucks, between Europe and the Middle East, Turkey will benefit from inclusion in the TEM network. Tourist facilities also hope to attract larger numbers of European tourists from the northwest and vacationing Arabs from the southeast.

Ports and Shipping. With 4,474 miles/7,200 km of coastline and intimate interrelations between land and sea in the west and northwest, Turkey has a long maritime history. The republic has maintained numerous ports, some active since ancient times, and also has sustained a vigorous maritime trade. In addition to numerous small ports for coastal shipping, Turkey operates four major ports and a score of secondary and minor ports for international trade. Although the tonnage handled varies from year to year, leading ports include Mersin, Istanbul, Iskenderun, and Izmir. Secondary ports from Alanya clockwise around Asia Minor to Trabzon are indicated on Map 21-2.

The total tonnage of general international cargo, excluding petroleum, loaded and unloaded through all Turkish ports exceeds that of any other Middle East country. Free zones were established at the two Mediterranean ports of Mersin and Antalya in the mid-1980s. Turkey operates the second-largest merchant marine fleet in the Middle East, nearly 870 ships; but their total deadweight tonnage is less than that of Iran and only one-sixth that of the fleet registered in Cyprus, which includes numerous tankers and other large ships using the Cypriot flag of convenience.

Airways. Turkish Airways (Türk Hava Yolları—THY), with more than 30 jet aircraft, is the fourth-largest airline in the Middle East. Turkey's 14 airfields with scheduled flights are second in the region only to the total in Saudi Arabia. There are, however, 30 major airports, including NATO airfields, notably Incirlik (near Adana), Izmir, and Karamürsel (near Izmit). International airports include Yeşilköy/Istanbul, Esenboğa/Ankara, Izmir, and Adana. Yeşilköy/Istanbul handles the fifth-largest number of passengers among Middle East terminals.

Trade

With its intermediate location, extensive coastline and numerous harbors, and range of resources, Asia Minor has historically engaged in extensive commerce and transit trade. Although some of the medieval trade routes from India, China, and East Africa ended at the Levant coast, others continued northward across Asia Minor to Trabzon or westward to the entrepôt of Constantinople or to lesser termini on the Aegean coast. European countries maintained active trade with the Ottoman Empire even as it declined.

During its early years, the Republic of Turkey had little more to export than agricultural products and specialty raw materials, such as meerschaum. By the late 1980s, manufactured products had mounted to more than two-thirds of the country's exports. Exploiting the Arab League boycott of Egypt for eleven years after 1979, Turkey increased its exports to Middle East countries as part of its expanding economic and political ties with its neighbors to the southeast—most of which were coincidentally formerly Ottoman imperial possessions. However, Turkey's persistent and vigorous efforts to strengthen relations with the EEC have directed 47 percent of exports to the EEC and attracted 38 percent of imports from the Common Market countries. All aspects of exports were sharply improved after the economic liberalization beginning in the early 1980s and after the Turkish lira was made fully convertible in early 1990.[16] One evidence is the escalation in the value of Turkey's exports from $2.28 billion in 1978 to $7.13 billion in 1984 and $11.6 billion in 1989. Turkey's imports have long exceeded exports, but recent improvement in the export picture has reduced the trade deficit.

Relations

Turkey's location at the intersection of strategic zones directs the country's attention in several different directions, and reciprocally, it is the focus of interest of at least a score of major powers and small states. Turkey avoided subjection to colonialism—quite the opposite—and now seeks to optimize its strategic advantages in multidirectional foreign relationships. Its policies during the past several decades have diminished resentment of its former imperialism and lessened traditional enmities, with the signal exception of relations with Greece.

Turkey's ramifying interests were particularly intensified in the early 1990s. Momentous developments in all three of the main sectors of Turkey's periphery have had a dramatic impact on the country's strategic equilibrium and relational patterns. These developments include the transformation of Eastern Europe in 1989–1990, the reverberating Gulf crisis initiated in August 1990, the disintegration of the Soviet Union in 1991, and the consummation of the Common Market in 1992. To the far northwest, Turkey continues to seek membership in the European Economic Community (EEC), which into early 1993 was still temporizing over Turkey's application partly because of the flawed Turkish human rights record both in Cyprus and among its own Kurds. Acceptance into the exclusive EEC—as with membership in NATO—is profoundly important for the country for several reasons. Inter alia, such acceptance would finally put the cachet on Turkey as a genuine "European" entity. Important economic benefits would also accrue to Turkey, certainly in trade but also in capital flow, labor mobility, tourism, transportation, and general development.

Less distant is the disintegrating Yugoslavia, formerly embraced in the Ottoman Empire, with Muslims of Bosnia expecting some concern on the part of Muslim Turkey, whence came the Islamic religion of Bosnia. Freshly rationalized relations must be evolved with other recently truly independent Balkan states, including Bulgaria with its nearly 1 million ethnic Turks, left over from imperial Ottoman days.

To the north and northeast, Turkey faces the fragments of the disintegrated former Soviet Union, still seeking geopolitical structure and direction. Turkey moved quickly in 1991–1992 to reach out to all the burgeoning republics in the area, but it especially pursued close relations with the new entities that are not only Muslim but also Turkic—Azerbaijan, Turkmenistan, Kazakhstan, Uzbekistan, and Kyrgyzstan. In June 1992, Turkey hosted in Istanbul a meeting of leaders of ten nations, including six former Soviet republics, who signed a declaration creating the Black Sea Economic Cooperation project. Similarly, Turkey has proposed a Balkan cooperative zone embracing Turkey, fragments of Yugoslavia, Albania, Romania, and Bulgaria.

Interactions with imperial Russia were a mainspring of Turkish foreign policy for centuries. As the relative strength of the two countries shifted over the years toward the Russians, the Turks turned to the British or the French in an effort to counterbalance Russian power. They later used links with Germany for the same purpose. Despite having earlier maintained neutrality during World War II, Turkey later declared war on the Axis and became a charter member of the United Nations, and Turkey and the Western powers allied against Soviet hegemonism after 1945. Thus, Turkey's membership in NATO and its relationship with the United States recall the earlier alignment of the Ottomans with Western powers to offset the strength of the Russians. With the straits a critical focus (see Map 11-7), Turkey, as the western segment of the Northern Tier and as a significant sector of the Eurasian Rimland, played a major geopolitical role during the cold war.

After Allied efforts to partition Anatolian Turkey ended in the mid-1920s, Turkey and Western European states reached an enduring détente. A member of NATO and the former CENTO, as well as of the Council of Europe, Turkey is also an associate member of the Common Market awaiting full membership. Although Turkey and the Council of Europe agreed to temporary separation after a 1980 military coup in Ankara, relations were later restored.

To the southeast, Turkey has expanded and strengthened economic and other relations with the rest of the Middle East, with which ties had been dormant for more than half a century. The common bond of Islam between Turkey and thirteen of the fifteen regional neighbors facilitates pursuit of common interests. Turkey has participated and played an active role in the Organization of the Islamic Conference and was host to the 1990 meeting.

Turkey's relations with its three contiguous Middle East neighbors are noteworthy, especially for their ups and downs. Links with Syria have never been warm, particularly because Turkey incorporated the Alexandretta (Iskenderun) area in 1938 (see Chap. 11). To compound the strains, Turkey's GAP developments are depriving Syria of increasing amounts of Euphrates water, thus diminishing the benefits of Syria's own Euphrates development projects. Nevertheless, as part of its early 1990s diplomatic offensive, Turkey held friendly talks with Syria on issues such as their 1987 water-sharing agreement and the problem of the Kurds.

Turkish-Iraqi relations are of signal importance to both parties, notably because of the oil pipelines from Iraqi fields to a Turkish export terminal. In addition, Iraq had turned increasingly, both economically and politically, to Turkey and Jordan during the 1980s as its outlets to the Gulf were blocked. When Iraq invaded Kuwait, Turkey inevitably joined the coalition against Iraq, shut down the pipelines and cross-border traffic, and allowed coalition warplanes use of bases in Turkey for attacks on Iraq. In return, Turkey received about $4 billion in grants and credits as compensation, mainly from Kuwait, Saudi Arabia, and Japan. Even so, the break in economic ties with Iraq had serious negative impacts not only for Turkey but also for Iraq. The long-range Kurdish problem continues to be a thorny issue in relations between Turkey and Iraq.

Intertwined with links between these two countries are ties between Turkey and Iran. During the 1980–1988 Iran-Iraq war, Turkey succeeded in maintaining mutually beneficial links with both combatants. It made the transition from the RCD to the ECO with Iran (see Chap. 11) and hopes to benefit from that association.

On the regional level, Turkey's most crucial problem in international affairs is its relations with Greece. Antagonism between Greece and Asia Minor is similar to that between Mesopotamia and the Iranian Plateau and also has ancient roots. Three developments in modern history are especially relevant: the Greek war of independence from the Ottomans in the early 1800s, the Greek-Turkish war of the early 1920s, and the conflict between Greece and Turkey over Cyprus after the early 1950s. The hostility over Cyprus carries over into the issue of the potential oil resources of the Aegean seabed, and further antagonisms focus on Exclusive Economic Zones, territorial waters, and a median line (see Chap. 11).

Turkey's primary ally in the West is the United States, which built ties to Turkey in 1947 through the Truman Doctrine, under which the United States in effect extended the Marshall Plan idea to Greece and Turkey. Under a series of bilateral agreements, U.S. economic and military aid to Turkey had reached $14.4 billion, of which $10 billion was military aid, by 1989. A large Point IV mission, later the United States Agency for International Development (USAID), coordinated civilian economic assistance. The Joint United States Military Mission for Aid to Turkey (JUSMMAT) and the Turkish–United States Logistics Group (TUSLOG) coordinated military aid and equipment transfers. For its part, Turkey accorded the United States access to more than a dozen major facilities, including military airfields and communications, naval, and intelligence-gathering facilities. More than 35,000 Americans were stationed in Turkey in the peak year of 1968. U.S.-Turkish relations cooled during the 1975–1978 U.S. embargo on arms supplies to Turkey as a sign of congressional disapproval of the Turkish invasion of northern Cyprus in 1974, but normal links were later revived.[17]

22

Iran: New Republic
on the Plateau

New State, Ancient Land

Iran's major rankings serve as reminders of the fundamental importance of the country: In the region, it is second in size, second in population, fifth in petroleum reserves, first in natural gas reserves, second in total area under cultivation, first in area under irrigation, second in wheat production, first in copper output, and otherwise a ranking producer (see tables in Chaps. 6, 7, and 8). Its natural gas reserves are second only to those of Russia, and its petroleum reserves may in fact well be second or third in the Middle East and in the world, although it was one of the earliest producers and has yielded billions of barrels since output began. Iran has been the core of Shii Islam for centuries and has appointed itself leader of the militant Shiism and even of militant Islam of the 1980s and 1990s. Ensconced as one of the strongest power foci in the Middle East (see Map 2-6), Iran has periodically demonstrated its viability and resiliency, the latest attestation coming in the Iran-Iraq war of the 1980s. Of especial historical-geopolitical significance is Iran's persistence in the concept of *Iran-zamin,* "the land of Iran." Somewhat comparable to the idea of *Greater Syria,* the concept is one of a broad area of former Iranian imperial domain, implanted Iranian culture, and historical Persian influence through millennia—an ancient relationship between a people and their cultural homeland.[1] Although contemporary sentiment regarding Iran-zamin may not reach the level of emotional irredentism, Iranian efforts to extend the Islamic fundamentalist revolution to neighboring lands suggest that the Iran-zamin idea is near the surface of Iranian revolutionary consciousness.

Certain aspects of ethnicity and terminology also suggest Iran's individuality. As one of the four states in the Middle East that is not Arab, Iran is the only major Middle East state whose national language is neither Semitic nor Turkic. Migrating Aryans brought their Indo-European language into the plateau in the second millennium BC and became the ancestors of the Persians and perhaps other peoples. The term *Iran* derives from "Aryan" and has always been preferred by the descendants of the Aryans as the general name for the area. Another toponym arose in the south-central part of the plateau. The local name Fars became the root for both "Farsi," the present designation for the main local language (Persian), and also the name "Persia," through consonant shift. The area was best known in the West as Persia until Reza Shah in 1935 demanded that "Iran" be applied to the state and the Western oil company operating there. Thus, the official name, Iran, is a reminder of the original Indo-European Aryans ("nobles") who laid the foundations for the future state. It is also a general term that includes all the peoples of Iran along with the Persians.

Entrenched in its high plateau, Iran has played a powerful historical role for more than 2,500 years. Since the evolution of a regional empire under Cyrus the Great, Iran has maintained a vigorous national base century after century, even while temporarily succumbing militarily and politically to Greeks, Arabs, Mongols, and others. Over the centuries, migrating peoples settled in the less populated mountain basins

IRAN

Long-form official name, anglicized: Islamic Republic of Iran
Official name, transliterated: Jomhuri-ye Eslami-ye Iran
Form of government: unitary Islamic republic with a single legislative house (Islamic Consultative Assembly)
Area: 636,372 miles^2/1,648,196 km^2
Population, 1991: 57,050,000. Literacy (latest): 62%
Ethnic composition (%): Persian 50.0, Azeri 23.0, Kurdish 9.1, Gilani 5.0, Mazandarani 3.0, Luri 2.3, Bakhtiari 1.6, Turkmen 1.5, Baluchi 1.0, Arab 1.0, Armenian 0.5, plus Qashqai, Afshar, Ilsavan (formerly called Shahsavan), and many splinter groups
Religions (%): Muslim 98.0 (Shii 90.5, Sunni 7.5), Christian 0.7, Jewish 0.3, other (Zoroastrian, Bahai) 1.0
GNP, 1988: $93.5 billion; per capita: $1,800
Petroleum reserves: 92.85 billion barrels
Main exports (% of total value, 1989): petroleum and petroleum products 92.6; carpets, fruits, nuts, hides 7.4
Main imports (% of total value, 1986): machinery and transport equipment 32.5; iron and steel 14.7; food and live animals 12.8; chemicals 9.7
Capital city: Tehran 6,042,584; other cities: Mashhad 1,463,508; Esfahan 986,753; Tabriz 971,482; Shiraz 848,289

and valleys, but, like the Chinese, Iranians assimilated many of the invaders and immigrants or tolerated other groups in isolated parts of the plateau. Periodically absorbing powerful new elements that refreshed and reinvigorated it, the vibrant Iranian culture persevered and preserved its essence.

The 1978–1979 Islamic Revolution brought numerous radical social changes in Iran, none more radical than the shift in the ruling class. Competing social groups have been a dynamic within the Iranian body politic for many decades: aristocracy, bazaar (merchants), clergy, tribal leaders, and army. Thought to be well under control, the clergy suddenly asserted itself in 1978–1979, and the Iran of the 1980s reversed the sociopolitical trends of the 1960s and 1970s. Peoples and environments once again renewed their traditional interaction in the human search for identity and control.

Iran enjoyed many years of generally good relations with the rest of the world before 1979. Its status as a pariah for more than a decade after that time sometimes obscures its long cultural traditions, enduring geopolitical significance, petroleum wealth, economic potential, and human resources. As is true in any political-geographical evaluation of a state, the short-term conditions must be balanced with the enduring factors. Such balancing is difficult in a Western estimate of Iran because of Iran's direct and indirect involvement in terrorism and other abnormal behavior after the Khomeini revolution of 1979. Nevertheless, the abiding factors in Iran's situation must be kept in focus, and those factors are emphasized in this chapter.

Plateau Palimpsest

The sequence of human occupance of Middle East lands over thousands of years is well preserved in the Iranian Plateau, and the antiquity of this settlement in Iran is neither inconsequential nor academic. Ruins and other evidence of ancient habitation are rarely out of sight in the more humid areas of the plateau. Numbering more than 250,000, archaeological sites in Iran include several Middle Paleolithic (Mousterian) sites from about 40,000 years ago, during the last glacial period. Thousands of tells containing successive Neolithic villages dot the valleys, piedmonts, and plains of western Iran. Also called *tepes* or *chegas* in Iran, mound sites of later villages are equally numerous,[2] and excavated examples have yielded elaborate pottery and ornaments of bronze, silver, and gold. On the flat Marv Plain (Marvdasht) before Persepolis, more than 1,000 tells have been enumerated, most appearing to date from 6000–5500 BC.

Following the succession of powerful early empires on the Iranian Plateau, the Arab Muslim invasion in the 630s introduced momentous changes in Iran. Although the collapse of the Sassanian Empire was at first staggering, a national revival demonstrated once again the Iranian vitality. Persian expertise, vigor, experience, and cultural vibrancy contributed to the effectiveness of the Umayyad Empire and then were major factors in the establishment of the Abbasid Empire in Mesopotamia, close to and associated with the Iranian core area. The Persian language diffused throughout the Middle East and exchanged hundreds of loanwords with Arabic, as well as with Turkish later on. Although Islam was cradled in Arabia and brought into the Fertile Crescent and Iran by Arabs, the Islamic civilization that evolved over the following several centuries was highly Persianized.

Iran suffered political fragmentation, cultural disruption, and physical destruction after the collapse of the Abbasid Empire in 1258; and Mongol and Tatar invasions under Genghis Khan, Hulagu Khan, and Tamerlane threatened Persian continuity and identity over three centuries. As in the seventh century, Iran absorbed and integrated disparate ethnic and cultural influences, preserved its "Persianality," and continued to thrive. This reinvigorated Iran incubated a late-sixteenth-century Persian golden age under the Safavid dynasty shah, Abbas the Great (1587–1629), whose lasting contributions to Persian culture are preserved in the splendid monuments of Esfahan.

Iranian power declined after Shah Abbas, and the Safavid dynasty ended in 1736, followed by the Zands until 1794. The mediocre Qajars, under whom Iran lost both vigor and territory, held the plateau until 1925, when Reza Shah founded the two-ruler Pahlavi dynasty and set the course for contemporary Iranian development. Because he refused to allow Iranian territory to be used by the Allies as a transit area for supplying the

USSR with war matériel during World War II, Reza Shah was forced by the Allies to abdicate and was replaced in 1941 by his young son, Mohammad Reza. Reigning during a period of development and modernization, Mohammad Reza Shah was ousted briefly by the nationalistic, anti-Western Mohammad Mossadegh between 1951 and 1953 but regained power with controversial U.S. assistance. He continued a strong reign and rule until the political-religious revolution led by the Ayatollah Khomeini forced him out in January 1979.[3]

A Theocratic Republic

Having sought political control in times past, Shii clerics joined lay factions in the 1970s to fight foreign influences and the wide domestic corruption and repression in Iran. After Ayatollah Ruhollah Khomeini and his clerical supporters had ousted the shah and his regime and had gained control, however, their methods were no less harsh than those of the earlier regime. The clergy proclaimed themselves, as God's representatives, divinely appointed to administer the state and thus justified both the revolution and their own methods of governing. To the clerics, there is only one party, the party of God; therefore, their political opponents are enemies of God. Such claims have been used periodically for centuries and have been adapted in other parts of the contemporary Middle East, from the Iranian-backed Hizballah in Lebanon to Jewish extremists in the militant Kach Party in Israel.

The revolutionary government ended a secular monarchy and established a theocratic administration, and the new politics required extensive domestic and international adjustments. National cohesion became a priority for the new government, and, although some ethnic groups in Iran reasserted their separatist tendencies, the government suppressed the tendencies and preserved national unity. Internationally, revolutionary Iran reoriented its foreign relations, repudiating Western (especially U.S.) political and cultural influences. The seizure of scores of diplomatic persons, including 53 U.S. embassy staff members on November 4, 1979, by Iranian extremists was an unprecedented violation of diplomatic protocol and international norms, and such actions isolated Iran globally. Release of the hostages after 444 days did little to improve world perceptions of Iran, since radical Shii fundamentalists in Iran continued to flaunt world opinion.

The outbreak of the Iran-Iraq war in September 1980 (see Chaps. 11 and 16) led to many casualties (estimated at 1 million for Iran) and great physical destruction. Southwestern Iran, like southern Iraq, suffered widespread damage, and Iraq conducted air raids and Scud missile attacks on several Iranian cities. Iran claimed in 1990 that by the time of the cease-fire in 1988, it had suffered $542 billion in damage and in another claim gave a figure of $1 trillion in damage. A UN team estimated damage at $97 billion.[4] Although Iraq received greater material and financial aid than Iran, the Iranians periodically received assistance at critical times, especially from Syria, Libya, Taiwan, and the People's Republic of China as well as from and through Israel and the United States, as was disclosed in the Iran-Contra congressional hearings in Washington in 1986 and 1987.

During the two years between the Iran-Iraq cease-fire and Iraq's invasion of Kuwait, the Islamic Republic of Iran achieved basic domestic stability, despite the eight years of bitter warfare—and, indeed, partly by using the war as a centripetal factor. During the same period, it made an unexpectedly smooth transition to a successor administration following the death of the Ayatollah Khomeini at age 87 in 1989. The new regime was more pragmatic and moderate than the extremist predecessor. The Iraqi invasion of Kuwait created a dilemma for Iran, which condemned Iraq but also disliked the United States and other anti-Iraq coalition members. Iran received a bonanza when Iraq finally accepted Iran's claims and conditions for an end to the eight-year Iran-Iraq war, primarily to obtain Iranian neutrality in the new Gulf crisis. By 1992, Iran sought to restore internal stability and to achieve external détente with a range of other states. Internally, it faced a chronic cleavage between the radical conservatives and the moderate pragmatists. Relations are discussed at the end of this chapter.

A Mountain-Rimmed Plateau

Iranian Landscapes

Variety and Contrasts. Even in a region of contrasts, the contrasts among Iranian landscapes are greater than those in any other Middle East country. Turkey and Israel display great variety, but only Iran has the range between lush, humid subtropical environments like the mountain-backed Caspian coast and totally barren, salt-encrusted deserts like the huge *kavirs* of Iran's interior basins. The country's landforms, climates, vegetation, and peoples are all of great variety.[5]

Landforms. The Iranian Plateau is a region of intermontane plateaus and mountains, with high and rugged mountains providing walls on three sides (Map 22-1). The land thus appears as a triangular bowl. The base of the low triangle extends from the northwestern corner to the southeastern corner, and the apex lies in the northeast near Mashhad. This basic form has influenced cultural evolution in the land from earliest times. Coastlands and mountains frame the borders of the contemporary state of Iran and have historically served as ramparts.

Iran is the central segment of the Tethyan geosynclinal belt that extends from Morocco to Indonesia. It is the eastern half of the Middle East's Mobile Belt or Fold Belt (see Map 3-2) and was compressed between the Arabian Shield and the Russian Platform during the long period of intense folding from Triassic to Pliocene and Pleistocene times. The Zagros and Elburz-Kopet mountains were folded and buckled upward as a result of this tectonic compression, embracing between them a relatively inflexible block, a denuded shield forming the vast interior *kavirs*. Iran today has so many mountains and high plateaus that its average elevation is an unusually high 4,920 ft./1,500 m.

Drainage. Reflecting Iran's primarily Mediterranean precipitation regime, runoff reaches a maximum in late winter and early spring during seasonal rains and the melting of snow. The Karun River, tributary to the Shatt al-Arab and Iran's largest river, has ten times as much flow in April as in October. Farther east, the Zayandeh Rud,

Map 22-1. *General map of Iran, with regional identification numbers,* ostan *("provincial") centers and other cities, highways, spot heights, and main mountain ranges.*

largest river in the Esfahan watershed, has a spring maximum discharge of 1,680 m³/sec with its load of meltwater but has less than 2 percent of that flow in late fall. Similarly, salty Lake Urmia, occupying a closed basin in northwestern Iran, covers one-third more area in May than in early October, since it receives snowmelt runoff from surrounding mountains in spring.

Large dams on several streams impound the seasonal runoff for use throughout the year, and many more dams are needed to increase the supply of water for irrigation purposes. Scores of smaller streams carry runoff from upper mountain slopes to piedmonts and alluvial fans on the inner sides of the many mountain chains and

then dissipate in the sands, gravels, and saline crusts of the interior basins. More than half of Iran's drainage area lies in interior basins, from the vast *kavirs* to pocket-sized valleys in the Zagros. It is, nevertheless, these interior streams that are exploited in thousands of cases by *qanat* systems for irrigation water. Table 4-1 shows the seasonality and yearly average of precipitation in the four main climate areas of Iran.

Pattern of Regions

The pattern of regional physical and cultural features in Iran reveals especially significant contrasts, and some understanding of the regional design aids in an appreciation of Iran's general character and problems. Several regional central places that are notably differentiated both historically and regionally and that are representative of their regions are included in the regional surveys.[6]

[1] Zagros Mountains and Gulf Coast.

As part of the southern arc of the great Alpine folding system, the Zagros Mountains extend northwest-southeast from the Turkish border for 1,000 miles/1,600 km to the Strait of Hormuz. Four parallel belts exhibit different lithology, structures, and landforms from west to east; and the southeastern Zagros features scores of salt domes, which pierce the entire folded sequence and form prominent landscape features in the desert climate.

It is in the four belts of the Zagros region that much of the population lives and most of the present and historical development of Iran has taken place. Winter precipitation intercepted by the considerable linear elevations provides irrigation water in the succeeding season. In the folds of the central-western Zagros are the great majority of the country's oil fields, and in the volcanic belt of the eastern Zagros are most of the country's metallic mineral deposits, along the interplate zone of contact. Most of Iran's major and more famous cities are nestled in the valleys or along the piedmonts of the Zagros folds and along the Gulf coastal plain west of the Zagros (Map 22-1).

In the northwest is Tabriz, Iran's fourth-largest city, a former imperial capital and now the provincial capital of Azerbaijan Ostan (Persian *ostan* = "province"). Its bustling old bazaar and mosques have the distinct atmosphere of a dominantly Turkic Azeri metropolis, but other ethnic groups also jostle one another on the crowded streets. The central Zagros valleys, basins, and eastern piedmont embrace several of the republic's traditional provinces—Kordestan (Kurdistan), Iraq-e Ajam, Lorestan (Luristan), Esfahan, and Khuzistan—and also several of its major centers, from Sanandaj and Qom in the north to Esfahan in the south. This group of cities includes former imperial capitals (Hamadan and Esfahan), noted carpet centers (Hamadan, Kermanshah [now renamed Bakhtaran], Qom, Kashan, Esfahan), contemporary industrial concen-

Figure 22-1. *Esfahan's great* Maydan-e Shah *(Royal Square), surrounded by intricately decorated monuments and facades. Esfahan was developed as a beautiful capital by Safavid shah Abbas the Great, who watched polo games on the original* maydan.

trations, and the important religious center of Qom. The status of Qom was enhanced after the Shii clergy gained power in 1979 and the Ayatollah Khomeini ruled like a sovereign from his home there. Esfahan especially preserves its former imperial status in its Safavid pavilions, picturesque main square, or *maydan* (Fig. 22-1), and blue-tiled royal mosque, Masjid-e Shah. Third-largest city in Iran, Esfahan is credited with half the beautiful sites of the world in the Iranian proverb *Esfahan nesf-e Jahan* (literally, "Esfahan is half the world").

In the southern Zagros, Shiraz is the main center. It is the fifth-largest city in Iran and is yet another of the western cities that has the special aura of a former imperial capital. Climatic and soil conditions give Shiraz a particularly good ecology for growing roses, and rose bushes crowd the hundreds of gardens that adorn the city. Two of Iran's most famous poets, Hafez and Saadi, are memorialized in impressive tombs in the city.

Iran's Gulf coast of more than 800 miles/500 km topographically and climatically repels dense human habitation and development. Along most of the shore, Zagros ridges rise precipitously from the Gulf, leaving no room for settlement. Elsewhere, marshy flats constitute the coast, and nowhere is fresh water plentiful. Nevertheless, Iran's very extensive oil operations in the southwest necessitate export facilities on the nearby Gulf coast and islands, and very considerable import needs require large-scale general cargo ports. The main terminal was developed on

Kharg (Khark) Island, 25 miles/40 km offshore, opposite Kuwait. Gulf cargo ports are Bandar-e Khomeini (formerly Bandar-e Shahpur) in the north, Bandar-e Bushehr (pop. 121,000) south of Kharg, and Bandar-e Abbas (pop. 202,000) on the Strait of Hormuz (Persian *bandar* = "port"). The coast, along which the provinces of Fars and Kerman reach the Gulf, is being more closely integrated with the rest of Iran but is still considered isolated. Indeed, some small towns along the coast have closer ties across the Gulf than with the interior of Iran.

[2] Elburz Mountains and Northeast Chains.

This region comprises not only the Elburz Mountain chain itself but also the eastern extension of the same compressional structures, as well as the piedmonts or forelands that lie north and south of the entire belt. The chain from the southwestern corner of the Caspian Sea to the northeastern corner of Iran beyond Mashhad is a segment of the northern belt of Alpine folding, splaying from the Zagros structures west of Tehran. Unlike the Elburz range proper, the eastern extension comprises several parallel ridges, which are usually referred to as the Kopet Mountains, the name of the northernmost ridge along the Turkmenistan frontier.

Averaging about 60 miles/97 km in width, the Elburz range has numerous summits above 12,000 ft./3,658 m. It culminates in the impressive symmetrical volcanic cone of Mt. Damavand, 18,600 ft./5,671 m, in the central Elburz, highest elevation in the Middle East. The steep northern slopes of the Elburz descend to the Caspian plain and to the shore, which lies 92 ft./28 m below sea level. On the opposite side, the southern slopes terminate at the plateau level, 5,000 ft./1,525 m at Tehran, so that the total relief is less than on the northern side. Several small glaciers give an indication of the elevation of the higher peaks. Except for a few high passes, traversed by three spectacular highways, the chain is a major impediment to transportation and to the flow of moisture-laden winds from the northwest. The Elburz are still building, as is indicated by the periodic sharp but rarely destructive earthquakes that strike Tehran. However, in the western El-

burz, a devastating earthquake struck June 21, 1990, causing 50,000 deaths and 100,000 injuries and rendering 500,000 homeless. Severe tremors have shaken areas across much of northern Iran as well as southwestern and eastern areas.

In northeastern Iran the folded Kopet ridges of northern Khorasan are appreciably lower than the Elburz proper and are more comparable to the folded Zagros. Open valleys are devoted to cereal cultivation and support a moderately dense population. Mashhad is the major city of the northeast. It is not only the second city of Iran but also, like Tabriz, a center of ethnic complexity, with Persians, Turkmen, Baluch, Kurds, Hazaras, and other peoples mingling in the bazaars and mosques. Turkmen especially bring their Bukhara-style carpets for marketing in Mashhad. Like Qom, Mashhad has one of the holiest shrines in Iran. The opening of the border between Iran and Turkmenistan and the other new republics of former Soviet central Asia in 1991 has produced an appreciable influx of visitors from these long-isolated lands.

The large population of the Caspian coast is distributed in numerous small towns and villages rather than in a few metropolitan areas. Rasht, in the west, is noteworthy, along with the port of Bandar-e Anzali (formerly Bandar-e Pahlevi). In the east are Gorgan and the port of Bandar-e Torkeman (formerly Bandar-e Shah). Several coastal towns are much-frequented resort centers, including Ramsar and Chalus.

The piedmont and foredeep south of the Elburz-Kopet belt support not only the metropolitan area of Tehran but also Qazvin to the west, the ancient city of Rey immediately south of Tehran, and a series of towns along the present Tehran-Mashhad railway, which follows the old Silk Road. A score of suburbs and former peripheral villages have coalesced to form greater Tehran, which sprawls along the alluvial fans on the southern side of the Elburz. About 20 percent of Iran's population resides in greater Tehran, which has an even higher percentage of the country's professional workers, office employees, and general labor force. Formerly, palaces, upper-class residences, and Western expatriates were concentrated on the upper slopes in northern Tehran, especially in the suburb of Shemiran (Fig. 22-2). These neighborhoods had first use of the water from the *qanats* that formerly supplied the city, and they were cooler because of their higher elevation. The city has an impressive concentration of government buildings, embassy compounds, banks, schools, and business establishments. Streets of the central business district have the most congested traffic of all Middle East cities, and the Tehran bazaar, in the crowded southern sector, is normally one of the major shopping centers of the Middle East and is especially noted for gold jewelry, carpets, and decorative brass and copper wares.

[3] **Eastern Highlands.** Several separate complex ridges form the eastern rim of the Iranian "bowl." Runoff from the ridges supports a few scattered villages, some of which include ruins of ancient settlements. At the southern end of the eastern highlands is Iran's only recently active volcano, Kuh-e Taftan. These eastern reaches of Khorasan, Iran's largest province, share a long, porous border with Afghanistan, most of which had been included in Iran-zamin for centuries. During the Soviet occupation of Afghanistan from 1980 to 1989, about 2 million Afghans sought refuge in eastern Iran. This frontier zone was brought under central government control only in the 1960s and is still occupied by a variety of ethnic groups that have only a tenuous relationship with Tehran.

[4] **Interior Basins.** This region is contained within the larger Iranian triangle. Although it includes several smaller basins, its two major depressions are Dasht-e Kavir in the north-center and Dasht-e Lut in the southeast (Persian *dasht* = "desert" or "plain").[7] The lowest part of the Dasht-e Kavir watershed is occupied by the Great Kavir (Persian *kavir* = "playa" or "salt flat"), an immense erosional surface with salt- and mud-filled depressions and extensive dune fields covering more than 20,000 miles^2/51,800 km^2. Dasht-e Lut (*lut* = "desert basin"), lowest sump in interior Iran, and only 672 ft./205 m above sea level, is somewhat smaller than the Great Kavir and is separated from it by a low divide. Dasht-e

Lut is quite different from the Great Kavir. Its weird surface is etched by wind into yardangs, alternating ridges and grooves, some as high as 195 ft./60 m, and the wind-eroded material is piled into dunes to the south and east.

Neither the great salt expanse making up the Dasht-e Kavir nor the rough Dasht-e Lut is inhabited or even utilized by nomads. Neither the soil nor the meager precipitation permits growth of perceptible vegetation, although desert bush survives on the higher parts of the basins and in the courses of seasonal streams. These barren interior basins are the least useful parts of Iran.

People: Demography and Ethnography

Population

With the second-largest population in the Middle East, Iran has far more people than all the other Gulf states combined, including Iraq and Saudi Arabia. Moreover, it has the region's most complex ethnic structure, both in the number of major groupings and in solid concentrations of those groupings. Its population of 56.3 million (1990) includes at least eight peoples numbering more than 1 million each and another half-dozen of approximately 100,000 to 1 million (see Table 6-3 and Map 22-2).

The areas with the most favorable environment for human occupation have long been densely populated: the Zagros valleys, Caspian coastlands, and inner piedmonts of the mountain frame. Along with the socioeconomic development and rising standard of living that began in the 1950s and faltered only in the late 1970s, Iran saw its net increase in population escalate to 46.3 per thousand, highest in the Middle East. Efforts initiated by the shah in the 1960s to slow the extraordinary birthrate were beginning to show modest results when the fundamentalist revolutionary regime reversed the government program. From a fairly high 2.9 percent population increase per year in the mid-1970s, the rate jumped to 3.9 percent—one of the world's highest—before the new regime reacted and again encouraged birth control. By early 1992, the growth rate was back down to 2.7 percent. Immi-

Figure 22-2. *Northwestern sector of Tehran, looking toward the snow-covered Elburz. Much of this development is post-1960 and was originally middle- and upper-income housing.*

gration and emigration play only a limited role in Iranian demographics, although scores of thousands of antirevolutionary Iranians, including Iranian Jews, left the country after the revolution.

Distribution. The western third of the country, including the Elburz range and the Caspian coast, contains more than 90 percent of the population. The remainder is distributed among Mashhad and the valleys of the northern Khorasan, the inner Zagros cities of Yazd and Kerman and their surrounding villages, and widely scattered concentrations in the southeast, including Bandar-e Abbas, Chah Bahar, Zahedan, and Zabol (see Maps 6-2 and 10-1).

Urbanization. As in other Middle East states, as well as in most developing countries, the shift from rural to urban areas in Iran has been pronounced. Whereas the urban population was only 30 percent of the total in the mid-1950s, it was 53 percent in the early 1990s. The urban increase notwithstanding, millions of Iranians continue to reside in more than 55,000 villages along the piedmonts and valleys of the countryside (see Fig. 10-1). Since the villages contain concentrations of agricultural population, the pattern of areal distribution of villages correlates with patterns of available runoff and of higher rainfall.[8]

Contributing to the urbanization is the steady sedentarization of nomadic peoples such as the Qashqai and Bakhtiari and the drift from the tribal areas into Tehran and other cities that offer economic mobility. Thus, the populations of Tehran, Esfahan, Shiraz, and Mashhad have more than quadrupled since 1956.

Peoples of the Plateau

Ethnic Complexity. As an ethnic mosaic, Iran is the most complex country in the Middle East. Although ethnic Persians (as distinct from Iranians in general) have played a prominent role in Iran's development, events have also been influenced by minority peoples occupying valleys and basins near the ethnic Persians. Both the location of Iran and its complex pattern of landforms have influenced the historical influx of various groups and the resultant ethnic pattern.[9]

Over the millennia, groups have invaded or migrated into the plateau from Asia Minor, the Caucasus, central Asia, and the Indian subcontinent. Once they found themselves south of the barriers of the Black Sea, Caucasus Mountains, and Caspian Sea, migrants were forced through the mountain-ribbed Iranian "throat" between the Caspian Sea and the Gulf. Some westward-moving peoples pushed on into and across Mesopotamia; others elected to settle in the basins of the rugged Zagros Mountains.

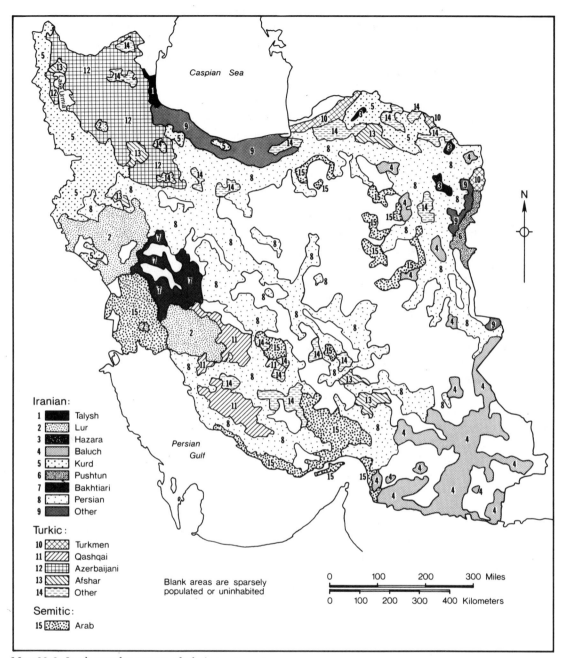

Map 22-2. *Iran's complex pattern of ethnic groups.*

The complexity of landforms, with elaborate patterns of parallel and sometimes interconnected linear valleys and irregular basins, imposed difficulties but also offered opportunities. There were opportunities for settlement, for survival for those who developed a water supply, and for protection from neighbors as well as from a central authority. Some early migrants have been partly or completely assimilated, but more than a score of peoples retain separate identities in exclusive territories, as do the Qashqai, Bakhtiari, and Lur. Several minorities maintain a tribal organization, thus structuring and protecting their culture. The remarkable preservation of minority languages provides a functional linguistic criterion to aid distinction among groups. In a few cases, religion becomes the main basis for particularity.

As a countertrend, modern communications and transportation, along with urbanization and education, have already begun to diminish tribal isolation and cultural distinctions. Increasing numbers of tribal leaders are being absorbed into the political establishment that their predecessors rejected. Minority members seeking better employment or other economic advantages learn Farsi in addition to their mother tongue, thus blurring the ethnic dividing lines. The central government, which a few decades ago used military force to subdue tribal separatism, now emphasizes employment for tribal members in government bureaus.[10] As they have for centuries, however, group identification and ethnic distinctions are inherent and unmistakable elements in Iranian cultural patterns and will remain so for the indefinite future.

Most of the peoples of Iran are discussed in Chapter 6 and are included in Table 6-3, hence only a few details need be added here to place them in more specific context. A few smaller groups are also mentioned. Map 22-2 shows the generalized patterns of the ethnic groups of Iran, and the identification numbers of the groups discussed are keyed to that map. Estimated percentages of the major groups are given in the summary data at the beginning of the chapter. Since no census has ever been taken of ethnic groups, and since official efforts have long been made to blur ethnic distinctions, statistics on the ethnic groups must be accepted as rough approximations.

Persians and Related Peoples. Persian (Farsi) is the principal language in a subfamily of Indo-Iranian languages that also includes Kurdish, Luri, Baluchi, Gilaki, Mazandarani, and several other tongues spoken by relatively small groups.

Although ethnic Persians (8) are the third-largest people in the Middle East and the largest single ethnic group in Iran, they are somewhat less than 50 percent of the country's total population. Persians are the most widely distributed of the Iranian peoples, but they are found especially in an almost unbroken broad ring around the interior basins. They comprise the great majority

of the upper class, the important government employees, and the economic elite.

The main concentration of Kurds (5) is in the Iranian segment of Kurdistan, in the western Zagros parallel to the Turkish and Iraqi borders. Mahabad, Sanandaj, and Bakhtaran (Kermanshah) are Kurdish centers. Like related tribes in Iran and Turkey, the Iranian Kurds have exhibited separatism, rebelling unsuccessfully in 1919, during World War II (the short-lived Mahabad Republic was broken up in 1947), and in 1979. The Kurds are mostly Sunnis and constitute the largest group of Sunnis in the republic.

The Baluch (4) are concentrated in the extreme southeastern corner of Iran and are the least economically and nationally integrated of the major minorities. The Baluch are still nomadic and are known for their hand-knotted Baluchi rugs.

Divided by the main concentration of the Bakhtiari (7), the Lur (2) have two concentrations in the central Zagros. Khorramabad is the center of the northern area, Lorestan; the oil center of Gach Saran lies on the southern edge of the southern concentration. The Bakhtiari, concentrated between the oil center of Masjed-e Soleyman and Shahr-e Kord, are considered the most powerful of the southern tribes. Making and marketing Bakhtiari carpets are important aspects of the tribal economy.

Secluded in high mountain valleys and basins in Khorasan (eastern Iran), a few tens of thousands of several tribal groups speaking Indo-European languages spill over from neighboring Afghanistan and the central Asian republics. A few other such groups live in scattered locations southwest and south of the Caspian. One of the largest is the Hazara or "Berberi" (3), living in and around Mashhad, who are a branch of a larger group in central Afghanistan. The Aimaq (9) include a score of tribal groups, a grouping that exemplifies the multiplicity of tribal divisions in this rugged area with its history of crisscrossing migrations.

Astride the northern segment of the Iranian-Afghan border live the Pushtun (6), who are also called Pashtun and are known farther east as the Pathan. Like the Hazara, they have migrated westward from their main concentration in central Afghanistan. A few tens of thousands of Tajik

(9) live in the northern part of the Zabol salient. West of the Caspian, on either side of the international border, are several thousand Talysh (1); along the southern Caspian coast and on the slopes above are the Gilani (sometimes Gilaki) (9) in the west, around Rasht, and the Mazandarani (9) farther east. The Gilani have several times taken separatist action, most notably during the establishment of a short-lived socialist republic after World War I.

Turkic Peoples. The Azeri, or Azerbaijani (12), the largest ethnolinguistic minority in Iran, speak a Turkic language but adhere to Shiism and other Persian cultural traditions. They are concentrated in relatively densely populated northwestern Iran, east of the Kurds and west of the Persians. Their center is Tabriz, but they also form a high percentage of the populations in Maragheh and Zanjan. While maintaining an Azeri identity and language, they join in Iranian nationalism as long as the central government accepts their informal autonomy. Their separatism was encouraged in the short-lived communist Tudeh Republic of Azerbaijan created under Soviet auspices at the end of World War II. Thwarting this Soviet effort was one of the first effective acts of the United Nations. More significantly revealing were the expressions of affinity after 1991 between the Azeris of Iran and those of the new Republic of Azerbaijan, successor to the former Soviet constituent republic. Long divided by a closed border, the two groups traveled back and forth after the collapse of the USSR. To the discomfiture of the Iranian government, the Azeris made several tentative declarations of hope for a union of Azeris in an enlarged independent state.

The Qashqai (11) have preserved one of the strongest nomadic traditions among the larger groups in Iran. They occupy two large areas in the Fars Province, one north of Shiraz and one to the south. With well-organized tribal confederations, the Qashqai have traditionally resisted central government control; and during the 1930s, the Iranian army disarmed the group and executed or imprisoned many tribal chiefs. The Qashqai periodically seek independence, as they did in the early 1960s, and separatism among

them reemerged in the early months of the 1979 revolution.

Turkmen (10), a tribally organized people, live in widely scattered groups in the northeastern mountains next to Turkmenistan. At one time they formed a strong military cavalry but are now nomadic pastoralists and settled farmers, known for hand-knotted carpets named after various descent groups—Tekke, Yomut, Salor, Saryk, and others. Their separatism, strong until the 1920s, reasserted itself after the 1979 revolution but was suppressed by the central government. Like the Azeris in the northwest, the Turkmen in the northeast have shown an affinity for their Turkic kinsmen in Turkmenistan across the newly opened border of the former Soviet Union.

The 50 or more Ilsavan (formerly Shahsavan) nomadic groups occupy a dozen scattered areas from the Aras River southeastward to the steppes south of Tehran. The Qajars (14) form an enclave among the Mazandarani on the southeastern corner of the Caspian Sea. Afshars (13) primarily inhabit several separate areas in northwestern Iran. Other small tribal Turkic groups are scattered chiefly in the mountains of Khorasan and in the more rugged areas east of Shiraz, especially the Teymurtash and Qaragozlu.

Arabs. More than 1 million Arabs (15) live primarily in Khuzistan, the plain at the head of the Gulf, which Arabs refer to as Arabistan ("land of the Arabs"). They also live in the southern Zagros interior and even in widely scattered areas northeast and east of the Dasht-e Kavir. Descendants of Arabs who invaded in the seventh century and of later settlers, the Iranian Arabs maintain their separateness and have not assimilated, although they are predominantly Shiis. Iran was concerned in the early 1980s that the Arabs of Iran might revolt and support Iraq in the Iran-Iraq fighting, but neither the Iranian Arabs nor the Iraqi Persians rose against their host governments.

Armenians and Assyrians. These two quite different peoples are grouped together as the two numerically significant Christian sects in Iran. The primarily Orthodox Armenians live in Tehran (about half), Tabriz, and Esfahan. As in Lebanon and Syria, they maintain their separate language, churches, and schools and have achieved marked success in professional and clerical positions in Tehran and in the Khuzistan oil fields.[11] The Assyrians are only one-tenth the number of Armenians and are concentrated west of Lake Urmia. They maintain their cohesion and preserve their Syriac vernacular and Nestorian Christianity.

Jews. Long resident in Iran, at least as early as the Babylonian Captivity, Jews were officially estimated in 1977 as numbering 90,000 but were probably more numerous. Many are merchants, especially rug dealers, in Tehran, Esfahan, Hamadan, and Shiraz. Iranian Jews have intermarried with Persians but preserve a Jewish identity in their own schools, synagogues, and social institutions. Influential under the shah, Jews have been subjected to discrimination under the revolutionary regime, as have Armenians, Bahais, and other minorities. About half of the Jews have emigrated, some to Israel but the majority of them to the United States.[12]

Refugees. Approximately 2 million Afghans who sought refuge in Iran during the Soviet occupation of Afghanistan were accommodated in camps and towns near the Afghan-Iran border as well as in the cities of Tehran, Mashhad, Birjand, and Zahedan.[13] Most of them were reluctant to return to Afghanistan even after the Soviet withdrawal in 1989 because of continued instability and fighting, and Iran sought international assistance to return the refugees to Afghanistan. Iran also received refugees from Iraq during the Iran-Iraq war when Iraq expelled more than 200,000 Shiis who it claimed were Iranians but who had been Iraqi citizens descended from Iranian immigrants to Mesopotamia several generations before. Other Shiis and Kurds fled Iraq in early 1991 to escape oppression by the Iraqis after their forced withdrawal from Kuwait.

Iranian Economic Patterns

Perspective

As in neighboring Gulf petroleum-producing countries, economic development and modern-ization have escalated in Iran since 1950. However, Iranian economic patterns exhibit comparatively greater complexity and subtlety of structure because of Iran's long economic history, early start in petroleum production, and combination—unique in the Middle East—of large size and large population with huge petroleum resources.[14]

Prior to development of the petroleum industry, Iran's traditional prosperity was based on a varied agriculture, trade, and widespread and artistic craftsmanship. Ordinary textiles, specialized hand-printed textiles called *qalamkar*, hand-knotted carpets, copper and brass items, decorated gold and silver items, enamel work, inlaid items, and hand-painted miniatures attracted buyers around the world. Although these traditional items form a negligible percentage of the country's present production and exports, demand for them remains high; and for some isolated tribal groups, such artisan sales provide much of the cash income. Also, these products, rather than petroleum, symbolize Iranian traditions and creativity. Agriculture continues to be a major sector in the Iranian economy and in many regions is the only economic activity of any significance.

Having assured himself in the late 1950s that petroleum had a vital role in the world economy and that Iran had a major place in the petroleum market, Mohammad Reza Shah pursued an almost frenetic program of economic development of his country. During the period 1960–1977, Iran's real annual growth of 9.6 percent was about double the average of other developing countries and was higher than the average of any other regional grouping of countries in the world. The very stable Iranian rial was virtually convertible.[15] Every sector received attention, especially physical infrastructure—roads, railroads, ports, airports, communications, industries, trade, urban development. However, when the shah concomitantly attempted to give Iran military superiority and to transform it into an industrial power, a modern welfare state, and a Westernized society, the effort became overloaded for the economic base. The social impact particularly elicited a backlash, and the Khomeini-led fundamentalist revolution reversed all aspects of the shah-initiated developments, especially the Westernization. However, the solidity of the physical and socioeconomic infrastructure was confirmed by the fact that the revolutionary regime was able to cope for several years by coasting on the shah's accomplishments, including the military buildup.

The revolutionary government's initial economic efforts will always be ambiguous because of the almost immediate impact of the Iran-Iraq war. The evidence is that the new regime had little comprehension of economic development. All major industries were taken from their private owner-managers and placed in state hands. Thousands of a wide range of establishments were confiscated from supporters of the previous regime. Banking was "Islamicized," so that loans were made interest free and the banks were unprofitable. Both internal and external circumstances constricted development. The external impacts were especially serious—the war with Iraq, sharp decline of oil prices, Iranian assets being frozen abroad, Western economic sanctions, and other blows. The GDP of the late 1980s was no higher than that of fifteen years earlier. The revolution prompted the exodus of entrepreneurs, managers, skilled professionals, and capital. The former privileged class was largely broken, but a new elite arose. The lot of the poor, for whom the revolution was theoretically launched, was not improved. Indeed, protests and riots by the unemployed poor broke out in June 1992 in a dozen cities from Khorramabad in the Zagros to Mashhad in the northeast corner.

By the early 1990s, in its first economic five-year plan (1989–1993), the more moderate regime that succeeded the Khomeini ideology was addressing economic realities. It was actively reprivatizing establishments, attempting to restore confidence in government policies, inviting selected foreign firms (notably excluding U.S. companies) to enter both the oil and industrial sectors, and seeking foreign financing for new industrial production, including automobile assembly. Also noteworthy is Iran's aggressive program of remilitarization, calling for an expenditure of $14.5 billion in 1992 (against $1 billion for

economic reconstruction). Suppliers include North Korea, Bulgaria, China, and Pakistan.

Agriculture and Water Control

Although only a limited proportion of Iran is naturally suitable for rainfed agriculture, human ingenuity over thousands of years has created a broad agricultural base for a large population. Finding, conserving, and channeling water to cultivable soil areas in linear valleys and along piedmonts were the essential challenge and the main accomplishment. Iran's agricultural productivity, supplemented by imports, remained sufficiently effective during the 1980s so that even under wartime conditions, the population suffered no widespread hunger. Despite the dominance of the oil sector in the national economy, 25 percent of the economically active population still engages in agriculture, which contributes 23 percent of the GDP.

As in Syria and Iraq, the large landowners and tribal leaders controlled huge areas before 1960, maintaining sharecropping agreements with peasants working the land. Indeed, landowners controlled entire groups of villages along with the land and the village inhabitants. Two major land reform programs transformed the system. One was the highly publicized "White Revolution" carried out by the shah in 1963; the other was the revolutionary government's land reform in 1982. The two reforms curbed the power of the large landowners and reduced the size of their landholdings.

Extensive areas in the northwest and northeast support rainfed cultivation and arboriculture, as well as specialty horticulture in the distinctive ecology of the Caspian coast. However, typical Iranian agriculture relies on water management. Although several irrigation techniques are now employed, the ancient system of tapping and distributing water through a network of *qanats* remains the most important (see Chap. 7). These underground water channels, revealed on the surface as a chain of wells, are ideally constructed in alluvial fans that absorb runoff from adjacent watersheds on higher slopes that have intercepted rain and snow. Scores of thousands of *qanats* in Iran, many constructed centuries ago

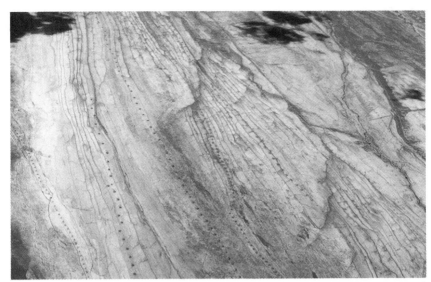

Figure 22-3. Qanats *on Iran's northwestern plateau. These underground tunnels with their surface chains of wells have been the standard Iranian irrigation method for millennia.*

and carefully maintained on northern and southwestern slopes, appear aerially as strings of beads on the long slopes of the fans (Fig. 22-3). Although all irrigated areas require local cooperation, *qanat*-watered basins demand an exceptionally high level of coordination and engender a complex and uniquely Iranian socioeconomic structure.

Crops. Nearly everywhere, except in the barren interior and southeastern corner, the dominant crops are wheat and barley, grown in both rainfed and irrigated areas. Much of the wheat is rough-milled to make the unusual Iranian bread: large, flat, and dimpled from being baked on hot pebbles in a large oven. Rice is the third major cereal, grown in paddies on the alluvial plains on the southwestern Caspian coast. Much of the excellent rice is consumed in the favorite national dish, *chelo kebab*—flattened, grilled lamb kebabs on a bed of rice. Wheat and rice production, nevertheless, fail to meet demand, necessitating substantial imports. Under the stresses of the 1980s, imports of cereals tripled over the decade 1978–1988. Potatoes are a fourth basic food grown in large quantities. Melons are grown everywhere, along with a wide range of vegetables. Also widely distributed are grapes used for raisins, table grapes, and in certain areas, wine.

Tree crops, common on the lower Zagros slopes, yield a wide range of nuts and fruits, with pistachios in great variety a particular specialty—Iran is the world's greatest pistachio producer. Almonds and walnuts also grow well in subhumid areas. Fruits, from citrus along the Gulf coast to apples in the higher elevations, include all but humid tropical varieties. A specialty crop, tea grows along the south Caspian coast in the same protected environment that produces rice and other subtropical crops. Tea is the popular social beverage in Iran, far surpassing coffee, and must also be imported to meet demand.

Grown on the Caspian coast and in favored locations in the southern Zagros, cotton and tobacco are major industrial crops. Both sugarcane and sugar beets have been expanded in acreage, and sugar mills process these crops at refineries in central and northeastern Iran. Opium poppies, once prohibited, are now being grown under government supervision, as in Turkey.

Livestock, Fishing, Forestry. Vast areas are well suited for the grazing of sheep and goats, and cattle raising is of increasing importance. Indeed, Iran ranks first or ties for first (with Turkey) among Middle Eastern countries in numbers of goats, sheep, and chickens and is second to Turkey in cattle. In addition to dairy products, cattle supply manure for fertilizer and for burning as domestic fuel (see Fig. 10-1). Fishing is important along the Gulf coast, along the Gulf of Oman, and on the Caspian Sea coast. Iranian Caspian fisheries are especially famous for their superior caviar, the roe of the large Caspian sturgeon. Already very limited and therefore expensive, the caviar supply is threatened by chemical pollution and by the fluctuating water level of the Caspian Sea. Although ranking behind several countries in amount of fish caught (see Table 7-3), Iran ranks second in the export value of fish because of its caviar sales. Iranian forests, particularly in the Elburz, are the only commercially productive forest areas in the Middle East other than those in Turkey.

Petroleum: A Major Producer

Iran became the first major petroleum country in the Middle East in 1908 with the discovery of the great Masjed-e Soleyman field in the folds of the middle Zagros, 100 miles/160 km north of the head of the Gulf (see Chap. 8). Oil has long played a dominant role in Iran's economy and has undergirded the country's economic development for several decades. In the late 1970s and in some recent years, the petroleum industry contributed nearly half of the national income and 98 percent of the value of exports. Such a major earner of foreign exchange—$15–18 billion in the early 1990s—supplies Iran with the hard currency to pay for large amounts of imports.

Iran is credited with petroleum reserves of 92.85 billion barrels, technically the fifth largest in the Middle East and in the world. However, claimed reserves of Iran, Iraq, Kuwait, and the UAE have leapfrogged one another over the years and may well prove to be roughly equal. Iran produced more than 6 million bpd in its peak year of 1974 before decreasing to a minimum of 1.37 million bpd in 1981 during the early years of the country's revolution and the Iran-Iraq war. Production returned to the 3.3–3.5-million-bpd level in the early 1990s and is planned to reach 4.5–5 million bpd by the mid-1990s. As in Saudi Arabia, coordinated production and reservoir conditions require only a minimum number of wells, with only 360 exploited in 1991. Some of the original wells are still producing thousands of barrels a day after 80 years.

Historical Note. The first concessionaire in Iran adopted the name Anglo-Persian Oil Company (APOC), changed in 1935 to Anglo-Iranian Oil Company (AIOC), and still later to British Petroleum Company (BP). The British government acquired a majority interest in the company in 1914 and expanded production and refining to meet the demands of both world wars.

One of the major crises in international oil industry history was the 1951–1953 dispute between the Iranian government under Prime Minister Mohammad Mossadegh and the AIOC. The crisis arose when the Iranian government rejected a draft agreement between the AIOC and Iran and nationalized the Iranian oil industry under the new National Iranian Oil Company (NIOC). During the dispute, Iranian oil sales fell to zero. In 1953, Mossadegh was displaced, and the way was clear for a completely new accord under which the former AIOC concession passed to a new consortium of British, Dutch, French, and U.S. companies.

Operating under NIOC supervision, the Consortium produced and refined most of the Iranian output for the next 25 years. However, NIOC also formed partnerships with several U.S., Italian, and Canadian companies in the late 1950s for exploration and production outside the original AIOC concession area, including offshore areas. NIOC attempted to be its own operator during the 1980s and succeeded in maintaining production, with limited assistance. By 1991, the government moved to accept foreign operators and exploration parties, despite its previous decade of isolationism. Such cooperation would without question be mutually beneficial and can be expected to expand during the 1990s.

Fields and Facilities. Most of Iran's oil fields are located in linear northwest southeast reservoirs paralleling the fold structures in the original discovery belt (Maps 8-2 and 22-3). Therefore, they are in the west-central Zagros north and south of Masjed-e Soleyman, in a 300-mile/485-km zone from Khorramabad in the northwest to near Shiraz in the southeast. Iran announced in December 1988 that the producing belt had been extended to southeast of Bushehr with the

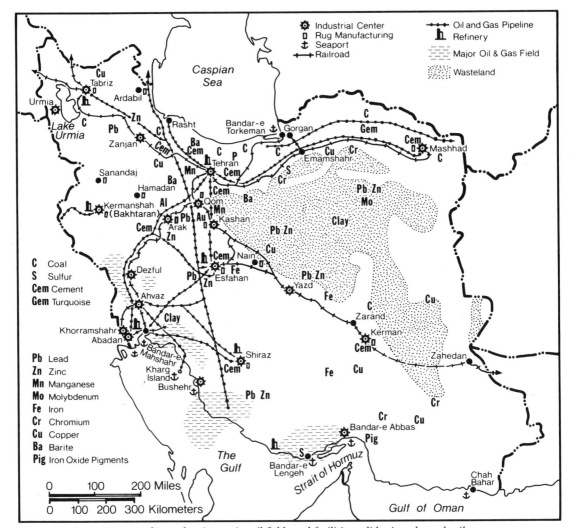

Map 22-3. *Economic map of Iran, showing major oil fields and facilities, solid minerals, and railways.*

discovery of a large field with 10 billion barrels of very heavy oil. By the early 1990s, 27 onshore fields were in production along with 11 offshore fields in the upper and lower Gulf. Only a few oil fields have been discovered elsewhere in the country (one north of Qom, for example), although gas fields are producing in the folded structures of the northern Khorasan.

Oil and natural gas pipelines form a dense network in the closely packed fields of Khuzistan and adjacent areas. Most of the lines feed the Kharg Island export terminal northwest of Bushehr, which in peacetime ranks with Ras Tanura and Juaymah in Saudi Arabia as being among the world's three largest export terminals. Numerous other lines normally carry feedstock to the refinery on Abadan Island, on the east bank of the Shatt al-Arab, which before 1980 was one of the two or three largest in the world, processing 600,000 bpd. Located within easy range of Iraqi warplanes, both the Kharg Island and Abadan facilities were very heavily damaged during the Iran-Iraq war but were actively being returned to normal operation in late 1992. Meanwhile, Iran's largest refinery is in Tehran, and others are in Esfahan, Tabriz, and Shiraz.

In addition to huge petroleum resources, Iran also possesses the second-largest nonassociated gas reserves in the world, 600.4 trillion ft.[3], exceeded only by those of the former Soviet republics, 1,750 trillion ft.[3] (the United States has gas reserves of 169.3 trillion ft.[3]). The wider distribution of gas in Iran compared to that of oil is an advantage for both domestic and industrial users. With such a surplus of gas, Iran in 1970 opened a 40–42-in./102–107-cm pipeline, IGAT-1, from its southwestern fields to northern Iran and onward into the southwestern areas of the former USSR. The 1978–1979 revolution halted construction on a second line, IGAT-2, from the Kangan gas field on the Gulf south of Shiraz to Astara, where the Azerbaijan border meets the Caspian Sea coast. Construction was finally resumed in 1992 under the aegis of the recently formed National Iranian Gas Company (NIGC). The IGAT-2 diameter is a huge 56 in./142 cm to Qazvin, northwest of Tehran, and 48 in./122 cm from Qazvin to Astara. Of the very large volume of gas pumped from the southwest, Iran plans to export 106 billion ft.^{3} per year to consumers in the Caucasus, Ukraine, and, increasingly, farther into Europe. Greater internal utilization of gas—for domestic, industrial, and power-generating purposes—is being vigorously encouraged.[16] Although Iran has lagged in the production of natural gas liquids and petrochemicals, its large natural gas reserves provide an incentive for development of such production in the 1990s.

Non-Oil Resources

Scattered mineral deposits, especially copper, were mined in ancient times on the Iranian Plateau. However, few commercially significant deposits had been identified in recent decades until modern technology, including space imagery, was applied to the exploration of the highly mineralized volcanic belt in Iran near the tectonic plate boundary along the inner Zagros. In this intensive study, geologists discovered one deposit after another—copper, iron, chrome, lead, zinc, manganese, coal, barite—approximately along the axis of the railway from Qom to Kerman. Numerous finds have been commercially exploited, some on a large scale. Iran possesses an array of mineral raw materials for eventual domestic use and export.

The most important discoveries were of copper, scattered along the entire length of the inner Zagros volcanic belt from the northwestern border to south of Bam in the southeast. The largest deposits are at Sar Cheshmeh, southwest of Kerman, which some Western engineers claim are the richest in the world. An integrated mining, smelting, and refining operation that is one of Iran's major projects has been under development since the early 1970s. Additional copper deposits near Yazd and farther northwest may later be exploited for processing at Sar Cheshmeh, and Iran hopes that copper-product exports will supplement foreign exchange earnings from petroleum.

Other metallic minerals found in quantity include ores of iron, chrome, zinc, lead, manganese, and antimony. A remarkable concentration exists near Bafq, southeast of Yazd, and the same area is the location of Iran's main iron ores and major deposits of lead-zinc ores, not far from large coal resources. Iron is transported to the Esfahan steel works by rail from Bafq, and still richer iron ore resources of 1.13 billion tons at Gol-e Gohar, south of Sirjan, are being mined to feed both the Esfahan and the Ahvaz plants. Several major chrome deposits south and southeast of Kerman yield ores for export.

Important nonmetallic minerals include coal; the largest deposits are northwest of Kerman, but more than a score of collieries also extend across northern Iran from Lake Urmia to Mashhad. Fine turquoise from Neyshabur, west of Mashhad, is used in a variety of locally crafted jewelry, although some turquoise is exported; inexhaustible supplies of salt occur in the numerous salt plugs near Bandar-e Abbas, with native sulfur from many of the same structures supplying an important export item; and kaolin, near Qom, is used in the large ceramics industry. Decorative tiles made with Qom kaolin are used in walls, floors, and even house facades, giving Iranian houses a distinctive appearance.

Industries

Industrialization of Iran, under the shah's initiative during the 1960s, proceeded on a scale that observers considered unrealistic. The emphasis on industrialization in the country's economic planning seemed to demand too much too fast. Plans produced large-scale projects with inadequate infrastructure, inducing Shii fundamentalist charges of "Westoxication" and anti-Islamic policies. Nevertheless, an appreciable number and variety of major industries were successfully established, from food processing to iron and

Figure 22-4. *Cheshmeh Ali, near Shahr-e Rey, south of Tehran. The water of this spring (lower left) has attracted settlers for millennia. For many decades carpets have been brought from all over Iran to be washed by local specialists in this mineral-free water. The rock slope above the spring serves as the drying rack for more than 100 carpets at a time.*

steel production to automobile assembly. Joint ventures with foreign corporations brought transfers of technology and training programs for Iranian labor, even though few ventures achieved planned production levels.

After 1978, few of the new industrial establishments sustained production as a result of the unreliable labor supply and shortages of raw materials, spare parts, and other inputs. The war with Iraq also skewed production and forced emphasis on wartime requirements. By the late 1980s, the government recognized the imperative need for industrial revitalization and the necessity to deregulate and deregiment the industrial sector. Privatization of at least one-fourth of the state-owned enterprises was in progress in the early 1990s, and selected foreign interests were cautiously being allowed to join the industrial development.

The industries of Iran are widely distributed in the western third of the country, including cities along the inner Zagros axis. Many of the manufacturing plants are concentrated around Tehran, and light industries and craft shops are found in dozens of towns and even villages. Major products include processed foods and beverages, cigarettes, home appliances, assembled au-

tomobiles, textiles, and machine tools. Iran is especially noted for its wide variety of hand-knotted Persian rugs, jewelry, metalwares, inlaid items, and decorated ceramic tiles (Fig. 22-4).

The Tehran region, including the western suburb of Karaj, is the dominant manufacturing focus of the country, including auto assembly plants, household appliance factories, and clothing factories. Esfahan, the second-largest industrial center, has the country's major iron and steel plant, cotton mills, and numerous small shops producing metal household items, including brass and copper trays. Tabriz, with a major machine tool plant, is the industrial center of the northwest. Arak, southwest of Qom, has Iran's only aluminum smelter, and about 80 percent of its output is exported. Still other cities with appreciable manufacturing plants are shown in Map 22-3, which emphasizes the concentration in the western third of Iran and the isolation of Mashhad in the far northeast.

Transportation and Trade

Land Routes. Economic development in the 1930s and even after World War II was inhibited by a limited infrastructure, and construction of a transportation net was both difficult and expensive. Terrain, climate, and distance combine to constrain construction of transportation routes, even if financing and engineering skills are available. By the 1980s, however, all cities had been integrated into a systematic highway network, well engineered and well constructed by European companies under contract. The net penetrates all parts of the country except the virtually uninhabited east-central interior basins (see Map 22-1).

The railway through the Zagros between Dezful and Qom was extended during World War II through Tabriz to the then Soviet border for the shipment of war matériel by the Allies to the Soviet Union. As part of the CENTO and RCD (Regional Cooperation for Development) railway from Istanbul to Karachi in Pakistan, a link was constructed to the Turkish border in the northwest and from Qom through Kashan and Yażd to Kerman. An extension is planned from Kerman to Zahedan to link with the Pakistani rail line to Quetta and Lahore. A separate line links Tehran and Mashhad along the southern piedmont of the Elburz and northern Khorasan mountains.

Ports. Despite a coastline of 1,555 miles/2,500 km from the Shatt al-Arab to the Pakistan border, Iran has surprisingly few good harbors for large port installations. Since the main population and development centered near the head of the Gulf even in antiquity, Iran's major ports lie in the arc from Khorramshahr to Bushehr; Bandar-e Abbas is an outlier on the Strait of Hormuz; and Chah Bahar (sometimes Bandar Beheshti) was developed during the 1980–1988 war as an outlet on the Indian Ocean for the southeast (see Map 22-3). The northern Gulf ports were further expanded during the 1960s and 1970s, although expansion could not keep up with utilization. Whereas Iraq's ports are concentrated along its narrow window on the Gulf, Iran had the wartime advantage over Iraq of having ports away from the focus of fighting and beyond normal air attacks. Bandar-e Abbas thus became a major general port. On the Caspian coast, Bandar-e Anzali (see Map 22-1) is the leading port for fishing and trade with the other Caspian Sea littorals.

Trade. Although in normal times Iran's imports include a range of contemporary industrial and consumer goods, the country's exports are overwhelmingly petroleum, petroleum products, and related items, by both volume and value, and Iran's oil exports became a crucial issue in the tanker war of the late 1980s. Petroleum customers vary appreciably from year to year, but regularly include Japan, the Netherlands, India, Germany, and Turkey. Imported products—machinery, iron and steel products, transport equipment, grains, textiles, and chemicals—come primarily from Germany, Japan, Turkey, and Britain. Weapons and ammunition have been a substantial share of imports during the last three decades, and armaments imports in 1992 approached the level reached under the shah in the 1970s. Despite its condemnation of the former regime for squandering Iranian wealth on weapons, the fundamentalist republican government was vigorously buying submarines from Russia, missiles from North Korea, tanks from several sources, and missiles and other arms from China, which also supplied nuclear technology.[17]

Regional and Global Relations

Long before petroleum was found in southwestern Iran, the Iranian Plateau played an important geopolitical role both locally and internationally. On the contemporary scene, Iran's geopolitical position and its place in world oil production require that the country seek a policy balance among the main foci of its interests: to the southwest, the Gulf states, specifically the Gulf Cooperation Council (GCC) but also Iraq; to the north, the new republics emerging from the disintegrated Soviet Union—those in both the Caucasus and central Asia, as well as Russia and the Ukraine; its longtime partners from the former Central Treaty Organization (CENTO) and Regional Cooperation for Development (RCD), Turkey and Pakistan; Western Europe, specifically the EEC but also such other important non-European trading partners as Japan; and, despite the mutual recriminations, the United States, which Iranian hardliners have labeled "the Great Satan" since 1978. Moreover,

Iran must seek this multifaceted foreign policy balance while trying to maintain a delicate internal equilibrium between militant, isolationist fundamentalists and pragmatic moderates.

By late 1991, Iran warily took steps to achieve a multilateral rapprochement and to reenter the international community after more than a decade of economic and political isolation. It liberalized trade, encouraged foreign firms to enter into joint ventures, invited foreign oil companies to participate in oil operations and exploration, moderated political rhetoric, influenced the release of all Western hostages in Lebanon, and restored many of its ruptured diplomatic relations. It restored ties with Western European countries, including the United Kingdom, for example, despite British indignation over Iranian death threats against Salman Rushdie, author of the allegedly sacrilegious novel *Satanic Verses.* U.S.-Iranian relations had not been restored by mid-1993.

For centuries prior to the breakdown of the Soviet Union in 1990–1991, Iran's grand strategy signified the fact that the state was geopolitically compressed between the dynamic spheres of interest and influence of imperial Russia and imperial Britain. Finding itself both goal and buffer, Iran achieved self-preservation by exploiting its dual role and playing one power against the other. After the rise of the Soviet Union and the advent of the cold war, Iran in the mid-1950s became a vital geopolitical player when the shah elected an anti-Soviet stance as a member of the Baghdad Pact/CENTO and the Northern Tier and as an overt ally of the United States. After 1979, Iran held both the Soviets and the West at arm's length until the collapse of the USSR. That collapse completely transformed—but did not eliminate—the geopolitical function of Iran.

New Eurasian Republics. In December 1991, Iran recognized eleven of the new successor republics and especially vigorously sought friendly relations with the republics of the Caucasus and central Asia. These areas are often thought of by Iranian nationalists as part of Iran-zamin and were mostly Iranian territory prior to 1826 west of the Caspian and 1876 east of the Caspian. They still preserve some Iranian cultural traits. Manifesting its interest in the emerging polities, Iran

promoted a new Caspian Council in early 1992 that links Iran, Turkmenistan, Kazakhstan, Azerbaijan, and Russia.[18] Both Turkmenistan and Kazakhstan are important in Iran's major Silk Route Project, linking Iran with China. Iran promoted and offered financing for rail links between Mashhad and Ashgabat (Ashkhabad), capital of Turkmenistan, and Dushanbe, capital of Tajikistan, and began work on the Mashhad-Sarakhs link in May 1992. Iran also championed membership of the central Asian republics in the Economic Cooperation Organization (ECO), the outgrowth of the RCD, created in 1964 with Iran, Pakistan, and Turkey.[19]

Regional. Although revolutionary Iran withdrew from CENTO in 1979 and thereby precipitated the organization's collapse, Iran maintained ties with Turkey and Pakistan and loosely continued participation in the RCD (now the ECO—see above). Communications with the West through Turkey were vital during the Iran-Iraq war. Iran tentatively planned an export oil pipeline through its Azerbaijan province to Turkey's Gulf of Iskenderun during the 1980s, but the plans were later abandoned.

Although relations between Iran and the GCC were strained from the beginning, since GCC states supported Iraq in the 1980s Gulf war, Iran moved rapidly to infuse cordiality into the relations after 1988 and especially after 1991. Ties were broken with Saudi Arabia in 1988 because of violence involving Iranians in Mecca, and although they were restored in March 1991, they were again strained a year later when the Abu Musa dispute resurfaced as Iran imposed its military control on the island in April 1992 and informed Sharjah that it would restrict travel to Abu Musa. Toward the northwest, Iran has maintained an incongruous link with Syria, which would logically have been expected to support the sister Arab and sister Baathist state of Iraq against the non-Arab, Shii state of Iran during the 1980s. The anomaly rests on the conflict between factions of the Baath party and competition for leadership of the Arab Mashriq. In return, Iran supports Syria's control of Lebanon. Iran's tortured war and subsequent turnabout relations with Iraq have been discussed earlier; however, worth noting is the fact that after Iraq's

1990 invasion of Kuwait and its offer to accept Iran's conditions for a peace treaty, the two antagonists resumed full diplomatic relations in October of that year.

Israel had reciprocal relations with Iran prior to 1979 through contracts for consulting and construction work on irrigation and other agricultural projects and through purchases of Iranian petroleum, delivered at Elat. In the post-revolutionary period, especially during the Iran-Iraq war, Israel has supplied Iran with weapons, at times with the cooperation of the United States. Officially, Iran denounces Israeli policies in the region as anti-Islamic. Israel periodically makes attacks on Iranian-backed Hizballah groups that operate against Israeli and Israeli-backed forces in southern Lebanon, including the Israeli-occupied so-called security zone.

Global. Britain's long-standing relations with Iran in both the political and economic spheres deteriorated after the 1951–1953 oil dispute. However, those relations were much better during the 1980s than those with other Western powers and were moderately cordial in the early 1990s. This was not the case with U.S. relations. After the U.S. Central Intelligence Agency assisted in restoring the shah to power in 1953, U.S.-Iranian cooperation lasted for 25 years, during which time this "island of stability" in the Middle East became the United States' "chosen instrument"—as it was referred to at the time. Huge quantities of military equipment—jet fighters, helicopters, tanks, artillery, naval craft—and related training programs equipped Iran for a leading military role in the Gulf. The U.S. position toward Iran inadvertently helped precipitate the downfall of the shah and the success of the Islamic fundamentalist revolution, as a widespread backlash emerged in Iran against the role of the United States. Following the unprecedented taking of American Embassy hostages in 1979 and the acrimonious break in U.S.-Iranian relations,[20] formal relations were still broken in mid-1993.

Epilogue

During the first half of 1993, the Middle East continued to exhibit (1) the perennial problems of the Arab-Israeli dispute, although they were rather subdued by the ongoing Middle East peace process; (2) the tangled aftermath of the 1990–1991 Gulf war; (3) the nettlesome manifestations of religious extremism, including ultraorthodox Judaism and Islamic fundamentalism; and (4) the endless round of competition for regional leadership. All of these were suddenly overshadowed in late August by the revelation of eight months of secret negotiations between representatives of the Palestine Liberation Organization (PLO) and the government of Israel. Seventeen rounds of talks, mostly in quiet areas of Norway, produced a Declaration of Principles providing for dramatic changes in the status of Gaza and the West Bank. Significantly, the preamble stated that the two parties "agree that it is time to put an end to decades of confrontation and conflict."

Subsequent to the revelations, there followed two weeks of institutional conferences and votes, then an exchange of letters of mutual recognition, after which Israeli leaders and PLO chairman Yasser Arafat met in Washington, D.C., and signed the accord in a historic ceremony on the White House lawn on September 13. Old enemies transcended decades of bitterness, shook hands, and promised a brighter future.

The accord provides for local elections for a Palestinian Council that would govern Palestinians in the West Bank and Gaza for a transitional period of not more than five years. The process would lead to a permanent settlement based on United Nations resolutions 242 and 338. Territorially, the interim period would begin with Gaza and the town of Jericho (see Map 15-1). A Palestinian police force would handle security among Palestinians, but Israeli forces would remain in the territories to handle security for the Israeli settlers and for the borders. Several agencies would deal with electricity, water, land, ports, trade, environment, and other concerns.

Deliberately left vague are such delicate problems as the future status of Jerusalem, refugee right of return or compensation, the future of Jewish settlements, and geographic links between the territories. Later agreements will have to spell out regulations for citizenship, travel, currency, bureaucracy, and similar arrangements.

The parties involved and outside observers were well aware that difficulties lay ahead of this first step. As expected, demonstrations against and in support of the accord took place in Gaza and Jericho as well as in Tel Aviv and Damascus. Some extremist Palestinians declared that the agreement betrayed Palestinian aspirations, and they threatened to assassinate chairman Arafat. Opposition Likud bloc leaders in Israel declared they would abrogate the agreement if Likud returned to power, and some extremist Jewish settlers in the occupied territories threatened revolt. Libya, Iraq, and Iran condemned the entire process, but the Arab League and the GCC approved the agreement. Jordan and Israel signed an Agenda for Peace on September 14, and the Israeli-PLO action obviously acted as a catalyst for further bilateral negotiations. Israeli Prime Minister Rabin stopped in Morocco en route home and conferred with King Hassan. The impact has already been great, and other ramifications are to follow. The declaration altered the political and psychological maps of the region, and they cannot be the same again.

An update glance at individual major players in Middle East affairs as of September 20, 1993, may start with Iraq, which continued to be neither fully defiant nor fully cooperative with regard to the United Nations resolutions and specific terms of the cease fire ending the Gulf war. After two years of first resisting and then relenting under pressure, Iraq remained under UN sanctions, unable to market any substantial portion of its potential 3-million-bpd petroleum production. However, the possibility that Iraq might be allowed to begin selling modest amounts of oil to obtain funds for humanitarian and reparations purposes precipitated a sharp drop in world oil prices in mid-1993. Despite the fact that its economy was in shambles, its financial reserves drained, its currency almost worthless, and its international standing low, Iraq still refused to accede to the full range of UN demands and in particular refused to accept the new UN-surveyed boundary with Kuwait. Iraq did, however, reluctantly accept the forced "no-fly" zones in the north and south. The June 26, 1993, U.S. cruise-missile attack on the Iraqi intelligence headquarters in Baghdad was declared by the new Clinton administration as a warning to Iraq that its reported plot to assassinate former president George Bush would not go unpunished. Even so, President Saddam Husayn maintained firm control over his country, a leader still in power but no longer powerful.

Iran, still viewed cautiously by most other governments, was under few constraints and continued periodically to engage in defiant rhetoric and to support certain violent actions. Noteworthy were the attacks by Hizballah (Hezbollah) in several areas; the most publicized of these were in southern Lebanon and northern Israel. Evidence accumulated that Iran was working to develop a nuclear capability and to reconstruct the powerful military establishment of the time of the shah that the revolutionary Khomeini-led clerics so vigorously condemned in the late 1970s. Increasing petroleum sales were expected to underwrite huge military purchases, although economic conditions were deteriorating in the country. Relatively moderate President Hashemi Rafsanjani was reelected in apparently open elections in June. Iran, unrepentant about the 1978–1980 holding of American Embassy hostages as well as other acts and threats of violence and terrorism, continued to be censured by the United States. It was considered by the Clinton administration to be a sufficient threat to U.S. interests and to Israel that in May 1993 an administration spokesman announced a policy of "dual containment" against Iraq and Iran.

Jordan and Yemen have both continued to suffer serious economic consequences as a result of their seemingly puzzling failure to participate in the UN coalition against Iraq in 1990. Highly dependent directly and indirectly upon financial support and good will of Saudi Arabia and Gulf amirates, the Kingdom of Jordan and Republic of Yemen appeared to some Western observers to have acted against their national interests in assuming their stances vis-à-vis Iraq. But the position of Jordan's King Husayn in regional crises is often one of moderation and mediation, and the intensive economic ties Jordan developed with Iraq during the 1980s added to Jordan's motivations. The emotional support of President Saddam shown by groups in Jordan—especially Palestinians—in 1990–1991 was a frustrated response to the resonant note he struck in his denunciation of Israel, U.S. support of Israel, and Western interference in Gulf affairs. By May 1993, in an altered environment, both the ailing king of Jordan and the public broke with Iraq, thereby improving the atmosphere for restoration of rapport between Jordan and its traditional friends. As in Yemen, democratic elections introduced fresh political air into the country, with another, still more open, round of elections scheduled in the kingdom in November 1993.

Yemen even more than Jordan faced desperate economic conditions in mid-1993. The 800,000 Yemenis expelled from Saudi Arabia—plus others from Gulf amirates—could not possibly be absorbed into the modest Yemeni economy, and Yemeni-Saudi relations remained at their nadir. One bright spot in the Yemen economic picture is the forecast that petroleum production will exceed 300,000 bpd by the end of 1993. It is of major political significance that in April 1993 Yemen held the freest multiparty elections in the history of the Arabian Peninsula.

Kuwait, the real victim of Iraq's aggression in 1991, has found that media coverage of other physical damage it suffered has deemphasized the trauma suffered by Kuwaiti social and political institutions. Although normal oil production was restored far earlier than was originally forecast, political reform and assurance of human rights have continued to be very slow in coming. At least some human rights abuses have been spotlighted and are in the process of being improved. In parliamentary elections in 1992, opposition groups made a strong showing, but even so suffrage was greatly restricted. The State of Kuwait was struggling in mid-1993 to regain a national identity and social integrity. Kuwait gave former president George Bush a hero's welcome in April 1993, but during his visit a plot to assassinate Bush was discovered and thwarted.

Saudi Arabia, key local player in the Gulf war and traumatized by its war experience, continues to relate to many of its neighbors on the basis of those neighbors' stances in the crisis: bitter animosity toward Iraq, resentment toward Yemen and Jordan, and appreciation and friendship toward the Gulf states and Egypt and especially toward the United States (and other coalition members). Al Saud rulers face a frustrating dilemma, partly of their own making, in the opposing pressures from the young progressives, on the one hand, who seek liberalization and democratization, and the militant Islamist fundamentalists, on the other hand, who want to abolish modernization and Westernization and to establish a theocracy. Announcement in 1992 of plans for an advisory body was implemented in late August 1993 by King Fahd's appointment of a 60-man consultative council. Economically, the kingdom has sought to regain a balance after the huge expenditures of 1990–1991 and has continued to gear up for a sustained high level of petroleum production (Saudi Arabia supplied 26 percent of U.S. crude imports in July 1993).

Egypt suffered an increasingly serious challenge from Islamist extremists during the first half of 1993. The moderate government of President Husni Mubarak is, at a different level, suffering opposite pressures similar to those mentioned for Saudi Arabia. However, the three dynamics in Egypt include steadily worsening economic conditions, especially for the poorest social groups; opposition from more militant Arab states (and active enmity from Sudan) because of Egypt's cooperation with the United

States and other coalition members in the Gulf war; and especially the systematic terrorism by extremist Islamist groups against the government and the tourism industry. Claiming that the government is corrupt and secular, the extremists have set off relatively small explosions in restaurants, streets, and tourist sites, achieving one goal of wrecking tourism. The terrorism by Egyptian and other extremists spilled over in the United States in the car bombing of the New York World Trade Center towers on February 26, 1993, and later allegations of a plot among related militants to conduct similar bombings elsewhere in New York. The Egyptian government arrested a large number of suspects after massive sweeps in Greater Cairo and after summary military trials executed more than twelve of the convicted terrorists. In mid-1993 Egypt badly needed enormous amounts of economic aid and needed to take comparable degrees of institutional actions (including family planning) to emerge from economic straits. President Mubarak played an important role in urging approval of the 1993 Israeli-PLO accord by other Arab states.

Turkey profited from its relative removal from inter-Arab conflicts and continued to play an increasingly significant role in regional affairs—not only in the Middle East but also in southeastern Europe and Central Asia. Despite a steady monetary inflation, the Turkish economy was expanding appreciably in mid-1993. The sudden death of energetic President Turgut Özal in April brought former six-time prime minister Süleyman Demirel to the presidency and U.S.-educated economist Tansu Çiller to the prime ministry, the latter as the second woman top official in the Middle East and second in the entire Muslim world. The new team is expected to continue the Özal-defined hope to make Turkey the central power in a region stretching "from the Adriatic to the Great Wall of China."

A major development in Turkey in the spring of 1993 was a resurgence in May of the cycle of violence between Marxist Kurdish rebels (PKK) and Turkish authorities after a promising two-month truce. During the truce the Turkish government moved toward liberalizing its restrictions against expressions of Kurdish ethnicity. But in late May, PKK rebels killed 33 Turks in an attack on a bus, and in response Turkish forces killed 125 Kurds. In retaliation, on June 24, Kurds in Europe attacked Turkish embassies, consulates, and airline offices. The violence heightened Turkey's Kurdish dilemma: If it took action against the rebels, it was accused of violating human rights; if it did not take vigorous action, the PKK could seize control of southeastern Turkey.

Kurds in Iraq continued to enjoy their greatest freedom in many decades. Having elected their own "parliament" and benefiting from the protection of the coalition forces under the "no-fly" zone rules, they approached the autonomy they have so long sought from the Baghdad central government.

Syria maintained a low profile during the period and even declined to react when Israel's attack on Lebanon in July 1993 caused casualties among Syrian troops. In the peace process, President Hafiz al-Asad stood firm on Syria's claim for the return of the Golan Heights.

Israel was readjusting to the return to political power a year earlier of the Labor Party under Prime Minister Yitzhak Rabin after fifteen years of Likud Party rule under prime ministers Menachem Begin and Yitzhak Shamir. The change brought two major policy shifts: a significant reduction in building new Jewish settlements in the occupied territories and an announced willingness to negotiate seriously in the regional peace process and to exchange land for genuine peace. Jewish immigration from the former Soviet lands slowed to a trickle. Even so, the United States agreed to the long-debated $10 billion loan guarantee for absorbing the immigrants, and Israel announced that the funds would be used for expanding the state's infrastructure and industrial capacity. In May 1993 former air force general Ezer Weizman replaced Chaim Herzog as president. Having been a "dove" for several years and having urged exchange of land for peace in the past, President Weizman was considered as complementing Prime Minister Rabin with regard to the peace process.

In another arena, the level of violence in southern Lebanon escalated to the highest in a decade when in late July 1993 Iranian-backed Hizballah guerrillas clashed with Israeli soldiers in an ongoing struggle over operations in the strip of Lebanese territory Israel occupies, partly by proxy, as a so-called security zone (see Map 13-1). By the time Israel ceased its bombing and artillery fire on July 31, more than 125 Lebanese had been killed, more than 500 wounded, and 250,000 had fled northward to escape the pounding. The Israeli army announced that two Israelis were killed by the Katyusha rockets. There was cautious optimism in late 1993 that the impetus toward peace would supersede the cycle of violence long typical of southern Lebanon.

Notes

Chapter 1

1. Cressey 1960.

2. See especially Pearcy 1964 (Pearcy was geographer, U.S. Department of State, at the time). Also relevant are Davison 1960 and Keddie 1972.

3. William B. Fisher 1978.

4. Beaumont, Blake, and Wagstaff 1988.

Chapter 2

1. Whittlesey 1929.

2. Whalen and Pease 1992. In line with the Arabian discoveries was the finding of a humanoid jawbone in 1991 near Tbilisi, Georgia, that was dated to 900,000 years ago. Another dating gave the bone an age of 1.6 million years. *New York Times,* Feb. 3, 1992.

3. A *tell* is termed a *tepe* or *chega* in Persian, *hüyük* in Turkish, and *kom* in Egyptian usage.

4. The Wendorf team found evidence that indicated, through laboratory dating, much earlier cultivation in the Nile Valley. See Wendorf and Schild 1980.

5. See Schmandt-Bessarat 1978 and other articles by her. See also the readable but scholarly Redman 1978, with its attention to environmental factors.

6. See Bibby 1969.

7. The original title of *Tales of the Arabian Nights* was *The Thousand and One Nights.* These charming stories, which include such familiar tales as those about Sindbad the Sailor and Ali Baba and the Forty Thieves, reveal many aspects of medieval Islamic culture. For good historical coverage of this period see Fisher and Ochsenwald 1990 and Hourani 1991.

Chapter 3

1. Technical terms not explained in the text are defined in the Glossary. See also the simplified geological time chart at the end of the book.

2. The theory of plate tectonics has been a major focus of earth science since the late 1950s. Simplified presentations are given in most leading atlases, and evolving aspects are discussed regularly in many journals, e.g., *Scientific American.* See the National Geographic Society 1983 and 1990. No single work in English covers the geomorphology of the Middle East, but see several studies listed in the Bibliography (Brown and Coleman 1972; U.S. Geological Survey 1966–1967, 1975, and 1989; Said 1962; and the very technical Dixon and Robertson 1984). Vita-Finzi 1986 is scientific yet readable and uses many examples and illustrations from the Middle East and North Africa.

3. El-Baz 1992, 74.

4. See Williams et al. 1991, El-Baz 1992, and Earle 1992.

5. Kreiger 1988 is a readable account of several aspects of the Dead Sea and has a very useful bibliography.

6. Both rivers are examined in detail in Kolars and Mitchell 1991. See also Naff and Matson 1984, 83–101.

Chapter 4

1. Factors and elements of Middle East climate are examined in Taha et al. 1981 and Rudloff 1981. Interesting data are in the Arabian American Oil Company n.d. (ca. 1978), which is unfortunately hard to find. Additional climate maps and diagrams are included in most good world atlases, including Espenshade 1990.

2. Mandaville 1990, quoting Saudi Arabia's Ministry of Agriculture and Water data.

3. Several sources describe the system, including Espenshade 1990.

Chapter 5

1. See Zohary 1962 and others of his many studies. Hills 1966 has general coverage of vegetation in arid lands. The interrelationships between plants and soils are also examined in Hills, and soils from an agricultural viewpoint are studied in Clawson, Landsberg, and Alexander 1971. Two sheets of the UNESCO "Soil

Map of the World" (1:5 mill.) cover the Middle East: VII-1 and V-2. A major new contribution to the flora of eastern Arabia is Mandaville 1990.

2. See Mandaville 1990, 16; Schulz and Whitney 1986; and Mandaville n.d.

Chapter 6

1. Of many useful studies of peoples, religions, and languages of the Middle East, a particularly helpful one is Weekes 1984, which has a bibliography for each people. Non-Muslims are included in Longrigg 1970, Bates and Rassam 1983, Eickelman 1981, and Gulick 1983. Hourani 1947 is dated but is still useful. Relatively up-to-date statistics of peoples within individual countries are given in the annual *Britannica World Data*.

2. Betts 1988 is a concise and useful study of the Druzes. For more details see Abu-Izzedin 1984.

3. For a popular account see Hitchens 1992. See also *Christian Science Monitor*, Jan. 25, 1993.

Chapter 7

1. J. D. Held 1979. Studies of Middle East land use that are more general include Clawson, Landsberg, and Alexander 1971, Askari and Cumming 1976, and Beaumont and McLachlan 1985. The crucial role of water is studied in Gischler 1979 and in Naff and Matson 1984. The UN's FAO *Production Yearbook*, published annually, is indispensable for production data.

2. For interesting discussions of Bedouins and camels see Dickson 1949, Arabian American Oil Company 1980, Bulliet 1975, and Hills 1966.

Chapter 8

1. Hundreds of sources cover various aspects of Middle East oil both in general and for respective producing states. PennWell's annual *International Petroleum Encyclopedia* (IPE) is very useful. (PennWell also publishes the *Oil and Gas Journal*.) Arabian American Oil Company 1980 and earlier editions are authoritative and available. Exxon 1984 is a handy, concise discussion with good maps. Danielsen 1982 looks at OPEC. Peterson 1983 examines regional oil and politics. For solid minerals, refer to the Bureau of Mines *Minerals Yearbooks*, especially *Middle East* 1989 and *Africa* 1989, which actually were published in 1992 and include information from 1990 and 1991. They also include some petroleum information. The discussion also embodies some material gathered directly in the field and not published elsewhere. For a readable best-seller account, see Yergin 1991.

2. Statistics on reserves and production differ among sources, and criteria for estimating reserves vary among companies and countries. "Proved" reserves are those that engineering evidence indicates can be commercially produced with reasonable certainty with normal techniques. "Probable" reserves are those whose existence is less well known but that are expected to be commercial in the future. Some companies also include "possible" reserves. A standard and available source is the annual *International Petroleum Encyclopedia*.

Most countries report reserves (and production) in barrels (bbl) of 42 U.S. gallons, but some report in metric tons (mt), and equivalents are not always precise. One mt is equal to 7.31 bbl of average gravity crude but may vary considerably with variations in gravity. Also, some information may be kept confidential, thus skewing other information.

Chapter 9

1. See *New York Times*, Sept. 8, 1992.

2. See Airport Operators Council International periodic reports and UN ICAO annual reports.

3. The material covered in this chapter has been the subject of scores of studies since the late 1960s. For a historical perspective, see Issawi 1982. Sayigh 1978 explores the economies in depth. Latest data on production, transportation, and trade are in *Foreign Economic Trends; Britannica World Data; World Factbook; Middle East and North Africa*; UN annuals; and *Middle East Economic Digest*.

Chapter 10

1. Several works on Middle East cities have appeared since the mid-1960s, most of which have been collections of papers given at conferences and symposia; for example, Saqqaf 1987 and Blake and Lawless 1980. Bonine 1977 contemplates the Islamic urban experience. English 1966 and Bonine 1979 focus on Iranian urban development, and Grill 1984 looks at Arabian Peninsula urbanization. Abu-Lughod 1971 examines Cairo. Ragette 1983 considers the reconstruction of Beirut. AlSayyad 1991 looks at the genesis of Arab Muslim urbanism.

2. Christaller's classical theory of central places, the most widely applied model for the study of the hierarchy of settlements, is of limited applicability in much of the Middle East. See Christaller 1966.

3. Vance 1977 takes a stimulating philosophical look at the city, primarily the Western urban phenomenon.

4. See Soffer and Minghi 1986.

Chapter 11

1. Mackinder 1904, which has been reprinted in several political geography studies. Sir Halford expanded and revised his thoughts in Mackinder 1919 and again in a 1943 *Foreign Affairs* article. An underrated challenge to Mackinder came in Spykman 1944. The Rimland challenge is discussed later.

2. The T. E. Lawrence saga was much celebrated during the 1920s and had a renaissance in the 1970s and 1980s. In the extensive literature about him, an excellent authorized biography is Wilson 1990, which places Lawrence in the context of the momentous events of the period.

3. See Howard 1963.

4. Ethnicity and the state have been examined in many studies. For one that focuses on the Middle East, see Esman and Rabinovich 1988.

5. Middle East state development has been analyzed in numerous recent studies. For examples, see Netton 1986, Salamé 1987, and Ben-Dor and Dewitt 1987.

6. Hartshorne 1950.

7. C. C. Held 1951.

8. Jones 1954.

9. The Iraq-Kuwait territorial dispute prior to 1990 is discussed in Long 1978, Kelly 1980, Crystal 1990, Bishku 1991, and Finnie 1992.

10. Details are given in Taryam 1987, which includes a useful bibliographical essay covering good sources on the islands and on the UAE.

11. The subject is examined from different viewpoints in dozens of studies, for example, Curtis 1981; Mortimer 1982; Voll 1982; Korany and Dessouki et al. 1984; Salamé 1987; Esman and Rabinovich 1988; and Andersen, Seibert, and Wagner 1990.

12. The Dreyfus trial is covered in numerous encyclopedias and histories of Zionism.

13. Aharon David Gordon, "Some Observations," in Hertzberg 1969. Other concepts of Zionism are discussed in Avineri 1981 and in some readings in Khalidi 1971. See also Selzer 1970.

14. Zangwill 1901.

15. The Balfour Declaration has been analyzed in many books and articles. The massive and authoritative Stein 1983 (a reprint of the 1961 edition), by a man associated with WZO, is the most detailed.

16. Figures are from Palestine Human Rights Center and *Christian Science Monitor,* Mar. 19, 1993. Three useful books on the *intifadah* are Peretz 1990, Schiff and Yaari 1989, and Nassar and Heacock 1990.

17. Begin 1977 includes an account by that author, who was commander of Irgun Zvai Leumi, the terrorist group that conducted the massacre. Begin was later prime minister of Israel. For a quite different version, see the report by the local Red Cross representative, Jacques de Reynier, in Khalidi 1971, 761–766.

18. Among several studies of the origins and ramifications of the Iran-Iraq war, an excellent one is Khadduri 1988. See also Chubin and Tripp 1988 and Karsh 1990.

19. The Gulf crisis and war were among the most intensively covered conflicts in history. Various daily and weekly news journals reported developments in minute detail. A useful, full chronology that condenses developments from reports in the *New York Times* and other media is given in the *Middle East Journal* 45, nos. 1, 2, and 3 (Winter, Spring, and Summer 1991). Also, the *Middle East Journal* 45, no. 1, has four excellent articles pertaining to the Gulf crisis.

20. Much of the information on Iraq's "eco-terrorism" is covered in media reports of the period, but a useful, concise report is Williams et al. 1991, which has excellent space imagery; see also Canby 1991 and Earle 1992.

21. See Howard 1974.

22. Kennan 1987 is a reprint of the widely read 1947 article and is accompanied by comments and a retrospect by that author.

Chapter 12

1. Devlin 1983 is a useful, concise survey of Syria. Khoury 1987 is an excellent account of Syria as mandate. Hopwood 1988 examines independent Syria's political and cultural evolution.

2. Syrians also celebrate May 17, the day on which the last French forces evacuated Syria.

3. See Batuta 1981, van Dam 1978, Van Dusen 1972, and N. N. Lewis 1949.

4. *New York Times,* Dec. 15, 1992.

5. *Foreign Economic Trends,* Syria, 91–19, Mar. 1991. See also Perthes 1992.

6. Data supplied by Syrian engineers at the Euphrates Dam during my visit on June 8, 1990.

7. See the excellent and detailed analyses in Kolars and Mitchell 1991.

8. For a partial explanation of U.S.-Syrian discord, see Little 1990. Syria blamed the United States for frustrating its progress because of periodic U.S. actions, overt and covert, that evidenced the incongruity of U.S.-Syrian interests and policies. Consonance was impossible between the Middle East's most anti-Israel and pro-USSR state and the world's most pro-Israel and anti-USSR power.

Chapter 13

1. Estimates of the Palestinian population vary widely for any country but especially for Lebanon (and, in the early 1990s, for Kuwait). The UNRWA estimate in early 1991 was 302,094, but Lebanese officials gave higher estimates (*Christian Science Monitor,* Apr. 8, 1991).

2. See also Cobban 1985, "Thinking About Lebanon."

3. See el Khazen 1985 and Bureau of Mines *Middle East* 1989 (1992).

4. Although the fighting in Lebanon was not across international boundaries and was "internal" or "civil" in many ways, one or another faction was continually and openly stimulated and supported by outside states and groups, especially Israel, Syria, Libya, Iraq, Iran, Saudi Arabia, and other Gulf states, not to mention most of the Great Powers.

5. N. N. Lewis 1953.

6. Ragette 1983 and *Christian Science Monitor,* Sept. 2, 1992.

7. Gulick 1967. Maps in the book show the differences between street patterns of the old city and modern developments.

8. Mikesell 1969.

9. Hudson 1971.

10. Many studies analyze Lebanon's problems leading to and during the civil war of the 1970s and 1980s, although readers must beware of some authors' biases. Useful are Haddad 1985, which is concise and philosophical but insightful; Khalidi 1979, by a moderate Palestinian intellectual; Rabinovich 1984, giving a moderate Israeli scholar's analysis; the entire issue of the *Middle East Journal* 38, no. 2 (Spring 1984); Friedman 1989 and Fisk 1990, two very good journalistic accounts, one American and one British; Gordon 1983, a concise general study of Lebanon, as is Salibi 1988; and Norton 1987.

11. See Sahliyeh 1986, Friedman 1989, Fisk 1990, and Rabinovich 1984.

12. See Kahan Commission 1983.

13. Even straightforward geographical writings on Cyprus by Cypriots show how viewpoints often differ sharply between Greek Cypriots and Turkish Cypriots. See Attalides 1979 for a moderate Greek Cypriot view. Denktash 1982 is an opposing view by the leader of the Turkish Cypriot community. See also the *Cyprus Country Study* 1980, the brief presentation in CIA 1973 for a concise coverage of the island before the emergence of north Cyprus, and Reddaway 1986. Stasis and Mavrocordatos 1989 is a secondary school–level book but is still useful.

Chapter 14

1. Useful for information on this period are G. A. Smith 1935, Naval Intelligence Division 1943, Baly 1957, and Aharoni 1967.

2. See Naval Intelligence Division 1943, R. Allen 1974, and Wilson 1987.

3. Tribalism is discussed at some length in *Jordan Country Study* 1991.

4. In addition to my own extensive field research during a score of visits to Jordan over 33 years, for this section I drew on Naval Intelligence Division 1943, Baly 1957 and 1987, Orni and Efrat 1971, and G. A. Smith 1935.

5. A handy, concise account of these sites is given in Khouri 1988.

6. See Salameh 1990, Kolars 1990, and Cooley 1984 and 1992.

7. Gubser 1983 is useful for information of this type. I should also like to thank the Jordan Information Bureau in Washington, D.C., for its extraordinary assistance.

Chapter 15

1. "Palestine" is universally used to apply to the general area between the Mediterranean Sea and the Jordan River and from Metulla in the north (at the northern tip of Israel) to Elat at the head of the Gulf of Aqabah.

2. Few of the hundreds of books on Israel focus on regional coverage. Survey of Israel (*Atlas of Israel*) 1985 is invaluable, and it is complemented by Orni and Efrat 1971. Also useful is Wolffsohn 1987 and the small but authoritative Israel Pocket Library 1973.

3. See Ashbel 1949.

4. Best coverage of this topic is Zohary 1962.

5. Israel's water problems are treated in many studies, but see Cooley 1984 and 1992; Kolars 1990; Dillman 1989; *Christian Science Monitor,* Mar. 14, 1990, Aug. 19, 1991, and Sept. 14, 1992.

6. *Near East Report,* Feb. 17, 1992, 44; and Dillman 1989.

7. University of Haifa geographer Arnon Soffer, quoted in *Christian Science Monitor,* Mar. 14, 1990. See also Dillman 1989.

8. See sections 3–5 in the Israel Pocket Library *Immigration and Settlement* volume. Sachar 1976, 395–424, gives slightly different figures. See also Friedlander and Goldscheider 1979.

9. See Sachar 1987, 833–835 and 232–234; *Israel Country Study* 1990, 88–91; and the Israel Pocket Library *Immigration and Settlement* volume, 59–61.

10. See the five-part series on Soviet Jewish immigration in the *Christian Science Monitor,* July 25–August 1, 1991.

11. See Arian 1989.

12. The problem is examined in Leslie 1971. See also Arian 1989, especially 22–24. Elazar 1989 examines the Sephardim in detail.

13. See Lustick 1980.

14. Compare Falah 1992 and Graicer 1992 re "mirror housing" and other discrimination. For discrimination in employment, see the *Jerusalem Post,* International Edition, Nov. 23, 1991.

15. Kahane 1981 voices a radical view but articulates demands by many Israeli extremists that all Arabs must be expelled from Eretz Yisrael. Kahane, who was formerly leader of the U.S. extremist Jewish Defense League, was assassinated in New York in 1991.

16. The Israeli economy requires close monitoring because of its rapid changes. Information is available in the *New York Times, Christian Science Monitor,* and *Washington Post* daily and in the weekly International Edition of the English-language *Jerusalem Post* and in the London *Economist.* The government's Israel Information Centre in Jerusalem publishes *Facts About Israel* annually, and good background is in the *Economy* volume of the Israel Pocket Library.

17. The subject is discussed in detail in *Israel* Country Study 1990, especially in Chapters 3 and 5; see also Black and Morris 1991, Hersch 1991, Cockburn and Cockburn 1991, and the Israeli government's annual *Facts About Israel.*

18. *Israel* Country Study 1990, 316; Cockburn and Cockburn 1991, 291–292; and *New York Times,* Mar. 14, 1992.

19. The revelations were widely covered in news media at the time. See Hersch 1991; Black and Morris 1991, 437–443; and *Israel* Country Study 1990, 317–318.

20. Fully reported in the news media during late 1986 and early 1987, the affair may be studied in Tower Commission 1987.

21. Collins 1990. The subject is examined in more detail in el-Khawas and Abed-Rabbo 1984, as well as in a six-part series in the *Christian Science Monitor,* June 20–21, 24–25, and 27–28, 1991. U.S.-Israeli relations are examined—praised or damned—in numerous studies. Safran 1978 is a widely used, detailed study for its time by a former Israeli who became a U.S. citizen and later advised Congress and other agencies on the Middle East. Spiegel 1985 is also an academic study of relations, examined administration by administration. Lenczowski 1990, written by a longtime scholar of Middle East affairs, looks at successive presidential policies also academically but from a somewhat differ-

ent viewpoint than Spiegel. Among his several well-balanced studies, Quandt 1986 focuses on the critical Camp David arrangements. Kenen 1981 gives a sympathetic view of the Zionist lobby in the United States. Mr. Kenen was, indeed, founder and longtime chairman of the American Israel Public Affairs Committee (AIPAC), the Israeli lobby in Washington, and editor of the AIPAC-associated *Near East Report.* A later editor of *Near East Report* recounts AIPAC's achievements in Bard 1991. An opposing view is Curtiss 1990, written by the editor of the *Washington Report on Middle East Affairs,* as is Findley 1989, by a former Republican congressman from Illinois whose reelection is widely considered to have been defeated by AIPAC-coordinated efforts. Opposing views on U.S.-Israeli relations are given in the weekly *Near East Report* and the American Educational Trust's monthly *Washington Report on Middle East Affairs.*

22. See Cockburn and Cockburn 1991 and *Washington Report on Middle East Affairs* 11, no. 5 (Nov. 1992): 12, 86.

23. See Aronson 1990, Benvenisti 1986, Nakhleh 1988, and Shehadeh 1985. Later coverage is found in *Israel* Country Study 1990. The several useful studies of the West Bank that appeared in the early and middle 1980s preceded Jordan's dramatic renunciation of ties with the West Bank in July and August 1988. Although economic details have changed, basic aspects are still relevant in Peretz 1986, Benvenisti 1984 (and his later reports), Elazar's two 1982 works, Day 1986, Sandler and Frisch 1984, Richardson 1984, and W. W. Harris 1980. Figures for the precise area of the West Bank vary among sources, depending upon segments included (East Jerusalem, Metropolitan Jerusalem, Latrun, "No Man's Land," Mount Scopus as well as West Bank proper).

24. Most data regarding the occupied territories must be treated with caution and should be cross-checked. As is shown in Table 6-1, *Britannica World Data 1991* gives a West Bank population of 908,000 for 1990, and the 1992 edition gives 960,000, presumably excluding East Jerusalem. *World Factbook 1990* gives 1,058,122 as the population for 1990. I have standardized in Table 6-1, but a population of more than 1 million for the area is a widely accepted figure; this includes Palestinians in East Jerusalem but excludes Jewish settlers.

25. Like data on Palestinians, those on Jewish settlers and settlements are problematic and are often minimized or maximized to suit a given purpose. Inclusion or exclusion of figures on East Jerusalem makes a huge difference. Israel insists that the East Jerusalem as enlarged unilaterally by Israel in 1967 is part of Israel itself, but the claim is rejected by the United

Nations and virtually all of its members except Israel. For recent data see *World Factbook 1990* and *Jerusalem Post,* International Edition, Feb. 1, 1992.

26. Nakhleh 1988 and *Christian Science Monitor,* Sept. 14, 1992.

27. Benvenisti 1984, 19.

28. See Gharaibeh 1985 and Nakhleh 1980, both of which have been overtaken by events consequent to King Husayn's disengagement from the West Bank.

29. Nakhleh 1988, 210.

30. *World Factbook 1990.* However, Anthony Lewis in the *New York Times,* Jan. 30, 1992, gives the number of Jewish settlers as 4,500, in spacious settlements with sidewalks, streetlights, running water, and, in one settlement, a horse-riding ring.

Chapter 16

1. The creation of Iraq is recounted in several studies (see Note 2 below), but the background given in Klieman 1970, Chapter 7, is especially relevant and includes the story of installing Faysal ibn Husayn as king of Iraq in 1921.

2. Among several good modern histories of Iraq see Marr 1985, Penrose and Penrose 1978, and Helms 1984. Several useful essays are included in Niblock 1982.

3. *Christian Science Monitor,* Mar. 25, 1991.

4. See *New York Times,* Jan. 24, 1993.

5. Discussed in Lees and Falcon 1952.

6. An intensive literature about the Kurds has developed during the past 25 years, especially in the early 1990s. Journalistic reports on the Kurds appeared daily during the spring and summer of 1991. More scholarly studies include Jwaideh 1960, O'Ballance 1973, Ghareeb 1981, Pelletiere 1984, Olson 1989, and Entessar 1992.

7. During field observations in Kurdistan in mid-1990, I visited the ruins of scores of the razed Kurdish villages and observed several of the new settlements. The sight left no doubt as to the scale of the project or about the government's determination to subdue the Kurds through reversing the geographical advantage.

8. The subject is well covered in Penrose and Penrose 1978.

Chapter 17

1. One of the first Saudi monographs on the country's archaeology is the elaborately illustrated al-Ansary 1982. Whalen and Pease 1992 discusses the Developed Oldowan tool findings.

2. The history of the interior of the Arabian Peninsula was little known until oil developments brought Arabia to world attention, and accurate, detailed his-

tory of the area is still limited. A useful concise account is in Arabian American Oil Company 1980. For more details, see Holden and Johns 1982. Some popular accounts are fanciful or spiteful.

3. See *New York Times,* Mar. 2, 1992, for a full discussion of the reforms, including provisions of the constitution. *New York Times,* Mar. 30, 1992, covers the king's announcement regarding elections. *New York Times,* Mar. 9 and Jan. 30, 1992, discuss the king's stand against militants of both extremes. *Christian Science Monitor,* Mar. 16, 1992, gives a critical evaluation of the reforms.

4. Coverage of Arabian regions and physical aspects is in Ministry of Agriculture and Water 1984; U.S. Geological Survey 1966–1967, 1975, and 1989; McKee 1979; Holm 1960; Brown and Coleman 1972; Brown 1972; Scoville 1979; Arabian American Oil Company 1980; and Farsi 1989.

5. Shamekh 1975 discusses Bedouins in the Qasim, and Altorki and Cole 1989 discusses development connected with Unayzah.

6. The readable Thesiger 1959 on the Rub al-Khali realm has become a classic.

7. The explosive and rapidly changing development of Saudi Arabia must be followed closely in relevant periodicals. It is well covered in the *Middle East Economic Survey* and the *Middle East Economic Digest.* The annual *Foreign Economic Trends* is excellent. Comprehensive statistics are given in the Kingdom of Saudi Arabia *Statistical Year Book.* Oil developments are given in Arabian American Oil Company 1980, Exxon 1984, Woodward 1988, Ali 1987, Nabir 1988, and *Aramco Annual Report.*

8. See the well-regarded Vidal 1955.

9. Although pro-Israel U.S. congressmen opposed the sale of 72 F-15s to Saudi Arabia in early April 1992, the issue of U.S. jobs in a tight election campaign led to a congressional compromise in September 1992, when a trade-off was arranged for Israel to receive both the much-debated $10 billion loan guarantee and also a broad offsetting transfer of weapons and technology. See *New York Times,* Aug. 13, Sept. 12, and Sept. 15, 1992.

Chapter 18

1. L. S. Amery, in his foreword to Wilson 1928, ix.

2. After development in the Gulf boomed, scores of studies on the subject appeared. For development and general coverage see Cottrell 1980, Anthony 1975, Long 1978, Niblock 1980, Crystal 1990, Zahlan 1989, *Persian Gulf States* Country Study 1984, and Netton 1986. Netton also contains an excellent essay on source materials. The Gulf Cooperation Council is analyzed in Twinam 1992.

3. Refer to Scoville 1979 and to Lorimer 1915.

4. Studies of the fabulous Gulf oil industry are also legion. Gulf petroleum is discussed in the studies already cited and also in Akins 1981, Penn Well's annual *International Petroleum Encyclopedia*, Exxon 1984, and Yergin 1991.

5. Many studies understandably link oil and Gulf security. In addition to the works cited in Notes 2 and 4, see Peterson 1983, Cordesman 1984, Ramazani 1979, Doran and Buck 1991, and Sindelar and Peterson 1989. Atherton 1985 pertains to the entire Middle East.

6. The classic work on the old Kuwait is the massive compendium Dickson 1949, followed by his *Kuwait and Her Neighbors.*

7. Crystal 1990, 39.

8. See Middle East Research Institute (MERI) report on Kuwait (1985), Al-Sabah 1980, Ffrench and Hill 1971, *Persian Gulf States* Country Study 1984, and Crystal 1990.

9. *Christian Science Monitor,* Mar. 19, 1991.

10. Return of stolen items is discussed in the *Washington Post Weekly,* Mar. 1, 1992, and *Christian Science Monitor,* June 17, 1991.

11. Among the many articles on the environmental catastrophe engendered by the oil spills and well fires in Kuwait, useful and easily available coverage, including ground photographs and space imagery, is given in Williams 1991, Canby 1991, and Earle 1992. An authoritative assessment with more perspective is given in *International Petroleum Encyclopedia* 1992, 222–229.

12. *Economist,* Feb. 29, 1992, 45; *New York Times,* Apr. 17, 1992; and *Christian Science Monitor,* May 29, 1992, which warns of the creation of "an irredentist rallying cry" if the new border is forced on Iraq.

13. Gulf Oil Corporation merged with Chevron (formerly Standard Oil Company of California [Socal]) in 1984.

14. The problem is examined in detail in Lesch 1991; and in articles in *Christian Science Monitor,* Mar. 26, 1991; Apr. 17, 1991; June 26, 1991; Aug. 2, 1991; and Feb. 27, 1992. See also French and Hill 1971, 1–50.

15. The main island was called al-Awal in the past, whence the name Awali for the oil field and oil town. Believed to have been the ancient Dilmun, Bahrain was the classical Tylos; and, to add to the confusion, the name Bahrain was long applied to eastern Arabia as well as to the islands.

16. See Brunsden et al. 1979. For a popular but useful illustrated account of Bahrain well into its current development, see Abercrombie 1979. For more detailed examinations, see Lawson 1988 and Nugent and Thomas 1985.

17. Bibby 1969. The finds are on display in the small but interesting Bahrain museum.

18. Clarke 1990 covers the history and status of Bahrain oil in minute detail and includes very useful appendixes and bibliography.

19. See the detailed Landsat images in Yehia 1983, which also includes sectional topographic and geologic maps of Qatar.

20. Batanouny 1981 gives good, concise coverage of the Qatar environment, as well as detailed scientific coverage of the flora. Yehia 1983 discusses and illustrates the *rawdahs* and coastal features.

21. Among the growing number of studies on Qatar, see Zahlan 1979, Crystal 1990, Moorehead 1977 (popular, with photographs), *Persian Gulf States* Country Study 1984, and Cottrell 1980.

22. Although "amir" and "amirate" are the preferred transliterations and are generally used in this book, "emirates" is more widely accepted in the name of the UAE and is, at the risk of some confusion, used in this specific application.

23. In addition to coverage of the UAE cited in Notes 2, 4, and 5 above, see Khalifa 1979, the MERI report on the UAE (1985), el Mallakh 1981, Peck 1986, Taryam 1987, and Zahlan 1989. Peck is concise and broad in scope and also has a handy list of references.

24. The traditional claim that the British assumed control of the Gulf to suppress Arab piracy is disputed in al-Qasimi 1988.

25. See *Economist,* July 13–19, 1991, 81–82, and July 27–Aug. 2, 1991, 67–68.

Chapter 19

1. These two peninsula rimland states were the last to receive intensive attention after the opening of the region but are now becoming the subject of an increasing number of studies. In Oman the present sultan is encouraging field research—see C. H. Allen 1987 (with references for further reading), Anthony 1976, Zahlan 1989, Dutton and Winser 1987, Janzen 1986, *Oman* 1989, and Mandaville n.d. The former PDRY (South Yemen) is discussed in Stookey 1982 and Bidwell 1983. Bidwell covers both former Yemens authoritatively. Steffen et al. 1978, on North Yemen, is highly geographical as well as demographic, Dunbar 1992 examines the unification of the Yemens. (Dunbar was U.S. ambassador to Sana at the time of the merger.) See also Dresch 1989.

2. *New York Times,* Feb. 5, 1992; and *Christian Science Monitor,* Feb. 19, 1992.

3. Since Oman has never had a census, this estimate could be highly inaccurate. A census is scheduled for 1993.

4. See Dunbar 1992.

Chapter 20

1. Egypt is one of the best-analyzed countries in the Middle East. Recommended studies of post-1952 Egypt include Waterbury 1983, Cooper 1982, Hopwood 1982, Harris 1988, Makram-Ebeid 1989, Lorenz 1990, and *Egypt* Country Study 1991.

2. Although technical in many aspects, Said 1962 is useful for the landforms of Egypt. Dr. Said was formerly director of the Geological Survey of Egypt. For the 1992 Cairo earthquake see *New York Times,* Oct. 13, 1992.

3. Details are given in Naff and Matson 1984 and in Gischler 1979.

4. Several studies of the Fayyum (often spelled Fayoum) are outdated or difficult to find, but see Hewison 1989.

5. The evolution of the Nile is well covered in Said 1981, which is less technical than Said 1962.

6. See Benedick 1979.

7. Nile water problems and some details of the High Dam are discussed in Naff and Matson 1984. See also Fahim 1981, Haynes and Whittington 1981, and Waterbury 1979.

8. The excellent Hobbs 1989 discusses the physical environment of the Eastern Desert and focuses on the Bedouins of the area.

9. See Chitham 1986.

10. Awad 1954.

11. Hobbs 1989 is an in-depth study of the Maaza.

12. See Farah 1986.

13. See the useful Abu-Lughod 1971.

14. See Moore 1986.

15. See *Foreign Economic Trends* for Egypt, Mar. 1990. Many of the current economic data discussed below are from this source.

16. Discussion and data are given in *Foreign Economic Trends* for Egypt, Mar. 1990, and detailed data are in UN FAO 1991.

17. See *International Petroleum Encyclopedia* 1992 and previous years, as well as *Foreign Economic Trends* for Egypt, Mar. 1990 and previous issues.

18. See Bureau of Mines, *Africa,* 1989 (1992), 66–78.

19. Lorenz 1990 gives an excellent discussion of the subject, including an introductory chapter entitled "The Geographic and Historical Setting."

20. U.S. aid to Egypt increased dramatically after Camp David and is analyzed in Weinbaum 1983.

21. See Quandt 1990.

22. See an insider's analysis of this subject in El Hussini 1987. The author was a commodore in the Egyptian navy.

Chapter 21

1. A good, readable discussion is in Dewdney 1971, which also covers the general geography of Turkey. For technical geology, see Brinkmann 1976. For technical tectonics, see Dixon and Robertson 1984, which reveals the enormous complexity of Asia Minor's structure.

2. See Section 3, Dixon and Robertson 1984.

3. These and other sites are covered in Bean 1968.

4. For a detailed, scholarly, yet practical study of the many archaeological sites in Turkey see Akurgal 1970.

5. Erinç and Tunçdilek 1952.

6. See Pitcher 1972, a superb historical geography of the Ottoman Empire with excellent maps.

7. B. Lewis 1968 is a standard work on the evolution of modern Turkey.

8. For opposing viewpoints on Turkish treatment of the Armenians, see Jernazian 1990 and Gürün 1985.

9. A detailed study is Kolars 1968.

10. This interesting phenomenon is traced in Karpat 1976.

11. An excellent guidebook on Turkey, intelligently written and superbly illustrated, is *Turkey* 1989.

12. Development is concisely covered in G. S. Harris 1985. For more details and later coverage see Schick and Tonak 1987 (Part 3) and Hershlag 1988.

13. Relevant figures are included in the MERI report on Turkey (1985) and in the *Foreign Economic Trends* for Turkey, Feb. 1991.

14. The rest of this section is based on briefings by officials of the Turkish State Hydraulic Works (DSI) at Atatürk Dam in 1990 and on Kolars and Mitchell 1991.

15. Much of this minerals information is adapted from the invaluable Bureau of Mines *The Middle East* 1989 (1992), 86–109, which was published in 1992 and covers 1990 and early 1991. Turkish government sources speculate that petroleum reserves may be 2 billion barrels, three times the amount usually credited to Turkey (p. 109).

16. The fall of the lira (pound) is illustrated by the fact that when I had my first temporary assignment to Turkey in 1958, the lira exchanged at 9 to $1. During my latest fieldwork in mid-1990, the rate was 2,618 to $1. In March 1993 it was 9,262 to $1.

17. See the *Turkey* Country Study 1988, G. S. Harris 1985, and *Foreign Economic Trends* for Turkey 1988, 1989, 1990, and 1991.

Chapter 22

1. See Limbert 1987, Chapters 1 and 2.

2. For a focus on Fars, see Summers 1986. For gen-

eral coverage of archaeological sites, see Matheson 1973.

3. Limbert 1987 covers these developments as well as Iran in general, including Iran-zamin.

4. See *Christian Science Monitor,* Jan. 1, 1990, and Amuzegar 1992.

5. An excellent, comprehensive coverage of Iran's geography is in W. B. Fisher 1968. A concise treatment is given in Limbert 1987, Chapter 1.

6. In addition to the standard Defense Mapping Agency 1985, see Adamec 1976–1988. Numerous place-names were changed by the revolutionary Iranian authorities (see A Note on Transliteration).

7. Detailed studies are in Krinsley 1970.

8. Two useful studies regarding Iranian settlements are Bonine 1979 and English 1966.

9. Concise discussion of peoples and their distribution is given in Limbert 1987 and *Iran* Country Study 1989.

10. This complex topic is insightfully treated in Cottam 1979.

11. So many Armenians were employed in the American Embassy in Tehran before 1979 because of their education and adaptability, that some wags referred to it as the Armenian Embassy.

12. *Economist,* Feb. 13, 1987.

13. *Economist,* Aug. 2, 1987; *Iran* Country Study 1989, 82–83; and *Christian Science Monitor,* May 30, 1991.

14. See Bonine and Keddie, 1981; Limbert 1987, Chapters 1, 5, and 6; and *Iran* Country Study 1989, especially Chapter 3.

15. The Iranian economy has been analyzed from many perspectives. One admirable book-length study is Amirahmadi 1990. A more recent, concise examination is Amuzegar 1992, which specifically compares the prerevolutionary and postrevolutionary conditions and from which much of the following is adapted.

16. *Economist,* Nov. 22, 1986; *International Petroleum Encyclopedia* 1992, 100–103; and *New York Times,* Nov. 7, 1992.

17. *New York Times,* Nov. 7, 1992.

18. *Economist,* Feb. 29, 1992.

19. Ramazani 1992.

20. For a penetrating analysis of these relations by a leading scholar, see Bill 1988.

Glossary

See Index for page number of main discussion of most terms. For names of geological time periods (Pleistocene, Cretaceous, etc.), see the geological time chart at the end of this glossary.

Abbasid: pertaining to the Muslim Empire ruled by the Abbasid dynasty from Baghdad AD 750–1258.

Allah: God.

Alluvial: pertaining to river-deposited materials, especially fine silt and silt-clay laid down on floodplains and deltas such as those of the Nile.

Amir (emir): commander, prince, ruler. May have, but need not have, territorial jurisdiction.

Amirate (emirate): realm of an amir. In lower Gulf, also called shaykhdom.

Ashkenazim: Jews from central or eastern Europe, directly or by descent.

Ayatollah: "rightly guided by Allah." Title of respect for upper-ranking Shii clergyman. One title for the late Ruhollah Khomeini, former Iranian revolutionary leader.

Ayn: flowing spring, open sinkhole water supply, or flowing artesian spring.

Baath: Arab Renaissance [Revival] Party, separate branches of which control the governments of Iraq and Syria.

Basalt: a common type of lava—dark, fine-grained, extrusive volcanic rock. In original molten state, flows readily from fissures; covers large areas of the Levant and western Arabia.

Basement (or basement complex): massive, very ancient igneous and metamorphic rocks, usually Precambrian, very complex and underlying sedimentary strata.

Bbl: barrel, barrels. Standard barrel of oil contains 42 U.S. gal. (34.97 UK or imperial gal.).

Bedouin: pastoral Arab nomad of the desert; corruption of Ar. for "desert dweller."

Bpd: barrels per day (usually oil production).

C°: temperature in degrees Celsius or centigrade. Temperature in C° = Fahrenheit° minus 32 times 5/9. Temperature in F° = C° times 9/5 plus 32.

Caliph: from Ar. *khalifah,* "successor"—i.e., successor to Muhammad as head of the community of Islam, the *ummah* (q.v.).

Cuesta: linear ridge with steep escarpment on foreslope and with gentle backslope. Asymmetry results from erosion of outcrop of gently dipping resistant stratum. Successive cuestas are prominent features of central Arabia.

Desert: any area with scanty rainfall, little vegetation, and therefore limited agricultural use. May be plain, plateau, or mountains at any latitude. Area in Koeppen's BWh group (see Map 4-3).

DFLP: Democratic Front for the Liberation of Palestine, one of the more aggressive Palestinian guerrilla groups.

Dhow: general term for several types of traditional coastal sailing ships plying the waters around the Arabian Peninsula and parts of Indian Ocean.

Diaspora: dispersion. Usually refers to the dispersion of Jews from Palestine after AD 70. Also, Jews now outside Palestine constitute the Diaspora. Palestinian refugees sometimes apply the term to their dispersion and community outside Palestine.

Dirah: traditionally accepted tribal range of the Bedouin tribe.

Diurnal: daily, occurring daily, or having a daily cycle; e.g., the range of high and low temperatures during a 24-hour period.

Dolomite: light-colored stratified sedimentary rock similar to limestone but high in calcium magnesium carbonate rather than the calcium carbonate of limestone.

Dunum: a unit of land area measurement common in Palestine and Jordan. Equivalency varies between 900 m^2 and 1,000 m^2 but is most commonly 919 m^2 (0.23 acre, 0.0919 ha).

Dwt: deadweight tons (maritime shipping).

EEC: European Economic Community (Common Market).

Enosis: union of Cyprus with Greece.

Entrepôt: center—usually a city and often a port city—that receives goods in transit, warehouses them, and reships them.

Ethnolinguistic: pertaining to a distinct people (ethnic group) whose distinguishing characteristic is especially language, although other criteria may also make them distinctive (e.g., Armenians).

Expatriate: one who lives in a foreign country. Many Europeans, Americans, and South Asians work and live in several Middle East countries as expatriates (informally called "expats").

Extrusive: pertaining to pouring out of molten rock (lava) onto the earth's surface, where it solidifies; opposite is intrusive (e.g., granite). *See* basalt.

Faluqa **(felucca):** traditional sailboat on the Nile and seas adjacent to Egypt, carries lateen sail.

Farsi: Persian, i.e., the language spoken by Persians.

al-Fatah (Fateh): palindromic acronym for *Harakat al-Tahrir al-Filastiniyya* (Palestinian Liberation Movement), a guerrilla group formed several years before the PLO. Power base for Yasser Arafat, one of Fatah's founders.

Fault: surface of fracture in rock involving vertical or horizontal (or both) displacement of rock on either side of the fault plane; result of tectonic strain in earth's crust. Faulting is a major cause of earthquakes (seismic crustal tremors). With horizontal shearing, a fault is left-lateral if displacement is to the left of an observer looking across the fault line. *See also* transform fault.

Fedayeen (*fidayyin*): From Ar. for "sacrificers," usually applied to Palestinian guerrillas or to Shii fundamentalist fighters.

Feddan: a unit of land-area measurement used in Egypt, equal to 1.038 acres or 4,201 m^2.

Feedstock: raw material for a processing plant, often applied to crude oil or natural gas for a refinery or petrochemical plant.

Fellah (pl. fellahin): roughly equivalent to peasant, from Ar. for "tiller of the soil."

Fertile Crescent: modern term for arcuate area extending from Gaza northward and northeastward across northern Syria and southeastward along Zagros piedmont (see Map 2-1), believed to be where Neolithic farming evolved.

Garigue: stunted evergreen dry scrub vegetation on limestone in drier areas of Mediterranean climate in Asia Minor and the Levant (cf. maquis).

Gawr **(gor, khor):** river floodplain, narrow coastal indentation, or flat-bottomed valley.

GCC: Gulf Cooperation Council, short form of Cooperation Council for the Arab States of the Gulf, formed in 1981 and including Saudi Arabia, Kuwait, Bahrain, Qatar, the UAE, and Oman.

GDP: gross domestic product, total value of goods and services produced by residents and nonresidents within a given country in a given year.

Gecekondu: Turkish for "built overnight," applied to spontaneous settlements built illegally on the peripheries of Turkish cities.

Geomorphology: "earth form," the earth science dealing with the origin and development of earth landforms; somewhat related to the older term "physiography."

Gneiss: coarse-grained crystalline rock usually with streaked or banded black-white-gray appearance. Is the product of dynamic metamorphism of granites and other igneous rocks. *See also* schist.

GNP: gross national product, total value of goods and services produced both from within a given country and from external (foreign) transactions in a given year.

Gondwana: a conjectured single landmass in Paleozoic times from which the southern continents are theorized to have been formed. *See* plate tectonics.

GOSP: gas-oil separator plant, an oil-field facility serving several producing wells to separate dissolved natural gas from the crude petroleum.

Graben: narrow, down-dropped block of the earth's surface bounded by parallel faults; related to rift valley. *See* rift.

Granite: intrusive igneous rock of various colors and grain size.

Hajj: the Muslim pilgrimage to Mecca, an obligation required in the Quran and one of the pillars of Islam.

Hamadah: a rock desert with barren, wind-scoured bedrock surface and little sand. There is an extensive *hamadah* where Arabia, Jordan, and Iraq meet.

Hamas: acronym for *Harakat al-Muqawama al-Islamiyya* (Islamic Resistance Movement), extremist group, one of several Palestinian resistance groups in West Bank and Gaza Strip.

Hammam: bath, bathing facilities, and/or toilet facilities.

Harem: quarters in a Muslim household set aside for women and children.

Hashimite: pertaining to descent from Hashim or the Hashimite clan, which included Muhammad's family and which was part of the Quraysh tribe; commonly pertaining to dynasty in Jordan and, before 1958, in Iraq.

Hectare: international unit of land area measurement, 10,000 m^2 or 2.47 acres.

Hegira (hejira): from Ar. *hijrah,* "flight"; the flight of Muhammad and his followers from Mecca to

Yathrib (renamed Medina) in AD 622, which marked the beginning of the Islamic calendar.

Hizb Allah (**Hizballah, from Arabic; Hezbollah, from Farsi**): Party of God, a group in Lebanon comprising Shii extremists who were involved in seizing hostages.

Horst: opposite of graben (q.v.); an uplifted block roughly paralleled by faults.

Igneous: pertaining to molten or formerly molten rock material, either extrusive (on the earth's surface) or intrusive (underground rock masses). Types include lava (extrusive) and granite (intrusive).

Imam: Shii religious or, sometimes, political leader; commonly, the leader of Muslim worship services; technically, one of the succession of Shii leaders who, beginning with Ali, are accepted by Shii as the legitimate successors of Muhammad.

Infitah: Ar. for "opening," i.e., economic opening in post-Nasserist Egypt.

Interfluve: linear area lying between roughly parallel rivers, e.g., the location of Baghdad between the Tigris and Euphrates rivers.

Intermontane: between mountains, usually a plateau between mountain ranges, e.g., the Anatolian and Iranian plateaus.

Intifadah: Ar. for "uprising," the rebellion of young rock-throwing Palestinians in the West Bank and Gaza Strip beginning in late 1987.

Iranian: pertaining to the country of Iran or to its citizens of whatever ethnic group (not equivalent to Persian).

Islam: "submission," the submission of the followers of Islam to the will of God (Allah).

Isobar: line on a map connecting points of equal barometric pressure.

Isohyet: line on a map connecting points of equal precipitation (see Map 4-2).

Isotherm: line on a map connecting points of equal temperature (see Map 4-1).

Jabal (jebel): Ar. for "hill," "mountain."

Jihad: Ar. for struggle on behalf of righteousness, especially within Islam; translation as "holy war" is rather ambiguous and focuses on only one aspect.

Karst: limestone or dolomite landscape subjected to carbonation-solution and having underground drainage, caverns, sinkholes, and other typical surface features.

Kavir: Pers. for "salt flat," "salt waste," "playa." *Kavirs* are numerous and extensive in eastern, interior Iran.

Kilometer: international unit of distance measurement equaling 1,000 m, 0.6214 mile, 0.5399 nautical mile.

Knesset: Israeli parliament.

Kufiyah: common traditional male Arab headdress, a large square of cloth folded diagonally and worn with straight edge over the forehead. Usually white in Gulf area, red checkered or black and white in the Levant, but colors and patterns vary among localities. Called *ghutrah* in Saudi Arabia.

Lava: extrusive igneous rock that flows onto earth's surface while molten. *See* basalt.

Levant: eastern Mediterranean coastal region, roughly the maximum area held by the Crusader states; comprising western Syria, Lebanon, Palestine, and western Jordan.

Lingua franca: a language or composite language spoken as a common tongue among several language groups in a given region.

Lithosphere: outermost shell of the earth's layers, 10–30 miles/16–48 km thick, comprising several rigid "plates" floating on the partly molten asthenosphere. *See* plate tectonics.

Littoral: of or pertaining to the shore (of seas or lakes).

Loess: fine, coherent, porous yellowish dust believed to have been picked up from barren areas by the wind and redeposited in amorphous layers nearby. Serves as parent material for fine-textured, deep, well-drained soils.

LPG: liquefied petroleum gas, primarily propane and butane, derived from NGL (q.v.).

Maghrib (Maghreb): Ar. for "west" and applied to the western Arab states in northwestern Africa: Morocco, Algeria, Tunisia, and sometimes Libya.

Majlis (mejlis): Iranian parliament, from general Ar.-Pers. term for gathering, gathering place, reception; hence, an official reception room or the occasion of a reception.

Mamluk: lit. "slave," but applied to Turkish and Circassian slave military oligarchy that ruled Egypt 1250–1517; also architecture and other aspects of the period.

Mandate: in the Middle East, a commission awarded by the League of Nations to Britain or France to administer an assigned territory toward timely independence; also the polity so administered under this commission (Palestine, Transjordan, and Iraq by Britain; Syria and Lebanon by France).

Maquis: a low evergreen scrub vegetation typical of better Mediterranean climate areas of western and southern Asia Minor and the Levant; includes oleander, rosemary, myrtle, and similar plants and is a higher-order plant association than garigue (q.v.).

Mashriq: Ar. for "east" and sometimes applied to the eastern Arab states in the Middle East as defined in this book. Less common term than Maghrib (q.v.).

Masjid: Ar./Pers. for "mosque."

Massif: general term applied to a compact upland mass.

Mawali: clients; non-Arab converts to Islam during early period of the Muslim conquests; soon outnumbered Arab Muslims (*ummah*, q.v.).

Maydan: Ar./Pers. for an urban open area or city square, typical of the traditional Islamic city.

Mesolithic: Middle Stone Age, sometimes called Epipaleolithic; transitional between Paleolithic and Neolithic periods and dated roughly 12,000–8,000 BC.

Metamorphic: pertaining to rocks whose original structure has been altered by great earth pressures (dynamic metamorphism) and/or by heat (thermal metamorphism), producing compact and resistant rock types (e.g., gneiss, schist, quartzite, marble).

Meter (metre): the basic international unit of measurement equaling 1,000 mm, 100 cm, or 3.28 ft.

Millet **(mil-let):** under the Ottomans, self-administered non-Muslim religious community (e.g., Jews, Christians), a logical extension of the early Muslim concept of "people of the book."

Mina: coastal inlet and, by derivation, port.

Minaret: tower associated with a mosque from which the call to prayer for the Muslim faithful is intoned at least five times daily by a muazzin (q.v.).

Monsoon: from Ar. word for "season"; the seasonal reversal of pressure and winds, especially across southern and eastern Asia; generally applied to rains typical of summer season in Asia and to winds in both summer and winter.

Muazzin (muadhdhin, muezzin): especially trained man who intones calls to prayer for the Muslim faithful from a minaret five times daily.

Muhammaden: loosely applied to follower of Muhammad, but preferred term is Muslim (q.v.).

Muslim: an adherent of Islam (q.v.), "one who submits"—to the will of God.

Neolithic: New Stone Age, beginning roughly 8,000 BC and ending 4,000–5,000 years later as copper and bronze came into use for implements.

NGL: natural gas liquids, derived from natural gas and yielding ethane, propane, butane, natural gasoline, and related substances.

Nomad. member of a social group that regularly migrates over a traditional realm in search of pasture for their flocks. Bedouins (q.v.) are the best-known true nomads of the Middle East.

OAPEC: Organization of Arab Petroleum Exporting Countries (see Chap. 8).

OPEC: Organization of Petroleum Exporting Countries (see Chap. 8).

Orogeny: a major tectonic process of fold-mountain building.

Orographic: pertaining to mountains; e.g., orographic rainfall is caused by the uplift, hence cooling, of humid wind blowing up a mountain slope—the process producing virtually all heavier rains in the Middle East.

PFLP: Popular Front for the Liberation of Palestine, extremist Marxist Palestinian group known for earlier aircraft hijackings.

Plate tectonics: theory that the earth's crust (lithosphere) comprises about six main and several other minor rigid "plates" that broke away from one main mass and are now "drifting" slowly in respective directions (see Chap. 3).

PLO: Palestine Liberation Organization, formed in 1964, which became the umbrella organization for Palestinian aspirations; Yasser Arafat, chairman. The PLO is acknowledged in most of the Arab world as the only legitimate representative of the Palestinian people.

Pluvial: rainy—pertaining to moister periods during the recent geological past, with such periods in the Middle East usually correlating with glacial advances and related climatic changes; opposed to alternating dry periods.

PNC: Palestine National Council.

Primate city: A city much larger—even many times larger—than any other city in the country and with a much greater range of economic and social activities. Term suggested by Mark Jefferson, 1939. Cairo, Baghdad, and Tehran are examples.

Ptolemaic: the Egyptian kingdom under the Hellenized dynasty of the Ptolemies, 323–30 BC.

Qanat: ditch, canal, tunnel; specifically, an underground tunnel-canal marked by a surface chain of wells; thousands of *qanats* are found on alluvial fans in Iran (see Fig. 22-3).

Qat: Catha edulis, a leafy plant grown on terraced hillsides in northern Yemen. *Qat* leaves are chewed by highland Yemeni men during afternoon hours for mild narcotic effect.

al-Quran (Koran): Ar. for "recitation"; Muslim holy scriptures, believed by Muslims to be the exact words of God revealed (or "recited") to the Prophet Muhammad through the angel Gabriel.

Ramadan: ninth month of the Islamic calendar, considered a holy month because Muhammad received the first revelations from Gabriel in Ramadan. During entire month Muslims are obligated to observe absolute fasting between dawn and dusk. Such fasting is one of the pillars of Islam.

Rift: a narrow linear trough between parallel faults or along linear fissuring, e.g., the Levant Rift, a segment of the great rift from northern Syria to southern Africa.

Riparian: pertaining to riverbanks, especially rights of access to the river ("riparian rights") or occurring along rivers ("riparian powers"). As noun, persons or polity along a river.

Sabkhah (subkha): a flat area of salty silt, whether a tidal flat, salt flat between dunes, or former tidal flat now cut off from the sea (see Fig. 5-2).

Sanjak: provincial administrative district of the Ottoman Empire, administered by a sanjak bey, later by a mutassarıf (e.g., Sanjak of Alexandretta).

Sassanian (Sassanid): pertaining to the Persian Empire or its ruling dynasty named after its founder, Sassan; empire lasted AD 227–651 (see Map 2-4D).

Saudi: concerning the central Arabian Peninsula dynastic family of Al Saud, the kingdom founded and ruled by members of Al Saud, or political policies of the dynasty; hence Saudi Arabia—Arabia of the Sauds.

Schist: fine-grained, foliated crystalline metamorphic rock of varying color. *See also* gneiss.

Sedimentary: formed of sediments—materials laid down usually in seawater but also in lakes and rivers or by wind—and usually stratified (e.g., limestone, shale, sandstone).

Seismic: pertaining to earth tremors or earthquakes.

Semitic: of or pertaining to the subfamily of the Afro-Asiatic language family that includes Arabic, Hebrew, and Aramaic languages; also pertaining to certain aspects of speakers of these languages, excluding racial characteristics.

Sephardim: technically, Jews from Spain or descended from Spanish Jews; by extension, "oriental" Jews (from North Africa, Middle East, and southern and central Asia).

Shah: Pers. for "king"; title of royal rulers of Iran until 1979.

Shariah: complex Muslim religious law and code of sociopolitical conduct and relations, derived primarily from the Quran and sunnah and secondarily from other traditions and opinions.

Shaykh (sheikh): lit. "elder," but specifically a term of respect and rank given to an Arab tribal leader; extended to the ruler of smaller states, which are then referred to as shaykhdoms (e.g., Bahrain, Qatar, also sometimes called amirates [q.v.]); further, by extension, a learned Muslim.

Shield: rigid mass of stable, ancient (Precambrian) rocks, usually greatly metamorphosed, forming the nucleus of a continent or subcontinent—e.g., the Nubian-Arabian Shield of the southwestern Middle East (see Chap. 3).

Shii (Shiite): from Ar. for "partisan," i.e., partisan of Ali, Muhammad's kinsman and son-in-law. Shiis believe Ali should have succeeded to leadership of the *ummah* (q.v.) upon Muhammad's death and that Ali and his several successors (Shii imams) are the only true heads of the *ummah*. See also Sunni.

Steppe: grassland, especially land of short grasses, thus indicating subhumid or semiarid climate (Koeppen BS); in the Middle East, transitional between desert and Mediterranean climate areas or other more humid areas.

Sultanate: realm of a sultan, a secular ruler equivalent to a king or other dynastic ruler.

Sunnah: *See* Sunni.

Sunni (Sunnite): Muslim who accepts the legitimacy of Muhammad's successors. So-called after "sunnah," the admonitions and examples of Muhammad regarding proper Muslim belief and conduct. *See also* Shii.

Suq: Ar. for "marketplace," comparable to Pers. "bazaar."

Tectonism (tectonic, tectonics): internal earth forces that build up, form, or deform the earth's surface or subsurface. *See* plate tectonics.

Tell: Ar. for "hill" or "mound," specifically a characteristic surface mound made up of accumulated layers of debris from successive human occupations of a settlement site over many centuries (see Chap. 2).

Transform fault: a fault zone involving mostly horizontal displacement along an edge of a tectonic plate, e.g., the San Andreas fault in California and the North Anatolian and East Anatolian transform faults; displacement along such faults periodically involves disastrous earthquakes.

Ulama (ulema): Ar. collective term for learned Muslim legal and religious leaders; theoretically, the ultimate repository of power in Saudi Arabia.

Umayyad (Omayyed): Arab Muslim dynasty of the Quraysh tribe and the empire it ruled from Damascus AD 661–750; also the dynasty's continued rule in Spain until 1030.

Ummah: Ar. for the community of Muslims, an especially important concept pertaining to Arab Muslims in the early decades of the Muslim conquests.

UNRWA: United Nations Relief and Works Agency, which since 1949 has operated emergency housing and food distribution for hundreds of thousands of registered Palestinian Arab refugees, usually in UNRWA-operated camps.

Vilayet: a province under the administrative pattern of the Ottoman Empire; term became crucial in post–World War I territorial settlements in the Levant.

Viticulture: cultivation of grapevines, almost a way of life in some specialized agricultural areas.

Volcanism (vulcanism): igneous activity processes in general, not just those associated with volcanoes; especially the processes by which molten materials and associated solids and gases are forced into the lithosphere or onto the earth's surface through craters or fissures. *See* basalt.

Wadi: widely used Ar. term for arid area stream basin (and, by extension, the stream), including major valleys and broad, hardly perceptible linear depressions, whether stream flow is perennial or periodic. Ar. for a major river (Nile, Tigris) is *nahr*.

Wahhabi: often misused term pertaining to reform puritan Muslim movement and group that evolved from the preachings of Muhammad ibn Abd al- Wahhab in the mid-1700s in central Arabia. Wahhabi puritanism is still strong in much of Arabia.

***Waq*f (wakf, vakf):** Muslim religious endowment or trust involving land or other property; widespread in Islamic world but decreasing in more secular states such as Syria.

Xerophytic: pertaining to specialized vegetation of arid lands. Special adaptations include deep or long roots, waxy leaves, and tough bark (see Chap. 5).

Zionism: Jewish nationalism stressing unity of Jews and creation and maintenance of a Jewish state in Eretz Yisrael (Land of Israel) in greater Palestine as a territorial base for Jewry.

EON	PERIOD		EPOCH	AGE	MILLIONS OF YRS AGO
CENOZOIC	QUATERNARY		Holocene (Recent)		0.01
			Pleistocene		1.6
	TERTIARY	Neogene	Pliocene		11.2
			Miocene		23.7
		Paleogene	Oligocene		36.6
			Eocene		57.8
			Paleocene		66.4
MESOZOIC	CRETACEOUS		Late	Maastrichtian	74.5
				Campanian	84.0
				Santonian	87.5
				Coniacian	88.5
				Turonian	91.0
				Cenomanian	97.5
			Early		144
	JURASSIC		Late		163
			Middle		187
			Early		208
	TRIASSIC		Late		230
			Middle		240
			Early		245
PALEOZOIC	PERMIAN				286
	CARBONIFEROUS				360
	DEVONIAN				408
	SILURIAN				438
	ORDOVICIAN				505
	CAMBRIAN				570
PRECAMBRIAN					
	ERA				
PROTEROZOIC	Late				900
	Middle				1600
	Early				2500
ARCHEOZOIC	Late				3000
	Middle				3400
	Early				3800

Geological Time Chart. *In this simplified geological time chart, Ages are shown only for the late Cretaceous, although Age subdivisions exist for all Epochs after the Middle Cambrian. The Middle East surface geology is dominantly Mesozoic and Cenozoic, although the Nubian-Arabian Shield is Precambrian. Western Gulf oil fields are mainly Jurassic and Cretaceous, whereas Iranian and Kirkuk fields are Paleogene.*

Bibliography

Bibliographical Note

The following list of references includes all the works cited in the Notes, a few other sources in English utilized in this book, and several additional works in English that are especially useful for a mid-level student or general reader. Most listings are reasonably available. More advanced sources and materials in languages other than English may be found in the bibliographies mentioned below.

The simplest way to stay abreast of the explosion of new literature on the Middle East is to refer to the listings in the quarterly *Middle East Journal (MEJ),* which includes reviews, short notices, listings of literature received, and a bibliography of periodical materials. The autumn issue has an annual index and lists the periodicals regularly surveyed for the bibliography. The *MEJ* entries may omit specialized geographical materials, most of which can be noted in one or another of the standard academic geographical journals (*Annals* of the Association of American Geographers, *Geographical Review, Professional Geographer, Geographical Journal,* and others). References and articles in both the *International Journal of Middle East Studies* and the *Middle East Studies Association Bulletin* are useful. The weekly *Economist* (London) and the daily *Christian Science Monitor* report regularly on Middle East affairs, as does the *New York Times.* More partisan but still useful are the *Jerusalem Post,* International Edition (weekly, in English), *Israel Economist, Journal of Palestine Studies,* and *Middle East Policy,* called *American-Arab Affairs* before March 1992. Every issue of *Aramco World* magazine covers some aspect of the Middle East. Several of the book references listed below have especially good bibliographies. Statistics may most easily be found in the Encyclopaedia Britannica yearbook's *Britannica World Data* and, more fully, in the standard United Nations yearbooks or other UN periodical statistical volumes.

Three especially useful bibliographical works are:

ABC-Clio Information Services. *The Middle East in Conflict: A Historical Bibliography.* Clio Bibliography Series no. 19 [annotated]. Santa Barbara, CA: ABC-Clio Information Services, 1985. 302p.

Atiyeh, George N., comp. *The Contemporary Middle East, 1948–1973: A Selective and Annotated Bibliography.* Boston: G. K. Hall, 1975. 664p.

Collison, Robert L., ed.-in-chief (individual compilers for each volume). *World Bibliographical Series.* Includes no. 2, *Lebanon;* no. 5, *Saudi Arabia;* no. 27, *Turkey;* no. 28, *Cyprus;* no. 29, *Oman;* no. 36, *Qatar;* no. 42, *Iraq;* no. 43, *UAE;* no. 49, *Bahrain;* no. 50, *The Yemens;* no. 55, *Jordan;* no. 56, *Kuwait;* no. 58, *Israel;* no. 73, *Syria;* no. 81, *Iran;* and no. 86, *Egypt.* Santa Barbara, CA: Clio Press, 1979–1991. Pages variable, from 162p. to 330p.

References

Abdulghani, Jasim M. *Iraq and Iran: The Years of Crisis.* Baltimore: Johns Hopkins Univ. Press, 1984. 270p.

Abdullah, Muhammad Morsy. *The United Arab Emirates: A Modern History.* New York: Barnes & Noble, 1978. 365p.

Abercrombie, Thomas J. "Bahrain: Hub of the Persian Gulf." *National Geographic* 156, no. 3 (Sept. 1979): 300–329.

———. "Arabia's Frankincense Trail." *National Geographic* 168, no. 4 (Oct. 1985): 474–512.

Abir, Mordechai. *Saudi Arabia in the Oil Era.* Boulder, CO: Westview Press, 1988. 247p.

Abu-Dawood, Abdul-Razzak S., and P. P. Karan. *International Boundaries of Saudi Arabia.* New Delhi: Galaxy Publications, 1990. 95p.

Abu-Izzedin, Najla M. *The Druzes: A New Study of Their History, Faith and Society.* Leiden: E. J. Brill, 1984. 259p.

Abu-Lughod, Janet L. *Cairo: 1001 Years of the City Victorious.* Princeton: Princeton Univ. Press, 1971. 284p.

_____. "The Demographic War for Palestine." *Link* 19, no. 5 (Dec. 1986): virtually entire issue.

Adamec, Ludwig W., ed. *Historical Gazetteer of Iran.* Vol. 1, *Tehran and Northwestern Iran;* vol. 2, *Meshed and Northeastern Iran;* vol. 4, *Zahidan and Southeastern Iran.* Graz: Akademische Druck-u Verlagsanstalt, 1976–1988. Vol. 1, 734p. + 62 p. maps; vol. 2, 708p. + 150p. maps; vol. 4, 480p. + 48p. maps.

Aharoni, Yohanan. *The Land of the Bible: A Historical Geography.* Trans. A. F. Rainey. London: Burns and Oates, 1967. 409p.

Airport Operators Council International (AOCI). "Worldwide Airport Traffic Report." Published periodically by AOCI, Washington, DC.

Ajami, Fuad. *The Arab Predicament: Arab Political Thought and Practice Since 1967.* New York: Cambridge Univ. Press, 1981. 220p.

Akins, James E. "The New Arabia." *Foreign Affairs* 70, no. 3 (Summer 1991): 36–49.

Akins, James E., et al. *Oil and Security in the Arabian Gulf.* New York: St. Martin's Press, 1981. 48p.

Akurgal, Ekrem. *Ancient Civilizations and Ruins of Turkey: From Prehistoric Times Until the End of the Roman Empire.* 2d ed. Trans. John Whybrow and Mollie Emre. Istanbul: Mobil Oil Türk, 1970. 375p. + 112p. photographs.

Ali, Sheikh Rustum. *Oil and Power: Political Dynamics in the Middle East.* New York: St. Martin's Press, 1987. 173p.

Allen, Calvin H., Jr. *Oman: The Modernization of the Sultanate.* Profiles: Nations of the Contemporary Middle East. Boulder, CO: Westview Press, 1987. 154p.

Allen, Richard. *Imperialism and Nationalism in the Fertile Crescent: Sources and Prospects of the Arab-Israeli Conflict.* New York: Oxford Univ. Press, 1974. 686p.

al-Ansary, A. R. *Qaryat al-Fau: A Portrait of the Pre-Islamic Civilization in Saudi Arabia.* London: Croom Helm, 1982. 147p.

AlSayyad, Nezar. *Cities and Caliphs: On the Genesis of Arab Muslim Urbanism.* Westport, CT: Greenwood Press, 1991. 196p.

Altorki, Soraya, and Donald P. Cole. *Arabian Oasis City: The Transformation of Unayzah.* Austin: Univ. of Texas Press, 1989. 260p.

Amirahmadi, Hooshang. *Revolution and Economic Transition: The Iranian Experience.* Albany: State Univ. of New York Press, 1990. 420p.

Amuzegar, Jahangir. "The Iranian Economy Before and After the Revolution." *MEJ* 46, no. 3 (Summer 1992): 413–425.

Andersen, Roy R., Robert P. Seibert, and Jon G. Wagner. *Politics and Change in the Middle East: Sources of Conflict and Accommodation.* 3d ed. Englewood Cliffs, NJ: Prentice-Hall, 1990. 331p.

Anthony, John Duke. *Arab States of the Lower Gulf: People, Politics, and Petroleum.* Washington, DC: Middle East Institute, 1975. 273p.

_____. *Historical and Cultural Dictionary of the Sultanate of Oman and the Emirates of Eastern Arabia.* Historical and Cultural Dictionaries of Asia no. 9. Metuchen, NJ: Scarecrow Press, 1976. 136p.

Antonius, George. *The Arab Awakening: The Story of the Arab National Movement.* New York: Hamilton, 1938. 471p.

Arabian American Oil Company (R. O. Williams, oceanographer). *Aramco Meteorologic and Oceanographic Data Book for the Eastern Province Region of Saudi Arabia.* Dhahran: Arabian American Oil Co., n.d. (ca. 1978).

Arabian American Oil Company (eds.: Ismail I. Nawwab, Peter C. Speers, and Paul F. Hoye; main research and writing by Paul Lunde and John A. Sabini). *Aramco and Its World: Arabia and the Middle East.* Dhahran: Arabian American Oil Co., 1980. 275p.

Arian, Asher. *Politics in Israel: The Second Generation.* Rev. ed. Chatham, NJ: Chatham House Publishers, 1989. 314p.

Aronson, Geoffrey. *Israel, Palestinians and the Intifada: Creating Facts on the West Bank.* London: Kegan Paul International (with the Institute of Palestine Studies, Washington, DC), 1990. 376p.

Ashbel, D. "Frequency and Distribution of Dew in Palestine." *Geog. Rev.* 39, no. 2 (April 1949): 291–297.

Askari, Hossein, and John Thomas Cummings. *Middle East Economies in the 1970s: A Comparative Approach.* Praeger Special Studies in International Economics and Development. New York: Praeger, 1976. 581p.

Atherton, Alfred L. "The Soviet Role in the Middle East: An American View." *MEJ* 39, no. 4 (Autumn 1985): 688–715.

Attalides, Michael A. *Cyprus: Nationalism and International Politics.* New York: St. Martin's Press, 1979. 226p.

Avineri, Shlomo. *The Making of Modern Zionism: The Intellectual Origins of the Jewish State.* New York: Basic Books, 1981. 244p.

Awad, Mohamed. "The Assimilation of Nomads in Egypt." *Geog. Rev.* 44, no. 2 (April 1954): 240–252.

Ayalon, Ami, and Haim Shaked, eds. *Middle East Contemporary Survey,* vol. 12: 1988. Published for the Dayan Center for Middle Eastern and African Studies, Tel Aviv Univ. Boulder, CO: Westview Press, 1990. 808p.

Bachrach, Jere L. *A Middle East Studies Handbook*. Rev. and exp. ed. Seattle: Univ. of Washington Press, 1984. 160p.

Baly, Denis. *The Geography of the Bible: A Study in Historical Geography*. New York: Harper, 1957. 303p.

_____. *Basic Biblical Geography*. Philadelphia: Fortress Press, 1987. 80p.

Bar-El, Raphael, and Ariela Nesher, eds. *Rural Industrialization in Israel*. Boulder, CO: Westview Press, 1987. 193p.

Bard, Mitchell Geoffrey. *The Water's Edge and Beyond: Defining the Limits to Domestic Influence on United States Middle East Policy*. New Brunswick, NJ: Transaction Publishers, 1991. 313p.

Barkey, Henri J. *The State and the Industrialization Crisis in Turkey*. Boulder, CO: Westview Press, 1990. 220p.

Basson, Philip, et al. *Biotopes of the Western Arabian Gulf: Marine Life and Environments of Saudi Arabia*. Dhahran: Aramco [Arabian American Oil Co.], 1979. 284p.

Batanouny, K. H. *Ecology and Flora of Qatar*. Doha: Univ. of Qatar, 1981. 245p.

Bates, Daniel, and Amal Rassam. *Peoples and Cultures of the Middle East*. Englewood Cliffs, NJ: Prentice-Hall, 1983. 288p.

Batuta, Hanna. "Some Observations on Social Roots of Syria's Ruling Military Group and the Causes for Its Dominance." *MEJ* 35, no. 3 (Summer 1981): 331–344.

El-Baz, Farouk. "Preliminary Observations of Environmental Damage Due to the Gulf War." *Natural Resources Forum* (Feb. 1992): 71–75.

Bean, George E. *Turkey's Southern Shore: An Archaeological Guide*. London: Ernest Benn, 1968. 188p.

Beaumont, Peter, Gerald H. Blake, and J. Malcolm Wagstaff. *The Middle East: A Geographical Study*. 2d ed. New York: Halsted Press, 1988. 623p.

Beaumont, Peter, and Keith McLachlan, eds. *Agricultural Development in the Middle East*. New York: John Wiley, 1985. 349p.

Begin, Menachem. *The Revolt*. New York: Nash Publishing Co., 1977. 386p.

Ben-Dor, Gabriel, and David B. Dewitt, eds. *Conflict Management in the Middle East*. Lexington, MA: Lexington Books, 1987. 323p.

Benedick, Richard Elliot. "The High Dam and the Transformation of the Nile." *MEJ* 33, no. 2 (Spring 1979): 119–144.

Benvenisti, Meron. *The West Bank Data Projects: A Survey of Israel's Policies*. Washington, DC: American Enterprise Institute, 1984. 97p. Updated periodically.

_____. With Ziad Abu-Zayed and Danny Rubenstein. *The West Bank Handbook: A Political Lexicon*. Boulder, CO: Westview Press, 1986. 228p.

Benvenisti, Meron, and Shlomo Khayat. *The West Bank and Gaza Atlas*. West Bank Data Base Project. Boulder, CO: Westview Press, 1988. 140p.

Betts, Robert Brenton. *The Druze*. New Haven: Yale Univ. Press, 1988. 161p.

Bibby, Geoffrey. *Looking for Dilmun*. New York: Knopf, 1969. 383p.

Bidwell, Robin Leonard. *The Two Yemens*. Boulder, CO: Westview Press, 1983. 350p.

Bikai, Patricia M. "The Phoenicians: Rich and Glorious Traders of the Levant." *Archaeology* 43, no. 2 (March/April 1990): 22–35.

Bill, James A. *The Eagle and the Lion: The Tragedy of Amerian-Iranian Relations*. New Haven: Yale Univ. Press, 1988. 520p.

Bill, James A., and Robert Springborg. *Politics in the Middle East*. 3d ed. Glenview, IL: Scott Foresman, 1990. 479p.

Bishku, Michael B. "Iraq's Claim to Kuwait: A Historical Overview." *American-Arab Affairs* 37 (Summer 1991): 77–88.

Black, Ian, and Benny Morris. *Israel's Secret Wars: A History of Israel's Intelligence Services*. New York: Grove Weidenfeld, 1991. 603p.

Blake, G. H., and Richard I. Lawless, eds. *The Changing Middle East City*. Croom Helm Series on the Arab World. London: Croom Helm, 1980. 273p.

Blake, Gerald H., and Richard N. Schofield, eds. *Boundaries and State Territory in the Middle East and North Africa*. Cambridgeshire, UK: Middle East and North African Studies Press, 1987. 167p.

Blake, Gerald, et al. *The Cambridge Atlas of the Middle East and North Africa*. New York: Cambridge Univ. Press, 1987. 132p.

Bobek, H. "Vegetation [of Iran]." Chap. 8 in Fisher, William B., ed., 1968.

Bonine, Michael E. "From Uruk to Casablanca: Perspectives on the Urban Experience in the Middle East." *Journal of Urban History* 3 (Feb. 1977): 141–180.

_____. "The Morphogenesis of Iranian Cities." *Annals* (Association of American Geographers) 69, no. 2 (June 1979): 208–224.

Bonine, Michael E., and Nikki R. Keddie, eds. *Modern Iran: The Dialectics of Continuity and Change*. Albany: State Univ. of New York Press, 1981. 464p.

Boustani, Rafic, and Philippe Fargues. *The Atlas of the Arab World: Geopolitics and Society*. New York: Facts on File, 1990. 144p.

Braun, Aurel, ed. *The Middle East in Global Strategy*. Westview Special Studies on the Middle East. Boulder, CO: Westview Press, 1987. 274p.

Brawer, Moshe, ed. *Atlas of the Middle East.* Prepared by CARTA, The Israel Map and Publishing Co., Jerusalem. New York and London: Macmillan and Collier Macmillan, 1988. 140p.

Brice, William C., ed. *An Historical Atlas of Islam.* Leiden: E. J. Brill, 1981. 71p.

Brinkmann, R. *Geology of Turkey.* New York: Elsevier Scientific Publishing Co., 1976. 158p.

Brown, Glenn F. "Tectonic Map of the Arabian Peninsula." Map AP-2. Jiddah: Kingdom of Saudi Arabia, Directorate General of Mineral Resources, 1972.

Brown, Glenn F., and R. G. Coleman. "The Tectonic Framework of the Arabian Peninsula." *Proceedings of the 24th International Geological Congress, 1972.* Section 3: 300–304.

Brunsden, Denys, et al. "The Bahrain Surface Materials Resource Survey and Its Applications to Regional Planning." *Geographical Journal* 145, no. 1 (Mar. 1979): 1–35.

Brynen, Rex. *Sanctuary and Survival: The PLO in Lebanon.* Boulder, CO: Westview Press (with Pinter Publishers, London), 1990. 255p.

Bulliet, Richard W. *The Camel and the Wheel.* Cambridge: Harvard Univ. Press, 1975. 327p.

Bureau of Mines, U.S. Department of the Interior. *Mineral Industries of the Middle East. Minerals Yearbook,* vol. 3. 1989 International Review. Washington, DC: U.S. Government Printing Office, 1989 (1992). 125p. (For Egypt, see *Mineral Industries of Africa,* 1984 [1992]. 315p.)

Burrell, Alison, ed. *Agricultural Policy in Jordan.* London: Ithaca Press, 1986. 147p.

Burrowes, Robert D. *The Yemen Arab Republic: The Politics of Development, 1962–1986.* Westview Special Studies on the Middle East. Boulder, CO: Westview Press (with Croom Helm, Kent, UK), 1987. 173p.

———. "Oil Strike and Leadership in South Yemen: 1986 and Beyond." *MEJ* 43, no. 3 (Summer 1989): 437–454.

Butzer, Karl W. *Early Hydraulic Civilization in Egypt: A Study in Cultural Ecology.* Chicago: Univ. of Chicago Press, 1976. 134p.

Cambridge Encyclopedia of the Middle East and North Africa. Trevor Mostyn and Albert Hourani, eds. Cambridge: Cambridge Univ. Press, 1988. 504p.

Canby, Thomas Y. "After the Storm." *National Geographic* 180, no. 2 (Aug. 1991): 2–32.

Carr, David. "Capital Flows and Development in Syria." *MEJ* 34, no. 4 (Autumn 1980): 455–467.

Central Intelligence Agency (CIA). *Issues in the Middle East: Atlas.* Washington, DC: U.S. Government Printing Office, 1973. 40p.

Chaliand, Gerard, ed. *People Without a Country: The Kurds and Kurdistan.* A. R. Ghassemlou et al. Trans. Michael Pallis. London: Zed Press, 1980. 246p.

Chaliand, Gerard, and Yves Ternon. *The Armenians: From Genocide to Resistance.* Trans. Tony Barrett. London: Zed Press, 1983. 125p.

Chitham, E. J. *The Coptic Community in Egypt: Spatial and Social Change.* Occasional Papers Series, no. 32. Durham, UK: Univ. of Durham Centre for Middle Eastern and Islamic Studies, 1986. 121p.

Christaller, Walter. *The Central Places of Southern Germany.* Trans. C. W. Baskin. Englewood Cliffs, NJ: Prentice-Hall, 1966.

Chubin, Shahram, and Charles Tripp. *Iran and Iraq at War.* Boulder, CO: Westview Press, 1988. 318p.

Clarke, Angela. *Bahrain Oil and Development 1929–1989.* Boulder, CO: International Research Center for Energy and Economic Development, 1990. 432p.

Clarke, John I., and Howard Bowen-Jones, eds. *Change and Development in the Middle East: Essays in Honour of W. B. Fisher.* London: Methuen, 1981. 322p.

Clawson, Marion, Hans H. Landsberg, and Lyle T. Alexander. *The Agricultural Potential of the Middle East.* Rand Corporation and Resources for the Future. New York: American Elsevier Publishing Co., 1971. 312p.

Cobban, Helena. *The Palestinian Liberation Organization: People, Power, and Politics.* Cambridge Middle East Library. Cambridge: Cambridge Univ. Press, 1984. 305p.

———. *The Making of Modern Lebanon.* Boulder, CO: Westview Press, 1985. 248p.

———. "Thinking About Lebanon." *American-Arab Affairs* no. 12 (Spring 1985): 59–71.

Cockburn, Andrew, and Leslie Cockburn. *Dangerous Liaison: The Inside Story of the U.S.-Israeli Covert Relationship.* New York: HarperCollins, 1991. 416p.

Cohen, Saul. *The Geopolitics of Israel's Border Question.* Jerusalem: *Jerusalem Post,* for the Jaffee Center for Strategic Studies, Tel Aviv Univ. Distributed by Westview Press, Boulder, CO, 1988. 124p.

Collins, Frank. "The True Cost of Israel." *Washington Report on Middle East Affairs* 8, no. 9 (Jan. 1990): 21, 55.

Cooley, John K. "The War over Water." *Foreign Policy* 54 (Spring 1984): 3–26.

———. "Middle East Water: Power for Peace." *Middle East Policy* 1, no. 2 (1992): 1–15.

Cooper, Mark N. *The Transformation of Egypt.* Baltimore: Johns Hopkins Univ. Press, 1982. 278p.

Cordesman, Anthony H. *The Gulf and the Search for Strategic Stability: Saudi Arabia, the Military Balance in the Gulf, and Trends in the Arab-Israeli Military Balance.* Westview Special Studies on the Middle East. Boulder, CO: Westview Press, 1984. 1041p.

Cottam, Richard W. *Nationalism in Iran.* Pittsburgh: Univ. of Pittsburgh Press, 1979. 376p.

Cottrell, Alvin, gen. ed. *The Persian Gulf States: A General Survey.* Baltimore: Johns Hopkins Univ. Press, 1980. 695p.

Country Studies: Area Handbook Series. Prepared for the Department of the Army by several agencies and with various editors. A study is available on every Middle East country (combined volume on *Persian Gulf States*), with fourth and fifth editions of studies of major Middle East countries published 1988–1991. Washington, DC: U.S. Government Printing Office.

Cressey, George B. "Qanats, Karez, and Foggaras." *Geog. Rev.* 48, no. 1 (Jan. 1958): 27–44.

_____. *Crossroads: Land and Life in Southwest Asia.* Chicago: Lippincott, 1960. 593p.

Crystal, Jill. *Oil and Politics in the Gulf: Rulers and Merchants in Kuwait and Qatar.* Cambridge Middle East Library, no. 24. Cambridge: Cambridge Univ. Press, 1990. 210p.

Curtis, Michael, ed. *Religion and Politics in the Middle East.* Westview Special Studies on the Middle East. Prepared under the auspices of the American Academic Association for Peace in the Middle East. Boulder, CO: Westview Press, 1981. 406p.

Curtiss, Richard. *Stealth PACs: How Israel's American Lobby Seeks to Control U.S. Middle East Policy.* Washington, DC: American Educational Trust, 1990. 192p.

Danielsen, Albert L. *The Evolution of OPEC.* New York: Harcourt Brace Jovanovich, 1982. 305p.

Davison, R. H. "Where Is the Middle East?" *Foreign Affairs* 38 (1960): 665–675.

Day, Arthur R. *East Bank/West Bank: Jordan and the Prospects for Peace.* New York: Council on Foreign Relations, 1986.

Defense Mapping Agency, U.S. Department of Defense. *Gazetteer of Iran: Names Approved by the United States Board on Geographic Names.* 2d ed. 2 vols. Washington, DC: U.S. Government Printing Office, 1985. 1827p. (Similar gazetteers have been produced by the Defense Mapping Agency for all major Middle Eastern countries, plus one for the Gulf states.)

Denktash, Rauf. *The Cyprus Triangle.* Boston: Allen and Unwin, 1982. 224p.

Department of State. *Background Notes.* Published for each country periodically. 4–12p. each.

Devlin, John F. *Syria: Modern State in an Ancient Land.* Profiles: Nations of the Contemporary Middle East. Boulder, CO: Westview Press, 1983. 140p.

Dewdney, John C. *Turkey: An Introductory Geography.* New York: Praeger, 1971. 214p.

Dickson, H.R.P. *The Arab of the Desert: A Glimpse into Badawin Life in Kuwait and Saudi Arabia.* London: George Allen and Unwin, 1949. 668p.

_____. *Kuwait and Her Neighbors.* London: Allen and Unwin, 1956. 627p.

Dillman, Jeffrey D. "Water Rights in the Occupied Territories." *Journal of Palestine Studies* 73: 19, no. 1 (Autumn 1989): 46–71.

Dixon, J. E., and A.H.F. Robertson, eds. *The Geological Evolution of the Eastern Mediterranean.* Published for the Geological Society. Oxford: Blackwell Scientific Publications, 1984. 824p.

Doran, Charles F., and Stephen W. Buck, eds. *The Gulf, Energy, and Global Security: Political and Economic Issues.* Boulder, CO: Lynne Rienner Publishers, 1991. 275p.

Dresch, Paul. *Tribes, Government, and History in Yemen.* Oxford: Clarendon Press, 1989. 440p.

Drysdale, Alasdair, and Gerald Blake. *The Middle East and North Africa: A Political Geography.* New York: Oxford Univ. Press, 1985. 340p.

Dunbar, Charles. "The Unification of Yemen: Process, Politics, and Prospects." *MEJ* 43, no. 6 (Summer 1992): 456–476.

Dutton, R., and N. Winser. "The Oman Wahiba Sands Project." *Geographical Journal* 153, no. 1 (Mar. 1987): 48–58.

Earle, Sylvia A. "Persian Gulf Pollution: Assessing the Damage One Year Later." *National Geographic* 181, no. 2 (Feb. 1992): 122–134.

Eickelman, Dale F. *The Middle East: An Anthropological Approach.* Englewood Cliffs, NJ: Prentice-Hall, 1981. 336p.

Elazar, Daniel J., ed. *Governing Peoples and Territories.* Philadelphia: Institute for the Study of Human Issues, 1982. 334p.

_____. *Judea, Samaria, and Gaza: Views on the Present and Future.* Washington, DC: American Enterprise Institute, 1982. 222p.

_____. *The Other Jews: The Sephardim Today.* New York: Basic Books, 1989. 236p.

Encyclopaedia Britannica, Inc. *Britannica World Data.* Part 2 of *Britannica Book of the Year.* Chicago: Encyclopaedia Britannica, Inc. Published annually.

English, Paul Ward. *City and Village in Iran: Settlement and Economy in the Kirman Basin.* Madison: Univ. of Wisconsin Press, 1966. 204p.

Entessar, Nader. *Kurdish Ethnonationalism.* Boulder, CO: Lynne Rienner Publishers, 1992. 207p.

Erinç, Sirri, and Necdet Tunçdilek. "The Agricultural Regions of Turkey." *Geog. Rev.* 42, no. 2 (Apr. 1952): 179–203.

Esman, Milton J., and Itamar Rabinovich, eds. *Ethnicity, Pluralism, and the State in the Middle East.* Published in cooperation with the Dayan Center for Middle Eastern and African Studies, Tel Aviv Univ. Ithaca, NY: Cornell Univ. Press, 1988. 296p.

Espenshade, Edward B., Jr. *Goode's World Atlas.* 19th ed. Chicago: Rand McNally, 1990. 367p.

Esposito, John L., ed. *The Iranian Revolution: Its Global Impact.* Miami: Florida International Univ. Press, 1990. 346p.

Exxon Corporation, Public Affairs Department. *Middle East Oil and Gas.* Exxon Background Series. New York: Exxon Corp., Dec. 1984. 40p.

Fahim, Hussein M. *Dams, People and Environment— The Aswan High Dam Case.* New York: Pergamon Press, 1981. 187p.

Falah, Ghazi. "Land Fragmentation and Spatial Control in the Nazareth Metropolitan Area." *Professional Geographer* 44, no. 1 (Feb. 1992): 30–44.

Farah, Nadia Ramsis. *Religious Strife in Egypt: Crisis and Ideological Conflict in the Seventies.* New York: Gordon and Breach, 1986. 135p.

Farah, Tawfic E., ed. *Pan-Arabism and Arab Nationalism: The Continuing Debate.* Foreword by James A. Bill. Boulder, CO: Westview Press, 1987. 208p.

Farid, Abdel Majid, ed. *The Red Sea: Prospects for Stability.* Published in association with the Arab Research Centre. New York: St. Martin's Press, 1984. 173p.

Farouk-Sluglett, Marion, and Peter Sluglett. *Iraq Since 1958: From Revolution to Dictatorship.* London: I. B. Tauris Paperbacks, 1991. 336p.

Farsi, Zaki M.A. *National Guide and Atlas of the Kingdom of Saudi Arabia.* Jiddah: Zaki M.A. Farsi, 1989. n.p.

Al-Farsy, Fouad. *Modernity and Tradition: The Saudi Equation.* London and New York: Kegan Paul International, 1990. 337p.

Fenton, Thomas P., and Mary J. Heffron, eds. *Middle East: A Directory of Resources: Organizations, Books, Periodicals, Pamphlets and Articles, Audiovisuals.* Third World Resource Directory. Maryknoll, NY: Orbis Books, 1988. 144p.

Fernea, Elizabeth Warnock, and Basima Qattan Bezirgan, eds. *Middle Eastern Muslim Women Speak.* Austin: Univ. of Texas Press, 1977. 402p.

Fernea, Elizabeth Warnock, and Robert A. Fernea. *The Arab World: Personal Encounters.* New York: Anchor Press, Doubleday and Co., 1985. 354p.

Ffrench, Geoffrey E., and Allan G. Hill. *Kuwait: Urban and Medical Ecology.* Geomedical Monograph Series no. 4, New York: Springer-Verlag, 1971. 124p.

Findley, Paul. *They Dare to Speak Out: People and Institutions Confront Israel's Lobby.* 2d ed. Westport, CT: Lawrence Hill, 1989. 390p.

Finnie, David H. *Shifting Lines in the Sand: Kuwait's Elusive Frontier with Iraq.* Cambridge, MA: Harvard Univ. Press, 1992. 221p.

Fisher, Sydney N., and William Ochsenwald. *The Middle East: A History.* 4th ed. New York: McGraw-Hill, 1990. 776p.

Fisher, William B. *The Middle East: A Physical, Social, and Regional Geography.* 7th ed. London: Methuen, 1978. 615p.

Fisher, William B., ed. *Cambridge History of Iran.* Vol. 1, *The Land of Iran.* Cambridge: Cambridge Univ. Press, 1968. 782p.

Fisk, Robert. *Pity the Nation: The Abduction of Lebanon.* New York: Atheneum, 1990. 678p.

Foreign Economic Trends (FET). Published periodically for each major country (annually in most cases) by the U.S. Department of Commerce from reports supplied by U.S. embassies.

Fraser, T. G. *The USA and the Middle East Since World War 2.* New York: St. Martin's Press, 1989. 221p.

Friedlander, Dov, and Calvin Goldscheider. *The Population of Israel.* New York: Columbia Univ. Press, 1979. 240p.

Friedman, Thomas L. *From Beirut to Jerusalem.* New York: Farrar, Straus, Giroux, 1989. 525p.

Geddes, Charles L., ed. *A Documentary History of the Arab-Israeli Conflict.* New York: Praeger, 1991. 461p.

Gharaibeh, Fawzi A. *The Economies of the West Bank and Gaza Strip.* Westview Special Studies on the Middle East. Boulder, CO: Westview Press, 1985. 182p.

Ghareeb, Edmund. *The Kurdish Question in Iraq.* Contemporary Issues in the Middle East. Syracuse: Syracuse Univ. Press, 1981. 223p.

Ghods, M. Reza. *Iran in the Twentieth Century: A Political History.* Boulder, CO, and London: Lynne Rienner Publishers and Adamantine Press, 1989. 296p.

Gischler, Christiaan E. *Water Resources in the Arab Middle East and North Africa.* MENAS Resources Studies. Based on a UNESCO working document. Cambridge: Middle East and North African Studies Press, 1979. 132p.

Goldschmidt, Arthur, Jr. *A Concise History of the Middle East.* 4th ed., rev. and updated. Boulder, CO: Westview Press, 1991. 465p.

———. *Modern Egypt: The Formation of a Nation-State.* Boulder, CO: Westview Press, 1988. 211p.

Gordon, David C. *The Republic of Lebanon: Nation in Jeopardy.* Profiles: Nations of the Contemporary Middle East. Boulder, CO: Westview Press, 1983. 171p.

Graicer, Iris. "Spatial Integration of Arab Migrants in a Jewish Town." *Professional Geographer* 44, no. 1 (Feb. 1992): 45–56.

Gregory, Barbara M. "U.S. Relations with Lebanon: A Troubled Course." *American-Arab Affairs* 35 (Winter 1990–1991): 62–93.

Grill, N. C. *Urbanisation in the Arabian Peninsula.* Durham, Eng.: Centre for Middle Eastern and Islamic Studies, Univ. of Durham, 1984. 113p.

Gubser, Peter. *Jordan: Crossroads of Middle Eastern Events.* Profiles: Nations of the Contemporary Middle East. Boulder, CO: Westview Press, 1983. 139p.

Gulick, John. *Tripoli: A Modern Arab City.* Cambridge: Harvard Univ. Press, 1967. 253p.

———. *The Middle East: An Anthropological Perspective.* Washington, DC: University Press of America, 1983. 244p.

Gürün, Kamvran. *The Armenian File: The Myth of Innocence Exposed.* New York: St. Martin's Press, 1985. 323p.

Haddad, Wadi D. *Lebanon: The Politics of Revolving Doors.* Washington Papers no. 114, published with the Center for Strategic and International Studies, Georgetown Univ. New York: Praeger, 1985. 154p.

Halliday, Fred. *Revolution and Foreign Policy: The Case of South Yemen 1967–1987.* Cambridge Middle East Library, no. 21. Cambridge: Cambridge Univ. Press, 1990. 315p.

Hammond Atlas of the Middle East: Geography, History, and Peoples. Maplewood, NJ: Hammond, 1991. 48p.

Harris, George S. *Turkey: Coping with Crisis.* Profiles: Nations of the Contemporary Middle East. Boulder, CO: Westview Press, 1985. 240p.

Harris, Lillian Craig, ed. *Egypt: Internal Challenges and Regional Stability.* Chatham House Papers, no. 39. London and New York: Royal Institute of International Affairs and Routledge and Kegan Paul, 1988. 116p.

Harris, William Wilson. *Taking Root: Israeli Settlement in the West Bank, the Golan, and Gaza-Sinai, 1967–1980.* Chichester, Eng.: Research Studies Press, John Wiley, 1980. 223p.

Hartshorne, Richard. "The Functional Approach in Political Geography." *Annals* (Association of American Geographers) 40, no. 2 (June 1950): 95–130.

Haynes, Kingsley E., and Dale Whittington. "International Management of the Nile—Stage Three?" *Geog. Rev.* 71, no. 1 (Jan. 1981): 17–32.

Heard-Bey, Frauke. *From Trucial States to United Arab Emirates.* London: Longman, 1982. 522p.

Held, Colbert C. "The New Saarland." *Geog. Rev.* 41, no. 4 (Oct. 1951): 590–605.

Held, Joanne D. [Cummings]. "The Effects of the Ottoman Land Laws on the Marginal Population and Musha Village of Palestine, 1858–1914." Master's thesis, Univ. of Texas, Austin, 1979. 225p.

Heller, Mark A. *A Palestinian State: the Implications for Israel.* Cambridge: Harvard Univ. Press, 1983. 190p.

Helms, Christine Moss. *Iraq: Eastern Flank of the Arab World.* Washington, DC: The Brookings Institution, 1984. 215p.

Hersch, Seymour M. *The Samson Option: Israel's Nuclear Arsenal and American Foreign Policy.* New York: Random House, 1991. 354p.

Hershlag, Z. Y. *The Contemporary Turkish Economy.* London: Routledge, 1988. 178p.

Hertzberg, Arthur, ed. *The Zionist Idea: A Historical Analysis and Reader.* Rev. ed. New York: Atheneum, 1969. 638p.

Hewison, R. Neil. *The Fayoum: A Practical Guide.* 2d ed. Cairo: American Univ. of Cairo Press, 1989. 115p.

Hills, E. S., ed. *Arid Lands: A Geographical Appraisal.* London: Methuen; Paris: UNESCO, 1966. 461p.

Hitchens, Christopher. "Struggle of the Kurds." *National Geographic* 182, no. 2 (Aug. 1992): 32–61.

Hobbs, Joseph J. *Bedouin Life in the Egyptian Wilderness.* Austin: Univ. of Texas Press, 1989. 165p.

Holden, David, and Richard Johns. *The House of Saud: The Rise and Rule of the Most Powerful Dynasty in the Arab World.* New York: Holt, Rinehart and Winston, 1982. 569p.

Holm, Donald August. "Desert Geomorphology in the Arabian Peninsula." *Science* 132, no. 3437 (Nov. 11, 1960): 1369–1379.

Hopwood, Derek. *Egypt: Politics and Society, 1945–1981.* London: Allen and Unwin, 1982. 194p.

———. *Syria, 1945–1986: Politics and Society.* London: Unwin Hyman, 1988. 193p.

Hourani, Albert H. *Minorities in the Arab World.* London: Oxford Univ. Press, 1947. 140p.

———. *The Emergence of the Modern Middle East.* Berkeley: Univ. of California Press, 1981. 243p.

———. *A History of the Arab Peoples.* Cambridge, MA: Belknap Press of Harvard Univ. Press, 1991. 551p.

Howard, Harry N. *The King-Crane Commission.* Beirut: Khayat, 1963. 369p.

———. *Turkey, the Straits, and U.S. Policy.* Baltimore: Johns Hopkins Univ. Press, in cooperation with Middle East Institute, 1974. 337p.

Hudson, James. "The Litani River of Lebanon." *MEJ* 25, no. 1 (Winter 1971): 1–14.

Hughes, Hugh. *Middle East Railways.* Harrow, Eng.: Continental Railway Circle, 1981. 128p.

Al-Humaidhi, Bader. "Twenty-Eight Years of Development Cooperation: The Kuwait Fund for Arab Economic Development." *American-Arab Affairs* 31 (Winter 1989–1990): 11–14.

Hunter, Shireen T. *Iran and the World: Continuity in a Revolutionary Decade.* Bloomington: Indiana Univ. Press, 1990. 254p.

El Hussini, Mohrez Mahmoud. *Soviet-Egyptian Relations, 1945–85.* New York: St. Martin's Press, 1987. 276p.

International Petroleum Encyclopedia (IPE). Published annually. Tulsa, OK: PennWell Publishing Co.

Israel Information Centre. *Facts About Israel.* Revised annually. Jerusalem: Israel Information Centre.

Israel Pocket Library. *Geography.* Compiled from material originally published in the *Encyclopaedia Judaica.* One of several volumes in this series (*Society; Religious Life and Communities; Immigration and Settlement; Economy;* and others). Jerusalem: Keter, 1973. 263p.

Issawi, Charles. *An Economic History of the Middle East and North Africa.* New York: Columbia Univ. Press, 1982. 304p.

————. *The Fertile Crescent 1800–1914; A Documentary Economic History.* Studies in Middle Eastern History. New York: Oxford Univ. Press, 1988. 502p.

Janzen, Jörg. *Nomads in the Sultanate of Oman.* Westview Special Studies on the Middle East. Boulder, CO: Westview Press, 1986. 315p.

Jernazian, Ephraim K. *Judgment unto Truth: Witnessing the Armenian Genocide.* New Brunswick, NJ: Transaction Publishers, 1990. 163p.

Jones, Stephen B. "A Unified Field Theory of Political Geography." *Annals* (Association of American Geographers) 44, no. 4 (Dec. 1954): 111–123.

Joseph, John, *Muslim-Christian Relations and Inter-Christian Rivalries in the Middle East: The Case of the Jacobites in an Age of Transition.* Albany: State Univ. of New York Press, 1983. 240p.

Kahan Commission. *The Beirut Massacre: The Complete Kahan Commission Report.* With an introduction by Abba Eban. Princeton, NJ: Karz-Cohl, 1983. 107p.

Kahan, David. *Agriculture and Water Resources in the West Bank and Gaza, 1967–1987.* Boulder, CO: Westview Press, 1987. 181p.

Kahane, Meir. *They Must Go.* New York: Grosset and Dunlap, 1981. 282p.

Kaikobad, Kaiyan Homi. *The Shatt al-Arab Boundary Question.* Oxford: Oxford Univ. Press, 1988. 184p.

Kark, Ruth, ed. *The Land That Became Israel: Studies in Historical Geography.* New Haven; also Jerusalem: Yale Univ. Press; also Magnes Press, Hebrew Univ., 1989. 332p. + plates.

Karpat, Kemal H. *The Gecekondu: Rural Migration and Urbanization.* Cambridge: Cambridge Univ. Press, 1976. 291p.

Karsh, Efraim. "Geopolitical Determinism: The Origins of the Iran-Iraq War." *MEJ* 44, no. 2 (Spring 1990): 256–268.

Keddie, N. R. "Is There a Middle East?" *International Journal of Middle East Studies* 4 (1972): 255–271.

Kedourie, Elie. *Politics in the Middle East.* Oxford: Oxford Univ. Press, 1992. 366p.

Kelly, J. B. *Arabia, the Gulf and the West.* New York: Basic Books, 1980. 530p.

Kenen, I. L. *Israel's Defense Line: Her Friends and Foes in Washington.* Buffalo, NY: Prometheus Books, 1981. 345p.

[Kennan, George F.]. "The Sources of Soviet Conduct." *Foreign Affairs* 65, no. 4 (Spring 1987): 852–868. (Originally published in this journal in July 1947, includes Kennan's updated comments.)

Keyder, Caglar, and Frank Tabak, eds. *Landholding and Commercial Agriculture in the Middle East.* Albany: State Univ. of New York Press, 1991. 260p.

Khadduri, Majid. *The Gulf War: The Origins and Implications of the Iraq-Iran Conflict.* New York: Oxford Univ. Press, 1988. 236p.

Khader, Bichara, ed. *The Economic Development of Jordan.* London: Croom Helm, 1987. 246p.

Khalidi, Walid. *Conflict and Violence in Lebanon: Confrontation in the Middle East.* Harvard Studies in International Affairs no. 38. Cambridge: Center for International Affairs, Harvard Univ., 1979. 217p.

————. "Lebanon: Yesterday and Tomorrow." *MEJ* 43, no. 3 (Summer 1989): 375–387.

Khalidi, Walid, ed. *From Haven to Conquest: Readings in Zionism and the Palestine Problem Until 1948.* Beirut: Institute for Palestine Studies, 1971. 839p.

Khalifa, Ali Mohammed. *The United Arab Emirates: Unity in Fragmentation.* Boulder, CO: Westview Press, 1979. 235p.

al-Khalil, Ali. "Lebanon and Its Future Development." *American-Arab Affairs* 37 (Summer 1991): 57–60.

Khalil, Samir. *Republic of Fear: The Inside Story of Saddam's Iraq.* Reprinted with new introduction 1990. New York: Pantheon Books, 1989. 310p.

el-Khawas, Mohamed, and Samir Abed-Rabbo. Foreword by Rabbi Elmer Berger. *American Aid to Israel: Nature and Impact.* Brattleboro, VT: Amana Books, 1984. 191p.

el Khazen, Farid. "The Lebanese Economy After a Decade of Turmoil." *American-Arab Affairs* no. 12 (Spring 1985): 72–84.

Kheirabadi, Masoud. *Iranian Cities: Formation and Development.* An Iran-American Foundation Book. Austin: Univ. of Texas Press, 1991. 160p.

Khouri, Rami G. *The Antiquities of the Jordan Rift Valley.* Amman, Jordan: Al Kutba, 1988. 151p.

Khoury, Phillip. *Syria and the French Mandate: The Politics of Arab Nationalism, 1920–1945.* Princeton, NJ: Princeton Univ. Press, 1987. 698p.

Kimmerling, Baruch, ed. *The Israeli State and Society: Boundaries and Frontiers.* Albany: State Univ. of New York Press, 1989. 301p.

Kingdom of Saudi Arabia. *Statistical Year Book.* Riyadh: Central Dept. of Statistics, published annually.

Kipper, Judith, and Harold H. Saunders, eds. *The Middle East in Global Perspective*. Boulder, CO: Westview Press, 1991. 359p.

Klieman, Aaron S. *Foundations of British Policy in the Arab World: The Cairo Conference of 1921*. Baltimore, MD: Johns Hopkins Press, 1970. 322p.

Kolars, John. *Tradition, Season, and Change in a Turkish Village*. Research Paper no. 82, Department of Geography. Chicago: Univ. of Chicago, 1968. 205p.

———. "The Course of Water in the Arab Middle East." *American-Arab Affairs* 33 (Summer 1990): 57–68.

Kolars, John F., and William A. Mitchell. *The Euphrates River and the Southeast Anatolia Development Project*. Carbondale: Southern Illinois Univ. Press, 1991. 325p.

Korany, Bahgat, Ali E. Hillal Dessouki et al. *The Foreign Policies of Arab States: The Challenge of Change*. 2d ed. Boulder, CO: Westview Press, 1991. 449p.

Korn, David A. *Stalemate: The War of Attrition and Great Power Diplomacy in the Middle East, 1967–1970*. Boulder, CO: Westview Press, 1992. 326p.

Kreiger, Barbara. *Living Waters: Myth, History, and Politics of the Dead Sea*. New York: Continuum, 1988. 226p.

Krinsley, Daniel B. *A Geomorphological and Paleoclimatological Study of the Playas of Iran*. Part I and Part II. Prepared for Air Force Cambridge Research Laboratories, U.S. Air Force, Bedford, MA. Washington, DC: U.S. Geological Survey, Department of the Interior, August 1970. Pt. 1, 329p.; Pt. 2, 486p.

Lacey, Robert. *The Kingdom*. New York: Harcourt Brace Jovanovich, 1981. 631p.

Lawless, Richard, ed. *The Middle Eastern Village: Changing Economic and Social Relations*. London: Croom Helm, 1987. 304p.

Lawson, Fred H. *Bahrain: The Modernization of Autocracy*. Profiles: Nations of the Contemporary Middle East. Boulder, CO: Westview Press, 1989. 150p.

Lees, G. M., and N. L. Falcon. "The Geographical History of the Mesopotamian Plains." *Geographical Journal* 118 (1952): 24–39.

Lenczowski, George. *The Middle East in World Affairs*. 4th ed. Ithaca: Cornell Univ. Press, 1980. 863p.

———. *American Presidents and the Middle East*. Durham, NC: Duke Univ. Press, 1990. 321p.

Lesch, Ann M. "Palestinians in Kuwait." *Journal of Palestine Studies* 20, no. 4 (Summer 1991): 42–54.

Lesch, Ann Mosely, and Mark Tessler. *Israel, Egypt, and the Palestinians: From Camp David to Intifada*. Foreword by Richard B. Parker. Indiana Series in Arab and Islamic Studies. Bloomington: Indiana Univ. Press, 1989. 298p.

Leslie, S. Clement. *The Rift in Israel: Religious Authority and Secular Democracy*. London: Routledge and Kegan Paul, 1971. 185p.

Lewis, Bernard. *The Emergence of Modern Turkey*. 2d ed. New York: Oxford Univ. Press, 1968. 530p.

Lewis, Norman N. "Malaria, Irrigation, and Soil Erosion in Central Syria." *Geog. Rev.* 39, no. 2 (April 1949): 278–290.

———. "Lebanon—The Mountain and Its Terraces." *Geog. Rev.* 43, no. 1 (Jan. 1953): 1–14.

———. *Nomads and Settlers in Syria and Jordan, 1800–1980*. Cambridge Middle East Library. Cambridge: Cambridge Univ. Press, 1987. 249p.

Lewis, Peter G. "The Politics of Iranian Place-Names." Geographical Record. *Geog. Rev.* 72, no. 1 (Jan. 1982): 99–102.

Limbert, John W. *Iran: At War with History*. Profiles: Nations of the Contemporary Middle East. Boulder, CO: Westview Press, 1987. 186p.

Little, Douglas. "Cold War and Covert Action: The United States and Syria, 1945–1958." *MEJ* 44, no. 1 (Winter 1990): 51–75.

Long, David E. *The Persian Gulf: An Introduction to Its Peoples, Politics, and Economics*. Rev. ed. Westview Special Studies on the Middle East. Boulder, CO: Westview Press, 1978. 174p.

Long, David E., and Bernard Reich, eds. *The Government and Politics of the Middle East and North Africa*. 2d ed., rev. and updated. Boulder, CO: Westview Press, 1986. 479p.

Longrigg, Stephen. *The Middle East: A Social Geography*. 2d ed., with revision and incorporation of new material by James Jankowski. Chicago: Aldine, 1970. 291p.

Lorenz, Joseph P. *Egypt and the Arabs: Foreign Policy and the Search for National Identity*. Boulder, CO: Westview Press, 1990. 184p.

Lorimer, J. G. *Gazetteer of the Persian Gulf, Oman, and Central Arabia*. 4 vols. Calcutta: Superintendent of Government Printing, 1915.

Lustick, Ian. *Arabs in the Jewish State: Israel's Control of a National Minority*. Modern Middle East Series no. 6. Austin: Univ. of Texas Press, 1980. 385p.

———. *For the Land and the Lord: Jewish Fundamentalism in Israel*. [New York]. Council on Foreign Relations Press, 1988. 256p.

McKee, Edwin D., ed. *A Study of Global Sand Seas*. U.S. Geological Survey Professional Paper 1052. Prepared in cooperation with the National Aeronautics and Space Administration. Washington, DC: U.S. Government Printing Office, 1979. 429p.

Mackinder, Sir Halford J. "The Geographical Pivot of History." *Geographical Journal* 23 (1904): 421–444.

_____. *Democratic Ideals and Reality: A Study in the Politics of Reconstruction.* New York: Holt, 1919. 266p.

Makram-Ebeid, Mona. "Political Opposition in Egypt: Democratic Myth or Reality?" *MEJ* 43, no. 3 (Summer 1989): 423–436.

el Mallakh, Ragaei. *The Economic Development of the United Arab Emirates.* New York: St. Martin's Press, 1981. 215p.

_____. *Qatar: Energy and Development.* London: Croom Helm, 1985. 184p.

el Mallakh, Ragaei, and Dorothea H. el Mallakh, eds. *Saudi Arabia: Energy, Developmental Planning, and Industrialization.* Lexington, MA: Lexington Books, D. C. Heath, 1982. 204p.

Mandaville, James P., Jr. "Plants [of the Oman Mountains]." In *The Scientific Results of the Oman Flora and Fauna Survey 1975.* A Journal of Oman Studies Special Report. Published by the Ministry of Information and Culture, Sultanate of Oman. n.d. Pp. 229–267.

_____. "Studies in the Flora of Arabia, XI: Some Historical and Geographical Aspects of a Principal Floristic Frontier." *Notes from the Royal Botanic Garden, Edinburgh* 42, no. 1 (1984): 1–15.

_____. *Flora of Eastern Saudi Arabia.* London: Kegan Paul International, 1990. 482p.

Manners, Ian R. "Problems of Water Resource Management in a Semi-Arid Environment: The Case of Irrigation Agriculture in the Central Jordan Rift Valley." Chap. 5 in Brian S. Hoyle, ed., *Spatial Aspects of Development.* Chichester, Eng.: John Wiley, 1974.

Marr, Phebe. *The Modern History of Iraq.* Boulder, CO: Westview Press, 1985. 382p.

Matheson, Sylvia A. *Persia: An Archaeological Guide.* Park Ridge, NJ: Noyes Press, 1973. 330p.

Mauger, Thierry. *The Bedouins of Arabia.* Trans. Khia Mason and Igor Persan. Paris: Souffles, 1988a. 139p.

_____. *Flowered Men and Green Slopes of Arabia.* Trans. Khia Mason. Paris: Souffles, 1988b. 189p.

Melamid, Alexander. *Oil and the Economic Geography of the Middle East and North Africa: Studies.* Ed. C. Max Kortepeter. Princeton, NJ: Darwin Press, 1991. 330p.

Merari, Ariel, and Shlomi Elad. *The International Dimension of Palestinian Terrorism.* JCSS Studies. [Jaffee Center for Strategic Studies, Tel Aviv Univ.] Jerusalem and Boulder, CO: *Jerusalem Post* and Westview Press, 1986. 147p.

Middle East and North Africa 1989. 35th ed. London: Europa Publications, 1988. 949p.

Middle East Research Institute (MERI), University of Pennsylvania. Reports on most major Middle East states, titled with respective state names. London: Croom Helm, mostly mid-1980s.

Middle East Review. 15th ed. Essex, UK: World of Information, 1988. 191p.

Mikesell, Marvin W. "The Deforestation of Mount Lebanon." *Geog. Rev.* 59, no. 1 (Jan. 1969): 1–28.

Miller, Judith, and Laurie Mylroie. *Saddam Hussein and the Crisis in the Gulf.* New York: Times Books Division of Random House, 1990. 268p.

Ministry of Agriculture and Water [Saudi Arabia]. In cooperation with the Saudi Arabian–United States Joint Commission on Economic Cooperation. *Water Atlas of Saudi Arabia.* Riyadh: Saudi Arabian Printing Co., 1984. 112p.

Mitchell, William A. "Reconstruction After Disaster: The Gediz Earthquake of 1970." *Geog. Rev.* 66, no. 3 (July 1976): 296–313.

Moore, Clement Henry. "Money and Power: The Dilemma of the Egyptian Infitah." *MEJ* 40, no. 4 (Autumn 1986): 634–650.

Moore, John Norton, ed. *The Arab-Israeli Conflict.* 3 vols.: 1 and 2, *Readings;* 3, *Documents.* Sponsored by the American Society of International Law. Princeton: Princeton Univ. Press, 1974. Vol. 1, 1067p.; vol. 2, 1193p.; vol. 3, 1248p.

Moorehead, John. *In Defiance of the Elements.* With photographs by Robin Constable. London: Quartet Books, 1977. 160p.

Mortimer, Edward. *Faith and Power: The Politics of Islam.* New York: Random House, 1982. 432p.

Mostyn, Trevor. *Major Political Events in Iran, Iraq, and the Arabian Peninsula 1945–1990.* Ed. Thomas S. Arms. New York: Facts on File, 1991. 308p.

Nabir, Mordechai. *Saudi Arabia in the Oil Era,* Boulder, CO: Westview Press, 1988. 247p.

Naff, Thomas, and Ruth C. Matson, eds. *Water in the Middle East: Conflict or Cooperation?* No. 2 in the Special Studies Series of the Middle East Research Institute (MERI), Univ. of Pennsylvania. Prepared for Defense Intelligence Agency, Dept. of Defense. A Westview Replica Edition. Boulder, CO: Westview Press, 1984. 236p.

Nakhleh, Emile A. *A Palestinian Agenda for the West Bank and Gaza.* Washington: American Enterprise Institute, 1980. 127p.

_____. "The West Bank and Gaza: Twenty Years Later." *MEJ* 42, no. 2 (Spring 1988): 209–226.

Nassar, Jamal R. *The Palestine Liberation Organization: From Armed Struggle to the Declaration of Independence.* New York: Praeger, 1991. 256p.

Nassar, Jamal R., and Roger Heacock, eds. *Intifada: Palestine at the Crossroads.* New York: Praeger, 1990. 347p.

National Geographic Society. *Exploring Our Living Planet*. Washington, DC: National Geographic Society, 1983. 366p.

———. *National Geographic Atlas of the World*. 6th ed. Washington, DC: National Geographic Society, 1990. 133p. + 135p. index.

Naval Intelligence Division [UK]. *Palestine and Transjordan*. Geographical Handbook Series B.R. 514. Oxford: Oxford Univ. Press for H.M. Stationery Office, 1943. 621p.

Netton, Ian Richard, ed. *Arabia and the Gulf: From Traditional Society to Modern States*. Totowa, NJ: Barnes & Noble, 1986. 259p.

Niblock, Tim, ed. *Social and Economic Development in the Arab Gulf*. New York: St. Martin's Press, 1980. 242p.

———. *Iraq: The Contemporary State*. New York: St. Martin's Press, 1982. 277p.

Norton, Augustus Richard. *Amal and the Shi'a: Struggle for the Soul of Lebanon*. Austin: Univ. of Texas Press, 1987. 238p.

———. "Lebanon After Taif: Is the Civil War Over?" *MEJ* 45, no. 3 (Summer 1991): 457–473.

Nugent, Jeffrey B., and Theodore Thomas, eds. *Bahrain and the Gulf: Past Perspectives and Alternative Futures*. New York: St. Martin's Press, 1985. 221p.

O'Ballance, Edgar. *The Kurdish Revolt: 1961–1970*. Hamden, CT: Archon Books, 1973. 196p.

Olson, Robert. *The Emergence of Kurdish Nationalism and the Sheikh Said Rebellion, 1880–1925*. Austin: Univ. of Texas Press, 1989. 229p.

Oman 1989. [Muscat]: Oman Ministry of Information, 1989. 151p.

Organski, A.F.K. *The $36 Billion Bargain: Strategy and Politics in US Assistance to Israel*. New York: Columbia Univ. Press, 1990. 315p.

Orni, Efraim, and Elisha Efrat. *Geography of Israel*. 3d rev. ed. Jerusalem: Israel Universities Press, 1971. 551p.

Parker, Richard B. *The Politics of Miscalculation in the Middle East*. Indiana Series in Arab and Islamic Studies. Bloomington: Indiana Univ. Press, 1993. 320p.

Pearcy, G. Etzel. "The Middle East—An Indefinable Region." Department of State Publication 7684. Washington, DC: 1964. (Updated from an article in the Department of State Bulletin, Mar. 23, 1959.) 12p.

Peck, Malcolm C. *The United Arab Emirates: A Venture in Unity*. Profiles: Nations of the Contemporary Middle East. Boulder, CO: Westview Press, 1986. 176p.

Pelletiere, Stephen C. *The Kurds: An Unstable Element in the Gulf*. Boulder, CO: Westview Press, 1984. 220p.

Pendleton, Madge, et al. *The Green Book: A Guide for Living in Saudi Arabia*. 4th ed. Washington, DC: Washington Middle East Editorial Associates, 1984. 253p.

Penrose, Edith, and E. F. Penrose. *Iraq: International Relations and National Development*. Nations of the Modern World. London: Ernest Benn, 1978. 569p.

Peretz, Don. *The West Bank: History, Politics, Society, and Economy*. Westview Special Studies on the Middle East. Boulder, CO: Westview Press, 1986. 173p.

———. *The Middle East Today*. 5th ed. New York: Praeger, 1988. 583p.

———. *Intifada: The Palestinian Uprising*. Boulder, CO: Westview Press, 1990. 246p.

Perthes, Volker. "The Syrian Economy in the 1980s." *MEJ* 46, no. 1 (Winter 1992): 37–58.

Peterson, J. E. *The Politics of Middle Eastern Oil*. Washington, DC: Middle East Institute, 1983. 529p.

Philby, H. St. John B. *Arabia of the Wahhabis*. London: Cass, 1977. (New impression of 1928 ed., with additions; one of Philby's several classic works on Arabia.) 422p.

Pipes, Daniel. *Greater Syria: The History of an Ambition*. New York: Oxford Univ. Press, 1990. 240p.

Pitcher, Donald Edgar. *A Historical Geography of the Ottoman Empire: From Earliest Times to the End of the Sixteenth Century*. Leiden: E. J. Brill, 1972. 171p. + 29 folded maps.

Polk, William R. *The Arab World*. Cambridge: Harvard Univ. Press, 1980. 456p.

Purser, B. H., ed. *The Persian Gulf*. New York: Springer-Verlag, 1973. 471p.

al-Qasimi, Sultan Muhammad. *The Myth of Arab Piracy in the Gulf*. 2d ed. New York: Routledge, 1988.

Quandt, William B. *Camp David: Peacemaking and Politics*. Washington, DC: Brookings Institution, 1986. 426p.

———. *The United States and Egypt: An Essay on Policy for the 1990s*. Washington, DC: Brookings Institution, 1990. 82p.

Quandt, William B., ed. *The Middle East: Ten Years After Camp David*. Washington, DC: Brookings Institution, 1988. 517p.

Rabinovich, Itamar. *The War for Lebanon, 1970–1983*. Ithaca. Cornell Univ. Press, 1984.

Rabinovich, Itamar, and Jehuda Reinharz, eds. *Israel in the Middle East: Documents and Readings on Society, Politics, and Foreign Relations, 1948–Present*. New York: Oxford Univ. Press, 1984. 407p.

Ragette, Friedrich, ed. *The Beirut of Tomorrow: Planning for Reconstruction*. Beirut: American Univ. of Beirut, 1983. 141p.

Rahman, Mushtaqur, ed. *Muslim World: Geography*

and Development. Lanham, MD: Univ. Press of America, 1987. 190p.

Ramazani, Rouhallah K. *The Persian Gulf and the Strait of Hormuz. International Straits of the World,* vol. 3. Alphen aan den Rijn, Netherlands: Sijthoff and Noordhoff, 1979. 180p.

————. "Iran's Foreign Policy: Both North and South." *MEJ* 46, no. 3 (Summer 1992): 393–412.

Reddaway, John. *Burdened with Cyprus: The British Connection.* London: Weidenfeld and Nicholson, 1986. 237p.

Redman, Charles L. *The Rise of Civilization: From Early Farmers to Urban Society in the Ancient Near East.* San Francisco: Freeman, 1978. 367p.

Reich, Bernard. *Israel: Land of Tradition and Conflict.* Profiles: Nations of the Contemporary Middle East. Boulder, CO: Westview Press, 1985. 227p.

Richards, Alan, and John Waterbury. *A Political Economy of the Middle East: State, Class, and Economic Development.* Boulder, CO: Westview Press, 1990. 495p.

Richardson, John P. *The West Bank: A Portrait.* Special Study no. 5. Washington, DC: Middle East Institute, 1984. 221p.

Rudloff, Willy. *World Climates.* With tables of climatic data and practical suggestions. Stuttgart: Wissenschaftliche Verlagsgesellschaft mbH, 1981. 632p.

Al-Sabah, Y.S.F. *The Oil Economy of Kuwait.* London and Boston: Kegan Paul, 1980. 166p.

Sachar, Howard M. *A History of Israel from the Rise of Zionism to Our Time.* Vol. 1. New York: Knopf, 1976. 932p. *A History of Israel from the Aftermath of the Yom Kippur War.* Vol. 2. New York: Oxford Univ. Press, 1987. 319p.

Safran, Nadav. *Israel: The Embattled Ally.* Cambridge, MA: Belknap Press of Harvard Univ. Press, 1978. 633p.

————. *Saudi Arabia: The Ceaseless Quest for Security.* Ithaca, NY: Cornell Univ. Press, 1985. 524p.

Sahliyeh, Emile F. *The PLO After the Lebanon War.* Westview Special Studies on the Middle East. Boulder, CO: Westview Press, 1986. 286p.

Said, Edward W., and Christopher Hitchens, eds. *Blaming the Victims: Spurious Scholarship and the Palestine Question.* London: Verso, 1988. 296p.

Said, Rushdi. *The Geology of Egypt.* Amsterdam: Elsevier, 1962. 377p.

————. *The Geological Evolution of the River Nile.* New York: Springer-Verlag, 1981. 151p.

Salamé, Ghassan, ed. *The Foundations of the Arab State.* London: Croom Helm, 1987. 260p.

Salameh, Elias. "Jordan's Water Resources: Development and Future Prospects." *American-Arab Affairs* 33 (Summer 1990): 69–77.

Salibi, Kamal. *A House of Many Mansions: The History of Lebanon Reconsidered.* Berkeley: Univ. of California Press, 1988. 247p.

Sandler, Shmuel, and Hillel Frisch. *Israel, the Palestinians, and the West Bank: A Study in Intercommunal Conflict.* Lexington, MA: Lexington Books, 1984. 190p.

Saqqaf, Abdulaziz Y., ed. *The Middle East City: Ancient Traditions Confront a Modern World.* New York: Paragon House, 1987. 393p.

Saudi Arabian American Oil Company. *Aramco Annual Report* (sometimes *Saudi Aramco Annual Report*). Published annually.

Sayigh, Yusif A. *The Economies of the Arab World: Development Since 1945. The Economies of the Arab World,* vol. 1. New York: St. Martin's Press, 1978. 726p.

Schick, Irvin C., and Ertugrul Ahmet Tonak, eds. *Turkey in Transition: New Perspectives.* New York: Oxford Univ. Press, 1987. 405p.

Schiff, Zeev, and Ehud Yaari. *Intifada: The Palestinian Uprising—Israel's Third Front.* Ed. and trans. Ina Friedman. New York: Simon and Schuster, 1989. 356p.

Schmandt-Besserat, Denise. "The Earliest Precursor of Writing." *Scientific American* 238 (1978): 50–59.

Schulz, E., and J. W. Whitney. "Vegetation in North-Central Saudi Arabia." *Journal of Arid Environments* 10 (1986): 175–186.

Scientific American. Special issue, *The Dynamic Earth.* 249, no. 3 (Sept. 1983).

Scott, Jamie, and Paul Simpson-Housley, eds. *Sacred Places and Profane Spaces: Essays in the Geographics of Judaism, Christianity, and Islam.* Contributions to the Study of Religion, no. 30. Westport, CT: Greenwood Press, 1991. 200p.

Scoville, Sheila A., ed. *Gazetteer of Arabia: A Geographical and Tribal History of the Arabian Peninsula.* Vol. 1, *A-E.* Graz, Austria: Akademische Druck- u. Verlagsanstalt, 1979. 742p.

Selzer, Michael. *The Wineskin and the Wizard.* New York: Macmillan, 1970. 241p.

Shamekh, Ahmed A. *Spatial Patterns of Bedouin Settlement in al-Qasim Region, Saudi Arabia.* Lexington: Univ. of Kentucky, 1975. 315p.

Shehadeh, Raja. *Occupier's Law: Israel and the West Bank.* Rev. ed. Washington, DC: Institute for Palestine Studies, 1985. 259p.

Shlaim, Avi. *The Politics of Partition: King Abdullah, the Zionists and Palestine 1921–1951.* [New York]: Columbia Univ. Press, 1990. 465p.

Sindelar, H. Richard, III, and J. E. Peterson, eds. *Crosscurrents in the Gulf: Arab, Regional and Global Inter-*

ests. For the Middle East Institute. London: Routledge, 1989. 256p.

Smith, Charles D. *Palestine and the Arab-Israeli Conflict.* 2d ed. New York: St. Martin's Press, 1992. 343p.

Smith, George Adam. *The Historical Geography of the Holy Land.* 25th ed. London: Hodder and Stoughton, 1935. 744p.

Smith, Pamela Ann. "The Palestinian Diaspora, 1948–1985." *Journal of Palestine Studies* 15, no. 3 (Spring 1986): 90–108.

Soffer, Arnon, and Julian V. Minghi. "Israel's Security Landscapes: The Impact of Military Considerations on Land Uses." *Professional Geographer* 38 (Feb. 1986): 28–41.

Spiegel, Steven L. *The Other Arab-Israeli Conflict: Making America's Middle East Policy, from Truman to Reagan.* Middle Eastern Studies, Monograph no. 1. Graduate School of International Studies, University of Miami. Chicago: Univ. of Chicago Press, 1985. 522p.

Spykman, Nicholas John. *The Geography of the Peace.* New York: Harcourt, Brace, 1944. 66p.

Starr, Joyce R., and Daniel C. Stoll, eds. *The Politics of Scarcity: Water in the Middle East.* Westview Special Studies on the Middle East. Washington, DC, and Boulder, CO: Center for Strategic and International Studies and Westview Press, 1988. 198p.

Stasis, Anastasios, and Michael Mavrocordatos. *Geography of Cyprus.* 3d ed. Larnaca: American Academy, 1989. 121p.

Steffen, Hans, et al. *Final Report on the Airphoto Interpretation Project of the Swiss Technical Cooperation Service, Berne.* Project carried out for the Central Planning Organisation, Sana. The major findings of the Population and Housing Census of February 1975. Zurich: Dept. of Geography, Univ. of Zurich, 1978. Two parts in 1 vol.: pt. 1, 164p; pt. 2, 231p. (Much of the same information appears in Hans Steffen, *Population Geography of the Yemen Arab Republic, Tubinger Atlas des Vorderen Orients,* suppl. ser. B. [Geisteswissenschaften], no. 39 [Wiesbaden: Ludwig Reichert, 1979], 132p.)

Stein, Leonard J. *The Balfour Declaration.* Jerusalem: Magnes Press of Hebrew Univ., 1983. 681p.

Stookey, Robert W. *South Yemen: A Marxist Republic in Arabia.* Profiles: Nations of the Contemporary Middle East. Boulder, CO: Westview Press, 1982. 124p.

Stronach, David, and Stephen Lunsden. "The University of California Berkeley's Excavations at Nineveh." *Biblical Archaeologist* 55, no. 4 (Dec. 1992): 227–233.

Summers, W. M. "Proto-Elamite Civilization in Fars." In Uwe Finkbeiner and Wolfgang Rollig, *Gamdat*

Nasr: Period or Regional Style? Wiesbaden: Ludwig Reichert, 1986. Pp. 199–211.

Survey of Israel. *Atlas of Israel.* 3d ed. Tel Aviv: Survey of Israel, 1985. Pages unnumbered.

Swagman, Charles F. *Development and Change in Highland Yemen.* Salt Lake City: Univ. of Utah Press, 1988. 200p.

Taha, M. F., et al. "The Climate of the Near East." Chap. 3 in K. Takahasha and H. Arakawa, eds., *Climates of Southern and Western Asia, World Survey of Climatology,* vol. 9. Amsterdam: Elsevier Scientific Publishing Co., 1981.

Taryam, Abdullah Omran. *The Establishment of the United Arab Emirates, 1950–85.* London: Croom Helm, 1987. 190p.

Taylor, Alan R. *The Superpowers and the Middle East.* Contemporary Issues in the Middle East. Syracuse, NY: Syracuse Univ. Press, 1991. 212p.

Thesiger, Wilfred. *Arabian Sands.* London: Longmans, 1959. 326p.

————. *The Marsh Arabs.* New York: Dutton, 1964. 242p.

Tower Commission. *The Tower Commission Report.* New York: Bantam Books and Times Books, 1987. 550p.

Turkey, 3d ed. Insight Guides. Hong Kong: Apa Publications, 1989. 404p.

Twinam, Joseph Wright. *The Gulf, Cooperation and the Council: An American Perspective.* Washington, DC: Middle East Policy Council, 1992. 294p.

United Nations, Food and Agriculture Organization (FAO). *Production Yearbook.* Rome: FAO. Published annually.

United States Geological Survey (USGS). *Geology of the Arabian Peninsula.* Geological Survey Professional Paper 560. A review of the geology of Saudi Arabia as shown on USGS Miscellaneous Geologic Investigations Map I-270 A, "Geologic Map of the Arabian Peninsula" (1963). Washington, DC: U.S. Government Printing Office, 1966–1967, 1975, and 1989. (This study consists of nine USGS Professional Papers in the 560 series, Geology of the Arabian Peninsula: A, "Arabian Shield," B, "Yemen," C, "Aden Protectorate," D, "Sedimentary Geology of Saudi Arabia," E, "Bahrain," F, "Kuwait," G, "Southwestern Iraq," H, "Eastern Aden Protectorate and Part of Dhufar," and I, "Jordan.")

Vance, James E., Jr. *This Scene of Man.* New York: Harper, 1977. 437p.

van Dam, Nikolaos. "Sectarian and Regional Factionalism in the Syrian Political Elite." *MEJ* 32, no. 2 (Spring 1978): 201–210.

Van Dusen, Michael H. "Political Integration and Regionalism in Syria." *MEJ* 26, no. 2 (Spring 1972): 123–136.

Vidal, F. S. *The Oasis of al-Hasa*. Dhahran: Arabian American Oil Co., 1955. 216p.

Vita-Finzi, C. *Recent Earth Movements: An Introduction to Neotectonics*. London: Academic Press, 1986. 226p.

Voll, John Obert. *Islam: Continuity and Change in the Modern World*. Boulder, CO, and Essex, UK: Westview Press and Longman, 1982. 397p.

Wagstaff, J. M. *The Evolution of Middle Eastern Landscapes*. Totowa, NJ: Barnes & Noble, 1985. 304p.

Waterbury, John. *Hydropolitics of the Nile Valley*. Syracuse: Syracuse Univ. Press, 1979. 301p.

————. *The Egypt of Nasser and Sadat: The Political Economy of Two Regimes*. Princeton Studies on the Near East. Princeton: Princeton Univ. Press, 1983. 475p.

Weekes, Richard V., ed. *Muslim Peoples: A World Ethnographic Survey*. 2d ed., rev. and enl. 2 vols. Westport, CT: Greenwood Press, 1984. 953p.

Weinbaum, Marvin G. "Politics and Development in Foreign Aid: US Economic Assistance to Egypt, 1975–82." *MEJ* 37, no. 4 (Autumn 1983): 636–655.

Wells, Samuel F., Jr., and Mark Bruzonsky, eds. *Security in the Middle East: Regional Change and Great Power Strategies*. Published in cooperation with the Wilson Center. Boulder, CO: Westview Press, 1987. 366p.

Wendorf, Fred, and Romuald Schild. *Prehistory of the Eastern Sahara*. New York: Academic Press, 1980. 414p.

Wenner, Manfred W., ed. *North Yemen: The Yemen Arab Republic After Twenty-Five Years*. Boulder, CO: Lynne Rienner Publishers, 1991. 185p.

Whalen, Norman M., and David W. Pease. "Early Mankind in Arabia." *Aramco World* 43, no. 4 (July-Aug. 1992): 16–23.

Whittlesey, Derwent. "Sequent Occupance." *Annals* (Association of American Geographers) 19 (1929): 162–165.

Wilkinson, John C. *Arabia's Frontiers: The Story of Britain's Boundary Drawing in the Desert*. London: I. B. Tauris, 1991. 422p.

Williams, Richard S., et al. "Environmental Consequences of the Persian Gulf War 1990–1991: Remote-Sensing Datasets of Kuwait and Environs." *Research and Exploration* (Special issue of National Geographic Society) 7 (1991): 1–48 (entire issue).

Wilson, Sir Arnold T. *The Persian Gulf: An Historical Sketch from the Earliest Times to the Beginning of the Twentieth Century*. London: George Allen and Unwin, 1928. 327p.

Wilson, Jeremy. *Lawrence of Arabia: The Authorized Biography of T. E. Lawrence*. New York: Atheneum, 1990. 1188p.

Wilson, Mary C. *King Abdullah, Britain and the Making of Jordan*. Cambridge Middle East Library. Cambridge: Cambridge Univ. Press, 1987. 289p.

Wolffsohn, Michael. *Israel: Polity, Society, Economy 1882–1982: An Introductory Handbook*. Trans. Douglas Bobovoy. Atlantic Highland, NJ: Humanities Press International, 1987. 302p.

Woodward, Peter N. *Oil and Labor in the Middle East: Saudi Arabia and the Oil Boom*. New York: Praeger, 1988. 195p.

The World Factbook. Published annually by the Central Intelligence Agency, Washington, DC.

Yapp, Malcolm. *The Making of the Modern Near East, 1792–1923*. London: Longman, 1987. 404p.

————. *The Near East Since the First World War. A History of the Middle East*. Ed. P. M. Holt. London: Longman, 1991. 526p.

Yehia, Mohamed Adel Ahmed. *Atlas of Qatar: From Landsat Images*. Doha: Centre of Scientific and Applied Research, Qatar Univ., 1983. 166p.

Yergin, Daniel. *The Prize: The Epic Quest for Oil, Money, and Power*. New York: Simon and Schuster, 1991, 917p.

Zahlan, Rosemarie Said. *The Creation of Qatar*. London: Croom Helm, 1979. 160p.

————. *The Making of the Modern Gulf States: Kuwait, Bahrain, Qatar, the United Arab Emirates and Oman*. The Making of the Middle East Series. London: Unwin Hyman, 1989. 180p.

Zangwill, Israel. "The Return to Palestine." *New Liberal Review* 2 (Dec. 1901): 615–634.

Zohary, Michael. *Plant Life of Palestine: Israel and Jordan*. New York: Ronald, 1962. 262p.

About the Book and Author

Despite the critical importance of the Middle East in U.S. and world affairs, *Middle East Patterns* continues to be the only comprehensive regional study of the area written by a U.S. geographer since 1960. This second edition retains the basic framework of its 1989 predecessor, examining the Middle East from a topical perspective and then from a regional, country-by-country viewpoint. A thoughtful consideration of the physical environment lays the groundwork for emphasis on cultural-political and geopolitical patterns, which are the essence of the study.

This completely updated edition includes 55 new photographs that have been added to 40 photographs retained from the earlier work. Several fascinating "then and now" photo pairs dramatically illustrate the development that has taken place in recent decades. Like the tables and graphs, the 61 thematic and regional maps were all especially created for the book: they have all been updated and are consistently styled, cleanly formatted, and easy to read.

An ideal midlevel text for courses in regional geography of the Middle East, the book is also valuable for courses in Middle East history, politics, comparative government, and economics. Its lively style makes the book an essential resource as well for specialists and general readers interested in the area. Those working in the Middle East with oil companies, other commercial organizations, and government agencies will find it especially informative.

Dr. Colbert C. Held is a retired Foreign Service Officer who was with the Department of State for eighteen years. Fifteen years were spent in the Middle East, with postings to embassies in Beirut and Tehran and to the American Consulate General in Dhahran, Saudi Arabia. He also held lengthy temporary assignments in every country in the Middle East. He has been Retired Diplomat-in-Residence at Baylor University since 1978.

Index